# Developmental
# Psychology

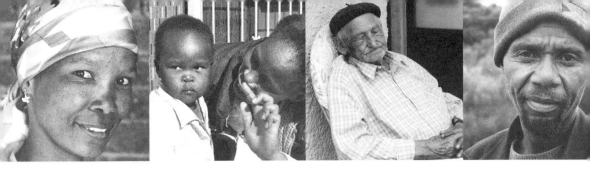

# Developmental Psychology

EDITORS:

DEREK HOOK

JACKI WATTS

KATE COCKCROFT

UCT
PRESS

**Developmental Psychology**

First published 2002

©UCT Press, 2002
PO Box 24309, Lansdowne, 7779

ISBN 1 919 713689

Copy editing by David Merrington
Indexing by Jan Schaafsma
Proofreading by Roelien Theron
Design and typesetting by Roelien Theron
Cover design by Catherine Crookes

Illustrations on pp. 57, 92, 107, 151, 176, 191, 201, 202–204, 209, 212, 218, 220, 247, 265, 294, and 313 by Belinda Karpelowsky, and pp. 19, 78, 122, 125, 136, 181, and 186 by Andre Plant
Photographs on pp. ii and iii by Cha Johnston and Michele Vrdoljak

Typeset in Granjon and Stone Sans
Printed and bound in South Africa by Creda Communications

# Contents

# Notes on contributors

**Kate Cockcroft** lectures in developmental psychology, cognitive psychology, and psychological assessment in the School of Human and Community Development at the University of the Witwatersrand. She has published in the fields of cognitive developmental psychology, educational psychology, and psycholinguistics. Her research interests in the field of cognitive developmental psychology centre on multilingualism, creativity, and learning disabilities.

**James Grant** graduated from the University of the Witwatersrand Law School with a B Proc LLB before embarking on postgraduate studies in psychology. His interest in moral psychology grew out his concerns with criminal responsibility. The moral reasoning of South Africa's worst serial killer to date, Moses Sithole, was the subject of his Honours dissertation. He now lectures in criminal law at the University of the Witwatersrand and is completing a research Masters in psychology concerning the interface between psychology, psychiatry, and the law on matters of criminal responsibility.

**Gill Haiden** is a lecturer in the School of Human and Community Development, University of the Witwatersrand. Her research interests include the development of gender identity, developmental and gender issues related to HIV/AIDS, and teaching and learning issues.

**Derek Hook** lectures in psychosocial developmental psychology in the School of Human and Community Development at the University of the Witwatersrand, Johannesburg. A co-editor of *Body politics: Power, knowledge and the body in the social sciences* and *Psychopathology and social prejudice*, he maintains a variety of research interests, stretching from the socio-political contexts of development, to the politics of identity and the fledgling field of critical psychology.

**Mambwe Kasese-Hara** is a lecturer in psychology at the University of the Witwatersrand; her main teaching and research interests lie in developmental and health psychology. She holds a PhD from Durham University, and an M Ed in Special Education from Manchester University.

**Catriona Macleod** completed her PhD at the University of Natal, and HDE, Honours and Masters in Educational Psychology at the University of Cape Town. She is currently employed as a senior lecturer in the Psychology Department of Rhodes University, East London. She teaches a large section of the undergraduate course on Developmental Psychology in this department, as well as an Honours course on Child Psychology and a module on interventions with children in the Counselling Psychology Masters programme. Her recent research has focused on feminist approaches to the study of adolescent sexuality and reproduction.

**Dr Lee Senior** is a clinical psychologist who holds a PhD from the University of the Witwatersrand. She has pursued her interest in children's emotional, social, and intellectual development through her work in private practice and within a remedial school environment, and has lectured in the area of personality development.

**Dr Jacki Watts** is a clinical psychologist and a senior lecturer in the School of Human and Community Development at the University of the Witwatersrand. She runs the Clinical Psychology Professional Training programme in the department and also runs a private clinical practice. Her interests are mainly within the arena of psychopathology, relating to its development and to clinical intervention problems.

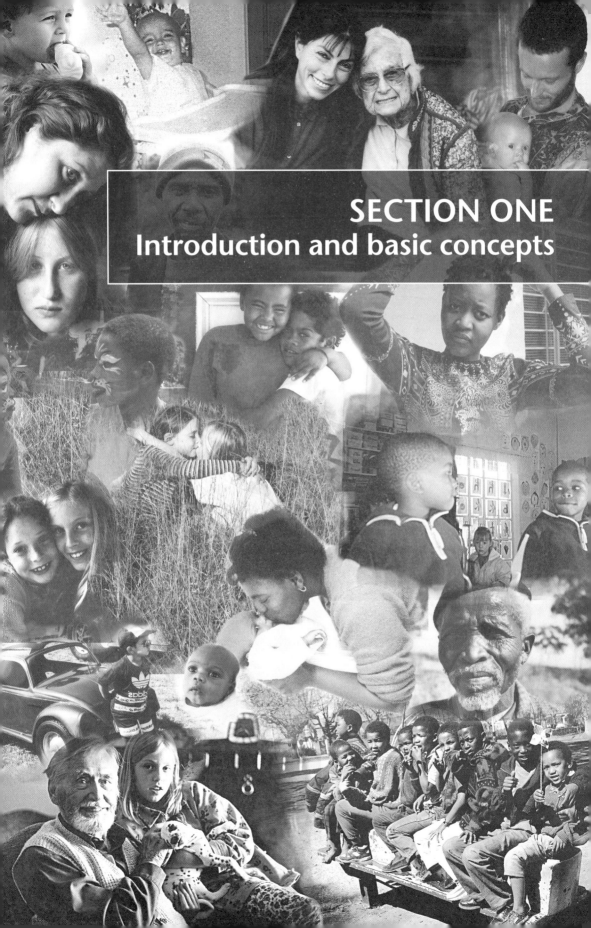

# SECTION ONE
## Introduction and basic concepts

# Psychoanalytic, cognitive, and psychosocial developmental psychology: The 'hows' and 'whys'

*Derek Hook*

---

This chapter introduces the 'hows' and 'whys' of developmental psychology under the following scheme:

1. The importance and power of developmental psychology.

2. The psychoanalytic, cognitive, and psychosocial domains in developmental psychology.

3. The learning approach and objectives in this book:
   ◆ Practical animation, rather than the mere learning or understanding of content.
   ◆ Appreciation of the learning 'tools' of theory, contextual specificity, and criticism.
   ◆ Personalising development theory.
   ◆ Learning outcomes.

---

## Orientation

There are four purposes in this chapter. First, it provides an introduction to developmental psychology. Second, it outlines this book's approach to the subject. Our intention in this is to mix theory, application, and critical thinking in almost equal measures, and so it is worth reflecting briefly on how we might mutually accommodate these diverse learning objectives. Third, this chapter introduces the basic aims and objectives of the book. A summary of learning outcomes provides a valuable set of goals to work toward. Finally, we suggest how this book may be used as a means of *applying* and *practising* rather than merely *reading* developmental psychology.

# Why study developmental psychology?

Developmental psychology is a foundational part of the greater domain of psychology. It enables us to explain a wide variety of psychological changes, both cognitive and social, which occur between birth and death. These various psychological changes are multifarious, and include insights into how children and adults learn, perceive, understand, recall, and process aspects of the world. Additionally, these changes are useful in helping us to explain how persons engage socially with their surrounding contexts, how they form identities, personalities, and even psychopathologies.

In short, developmental psychology is intricately connected to, and contributes to, many other sub-disciplines in psychology. Cognitive developmental psychology informs many theories of learning, memory, language acquisition, and intelligence, for example. Similarly, psychosocial and psychoanalytic developmental psychologies inform theories of personality, interpersonal relations, identity, morality, psychopathology, and social theory more generally.

So, if we want to think practically about educational issues, about how best to teach children, for example, or about clinical interventions, about how best to conceptualise and understand a person's personality, or their apparent psychopathology, developmental theory proves to be a very valuable tool.

## The importance of developmental psychology

Developmental psychology also has its uses beyond the strict confines of psychology itself. As Burman (1994, 2) notes, developmental psychology plays a huge – although not always obvious – role in our day-to-day lives:

> Developmental psychology, more than any other variety of psychology, has a powerful impact on our everyday lives and ways of thinking about ourselves. Its effects are so great that they are often almost imperceptible, taken-for-granted features about our expectations of ourselves, others, parents, children and families.

Developmental psychology is a very important source of institutional knowledge about children across various ages. On what basis, for example, do we decide when preschoolers are actually ready for school; how do we decide when a child should fail a standard, or be put back a year; how do we decide what behaviour is or is not problematic for a certain age? (Of course, developmental psychology is also the instrument for intelligence and various other psychometric assessment tests.) Moreover, it is also something of a lens through which we understand what it means to be a child, an adult, an infant, a mother, etc. In other words, developmental psychology influences both formal, institutional, and less formal, or commonplace, social understandings and values. All of these levels of knowledge are powerful. The former, for example, might influence national or governmental decisions about schooling, or about health policy. The latter influences notions of parenting, how we might understand, care for, communicate with – and even *discipline* – children.

*Developmental psychology has a powerful impact on our everyday lives and our ways of thinking about ourselves; it influences even our most basic conceptions of ourselves, others, parents, children, and families. It is a very important source of institutional knowledge, particularly in education, about children across various ages.*

Developmental psychologists therefore hold a great deal of power and influence, and as such, the old adage is true: 'With great power comes great responsibility'. This book will aim to impress upon its readers not only the overall gravity of developmental psychology's research and theory, but also, and perhaps more important, the imperatives of attaining a broad and critical knowledge base in the area.

### 'Developmental psycholog*ies*': the range of developmental psychology

There are any number of spheres of human development, including those of *physical development*, *cognitive development*, and *psychosocial development*. As Featherman puts it, developmental changes over the lifespan 'arise from a mixture of biological, psychological, social, historical and evolutionary influences and their timing across the lives of individuals' (cited in Craig 1996, 7). These spheres of development are intertwined and are mutually dependent; they intersect and combine in complex ways. They cannot be separated from one another. A child who has hearing loss, for example, may be at risk of delayed language development (Papalia, Olds, and Feldman 1998). Likewise, in puberty, dramatic physiological and hormonal changes affect the developing sense of self, just as in older adults physical changes in the brain may cause intellectual and personality deterioration (Papalia, Olds, and Feldman 1998).

## Three principal domains of development

Some theorists have conceptualised development as occurring within three principal domains: physical, cognitive, and psychosocial. Following Craig (1996), the *physical domain* refers to physical characteristics like size and shape (and height and weight) and changes in brain structure, as well as sensory capacities and motor skills (like walking, talking, and learning to write). The *cognitive domain* involves all mental abilities and activities and even the organisation of thought (including changes in perception, memory, reasoning, creativity, and language). The *psychosocial domain* refers to personality characteristics and social skills – the individual's unique style of behaving and responding emotionally to social circumstances. (This involves interpersonal skills, the self-concept, and various social abilities that might be thought to include certain psychoanalytic conceptualisations of development.)

In this book we specify a fourth principal domain – the *psychoanalytic domain* of development. Our focus will be on the psychoanalytic, the cognitive, and the psychosocial domains and it will hence be useful here to provide more detailed definitions of these three areas.

## Psychoanalytic approaches to development and personality

Psychoanalytic assumptions of personhood, while still of major theoretical importance in the greater field of psychology, appear to have fallen by the wayside in many undergraduate developmental psychology curricula. This is a situation that the authors of this book would like to see rectified. Section Two of this book includes accessible introductions to psychoanalytic theory (and the historical conditions underlying its emergence) and to the concepts and work of the major figures in that field, namely Freud, Klein, Jung, Winnicott, and Lacan.

Psychoanalytic theory, in brief, focuses on the intra-psychic dynamics of individuals. It prioritises the role of the unconscious and the 'nuclear' nature of childhood events as defining the subsequent personality structure of the individual. Understandings of psychopathology – of 'how things can go wrong' in development – are also of central importance to psychoanalytic developmental theory.

## Defining cognitive developmental psychology

An essential part of development concerns how our mental abilities change with maturation and learning. This is called cognitive development. Cognition refers to the act or process of knowing, and cognitive abilities include intelligence, memory, language, perception, attention, and problem solving. The focus of cognitive psychology is not on what is known, but rather on how information is received, organised, and changed. Cognitive development is concerned with how we process information at different stages in our lives. Section Three of the book – on cognitive development – will cover the development of intelligence, language, and memory from infancy to adulthood. These mental abilities will be discussed in the context of the three main theoretical approaches to cognitive development, namely Piagetian, social context, and information processing.

## Defining psychosocial developmental psychology

Psychosocial psychology refers to a person's sense of identity and self, to their sexual, moral, and psychological growth, *within a particular socio-cultural context*. It refers to the way individuals relate to and understand others around them in the interpersonal sphere, to the individual's unique style of behaving and responding to social circumstances. As such it also includes questions of *emotional* development. These are the unique qualities that make us what we are, and that underwrite the nature of the human condition. It is largely on the basis of these developing social interactions and adaptations that we come to possess our own personal values, idiosyncrasies, personalities, and, sometimes, psychological mal-adaptations and problems.

Section Four of this book presents the (by now) classic psychosocial theories of development: attachment theory, Erikson's psychosocial account of development, and conceptions of moral development – as well as more contemporary socio-political theories including those of Bronfenbrenner and theories of gender identity. These latter theories – discussed in Chapters 17 and 18 – represent a significant advance on the earlier psychosocial approaches by engaging more directly with overtly political issues of socio-historical context.

Section Five of the book examines issues of particular pertinence *to the Southern African context*. In Chapter 20 we consider issues of race, cul-ture, and psychological theory. We ask how psychological theories of human development have been influenced by culture and ethnicity and, perhaps more important, we ask how developmental psychology may begin to deal with these issues so as to avoid bias and drawing erroneous conclusions. These are questions that reflect on the capacity for psycho-logy as a social science that is concerned with peoples of various cultural, ethnic, and socio-economic backgrounds, particularly in sub-Saharan Africa. Chapter 21 presents a metatheoretical overview of a variety of central terms, debates, and tensions within contemporary developmental psychology and how they apply to current Southern African socio-polit-ical priorities.

## The approach and objectives of this book

This book has three basic and paramount objectives. The first is to *bring together typically disparate sub-disciplines of psychology* in a single book – hence the inclusion of cognitive, psychosocial, and psychoanalytic sec-tions, each edited by an expert in these respective domains. Treating these sub-disciplines as ostensibly separate subjects leads, in the view of the authors, to an artificially fragmented overview of development – a per-spective that lacks the integrating synthesis necessary to offer novel explanatory links *across* such approaches. While each of these sections is semi-autonomous – allowing lecturers to use any one section without necessary reference to the others – it is our hope that the material be taught in conjunction, so that students may gain a 'holistic' overview of human developmental psychology.

The second objective of the book is to enable readers to *practice* the material they are learning, rather than merely *review* it, or simply *read* it. We hope that the book will *animate* the subject of developmental psy-chology, providing the opportunity for learners to *practice* and *apply* the theory, to try their hands at actually *doing* as opposed to simply *under-*

*standing* what has been said. We have a series of strategies for this objective, which we will discuss presently.

Our third – and perhaps most important – objective is best presented as a goal: *to get students to apply fundamental developmental theories and notions to real-world situations in critical, ethical, and illuminating ways.* This overarching objective emphasises the roles of theory and context, and it is important that we elaborate briefly on each of these.

## The importance of theory

Theories are a foundational aspect of the discipline of developmental psychology. They are *tools* that enable us to organise and make sense of a wide range of developmental information that may otherwise have remained incoherent. Rather than meticulously *record* all the details of development in a specific and isolated environment, and hence offer only reflections *on what has gone before*, within a limited sphere, we want a more adaptable and mobile approach, a more forward-looking orientation that possesses a greater explanatory power *across* certain contexts.

Put differently, we want not only to suggest explanations for certain psychological occurrences in development *that has happened*, we also want a reasonable basis from which we may attempt to predict certain developmental outcomes *still to occur*. Likewise we need explanatory tools that we can apply in a variety of contexts, so that we can *move between different levels of explanation, and different spheres and locations of influence*. For all of these reasons then, this book aims to provide a thorough and detailed explication of a variety of important developmental theories, and to do so both faithfully and critically.

## The importance of context

Although theories of development do give us a certain amount of explanatory power, they are not infallible, and need to be constantly tested, revised, and updated. Theories are only useful to us as long as they accurately and usefully *and ethically* expand our power to explain, predict, and analyse critically. Indeed, should a theory fail in these respects, then it is time to reformulate or adapt the theory, if not to do away with it altogether. Similarly, while one theory may be well designed to explain one aspect of human behaviour, it may need to be complimented with other theories if various aspects of behaviour are to be properly accounted for. By assimilating more than one theory we become able to analyse behaviour from more than one frame of reference; we become able to assess different theories and to see the value of competing explanations. (In this connection, readers will note that several of the book's accompanying practical exercises will require them to consider how different theories of development may be used in conjunction, or, alternatively, in contrasting opposition.)

One should be very careful, therefore, in singing the praises of the *unconditional* application of theory. The wanton application of theory is in fact very dangerous, not only in the sense that it may give us false – or ideologically unsound – representations of what development is, or should be, but also in the sense that such inaccuracies may be profoundly detrimental to those people being studied or ostensibly 'helped' by the application of developmental psychology. For example, the unconditional application of theory can lead to the entrenchment of certain question-able political values, such as occurs in the negative stereotyping of disem-powered or historically disadvantaged groups.

This will be an important ongoing theme across the book – an aware-ness of the effects of irresponsibly reproducing supposedly 'universal' cat-egories across cultures and contexts. (Examples of this would be the imposing of white, masculine, capitalistic, American, or Eurocentric norms in African environments, or male or heterosexual values as the standards for female or homosexual development.) Such an unmediated or unethical use of theory may most certainly serve the social status quo (that is, dominant-power interests), by actively disempowering and mar-ginalising certain sectors of society. This is a tendency that we should, at all times, be highly conscious of and attempt to avoid.

## The specifics of 'here and now'

What we are saying, essentially, is that it is vital for us to develop an eye for specificity, because, quite frankly, not to do so, to implement certain developmental generalisations in *inappropriate* contexts, is to risk damag-ing the very people developmental psychology is supposed to help. What this book suggests, therefore, is that it is vital for us, in our engagements with developmental psychology, to remain acutely aware of the specificity *of the time*, *the place*, *the culture* and *the socio-political environment* of the development we are studying. This is a vitally important goal, and par-ticularly so in the case of a country with the socio-political history of South Africa, where we can never make the assumption that develop-mental contexts have been the same for white and black South Africans. (One need only think of the differentiated developmental facilities, resources, or institutions accessible to different sectors of society in apartheid South Africa.) These differences are important not only within South Africa, but also between South Africa and the various 'first world' locations where so much developmental psychology is produced.

We have to face up to the prospect that development 'here and now', so to speak, may be significantly different from development anywhere or anytime else in the world. The idea here is that social development in South Africa in the years 2001, 2002, 2003, and so on, might be a *distinct* and *unique* sphere of development, which we should be wary of making generalised assumptions about, and which may not best be understood through a simplistic application of generic European- or United States-centred models of development.

A useful tip here is to be as attentive as possible as to how our current location, in post-apartheid South Africa, in the first years of the new mil-lennium, is *different to any other period in history*. We should, in this way, consider how different our current context is to those of other societies and cultures across the world. In other words, we may find it profitable to emphasise how the *familiar*, the *common-place*, the *ordinary* in our day-to-day lives may in fact seem *unfamiliar*, *extraordinary*, *or strange* to some-

PHOTO: CHA JOHNSTON

*The approach of this book suggests that we need to be acutely aware of the specificity of* the time, the place, the culture, *and* the socio-political environment *of the development we are studying.*

one exposed to it for the first time. In this way we may become more attuned to those fine and yet insidious contextual details that may in fact influence social psychological development in profound ways.

## Separating and combining context and theory

One might rightly observe that utilising generalisable theory on the one hand, and developing an appreciation for the specifics of 'here and now' on the other, seem to be conflicting objectives. In many ways they are. However, a little of each, in our view, would seem vital in practising good developmental psychology.

The two approaches can be used in *complimentary* ways. This entails the continual application of *theory to context* and of *context to theory*, allowing each to illuminate the other. The rationale for this is in emphasising how theory may most effectively be used in conjunction with the specifics of context – just as context may most effectively be used in conjunction with the depth of theory.

Alternatively, the two approaches can, and in some ways *should*, be used to oppose, challenge, and critique one another (challenging theoretical explanations on the basis of context, and contextual explanations on the basis of theory). The rationale for this lies in an appreciation of the *limitations of theory used outside of context*, and an appreciation of *the limitations of context used outside of (any) theory*.

Students should be able to utilise both theoretical and contextual levels of explanation in developmental psychology, either separately or in combination. In the latter case, you should be able to use them as complementary approaches that provide different levels of explanation for phenomena, or alternatively, as approaches that critically reveal one another's limitations.

## The value of criticism

No academic discipline can adequately adapt and develop without criticism levelled at itself, both from within and from without. If we are not prepared to rejuvenate and refresh the field in which we are working, then it will atrophy, and lose its general efficacy and explanatory power. The need for a strong critical (and self-critical) tradition is all the more urgent when an ethical imperative is involved, that is, when we are working in a discipline that affects the lives of real people. Learning to formulate criticism of the theories or the practices of developmental psychology is a key objective of this book, which in part may be facilitated through the opposing of theoretical and contextual approaches.

## Applying theory and context

This workbook is designed to be used in conjunction with a series of critical thinking tasks. As we have prioritised the *application* of context and theory, a central case study has been provided in Chapter 3 in which to practice this. The case study presents the developmental history of the South African serial killer Kobus Geldenhuys. It is hoped that this task will help to make theory, along with a feel for contextual specificity, appear practicable, adaptable and performable, rather than letting either of these atrophy by knowing something merely 'within the pages of a book' or within the confines of a very delimited social context.

## Your own development

Our approach in this book is to encourage you to personalise your understanding of development with reference to your own life experiences. For this purpose we have included a project in which you begin your own 'developmental map', or 'developmental diary'. This is a project that should be selectively undertaken – clearly not all developmental theory allows for any easy (or comfortable) application of one's own life details. There is little doubt that not all memories of our own early development are necessarily pleasant. In this sense, this 'developmental diary' project is not meant to lead to a kind of 'self-therapy' or to a confrontation of past events – rather it is meant to help readers assimilate the theoretical material by reflecting on how it may or may not pertain to their own lives.

PHOTO: CHA JOHNSTON

*One learning strategy proposed by this book is focusing on your own development by keeping a developmental journal, in which you map how certain aspects of developmental theory may have pertained to your own life.*

# Conclusion

This chapter has introduced the 'hows' and 'whys' of developmental psychology as it will be presented and hopefully *applied* by the reader in working through the book. The overarching rationale, structure, and contents of the book have been indicated, as well as its pedagogical aims and learning outcomes. We have intimated the basic importance and power of the discipline of developmental psychology, before giving brief definitions of the psychoanalytic, cognitive, and psychosocial domains in developmental psychology. We have examined the importance of theory and contextual specificity as learning tools. The chapter concludes with a series of practical suggestions that will enable you to animate and personalise the material you engage with.

## Learning outcomes

The following list of learning outcomes for this book will help you monitor your progress across the course. After reading this book, you should:

◆ Be able to explain key concepts, debates, and theories in developmental psychology.

◆ Be able to apply developmental theories to explain human behaviour, including your own, in critical, ethical, and insightful ways.

◆ Be able to critically evaluate and compare theories.

◆ Be aware that all theory is contested and contextual.

◆ Understand diversity in human development.

◆ Know the importance and power of developmental psychological explanations in the understanding of human and social behaviour.

◆ Be able to practice and apply developmental psychology – rather than merely reading or understanding it – through the personalisation of developmental explanations or through thorough engagement with detailed case study documents.

◆ Understand the value of developmental theory as a generalisable explanatory tool that may be conditionally applied across contexts.

◆ Know the importance of the socio-political, historical, and cultural context in which development occurs.

◆ Understand the South African developmental context.

◆ Be critically aware of the shortcomings and dangers of the misapplication of developmental theory; that is, understand the general limitations of theory outside of context.

◆ Be aware of the immobility or limitations of contextual-level explanations without the depth and generalising force of theoretical explanation; that is, understand how context may be used in conjunction with theory.

# Critical thinking tasks

## 1) Heightening sensitivity to age

Imagine as clearly and in as much detail as possible one or both of your parents when they were eighteen years old. It might be useful to consult old photographs. Imagine them at that time, just leaving (or having already left) school, deciding on a career, looking for a girlfriend or boyfriend. Imagine the kinds of things they do, their likes and dislikes, their friends, their favoured activities, social and otherwise. Try and get as clear and vivid a sense as possible of that time, its unique history, its social conditions and so on. In what ways do you think your parents at that age would be like you, and in what ways not. How, if at all, does it change your perception of them for you to be older than them? What kind of comparisons can be made between that time and this time, between your parents' living conditions and habits then, and yours now? How do these comparisons sensitise you to historical and social contexts of development?

Now imagine someone with whom you have had conflict, or someone – preferably older – who has treated you unfairly at some time. Imagine them as a toddler, or as an infant. How, if at all, does this change things? How does the power balance implicit in either of these cases change when the people involved are far younger? Now imagine yourself as old, as a grandmother or a grandfather, now retired. You are walking with a stick; it's painful to walk, and it takes you a long time to get where you're going. You feel very reliant on others, even though you wish you didn't. Your hearing and sight are not what they used to be. You see a bunch of university students, second-year psychology students is your guess, going past you, what do you think? What does the eighty-year-old version of yourself think of your current self?

The purpose of these exercises is to try and 'free us up' from being stuck – in how we think about others – and in the age we are now. The purpose here is to remind ourselves of the fact that we were all helpless infants once, that we were all in the womb before that, that all of us were born, that we were all adolescents once, and that the majority of us will, hopefully, be old one day. By the time most of us die we will have had a turn at being a wide variety of ages. Often we seem to work on the irrational assumption that in many ways we have been as we are for a long time, and that we will be as we are today for a very long time. That's not really true; we are aging and changing all the time. Our age and our age-related experience continually impact upon how we think about the world and ourselves. Our ages inform our identities in very fundamental ways. The overall purpose of this set of exercises is to heighten our sensitivity to age, to illustrate how we stereotype certain age categories in certain ways, and to suggest how age works as a central factor in power relations.

## 2) Starting your own developmental journal

Try and collect a series of photographs of yourself at different ages. Start a scrapbook, label it your 'developmental journal' and stick these photographs (or copies of them) into the book in a chronological order. Try and write brief personal descriptions of what you felt it was like to be certain ages. You might want to involve distinctive memories, or events related to you by your parents. This 'journal' will prove useful in allowing you to illustrate with your own life experiences the developmental theories that we are going to examine.

## 3) Reflecting on benefits and limitations

Reflect briefly on the benefits and limitations of both exclusively theoretical and contextually-specific approaches to developmental psychology.

# 2

# Basic concepts and principles in developmental psychology

*Derek Hook and Kate Cockcroft*

---

This chapter presents certain fundamental concepts in the study of human development. It also covers the following debates and controversies in the theory of developmental psychology:

1. Stability versus change.

2. Life-span perspective.

3. Nature versus nurture.

4. Continuity versus discontinuity.

5. Ontogeny and phylogeny.

6. Critical periods.

7. Non-normative and normative influences.

---

## Introduction

This chapter provides a grounding in certain of the important ideas and debates in contemporary developmental psychology. It provides a basic conceptual vocabulary for human development and it enables the reader to relate different theories to one another. We examine a series of theoretical tensions, debates, and concepts within the field before asking two critical questions: does theory follow development or does development follow theory, and is psychological development a political phenomenon?

# Debates within developmental psychology

## Stability versus change

Earlier psychological theory supposed that personality was fundamentally shaped during the early childhood years and remained, in relative terms, the same thereafter. The modern approach in developmental psychology differs from this (largely Freudian) view that the first five years of childhood influence people permanently. According to the modern view children are not passive recipients of environmental influences, but are active themselves in influencing and moderating these environmental factors. As Louw, Louw, and Schoeman (1995, 491) emphasise, '[t]his does not mean that there is no underlying continuity regarding certain characteristics such as basic temperament, but rather that children do not have to be passive reflections of their environment'. This debate has lost much of its importance since the advent and dominance of the **life-span perspective**.

**Life-span perspective.** An approach to human development which examines changes at all ages, through adolescence and adulthood, to late adulthood, up until death.

## The life-span perspective

The life-span perspective is one of the basic approaches of current developmental psychology. Whereas many earlier approaches strongly prioritised the first six years of life as a blueprint that would determine the pattern and course of an individual's life thereafter, most contemporary approaches in developmental psychology – including the life-span perspective – examine the entire life-span from birth right up to death. Researchers look at the ways in which changes can and do occur at all ages, through adolescence and adulthood, to late adulthood, up until death. Development is not something that only happens to children. As Sears and Feldman (cited in Santrock 1999, 8) suggest:

> The next five or six decades [after childhood] are every bit as important, not only to those adults who are passing through them but to their children, who must live with and understand parents and grandparents. The changes in body, personality, and abilities through these later decades are great. Developmental tasks are imposed by marriage and parenthood, by the waxing and waning of physical prowess, and of some intellectual capacities, by the children's flight from the nest, by the achievement of an occupational plateau, and by retirement and the prospect of final extinction. Parents have always been fascinated by their children's development, but it is high time adults began to look objectively at themselves, to examine the systematic changes in their own physical, mental and emotional qualities, as they pass through the life-span, and to get acquainted with the limitations and assets they share with so many others of their age.

### The advantages of the life-span perspective

If we study development with the object of facilitating health and avoiding problems, then clearly the study of aging must be just as important as the study of growth. Indeed, aging is often accompanied by problems of loneliness, bereavement, depression, and by a lack of social networks,

PHOTOS: CHA JOHNSTON

*The life-span perspective examines developmental psychology across the entire life-span from birth to death. It means that researchers look at the way changes can and do occur at all ages, through adolescence and adulthood, to late adulthood and old age, up until death.*

supports, and relationships. Each of these problems represents a valid focus for developmental psychology.

A further important feature of the life-span approach is that it recognises the importance of social setting and historical situation (Gormly 1997). In addition, rather than believing that behaviour is fixed and unchanging after childhood, the life-span perspective considers that helpful changes and benefits can be implemented at any developmental stage. In this respect it is a useful complement to clinical psychology through its assertion that one can intervene and facilitate beneficial change within individuals *at any age*.

## Characterising the life-span approach

According to Baltes (cited in Santrock 1999, 10), the life-span perspective has seven basic characteristics. These are explained as follows.

- ◆ *Development is lifelong:* development occurs across the full life-span of the individual, including both growth and aging, gains and losses, all of which interact in dynamic ways.
- ◆ *Development is multidimensional:* biological, socio-emotional, and cognitive aspects overlap within development; for example, intelligence contains many overlapping components such as abstract, spatial, social, and nonverbal intelligence.

# The riddle of the ship of Theseus

Theseus was the captain of an old ship that he loved dearly, and that he had sailed for many years. His ship was dilapidated though, and badly in need of repair. Unfortunately however, Theseus did not have much money. What he opted to do was slowly repair the broken parts of the vessel, when he had the money. His friends often asked him if he dreamed of a new ship as complete and sturdy as his own ship was flimsy and in need of repair. Theseus always laughed at this, saying that he would never want a new vessel, because he very much loved his own ship, and felt very loyal to it. Nevertheless, he made repairs when he could afford to do so. First he bought new sails. Then he pulled down the old wooden mast and replaced it with a fibreglass substitute. He ran short of money for a while, and could not make many more changes.

A few months later, however, he inherited a substantial amount of money, and was able to replace many of the broken parts of the ship. The first thing to go was the old rudder and the old anchor; they were replaced with newer and far more sophisticated pieces of equipment. He changed the wooden floor of the vessel for a stronger lighter substance. In time he even lengthened the boat, and exchanged the sails for a rudimentary engine.

Eventually the ship looked totally different to the vessel he had begun with – in almost every way. His friends would joke with him, teasing him that he now had a new ship after all. Theseus was always dismissive of these jokes, saying that despite many changes it was still his original boat, in all the ways it counted most. Several years later it came to pass *that every original element of his boat had been replaced* – not one tiny part of the original vessel remained. One of Theseus's friends brought this to his attention, and again asked him: 'Do you still believe that is your original ship?' Theseus could not answer him.

What would your answer be? Is this still the original ship, or is it a totally different vessel? Reflect on how this story might be an effective analogy for personal development across the life-span. To what extent do our bodies, our identities, our personal psychologies change over the life-span? Do we remain the same person before and after birth, before and after puberty, after the birth of a child, after the death of a parent? How much do we change across our life-span?

♦ *Development is multidirectional:* some dimensions of development may increase or grow while others decrease. Wisdom, for example, may increase while mental agility may decline.

♦ *Development is plastic:* depending on an individual's life conditions, development may take many paths and there is often potential for change. For example, the reasoning abilities of older adults may be improved through training.

♦ *Development is embedded in history:* historical conditions are very important. For example, the career orientation of many thirty-year-old females today is very different to those of women forty years ago; similarly the career orientation of many black South Africans today is certainly different to those of black South Africans forty years ago.

♦ *Development is multidisciplinary:* sociologists, psychologists, linguists, anthropologists, medical researchers, and neuro-scientists all study human development from different perspectives.

◆ *Development is contextual:* individuals continually respond to and act on various contexts which in turn influence them. As stated by Baltes, 'individuals are changing beings in a changing world' (cited in Santrock 1999, 10).

## Nature versus nurture

**Heredity.** Those inborn characteristics which we inherit through our genes from our parents.

**Nativism.** The viewpoint that our characteristics and abilities are chiefly determined by our inborn characteristics (often also referred to as genetic determinism). This represents the nature side of the nature-nurture debate.

**Genetic determinism.** See nativism.

**Environmental determinism.** The view that environmental factors exert the greatest influence on human development. This represents the nurture side of the nature-nurture debate.

The question of nature versus nurture is an ongoing debate within developmental psychology. The viewpoint of 'nature' – that our characteristics and abilities are chiefly determined by **heredity** (inborn characteristics) – is often referred to as **nativism** or **genetic determinism**. On the other hand, the view of 'nurture' – that environmental factors are predominant in development – is known as **environmental determinism** (Louw *et al.* 1995).

Although this debate has raged for centuries, the majority of contemporary developmental psychologists have come to accept the fact that the interaction between heredity and environmental influences is so complex that it is senseless to regard one of the two as more important (Louw *et al.* 1995). Indeed, given this complexity, one often gets the feeling that behind every genetic (or nature) explanation one should look for the influences of environment (nurture), and behind every environmental explanation one should look for the influences of nature. In this regard, to paraphrase Gormly and Brodzinsky (in Louw *et al.* 1995, 490), the critical question in development these days is not which factor – heredity or environment – is responsible for behaviour, but how these two factors interact so as to propel us along our developmental paths.

There is no doubt that the separate roles of these two factors blur all too quickly in practice. As Papalia, Olds, and Feldman (1998) note, people change their world even as it changes them: a baby girl born with a cheerful disposition, for example, is likely to get positive reactions from adults, which strengthens her trust that her smiles will be rewarded and motivate her to smile more. Likewise, despite the fact that there is growing evidence that language acquisition is an innate capacity exhibited by children, the role of nurture, or the lack of nurture, as in the case of the Wild Boy of Avyron, can effectively extinguish these abilities. (The 'Wild Boy of Avyron' was discovered at the age of twelve in a forest in France by hunters. Despite five years of intensive teaching, his educator, ontologist Jean Itard, never succeeded in teaching the boy more than just a few simple words.)

### The complexity of nature/nurture interactions

To accept the complexity of nature/nurture interactions is to accept that their effect on the individual will differ from person to person and as such there can be no fixed formula for predicting the effect of heredity or environment upon a specific person (Louw *et al.* 1995). This does not mean, however, that both factors can be assumed to play *an equal role* in all stages of development. According to Gormly (1997), certain behaviours, such as walking, can best be explained by the process of maturation that is guided by our genetic blueprint. Likewise the universal first actions of a newborn baby, gasping to fill its lungs and then crying to announce its arrival, may be seen as predominantly instinctive (Craig 1996). As Morris and Maisto (1998, 392) note:

> Research has disproved the old idea that **neonates**, or new born babies, do nothing but eat, sleep, and cry, while remaining oblivious to the world ... newborns come equipped with a number of useful reflexes ... such as those that control breathing ... Some enable babies to nurse. The rooting reflex causes them to turn the head toward the touch of a nipple on the cheek and grope around with the mouth ... the swallowing reflex enables them to swallow milk and other liquids without choking ... The grasping reflex causes newborns to cling vigorously to an adult's finger or to any other object placed in their hands. The stepping reflex causes very young babies to take what looks like walking steps if they are held upright with their feet just touching a flat surface.

*Is the ability to mimic expressions an innate instinctual capacity in infants? Much current research would suggest that it is.*

Many of these reflexes seem fairly instinctual, but there are other, surprisingly complex, kinds of behaviours that appear to be universal for babies and that seem to go beyond the categories of the reflexive or the purely instinctual:

> babies are ... capable of ... imitating the facial expressions of adults. If an adult opens his or her mouth or sticks out his or her tongue, newborn babies often respond by opening their mouths or by sticking out their tongues ... When this ability to imitate was first noted in newborns, psychologists could hardly believe it. How could babies carry out such complex responses at an age when they have no idea how their own face looks, much less how to make specific facial expressions? (Morris and Maisto 1998, 392).

In addition to these 'preprogrammed' universal tendencies observed in babies, recent evidence also suggests that they are active in the womb, sucking their thumbs, swinging from their umbilical cords, and squeezing and releasing these to moderate their oxygen flow. These findings suggest that environmental factors may occur even in prenatal periods.

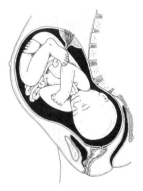

## Continuity versus discontinuity

Does developmental growth follow a slow, cumulative, and gradual pattern (as, for example, a huge tree develops from a tiny seedling), or does growth rather take place in clearly differentiated stages, (as a larva transforms into a moth) (Louw *et al.* 1995)? Psychological theories differ on this issue. Some see development as a slow and even process during which experiences gradually accumulate to make changes possible; others regard development as a series of genetically predetermined stages or steps in which each stage differs qualitatively from the previous one (Louw *et al.* 1995). Consequently, development may be understood as either predominantly continuous or discontinuous.

A second aspect of the continuity-discontinuity debate concerns the nature of developmental changes: are they qualitative or quantitative?

**Figure 2.1** Children act on their environments virtually from conception. In scans, foetuses have been seen swinging from their umbilical cords, performing somersaults and sucking their thumbs.

**Neonate.** A baby in the first month of life.

# If I were in the womb, what would it be like?

If you or I were in the womb what would it be like? Well, it would be like being in the middle of someone else's body. Their heart, which is bigger than you, would be thundering away. Around you would be metres and metres of arteries and veins filled with some else's blood. How would you get any peace, when above you, two cavernous lungs worked day and night? Worse still, right next to you would be the biggest distraction of all ... [the stomach]. Three meals a day and who knows how many ice-cream and gherkin sandwiches have got to go somewhere. And to top it all, you would be growing all the time ... (Dale, De'ath, Evans, Thompson, Georgi, and Spencer 1998).

In other words, the world inside the womb is anything but simple, serene, silent, and devoid of stimulus.

The real world inside the womb is dynamic and bustling ... Instead of lying quietly ... [the fetus] is having a go at a kick, or even a somersault. It gulps, and swallows up to half a cup of amniotic fluid every day. From quite early on it sucks its thumb, a habit which may take years to break .... (Dale *et al.* 1998).

This is part of what we know of the foetus around the time of mid-pregnancy.

But what does it know? By this time it has begun to develop the basics of all five senses, although at this point they are totally blurred:

Instead of having separate senses ... [it seems] ... that a fetus's senses are much less distinct. Sounds, for instance, may be 'felt' through the skin, as well as heard by the ears. Likewise, changes in the fluid which surrounds the fetus will be as much smelled as tasted. Sounds from the outside world will be filtered through the mother's body. So although no doubt a fetus will be familiar with the sound of its mother's voice, this voice will sound, relative to our own ears [somewhat] ... distorted (Dale *et al.* 1998).

It is for these reasons that infants are said to have some familiarity with their mother's voice, even before they are born. Similarly, it is for these reasons that rhythmic sounds, such as a vacuum cleaner or music, often prove soothing to newborns after birth – even if they are fairly loud – because they remind the child of the womb. Indeed, in the womb, the volume of noise around the fetus is able to reach the formidable level of ninety-five decibels with each beat of the mother's heart.

**Source:** *The Human Body*, BBC Films in association with the Learning Channel (Dir. Dale, De'ath, Evans, Thompson, Georgi, and Spencer 1998).

---

**Quantitative changes.** Changes in degree or amount, for example, changes in height or weight.

**Qualitative changes.** Changes in kind, structure or organisation, which make a fundamental difference to the individual. For example, the preverbal infant is qualitatively different to the toddler who can speak.

**Quantitative** changes are changes in degree or amount. For example, children's memories improve gradually with each passing year, particularly as they acquire increasing knowledge about the world which provides contexts for remembering past events or information. On the other hand, **qualitative** changes are changes in kind, structure or organisation, which make a fundamental difference to the individual. For example, the young prelinguistic infant is qualitatively different to the preschooler who can speak well, and the sexually mature adolescent is fundamentally different from a peer who has not yet reached puberty (Shaffer 1996). Continuity theorists tend to regard developmental changes as gradual and quantitative, whereas discontinuity theorists regard these changes as more distinctive and qualitative (Shaffer 1996).

Discontinuity theorists propose the existence of different developmental stages, each stage characterising a fundamentally different phase of life, and each stage having a unique set of skills, abilities, emotions, and behaviours.

## Ontogeny and phylogeny

An important aspect of developmental psychology is that it applies both to the individual development of the specific child or person as well as to the developmental norm for a wider group of people. This distinction between individual development (**ontogeny**) and group or 'species' development (**phylogeny**) is often a controversial one. Developmental norms refer to the average ages of certain phenomena – the first word, the age at which children begin to walk, etc. It is important to emphasise, however, that these are merely averages and not absolutes. As Papalia and Olds (1998, 6) note:

> Although people typically proceed through the same general sequence of development, there is a wide range of individual differences. Only when deviation from a norm is extreme is there cause to consider a person's development exceptionally advanced or delayed.

Because people differ so widely in height, weight, and build, in constitutional factors such as health and energy level, and in emotional reactions, there can be great deviance from norms across individual levels of comparison. It is important to note here that individual differences also increase as people grow older. Whereas many changes in childhood seem tied to maturation of the body and brain (the unfolding of a definite sequence of physical changes and behaviour patterns), later life changes are more contingent on life experiences (Papalia and Olds 1998).

**Ontogeny.** Application of developmental psychology to the understanding of the individual development of the specific child or person.

**Phylogeny.** Application of developmental psychology to the understanding of a wider group of people, or 'species' development.

**Critical period.** A specific time during development when a given event has its greatest effect.

## Critical periods

Another important concept in developmental psychology is that of **critical periods**. A critical period is a specific time during development when a given event has its greatest impact. Lenneberg, for example, proposed a critical period – before puberty – for language development. As another example, some ethologists believe that the first three years of life are the critical period for the development of emotional and social responsiveness in humans (Papalia and Olds 1998). The concept of the critical period expresses the crucial nature of timing, and specifies a time-span when – and only when – a particular environmental factor can have an effect (Craig 1996).

For example, if a pregnant woman who lacks immunity for rubella is exposed to the virus 2 months after conception, severe birth defects such

PHOTO: KATE COCKCROFT

*While two children may be the same chronological age, their 'readiness' for various aspects of development can differ considerably.*

as deafness, or even … miscarriage … may result. If however, that same woman is exposed 6 months after conception, the virus will not affect her developing baby (Craig 1996, 10).

The application of the idea of critical periods to developmental psychology is a controversial one, however. Although evidence for critical periods of physical development is undeniable (especially in the case of foetal development), for other aspects of human development the concept seems less relevant. Indeed, while the human organism may be particularly sensitive to certain psychological experiences at certain times of life, later events can often reverse the effects of early ones (Papalia and Olds 1998). What may be more important is the concept of **readiness**, or the point at which an individual can be said to have matured sufficiently to be capable of a particular behaviour (Craig 1996). For example, some eleven-year-old children are obviously in the concrete operational stage as evidenced by their thinking, while other children of the same age may have matured cognitively to a point where they are 'ready' to understand and use the qualities of thinking that define the formal operational stage.

**Readiness.** The point at which an individual can be said to have matured sufficiently to benefit from a particular learning experience.

**Normative.** An event is normative when it occurs in a similar manner for most people in a given group, for example, physical changes such as puberty or menopause.

**Non-normative.** These are unusual events that have a significant impact on an individual's life.

**Cohort.** A group of people born during the same historical period.

## Normative and non-normative influences

The last in this series of important concepts for developmental psychology are **normative** and **non-normative** influences.

An event is normative when it occurs in a similar way for most people in a given group. Normative age-graded influences are highly similar for people in a particular age group. They include biological events (like puberty and menopause) as well as cultural events (such as entry into formal education and retirement from paid employment). Normative history-graded influences are common to a particular **cohort**, which is a group of people who share a similar experience, in this case, growing up at the same time. Non-normative life events are unusual events that have a

*Normative history-graded influences are common to a particular cohort, that is, to a group of people who share a similar experience – in this case, growing up at the same time.*

PHOTO: CHA JOHNSTON

major impact on individual lives. They are either typical events that happen to a person at an atypical time of life (such as the death of a parent when a child is young) or atypical events (such as being in an airplane crash or having a birth defect) (Papalia and Olds 1998, 7).

# Does development follow theory, or does theory follow development?

The assumption in much developmental psychology is that one is studying, in a naturalistic fashion, what one observes 'out there' in the developmental world of children and adults. The idea is that the developmental theories and explanations that we formulate follow observed development. This is an assumption that we need to be particularly critical of, since there is always the possibility *that our given preconceptions influence how we observe the world*.

Take for example the idea of perceived gender differences in the development of little boys and girls. Erikson 'observed' a variety of differences in the apparently gendered behaviour of boys and girls. He claimed that boys, left to play in a sandpit, were prone to build towering, phallic-like structures. Girls, by contrast, would build hollow, enclosing, womb-like structures (Erikson 1963). Erikson is clearly showing his psychoanalytic loyalties here. One cannot help wondering whether his dedication to certain of these psychoanalytic ideas is affecting how he observes the world, not only in terms of how he understands *what* children are building, but also in terms of how he perceives gendered difference between what boys and girls do. Therefore we must ask: Is Erikson correctly observing a gender difference, or is he already, on the basis of prior assumptions, perceiving little boys and little girls differently?

This presents a philosophical problem: at what point are we truly observing what is out there (as a way of building explanations and theories), and at what point are we already drawing implicitly on preconceived explanations and theories (in our act of perception)? The implication here is that we need *always* to be aware of how our prior conceptions influence our perceptions of the world. This is the reservation we need to keep in mind: *maybe rather than producing knowledge we are merely reproducing certain ideological viewpoints*. This is particularly important in developmental psychology, where, as previously mentioned, the knowledge of psychologists has a very real and concrete bearing on the lives of people. If we reproduce various forms of prejudice or discrimination in the scientific knowledge we are producing, then clearly we are participating in forms of social injustice, in an inequitable 'science' that selectively disempowers certain members of society.

## Is development a political phenomenon?

The speculation above leads logically to, and also helps to answer, the question of whether development is a political phenomenon. The point

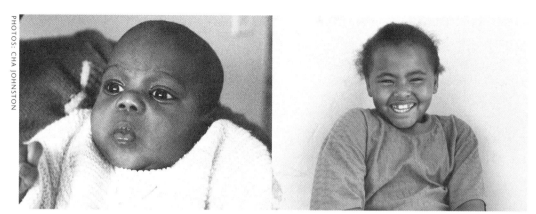

*What is normal behaviour for a five-month-old child? How should one raise a little girl as opposed to a little boy, and why?*

of the discussion above is that certain political notions (political in the sense of power relations) permeate even our most basic understandings of the 'natural' world. Political discourse is an active part and even forms the basis of what we think is natural. How we understand gendered norms of development, as in the example from Erikson, has an important bearing on what we think is appropriate behaviour for men and for women. But what is 'natural' or 'appropriate' behaviour for women? How do we use such notions, what do they mean, and what sector of society do they selectively empower or disempower? What is normal behaviour for a five-month-old child? How should one raise a little girl as opposed to a little boy, and why? These are some of the many important and critical questions to be aware of – how, and in what ways, may the knowledge we produce in developmental psychology serve certain political functions, and how may it implicitly be motivated by political considerations?

## Considering the contexts within which development occurs

The contextual approach holds that development must be understood in terms of the total setting or context in which it occurs. Behaviour cannot be understood outside of contexts. The individual cannot be understood in isolation from her or his environment, and development must be seen as a dynamic and changing process in which the individual and the environment continuously interact (Gormly 1997).

### Implications of the cultural context for developmental psychology

Culture presents a particularly broad but incisive context for development. As defined by Santrock (1999, 13), culture entails 'the behaviour patterns, beliefs and all other products of a particular group of people that are passed on from generation to generation'. The following example from Papalia, Olds, and Feldman (1998, 9) gives a specific illustration of this:

# Contexts for development

Contexts for development may be understood as follows:

◆ *biological context:* health and physical status,

◆ *social context:* family network, friends, peers, and colleagues,

◆ *cultural context:* the dominant culture in which the subject grows up,

◆ *historical context:* the times in which the subject grows up,

◆ *economic context:* the subject's financial and work environment, and

◆ *intellectual context:* the subject's ability to deal with new challenges (Gormly 1997).

When adults in the Kpelle tribe in central Liberia were asked to sort 20 objects, they consistently sorted on the basis of functional categories ... Western psychologists associate functional sorting with low levels of thought; but since the Kpelle kept saying that this was how a 'wise man' would do it, the experimenter finally asked, 'How would a fool do it?' He then received the 'higher-order' categories he had expected – four neat piles with food in one, tools in another and so on.

The lesson here is that we must be cautious about adopting or believing in universals when studying development; what is normal or natural for one cultural group is quite extraordinary for another. Therefore it is important to consider cultural differences when assessing the development of an individual child or adult. In this regard, cross-cultural studies are valuable in comparing the norms of one cultural group with those of another. They help us to determine which kinds of development are similar across cultures, which are universal, and which are neither, but are culture-specific.

Of these two examples from Papalia, Olds, and Feldman (1998, 9), the first presents an apparent cultural universal, and the second illustrates a cross-cultural comparison:

> ... no matter where children live, they learn to speak in the same sequence, advancing from cooing and babbling to single words and then to simple combinations of words. The sentences of toddlers around the world are structured similarly, though the words might vary. Such findings suggest that the capacity for learning language is inborn. On the other hand, culture can exert a surprisingly large influence on early motor development. African babies, whose parents often prop them in a sitting position and bounce them on their feet, tend to sit and walk earlier than American babies ...

## Ethnicity and gender as aspects of the cultural context for development

Santrock (1999) emphasises ethnicity and gender as two important dimensions of culture that exercise a powerful effect on the development of individuals.

# Did you know? Some interesting facts about early child development

◆ The human baby at birth is less matured than any other species. In the first few months after birth the human newborn seems woefully inept; other animals get up and walk within seconds of being born, but the human infant can barely control its own twitching limbs.

◆ Babies have certain instinctual skills that adults have lost. For example, all babies can swim from the moment they are born – they instinctively kick to propel themselves forward in water. Water flows through their gaping mouths into their stomachs where their lungs shut off automatically, protecting them from drowning. No one is exactly sure why babies have this skill; it may be an offshoot from their time in the womb, or an 'evolutionary echo' from our distant amphibious past.

◆ Babies have already had a certain amount of kinaesthetic experience in the womb; it is here where they first start learning to move about.

◆ Even above the constant 'roar' of the mother's heartbeat, the *in-utero* child hears, and reacts to, its mother's voice. At this early stage there is even some rudimentary interaction between mother and child. This interaction between the baby and its surroundings fuels the baby's own development. Although babies are not simply 'pre-wired' to become human, they are in a sense 'programmed' to seek out the experiences that will transform them.

◆ Babies trigger their own birth. Once the baby is ready to survive in the outside world, it releases a hormone into its mother's bloodstream and the resulting muscular spasms lead to the birth process. Birth is even more traumatic for the baby than it is for the mother. The child's adrenalin levels are twice that of hers, even higher than that of an adult experiencing a heart attack.

◆ In the first few minutes after birth, the newborn infant's senses are bombarded with new sights, sounds, and feelings. Within the first few hours after birth infants can mimic certain facial expressions; this is not conscious mimicry, but babies are able to translate what they see into similar actions on their own part. Imitation is one of the best learning strategies babies have.

◆ The brain of the newborn human child is less organised at birth than the brains of virtually every other species. This sounds like a handicap, but in fact it is a great advantage. Because human babies' brains are flexible, essential connections between cells can develop as a result of a baby's experience and so facilitate the process of learning.

◆ Although newborn infants are physically helpless, they are equipped with an 'inbuilt' skill to control others: their (generally) cute appearance and behaviour and, importantly, their crying help ensure that they soon become the centre of family life. Crying is, in fact, the key to the survival of infants; it triggers a physiological response that their mothers find near impossible to ignore, and which (among other factors) stimulates their mothers' breasts to produce milk. Crying is more than a 'meal-ticket' for babies; they cannot experience the world by themselves as yet, and for now others must 'bring the world' to them. Crying, then, is also the key to early learning.

(continued)

◆ At three weeks, a baby's most active muscles are those that control its eyes. Vision, however, is still less than perfect; the baby can pick up only the strongest of contrasts, and can make out only objects that are less than a metre away. Because the baby has not yet combined the bifocal images of its two retinas, at first it sees everything in double. Its eyes are drawn to moving objects; this sensitivity to movement draws the baby to look at those things which best stimulate the developing visual areas of the brain. This rudimentary vision is ideally designed to study moving, high-contrast human faces. In the first two months, babies are 'programmed' to search out and stare at the human, because it is from people that they learn the most.

◆ Just as babies' eyes are 'programmed' to seek out human faces, so their ears are drawn to the sound of voices. Infants are so attuned to human speech that they are able to recognise their mothers' voices within the first week after birth. In this way it is not unusual that comfort for infants often comes in the form of a mother's soothing voice.

◆ Within weeks of birth, babies are said to be able to tell the difference between one language and another (their brains register familiar streams of words). Babies are able to pick out the patterns and intonations that make their own language different from others. Moreover, at eight weeks, infants are said to prefer the sound of their native tongue to other languages.

**Source:** *Baby It's You*, Channel 4 Television Films (Dir. Klein and Hickman 1994).

He defines ethnicity as 'based on cultural heritage, nationality characteristics, race, religion and language'. These qualities are important to bear in mind in understanding development, although, as he warns, their influence is more useful in fixing a heterogeneous, rather than a stereotypical, conception of a group.

He defines gender as 'the socio-cultural dimension of being female or male' (1999, 14) and goes on to warn that few aspects of our development are more central to our identity and social relationships than is gender. (For a more detailed discussion of gender identity, see Chapter 18 on gender identity formation.)

# Conclusion

This chapter has provided a brief overview of important concepts and tensions in the study of developmental psychology. These basic concepts and debates are certainly worth reflecting on, both on a personal level, and as a critical lens through which developmental theory can be analysed and applied. This chapter has maintained a largely metatheoretical focus in order to survey key debates in the field of developmental psychology. Our object in this has been to extend the reader's conceptual vocabulary in this field, and to provide a basis with which to engage, compare, and relate within context the various theories of development presented in the chapters that follow.

# Critical thinking tasks

1) With reference to one of the theorists discussed in this book, explain how the cultural perspective of that theorist and of the people he or she studied could have affected the theory that was subsequently developed.

2) Choose one of the theorists discussed in this book, and describe that theorist's particular standpoint with regard to the major debates in developmental psychology (that is, stability versus change; nature versus nurture; continuity versus discontinuity; ontogeny and phylogeny; critical periods; and non-normative and normative influences).

3) If you have opted to keep a 'developmental journal' as suggested at the end of Chapter 1, try and provide illustrations in your journal of certain of the key concepts described above, such as critical periods, normative versus non-normative developmental influences, or natural versus nurtural factors of development.

# Case study: The developmental history of Kobus Geldenhuys, the 'Norwood killer'

*Derek Hook*

This chapter presents a detailed case study of the developmental details of the infamous Norwood serial killer Kobus Geldenhuys. It thus provides a real-life, context-based, South African application for the more theoretical chapters to follow. In doing this it will also serve to highlight a number of broader developmental influences in the South African context. The case study considers the following aspects:

1. Geldenhuys's family dynamics.

2. Questions of attitudes towards women and sexuality.

3. Resentment and punishment within the family.

4. Social isolation and loneliness.

5. Exposure to violence.

6. Personal and familial conflict.

7. Rape and its relationship to issues of power.

8. The details of Geldenhuys's crimes.

The chapter ends with a series of critical thinking questions designed to help learners consider the multidimensionality of developmental psychological influences, as well as the broader applicability of several of the above themes to the South African context.

# Introduction

This case study has been assembled from a variety of different sources. The prime data source has been an unpublished criminological investigation conducted by Irma Labuschagne (2000), a data source complemented by a talk given by her in 1999 (Labuschagne, personal communication 1999). Other sources include news and print media (Lazarus 1993a; 1993b), and a documentary film entitled *Criminal Minds* (Dir. Morris 2000). South African serial killer 'profiler' Micki Pistorius has also proved an important source of information on Geldenhuys, both in interview (Pistorius, personal communication 2000a) and in her publications (Pistorius 1999; 2000b).

Kobus Geldenhuys, the notorious Norwood serial killer.

Irma Labuschagne, the consulting criminologist on the Geldenhuys case.

# Critical and ethical research concerns

While it is true that researchers of any sort should remain critical of even their basic 'raw material' data – and readers should be critical even of the current case study – there is much about the following case study to recommend it as a powerful vehicle through which to apply developmental theory, so much so that Labuschagne (in Morris 2000) recommends it as a learning tool.

A final introductory remark concerns the ethics of making published use of case study details. It is imperative that developmental psychology researchers always respect the confidentiality and privacy of their subjects' clinical material. The information that follows presents rather a special case, however, because most of it has already been presented not just in public forums, but also in a mass media context. (See Lazarus 1993a; 1993b and Morris 2000).

Furthermore, all the details of Labuschagne's criminological evaluation have been heard in open court, and therefore already belong to the public domain.

# The case study

## Geldenhuys's family dynamics

Kobus Geldenhuys grew up in a disciplined and God-fearing household. The only son of a strict, controlling mother and an introverted, subservient father, he was raised in an environment where frequent physical punishment appeared to be the norm. His family background appeared, for the most part, to be structurally normal, although there were some signs of dysfunction. Geldenhuys's parents had, at the time of his conviction, been married almost thirty years. His father had worked as a meter-reader for the City Council of Benoni, and his mother had worked as a cook at the Service Centre for the Aged.

There was little doubt that Geldenhuys's mother was the dominant figure in the family; her husband took a more soft-natured and reserved role in their son's upbringing. It seems that Geldenhuys was a largely normal toddler. However, an interview with a family friend revealed a problem that appears to have arisen in Geldenhuys's childhood: when he was two years old, his mother believed that 'little men' had told her she must kill the child (Labuschagne 2000). Mrs Geldenhuys had apparently claimed that at one stage she had believed that Satan was attacking her and she had visited her clergyman to drive him out (Labuschagne 2000). Although there are conflicting reports, it seems that the mother experienced similar paranoid delusions again after her son's arrest.

## An undemonstrative family environment

On the whole, the marriage and the parents' relationship with their son appeared to be relatively happy, despite seeming to be emotionally undemonstrative. In this regard Geldenhuys said the following:

> My mother would ... [infrequently] show ... [me] her love. Now and then ... my father would kiss her. My father would not say that he loved me. My father is a quiet person. Since my primary school days my mother was very strict and I cannot remember her saying that she loved me, but if I was ill, then ... [she took care of me] ... and I could see she loved me. Since my high school days, my mother ... would ... wrestle with me. This may have been the manner in which we showed love. She also liked to show me to people that I did not know. I did not like that. On a day after I had left school, I asked her if she would still show me off to people when I was 52 years old. And she said to me yes (Labuschagne 2000, 2).

It seems thus that Geldenhuys grew up in an unaffectionate environment, believing that he could not really speak to his parents about his problems. There was, as is suggested above, no doubt that the religious Mrs Geldenhuys was the head of the family. She insisted that the family attend church without exception every Sunday. She served as a Sunday school teacher for several years.

## Attitudes towards sex and women

As Geldenhuys got older his mother warned him that women were evil and sinful, and that he should stay away from them wherever possible. She also told him that any kind of sexual activity, including masturbation, was wrong and punishable, and that God 'was always watching him'. She demanded that he only bath and use the toilet with the door open so that she could watch him, and be sure that he did not masturbate. As a result of various parental restrictions, Geldenhuys enjoyed little, if any, personal privacy in his upbringing, and his social life was largely restricted to family interactions. He had few, if any, friends and it seems that he felt lonely and isolated. His mother frowned upon the prospects of him socialising with schoolmates, and particularly with girls, whom she felt would tempt him into sex. Even when he tried to get away from home on 'Voortrekker' camps, his mother would insist on accompanying him.

Although he was almost constantly under his mother's eye, Geldenhuys recalled one particular incident when she had to leave the house unexpectedly on account of an emergency. She was gone for a few hours, and returned to catch him in the act of masturbating. She was livid and reprimanded him. Labuschagne (1999) claimed that Geldenhuys's mother had threatened him with 'extremely dire consequences', and that this incident had had a profoundly disturbing effect upon him. Speaking of the taboo on sexual matters, and of how he received no sexual guidance from his mother or father, he refers to this incident:

> My mother did not tell me about these things. When I became engaged, all that I was told was that a woman's body is pure and that it should be cared for. I found everything out of books and at school I heard of certain things, such as masturbation. Once my mother caught me doing that in the bathroom and she said that she was going to tell my father. But he never did or said anything. I was afraid to do anything with girls because of what could happen. I wanted to do it, but I was scared. I did it the first time with my fiancée (Labuschagne 2000, 2).

## The crimes and sentencing of Kobus Geldenhuys

Twenty-five-year-old lance-sergeant Jacobus Petrus Geldenhuys of the South African Railway Police was arrested in late 1992. He was convicted of fifteen crimes, including five counts of murder, and three of rape and of attempted rape, committed in Norwood, Brakpan, and Benoni between May 1989 and July 1992 (Smuts 1993a; 1993b).

He was sentenced to death five times by Mr Justice T. D. Cloete in the Rand Supreme Court on 24 September 1993, but his life was spared following the abolition of the death penalty (Meyer 2001). He is currently serving five life sentences in the Boksburg prison.

The details of his crimes were as follows. On 5 December 1989 he strangled a young twenty-one-year-old woman and subsequently burnt her body. Almost a year later, on 6 November 1991, he raped a thirty-seven-year-old woman, stole her car, and left it at the Norwood police barracks. A few weeks later (26 November) he raped a sixty-eight-year-old woman, also in Norwood, and stole approximately R50 from her, allegedly leaving her with the words, 'Goodnight, sleep well' (Morris 2000).

On 16 and 30 December – exactly two weeks apart – he raped and then shot in the head two twenty-seven-year-old-women, both in Norwood. One of these victims was found dead in her bathtub. Sometime later, on 7 May 1992, he shot and killed a seventy-four-year-old victim in Brakpan. His last victim was also his youngest, a sixteen-year-old girl whom he raped and killed behind his parents' Benoni home (15 July 1992).

## Punishment and resentment

There are conflicting reports over the extent of the physical nature of the parental discipline Geldenhuys was exposed to as a child (in other words, as to whether he was or was not what one might classify as an 'abused child'). What is not in doubt is the fact that it was always his mother who meted out punishment. Mrs Geldenhuys admitted that she did often 'give her son a hiding' because of his poor school marks (Labuschagne 1999). Her feelings, though, were that it was better to reprimand her son verbally where possible, as he became extremely anxious when threatened with violence; in fact she felt that 'as a child he could not handle aggression' (Labuschagne 1999).

It seems that Geldenhuys felt a 'great gap' in his life because he was an only child, and on various occasions expressed the wish for brothers and sisters (Labuschagne 2000). Not only was Geldenhuys's relationship with his parents undemonstrative, it was also one of little communication. For instance, he was never told that his mother had had two miscarriages; he did not know the dates of his parents' birth, nor when they were married. Furthermore, Geldenhuys seems certainly to have felt that his mother exercised pressure on him. He also reputedly had very negative feelings about her always showing him off and bragging about him. Although he did not express it, it does appear that to a degree he felt a measure of anger towards his mother (Labuschagne 2000). At this time (when still at school) he was indulging in petty theft, stealing small amounts of money here and there for the 'adventure' of it. He tells for instance that from Standard 3 on, he stole money out of his mother's purse.

It seems that Geldenhuys's mother had handled his financial affairs from a very early age, and that he was not very responsible with money generally. A friend mentioned the fact that even directly after payday, when he had started work, Geldenhuys generally didn't have any money. The same friend reported that the happiest time in Geldenhuys's life was when his parents had moved to the Cape and Geldenhuys stayed behind and boarded with the police chaplain: ' … he then got out of his mother's surveillance a bit, and could make his own decisions' (Labuschagne 2000, 4). When he matriculated with the bare minimum needed to pass, and with little visible ambition, his mother forced him to join the Railway Police, something he was very unhappy about:

> I would not have been a policeman, because I went to a trade school. But when I came out, there was no work. I went out looking for work, but everyone just promised they would telephone. I was called up at the second intake of the armed forces and I wanted to go to the navy. Then my mother saw that I found no work, she decided I should go to the Railway Police. A week after I started there, the papers came calling me up to the navy. But then I could not go. I felt very bad about that, because I badly wanted to go (Labuschagne 2000, 5).

## Social isolation and loneliness

Although Geldenhuys's railway police job was generally unchallenging, it allowed him to travel overseas where he gained access to a huge variety of pornography, not at the time available in South Africa. He wasted little time in amassing an extensive collection of pornographic magazines and videos. He was also able to go out and dance at nightclubs, something he never did at home:

> In SA I never danced nor attended a disco. When I was in Taipei I did go once, and even danced. Once there, it was very nice, the people are so sympathetic and chat to you even though they come from Japan and Korea – it was interesting (Labuschagne 2000, 5).

The other 'advantage' of Geldenhuys's job was that it kept him largely alone, and the antisocial tendencies he exhibited as a child appeared to become more pronounced as an adult, particularly in South Africa, despite his apparent greater sociability overseas. (In fact, if there was one feature that unified all the different accounts and descriptions of Geldenhuys's life it was that of being a loner, an introvert who never really made friends, who kept to himself, maintaining a constant social isolation.)

Now living on his own, Geldenhuys had the freedom to indulge many of the sexual desires he had been denied whilst living with his parents, and spent most of his free time watching violent or pornographic videos and playing video games. Both his parents and his pastor confronted him about the nature of the pornographic material that he collected, but he resisted any attempts to get rid of the material.

## A love interest

In 1989 Kobus met a mentally handicapped girl at a church function; the two began a romantic relationship and soon became engaged. It was clear that the two were very much in love; they would swap love letters, spend hours in one another's arms, and watch videos together. He even stole a CD player and a number of CDs as gifts for her. Asked to give a written response about the relationship he had with this girl, Geldenhuys had the following to say:

> I love her very much. She radiates love. She likes to give little hugs ... we wrote and gave each other letters. In each other's presence ... we held each other so that we were not parted from one another until the time she had to leave (Labuschagne 2000, 8).

Kobus described her as 'a wonderful girl', and one of his regrets for his later actions was that he would no longer be able to pursue this relationship. By all indications she was the only person whom Kobus felt comfortable with, in whom he felt he could invest and share himself.

It appears, furthermore, that Geldenhuys was always gentle towards his fiancée, and was never, particularly in sexual matters, aggressive towards her. Questioned as to whether he ever considered raping his lover, he answered thus:

> No, I feel completely different towards her. Look, when I wanted to make love with her, I asked if she would. If she said no, then I left it, and if she said yes, then we did so. If she said no that was okay, and I had no problem with it. I did not feel angry or thought we could have done it or whatever. I never felt 'to hell with her' (Labuschagne 2000, 8).

## Conflict with his fiancée's father

Geldenhuys's lover confirmed that he was never sexually aggressive towards her. She felt their sexual relationship was normal and that they fitted well together. Her parents accepted him for their daughter's sake, but they were troubled about the fact that he showed no real ambition. Her father felt that Geldenhuys 'wasted a lot of time that he could have used more constructively' (Labuschagne 2000). Similarly they were afraid he would be just 'a loafer who would never achieve anything' (Labuschagne 2000). They were also upset about the fact that he evidently had no friends and was apparently too dependent on their daughter. Nevertheless, they were extremely shocked after hearing of his conviction for murder and rape. They had considered him to be soft natured, yielding, and well mannered, with no signs of the aggression or anxiety within him (Labuschagne 2000).

It certainly seems that Geldenhuys had felt inferior in the company of his fiancée's parents. Asked about his fiancée's father he replied:

> Her father is a terrible perfectionist. We were engaged and every-thing and would wed. Just before that, [he] ... told me on the tele-phone that I should get my own flat and that I should write my sergeant's exams ... [W]hen I asked him if [I could marry his daughter] ... he did not [answer] ... but then ... asked me what was my problem, why didn't I write the exams ... you know, all these things. So I said to him, oh, let's leave it all. Then I [put the phone down on him] ... Then he went and cancelled everything, the wedding and so forth (Labuschagne 2000, 10).

## Exposure to violence

At about this time the Railway Police were incorporated into the South African Police. Kobus had to adapt his job accordingly and perform a far more traditional policing role. He was issued with a standard firearm. He found the transition very difficult however, partly because he had more

*Geldenhuys was a member of the internal stability unit in Alexandra – where he both witnessed and presumably participated in the perpetuation of violence in the township.*

PHOTO: NIC BOTHMA/AFRICA PHOTOS

social contact with his peers, and partly because he became a member of the Internal Stability Unit in Alexandra and was exposed to a great deal of township violence, both as a witness and presumably as a participant. He was very unhappy and had a negative and anxious outlook during his term in Alexandra. He could not fit in, and again felt lonely and alienated. During interviews it was established that he could not deal with the 'terrible things' that he saw there (Labuschagne 2000).

Although largely keeping to himself at the police barracks, Kobus did begin drinking with work colleagues. Despite this, he was unable to speak of the trauma he experienced on an almost daily basis, and continued to find it difficult to adjust to his new situation. Tellingly, after his conviction, Geldenhuys was to be diagnosed as having a schizoid personality disorder. Schizoid personalities are said to be those kinds of people who have a great deal of difficulty adjusting to new situations, or integrating with people, who almost always choose to follow solitary activities if they have the choice, and who show emotional coldness, detachment, or 'flattened affect'.

## The rapes begin

This seemed to be a time of particular tension and difficulty for Geldenhuys; the difficulties of his work environment, the ongoing exposure to violence, and the conflict with his fiancée's father all appeared to overlap at this point. All of these demands were, apparently, to prove too much for him. Around this time his antisocial behaviours spiralled from petty theft and suburban crime to calculated rape, a crime that he described as a kind of 'adventure', and as something he could not 'bring himself to stop'.

He happened upon his first victim, a domestic worker, while he was breaking into the back garden of a Norwood house, looking to steal money. He claims that he hadn't been aware that she had been there, and that he only killed her to prevent her from screaming for help. He killed her by brutally beating her to death with a brick. After this he set her, and her room, on fire. He described the event in the following way:

> [She saw me breaking in and] ... began screaming. I ran up to her and gripped her throat ... Then I decided to murder her ... Afterwards I went to vomit because I felt dirty. I felt numb in my arms. I knew they would catch me. I knew very well that what I did was wrong. I got scared. But after that, when I heard that she was dead, I felt relieved (Labuschagne 2000, 13).

After this incident Geldenhuys embarked on a series of rapes. All of these crimes were committed within a two-kilometre radius; the homes of each of these victims could easily be made out from the roof of the police barracks where he lived. In the first week of November 1991 Geldenhuys raped a woman in a block of flats directly adjacent to his police barracks. He stole a small amount of money and also took her car. Presumably because it was dark (he committed the crime in the early hours of the morning), and because he felt that his victim had not seen his face, he did not kill her. Less than three weeks later he struck again, again breaking into the victim's flat while she was asleep. He bludgeoned his sixty-eight-year-old victim on the head with the back of his gun before raping her, allegedly leaving her with the words, 'Good night, sleep well' (Morris 2000).

## Cultural fascination with the serial killer as 'super anti-hero'

There has been a virtual explosion of interest in the serial killer as a kind of cult anti-hero. Popular films and literature that focus on this enigmatic figure, whether of a fictitious or documentary nature, abound. One thinks of Thomas Harris's best-selling novels *Hannibal* and *Silence of the lambs*, which were so successfully converted into Hollywood blockbusters, as exemplars of this trend. Kobus Geldenhuys himself has featured in a variety of television shows, newspaper articles, and research projects (see Labuschagne 2000, Lazarus 1993a; 1993b, Macfarlane 2001, Meyer 2001, Morris 2000, Pistorius 1999; 2000, Smuts 1993a; 1993b).

It is interesting to consider why we find these figures so fascinating. Perhaps part of the reason for this is that their actions seem so incomprehensible, so utterly reprehensible in a modern era where self-restraint, self-control, and the ability for moral and empathic behaviour are so highly valued.

Serial killers are also of much interest within South Africa, particularly considering that (according to Micki Pistorius, an FBI-trained South African 'profiler') South Africa boasts the world's highest rate of serial killers per capita after the United States of America. Perhaps this has something to do with the country's 'culture of violence', where violence is somehow perceived as a sanctioned means of responding to social problems. (One thinks for example of the violence that characterised both the apartheid state and resistances to it as well as the country's high incidence of brutal crime.) What is

perhaps more disturbing is that the frequency of serial killing in South Africa and the profile of the typical serial killer's victim seem to represent a broader pattern of social oppression and violence. It is black women – seemingly the most disempowered sector of South African society – that feature most prominently among the victims.

Psychology seems to offer two general explanations for serial killing: developmental disturbance (such as childhood trauma, an abusive upbringing) and antisocial personality disorder (what used to be referred to as 'psychopathy' or 'sociopathy'). These explanations are often considered jointly in trying to account for the actions of serial murderers.

Seltzer (1998) interestingly suggests another explanation – that of media representation. For him many serial killers become part of the process of their own representation in the media (the most striking South African example is that of Moses Sithole, who directly and telephonically contacted a Johannesburg newspaper to report his activities). Such attempts at self-representation, at recording and documenting their acts, at becoming an infamous iconic social figure, should, he claims, be factored into any attempts to explain such behaviour (Seltzer 1998).

While it seems that there is no easy answer as to why serial killers command so much fascination and curiosity, there seems little doubt that serial killing as a favoured media and cultural representation will not vanish soon.

## Rape leading to murder

Although Geldenhuys denied having deliberately 'picked' his victims beforehand, there is some evidence to suggest that he had visited certain of them previously, posing as the concerned policeman (Morris 2000). Geldenhuys was to rape yet another woman, again in a Norwood flat, in early December of 1991, before using his firearm to commit murder. On 30 December 1991 he raped a woman, smoking a cigarette after the act, before running her a bath. Having forced her in the bath he shot her, point-blank, in the head. It seems that his resorting to murder was a result of his fear of being identified by his victims. In fact, according to Irma Labuschagne (1999) he had, perhaps not surprisingly, seen one of his earlier victims at the police station at which he worked. This event made him realise that he would need to be more 'careful' in his crimes. From now on he would rape only when armed; he would later say that it was only the fact that he had access to a weapon that gave him the 'guts to carry on'.

It is an important fact that the rapes did not always lead to sexual gratification on Kobus's part; he certainly did not always ejaculate, or even have successful penetrative sex with his victims. This fact seems to suggest that the crimes were more about rage, fury, and power than they were about attaining sexual pleasure. Labuschagne (1999) views him as a 'power rapist', and claims that:

> With the rapes ... those few seconds ... were the only times in his life where he felt he had control ... he was [caught in a] ... continuous searching for a feeling of being in control ... he was a power rapist. Had he not been arrested he would still be doing it.

## Trying to account for the murders

As is mentioned above, Geldenhuys claims not to have selected his victims according to any specific sexual criteria. The largely discrepant ages of the victims seem to in part corroborate this claim. Geldenhuys's actions after committing rape were often erratic, contradictory, and difficult to account for. On one occasion he even parked a victim's car outside the Norwood police station, despite the fact that it had been reported stolen. Often he would offer his victim a cup of coffee, or even give her a blanket. (On one occasion, as illustrated above, he even offered to run the victim a bath). However, if the victim tried to turn the light on, or got a good look at his face, or made any kind of attempt to escape, he would kill her by shooting her point-blank between the eyes. He said that the thing he enjoyed most about the murders was the star-shaped indentation left by the firearm when it was pressed against the victim's forehead (Pistorius 1999).

The contradictory nature of Geldenhuys's actions seems to be reflected in varying perceptions of him. Labuschagne (1999) notes how she found radically different perceptions, according to whom she asked, in how his work colleagues viewed him. She noted this disparity in her own observations of him. On the one hand, she claimed he came across as gentle and friendly and shy and timid; on the other hand, he had committed deeds of brutal savagery. Although it seemed that he was fully aware that his actions were wrong, he seemed to show very little emotional insight into what he had done (Labuschagne 2000). He would speak readily of his crimes, repeating certain phrases like an automaton: 'I knew that what I did was wrong'; 'I kept no record of it'; 'I knew they would catch me', or 'I was afraid they would catch me'. But when speaking of the crimes he would show no emotion or any real, visible signs of remorse or empathy. In fact, he seemed to show very little insight at all into the nature of his crimes, as is apparent in the following dialogue with Labuschagne:

Q  When you raped a woman the first time, did you genuinely enjoy it?
A  I think it was more for the adventure – I actually don't know.
Q  Now think carefully – which was better; the fact that a woman was afraid of you, or the fact that you had sex with her?
A  I think it was more the adventure.
Q  What does adventure mean to you?
A  That you must do it ... stealthily ... and she is strange. What her attitude will be, and so on.
Q  Did you feel bad if you could not penetrate?
A  No, not at all. I wasn't angry because I didn't get it right. When I felt that I could not penetrate I really did not feel bad. I did 'come' in my underpants after I pulled them up. So then I shot her and just left.
Q  Did it matter to you how she looked?
A  No. One woman that I raped was in her 80s; no wait, 60 or 70 – so you can see for yourself that I did not know how the person looked. All I know is that it was a woman.
Q  Did you ever feel in your head that something is 'out of control'?
A  Yes, while I was doing it, then the thought came. Look, I was now living on my own. OK, and now that the night came, now I must get out of here, then you walk around and you see there's a light, and you see there's a woman, and then you actually go to rob, you know, steal money. And then later, then you think, no, you are going back to rape. But not during the day, I did not get that feeling. It happens when I feel, no, I've had enough now of watching TV, or whatever.
Q  When you raped, did you get the same kind of erection as when you slept with your fiancée?
A  It's altogether, altogether different. It's definitely, definitely not the same. I would, yes look, ... sometimes I did well, uhm, ... get an erection, and sometimes again not.
Q  What did you actually get out of raping?
A  (Weeping) I ... no, I don't know ... I just do not have that answer.
Q  If it was just sex, you could have gone to an escort agency.
A  Yes ... because, look ... there were many opportunities to do this, specially overseas where I saw so many of these things, and in Germany I even went to the strip shows and the prostitutes that stay in the apartments; and do you know, it just didn't attract me – to actually have sex with such women.

Q  So, if you say it wasn't sex that you were looking for, what do
   you think it was?
A  I do not know ... how to answer that question.
Q  You are really not stupid. You were a policeman, you knew
   you were doing something terribly wrong. What ... drove you?
A  Yes, yes. Did I then feel as if I was in ... control? Or boss?
Q  Did you sometimes feel you were not in control?
A  Yes, I can only say that the weapon gave me the guts to actu-
   ally do it again.
Q  And if you did not have a weapon?
A  Then I would not have done it. Then I would probably have
   stuck to stealing small change, or something like that.
Q  The weapon gave you the guts – but what is this 'something'
   that let you do it?
A  ... [I can't explain] ... you know these things more than I do ...
   life's problems maybe ... maybe I can't get along with life's
   standards and that's why ... everything just happens to me. I
   wanted to go to the navy, and when I got the chance I could
   not go. And my fiancée's father ... that's about the closest that
   I can think of ...

## After the crimes

Geldenhuys acted differently after various murders. In one case he had
to wait for a considerable period of time in a (dead) victim's flat before
leaving – he was afraid that someone might have heard the shot and
he did not want to walk around the streets. He claimed that if someone
had heard the shot and entered the premises he would have killed them
too. On other occasions he would go and play video games, 'probably to
forget, I don't actually know' (Labuschagne 2000, 14). He was never
physical after such deeds. He usually partook later of a meal and did not
think about it again – until 'it' began again. He claimed in fact that, in the
course of time, he had realised that he could not stop his actions. He said
that he considered giving himself up, particularly when he saw something about the so-called Norwood rapist on TV. About this he says:

> I read nothing about it in the papers, but I did see the story that
> they read in the TV news. I got such a warm feeling and I got so
> scared. My heart began to beat faster, and so on. I wanted to stop
> after the second incident in Norwood. I knew, no, now I must
> stop, I should shoot myself or whatever, I don't know. I felt very
> scared. First I waited that they would come and knock on my
> door, so I put my firearm beside me on the table, you know, in
> case somebody should come, then I would shoot myself. I did not
> really want to do it, but if it happened at that time that somebody
> should come, then I probably would have. Or maybe not. I was
> very uncertain. After the fourth incident in Norwood, ... [the
> police] ... said we must all be in the TV room at a certain time on
> a certain day. They were going to take fingerprints and so on, and
> then I decided, no, I'm going to give myself up. If they came, I
> would say, ok it's me. But then they didn't come and so I left it.
> Then I moved out of Norwood as I saw I just wanted to get away
> from the problem (Labuschagne 2000, 15).

Geldenhuys claims that should he have been married on the date initially set with his fiancée, he would have stopped all his criminal activities. At other times he professes that he cannot be sure that would have been the case, and that he frequently had feelings of being unable to control himself – that 'it would begin again' despite all his efforts to stop. In her closing recommendations Irma Labuschagne, the consulting criminologist, asserted her strong belief that should Geldenhuys ever be freed, he would without doubt commit the same actions, and that he should therefore be imprisoned for life.

# Conclusion

How can we account for the actions of Kobus Geldenhuys? What is it that leads an individual to commit such brutal acts of violence? Could significant changes in his developmental history have prevented all of this from happening? Would a developmental psychologist have been able to predict these actions should s/he have had a reasonable knowledge of Geldenhuys's developmental history? Can developmental psychology even begin to start posing answers to these difficult questions? The chapters that follow will consider some tentative answers to these questions.

One of the objectives of this chapter has been to impress upon learners the complexity and the multidimensionality, of developmental influences. If we look closely at the content of the case study we can find evidence not only of possible intra-psychic, psychosexual or object-relational (that is, psychoanalytical) motives behind Geldenhuys's acts, we can also spot notable psychosocial, cognitive, and possible socio-political influences.

## Critical thinking tasks

1) What are the main themes in Geldenhuys's story? Put differently, what, in your opinion, are the main factors that seem to have played a role in motivating Geldenhuys's actions? Are many of these factors typical of the South African context? Which ones are, and in what ways are they? Illustrate your answer with examples.

2) While considering the various factors above, consider how you might be able to divide them between the broad areas of cognitive, psychoanalytic, and psychosocial developmental influences on development. How interconnected are these themes, in your opinion?

# SECTION TWO
## Psychoanalytic approaches to development and personality

# A basic introduction to psychoanalytic thought

*Jacki Watts*

---

This chapter will consist of the following broad sections:

1. A brief historical introduction to Freud, Klein, Winnicott, and Jung, the main theorists discussed in Section Two.

2. A discussion of the developmental assumptions that underpin the theories of this section.

3. A genealogy of developments within the field of psychoanalytic thinking.

---

## A brief historical introduction

This chapter offers a brief historical contextualisation of the emergence of perhaps the predominant psychoanalytic theorists of the last century, Freud, Klein, Jung, and Winnicott. We also present certain of the basic psychoanalytic assumptions important to the study of development, which will provide a foundation for the chapters to follow. After looking at the importance of childhood in development, at the normal/pathological distinction, the notion of the unconscious, and the value of stage-based theories, we will conclude with a brief critique of certain of these notions.

### A bit of Freud

Austria at the turn of the twentieth century was a prosperous country ruled by the Hapsburg dynasty. Franz Joseph became head of the dual Austro-Hungarian monarchy in 1867 and it was only with the assassination of his nephew in Sarajevo in 1914 and the start of World War 1 that the prosperity and dominance of Austria came to an end. In 1900, at the time of the publication of Freud's *Interpretation of dreams*, Vienna was the seat of European culture and beauty. Austria is a predominantly Catholic country. At the turn of the century, Jews in Vienna were an often-persecuted minority. It is significant to note that virtually all the early pioneers of psychoanalysis were European Jews who suffered various forms of persecution and discrimination. Freud and Klein grew up in a society that was basically anti-Semitic. In the year of Klein's birth, 1882, the German-Austrian student fraternities passed the Waidhofer Resolution that declared that every human being with Jewish blood in its veins was born without honour and must therefore lack in every decent human feeling. It was in this culture that psychoanalysis found its home. Grosskurth (1986) describes the role of psychoanalysis as becoming, for many Jews, a religion with its own rites and demands of unswerving loyalty. Freud's elaborations of the workings of the unconscious and the role of repression and aggression provided conceptual tools with which to grapple and try to understand the suppression experienced by the Jews at this time.

Sigmund Freud (1856–1939) managed to build around him an inner circle of supporters of psychoanalytic ideas. He was the undisputed leader of this group, but the group was not without its tensions and rifts between Freud and various members. Gay (1988) provides a well-researched biographical account of Freud's life and the various intense relationships and tensions that characterised his life. Karl Abrahams and Sandor Ferenczi were influential members of Freud's inner circle, which also included Otto Rank and Carl Jung. This inner circle radically influenced the Western world's concepts of art, culture, and how we view the nature of man. No longer could the Western world see itself as guided by rational, conscious, exclusively higher and noble principles. What psychoanalysis brought into focus was the layering below the surface of conscious experience and motivation. It explored the seemingly irrational behaviours of neurosis. What the psychoanalytic circle uncovered were the meanings lying within the symptoms of experiences such as hysteria, obsessive-compulsive behaviour, and anxiety states. Psychoanalysis demonstrated the importance of childhood for the subsequent development of the psychic life of the individual. It also pointed to the role of psychic life in structuring the development of personality. The Inner Circle generated the core of psychoanalytic thinking of the time.

## A bit of Klein

Melanie Klein (1882–1960) was born in Vienna at a time when Freud was already working as a neurologist. While Klein had an ultimately productive life, there were a number of tragedies and deaths. These included the deaths of a sister, her brother, her own son, and her analyst of many years, Karl Abrahams. Her life was fundamentally changed, however, upon reading Freud's *Interpretation of dreams* (1900) in 1914. From that time on she immersed herself in psychoanalytic thinking. Grosskurth's biography (1986) describes a dynamic but difficult woman who not only had to deal with much tragedy in her life but also much opposition to her ideas. She appears to have been a woman who inspired fierce loyalty and equally fierce antagonism, both from her colleagues and her own family, particularly her daughter, Melissa. Klein had two long analyses, one with Abrahams and the other with Ferenczi. (It is interesting to note that while a personal analysis is a prerequisite to becoming a psychoanalyst, Freud himself did not undergo an analysis. He undertook this himself through an intensive analysis of his dreams.) With the encouragement of these men, and Ernest Jones in England, Klein pioneered the psychoanalytic treatment of children through play therapy.

In 1925 Klein went on a lecture tour to Britain. Her ideas were met with enthusiasm, mainly because Ernest Jones was already working in conceptual areas that were in harmony with her own. Jones had a tempestuous relationship with Freud, so it is thus not surprising that he would welcome Klein's presence. Klein returned to Britain the next year and stayed until her death in 1960. By the time Freud and his daughter Anna arrived in Britain in 1939 (Jones assisted them to flee the Nazi threat), Klein had established an influential presence. The meeting of these two powerful theoretical positions resulted in a theoretical rift that divides the psychoanalytic community to this day. There was both a personal and a theoretical struggle between Klein and Anna Freud. Anna Freud was also working with children. Her work was strongly influenced by Freud by whom she had been analysed. Anna Freud maintained that one could not work within **transference** with children, as they were still too dependent upon real parents. Klein maintained that spontaneous transference arose towards the therapist and had to be dealt with through neutral interpretation of the dynamics of the phenomena. Klein was also postulating ideas about the richness of the internal world of infancy that Classical Freudians were finding difficult to stomach.

During this time many creative advances in theoretical understanding were made by Klein and her followers. This group did, however, seem to be overly concerned with issues of legitimacy. Klein and her immediate followers were at pains to demonstrate their allegiance to Freud. As a result, for quite a while her work was not viewed in its own right, with an objective evaluation of the strengths and weaknesses of her theory. Rather her concepts were evaluated by the degree to which they did or did not accord with Freud's conceptualisations. Such comparisons are futile for her theories were concerned with different aspects of psychic functioning. However, it was due to Klein's struggle to gain acceptance from Freud that the metapsychological differences between their theories were missed for a number of years.

**Transference.** The repetition, in adulthood, of infantile prototypes of self-and-other relations and instinctual wishes towards others. Psychoanalytic cure is based on the identification of the transference and its interpretation.

## Some Winnicott

Donald Winnicott was the cherished son of an upper-class British family. His father, Sir Frederick Winnicott, was the Lord Mayor of Plymouth. Winnicott was the youngest child, with two elder sisters who were devoted to him. He was an excellent scholar and athlete, growing up to be a handsome, cultured, and enigmatic man. He started his career as a paediatrician and maintained an interest in children throughout his life. As a theorist he devoted his life to exploring the implications and importance of the bond between mother and child. He entered the British Psychoanalytic Society at the time of its most creative and open debates.

**The Bloomsbury group.**
A literary, artistic, and intellectual circle of friends who met at one another's homes in and around the Bloomsbury area of London in the early decades of the twentieth century. At its core were the sisters Vanessa Bell and Virginia Woolf. It also included the novelist E. M. Forster, the artist and critic Roger Fry, John Maynard Keynes, the influential economist, Victoria Sackville-West, the poet and writer, and Lytton Strachey, the biographer. In its broad artistic and philosophical range, the Bloomsbury group had a profound influence on English cultural life.

Ernest Jones (who invited Klein to lecture in London) was then president of the Society. James and Alix Strachey, and Adrian and Karen Steven represented the **Bloomsbury** influence. (The first of Winnicott's two long personal analyses was with James Strachey.) Other influential people at the time were John Rickman and Sylvia Payne, who worked with shell-shocked troops from World War 1. There were also those who were to become loyal to the Kleinian tradition: Joan Riviere, Susan Isaacs, and Paula Heimann, among others. (Winnicott had his second analysis with Joan Riviere.) The arrival of the Freud family in 1939, and the ensuing conflict with Klein, was to change the quality of the debates to a more intense and acrimonious level.

Winnicott appears to have remained aloof to these 'intrigues', remaining a profoundly individualistic person. He gave innumerable talks to a wide-ranging cross-section of people, from social workers, for instance, to clergymen, to mothers themselves. He preferred these forums where he could engage with his audience rather than the more cerebral discussions of academia and psychoanalysts. Winnicott never aligned himself with either party in the Freud and Klein wrangles, remaining clinically objective, and providing the model for the independence and creative thinking that characterises the Middle or Independent tradition. He was to have a profound effect in influencing this branch of psycho-analytic thinking. Winnicott's writing is poetic and deceptively easy. You are left with the taste of an idea but it is up to you to grapple and strug-gle with the concepts to appreciate fully the richness and complexity of his thoughts. (Read Kohon (1986) for a sample of these theorists.)

## A little bit on Jung

Carl Gustav Jung was born the son of a minister, on 26 July 1875. He died on 6 June 1961 at the age of eighty-five. Within his extended family many uncles were also ministers, and religion was therefore an important influence in his life. Jung is probably best known for his fall-out with Freud and for his development of theory that later came to be known as Analytical Psychology. The issues he dealt with in his theory arose in part from his own personal background, which is vividly described in his autobiography, *Memories, dreams, reflections* (1963). After his rift with Freud it is thought he experienced a period of **psychosis**. He retreated from social interaction for a time, living the life of a hermit. During this time he explored his experiences through making sculptures and seeking symbols to capture the nature of his psychic journey. This was an act of courage and faith in the resilience of the psyche. The resolution of this experience, together with the fact that throughout his life Jung experi-enced periodic dreams and visions with striking mythological and reli-gious features, had a profound influence in shaping his interest in myths, dreams, and the psychology of religion. For many years Jung felt he pos-sessed two separate personalities: an outer public self that was involved with the world of his family and peers, and a secret inner self that felt a special closeness to God. The interplay between these selves formed a central theme in Jung's personal life and contributed to his later empha-sis on the individual's striving for integration and wholeness.

**Psychosis.** Generally considered to be the extreme of mental illness. The consciousness becomes flooded with unconscious contents, so that the ego is partially or completely overwhelmed, thus losing contact with external reality.

Jung initially studied archaeology, confirming his interest in and profound knowledge of ancient cultures and myths. He later completed his medical training in Basel and spent these early years in practice at the Burgholzli Mental Hospital in Zurich, where he conducted studies in word association. These association tests were important to the development of Jung's thought. He discovered that words clustered together around certain ideas or themes, and that it was possible to identify which of these themes were anxiety provoking to the participants. This work demonstrated the workings of the unconscious meanings of words. Thus it was not surprising that Jung was deeply influenced by Sigmund Freud's writings on mental illness and dreams. From 1907 to 1913 Jung maintained close ties to Freud, and in 1911 he became the first president of the Internationale Psychoanalytische Gesellschaft (International Psychoanalytic Association). During this time Jung was seen as the 'heir apparent', the natural successor to Freud as theoretical leader of the psychoanalytic movement. However, their relationship began to deteriorate, over personal and theoretical disputes. The principal theoretical disputes were concerned with the significance of sexuality and spirituality in human life. These disputes finally led to the breakdown of the relationship in 1913.

Freud was an extremely powerful and influential man in the psychoanalytic world. (We have seen how his influence led Klein to expend so much energy on demonstrating her loyalty and allegiance to his theories, even though her ideas were strikingly original in their own right.) Jung's break with Freud was a significant event in the lives of both men. Their relationship remained unresolved and the rift seems to have resulted in a lasting inability to integrate across their theoretical divide.

# Key psychoanalytic developmental assumptions

This section discusses five specific assumptions that underlie psychoanalytic theorising. Without being familiar with the theories, this section may be somewhat difficult. Once the whole chapter is completed it would be worthwhile to come back to this section to re-integrate the concepts into your more complex understanding of the theories. Each of the theorists covered in the section has a particular way of engaging with these assumptions. Thus, while they hold to the validity of the assumptions, they formulate them in ways that are unique to their theories. This is because each of the theorists has a slightly different focus in their theorising: Freud focuses on childhood, Klein on infancy, and Winnicott on the mother/infant unit, while Jung theorises on adulthood and Lacan on the child within a symbolic system. It is inevitable that they would see the same phenomena from different viewpoints. The language of each theorist allows a different understanding of perhaps the same phenomena as well as offering descriptions of different phenomena. As an example, both Freud and Klein look at instinctual life but each has provided a language that allows us to see the phenomena from different perspectives.

PHOTO: CHA JOHNSTON

*Psychoanalytic theory is concerned with the development of personhood.*

**Phantasy.** The mental correlate of the instincts. That is, phantasy is the mental activity that is mutually bound up with the instincts and gives them a mental representation (Isaacs 1948).

**Psychopathology.** Mental functioning that is deemed abnormal as judged by the norms of the subject's culture and society. In studying psychopathology one is concerned with understanding the origin, development, and characteristics of its various manifestations.

## The significance of childhood

All psychoanalytic theories observe the significance of childhood in the development of personality. Childhood is seen as the developmental period when the child is most vulnerable to the influences of social, cultural, and family demands. It is also the time when the human organism is still in its most formative stage and is developing ways of coping with both external and internal demands. By internal we mean physiological demands such as hunger, cold, discomfort, satiation, as well as emotional demands such as fear, rage, neediness, and love. Psychoanalytic theories propose that it is during childhood that the interface between culture and physiology is at its most significant. The infant comes into the world as a bundle of sensate experiencing, that is, the baby is only an experiencing body without the cognitive or emotional capacities to make sense of this experience. This initial state has to be organised into some form of coherent experience that has meaning for the infant and the developing child. Each of the theorists in this section hypothesises certain routes by which meaning is achieved. Each focuses upon certain elements of development, which elucidate certain developmental achievements.

Freud postulates that the progressive physiological complexity of the child's development interacts with cultural prohibitions (in Richards and Dickson 1977). This process leads to an evolution whereby the child comes to progressively harness and curb his or her instinctual nature, eventuating in a mature capacity to love and work. Klein (1946) proposes that the infant, initially encapsulated within an internal world of **phantasy**, is faced with the task of moving from this internal world into a world of shared reality. Klein's focus is on early infancy and the internal processes that occur to lay the foundations for future cognitive and emotional capacities. Winnicott (1958) theorised around the significance of the mother/child bond. He saw this bond as essential to the future capacities of the child to integrate and be able to relate to others in mature and fulfilling ways. Jung (1986) also asserted the importance of childhood. He felt, however, that this terrain of theoretical understanding had been well documented by Freud. Jung's focus was on development during adulthood. He postulated that significant developmental challenges faced humankind throughout life and these were the challenges involved in the journey of individuation, a universal development towards integration of the personality. Lacan (1977) postulated that it was important to understand how the symbolic world of language and culture acted upon the child and imposed an alienation from the self that the child can never overcome.

## Normal and pathological development

Psychoanalytic theory arose from work with pathological functioning. This theory derives from work within the clinical field and work with individuals who are struggling or suffering with various states of psychic pain (**psychopathology**). One could argue then that these theories are only apposite to pathology. Certainly, psychoanalytic theories have given clinicians the understanding and insight to treat psychological conditions that had previously been considered untreatable. For example, **psychoanalytic psychotherapy** is the treatment of choice when one considers conditions such as **personality disorders**. Freud's theoretical paradigm is concerned with Oedipal disorders, which are termed neuroses. Post-psychoanalytic theory has offered insights into pre-Oedipal disorders. These have come to be seen as disorders of the development of the self. Psychoanalytic theory, in considering the development of pathology, has inevitably offered clinicians and theorists the opportunity to see very clearly those contexts which foster development of children and those which lead to pathology and psychological damage. In this sense, through psychoanalytic theory, one is able to trace both 'normal' and pathological development. The theorists covered in this section all postulate that there are certain optimum conditions that foster psychological growth. Freud (in Richards and Dickson 1977) and Klein (1946) tend to focus on the internal world and conditions that impede or foster **psychic development**. Winnicott (1958) focuses on what is required from the primary caregiver to foster the child's optimum development. Within this context he analyses those conditions that lead to compromises in the child's development. Jung (1986) traces the processes whereby integration and balance between opposing forces lead to integration of the personality. Each theorist, in postulating a theory of pathology, also postulates a theory of normal development and the conditions necessary to foster this development.

## Stages of development

All psychoanalytic theories see development as proceeding through a sequence of stages. Freud postulates that the child develops through the psychosexual **stages**, with each stage heralding a more mature and advanced capacity to integrate instinctual life in the service of mature heterosexuality (Richards and Dickson 1977). Klein (1946) postulates two primary intra-psychic **positions** through which the infant must pass. These positions will provide the matrix through which the person will interact in the world. The paranoid-schizoid position is the more immature position and underlies pathological states, while the depressive position informs more mature capacities for interpersonal relating. These two positions provide the foundation, as it were, of the internal world. Upon this foundation the negotiations of the psychosexual stages occur. Thus if the subject is within the paranoid-schizoid position, one would expect that there would be difficulties in negotiating the psychosexual stages. Winnicott has formulated his theories upon those of Freud and Klein, and therefore he does not articulate the idea of stages or positions as such. Rather, his focus is on the notion that the infant goes through a sequence of developmental needs, which must be attended to by the mother or primary caregiver. He examines this sequence of needs and the implications of the quality of care given to these needs (Winnicott 1958). Jung (1986) postulates the possibilities of tensions between opposing archetypal

**Psychoanalytic psychotherapy.** A modification of psychoanalysis. Whereas psychoanalysis is based upon at least thrice weekly sessions, which are only transference based, psychoanalytic psychotherapy is conducted less often and (while transference based) it also deals with reality-based interventions.

**Personality disorder.** Deeply ingrained and maladaptive patterns of relating to, thinking about, and perceiving the world and oneself. These patterns lead to impairment in functioning and distress in the individual. Personality disorder can often be diagnosed by late latency or adolescence. The disorder continues throughout life unless treated. Personality disorders are also termed disorders of the self. Long-term psychoanalytic psychotherapy is the treatment of choice.

**Psychic development.** The process whereby the mental life of an individual becomes constituted to be able to function within both internal and external reality.

**Stages.** Development that is built upon and dependent on the attainment of prior developmental aspects.

**Positions.** Independent phases that can be returned to at various times throughout development.

energies and sees development as the progressive integration of these archetypes. (Remember that his focus is on adulthood, and that he felt that the development of the child had been thoroughly addressed by Freud himself.)

## The role of the unconscious

Psychoanalytic theories all maintain the view that our psychic motivation stems largely from **unconscious** forces. This is not to say that we are incapable of conscious, rational thought and higher moral reasoning. What the theories propose is that humans are more than these conscious, rational capacities. The infant is born into a state of unconsciousness. The infant is also essentially an instinctual being, that is, one who knows the world through his or her bodily experiences – feeding and defecating – and his or her primitive capacities for love and hate. This aspect of the unconscious remains with us. The unconscious is primarily an area of instinctual functioning which influences behaviour through the prompting of primitive instinctual psychic experience. All the theorists maintain this notion that we are born with a primary area of psychic functioning which is unconscious. This area of psychic functioning can never become known directly and is only known about through its influences on our daily life. This understanding helps to address questions such as why we so often marry someone who is like one or both of our parents, why we undermine ourselves when we so want to succeed, or why an abused child marries an abusive partner. The unconscious is at work in all those times when our motivations for behaviour seem so strange.

Psychoanalytic theory postulates a vast array of instinctual energies. Freud focuses on two, the sexual and the aggressive energies. Isaacs (1948) a working colleague of Klein, postulated that phantasy was the mental correlate of the **instincts**. This concept opened the door to understanding the relational quality of instinctual life. By this is meant that instinctual life is lived in relation to others. Post-Freudians have postulated, in opposition to Freud, that the instincts have a very specific aim. All instinctual life is lived in a phantasy self-and-other relational matrix. Emotions such as greed, envy, terror, paranoia, love, and guilt are all possible unconscious instinctual psychic motivations. Jung (1986) goes further to hypothesise that a person has access to the 'collective unconscious', an innate reservoir of archaic knowledge about being human. An individual is connected to this collective reservoir through the operation of the complexes, the personalised link to archetypal energies. These concepts will be explained and discussed in further chapters of Section Two.

A destructive aspect of unconscious functioning is also postulated. Throughout the ages, humans have attempted to harness their instinctual natures. This has led to them being able to live with others in increasing levels of consciousness and civilisation. This process seems to have been bought at a price. While governments advance humanitarian principles and notions of civilised, rational interactions between races and nations, never before has humankind had such capacities for worldwide destruction and mass exploitation. What we see is that the more conscious and moral certain nations become, the more their aggressive and greedy needs

**Unconscious.** Denotes all those contents that are not in consciousness. It can also denote contents that have been repressed.

**Instinct.** A dynamic process consisting of a pressure of energy that stems from the source, a bodily state of tension, such as hunger. The instinct directs the organism towards the discharge of such tension. The object, such as food, allows the instinct to achieve its aim.

PHOTO: CHA JOHNSTON

*The realm of the dream world and the unconscious underpins all psychoanalytic theory.*

become hidden from consciousness. They are repressed and kept hidden through various processes which we call defences. The child develops in a similar fashion. As the child matures and becomes socialised, so the more primitive and 'unwanted' aspects of normal behaviour are relegated to the unconscious. Our awareness of these unwanted aspects is dealt with through the operation of defences, a concept we will discuss later in the section. Thus psychoanalytic theory postulates two aspects to the unconscious: an innate and universal operation of psychic motivation based in bodily instinctual life, as well as those aspects of human functioning which are deemed unacceptable. These aspects become relegated to the unconscious due to the inevitable socialisation of our instinctual natures.

## Cognitive and emotional development

We have briefly considered how Freud looks at the operation of the instincts within psychosexual development. We have also briefly considered how Klein perceives the relational qualities of her two intra-psychic positions, how Winnicott emphasises the role of the mother and her care of the infant, and how Jung considers the work of the archetypes and the complexes that give access to the collective unconscious. These assumptions lay the foundation for what is perhaps the major assumption of psychoanalytic theory: that the quality of resolution of these prior conditions lays the matrix for our future emotional and cognitive capacities. The quality of resolution would indicate the degree to which we are capable of living relatively free from the pathologies of our unconscious inner worlds. Where our childhood experiences have left fixations and unmet developmental needs, we will be compromised in letting go of these unconscious influences. Where we are relatively free of fixations and have experienced 'good-enough mothering' (Winnicott, 1958) we will be relatively capable of emotional and cognitive autonomy in both our internal and external worlds.

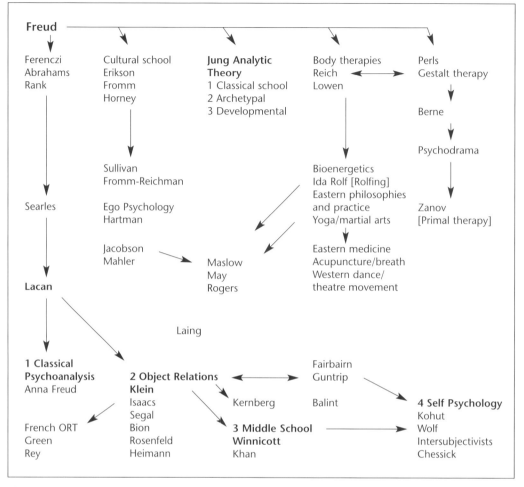

**Figure 4.1** A genealogy of dialogues and developments in psychoanalytic thinking.

## Critique of psychoanalytic assumptions

The critique of psychoanalytic assumptions applies across the spectrum of theorists we have covered in this chapter. Each theorist will have areas that attract critique yet there are general critiques that apply to all. The foremost of these is the claim that psychoanalytic theory is unscientific.

It is claimed that most aspects of the theory lack experimental support and that the theory is unverifiable according to normal scientific standards. This is a particularly dated critique, which fails to acknowledge the enormous amount of research data gathered over the years in support of psychoanalytic claims. This data comes from a wide range of research interests, from infant observation, to neurological research, to clinical case studies. All these fields offer wide-ranging support for the importance of childhood, for the role of parenting, and for the significance of unconscious motivations in innate emotional capacity and in adult personality functioning. Look at the following chapter on Freud for a more elaborated discussion of these issues.

A more difficult critical claim concerns the deterministic nature of psychoanalytic theory. The claim is made that the theory suggests psychological development of the individual to be largely complete by the time of puberty and that the individual is then imprisoned by his or her developmental history. A way to think about this claim is to consider that the theory is deterministic about the development of psychic apparatus during certain times and conditions. However, it is not so when one comes to the particulars of an individual's life. The theory is not predictive. All it claims is that at certain developmental stages, certain developmental achievements occur, which lead to the maturing of the human organism.

Clearly all theory is worthy of critique. Nevertheless, one's critique must respond to the current state of the theory.

# Recommended reading

Freud, S. (1977). 'Three essays on the theory of sexuality'. In A. Richards and A. Dickson (eds), *The Penguin Freud Library. Volume 7 on sexuality: Three essays on the theory of sexuality and other works.* London: Penguin.
*(Freud lays out his theory of infantile sexuality in ways that make the theory accessible.)*

Gay, P. (1988). *Freud, a life for our times.* London: Papermac.
*(A wonderful insight into the life and times and the theory of Freud.)*

Grosskurth, P. (1986). *Melanie Klein. Her world and her work.* London: Jason Aronson.
*(A thorough biography of Klein. Gives insight into her life and motivations and gives human drama to her theory.)*

Isaacs, S. (1948). 'The nature and function of phantasy'. In M. Klein (ed.), *Contributions to psychoanalysis, 1921–1945.* London: Hogarth Press.
*(The first exposition of the Kleinian position on phantasy. Rather long-winded but definitive for the serious student.)*

Jung, C. G. (1963). *Memories, dreams, reflections.* London: Routledge & Kegan Paul.
*(An autobiography that gives one a personal glimpse of how Jung thought about his life.)*

Jung, C.G. (1986). *Analytic psychology: Its theory and practice.* London: Ark Paperbacks.
*(A very readable overview of Jung's theories. It is based upon his lectures to the Tavistock.)*

Klein, M. (1946). 'Notes on some schizoid mechanisms'. *International journal of psychoanalysis, 27,* 99–110.
*(Her definitive paper. It may be a bit hard but well worth the effort to serious students.)*

Kohon, G. (ed.) (1986). *The British school of psycho-analysis: The independent tradition.* London: Free Association Books.
*(This collection has some wonderful essays, which illustrate the creativity characteristic of the Independent tradition.)*

Lacan, J. (1979). *The four fundamental concepts of psychoanalysis.* London: Penguin.
*(A difficult read, but for the serious student it covers Lacan's reading of four of Freud's basic concepts.)*

Segal, H. (1964). *Introduction to the work of Melanie Klein.* New York: Basic Books.
*(One of the best overviews of Klein's work.)*

Winnicott, D. W. (1958). *Collected papers: Through paediatrics to psycho-analysis.* New York: Basic Books.
*(As always, a wonderful experience.)*

# Critical thinking tasks

1) Once you have reviewed the whole of Section Two, consider in what ways the theorists covered may offer complementary and/or divergent views of development.

2) Is the period of childhood – in your opinion – really as significant for personality development as psychoanalytic theorists argue it is? Motivate your answer with reference to your own experiences.

3) Give careful thought to the concept of the unconscious; what evidence can we find for the existence of this 'area' or aspect of psychological functioning? Again refer to personal references drawn from your own life.

4) If you were formulating a theory of development, what assumptions would underlie your theory?

5) What do you think are the strongest critiques of the psychoanalytic approach and why?

6) Give some thought to how the basic psychoanalytic principles discussed above inform the clinical practice of psychoanalysis.

# Freud's psychoanalytic theory of development and personality

*Derek Hook and Jacki Watts*

This chapter will cover the following of Freud's major concepts:

1. The notion of unconscious functioning.

2. The nature of infantile and adult sexuality.

3. The basic theory of psychosexual development.

4. The conceptualisation of the Oedipus complex.

5. The topographical and the structural models of the mind.

6. The role of defences.

7. Conceptions of psychopathology.

8. The role of dreams in Freud's theory.

9. A critique of his theoretical contributions to understanding human personality and development.

## Freud, psychoanalysis, and developmental psychology

Freud's psychoanalytic thinking has had an enormous impact, not only in terms of its clinical importance within the realm of treating mental distress or psychopathology, but also in terms of its impact on critical and intellectual ways of thinking, of analysing and explaining cultural phenomena in the twentieth and twenty-first centuries. Freud's theories are also important in that they propose an understanding of a basic structure for normal personality development.

Sigmund Freud

They thus offer a broad framework through which to trace the aetiology of psychopathology. For these reasons his theorising is strongly tied to the pragmatics of clinical application. Another reason why Freud's theories are so useful is that they strive for a balance between biological and social factors of development, seeing man within his bio-psycho-social context. Freud saw that neither socio-cultural nor physiological factors could be dropped from developmental theory, as they work in tandem to determine the individual's unique personality and particular psychological problems.

**Psyche/psychic.** Initially used to indicate the 'soul'; now used to designate the psychological, or the mental. Often contrasted with soma, meaning the body.

## The concept of the unconscious

**Unconscious.** Term used to designate those mental processes and contents not knowable to the individual subject. More specifically, the unconscious is a region of the mind that operates autonomously and plays a crucial role in mental (psychic) functioning. It has its own mode of expression and steers us into behaviours and emotions for which the motivations are unknown to our conscious mind. This region influences our everyday behaviours and, significantly, this region is implicated in the formation of neurotic symptoms. The unconscious contains a massive store of memories, impulses, wishes, and fantasies.

Freud was not the first to discuss the operation of an unconscious dimension. In fact he was working within a well-established tradition himself but history now places his conceptualisations as the beginning of an amazingly wide and profound development within both psychology and culture generally. What was new was Freud's insistence that understanding the unconscious was the Rosetta stone to understanding the human **psychic** life. There were a number of different phases in the development of his thinking – his work under Charcot, his attempt at the 'Project for a Scientific Psychology', his attempt at postulating a physiological model of psychic functioning, his work with hypnosis, dreams, and psychopathology. All these phases culminated in a broad and amazing theory postulating a particular understanding of the operation of the mind.

He postulated that psychic functioning could not be reduced to what is conscious. His work suggested to him that there is a region of the mind that operates autonomously, playing a crucial role in mental (psychic) functioning. This region of the mind, Freud postulated, has its own mode of expression. It steers us into behaviours and emotions for which the motivations are unknown to our conscious mind. This region influences our everyday behaviours and, significantly, it is implicated in the formation of neurotic symptoms. This region of the mind he termed the **unconscious**.

The contents of the unconscious are not inherently different to consciousness. This is an important point because it is a common error to

## Freud's conception of instincts

Instincts are traditionally considered to be hereditary patterns peculiar to animal species. They are unvarying across members of the species, they unfold developmentally, they are generally resistant to change, and they appear to have a purpose. In Freud's postulation, the instinct (*trieb*) is a dynamic process involving a source – a pressure of energy such as the bodily stimulation one feels with hunger or sexual arousal – and an aim, which will eliminate the tension produced by the source. It is through the object, such as food or a sexual object, that the instinct may obtain its aim.

assume that the contents of the unconscious are appalling, horrendous, dangerous **instincts** which, if allowed out to play, would destroy one. This is not so. Rather, it is socialisation that has imposed the need for some feelings and actions to remain unconscious to our functioning. These feelings and actions are associated with our natural instinctual life – our inborn patterns of behaving towards certain stimuli. These may be sexual and aggressive feelings. Social living dictates that some of this material needs to remain unconscious to safeguard the coherence of the society. It is upon this premise that Freud postulated our development towards a relatively civilised state.

**Instincts.** The biological and inborn physiological needs of the infant.

**Soma/somatic.** The body/of the body.

## Trieb

In considering the conditions that might render psychic material unconscious, Freud postulated the operation of the instinct or drives. Freud wrote in German, using the terms *instinkt* and *trieb*. English translations have used the term *instinct* for both these terms, leaving the risk of confusing the two meanings that Freud intended. In his writing they are used in quite distinct ways. *Instinkt* is used in the classical sense of animal instinct, such as an instinctual recognition of danger, whereas his use of *trieb* designates a dynamic, that is, the instinct has a source, an aim and an object. His concept of *trieb* has commonly come to be termed instinct. It is this simplification that has led to the common misunderstanding of the lay person in stating that for Freud 'sex is all'. This is not so at all. It is instinct as designated by *trieb*, which underlies Freud's complex understanding of psychic motivation.

The instinct has its source in the bodily sensation, such as an oral need. The aim of the instinct is then to discharge the state of tension created by the need, either through eating, drinking, talking, smoking, or screaming, etc. The object is the means by which this may come about, for example food, cigarettes, drugs, or words.

The popular view of sexuality is that it means heterosexual genital contact. In his study of perversions and infantile sexuality, Freud postulates the infant in an initial polymorphous state, that is, infantile sexuality occurs in several distinct forms – oral, anal, phallic, and genital. This state is merely concerned with the aim of eliminating tension at the **somatic** source. The source could be oral, anal, or phallic. The instinct would thus attach itself to any object that resulted in satisfaction. Fixations at this stage of polymorphous infantile sexuality could lead to what Freud defines as *perversion* in adult sexuality. What he demonstrates in his study of sexual perversion is that the object is variable. It is chosen because of the vicissitude of the person's history and where the fixation may lie.

In the relative normal development of sexuality, the aim of the instinct only becomes subordinate to the genital zone at the end of a complex evolution through childhood. This evolution is dependent upon biological maturation but its course is influenced by complex forces of repression that may result in fixation at any of the psycho-sexual stages. Thus one can see that in and of itself, the instinct has no moral rightness or wrongness about it. The polymorphous nature of infantile sexuality is pressured through the progressive demands of socialisation into a genital state and the variable infantile motivations inherent in the instinct are repressed into the unconscious (Laplanche and Pontalis 1973).

Significantly, an intimate relationship exists between the growth of consciousness and the growth of civilisation. Consciousness has allowed greater control over instinctual life. Thus most of our instinctual urges have become repressed in one way or another. We value measured living – not too much food, sex, or pleasure. The natural unconscious instincts of the baby, when they surface to consciousness, have to be repressed in the interests of the social world. Our instinctual life, in and of itself, is not 'bad' but it is the need to live with others that requires the need to control this life. This has left us fearful of our instinctual nature.

# Infantile and adult sexuality

Because he came to the study of human psychology through psychiatry and medicine, it is understandable that Freud was always keen to emphasise a strong biological current in human development. In fact, for Freud, the story of human development can largely be traced through the various primary bodily functions of the infant, functions which are necessary for its survival, and which also provide a powerful focus of socialisation in the first few years of life. Freud's theory of development is one that requires us to suspend many of our normal assumptions about childhood and sexuality. For instance, the ways in which we typically discuss and understand human sexuality are too narrow for Freud. For him, human sexuality is about far more than merely penetrative genital sex between heterosexual partners.

Because Freud maintains that **sexual instincts** are as present and as active in infants as they are in adults and that infants are sexually active beings from day one (Freud 1977), we need to qualify what he means by infantile sexuality and to clarify the crucial differences between this and adult sexuality. First, where infantile sexuality revolves around the pleasurable stimulation of any of the **erogenous zones** of the body, adult sexuality is predominantly focused only on the genitals. (Erogenous zones are those parts of the body that are tied to necessary somatic (physical) functions (eating, excreting, urinating). They are the sources of both tension and pleasure for the individual. There are three basic erogenous zones: the mucous membranes of the mouth, the anus, and the genitals. The stimulation of the mouth leads to oral pleasure (sucking, smoking, eating), the emptying of the bowels produces anal pleasure, and the rubbing of the penis or vagina leads to genital pleasure).

Unlike adults, infants have no necessary focus on their genitals as the most important source of pleasure. Because of this lack of differentiation, Freud suggests that infantile sexuality has not properly defined its **sexual aim**, in other words the specific sexual act towards which one's sexual instinct is particularly drawn is not defined. As a result, any one of a variety of activities that provide bodily sensations of pleasure – such as looking, touching, and even the exchange of pain – can be the sexual aim for the infant. Infants, therefore, are **'polymorphously perverse'** (Freud 1977). This term indicates that they have no hierarchies or ordering of sexual instincts. Mature sexuality, by contrast, requires that the adult should subordinate all the other sexual instincts (for oral, anal, and visual

**Sexual instincts.** The inborn dynamic drive, located in the id and physiologically based, that urges one to find gratification in a sexual object. In Freud's view, this instinct is meant to serve the procreation of the species.

**Erogenous zones.** Those parts of the body that are tied to necessary somatic (physical) functions (eating, excreting, urinating) and that are the sources both of tension and of pleasure for the individual. There are three basic erogenous zones, the mucous membranes of the mouth, the anus, and the genitals.

**Sexual aim.** The specific sexual act towards which one's sexual instinct is particularly drawn. As an example, any of a variety of sexual activities, such as looking, touching, or even the exchange of pain, can initially be prioritised as the sexual aim for the infant.

**Polymorphously perverse.** The phrase Freud uses to describe the sexuality of the infant before it has been hierarchised into component instincts (oral, anal, and phallic) under the subordination of all other sexual instincts to the priority of penetrative genital sex.

PHOTO: CHA JOHNSTON

*In Freud's view we are born neither innately heterosexual nor homosexual; instead, we are all innately bisexual.*

satisfaction) to the sexual priority of penetrative, genital sex. This does not mean that all our other sexual instincts disappear as we reach mature sexuality. Oral and anal sex (and visual stimulation) still remain potentially pleasurable for adults; it is just that these sexual pleasures generally become subordinated, as 'foreplay' activities, to the priority and focus of genital sex.

The second important difference between infantile and adult sexuality is that the infant, unlike the adult, has not channelled the sexual instincts towards a specific **sexual object** (Freud 1977). Freud used this term to denote one's preferred type of sexual partner, the person whom one finds sexually attractive. Freud maintains that settling on a secure object-choice is a characteristic only of mature adult sexuality. Thus the infant is not only polymorphously perverse but also inherently **bisexual**. The infant has no innate predisposition to any one gender as more sexually desirable. For Freud, in short, there is no genetic preprogramming

**Sexual object/object-choice.** Freud's term for one's preferred type of sexual partner or the person whom one finds most sexually attractive.

**Bisexuality.** Having no sexual preference for either exclusively male or female categories of object-choice.

## 'Perversions'

Perversions specifically denote deviations of the sexual instincts. It refers to the whole of psychosexual behaviour that accompanies atypical means of obtaining sexual pleasure. Perversion is said to be present in adults when:

1. Orgasm is reached with other sexual objects than through coitus with the opposite sex. These could be, among other forms, homosexuality, paedophilia, and bestiality.

2. The orgasm is subordinate to certain other extrinsic conditions that may of themselves bring about sexual pleasure. These could be, among other forms, fetishism, transvestism, voyeurism, exhibitionism, and sado-masochism (Laplanche and Pontalis 1973).

*For Freud infantile and adult sexuality are qualitatively different. Freud believed, against the dominant views of the time, that sexual instincts were powerfully present in children.*

making the infant male prefer females, or the female prefer males. Sexual preference, the making of a stable object-choice (be it heterosexual or homosexual), is thus only an outcome of the process of psychosexual development.

The fact that the infant has no in-built object-choice is supported by Freud's contention that the infant will form an erotic attachment to whoever nurses, cares for, and feeds it in the earliest months of life. Typically this is the mother, and significantly, infantile sexuality obeys no sexual taboos against incest. In fact, Freud claims that infantile sexuality is innately incestuous, and the sexual desires of the child for one or both of the parents are so strong that they need to be resolved in the Oedipus complex, which we will presently describe in more detail. Freud has hence formulated the broad differences between the beginning points of infantile sexuality and the (ideal) end points of adult sexuality. This picture corresponds to the more general progression of human development from the infant in the un-socialised, amoral state of nature, to the adult in the socialised, moral state of culture. We can now go on to 'fill in the gaps' that connect infantile sexuality to adult sexuality.

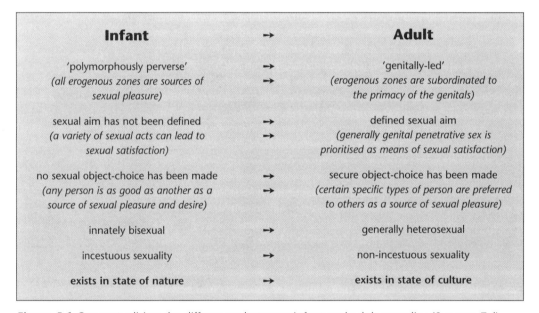

| Infant | → | Adult |
|---|---|---|
| 'polymorphously perverse' *(all erogenous zones are sources of sexual pleasure)* | → → | 'genitally-led' *(erogenous zones are subordinated to the primacy of the genitals)* |
| sexual aim has not been defined *(a variety of sexual acts can lead to sexual satisfaction)* | → → | defined sexual aim *(generally genital penetrative sex is prioritised as means of sexual satisfaction)* |
| no sexual object-choice has been made *(any person is as good as another as a source of sexual pleasure and desire)* | → → | secure object-choice has been made *(certain specific types of person are preferred to others as a source of sexual pleasure)* |
| innately bisexual | → | generally heterosexual |
| incestuous sexuality | → | non-incestuous sexuality |
| **exists in state of nature** | → | **exists in state of culture** |

**Figure 5.1** Conceptualising the differences between infant and adult sexuality (Sue van Zyl).

## Psychosexual stages of development

We have established that the infant is a sexual being that receives sexual pleasure through the stimulation of its various erogenous zones. We have also established that these zones are bound to vital physical functions that the infant needs to perform in order to survive. The child experiences the build-up of tension in these zones, for example, a full bladder, or the need for food. Subsequent relief of these tensions leads to the child's experience of pleasure. It is worth emphasising here that the infant receives these pleasures on a daily basis through the routines of feeding, being washed, cleaned, and nursed. In line with the idea of the **libido** being 'schooled' is Freud's postulation that, although each of the erogenous zones may be pleasurably stimulated from the beginning of life onwards, different zones dominate at different times of the infant's life. He also postulates that different and important socialising challenges are tied to each of the zones. In this way it makes sense to speak of developmental stages. Each stage requires the infant to complete an adaptive activity, which will contribute to the biological maturity of the child, and will also have a foundational influence on the child's emerging personality.

The transition from one zonal stage to the next is not always smooth. If the developing child does not properly resolve the specific developmental challenge of each stage, then a certain amount of the libido becomes permanently invested in these zonal stages. Freud (1977) calls this process **fixation**. The result of fixation is that less libidinal energy is available to deal with the conflicts in the later stages. The successful resolution of later stages then becomes more difficult. Various psychological problems and personality traits may result from fixations at certain stages of psychosexual development. Fixation can occur because the child was overindulged in a certain stage and does not wish to move on. An example might be a child who is overfed and finds weaning a difficult time due to the satisfying relationship to the breast. Fixation might also occur because a child was frustrated in having the psychosexual needs of the stage adequately satisfied. In such a case, neither the biological needs nor the emotional needs of the child have been adequately resolved. These ideas will become clearer as we continue. It is important to emphasise that the work of the instincts, their satisfaction, and the fixations that might arise are processes that are completely unconscious.

## The oral stage (birth to eighteen months)

The oral stage is the first stage by virtue of the fact that feeding is the primary function of the child at this age. Most of the infant's interaction with the world at this time occurs through the mouth. The mouth is the source of pleasure, through tasting, licking, and sucking. Freud claims that at this stage, sexual activity has not yet been separated from the ingestion of food. The mouth is also the means through which the child may best be soothed, by giving it a bottle or the breast to suck on. At this stage it is also true to say that the mouth is an exploratory instrument and is in many ways the primary means through which the infant establishes contact with the outside world. As Maier (1988) claims, infants essentially meet their society orally.

Each stage has a passive and an active component, or phase. In the oral stage, the first component is passive, the **incorporative phase** (sucking), which shows the

**Libido.** The sum total of all of an individual's various and combined sexual instincts, which are inborn.

**Fixation.** The outcome of a child's failure adequately to resolve and move on from a specific developmental challenge during the psychosexual stages, when a certain amount of the libido becomes 'stuck', permanently invested in a particular stage. This leads to the development of certain personality dispositions.

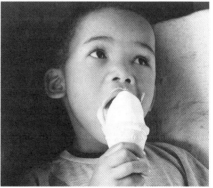

*Although the oral stage predominates between birth and eighteen months as a source of pleasure and a means of exploration, it continues to be a powerful focus throughout childhood.*

PHOTOS: CHA JOHNSTON

An oral fixation might manifest in an individual gaining an inordinate amount of pleasure from oral stimulations, such as smoking, eating, drinking, kissing, or even talking.

Freud maintains that incorporation is the basis for the psychological function of identification. The example Freud gives is of thumb sucking, where the child substitutes part of its own body for the nipple.

extent to which the infant is helpless, dependent, and limited to 'taking in' the outside world. Freud maintains that incorporation is the basis for the psychological function of **identification**, whereby a part of the outside world is taken into the individual as a way of making it part of them and as a way of making them more self-sufficient. The example Freud gives is of thumb sucking, where the child substitutes a part of its own body for the nipple. The second phase of the oral stage is an active one, the **sadistic phase** (biting). It occurs as the infant begins teething and here pleasure becomes linked to the destructive activities of chewing and biting. This is also the point at which the infant begins eating solid foods. The sadistic qualities of this phase are epitomised in the action of biting the breast. A variety of aggressive tendencies may be linked to this developmental phase.

As weaning is a goal of the oral phase, it becomes increasingly important for the child to let go of the mother and to become less reliant upon oral gratification, which is a need that will inevitably be frustrated. A number of personality traits may stem from the quality of resolution of this phase. Such traits reside along the continua of dependence-independence, trust-mistrust and optimism-pessimism. Unsatisfactory resolution results in fixation at the more 'negative' ends of these continua. It is not difficult to identify the qualities of 'oral characters'. These are the people that relate to the world orally and who are more preoccupied than others, with the pleasures of eating and drinking (or the avoidance of eating, such as anorexia nervosa). They may have preference for oral types of sexuality such as kissing, cunnilingus, or fellatio. They may also choose to reduce tension by smoking, drinking, or nail biting (Abraham 1927). Gullibility – the tendency to 'swallow everything you're told' – also derives from this phase of development (Carver and Scheier 1988).

**Incorporative phase.** The first part of the oral stage, when the infant is helpless, dependent, and limited to 'taking in' the outside world. Freud maintained that incorporation was the basis for the psychological function of identification, whereby a part of the outside world is taken within the individual as a means of making it part of them.

**Identification.** The process whereby a subject adopts one or more attributes of another subject for her- or himself.

**Sadistic phase.** The second part of the oral phase where the infant begins teething and where pleasure becomes linked to the destructive activities of chewing and biting.

## The anal stage (eighteen months to three years)

During the anal stage the focus is on the anus as the erogenous zone. Again, this stage of development involves first an active, then a passive phase. To begin with, the aim is simply to eject the object, to destroy it, and 'be done with it'. This is the passive phase of the anal stage where the child concedes to parental demands, and 'gives away' or 'sacrifices' the faeces as a 'gift'. This phase of the anal stage is often accompanied by encouragement, reward, and praise from the parents. The child is thus convinced of the value of producing 'things' at the 'right' time and place.

Freud suggests that this provides the basis for adult productivity and creativity, or the converse of obsessive anxieties over production.

The second and active phase of the anal stage relates to the retaining of faeces, to 'holding back', and to the defiance of parental wishes. The child has now learnt sphincter control and is able to increase its own sexual pleasure by withholding faeces. The defiance in this 'holding back' provides for the possibility of a change in the child's character. The child not only wants to decide for itself, but for others too. It wants to own, to dominate, and to punish others. Hence this stage of zonal development may be linked to dominating and controlling dispositions in later life.

The refusal of the child to 'deliver' faeces may lead to negative parental reactions such as scolding and punishment, to which the child may react in two ways. If it responds by withholding the faeces and urine, then **anal retentive traits** develop. Fixation at this stage can be seen in personality traits such as excessive orderliness, stinginess, and stubbornness. Alternatively, the child may rebel by forcefully excreting, which may lead to **anal expulsive traits**. Fixation at this stage can be seen in personality traits such as cruelty, hostility, and messy and destructive behaviour.

## The phallic stage (three to five years)

The necessities of urination and washing of the genital areas make it inevitable that children will notice the pleasure associated with these body parts. Freud (1977, 88) observes that 'scarcely a single individual escapes' some kind of **infantile masturbation** in this phase. This masturbation is of a non-orgasmic type. Up until this point of psychosexual development, sexual desire is largely **auto-erotic**, which is to say that sexual pleasure can, to a large extent, be achieved through self-stimulation, such as thumb sucking. Although the primary caregiver has been a central figure in the sexual life of the child up until now, it is only really at this **phallic stage** of development that sexual urges and desires towards a sexual object come to focus strongly on one external object, which, invariably, is this person. This developing sexual desire for the caregiver grows increasingly strong, and it is this that leads the child into the Oedipus complex, which we shall discuss presently.

The phallic stage is characterised by the interest that children now show in their genitals. In boys, in particular, Freud claims, it is this organ (the penis) that best represents the child's instincts for knowledge, through its proneness to excitement and the wealth of sensations that it is capable of. Freud maintains that the drive for knowledge generally springs from this stage of development. Children are very curious about the sexual differences of the genders and about 'where babies come from'. This is the time of games such as 'you show me yours and I'll show you mine', which manifest the **scopophilic drive** of this stage (the desire to see another's sexual organs). The scopophilic drive manifests in active and passive guises as **exhibitionism** (the sexual desire to show one's genitals to another) and **voyeurism** (the desire to see other people naked or engaging in sexual activity) respectively.

It is at this stage also that girls and boys discover their anatomical sexual differences. Following the perspective of the little boy, Freud claims

**Anal retentive traits.** Particular fixation at the oral stage leading to personality traits such as excessive orderliness, stinginess, and stubbornness.

**Anal expulsive traits.** Particular fixation at the oral stage leading to personality traits such as the tendency to be cruel, hostile, messy, and destructive.

**Infantile masturbation.** Non-orgasmic, pleasurable stimulation of the genitals.

**Auto-eroticism.** Early quality of sexual development in which sexual pleasure can, to a large extent, be achieved through self-stimulation.

**Phallic stage.** Phase of psychosocial development where the erogenous focus in boys is on the penis, and in girls on the clitoris.

**Scopophilic drive.** The desire to see another's sexual organs, manifesting in active and passive guises respectively as exhibitionism (the sexual desire to show one's genitals to others) and voyeurism (the desire to watch other people naked or engaging in sexual activity).

**Exhibitionism.** The sexual desire to show one's genitals to others.

**Voyeurism.** The desire to watch other people naked or engaging in sexual activity.

that it is his assumption that all other living beings possess a penis similar to his. Inevitably though, the boy discovers that girls lack a penis and apparently, before long, the girls discover this absence. The childhood reaction to this discovery in boys is one of fear, the fear that they might lose their penis, that 'someone might take it away'. In girls the reaction is of jealousy; they see the little boy has something that they do not, and they instantly want it. These are the two respective bases for the formation of **castration anxiety** and **penis envy**. Castration anxiety in males is where there is either a literal or a figurative fear of, in some way, losing the penis, or manhood generally. Penis envy in females is the desire to possess a penis, or to attain a certain masculine status. Both of these phenomena will be discussed in more detail in relation to the Oedipus complex.

There are a number of reasons why Freud's hypothesis about the significance of having or not having a penis is valid. Having or not having a penis is permeated with cultural values and meanings. In patriarchal societies men have greater power, and little boys are accorded more importance than little girls. Girls may even be killed at birth. The rise of Feminist thought attests to the theorising that has attempted to understand the dominance of the male. However, the significance of the penis is not wholly determined by culture. The value of having a penis is also supported by a diverse range of influences. Consider, for example, issues of active and passive behavioural roles where the act of penetration by the penis, by definition, implies greater power than the more passive act of incorporation by the vagina. Judgements around absence and presence are also made where the having of something is always preferable to the not having of it. There are also judgements around size where bigger or more noticeable is also always better. It is understandable that male genitals are seen as preferable to the discreet or smaller sexual organs of women. There are also the questions of convenience and ability, as in being able to urinate standing up.

The active-passive polarity of this phallic stage corresponds to the penis versus non-penis, male-genital versus castrated polarity, or put more simply, to the distinction between presence and absence. For Freud this presence-absence distinction has important ramifications for the way children come to understand their gender roles in society, and how they come to be gendered into an active position or a passive position. The parental 'training' that accompanies this stage is the prohibition around masturbation and appropriate sexual behaviour. The prohibitions may or may not be accompanied by threats of punishment. We will discuss the implications of the prohibition as part of the Oedipus complex.

## Latency (five years to puberty)

After the turmoil of the Oedipus complex, and its hopeful resolution, the child enters a period of relative calm where sexual and aggressive instincts become fairly inactive. The calmness of latency is largely the result of the large-scale use of the **defences** of **repression** and **sublimation**. These have been required to bring to an end the Oedipus complex and institute a rudimentary superego, which we will describe later. Sublimation refers to the situation where the build-up of sexual and

**Castration anxiety.** The literal or figurative unconscious fear in males of in some way losing one's penis, or one's manhood generally.

**Penis envy.** The literal or figurative unconscious desire in females to possess one's own penis, or to attain a certain masculine status.

**Defences.** The multiple processes which protect the ego from real or imagined threats, and whose ultimate function is to keep unconscious material out of conscious awareness. Defence mechanisms may be used to channel or control the forces that may otherwise lead to neurosis. Defences typically act as a compromise between wish and reality.

**Repression.** The mechanism through which unacceptable or disturbing impulses or ideas are kept by the ego out of the conscious part of the mind.

**Sublimation.** The situation where the build-up of sexual instincts is expressed in socially acceptable ways, like the making of art, the dedication of one's life to religion, or the search for knowledge.

aggressive instincts is expressed in socially acceptable ways, such as running instead of fighting, the making of art, the dedication of one's life to religion, or the search for knowledge (Freud 1977). Repression refers to the mechanism that keeps unacceptable or disturbing impulses or ideas out of consciousness (Freud 1977).

Sublimation is considered the most mature and productive defence mechanism. Freud considers the period of latency a necessary condition for our aptitude to develop 'higher civilisation'. Significantly, the form or aim of the sublimation will be culturally prescribed. In one culture, sublimation may take the form of stringent devotion to religion; in another it may take the form of dedication to a well-paid and demanding corporate sector job.

Given that sexual and aggressive instincts are far more moderate at this stage of development, the child has the opportunity to turn its attention to other pursuits. This is not so much a time where conflicts are confronted, or new traits developed, but rather a time where children begin to consolidate. The consolidation is based upon the breadth and quality of earlier experience related to the developmental stages already completed. Parental identifications picked up in the phallic stage, for example, may now be complemented with other important social or authority figures. The period of latency is also when children really learn to feel love for those who have taken care of them throughout their childhood. As Freud (1977, 146) puts it, 'All through the period of latency children learn to feel for other people who have helped them in their helplessness, and who have satisfied their needs, a love which is on the model of, and a continuation of, their relation as sucklings to their nursing mother.' It is here that love becomes a part of the sexual instincts.

Whereas previously nature (physiology) has been the dominant force in the child's psychosexual development, with the advent of the Oedipus complex, and onwards, the force of culture now begins to be dominant in the psychosexual life of the individual.

## The genital stage (puberty onwards)

As latency draws to a close with the arrival of puberty, sexual and aggressive urges once again come to be influential. Conflicts encountered at previous developmental stages may occur again, this time within the broader demands of culture. The ability to deal with and resolve such crises is important to the eventual identity of the adolescent. Adult sexual desires begin to become apparent in the individual, but although the adolescent is sexually mature in the biological sense, the act of sexual intercourse is not yet socially acceptable. Other means of gratification are therefore sought, and masturbation and sexual fantasy become increasingly important preoccupations of the individual.

Great physiological changes accompany this final stage of development: menstruation in girls, and the capacity for erection in boys. These changes prove very important in adapting infantile sexuality to its final, normal, adult shape. If all the prior psychosexual stages have been properly negotiated and no strong fixations have developed, the individual generally enters this stage with the sexual instincts powerfully focused on the genital organs. The auto-erotic sexual instincts now become absolutely directed towards a sexual object and the separate and partial component instincts of the various erogenous zones combine in subordination to the primacy of the genital zone. The pleasures of the other erogenous zones will generally now be little more than 'fore-pleasures' to the overriding focus on penetrative heterosexual genital intercourse.

The Oedipus complex has been instrumental in instituting a non-incestuous, (generally) heterosexual, **genitally-led** eroticism that serves the purpose of reproduction. Also of great importance is the fact that the sexual instincts become absolutely directed towards a sexual object. Instead of being preoccupied with one's own sexual gratification, the individual now develops the desire to share mutual sexual gratification with someone else.

**Genitally-led.** The phrase Freud uses to describe the sexuality of the adult after the various component sexual instincts have been subordinated under the sexual priority of penetrative genital sex.

Whereas the phallic stage was dominated simply by the sensory organ stimulus of the penis and the clitoris, the genital stage is dominated by the goal of orgasm through a particular form of stimulation of the penis and the vagina. The overarching sexual aim of this final phase is, for the male, to penetrate the vagina with his penis, and for the female, to be penetrated in the vagina by the penis. The ability to achieve full and free orgasm with a heterosexual partner on an equal basis is an important foundation for intimate relationships and life-partner choices from here on. By now, individuals are able to share erogenous pleasure with others in a warm and caring way, to be concerned for them, to feel love for them.

Individuals generally now have better control over their sexual and aggressive instincts and have been transformed from the self-centred and pleasure-seeking infant into the well-socialised and caring adult. As we know, not all people succeed in properly entering the genital stage. Many of us have less than adequate control over our sexual and aggressive instincts and are also unable to gratify our sexual desires in a completely satisfying and acceptable way. So although the genital stage represents the perfect culmination of psychosexual development it is, in many ways, more of an ideal to strive for than an end that may be taken for granted (Fenichel 1945).

## Concluding the psychosexual stages

In concluding this section it is important to emphasise that any obstruction to the resolution of a particular psychosexual stage will lead to the development of psychosocial problems. In this sense, Freud's 'developmental map' is not only about tracing normal development, but is also a way of tracing the origins of psychological problems in patients. This reflects the fact that his developmental psychology was very much designed around the needs of clinical treatment. The other point that bears repeating is that each zonal stage is distinguished by an active-passive polarity. What this means is that there is broad latitude as to how an individual might negotiate these stages. For Freud these polarities largely correspond to the masculine-feminine polarity of patriarchal societies, where males are generally accorded active and dominant roles, and females are restricted to passive and submissive roles. In this connection Freud's work has become an important focus for people working in the field of gender issues, both in the sense that he seems to offer an under-

# Is Freud homophobic?

It is important to be clear about Freud's views on homosexuality. For Freud (1977) homosexuality is not abnormal in the morally evaluative or stigmatised sense of the term. He claims in fact that:

> Psychoanalytic research is most decidedly opposed to any attempt at separating off homosexuals from the rest of mankind as a group of special character. By studying sexual excitations other than those that are manifestly displayed, it has found that all human beings are capable of making a homosexual object-choice and have in fact made one in their unconscious (Freud 1977, 56).

This in fact is an extraordinarily progressive view on homosexuality, particularly considering the predominance of conservative attitudes towards sexuality in late nineteenth-century Western Europe when Freud was writing. Indeed, Freud (1977) rejects outright the notion that sexual deviation should be couched in terms of 'degeneracy' or 'disease', or that the term 'perversion' should be used as a term of reproach. For Freud (1977), every individual's sexuality, like their psychological adjustment more generally, deviates somewhat (however slightly) from the ideal norm. There is, in his words, 'no healthy person that fails to make some addition that might be called perverse to the normal sexual aim' (Freud 1977, 74).

If we consider how different and idiosyncratic each individual's path through the zonal stages and the Oedipus complex *must be*, we then start to appreciate that each instance of sexuality is in some way distinct. In fact, considering the challenges that Freud sees confronting the task of 'nomal' sexual development (the transformation of the auto-erotic, incestuous, polymorphously perverse, and bisexual instincts, not to mention the resolution of the Oedipus/Elektra complex), it is almost a miracle that any vaguely 'normal' sexuality emerges at the end of a child's development.

Nevertheless, it is undeniable that although Freud can explain the occurrence of the homosexual object-choice, he cannot avoid seeing it as in some ways deviant or aberrant. For Freud (1977), homosexuality stems from three principal sources: 1) a narcissistic object-choice, where one takes one's self, or one's own sex as an object of sexual desire, 2) a problematic negotiation of the Oedipus complex, where the individual comes to both desire, and identify with, the same sex (rather than desiring the opposite sex and identifying with the same sex, as occurs in the successful resolution of the Oedipus complex), or 3) an early fixation which has prevented the individual from attaining the full genital psychosexual stage of development.

It is important to note that homosexuality is not necessarily psychopathological for Freud; it is only psychopathological for the individual if they experience their object-choice as conflictual on the level of personality (meaning that there is ego/superego conflict attaching to the object-choice). For Freud, it is possible to be a well-adjusted and non-psychopathological homosexual. Moreover, it should be noted that Freud's theory is led by the evolutionary priority of species-preservation. In this way he is insisting that nature (and following from it, culture) demands that heterosexual, penetrative, genital sex be the norm within society, for this, until very recently, was the only way in which the reproduction of the species could be assured (Freud 1977).

Ultimately, however, despite the above arguments, there is now general and widespread support for the view that describing homosexuality in terms of deviance, abnormality, aberrance, and particularly psychopathology, is unavoidably derisive, value-laden, and a damaging approach to a healthy and loving form of sexuality. From this claim it is very difficult to rescue Freud.

standing of how the influence of gendering affects development, and also, paradoxically, how Freud himself is seen as yet another example of how the rights and powers of women are systematically marginalised within society.

# The Oedipus complex

The Oedipus complex is perhaps the central challenge to the socialisation of infantile sexuality. Freud saw this drama taking place in the phallic stage of development, and named it after a famous tragedy in classical Greek drama, *Oedipus Rex*. In the play Oedipus, the heir to the Greek throne, is born under a curse and, as a result, is given away at birth by his parents. Oedipus grows up, unaware of his true identity. As an adult he unknowingly meets his father, challenges him, and kills him in a sword fight. Subsequently Oedipus meets his mother, and again unknowingly, sleeps with her. After he discovers what has really happened, that he has killed his father and slept with his mother, he punishes himself in an agonised fit of remorse by putting out his own eyes. The reason that Oedipus Rex is such a great and archetypal story, says Freud, is that it is the story of all of us. We are all destined, 'cursed', to direct our first sexual impulses towards our mothers, and our first unconscious jealous and murderous thoughts towards our father. Similarly, passing through this process involves guilt and self-punishment. It is vital to emphasise that this all happens at a deeply unconscious level. In fact these desires are so shocking that they need to be strongly repressed, that is, kept in the unconscious part of the mind and prevented from rising to the level of conscious awareness. How we attempt to prevent these unconscious aspects from rising to consciousness will be looked at in the next section – the structure of the mind.

The complex manifests somewhat differently in boys and girls (in the case of girls this complex is often referred to as the Elektra complex, after another Greek character who persuades her brother to kill their mother). Given this difference, it is better to deal with the two separately.

The boy child enters the Oedipus complex loving his mother and desiring her as his sexual object. This is because it is generally she who cares for, cleans, and feeds him, thus stimulating his erogenous zones. Freud maintains that the father stands as a challenge to the boy's desires to have the mother, and to have her all to himself. As a consequence the boy starts to develop jealousy and strong resentment and hatred towards the father. These unconscious feelings of hostility can become very strong, in fact even murderous, and they eventually induce feelings of guilt in the child. The child also begins to suspect that the father will take concrete steps to prevent him from acting on his desire for his mother.

## Castration anxiety

It is important to reiterate that the Oedipus complex overlaps, and is an integral part of, the phallic stage, that period when children are insatiably curious about others' genitals. It is around this time that the boy has the experience of seeing a girl – or for that matter his mother – naked, and notices that they do not have a penis. This, according to Freud, has an enormous effect on the little boy, who begins to think that he could lose his penis as well. The boy automatically assumes that the female must once have had a penis and that they have been castrated, that someone has 'taken it away'. The fear of losing his penis develops into what Freud calls castration anxiety: the fear that the father will take away, or 'cut off' the boy child's penis to prevent him from making sexual advances towards the mother. Castration anxiety is aided and abetted by the prohibition that Freud assumes is placed by parents on the little boy's attempts at masturbation, and from the implied threats ('We'll cut it off') stemming from that prohibition.

Castration anxiety eventually causes the boy to give up his mother as a sexual object. He realises that he cannot have her and that his father will not allow him to. The child then takes the next best option, which is to identify with the father. By identifying with the father (who is physically like him by virtue of the fact that he too has a penis) the little boy feels protected, feels that the father is less likely to harm him. This identification also helps the boy get past his ambivalent feelings towards the father, who is no longer an enemy, but is like him. One can see how a boy's father in this way becomes an important role model for the child. Freud holds that this identification has important implications for the development of the superego, which we shall come to presently. Importantly also, this identification allows the boy to have vicarious access to the mother by imagining that he is the father. Ultimately, however, perhaps the most important aspect of this identification is that the little boy realises that the mother is 'off limits' to his sexual desires; he realises that he cannot have her, but that he can have another sexual object like her, another female, and preferably one who resembles the mother in some way.

Therefore there are two vital psychological processes that must occur if the Oedipus complex is to be resolved: identification with the same-sex parent and the giving up of the opposite-sex parent as an object of desire, which leads to the substitution of that opposite-sex parent by another similar object. One of the functions of the Oedipus complex is to separate identification and desire. Failure to separate these two processes, that is, desiring and identifying with the same parent, leads, in Freud's view, to homosexuality.

## The female Oedipus complex and penis envy

The girl child starts the female version of the Oedipus complex in the same way that the boy starts the male Oedipus complex, by desiring the mother. For Freud the psychosexual development of the girl is always more problematic and less stable than that of the boy. Freud maintains that the girl has to switch from different erogenous foci, from the phallic (clitoral focus) to the genital (vaginal) stage. Freud maintains that mature genital sexuality in a woman is attained through vaginal, not clitoral, satisfaction. (Sexology research, however, indicates that this is largely a fallacious distinction.) Further, the girl has an extra step to make in the

Oedipus complex. Whereas the boy remains desiring the mother or her substitute, the girl needs to shift from desiring the mother to desiring the father. Freud accounts for this with what he calls penis envy, which is much like the girl's equivalent of castration anxiety. Like the boy child, the little girl sees a naked member of the opposite sex, usually the father. In the instant she sees the penis, as Freud (1977) puts it, she wants it. She turns against her mother in disgust, blaming her for not giving her one, or worse yet, assuming that she had one, and that the mother has cut it off.

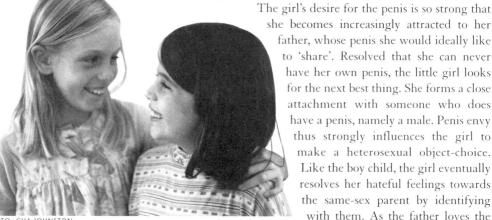

The girl's desire for the penis is so strong that she becomes increasingly attracted to her father, whose penis she would ideally like to 'share'. Resolved that she can never have her own penis, the little girl looks for the next best thing. She forms a close attachment with someone who does have a penis, namely a male. Penis envy thus strongly influences the girl to make a heterosexual object-choice. Like the boy child, the girl eventually resolves her hateful feelings towards the same-sex parent by identifying with them. As the father loves the mother, identification with the mother affords her the vicarious outlet for her sexual desires for the father.

PHOTO: CHA JOHNSTON

*Both because little girls have to take an extra step in their development through the zonal stages, and because their first sexual object is the mother, Freud concludes that women move far more easily between homosexual and heterosexual object-choices than do men.*

The girl does eventually discover a physical substitute for a penis: a baby. In this way Freud offers an explanation for the strong desire of many women to have a child. Of course the desire to have a child (and preferably a boy child, with a penis) also entails the need for the woman to incorporate a penis into her body, so as to get pregnant. This itself is a desire driven by penis envy. Ultimately this capacity to bear children is something that cements the bond of identification between mother and daughter.

## The longevity and universality of the Oedipus complex

Castration anxiety and penis envy remain strong unconscious motivational forces throughout the lives of males and females. Fixations developing during the phallic stage (which overlaps with the Oedipus complex) may lead to men trying their utmost to 'prove' that they have not been castrated by siring many children, or sleeping with many women, or more symbolically, by being very ambitious in their careers. Similar fixations in women may lead to their exhibiting penis envy in very overt ways, by being flirtatious for example, and seductive with many men. Moreover, in Freud's view, both of these processes (castration anxiety and penis envy) have powerful effects on the morality of males and females respectively. Because males have learned, through fear of castration, a healthy respect for moral law, and because they have strongly identified with the male father figure, who in patriarchal societies is largely the one 'in charge', they have a far stronger regard for

*Relationships between the young child and the opposite-sex parent take centre stage during the Oedipus complex.*

moral law and order than women. (This will be explored in more detail as we progress.)

The Oedipus complex offers an important explanation of how the child moves from incestuous to non-incestuous sexuality and from having no object-choice to having a secure object-choice. Freud claims that the occurrence of these complexes is universal, and that they are universally necessary precisely because they prevent the development of incestuous sexual relations within families and promote the preservation of the species by 'schooling' the sexual instincts of children towards members of the opposite sex. Incest is taboo in every society, says Freud, just as heterosexual sex is the predominant form of sexual interaction in every culture.

# The structure of the mind

Having examined the workings of the psychosexual stages and the Oedipus complex, it is now important to consider briefly Freud's theory of the structure of the mind. Freud developed two models of the mind, the earlier **topographical model** and the later **structural model**. This later model is useful in understanding how the unconscious can work at the level of not only the *id*, but also the *ego* and the *superego*.

At its most basic, the mind may be thought of as comprising two fundamental regions, one which is conscious and one which is unconscious. (Freud also postulates a third region: the preconscious.) The conscious part of the mind contains all those thoughts, feelings, and behaviours you are aware of at the moment. All psychoanalytic theorists hold to the view that consciousness is always infiltrated and influenced by the unconscious. Thus while we may assume ourselves to be conscious, even this experience of consciousness is suffused with unconscious material. Consciousness relies upon making connections with the world of language and consensual reality. Thinking from the conscious system main-

**Topographical model of the mind.** Freud's first 'mapping' of the mind, in which the mind is divided into three basic sections, the conscious, the preconscious, and the unconscious.

**Structural model of the mind.** Freud's later adaptation of the original topographical model of mind. The structural model includes the understandings of the ego, the id, and the superego. These are the basic components of personality functioning, and it is their complex interaction that produces human behaviour. If the first topography of mind outlined the 'territories' of the mind, the second topography outlines the central 'players' (or 'agencies') within the mind, adding a dynamic, or interactive, explanation to a descriptive explanation of the mind.

# Is Freud a chauvinist?

Many feminist writers have taken exception to the way Freud has characterised women (Horney 1967; Chodorow 1978). The focus of the feminist critique of Freud is often the notion of penis envy, which sees women as haunted throughout their lives by feelings of emptiness and jealousy stemming from their earlier 'castration'. The implication of this idea is that women will always in some way be inferior and that they will always (however unconsciously or consciously) want to be like men, or want to possess men. In many ways this seems a demeaning and unbalanced view of women, which portrays women from an insulting, and irredeemably masculine point of view. It is also a point of view that serves male interests (take, for example, the idea that women want, because of penis envy, to incorporate the penis into their body through intercourse).

Similarly, the idea that women do not experience castration anxiety, and therefore do not develop as powerful a superego as do men (see below), paints a picture of women as less moral and far more likely to disturb the moral order than men.

In Freud's defence, it should be noted that he lived in a very different historical and cultural era to our own, where equal rights and equality were in no way as prioritised as they are now. In this way, rather than being automatically sexist, Freud has shown us how certain psychosexual developments and anatomical distinctions came to be particularly culturally-loaded in the era in which he lived. In fact, Freud (1977) does suggest that what is important in the little girl's valuation of, and desire for, the penis is not merely her perception of the penis in isolation, but the social perception of the desirability of the penis.

Perhaps Freud then, rather than demeaning women, was simply an astute reader of culture, who effectively integrated the dominant patriarchal values of his time into his theory so as to expand its explanatory power. In fact, one might suggest that Freud's theory is particularly culture-sensitive, in the sense that penis envy adequately reflects the female desire to possess and attain all the rights and privileges that men had, and to a certain extent still have, as their prerogative. If this is the case, then Freud is largely 'off the hook' for being a sexist, but then his theory must be considered to be limited in the sense that it should not uncritically be applied to such different socio-cultural eras as our own.

Similarly, we must ask serious questions about if and how this theory should be applied, particularly if it perpetuates disempowering and demeaning stereotypes of women. Peterson (1980) has humorously mocked the idea of penis envy by suggesting that today men seem to exhibit what she calls 'vagina envy'. This idea makes a certain amount of sense when one considers that female anatomy enables women to bear children, an ability that, in some cultures, makes women more socially powerful than men. In Western 'First World' societies, however, it may be argued that this ability is considered to disempower women, to put them at a disadvantage in a professional working environment.

Although there is little doubt that certain of Freud's theories and understandings may be seen as demeaning to women, it is worth noting that his work, and that of psychoanalysis more widely, has become an important basis from which certain feminists, such as Juliet Mitchell, have engaged critically with issues of gender and patriarchal power.

tains the relations between words and meaning. What is significant is that, while the word relates to the meaning in consciousness, it is always also related to the meaning in the unconscious level. This link is made through a chain of associations. This understanding has allowed the development of the talking cure, where it is understood that by listening to the latent (hidden) meanings of the client's words you are given access to unconscious material. An example might be a client who discusses having seen a violent film, where the murderer is caught. You know that she is struggling with violent anger towards her husband and so you might hypothesise to her that she would like to harm her husband but is afraid that she would be punished. The client might be articulating his or her thoughts from the level of consciousness but the assumption is made that this conscious content is informed by unconscious motivations.

## The topographical model

In Freud's conception of the regions of the mind, the preconscious has a fluid boundary with consciousness, in that the content of the preconscious system can be conscious at one time and unconscious at another.

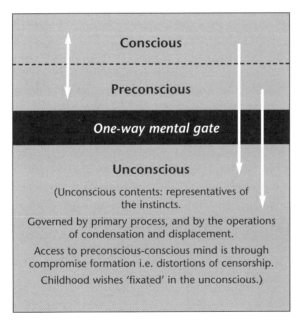

**Figure 5.2** Freud's topographical model of the mind, which divides the mind into conscious, preconscious, and unconscious parts. Note that whereas material can pass relatively freely between conscious and preconscious portions of the mind, unconscious material cannot pass freely into consciousness (hence the idea of the one-way gate). It is only under special conditions that any unconscious material can impinge upon the conscious mind. Dreaming is one such special circumstance, where especially disguised and moderated unconscious material is able to have some entry into the preconscious. Because the individual is asleep, this material does not impinge directly on consciousness.

**Ego.** The 'executive' or adaptive agency of the mind that mediates between the demands of reality, the superego, and the id. The ego arises from the needs to master instinctual impulses and to operate independently of parental figures, and from the self-preservative imperative for the id to adapt to the conditions of objective reality.

**Id.** The original and structural component of personality, the id is the 'instinctual bedrock' that the child is born with, and upon which their eventual personality will be built. The id is entirely unconscious and is strongly tied to the biological needs of the child. It supplies the 'psychical energy' that drives the mind and can in this way be thought of as the 'engine' of personality.

**Superego.** The last part of the personality to develop, the superego arises as a result of the resolution of the Oedipus complex, and is largely the product of the internalisation of parental authority, although it involves also the influence of other authority figures and of social values more generally. It is the superego that determines what is right and wrong for the moral individual.

**Pleasure principle.** The regulating ideal of the id, being that all instinctual urges should be satisfied immediately.

The preconscious part of the mind works continually to keep unconscious material, the true motivation and impetus behind most of our acts and behaviours, repressed and hidden. Note that whereas material can pass relatively freely between the conscious and preconscious portions of the mind, it can only pass freely *into* the unconscious portion of the mind. That is, unconscious material cannot pass freely into consciousness. Exceptions are when unconscious material is allowed some penetration into the preconscious part of mind. These could appear as slips of the tongue, jokes, dreams, and the emergence of neurotic symptoms.

The content of Freud's unconscious (that is, the *dynamic* unconscious) is twofold. The unconscious contains the innate instinctual drives, our sexual and aggressive strivings. These strivings form the basis of our instinctual life. These innate instincts are not personal drives, they are part of our nature as human beings. From an evolutionary perspective, we need to have sex to keep the species going, and we need to defend ourselves to stay alive. The unconscious, however, also contains repressed instinctual material. Throughout the psychosexual development of the child, the innate instincts take on a personal dimension. The child wishes to love his or her mother and kill his or her father. These desires are just too shocking and the child represses them into the unconscious. In Freud's theory, these repressions are adaptive, leading to identifications with the same-sex parent and a healthy heterosexual life. Thus the concept of the unconscious articulates Freud's understanding of how we are able to curtail the press of our instinctual nature, where instead of living out our 'animal nature', in other words fighting and raping, we are able, some of the time, to be civilised, controlled, and adaptive in our lives.

## The structural model

Freud later adapted his first topography by adding his understandings of the **ego**, the **id**, and the **superego**. These are the basic components of personality functioning, and it is their complex interaction that produces human behaviour. Where the first topography of the mind outlines the 'territories' of the mind, the second model outlines the central 'players' (or 'agencies') within the mind, adding a dynamic, or interactive, explanation to a descriptive explanation of mind.

## The id

Freud claims that the id is the original component of personality; it is the 'instinctual bedrock' with which the child is born and upon which its eventual personality will be built. The id is entirely unconscious and is strongly tied to the biological needs of the child. It supplies the 'psychical energy' that drives the mind and can in this way be thought of as the 'engine' of personality. The id is regulated by the **pleasure principle**, that is, by the idea that all needs (for example hunger, or the need to urinate) should be satisfied immediately. According to the pleasure principle we should eat at the first feelings of hunger, or should seek sexual gratification at the first twinges of sexual arousal. If such needs are not satisfied quickly, then there is a resulting build-up of pressure, which the child

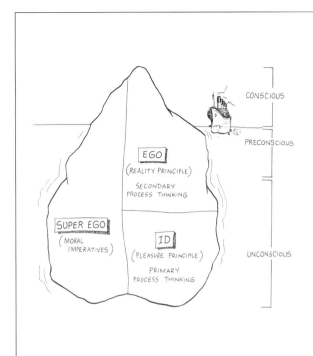

CONSCIOUS

PRECONSCIOUS

EGO
(REALITY PRINCIPLE)

SECONDARY
PROCESS THINKING

SUPER EGO
(MORAL
IMPERATIVES)

ID
(PLEASURE PRINCIPLE)

PRIMARY
PROCESS THINKING

UNCONSCIOUS

**Figure 5.3** Freud's structural model of the mind. Freud often likened the structure of mind to the proportions of an iceberg, dramatising the size difference between ego and id by noting that the ego was proportionate to the tip of the iceberg that juts out above the surface, while the id was proportionate to the large area of the iceberg that remained submerged. Note how the first topography of mind has been transposed on this structural model, and that, whereas the id is completely unconscious, the ego has conscious and preconscious aspects, and the superego straddles all levels. The preconscious is that part of the mind, which, in the iceberg metaphor, is just beneath the surface of the sea.

experiences as discomfort (un-pleasure). It is this discomfort that the pleasure principle hopes to avoid. The pleasure principle is clearly problematic, however, especially if one considers what would happen to us if we went around acting on our slightest desires, demanding gratification in the most immediate fashion. The pleasure principle, in short, does not take into account what might be the outcome of acting in such ways; it is unconcerned with what is rational or appropriate.

The id's main mechanism for dealing with the build-up of tension is called the **primary process**. The primary process involves the conjuring up of a mental image that would provide **hallucinatory gratification** of the instinctual need that is building up. The hungry child may imagine the mother's breast, just as we might imagine a fantasy image of something that we desire sexually, or the image of a person close to us whom we have not seen for a long while. This experience of generating an image that would fulfil a pressing need is termed **wish fulfilment** by Freud, and it is the basis of dream activity. Wish fulfilment activity does not bring about a real end to the need in question. No matter how much a hungry person imagines food, that imagined food will not satisfy their hunger. This is yet another demonstration of how the id, and the pleasure principle, do not take reality into account in their functioning.

**Primary process.** The id's main mechanism for dealing with the build-up of tension. The primary process involves the conjuring up of a mental image that would satisfy the instinctual need that is building up.

**Hallucinatory gratification.** The conjuring up of a mental image that would provide some (limited) satisfaction of the instinctual need that is building up.

**Wish fulfilment.** The experience of generating an image that would fulfil a pressing need and the basis of dream activity.

## The ego

As the child gets older, it becomes increasingly important that she or he is able to adapt to objective reality as this is vital for the survival of the child. It is because of this need that the ego develops. The ego then arises out of the inadequacy of the id, as a 'negotiator' between the id and the requirements of external reality. The ego develops out of the id, and it harnesses part of the id's energy for itself. Thus part of the ego is also unconscious. However, because the ego is also involved with transactions with the outside world, it needs also to exist in the conscious and preconscious levels of the mind.

**Reality principle.** Regulates the ego, and aims to adapt the instincts and impulses of the organism to the state and conditions of the objective and external world.

The ego is regulated by the **reality principle**, which is the idea that behaviour must adapt to the state and conditions of the external world rather than just obeying the instinctual needs and urges arising from within the individual (Freud 1991). The reality principle introduces the standard of rationality into behaviour and leads one into considering the consequences of one's actions within a certain environment. Rather than obeying the pleasure principle, to steal food, for example, when we are hungry, the ego alerts us to the fact that such an act may well have undesirable consequences. The ego attempts instead to delay gratification and to redirect the individual to attain food in a more appropriate or legal manner.

Delaying gratification to a more opportune, safe, sensible, or later time is hence one of the overriding functions of the ego. In this respect the ego relies on the **secondary process**, which finds a match between unconscious and external factors. This entails matching the image of what is desired, which stems from the unconscious hallucinatory image of the primary process, to a real and achievable perception of that object in the world (Freud 1991). It is this ability for realistic thought, claims Freud, which enables the ego to come up with plans of action for the satisfaction of its needs. The ego can weigh up such plans, and decide which will work and which will not, a process known as *reality-testing*. It is in this way that the ego is the home of intellectual processes and problem solving within the individual.

**Secondary process.** The secondary process finds a match between the image of what is desired (from the primary process) and a real and achievable perception of that object in the world. It is the basis of problem-solving behaviour and intellectual activity.

We must be careful not to assume that the ego is the same as the 'self'. Although the ego is that part of the personality structure that is best adapted to the constraints of external reality, it is still just one of the dynamic agents that make up the personality. It is the sum of these dynamic agents that constitutes the 'self' of the individual. Another important aspect of the ego is that it is amoral. We cannot assume that the ego is 'all good', just because it affords us some control over the id. In fact, the ego has no moral sense and spends a good deal of time deceiving us, particularly about the unconscious stimuli coming from the id. In fact the ego itself would be unconcerned with dishonesty and with allowing the pleasure principle to 'go wild' as long as there is no chance of the individual being caught or reprimanded for these actions. There is another agent that takes care of the moral aspects of our personality, the *superego*.

**Ego-ideal.** The positive side of the superego, the ego-ideal stems from the individual's identification with their same-sex parent, but embodies more generally all of the highly-respected values and standards of excellence that the child has inherited from both parents. Strong-felt moral standpoints come from the ego-ideal, and one feels a sense of pride and identity when one engages in behaviours that are congruent with the ego-ideal.

## The superego

The superego is the last part of the personality to develop. It arises as a result of the resolution of the Oedipus complex and is largely the product of the internalisation of parental authority. It also involves identification with the influence of other authority figures and of social values more generally, such as religion. It is the parents initially who determine what is right and wrong for the child. Identification with these parental roles allows the child to act increasingly in a moral fashion and to develop the superego. The superego has both positive and negative sides, both of which stem from the finalisation of the Oedipus complex. The positive side of the superego is called the **ego-ideal**. It stems from identification with the same-sex parent as well as embodying more generally all of the highly-respected values and standards of excellence that the child has inherited from both parents (Freud 1991). Strongly-felt moral standpoints come from the ego-ideal, and one feels a sense of pride and identity when one engages in behaviours that are congruent with the ego-ideal.

The negative side of the superego develops from the threat of punishment that parents use to discipline their children. This aspect of the superego is called the **conscience**, and it consists of a collection of rules and prohibitions about what is and what is not allowed. If an individual indulges in bad acts or thoughts, the superego punishes them with feelings of guilt. (Freud suggests that because males have a very severe and frightening form of prohibition in the form of castration anxiety, they have a more fully developed superego than do women.) If, for whatever reason, an individual does not properly develop a superego, they will lack respect for social laws and order. People suffering from antisocial personality disorders (once called 'sociopaths' or 'psychopaths') have insufficiently developed superegos.

The primary function of the superego is to inhibit and squash any unconscious impulse of the id. It also tries to make the ego act in a moral way, to take moral as well as rational considerations into account when deciding how to act in a certain situation. Last, the superego tries to guide the person towards perfection in what they say, do, and think. In this regard the superego is a hard taskmaster. It is not realistic but perfectionistic in the demands it makes upon the ego, and it can be vindictive and even sadistic in punishing the ego when it acts in a wayward manner. The superego operates on all levels of the mind, conscious, preconscious, and unconscious.

> **Conscience.** The negative side of the superego, which develops from the threats of punishment that parents use to discipline their children. It consists of a collection of rules and prohibitions about what is and what is not allowed. If an individual indulges in bad acts or thoughts, the superego punishes them with feelings of guilt.

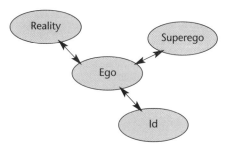

**Figure 5.4** The ego as the 'slave with three masters' has to mediate between the often conflicting demands of the id, the superego, and external reality.

## The dynamic interaction of id, ego, and superego

Having briefly sketched the three agencies of the mind one can see that the ego has a difficult task in attempting to balance the demands of the superego and the id, and to keep them both congruent with the conditions of external reality. Conflict is unavoidable. This is easy to see if one considers how strongly opposed the objectives of the id and the superego actually are. How well the ego copes is dependent upon **ego strength**. Ego strength is the term that has been used to describe the ability of the ego to moderate, and deal with, the effects of these opposing forces (Freud 1991). The more ego strength one has, the more one is able to deal with these competing pressures. Conversely, the less ego strength one has, the more one is at the mercy of these conflicting forces. The clinical objective

> **Ego strength.** The term used to describe the ability of the ego to moderate, and to deal with, the effects of the opposing forces of the id, the superego, and reality.

**Signal anxiety.** This term indicates one of the prime functions of anxiety, namely the alerting of the ego to a potential (unconscious) id discharge.

**Defence.** Mechanism that acts to reduce or eliminate any excitation liable to threaten the integrity and stability of the psyche.

**Compromise formation.** The form taken by repressed material in order for it to be admitted into consciousness. The repressed idea becomes so distorted as to be unrecognisable. Thus both the unconscious wish and the demands of the defence can be satisfied.

**Symptom.** The (neurotic) compromise formation taken by repressed material in order for it to be admitted into consciousness. Symbolically, the wish of the id is allowed, hence satisfying the id, while at the same time it is not allowed, hence satisfying the superego. The symptom both hides and reveals the psychic conflict.

**Neurosis.** An emotional disorder; the displaying of emotional distress via the formation of a symptom. It is a functional disorder – a conflict phenomenon involving the thwarting of an instinctual urge. Neurosis is understood as a psychogenic state.

for an individual should thus be to increase their ego strength so that there is a healthy balance between the forces of their personality.

# Defences

Given that one of the ego's main tasks is negotiation between the id's demand for discharge and the superego's censorship, the ego must have a means of doing this. Freud postulated that anxiety operates to assist the ego in this task. One of the functions of anxiety is to alert the ego of the danger inherent in the press of the id for discharge. This is **signal anxiety**. The ego responds to the anxiety by harnessing the mechanisms of defence. At an unconscious level the mechanisms of **defence** are more or less integrated into the ego and act to reduce or eliminate any excitation that is liable to threaten the integrity and stability of the psyche. Repression is the corner stone of the defences, with all other defences arising out of its workings. Repression smothers or 'censors' awareness of the forbidden desire. Once this has happened other defences may come into play if additional protection is needed.

Consider a situation where someone is very angry. The individual may repress the anger, and if this defence is successful, the experience of anger will be buried in the unconscious. However, if the anger was so great or the ego did not have sufficient resources, then the repression may be only partly successful and the emotion of anger continues to press for discharge. The defences used to provide additional protection could range from immature, infantile level defences such as *denial* (I am not angry), *projection* (It is you who is angry), *reaction formation* (I am inordinately peaceful), to more mature forms of defence such as *intellectualisation* (One is only angry when there has been a sufficient amount of frustration to warrant an amount of tension release) to *rationalisation* (I am only angry because you provoked me). The defence of *sublimation* is a constructive defence, allowing one to channel, rather than repress, sexual and aggressive energies into socially acceptable forms such as sport, arts, learning, and love. Thus rather than being consumed with the anger, you go for a run or complete an amount of work.

# Pathology and neurosis

Defences may not be able to cope with the pressure of the instinctual wish. This may be due to the intensity of the urge or a weak ego structure. In this event, the ego is forced to form a compromise between the id and the superego. This is a **compromise formation**, which safeguards against being overwhelmed by the id as well as satisfying the superego demands. The compromise formation is the form taken by the repressed material (such as anger or sexuality) in order for it to be admitted into consciousness. Thus the compromise formation is the formation of a **symptom**, which we call neurotic behaviour. The symptom, for example obsessive behaviour, is a symbolic expression. Symbolically, the wish of the id is allowed, hence satisfying the id, while at the same time it is not

# Types of defences

A defence mechanism is a specific, unconscious, intra-psychic adjustment that occurs in order to resolve emotional conflict and to reduce an individual's anxiety. A defence can be called a mental mechanism, an ego defence mechanism, or an adjustive technique. A few of the major defences which have been identified are:

**Repression:** the involuntary and automatic placing of unacceptable impulses or feelings or images into the unconscious. That is, an unconsciously motivated forgetting.

**Suppression:** the voluntary, intentional putting of unacceptable feelings, etc. into the preconscious. In other words, intentional forgetting.

**Regression:** the unconscious return to an earlier level of emotional functioning.

**Reaction formation:** behaviour or attitudes that are the opposite of unacceptable conscious or unconscious impulses.

**Identification:** the unconscious adoption or internalisation of the personality characteristics of another person, usually the attributes that are admired or envied, but can also be those which are feared.

**Fixation:** the arrest of maturation at an immature level of psychosexual development.

**Introjection:** the symbolic internalisation or assimilation of another person who is either loved or hated.

**Projection:** attributing, to another person or object, one's own thoughts, feelings, or unacceptable impulses.

**Rationalisation:** an unconscious mechanism, which can be thought of as retrospective justification. One gives acceptable motives to what essentially does not have recognisable motives.

**Idealisation:** overestimation of the qualities of another, while **devaluation** is the underestimation of such qualities.

**Intellectualisation:** using intellectual concepts and words to avoid experiencing or expressing emotions.

**Dissociation:** the unconscious detaching of certain behaviour patterns from their normal patterns of behaving. An example might be depersonalisation.

**Sublimation:** channelling unacceptable instincts into socially acceptable activity.

allowed, hence satisfying the superego. The symptom both hides and reveals the psychic conflict.

**Neurosis** is an emotional disorder. Thus when we speak of a neurotic we mean someone who is displaying emotional distress via the formation of a symptom. The symptom could range from anxiety, panic attacks, depression, and lying, to promiscuity. The psyche is amazingly creative in both hiding and revealing the nature of the emotional pain with which the person is struggling. Neurosis is understood as a **psychogenic** state. This is an illness caused by psychological factors. Neurotic symptoms may indicate conflict over something already done. A classic example

**Psychogenic.** Term used to signify that illnesses and symptoms are of a mental origin.

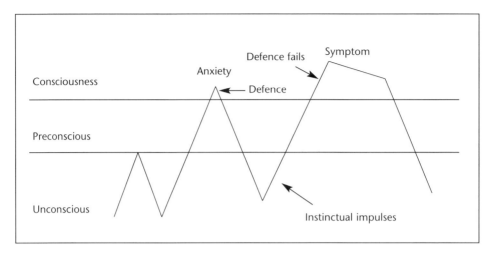

**Figure 5.5** Model of symptom formation. The model shows the experience of signal anxiety indicating the press of instinctual impulses. Defences are then brought into operation, which, being successful, reduce the anxiety and push the instinctual impulse back into the unconscious. When the defence is not effective, then the impulse continues to press for discharge into consciousness and a symptom develops in order to hide the meaning of the impulse from becoming known to consciousness.

**Hysteria.** Inability to successfully repress instinctual sexual desires that results in a variety of somatic complaints, such as blindness and paralysis, which have no basis in physiological impairment.

**Dream-work.** The multiple processes through which the latent content is transformed into the manifest content of a dream. Condensation and displacement are vital mechanisms of the dream-work.

**Latent content.** The unconscious content of a dream as revealed by interpretation.

**Manifest content.** The surface meaning of the dream; the content as reported by the dreamer.

is Lady Macbeth's compulsive attempts to clean her hands after the murder of the king. By compulsively washing her hands, she betrays her murderous desires (the id) as well as satisfying the superego demand for punishment, the hand washing. The conflict may also be over something that is unconsciously wished for but not done in reality. Freud's work with **hysteria** revealed that an inability to successfully repress instinctual sexual desires resulted in hysterical symptoms. These were *somatic* complaints such as blindness and paralysis, which have no basis in physiological impairment. The symptom can be traced as symbolically expressing the psychic conflict, for example, paralysis of the hand that had been touched by the desired man. In the symbolism of the paralysis, we see that while the touch is desired, the paralysis precludes the pleasure.

## Dreams

Freud (1978) saw dreams as expressions of unconscious wishes. Hence dreams allow a certain amount of instinctual discharge, releasing instinctual pressure in the form of instinctual wish fulfilment. Given that Freud's theory revolves around the notion of unconscious material surfacing into consciousness, dreams have a special relationship to consciousness. This relationship is mediated by the censorship of the ego. To allow access to the dream material, the ego is involved in the operation of what Freud terms **dream-work**. The dream-work undertakes to disguise the unconscious meaning of the dream (the **latent content**). The result is that consciousness has access to the dream, but only in its surface meaning, or **manifest content**. The manifest dream, which is

## Did you know? The relationship between neurosis and the superego

The development of neurosis is linked to a harsh superego. Thus oppressive and critical child-rearing practices are more likely to induce the development of neurotic behaviour. Psychopathy, on the other hand, is linked to ineffective superego functioning. Thus harsh, cruel, neglectful or disinterested child-rearing practices, which inhibit the possibility of the child identifying with suitable and loving authority figures, have serious consequences. These authority figures should symbolise the moral values of the society. However, either through their poor treatment of the child or their own lack of superego functioning, they compromise the child's capacity to develop a strong and healthy superego.

Such developmental circumstances are more likely to induce psychopathic behaviour. A psychopath is someone who exhibits antisocial behaviours and is indifferent to morality. There is a distinct film genre that gives excellent portrayals of psychopathic functioning. Some examples are David Lynch's *Blue Velvet*, *Wild at Heart*, and *Lost Highway* and Quentin Tarantino's *Pulp Fiction*, *Reservoir Dogs*, *True Romance*, and *Natural Born Killers*. Danny Boyle's *Shallow Grave* also provides an interesting unfolding of psychopathic behaviour.

remembered in consciousness, is sparse in comparison to the richness of the latent content. The ego disguises the dream principally through the processes of **displacement**, **condensation**, and **symbolism**, which operate as follows.

◆ Displacement occurs when the meaning of an image or idea becomes detached from the image and is passed onto or displaced onto another image or images. The new image is related to the first idea through a chain of associations. The classic example would be dreaming of a steeple or a cigar, which could be interpreted as the penis having become displaced onto the image of the steeple or cigar.

**Displacement.** Unconscious process through which the meaning of an image or idea becomes detached from the image and is passed onto or displaced onto another image or images.

**Condensation.** Unconscious process through which two or more ideas or images combine into one.

**Symbolism.** The figurative representation of an unconscious idea, conflict, or wish.

PHOTO: CHA JOHNSTON

*Dreams, for Freud, are 'the royal road to the unconscious'.*

◆ Condensation is an unconscious process whereby two or more ideas or images combine to form one symbol. An example may be the image of a church, which for a particular individual stands for the spirituality of God, the strictness of the father, and the protection of the mother.

◆ Symbolism is the figurative representation of an unconscious idea, conflict, or wish.

In his *Interpretation of dreams* (1900/1978), Freud proposed a model for understanding dreams as the censored wish fulfilment of the id strivings. In a process that is similar to the formation of neurotic symptoms, the manifest dream becomes the conscious compromise of the unconscious wish. The mechanisms of displacement, condensation, and symbolism, as well as the operation of the other defences, result in the compromise – the manifest dream.

## The practice of psychoanalysis

Psychoanalysis is based upon the premise that the patient is always communicating at an unconscious (latent) level to the psychoanalyst. In fact all psychoanalytic psychology holds to the idea that all our conscious thought processes are linked to unconscious meanings and motivations. Freud discovered that by remaining neutral and listening to these communications, the latent meanings were revealed. The method employed is that of free association. The patient is encouraged to speak without censorship about whatever comes into his or her mind. By remaining neutral and observing, the psychoanalyst can note when free association becomes difficult for the patient. These are the nodal points at which internal censorship has occurred. Over a period of time, these nodal points of censorship start to cohere around the fixation issues of the patient. It is also observed how the patient attempts to draw the analyst into certain repetitions of the past (the repetition compulsion). Through these attempts to repeat and heal the past, it becomes clear where and why there is fixation at certain psychosexual stages. As the analyst comes to understand these meanings, he or she is able to offer interpretations about the unconscious operation of the patient's psyche.

## Critiques of Freud's developmental theory

Theories are an important way of coordinating and explaining developmental phenomena, and of making sense of the world. However, if theories have serious shortcomings, or are applied indiscriminately across too wide a diversity of contexts, then they can in fact limit the understandings one has of the world and prevent one from looking for different answers. Freud's theory of psychosocial development has certainly been an enormously important one within the history of psychology and psychoanalytic thought but, like any other theory, it requires critical evaluation.

# A fictional vignette

Henry is twenty-eight and presents himself for psychotherapy with a number of obsessional complaints. These include that he is not able to leave the house without first washing his hands for about an hour. He has become seriously constipated. He also has never been able to have sex with a woman because he is repulsed by how dirty it is. It is revealed that Henry's father left the family when he was about two and a half years old – at the time his mother started his toilet training. His father moved in with a woman whom Henry's mother referred to as 'the whore'. Henry has an enmeshed (overly close) relationship with his mother and the two of them have lived alone since the father left. Neither Henry nor his mother has had any significant relationship outside of their mother and son unit. His mother is a very religious and controlling woman. She instilled into Henry the idea that he must be a 'good, clean boy'. She gave him regular enemas to ensure that he was 'clean inside'. It is further revealed that Henry has recently met a woman at work to whom he finds himself attracted. There is great difficulty and shame in revealing that he has been having sexual thoughts about this woman and masturbating into his mother's panties. These activities leave him feeling dirty and ashamed.

## Character diagnosis
Analysis of the clinical material suggests that Henry has strong anal personality traits stemming from fixation at the anal stage of psychosexual development. His infantile attempts at autonomy became identified with the needs of the mother for cleanliness. He also became her substitute love object. Her controlling and intrusive attitude towards him left him with passive anal retentive tendencies and an inability to assert his separateness. His initial struggles and failure to attain autonomy are symbolised in the mother's frequent invasive attempts to empty and control his 'bad' insides. Henry is left with pathological fantasies of the dirtiness of his insides (his dirty urges) and with anal retentive attempts to control these instinctual urges. The anal fixation has precluded him from attaining full genital sexuality. His sexuality is still of an infantile nature, with the sexual aim satisfied through a fetish.

## Neurotic dynamics
The neurotic symptoms (hand washing, constipation, and fetishism) arose as a consequence of Henry's weakened ego being unable to negotiate between the id's demand for sexual discharge and the severity of the superego's prohibition. Henry's superego identification appears to be based upon his mother's moralistic and sadistic attitude towards bodies and sexuality, viewing instinctual life as dirty and bad. Henry's attempt at sublimation, the move to masturbation fetishism, was not a successful enough compromise to the superego. In fact it only served to increase the tension, with the masturbation providing evidence of the 'dirty contents' of the insides of his body. All other defences having failed, the symptom formation of hand washing and constipation served as the compromise between the id and the superego. The constipation prevented any discharge of dirty contents and the hand washing cleansed and punished the dirty act of masturbation. Both these symptoms reveal the hidden desires to discharge aggressive and sexual impulses towards the mother. The use of her panties highlights his fixation on the mother as the love object. The symptoms also hide the nature of the psychic conflict from Henry's consciousness.

## Lack of verifiable scientific evidence

One of the most frequently heard criticisms of Freud, and of psycho-analysis in general, is that the theories lack experimental support, and are unverifiable by the normal methods of science (Erdelyi and Goldberg 1979). In terms of the normal criteria of science, it is claimed that psycho-analytic theories cannot be thought of as scientifically true and from a scientific point of view may even be considered to be unfalsifiable. This means that there is no reasonable way to dispute them (just as there is no reasonable way to dispute something like astrology).

There are a few ways of answering such criticism. Good science does not claim that only what is directly measurable is accessible to scientific investigation. For example, while we cannot 'see' the unconscious, we are certainly able to observe its influence. Further, in terms of Freud's theo-ries being unfalsifiable, let us assume that he is wrong about the function of dreams as allowing instinctual discharge. If you then deprived a per-son of dream sleep it should have no effect on them. Yet research within cognitive neuropsychology indicates that when someone is deprived of dream sleep, they suffer the exact consequences that Freud postulated. There is a build-up of tension and the development of neurotic symptoms (Solms 1995). Thus it would seem that as we become more sophisticated, both in conceptualising research and science and in our methods of inves-tigation, Freud would stand up well to scientific scrutiny.

While it may be true that we cannot verify all of Freud's theorising, certainly many aspects of the theory have been researched and verified. To name a few areas, cross-cultural research indicates the operation of Oedipal taboos, infant observation endorses the innateness of certain aspects of personality, and even cognitive and social learning theorists have come to promote the idea of unknown internal motivations influ-encing behaviours. Advances in cognitive neuropsychology have brought about a better understanding of the significance of dreams and have sup-ported Freud's postulations about the function of dreams (Solms 1995; Solms and Saling 1990).

## Cultural bias

A second very general criticism of Freud is that his theories emerge from a particular socio-cultural and historical location and hence exhibit a strong cultural bias (Cloninger 1996; Nolen-Hoeksema 1988). In Europe at the end of the nineteenth century, when Freud wrote, men had far greater powers and importance within society than did women. Likewise, homosexuality was strongly frowned upon. The critique sug-gests that it remains open to speculation as to what extent these political and social contexts have permeated Freud's theories and limited the degree to which they may be universally applied. (Freud himself consid-ered his theory to be universally applicable.)

Problems of cultural bias need to be taken seriously and researched to investigate the validity of their claims. Certainly some feminist writers have taken Freud's theories as the lens through which to analyse and understand the reality of political and social gender imbalances. These understandings have not only been applied to 'First World' countries but to gender relations generally and to the deeply unconscious motivations for such gendered relations.

It may also be tempting to agree that Freud's emphasis upon sexuality was a product of his time in history. However, psychoanalytic thinking today still prioritises the body as the vehicle through which the infant engages with the world. All the theorists in this book place the body and the way it relates to the world as the basis through which meaning and personality are given coherence.

## Deterministic and reductionist trends

A final critique comes from humanistic psychology, which sees Freud's view of the unconscious as the force that drives our actions and largely determines who and what we are, as a restrictive and overly deterministic view. They claim that this view allows little latitude for change or for meaningful agency within individuals and reduces the finest qualities of human achievement to unconscious instinctual motivations. This critique comes from within a tradition that has rejected the notion of human beings having the capacity for innate aggression. Humanistic views of people are imbued with optimism but are challenged to account for the widespread horror that has characterised much of humankind's history. Freud's theorising arose within a context of racial hatred and two world wars. He was forced to theorise the possibility of understanding such behaviour and motivation. Humanistic views appear loath to make human beings responsible for the horror of which they are capable in the way that Freud was brave enough to do.

This criticism does not take into account Freud's basic principle, which is about the dynamic nature of the psyche. The psyche is always attempting to negotiate and re-negotiate itself in relation to both external and internal realities. It is only in psychosis that external reality does not impact upon the ego's negotiations with the demands of our social and cultural milieu. What Freud postulates is that where there has been fixation, the conflictual aspects of the fixation will influence the ways in which ego negotiations operate. Freud does not hypothesise men or women as encapsulated psychic automatons that act only from internal motivations. These motivations are always in contact with the demands of external reality, except, as mentioned, in psychotic states.

PHOTO: MICHELE VRDOLJAK

*How relevant is Freudian theory to South Africa in the twenty-first century? Cultural bias is one of the most frequent criticisms of Freud's psychoanalytic theory.*

# Some replies to critiques of Freud

In assessing the cogency of any criticism, it is useful to identify and examine the assumptions that underlie the specific criticism. This will reveal the philosophical context from which the criticism is launched, and provide a basis for establishing the relative power of the criticism to render a theory unsubstantiated, irrelevant or invalid.

## 1. Freudian theory is unscientific

This is probably the most common criticism of Freudian theory. It is claimed that most aspects of Freud's theory lack experimental support, thus rendering it scientifically unsubstantiated. In addition, since the theory is claimed to be unverifiable according to normal scientific standards, it is regarded as inherently unscientific. A closer look at the assumptions underlying these criticisms reveals the presence of an empiricist epistemology, where the truth or factual nature of a theory depends exclusively on directly measurable empirical evidence. There are a number of ways in which to think about this criticism:

♦ Recent research studies (for example Western 1998; 1999) indicate that many Freudian concepts are now supported experimentally, including the function of dreams, the existence of unconscious cognitive, affective, and motivational processes, the operation of Oedipal taboos across different cultures, and the innateness of certain aspects of personality.

♦ Even if there were no experimental support for aspects of Freudian theory, good science does not claim that the only criterion for scientific evidence is the directly measurable phenomenon. The empiricist approach is only one among many in the debate around what constitutes scientific evidence. Consider the theory of gravity as an example – the only evidence for gravity (an intangible causal agency) is the tangible effect it produces. Gravity itself is thus not directly measurable, and can

only be evidenced by its effects. Yet the theory of gravity has the status of a fully credible scientific theory.

♦ The same consideration can be applied to Freud's theory of the unconscious or of the psychical apparatus. There is no directly measurable evidence for either, but the visible effects can be accounted for by invoking Freudian theory.

## 2. Freudian theory is culturally relative

A consistent criticism of Freudian theory is that it is steeped in nineteenth century socio-cultural and political thought and as such is more of a biased intellectual legacy from a particular historical period than a universally applicable theory. In particular, Freud's view of human sexual development is regarded as a product of the restrictive Victorian attitude towards sex that was common during that era.

The perspective that culture determines thought has recently been restated with the rise of post-modern theory, which claims that reality is socially constructed via language and culture. In terms of post-modern theory, there are no universal realities, only contextual ones, and thus Freudian theory is only a representation of a cultural discourse of that era. The fundamental assumption underlying this perspective is that reality is culture- and language-dependent and not objectively defined. In assessing the validity of this view, consider the following points:

♦ Cultural bias may well inform some aspects of Freudian theory, but this issue needs to be evaluated in terms of current cross-cultural research,

(continued)

which seems to support aspects of Freudian theory (Western 1998; 1999).

◆ Current psychoanalytic thinking still prioritises the body as the vehicle through which the infant engages the world, and by which meaning and personality are given coherence. Infant observation studies support the notion that the infant comes to understand itself initially through the body.

◆ Even if there were no empirical support for the universal applicability of Freudian theory, this would not necessarily demonstrate its inherent cultural bias. Consider the following problem: to hold that there are no universally applicable conditions is itself a universal statement, and therefore a contradiction in terms. We must acknowledge at least the possibility of universally applicable conditions if we are to remain logically coherent, and so entertain the possibility that Freudian theory is universally applicable.

### 3. Freudian theory is deterministic

This criticism stems from the perception that Freud regarded the psychological development of the individual to be largely complete by the time of puberty. By this measure, the individual is imprisoned by her or his developmental history and significant change is impossible. The assumption that underlies this criticism is that human development is not determined only by prior events, nor can it be reduced to instinctual biological drives. The problem with this criticism is that it fails to take full account of Freudian theory, and thus misrepresents the theory to a certain extent. Consider the following aspects of Freudian theory:

◆ Freudian theory is deterministic about the development of the psychic apparatus (id, ego, and superego), but not about the particularities that transpire in an individual's internal and external

experience of life once these structures are in place.

◆ The contents of the psyche are unique to each individual, even though the basic structure of the psyche is the same for all.

◆ The dynamic nature of the psyche means that an individual is always negotiating and re-negotiating the self in relation to both external and internal realities. The instinctual motivations are always in contact with the demands of external reality and always tempered by cultural injunctions. Thus internal psychological processes (such as sublimation, defences, or associations) occur continuously throughout the life-span in response to external realities and these processes produce changes in behaviour, cognition, and affect.

Freudian theory can therefore be described as deterministic at the level of psychic structure, but not at other levels of functioning.

### 4. Freudian theory reduces human activity to biological instincts

This criticism comes from the Humanist tradition, which rejects Freudian theory on the grounds that it reduces the finest qualities of human achievement to unconscious instinctual drives and, by so doing, fails to account for human agency and choice as a factor in psychological development. The underlying assumption here is that human beings naturally tend towards growth and self-actualisation and consequently the capacity for aggression is not innate, but a response to the environment. In assessing the validity of this perspective, it is useful to consider the following points:

◆ Freudian theory does postulate a hidden relation between human behaviour and motivation, namely unconscious instinctual drives. Yet this does not imply that

(continued)

all human endeavour is reduced to instincts. Freudian theory places great emphasis on the role that culture (external reality) has in curtailing and modifying these instincts (including aggression), in the service of making communal life possible.

◆ If human aggression is only a response to the environment, there must be an innate capacity for people to be aggressive, much as there is an innate capacity for the acquisition of language. This capacity for aggression can partly explain the widespread horror and destruction that has characterised the history of humankind since the dawn of time. By rejecting the notion of innate aggression, the Humanist perspective fails to hold humankind responsible for the horror of which it is so obviously capable. —*Sue Williamson*

# Recommended readings

Appignansi, R. and Zarate, O. (1992). *Freud for beginners.* New York: Icon.
*(True to its title, this text utilises an impressive spread of illustrations, in a near comic-book format, to lead its readers through the theory and history of Freudian analysis. Recommended.)*

Freud, S. (1977). 'Three essays on the theory of sexuality'. In A. Richards and A. Dickson (eds), *The Penguin Freud Library. Volume 7 on sexuality: Three essays on the theory of sexuality and other works.* London: Penguin.
*(A collection of the classic papers that laid the foundations for Freud's distinction between adult and infant sexuality and the theory of the psychosexual stages.)*

Freud, S. (1978). *The interpretation of dreams.* London: Penguin.
*(A fascinating read. Shows Freud at his most accessible. How he develops his concepts is intriguing. This book covers most of the outline of his understanding of the unconscious.)*

Freud, S. (1982). *Introductory lectures on psychoanalysis.* London: Hogarth Press.
*(Freud is very easy to read and this volume introduces you to the basic concepts of psychoanalysis.)*

Gay, P. (1988). *Freud: A life for our time.* London: Papermac.
*(A wonderful tale which traces Freud's life and theoretical developments. There are also some intriguing accounts of the intense relationships Freud made with certain people.)*

Laplanche, J. and Pontalis, J. B. (1973). *The language of psycho-analysis.* London: Hogarth Press.
*(An academic read, defining psychoanalytic terminology.)*

Osborne, R. (1993). *Freud for beginners.* London: Writers and Readers.
*(Rival publication to Appignansi and Zarate (1992). Also recommended.)*

Storr, A. (2000). *Freud: A very short introduction.* Oxford: Oxford University Press.
*(A very concise 'primer' to Freudian psychoanalysis that can be read in an hour or two. It usefully blends anecdotes from Freud's own life with explanations of key theoretical terms and principles.)*

Western, D. (1998). 'The scientific legacy of Sigmund Freud: Toward a psychodynamically informed psychological science'. *Psychological bulletin,* 124 (3), 333–371.

Western, D. (1999). 'The scientific status of unconscious processes: Is Freud really dead?' *Journal of the American Psychoanalytic Association*, 47 (4), 1061–1112.

Wolheim, R. (1977). *Freud.* Glasgow: Fontana/Modern Masters.
*(Nearly a classic in its own right, Wolheim's slender volume does an admirably succinct job of accurately tying together the main theoretical strands of Freud's thought.)*

# Critical thinking tasks

## Specific tasks

1) Accepting that the introductory case study provides us with only limited evidence, is there any indication that Kobus Geldenhuys was fixated at a particular stage of his psychosocial development? Is it possible to relate any of his particular adult behaviours to such a fixation? What are the possible personality characteristics that he may have acquired in the course of his development across the various psychosexual stages?

2) The Geldenhuys case study suggests that this person grew up with no strong male authority figure or role model. How would this impact on his development through the Oedipus complex? Furthermore, in later writings Freud suggests that the Oedipus complex may draw on characters beyond the immediate parents in fulfilling important Oedipal roles. Malinowski (1927) for instance found that Trobriand Islanders had a far more respectful, fearful, and potentially hostile relationship with their maternal uncles than they did with their fathers. Does it appear in Geldenhuys's case that a key Oedipal character may have existed outside his own immediate family? Who would this character have been, and how may they have impacted on his personal resolution or non-resolution of the Oedipal complex?

3) Freud contends that the ego is a 'slave of three masters'. Apply this statement to a careful consideration of Geldenhuys's personality structure as exhibited in his murderous actions.

4) Do you feel that Freud's idea of penis envy and his general portrayal of women within his developmental theory are reasonable? Explain your answer.

## General tasks

1) Having worked through this explanation of Freud's developmental theory, write an essay that will attempt to account for the criminal actions of the murderer and rapist Kobus Geldenhuys. Make thorough reference to the details of the case study in Chapter 3, and be sure to involve the zonal stages of development, the Oedipus complex, and the ego/id/superego structure of mind in your answer.

2) In what ways do you think Freud's theory might be limited? If you have completed the case study questions above, refer specifically to any possible limitations in accounting for the actions of Geldenhuys. Are there gaps in the theory that need to be filled, and if so, what are they?

3) Give some thought to how Freud's developmental theory applies to your own life. Do you think that it helps explain much about you? If so, what, and how? If you feel that Freud's theories are not able to explain significant aspects of your life, reflect on why you think this is so.

# Klein's object relations theory of development and personality

*Jacki Watts*

This chapter will explain Klein's theory of object relations, focusing upon the following areas:

1. Introductory concepts.

2. Theoretical focus.

3. Psychological birth and selfhood.

4. The concept of an internal world.

5. The role of phantasy.

6. The concept of psychic structure.

7. Innate capacity.

8. Paranoid-schizoid and depressive positions.

Melanie Klein

## Introductory concepts

In this chapter we examine the ideas of Melanie Klein whose work resulted in the development of object relations theory. This first section introduces the key concepts of the **intra-psychic** world, phantasy, and object relations

### The intra-psychic world

The term intra-psychic refers to the *internal world* of experience, that is, the activities of the mind. Klein's theory is based upon a model of intra-psychic functioning that postulates that the infant's physiological life provides the stimulus for primitive cognitive or mental functioning. Thus she prioritises the stimulation of the body (in other words the instincts), as does Freud. However, where Freud conceived a drive model of conflicting instinctual urges as the model of psychic functioning (Greenberg and Mitchell 1983), Klein's theory postulates a relational model of psychic functioning.

Klein's focus is on the content of the intra-psychic world. She postulates that this content is made up of **phantasy** relations that mirror or reflect the physiological state of the infant.

**Intra-psychic.** The internal world of emotional or mental functioning.

**Phantasy.** The mental correlate (equivalent) of the instincts.

## Phantasy

Phantasy refers to the intra-psychic experience of unconscious relations between good and bad experiences. It is postulated to be the mental correlate (the equivalent) of instinctual life (Isaacs 1948). Phantasy is the term used to denote the most primitive origins of thought. Klein (1932) postulates that we have innate knowledge of certain images, such as the breast, and it is these innate images that constitute the origins of thought. Phantasy is the reservoir of innate unconscious images and knowledge, which has been built up as a result of phylogenetic inheritance.

## Object relations

In phantasy the infant is able to develop an awareness of the breast. It is also in phantasy that the infant has a relationship with the breast. Such relationships are innate to our capacity to be human. Thus the experience of the body is linked to innate knowledge about what the body is experiencing. This concept is central to object relations thinking and will be explored in detail later.

Klein's concepts introduced a way of understanding the individual that has led to creative and innovative advances in post-Kleinian writings about the quality and nature of our personalities. Object relations thinking has provided the major impetus for understanding the development and treatment of **pre-Oedipal** personality structures, such as borderline and narcissistic personality disorders.

**Pre-Oedipal.** The time, in Freudian terms, which is focused upon the oral and anal stages. It is the time when the child is still within a dyadic focus (the mother), and has not as yet come to see the father and mother as conflictual objects to love. These conflicts arise with the Oedipal stage where loving the mother and father is no longer an uncomplicated affair.

Freud's focus had been on the importance of Oedipal issues (a **triadic**, three-person, conflict model of understanding intra-psychic functioning). His interest was in the importance of psychosexual drives in the development of the personality and of neurosis and, of course, on the nature of the unconscious. Freud's contribution to understanding development and pathology lay in his focus on the psychosexual stages and the child's eventual resolution of the Oedipal situation – of the three-person relationships between parents and child. Object relations theory focuses on the first years of development, where the infant is primarily involved in a two-person interaction, or a **dyadic** relationship. The focus is thus on early primitive mental operations, which are postulated as largely biological in origin. These early primitive mental operations have a fundamental impact on the development of the quality and nature of our intra-psychic relational object phantasies and hence on our interpersonal perceptions of the world and others. What Klein (1946) postulates is that the quality of our intra-psychic object relations will provide the lens through which we are able to see and interact in the world and with others and our self.

**Triad.** A three-person relationship such as the relationships that characterise the Oedipal situation – mother, father, and child.

**Dyadic.** A dyadic relationship refers to a relationship of two.

# Theoretical focus

Klein's work was with young children, the youngest being two years old. From these analyses she worked backwards to capture the significance of the experiences of early infancy. This method of theory building followed the route pioneered by Freud. Freud had pieced together a theory of the significance of childhood psychic development by working backwards from the free associations and symptoms of adults.

Initially in working with children, Klein was faced with the limitations of the language of children. By chance, she came to conceptualise play as giving us access to the internal unconscious world of children – the **manifest symbolic representations** (Klein 1926). Manifest symbolic representation refers to the idea that what we see the child doing in play is a symbolic representation of latent (that is, unconscious) meanings. (This is equivalent to the free association of adult patients in psychoanalysis that provides clues to latent, unconscious meanings.)

The world of children is made up of unconscious conflicts and wishes. **Play therapy** allows the working through of the conflicts and wishes associated with significant others in the child's life. Material from these therapies led Klein to make theoretical formulations about the nature of the early psychic life of infants. The psychoanalytic play process revealed how the child is continually engaged in sifting ideas about self and others. This information led Klein to closely examine the child's self-other **configurations**. (This is a term used to denote an intra-psychic relational meaning. In our phantasy life we construct images (objects) of self and significant others in continually changing patterns of relationships with each other, which are not necessarily related to the reality of our external circumstances. These configurations inform our perceptions of external reality and explain how, in some circumstances, we can be so wrong about what is happening around us.) Klein postulated that play revealed these configurations as patterns of internal relationships with phantasy *objects*. The nature and function of these internal, unconscious object relationships was to hold her theoretical interest for most of her life. (The concepts of phantasy and objects will be further explored later.)

Klein's concern was to understand the preverbal, precognitive world of the infant's experience (Klein 1975a; 1975b). The infant's world is initially a world of only sensate experience. It is through the experiences of the body that the infant makes contact with the world. For the infant, there is a seamless experiencing, where self and world are experienced as one with no boundaries or edges marking where the baby's body stops and the other person or the world starts. There is little cognitive ability, and at this stage certainly no interpolated 'I' to mediate cognition. To capture this infantile experience is clearly very difficult, which is why the language of object relations theory is sometimes odd in that it is trying to grasp, in language, what essentially has no language.

Klein examines the processes through which the infant – initially an undifferentiated bundle of **pre-personal needs** – evolves into a unique person, with a distinct character, personality, and way of relating both to the world and to her- or himself. The means through which Klein

**Manifest symbolic representations.** The readily seen symbolic presentation of something else such as a person, an idea, or an image. The remembered dream is a manifest symbolic representation of the unconscious images.

**Play therapy.** The psychoanalytic method of intervention that is used with children. The play is seen as the equivalent of the free associations of adults in psychoanalysis in revealing unconscious material.

**Configurations.** The composition of internal object relations, which consist of characteristic self-other representations. In other words, how we experience ourselves and others.

**Pre-personal needs.** The time in early infancy when the infant is not cognitively aware that his or her needs are experiences of his or her own body. Rather these experiences are felt as impersonal experiences, which merely happen to the infant.

explored this focus was through play. The play of the children in analysis revealed a complex set of phantasy relations both with the self and with significant others – the self-other configuration.

## Psychological birth and selfhood

Psychodynamic theorists agree that the attainment of selfhood or personhood is a developmental achievement and not a biological given. This is not the same as physical birth. Some individuals never achieve a sense of stable selfhood, but are left feeling that their existence is dependent upon certain conditions for survival. This is understandable when we consider that selfhood emerges gradually out of the infant's initial state of total dependence upon the mother.

**Primary narcissism.** The first relationship that the infant is capable of having. It is the relationship to the self.

Like Freud, Klein held that early experience is characterised by the qualities of **primary narcissism** and **omnipotence**. This means that in the infant's initial early experience, the infant is both the centre of the world, and the world. The infant is all. This is the state of primary narcissism. Omnipotence is the infant's sense of making the world happen. The infant does not have the cognitive capacity for a sense of person, place, and time, neither is there a sense of people and events separate from the infant. Rather, 'things' happen as an extension of the infant, through its own omnipotence. The breast does not appear of its own volition; rather it is the infant's need of the breast that makes it appear. Thus, initially, the infant is *lived through* the experiencing of his or her body in a fundamentally unconscious way. Psychological birth is that journey whereby the infant moves from an unconscious, **solipsist** state, to engagement with outside realities. This is a journey fraught with attacking demons and dragons, and warm, nurturing breasts.

**Omnipotence.** The initial state of the infant where the experience is of unlimited power. For instance, the breast comes because the infant makes it come.

**Solipsism.** The belief that the self is all that there is or that one can know.

## The concept of an internal world

Early intra-psychic experience is concerned with the task of separating out the various emotional experiences that accompany bodily states, hence the phrase, the infant is *lived through* the experiencing body. Feeding can be a pleasurable experience as well as one fraught with conflict. A feed can be a good feed or a bad feed. Similarly, defecating could be the giving of good things, or the expelling of bad things. Because the infant has no cognitive ability to conceptualise inside/outside, me/not me, the infant can only know of these good and bad experiences in the most basic terms, that is, in terms of the pleasure or un-pleasure of the body experiences. Thus the infant experiences good and bad 'bits' in relation to bodily experience. Typically, a good feed will result in a good bodily feeling and the experience of taking in a good bit – the good breast. As such the 'breast' is not a person but an experience. A bad feed results in an experience of a bad feeling. This feeling is like taking in a bad bit – the bad breast.

It is important to note that, at this stage of development, 'bits' of experience are experienced as if they were bits (or parts) of the infant. This is due to the infant's limited cognitive ability to distinguish me/not me. Pleasurable and un-pleasurable bodily experiences are thus experienced as concrete bits or parts of the infant, as well as **objects** that have good or bad intent towards the infant. Klein (1946) termed this the experience of **part objects**.

Klein (1946) postulates that from birth, the intra-psychic life of the infant is concerned and taken up with its relations to these good and bad experiences (or part objects). One can see that to speak of relations to people is much too complicated given the infant's limited cognitive abilities. The infant can only have phantasy relations to parts of bodily experience.

## Part object relating

A baby who is hungry has the experience that there is an object that is attacking. Thus the experience is one of being attacked and having to defend him or herself from this attack. Adults also have this experience. Some adults who are paranoid do not consider that what is happening to them may be normal or even of their own doing. They will have the experience of being attacked by the world and having to defend themselves from these attacks. Thus a paranoid person who has someone cancel a date will experience the cancella-

tion as being a personal attack against him- or herself. They will feel compelled to attack back or to withdraw thus protecting themselves from further attack. They will not be able to see that the cancellation may have been within the natural course of events and had no particular personal meanings attached to it. The person who cancelled will be experienced as a hated part object that is attacking; they will not be remembered as the person who only minutes before the cancellation was desired and liked.

**Objects.** The word used by Freud and object relations theorists to convey the idea that the infant, while relating to people in external reality, is internally not yet capable of relating to real people. Instead the infant relates to a phantasy construction, which is the object of the person.

**Part objects.** State in which the infant is unable cognitively to apprehend real people, or apprehend whole objects. Objects can only be experienced in terms of their functions, such as the breast instead of the mother.

## The role of phantasy

The term 'phantasy' is used to denote the kind of relations that occur in object relations. They are not fantasies or daydreams, neither are they concerned with the reality principle. Rather, phantasy is postulated to be the reservoir of innate, unconscious images and knowledge, which has been built up as a result of phylogenetic inheritance. Isaacs (1948) elaborates the concept of phantasy as constituting the basic substance of all mental processes – that from birth some mental activity is operating. The level is, however, too primitive to think of it as constituting 'thinking'. Thus the term phantasy denotes this first mental activity. As such, phantasy is the psychic or mental representation of the instincts (the bodily experience). Freud had postulated that psychic motivation results from the instincts libido and aggression, later the *life* and *death instincts*. What Isaacs postulates is that phantasy occurs concomitantly with instinctual life and forms the psychic (mental) content of the instinct. Psychic motivation was thus moved out of the arena of Freud's drive model and firmly located into a relational model of psychic functioning. In other words, it is our relational needs that inform our psychic functioning rather than our instinctual urges. Phantasy thus came to be seen as the primary mental activity and the primary content of all thought. There is no impulse or instinctual urge that is not experienced also as unconscious phantasy. All thought, however rational, is seen to be based in unconscious phantasy. It is this concept that underlies the psychoanalytic understanding that every action and thought has significance and that even feelings of emptiness are rich with unconscious meanings.

## The concept of psychic structure

It is important to emphasise that there is no such place in the brain as the psyche. Rather, by psyche we mean a mental process that progressively builds up through cognitive development and makes possible the ability to think, feel, and have a mental life. This process is conceptualised as the building of psychic structure, the gradual building up of the contents of an internal object relations world and the particular quality of these relations. Early physiological experience and the accompanying phantasy relations lay the foundation for an individual's particular psychic life. How this happens is initially through **introjection** and **projection**. The earliest interactions that the child has with the world are through:

> **Introjection.** The taking in of experiences. In psychoanalytic terms it refers to the internalisation of the parental figures and their values.

1. Introjection of the world through the senses. This process is the internalisation of the world through the physiological processes of the body, such as feeding.
2. Projection, which occurs when unwanted or even valued bodily sensations are projected out. This occurs also through physiological processes of the body, such as defecation or screaming. With feeding the infant takes in (introjects) the good or bad milk. With defecation the infant expels (projects) what is either good or bad. These physiological experiences occur concomitantly with phantasy. In phantasy there is introjection of the good or bad part object or the expulsion of the good or bad part object. Internalisation and the building of structure are brought about through the continual interplay between introjection and projection of good and bad. A good introject leads to the development and internalisation of good phantasy objects, the good breast, good babies, good penis. A bad introject leads to the development and internalisation of bad phantasy objects, the bad breast, etc.

> **Projection.** A mental mechanism by which the infant expels unwanted or terrifying aspects of his or her internal world. In Kleinian theory, projection is initially a developmentally normal mechanism that assists in the safe keeping of the good object. With development, its use comes to be associated with a defence mechanism whereby one's own traits and emotions are attributed to someone else.

The quality and content of the ongoing process of the infant's projection and introjection builds up the basic contents of the psychic structure of the personality. The quality of the phantasy relations between our good and bad objects or introjects – which are inevitable aspects of development – determines how well we negotiate our concept of self and our relations to others.

This history of early intra-psychic object relating determines the scenario, as it were, of what will be available to be experienced. Out of all the possible and potential ways of being and experiencing in the world, the contents and quality of our early object relations lay down a matrix for our psychic structure. It is through this **matrix** that a particular life can be lived. This unconscious matrix provides the patterns that allow for what is experientially available to be experienced by that individual.

This concept is similar to the Lacanian notion that the unconscious is like a language. It is through language that we are able to be aware and conceptualise. Without a language that offers this ability we are unable to

> **Matrix.** The determining factor which has the power or quality of deciding an outcome or process. Thus the phantasy object relations act as the matrix, or the power, that will determine how we see the world.

conceptualise our experience. Consider that Eskimos have numerous words to describe the various qualities of snow. These words offer them the opportunity to see a number of different and discriminating aspects of snow. A non-Eskimo, with only the word snow to describe or speak of snow, is not able to make these discriminations.

The implication for development is enormous. An infant whose experience may have been of neglect and consequent physiological deprivation, may have an unconscious object relational world that is only about neglect and deprivation. They may then, as a consequence, be dominated by unconscious phantasies of murderous destruction and paranoia about the world. The personality structure of such an individual may have difficulties with impulse control over disappointments and with trust in self and others. An infant with *good-enough* mothering (Winnicott 1958) will have an internal world that contains loving and balanced measurements of love and hate. They would not be dominated by murderous destructive phantasies. Their personality structure will have attained an ability to tolerate disappointment and frustration and allow trust in self and others. In other words, their psychic structure would be built up by sufficient internalisation of 'good' object relational configurations.

## Innate capacity

Klein's major focus is on the intra-psychic world. While she acknowledges the role of the environment (the mother) in influencing this capacity, it was only in the last phase of her career that she started to explore the implications of external influences. This focus arose because of the growing interest in infant observation in Britain. Klein was greatly influenced by Freud's concepts of the *life* and *death* instincts. She saw these instincts as being the prime motivators for the anxieties that characterise internal object relations. Libidinal and aggressive phantasies are seen as the direct mental/psychic representations of the life and death instincts (Klein, 1946).

Klein saw *aggression* as a fundamental human potential, in the same way as she saw *love*. Love and aggression are constitutional givens. Klein (1957) postulates that the level of normality and stability of psychic structure is dependent upon the child's **constitutional** or **innate** capacity for aggression and love. The infant has a genetic potential for greater or lesser capacities to love or hate. This varies from infant to infant. This means that love and hate are the basis of our motivational life or, once again, that our psychic motivation is *relational*. Our need to live, which is seen as a relational need, is co-existent and in continual tension with our need to die, which we are doing from the moment of birth.

The death instinct is operative from birth. The infant therefore suffers from **paranoid** anxieties and attempts to deal with these anxieties through **schizoid** mechanisms, which consist of *splitting* and *projective* defences. The operations of the life and death instincts are important in Kleinian theory and underpin the idea that behind all psychic motivation is an element of aggression. The implication of this concept is that a

**Constitutional/innate.** Aspects that exist at birth but are not hereditary. They are acquired during foetal development. An example is the level or amount of innate aggression in the infant.

**Paranoia.** State of mind characterised by feelings of being persecuted. In the paranoid-schizoid position, for instance, paranoia is the primary anxiety that the infant, and later the adult, is under threat.

**Schizoid.** A way of being in relation to others that is characterised by withdrawal and an inability to form close relationships.

psychoanalysis is not complete until the aggressive components of the psyche have been analysed. Klein's conceptualisations facilitated a way of understanding some of the anomalies of human behaviour. An example is an individual who in reality is talented, attractive, and admired but whose internal phantasy object relations are suffused with aggressive impulses, leaving them feeling worthless, unattractive, and empty.

Later object relations theorists took more note of the impact of external reality. Theorists such as Wilfred Bion (1962; 1967) elaborated the fundamental role of the mother in facilitating the child's capacity to think, and Winnicott (1958) elaborated a theory of the mother-infant unit as the basis of the development of a self.

## Envy

Envy is seen as a particularly malignant form of aggression (Klein 1957). In all other forms of hatred, aggression is directed towards the bad object. The bad object is hated because it is seen as persecutory and/or withholding. It is seen as persecutory largely because it contains the projections of one's own sadism. When we hate someone it is because we have projected a part of our selves that we hate. This is not to say that he or she may not be an objectionable person. However, it is through the mechanism of projection that we invest emotionally in that person. The hated person is invested with aspects of our own split-off hated parts. We are linked through the operation of projection, this is why we experience the emotional involvement or reaction. As an example, you may hate someone because they are lazy. The interpersonal dynamic would suggest that laziness is part of yourself, which you have denied or split off. If laziness were not a split-off aspect of yourself you would probably not have any particularly strong feelings about the lazy person. Thus, once you have come to terms with split-off or denied aspects of your psyche there is no energy or need to hate the other person.

Envy, however, is different to hatred. It is directed towards the good object. It hates the goodness that is possessed by the good object and wishes to destroy the very goodness that it envied. Klein (1975b, 56) makes some interesting distinctions between envy and greed and jealousy:

> In greed, destruction is a consequence of greed, not a motive. In jealousy, destruction is directed towards a third. Jealousy occurs in triadic, three person, relationships. You are jealous that a third person has the goodness of a special other. You want the goodness for yourself and hate the third. Siblings are jealous of the love a mother may give to one of the other siblings, wanting it all for themselves. In envy, destruction is the motive. In envy there is a dyadic, two person, relationship where you wish to destroy the goodness of the other. Thus in envy, a sibling would hate the mother rather than experience jealousy of another sibling.

## Positions

Klein postulated the concept of **positions** rather than **stages**. The concept of positions emphasises that there is a process that persists throughout

**Positions/stages.** In Kleinian terms, *positions* refer to a particular arrangement of object relation configurations to which one returns depending upon developmental and contextual issues. For example, a person in the depressive position may return to the paranoid-schizoid position if there is trauma in their life. A person in the paranoid-schizoid position may move to the depressive position by working through various psychological conflicts. Freud's *stages* refer to distinct time periods which are sequential and which affect the quality of the next stage.

life. Klein (1946) postulated two positions, an early paranoid-schizoid position and a depressive position. The depressive position never fully supersedes or overcomes the paranoid-schizoid position and throughout life we may oscillate between the two. These positions provide the phantasy contents or object relational dynamics that constitute the matrix through which we will negotiate our intra-psychic and interpersonal relations to the world.

## The paranoid-schizoid position

The paranoid-schizoid position is the earliest position, occurring from birth to approximately three months. In the infant's experience, pleasure (satisfaction) and un-pleasure (frustration) experiences are either good or bad bodily sensations. An experience is either good or bad, there is no grey or in-between in paranoid-schizoid functioning. Sensations are experienced as objects, as things in themselves. This is because there is little cognitive ability to conceptualise the experience. We could speak of the infant experiencing what feels like something that is happening, a body experiencing an experience. This is part object experiencing. For example, hunger would be a part object experience for the infant. The infant would not know that it was his or her hunger or even that it was hunger. It is an experience. Similarly, the mother's breast is a part object. Either it is a good object because it has brought pleasure and good milk or it is a bad object because it has withheld or has been an absent breast. The infant cannot cognitively know about the breast being the same good and bad breast.

PHOTO: CHA JOHNSTON

*Paranoid-schizoid functioning is characterised by a feeling of alienation and fragmentation.*

Un-pleasure (frustration) is experienced as persecutory due to the operation of the death instinct. In the early omnipotent state frustration is experienced as an attacking object. The pain in the hungry baby's tummy is an attacking concrete object. The attack must be defended against. This is achieved through the defence mechanisms of projection and splitting. However, the projection increases persecutory anxiety due to the increasing fear of the return of the bad through **re-introjection**. The function of splitting (splitting the good from the bad) allows the good to be protected from aggressive attack by splitting it off to safety.

**Re-introject.** Psychic aspects that had initially been projected. They are then re-incorporated into one's inner world.

While part objects prevail, the infant's phantasy relations are dominated by paranoid anxieties. There is anxiety about the potential dangers of the bad objects. By keeping the part objects split and separate the infant is able, in phantasy, to keep the bad part objects separate and isolated from the good part objects. The paranoid-schizoid position is characterised by paranoid anxieties and by the most primitive mechanisms of splitting, projection, and denial. Splitting has two functions. One is as a defence mechanism, which keeps good and bad separate. The other is as a normal mechanism of development. It is through successful splitting, keeping the good safe from attack, that the infant can accumulate 'good' experiences. This accumulation allows the infant to develop a psychic

## A case of envy

Mary is a successful accountant. She has a husband and two children yet she is unhappy with her life and feels that she always has to prove that she has the best of everything. Consequently she pushes both herself and her family to be the best at everything and is most upset when this does not happen. Significantly, when it does happen and she could enjoy the success, she is even more unhappy, feeling that it was all worthless and not satisfying. The dynamic here is that she is envious of the good of things and when she achieves the good, she destroys its meaningfulness

and is left feeling empty and greedy. Developmentally, Mary had a sister who was her mother's favourite. The two girls were not that close as children but managed to get along well enough. In relation to the mother, Mary was a rebellious child. She behaved as if she did not care about her mother and went out of her way to upset her mother. Klein would propose that Mary's innate capacity for envy was evoked by her relationship with her mother. A child, with less envy, would perhaps have directed her aggression, in the form of jealousy, towards the sister.

structure that is stable, with a coherent ego, able progressively to survive attack and acquire a continuity through time.

The operation of envy undermines development, with serious consequences. Splitting is a necessary and healthy aspect of development, but due to the operation of envy, however, the good object is no longer safe from attack. The good object is attacked in phantasy in an attempt to destroy the envied good. Splitting is then no longer an effective method for protecting the good object. In consequence, persecutory anxiety increases because clearly there can be no good, only bad. Envy destroys hope because the very goodness inherent in hope is destroyed. You will notice that envious people are also paranoid people who find little good in the world.

## The depressive position

With cognitive development, the infant's awareness that the good and the bad breast are one begins to occur. This is the beginning of **whole object** relating. When whole objects come to dominate, the nature of the anxieties change to depressive anxieties. The greater cognitive capacities of the infant facilitate the recognition that the good and bad objects are one and the same. Anxieties then cluster around guilt over the damage done to the good object. Guilt leads to attempts at reparation for the damage done. This is the essence of the depressive position: to tolerate ambivalent feelings towards one and the same object, that is, to love and hate the same object and to allay guilt through attempts at reparation.

Where reparation is successful, healthy development occurs, with the individual negotiating the various developmental stages through the matrix of the depressive position. (These are the stages postulated by, for example, Freud and Erikson.) Throughout life we will continue to negotiate our ambivalence and the fact that we both love and hate the ones closest to us. Under times of stress or trauma we will revert to the more

**Whole objects.** Internal representations of object relations that have become more cognitively sophisticated and which are able to incorporate the image of the whole object – the mother and not merely her breast. We would still speak of objects, as the phantasy world does not entail reality-based cognition of other people and ourselves. Rather this world is pervaded by phantasy representations that reflect the infantile needs, desires, and conflicts of the primitive mind. These part or whole object relational matrixes inform all future adult rational thought.

*Functioning within the depressive position allows you to commit to relationships and to negotiate your love and hate for your partner with compassion.*

primitive modes of functioning of the paranoid-schizoid position and our paranoid anxieties will come to the fore again.

Successful negotiation of the depressive position does not mean that one must be depressed or have had a depression to be healthy. Rather, what is meant is that the dynamic components of loss – loss of the good object and a capacity to mourn, to feel guilt and concern for the other, and to desire to make reparation (or to love another) – are integrated into the personality. Integration is never complete and the individual may oscillate between the two positions depending upon the particular context of his or her life.

Unsuccessful integration results from unsuccessful reparative attempts. The child is left with the phantasy that the damage done to the good object was too great to repair. The despair in this awareness leads to two alternatives:

1. There will be a retreat to the paranoid-schizoid level of functioning with an increase in paranoid anxieties.
2. There may be a retreat to what Klein (1948) termed the manic defence. The manic defence involves omnipotent denial of the damage done and denial of anxiety. A manic defence is commonly seen in everyday life where people cope by denying the seriousness of situations. It also underlies the structure of manic-depressive states. Klein thus postulates that unsuccessful reparative attempts have serious implications for the development of a pathological personality structure.

For Klein (1948) all psychopathology originates from a failure to achieve reparation and from the subsequent retreat to more pathological or infantile internal object relations.

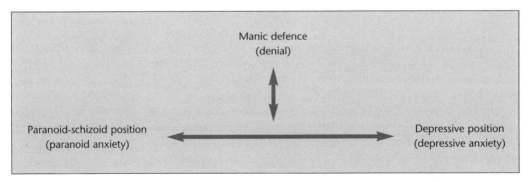

**Figure 6.1** Diagram of movement between positions and development of pathology.

# Critique of Kleinian theory

Klein has given centrality to the constitutional nature of aggression. However, later theorists have questioned this role to varying degrees. The Independent School and Self Psychology see aggression as a result of environmental failure. This approach suggests that it is the failure that invites an aggressive response and the subsequent development of object relations. This critique, by definition, must still hold to the notion that aggression is an innate possibility. Support for either position appears to depend upon the theoretical frame of reference. Theory appears to dictate the findings, with each position claiming evidence for its postulations.

A similar argument applies when thinking about the function of envy. A coherent critique of innate aggression and envy sees manifestations of aggression and self-destructive phenomena as arising from a number of other possible factors:

1. inevitable frustration of an infant's intense greedy neediness,
2. inevitable failures of good-enough mothering, and
3. the primitive nature of the infant's cognitive abilities.

*Towards the end of her career Klein started to prioritise the relationship to the real mother.*

In other words, the intense neediness and dependence of the infant mean that inevitably mothering will fail. Perhaps it is important to understand that Klein's theory does not stand or fall on the ground of the innateness of aggression. What her theory demonstrates, in clinical practice, is the central role played by aggression in the development of destructive self-other phantasy object relations.

Klein has also been criticised for seeing love and hate as not only the central, but the exclusive, thematic concerns of the human psyche. The conceptualisation has been seen as too narrow. The point is probably that Klein's focus was only on the first year of life. Within this time, the cognitive abilities are very limited and her postulation is that the infant can only be concerned with the most primitive and basic of human emotions, which are love and hate.

In relation to real parenting, Klein appears to see the impact of the parents as uniformly positive, and while she acknowledges some parental states such as depression in the mother, she does not build the implications of these states into her theory. The origins of pathology seem to lie in the infant's own aggression. Klein has, however, made enormous contributions to psychoanalytic thought. Her theorising has opened up the possibility of intervention in severe pathologies such as psychotic states – for example schizophrenia – as well as self-pathologies such as borderline and narcissistic conditions.

PHOTO: CHA JOHNSTON

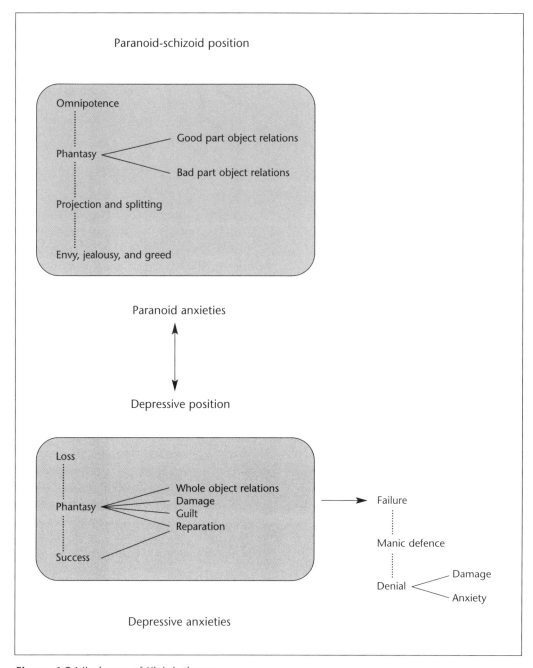

**Figure 6.2** Mind map of Klein's theory.

# Recommended reading

Bion, W. (1962). *Learning from experience.* New York: Basic Books.

Bion, W. (1967). *Second thoughts.* New York: Jason Aronson.
    (*Bion is one of the most prominent object relations theorists. He is difficult and challenging. To consider yourself a serious student you will have to read him at some stage. These two books cover his theorising about the role of the mother and the processes involved in the development of thought.*)

Greenberg, J. K. and Mitchell, S. A. (1983). *Object relations in psycho-analytic theory.* London: Harvard University Press.
    (*A scholarly but readable examination of the theoretical developments among the post-Freudian theorists. Covers theorists such as Klein and Winnicott to Kohut and Kernberg, among a number of other significant figures.*)

Grosskurth, P. (1986). *Melanie Klein: Her world and her work.* London: Jason Aronson.
    (*A thorough biography of Klein. As the title implies, the book gives access to Klein's life and motivations and gives human drama to her theory. This is the only complete biography on Klein. It is an excellent read.*)

Isaacs, S. (1948). 'The nature and function of phantasy'. In M. Klein (ed.), *Contributions to psycho-analysis, 1921–1945.* London: Hogarth Press.
    (*The first exposition of the Kleinian position on phantasy. Rather long-winded but definitive for the serious student.* Contributions to psycho-analysis *contains a collection of papers from the greats of early Kleinian theorising. It is interesting, both from an historical point of view and for laying the foundations of Kleinian thought.*)

Klein, M. (1926). 'The psychological principles of early analysis'. *International journal of psycho-analysis*, 8, 25–37.

Klein, M. (1932). *The psycho-analysis of children.* London: Hogarth Press.

Klein, M. (1946). 'Notes on some schizoid mechanisms'. *International journal of psycho-analysis,* 27, 99–110.
    (*Her definitive paper. It may be a bit difficult but well worth the effort as it summarises her most salient concepts and gives an overview of the two positions.*)

Klein, M. (1948). 'Mourning and its relation to manic-depressive states'. *Contributions to psycho-analysis, 1921–1945.* London: Hogarth Press.

Klein, M. (1957). *Envy and gratitude: A study of unconscious forces.* New York: Basic Books.

Klein, M. (1975a). *Love, guilt and reparation and other works, 1921–1945.* London: Hogarth Press.

Klein, M. (1975b). *Envy and gratitude and other works, 1946–1963.* London: Hogarth Press.
    (*These two 1975 collections of papers cover the essential concepts explored by Klein.*)

Kohon, G. (ed.) (1986). *The British school of psycho-analysis: The independent tradition.* London: Free Association Books.
    (*Has some wonderful essays from the Independent School and an informative introduction that details the development of the Middle School, also known as the Independent School.*)

Segal, H. (1964). *Introduction to the work of Melanie Klein.* New York: Basic Books.
    (*One of the best overviews to the work of Klein.*)

# Critical thinking tasks

## Specific tasks

1) Is there any indication that Geldenhuys was functioning from the paranoid-schizoid position? Write an essay that illustrates how Klein's theory might account for the criminal behaviour of Geldenhuys. Pay particular attention to the operation of such phenomena as splitting, denial, idealisation, or any of the other characteristics of the paranoid-schizoid position.

2) In what ways do you think Klein's theory might be limited? If you have completed the case-study question above, make specific reference to any limitations in the theory in accounting for the acts of Geldenhuys. Are there gaps in the theory that need to be filled, and if so, what are they?

## General tasks

1) Organise an infant observation over a period of about six weeks. In the observation, be sensitive to the baby's responses to the world around him or her. See what deductions you can make about the internal experience of the child.

2) Splitting and projection are two defence mechanisms that are quite easy to see in operation. While they are characteristic of the paranoid-schizoid position, they also occur in the everyday functioning of people who operate mostly in the depressive position. Try to identify instances of splitting – when a situation or an emotion is split – for example, 'I am good and they are bad'. What do you understand about the need to behave in this way? You might also see instances of projection, when the subject attributes to others her or his own personality traits or emotions. It might be more difficult to see splitting and projection operating in yourself because of their unconscious function, but you might be able to become aware of engaging in such defences.

# Donald Winnicott

*Jacki Watts*

This chapter consists of the following sections:

1.  A general introduction to Winnicott.

2.  Winnicott's focus; psychological birth; personhood.

3.  Impingements and appropriate failure.

4.  The process of un-integration to integration.

5.  Holding.

6.  Primary maternal preoccupation.

7.  The role of the father.

8.  Good-enough mothering.

9.  Transitional phenomena.

10. The true and false self.

11. Critiquing Winnicott.

Donald Winnicott

## Introduction

In this chapter we examine Donald Winnicott's contributions to understanding the significance of the mother and infant bond. Winnicott's sense of the importance of this relationship is fundamental to his understanding of the development of the individual. He explores how the quality of this relationship between mother and infant influences the degree to which one can become a person. We look at Winnicott's concept of the development of *personhood*, which reflects his remarkable creativity and genius. Theorists had previously taken it for granted that one was a person.

**True and false self.**
Concepts based in the experiencing body. The true self is based upon what is true about sensate experiencing, i.e. id or instinctual needs. If we are able to remain in touch with this level of integrity with the body we are living close to the true self. Body integrity would mean that we are in touch with our emotional lives, with our passions and hatred. We manage to live them in ways that have integrity for our lives as well as being appropriate within social contexts. The false self means that we have had to abandon the integrity of the body. We had to adapt to the demands and needs of external reality such as the mother's need for the child to be clean all the time. In the adaptation, the false self loses touch with the body and complies with an external truth: 'I am not a normal child who likes to mess, I am a clean perfect child'.

**Intra-psychic.** Mental activity that occurs within the personality.

**Interpsychic.** Psychic activity that involves relations between people.

**Free association.**
Speaking about the first things that come into your mind without censoring them. Psychoanalysis is based upon this method as it becomes clear when it is difficult for the patient to speak. These are the times when conscious or unconscious censorship is at work.

Winnicott did not. He suggests that we *become* persons, and that we can only achieve this given the necessary environmental provisions and innate potential. He would suggest that some people do not become persons but remain extensions of others, that is, *false selves*. We shall explore his conceptualisations of **true and false self** development.

Winnicott's writings, while stemming from a Kleinian base, shifted psychoanalytic emphasis from the **intra-psychic**, to the **interpsychic**, or the interpersonal realm. Within this focus, his exploration of the mother-infant relationship has provided invaluable insight into infant development. His understanding of the role of the mother has also provided a model for therapeutic intervention. The classic **free association** of Freudian analysis is indicated for intervention with neurotic conditions, but it is not applicable in **personality disorders**. Individuals with personality disorders cannot withstand the frustrations and lack of gratification that occur in a psychoanalytic analysis. While the advances offered by Kleinian theory have opened avenues for intervention with **self-pathology**, Winnicott's model has suggested a new metaphor for psychotherapy intervention. This model is based upon modification of the strict psychoanalytic method and offers a focus on certain specific aspects of the relationship between therapist and client. It allows the individual to re-visit, within the relationship to the therapist, the early damage of the pre-Oedipal development stage.

# Winnicott's focus

Winnicott (1945; 1960), like Klein, was concerned with examining the processes through which the little bundle of sensate experiencing becomes a person. Winnicott focused upon the relationship between the mother and the infant. While guided by Klein's (1946) understanding of the internal phantasy world of the infant, he gave central importance to the reality of the external mother. Winnicott saw the mother as influencing both the extent to which one could *become a person* – that is, living one's life in relation to one's *true self* – and the *stability of the person*. We shall discuss the idea of the true self presently. (Winnicott's term 'mother' refers to the real mother of the child. However, the term can also be applied to the function served by the primary caregiver. This extended understanding of the term has implications for South Africa where a large proportion of children are reared within extended family contexts.)

## Psychological birth and personhood

Freud took the entity, or even the existence, of the 'person' of the individual for granted. This was not the case with Winnicott. He was fascinated with what enabled the making or 'becoming' of the person. Winnicott was foremost a paediatrician and he saw the mysteries of the mother-infant bond as fundamental to understanding what was involved in becoming a 'person'. Winnicott coined the famous clinical understanding that there is no such thing as an infant; there is only a mother *and* infant. This formulation means definitively that, where there is an infant, there is maternal care (1956). If maternal care is not there, there is no infant – the infant will die. What is unique about Winnicott is that he took this obvious fact and explored its implications in a creative and distinctive way. The basic understanding is that initially the infant is in a state of **omnipotence**. It does not have the cognitive capacities to understand that the world and the mother are separate entities. Rather, for the infant, the world and the mother are products of his or her own making. This experience is an aspect of the infant's initial **hallucinatory relationship** to the world and people. The world and the infant are all one. Through this experience the infant's **grandiosity** and **wish fulfilment** remain intact, safeguarding the stability of the infantile ego.

## Impingement and appropriate failure

The distinction that Winnicott makes between **impingement** and **appropriate failure** is central to his understanding of the role of a *good-enough* mother (Winnicott 1958). Winnicott maintains that the initial state of the infant's ego is one of fragility and fragmentation. In this state, the ego cannot tolerate impingements. An impingement is experienced when the mother acts towards the infant as if the infant were able to tolerate degrees of frustration and separateness from her, which it is not capable of tolerating. Winnicott defines this experience as a demand made by the environment (that is, the mother), which the infant is unable to meet due to the unintegrated state of the infantile ego. The experience is a demand made upon the infant to be able to be separate from the mother and to be able to react to this separateness. Remember that psychoanalytic theory sees the infant's experience as initially an omnipotent state where the infant and the world are experienced by the infant as one and where there is no need for the infant to have to react. The need for the infant to

**Personality disorders.** Enduring, maladaptive ways of relating in the world that affect perceptions, thinking, and interpersonal relations. Individuals who are personality disordered struggle with damage to their personality structure; as such they have not fully developed their 'personhood'. Developmentally, such individuals have not had optimum conditions to develop stable personality structures. They struggle with problems of the 'self'.

**Self-pathology.** Personality pathology that results from disruptions prior to the Oedipal years. The disruption occurs due to compromises within the infant/mother/primary caregiver relationship. These disruptions lead to unstable development of the child's sense of self.

**Omnipotence.** State of believing that one has unlimited powers.

## Effects of impingements

An example of an impingement is a hungry infant who is not fed. The child will experience the hunger as a threat or an outside demand that threatens his or her cohesion. There is not the cognitive ability to know what the experience is, or that eventually the mother will come to feed the child. For the infant, the demand is terrible and life threatening. The lack of feeding makes a demand upon the child for frustration tolerance that the infant is incapable of meeting. The child will reach a peak of desperation, and then when the feeding does not come, will fall into despair. Winnicott (1952) refers to this experience as nameless dread. Many adults are familiar with the anxiety of what is essentially associated with *nameless dread*. It is an experience of an acute anxiety that one will fall to pieces. This experience stems from such early impingements when the child was unable to cope with the experience of separateness from its mother. With such experiences, the infant must deny its hunger and the infant begins to develop compliance to the outside world. This is a *false self compliance*.

**Hallucinatory relationship.** A false sensory perception that is not based upon reality. In terms of infantile development this is an extremely important experience as it safeguards the infantile ego from fragmentation.

**Grandiosity.** The exaggerated belief in one's own importance or power. In infantile terms this is an essential experience for the infant as it allows a safeguarding of the infantile ego against its own reality-based helplessness.

**Impingement.** Demand made by the environment (the mother) upon the infant to be separate from her. The infant is unable to meet the demand due to the unintegrated state of the infantile ego.

react indicates that there has been maternal failure to meet its needs. In short, there has been impingement.

Impingements have serious implications for the development of the infant. Demands upon the infant to react to the environment result in the ego *falling to bits*. The demand to react to separateness comes at a time when there is not sufficient infant ego strength to sustain the reaction. Thus the reaction results in a loss of cohesion and the experience of 'falling to bits'. If the demand is persistent, the infant then has a need for some armour. 'The infant that is disturbed by being forced to react is disturbed out of a state of *being*' (Winnicott 1960).

Winnicott does not imply that the pair must always have this mother-infant unit whereby the infant can live in a hallucinatory relationship. Rather, he proposes that failure must occur but that it must occur within specific parameters (Winnicott 1960). He terms this kind of failure, *appropriate failure*. As the infant develops there must be the experience of separateness from the mother. This experience of separateness allows the infant to develop a sense of its own being as a separate and independent person in the world. These experiences must, however, be appropriate to the capacity of the infant ego to experience separateness. When this is so the infant can experience his or her separateness from the environment as building up the ego.

Therefore, providing that the environment is sensitive to adapting to the needs of the infant's experience of *going-on-being* – not putting the infant in the situation where it will 'fall to bits' – the demand for separateness will not be *impingement* but will be *appropriate failure*.

## Is birth an impingement?

Winnicott did not see birth as an impingement upon the infant. He saw birth as something for which the infant has been innately prepared. He was too much of a pragmatist to hold that something as natural and normal as the birth process could be construed as traumatic for the infant. It is not the actual birth that constitutes the impingement; rather it is the way that the environment may fail the infant. This could occur through the alienating processes that characterise modern gynaecological hospitals, or through the nature of the mother's bonding with her infant in the first days after birth.

**Wish fulfilment.** State in which the wish seems to have been fulfilled in imagination. Thus dreams, symptoms, and hallucinations are all wish-fulfilment in which the wish has found expression.

# The process of un-integration to integration

Integration into personhood is a developmental achievement. Winnicott (1945) saw the infant as having at first an **unintegrated personality**, a *primary un-integration*. This state is characterised by total dependence upon the mother. Winnicott (1958) proposed that it is the mother who provides the ego support necessary for the infant's fragile ego. This maternal ego support allows the infant to live and develop, despite its helplessness. Where this support is missing, integration will not occur, resulting in various degrees of pathology. Where the maternal ego support is compromised, some integration of the infantile ego will occur, but the infant's ego will also be compromised. This will be due to its need to react to the failures of the mother (her impingements). In this case the integration is based on a false self integration.

The infant must react and adapt to the failures of the mother, and it is through this reaction and adaptation that the true self of the person either becomes hidden or does not exist (Winnicott 1960). It is no wonder that we are often so ambivalent about our mothers. For a critical period of our lives, it is they who keep us alive. In consciousness we are grateful to people to whom we owe our lives, but at an unconscious level it is much more complicated. Many cultures have rituals and beliefs about what is involved when someone saves your life. In psychotherapy we see the psychological implications of this dependence and the ambivalent feelings of gratitude and resentment that an adult child might feel towards their parent.

# Holding

**Holding** is a fundamental concept (Winnicott 1958). By *holding* he means the quality of the mother's provision of infant care. Without *holding* the inherited potential of the infant cannot come into being. The quality of the mother's holding has a fundamental influence upon the actualisation of the infant's selfhood. Winnicott means by this that literally the infant cannot start to *be*, except through the *holding* of the mother. The quality of the infant's *being* will be largely dependent upon the quality of the mother's holding capacities. For the infant, where holding confirms the *aliveness* of its body, it has experiences of the *aliveness of the true self*. This means that the infant then has an experience of existing. Thus infant care, or holding, which confirms the bodily experience of the infant rather than substituting the mother's experience, results in experiences of existing. An example that illustrates this concept is an infant who is fed when hungry. The feeding – that is, holding – will confirm the experience of the body. On the other hand, a hungry child who has his or her nappy changed will not have the experience of the body confirmed.

Winnicott maintains that holding is based upon **empathy** and not upon understanding. Thus Winnicott's concept of mothering has nothing to do with intelligence or education. Good mothering is about a mother's capacity to *feel* her way appropriately into her child's experience. Winnicott (1958) classifies holding into three stages:

1. Absolute dependence, where the infant is totally dependent upon the quality of maternal care and has no means of controlling what is well or badly done.
2. Relative dependence, where the infant gradually becomes aware of the details of maternal care. The infant begins to experience the

**Appropriate failure.** Failure of the environment (the mother), under the controlled conditions of holding, to meet the infant's needs. This kind of failure is necessary in order to stimulate the infant's development of an active and positive sense of separate being, leading to a sense of 'me' and 'not me'.

**Unintegrated personality.** The state of the infant's early ego development. The infant's ego is not able to function as a separate ego but relies on the mother for containment and auxiliary ego containment.

**Holding.** The quality of the mother's provision of infant care.

**Empathy.** The ability to understand and enter into the feelings of another.

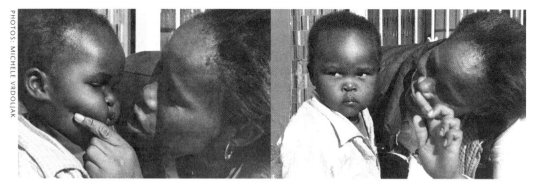

*Mediating meaning. The mother introduces the world to the child. She does this by appropriately interpreting the child's experience, i.e., by responding to the true self of the child. In this way she mediates meaning.*

mother as possibly separate and can start to relate the mother's activities to its own personal impulses.

3. Approaching independence, when the infant can start to do without actual care.

These three stages of holding are supported by the infant's growing cognitive capacities. The infant can begin to rely upon memories of care. These memories form the basis of the infant's introjection of the details of care. This means that the infant learns about caring through taking in the model of care given by the mother. Clearly, failure of maternal care will affect the quality of the infant's sense of care and compromise both the *introjection* of care that is available to the infant as well as the confidence that the infant can have in the environment.

## Primary maternal preoccupation

Winnicott maintains that for a mother to be able to do all the things that are required of her to be a mother, a special characteristic is required, which he formulates as **primary maternal preoccupation** (Winnicott 1958). He conceptualises this as occurring during the last period of her pregnancy and a few days to a couple of weeks after the birth of the child. This is an innate, natural state of the mother whereby her world becomes focused on the child. It is a state where the mother is *primarily preoccupied* with her infant. The mother and infant form a psychological *oneness*. The mother is able to feel her way into the **body-needs** and later the **ego-needs** of her infant.

The distinction between body- and ego-needs is an important one in psychoanalytic theory. Body-needs and ego-needs refer back to Freud's distinction between the id and the ego. *Body-needs are id needs.* The child needs to have its id needs attended to for it to be *contained* and appropriately nurtured. If these needs are not met the child will be overwhelmed and 'fall to bits'. However, with the development of the child's cognitive capacities, the id needs have to become contained by the ego. Initially it is the mother's ego that provides this auxiliary function. Her ego contains the id needs of the child. With development the child learns – *gradually,*

**Body-needs and ego-needs.** Concepts that refer back to Freud's distinction between the id and the ego. Body-needs are id needs. The child needs to have its id needs attended to for it to be contained and appropriately nurtured. If these needs are not met the child will be overwhelmed and 'fall to bits'. However, with the development of the child's cognitive capacities, the id needs require to become contained by the ego. Initially it is the mother's ego that provides this auxiliary function. Her ego contains the id needs of the child. With development the child gradually learns, through appropriate failure, that it is able to take on the functions of the mother's ego and contain its own id needs. The mother must provide an appropriate model of containment, which the child is able to introject.

*at its own pace*, and through appropriate failures on the mother's part – that it is able to take on the functions of the mother's ego and contain its own id needs. It is vitally important initially, in the first few days of life, that the mother provides this *containment*. She does this, according to Winnicott, through *primary maternal preoccupation*. Winnicott represents this state as an illness, a form of psychosis, whereby the mother is able to relax her psychological boundaries and become fused with the infant. It is important that the mother is able to experience this state, and for this she must be psychologically healthy enough; she must have the necessary ego resources to allow herself to be fused with the infant. In this state of primary maternal preoccupation she is able to identify with the baby. She can make sense of the cries and bodily gestures of the baby and translate these sensate experiences into meaningful experiences. This capacity for primary maternal preoccupation allows the mother either to bring or not to bring meaning to the child's experience. If the mother's reaction (her *holding*) matches the bodily experience of the infant, she brings meaning to experience. She feeds when the infant is hungry; she warms when the infant is cold. How a mother knows these things about her infant is through her ability to be attuned to her infant, to be in a state of primary maternal preoccupation.

If the mother can be in this state and adapt appropriately to the needs of the infant, there is little disturbance and need for reaction. The infant's existence remains intact and relatively seamless. When the mother gets it right, there is no awareness of the mother, and the infant's developmentally needed state of omnipotence remains intact. Where a mother is not psychologically healthy enough to move into a state of primary maternal preoccupation, the result is that she enforces impingements upon the infant. She substitutes her own needs and understandings onto the id needs of the infant. When this happens the id experiences (the body experiences) of the child are not given meanings that refer to or make sense of the child's experience. The result is that the potential aliveness of the body is killed and the child must then adapt to the meanings imposed by the external world to understand his or her experience. Should this happen, it comes at a time when the infant is least able to cope with such failure, that is, in the first few days of life. The impingements interrupt the *going-on-being* of the infant and produce the threat of annihilation. For Winnicott (1945) the fear of annihilation is the most primitive anxiety.

PHOTO: CHA JOHNSTON

*Primary maternal preoccupation. For the last few weeks of pregnancy and the first few days after birth, the mother loses her interest in the outside world and becomes preoccupied with the baby.*

**Primary maternal preoccupation.** Innate, natural state of the mother whereby she is primarily preoccupied with her infant. She is able to form a psychological 'oneness' with the infant and feel her way into the body-needs and later ego-needs of her infant. Winnicott speaks of this time as an illness, a form of psychosis, whereby the mother is able to relax her psychological boundaries and to become fused with the infant.

## Eating disorders

It is a common experience of people with eating disorders to use food to calm or comfort themselves. They have learned to see food as a substitute for emotional holding. Developmentally we can postulate that in their childhood their mothers were either anxious or unable to meet their emotional needs. Instead food was given as a substitute. Thus, for example, the anxious or lonely baby is related to and treated as the hungry baby. The child then comes to associate emotions with feelings of needing to eat.

The basis of the establishment of a stable ego is a sufficiency of the experience of going-on-being. For the infant, the possibility of this state of going-on-being is totally dependent upon the quality of the mother's management of infant care, that is, her capacity to hold the infant's id and developing ego-needs.

## Role of the father

PHOTO: JACKI WATTS

Apart from the mother's own psychic conflicts which may compromise her capacity for primary maternal preoccupation, the mother also needs, during this period, the strong containment of the environment. This containment facilitates her ability to become preoccupied with the infant. It is in this capacity that the father plays a fundamental role. He provides the safety and containment for the mother that allows her to relax her psychological boundaries and become devoted to and fused with the infant, providing perfect attunement, or matching of the infant's needs. Together the parents form the parental dyad, which is the macro containment of the infant.

*Fathers act to contain the family unit. The symbol of the father conveys his strength, which allows the mother to surrender her own ego strength to merge with the baby.*

## Good-enough mothering

Winnicott postulates mothering as a process, which matches the changing needs and cognitive development of the infant. While a period of almost perfect attunement – that is, the state of primary maternal preoccupation – is necessary for the infant's initial development, this harmony between infant and mother needs to come to an end. If the mother continues in this state and continues to pre-empt the infant's needs, the infant will not have the opportunity of experiencing where the mother leaves off and the infant itself begins. The infant must begin to have experiences that define it as an entity, separate from the mother. For this to happen, the mother must begin to *appropriately fail* in meeting the infant's needs. Winnicott points out that it is 'appropriate' failure that is needed, not impingements. These failures give the infant slow, measured, small doses of frustration and anxiety. This anxiety begins to disrupt the infant's omnipotence in ways that do not threaten it with annihilation. The infant begins to experience that it is not the whole world. Appropriate failure disrupts this omnipotent phantasy, forcing upon the infant experiences that start the rudimentary distinctions between *me* and *not me*, between *inside* and *outside*. Appropriate failures allow the infant to come slowly to experience an outside reality over which it does not have omnipotent control. Each failure results in bodily tensions and experiences of relative terror and disintegration. Survival of each of these experiences leads to a growing stability and trust in a sense of going-on-being. These experiences allow the infant to experience separateness from the mother without being overwhelmed by it. For this developmental transition to occur appropriately, Winnicott (1960) postulates the concept of the **good-enough mother**. Such a mother is attuned to her infant and will fail the infant appropriately to enhance her child's growth.

**Good-enough mothering.** The mother's capacity to fail appropriately in meeting the infant's needs. Winnicott makes the point clear that it is 'appropriate' failure that is needed, not impingements. These failures give the infant slow, measured, small doses of frustration and anxiety. These experiences allow the infant to experience separateness from the mother without being overwhelmed by the experience.

As the initial experience for the infant is that it is both the world and the creator of the world, the mother has the very important role of upholding this phantasy. She does this initially in a state of primary maternal preoccupation. The good-enough mother only slowly disillusions the infant with appropriate failure, keeping the infant from 'falling to bits', or 'disintegrating'. The infant's initial sense of omnipotence is a vital stage of its initial sense of going-on-being and psychic growth. The good-enough mother has an intuitive knowledge of this state and does not challenge or disrupt the infant's omnipotence. The mother who is not 'good-enough' induces traumatic and inappropriate failures that lead to traumatic breakdowns of omnipotence and the infantile experience of 'falling to bits'.

A few possible situations which could constitute inappropriate failures for the infant range, for example, from the hospitalisation or death of the mother soon after birth to a mother who may be incapable of primary maternal preoccupation due to psychiatric illness or self-pathology. In such instances there may be premature failure of the mother-infant bond with the infantile ego falling into fragmentation. When the infantile ego is not contained by the mother the result is a traumatic breakdown of the infant's sense of omnipotence. The ego is forced to react to separateness and this leaves the infant with an untenable break in its sense of going-on-being. These breaks may manifest in the adult as feelings of terror, of falling forever, of a never-ending black hole. Such symbols represent the infantile experience of disintegration and fragmentation. The most severe failure may result in psychosis. Winnicott (1974) maintains that the clinical fear of breakdown is the fear of a breakdown that has already been experienced in infancy.

# Transitional phenomena: transitional space and the transitional object

The basis of our capacity to be alone – a state where we are secure in our existence and our ability to survive – is built upon early experiences of being alone in the presence of a mother who *holds* the emotional life of the infant, knowing when not to impinge upon the infant (Winnicott 1958).

This capacity to be alone is fundamentally important in the development of a creative capacity and the formation of symbolic thought and activity. How this state is achieved is a question that concerns most object relations theorists. They consider the process by which the infant moves from a solipsistic internal world to a world of shared reality, from a sense of self as one with the world to a sense of self as separate and distinct from others and yet connected to the social and cultural domain. Winnicott (1951) postulates the importance of **transitional space**. This is the *space* available to the child who is allowed to experience the capacity to be alone while in the safety and containment of the mother. In this space the child plays with an area of experiencing which is about neither *me* nor *not me*. It is a kind of daydreaming where the infant can play with creating and

**Transitional space.** The 'space' available to the child who is allowed to experience the capacity to be alone when in the safety and containment of the mother. In this space the child plays with an area of experiencing which is about neither 'me' nor 'not me'. It is a kind of daydreaming where the infant can play with creating and destroying the first 'me-not me' object – the transitional object.

PHOTO: MICHELE VRDOLJAK

*The baby's transitional object acts as the first* me-not me *object. It facilitates the child's development into an external world of reality.*

**Transitional object.** The first object that is both 'me and not me.' This transitional object is often the infant's teddy bear, or thumb, or the corner of a favourite blanket.

destroying the first *me-not me* object – the transitional object (Winnicott 1951). The **transitional object** is the first relationship the child has with an object that is both *me and not me*. This is often the infant's teddy bear, or thumb, or the corner of a favourite blanket. The character Linus in the *Peanuts* comic strip carries his blanket around with him – this is his transitional object. The *good-enough* mother senses that this object is special to the infant and will make sure that it is always available.

The infant will start to relate to an object in a particular way that reveals two contrasting impulses – to love and to destroy. The object is used both to soothe the infant, for example, to suck on when going to sleep, as well as to be destroyed, in being pulled and dragged around. In *phantasy*, the infant both loves and destroys the object. The object's survival and its non-retaliation allow the infant to play with its own loving and destructive urges and in this way the object provides the bridge – the *transitional space* – between what is phantasy and what is reality. The object, by being both loved and destroyed, by being both *me* and *not me*, and (importantly) by surviving the intensity of these emotions, facilitates in negotiating the space between inner reality and external reality, for the development of symbol formation. The object survives attacks of love and hate. It promotes a distancing between emotion, action, and rudimentary thought and the sense of *me-not me*. The object comes to stand for or *symbolise me-not me*, rather than *being me-not me*. The object also comes to stand for the emotions and/or the actions. In this way the first rudimentary symbol formation occurs.

Winnicott (1951) postulates that transitional space is vital for play and aliveness. It is the space where the child is able to play with potential. For the child to be able to use transitional space, the child needs to have had the experience of the safety of non-impingements. As we have seen, this means being able to be with the mother who will allow the infant just to be, without impinging upon it. In these periods, the infant has rhythms of de-integration (sleep or daydreaming) and integration (wakefulness). These rhythms, which coincide with the rhythms of the body, are the

*The capacity to be alone. The mother, by facilitating sufficient experiences of integration and de-integration, gives the infant the opportunity to acquire a stable sense of the true self without impingements. These kinds of experiences develop into the capacity to be alone.*

PHOTO: CHA JOHNSTON

material substance of true self experiencing. The accumulation of these bodily experiences coheres the *going-on-being* of the infant's sense of self. It is these experiences that result in our taken-for-granted confidence in being able to survive and to be alone without feeling that we will disintegrate. The importance that Winnicott accords transitional space is seen in his postulation that transitional space is the seat of a culture's creativity.

As adults we still need moments when we can *play in transitional space*. Most of us will know the experience of rejuvenation that comes from having 'time out', when we can be alone with ourselves. This may come from just *being* or from creative activities – a trip to the mountains, a walk in a garden, listening to music, painting, creating, etc.

## The true self and the false self

Winnicott (1960) postulates that the *true self* is based in the experiencing body. The true self is based upon what is true about sensate experiencing, that is, the experiencing of id or instinctual needs. If we are able to remain in touch at this level of integrity with the body we are living closely to the true self. Body integrity would mean that we are in touch with our emotional lives, with our passions and hatred. We manage to conduct our emotional lives in ways that have intra-psychic integrity as well as being appropriate within social contexts. At the earliest stage, a mother who accurately reflects the sensate experiences of her infant accurately reflects the true self experience of the infant. The way she cares for (holds) her infant brings meaning to the child's experience. A good-enough mother brings to the child those meanings that accurately reflect the experiences of the child. Thus an infant who cries because it is hot is made cooler when the mother has related accurately to the true 'hot' self of the child. If the infant is given the breast, instead of being made cooler, the mother has imposed her own meanings on the infant's experience. She has *impinged* upon the true self of the infant. In this impingement she has imposed a false 'hungry' self onto the child. When the mother does not respond to the true self experiencing, the child has no option but to *adapt to the false self expectations* of the mother.

Throughout development, the environment will inevitably not respond accurately to the experiences of the child. Such perfect response would damage the child in the same way that continued perfect anticipation of the child's needs damages the child. In a social world it is also necessary for the child to adapt to the social demands of the environment. Thus it is both necessary and natural that the child should develop a degree of *false self functioning* to curb and channel its instinctual life. If it did not do this it would be impossible to live with, being demanding, selfish, and intent upon satisfying its own needs. The false self may, at this benign level, provide adaptation to social requirements. Thus, at a healthy level, the false self can act to protect the true self by enabling the individual to conform to social norms. At more severe levels of adaptation, the false self acts to protect the true self from the impingements of a failing environment.

*The false self develops in response to adaptations to environmental demands. Hence the puppet symbolises the false self responding to environmental stimuli.*

There will be degrees of severity in the development of the false self, depending upon the severity of the impingements to which the child must adapt. Winnicott postulates that there is a *continuum of false self development*. Normality is where the false self acts to allow smooth passage through the world, as it were, by inducing appropriate and socially acceptable ways of expressing love and hate and other forms of acceptable behaviour.

Further along the continuum the false self may protect the true self from harm. For example, where a family may covertly forbid independence and separation, the false self will comply and adapt to these demands, while the independence of true self may lie dormant. An example may be the young woman who has been an 'A grade' student at school, devoted and obedient, and dependent upon her parents. Throughout her childhood and adolescence she has adapted to the demands of the family in return for their acceptance. Were she to rebel she would be abandoned or seen as a disgrace to the family. When she arrives at university, she 'goes wild' and attempts to liberate her true self by trying to be true to her own needs.

At the pathological end of the continuum the false self acts as if it were the real person. Adaptation has become complete. In such cases Winnicott suggests that the person does not, as yet, exist. The functioning of the individual is made up of adaptations to the demands of the environment. The individual is purely an adaptation to whatever the demands of the early environment have been. He or she is not a *person* in his or her own right. In such cases, psychotherapy would need to provide a context for the individual's regression to a state of dependence. Working through this state of regressed dependence would allow the false self to give up its **protection** to make way for the developing true self.

**Protection.** Winnicott is quite idiosyncratic about language usage and it would seem that his intention was to see the false self as a protection in all its positive and negative senses. Thus the word has a much broader meaning than the Freudian 'defence'.

# Critiques of Winnicott

A major critique of Winnicott is concerned with his writing style. While he claims to be within the psychoanalytic paradigm, it is difficult to find

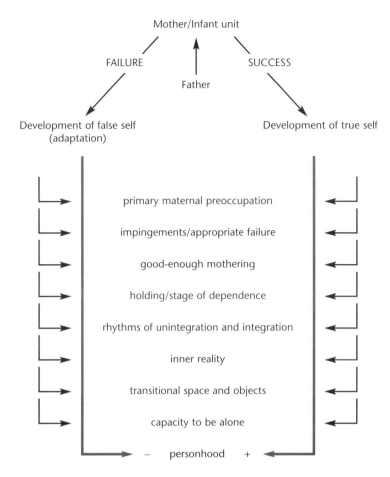

**Figure 7.1** Mind map of Winnicott's theory.

evidence, within his theory, of adherence to fundamental psychoanalytic concepts. Thus while he claims to adhere to psychoanalytic assumption, his theory is formulated as a unique and original interpretation of traditional theory.

Further, his concepts are often so beautifully written that they lack theoretical rigour. As such they run the risk of being meaningless when placed against other more theoretically 'tight' formulations. An example of this problem is his conceptualisation of the self. While the concept of self is used extensively in psychoanalytic theory to denote the totality of the personality structure, Winnicott's use implies that the self is possible only contingent upon the quality of the mother's care. Such a formulation has clinical usefulness as it reflects the experience of many clients who feel that they do not exist because of the quality of maternal abandonment that they experienced. However, in terms of the development of psychic structure, the formulation is meaningless. Psychic structure and the self will develop regardless of the quality of maternal care.

Another example is Winnicott's concept of transitional phenomena. The concept is innovative but adds little within the context of a coherent theory of object relations development. The transition from merged unit to separateness can be accounted for in more theoretically rigorous ways, as we may see, for example, in Klein and Freud. It would appear that Winnicott's theoretical formulations are a challenge to traditional conceptualisations of personality development. However, his theory is meaningful for the experiences of clients and practitioners in psychotherapy, as he appears to articulate the development and the experience of *personhood* in creative and facilitative ways.

## Recommended readings

Goldman, D. (ed.) (1993). *In one's bones: The clinical genius of Winnicott*. London: Tavistock.
(*A collection of papers by Winnicott and others that highlights the range, creativity, and unique contribution of Winnicott.*)

Kohon, G. (ed.) (1986). *The British school of psycho-analysis: The independent tradition*. London: Free Association Books.
(*A wonderful introduction to the writings of some of the Independent tradition theorists. You will get a good sense of the way they think about their work and their patients.*)

Winnicott, D. W. (1958). *Collected papers: Through paediatrics to psycho-analysis*. New York: Basic Books.

Winnicott, D. W. (1964). *The child, the family and the outside world*. London: Penguin.

Winnicott, D. W. (1965). *Maturational processes and the facilitating environment*. New York: International Universities Press.

Winnicott, D. W. (1971). *Playing and reality*. New York: Basic Books.
(*These four books provide the essential coverage of Winnicott's concepts. They are all highly readable and, for books on theory, most enjoyable. Be aware that Winnicott's idiosyncratic style is deceptively easy.*)

## The concepts covered in the chapter are drawn from the following papers:

Winnicott, D. W. (1958)[1945]. 'Primitive emotional development'. In *Collected papers: Through paediatrics to psycho-analysis*. New York: Basic Books.

Winnicott, D. W. (1958)[1951]. 'Transitional objects and transitional phenomena'. In *Collected papers: Through paediatrics to psycho-analysis*. New York: Basic Books.

Winnicott, D. W. (1958)[1952]. 'Psychosis and child care'. In *Collected papers: Through paediatrics to psycho-analysis*. New York: Basic Books.

Winnicott, D. W. (1958)[1956]. 'Primary maternal preoccupation'. In *Collected papers: Through paediatrics to psycho-analysis*. New York: Basic Books.

Winnicott, D. W. (1965)[1960]. 'The capacity to be alone'. In *Maturational processes and the facilitating environment*. New York: International Universities Press.

Winnicott, D. W. (1965)[1960]. 'Ego distortions in terms of true and false self'. In *Maturational processes and the facilitating environment*. New York: International Universities Press.

Winnicott, D. W. (1965)[1960]. 'The theory of the parent-infant relationship'. In *Maturational processes and the facilitating environment*. New York: International Universities Press.

# Critical thinking tasks

## Specific tasks

1) How might Winnicott's theory provide a way of understanding the behaviours and motivations of Geldenhuys as described in the case study? You would need to know about his mother and the quality of maternal care he received as a child.

2) Would you consider Geldenhuys's behaviour a false self adaptation to environmental impingements? How would you justify your answer?

3) Consider the hypothetical case of a sexually abused child who is prematurely forced into sexuality and becomes promiscuous. How would you explain this development into promiscuity in Winnicott's terms?

## General tasks

1) Consider in what ways you may be acting from a false self position. Remember that the false self is largely an unconscious way of being in the world, but it is possible to have some knowledge of when we act in ways that are adaptations to the demands of those around us.

2) Take a survey of people to find out how many of them had transitional objects in their childhood. Find out what the objects were and what happened to them. See if your findings fit Winnicott's theory of transitional phenomena.

3) Observe two mothers, one whose baby is only a few days old, and the other whose baby is a few months old. Observe and make notes about the differences between the ways they react to their infants.

# 8

# Jung's analytic theory of the development of personality

*Jacki Watts*

This chapter presents an overview of Jung's psychoanalytic theory of self and personality. It covers the following of his major concepts:

1. The psyche (consciousness, the personal unconscious, and the collective unconscious).

2. Complexes.

3. Archetypes.

4. Opposites.

5. Psychic activity.

6. Pathology (the concepts of inflation, participation mystique, neurosis, and alienation).

7. The hierarchy of archetypes (the concepts of persona, shadow, animus/anima, and self).

8. The role of the self in individuation.

9. Stages in the individuation process and some archetypal themes.

10. Personality types and their functions.

11. Theory of symbols.

12. Some ideas about analytic psychotherapy.

13. Dreams from an analytic perspective.

Carl Jung

# Introduction

Jung's theoretical break from Freud arose from differences between the two men over the role of spirituality in the human psychic world. Jung was well aware of the significance of childhood for the formation of personality. In fact, he confirmed that Freud had clearly mapped out the psychology and the appropriate intervention when the problems of the individual start with problems of separating from the influence of home and parents (Jung 1983). However, we shall see that the issue of spirituality presents a major difference between Freud and Jung. We shall see that a spiritual dimension is important to an overall understanding of Jung's view of humanity and his conceptualisations of psychic motivation and growth.

Central to Jung's theory is the concept of the **individuation of the self** as an innate process. Jung sees all of humankind as located within a shared experience of humanness and guided by a universal collective unconscious. He sees the individual, within this context, as having an innate need to seek growth. Growth occurs due to the workings of the self, which has access to the wisdom of our collective unconscious. This wisdom becomes accessible to us through our dreams and the symbols of our culture.

Individuation is a lifelong process that is never completed. We start life with the self as the centre. The self is both the centre and the goal of life. Throughout development the self unites and organises our experiences towards its goal of progressive integration and wholeness. The soul is an important concept in Jung's theory, and appears to be the same concept as the self – Jung sees the self as the closest we come to an experience of God. This short description indicates how central spirituality is in Jung's thinking. We shall go on to examine these ideas and illustrate his theory of individuation.

# Psyche

Jung (1983; 1986) was concerned almost exclusively with the psyche. **Psyche** is a term used by all dynamic theorists. It signifies the idea that the

*'We become what we dream ... We achieve in reality, in substance, only the pictures of the imagination.'*

Lawrence Durrell

**Individuation.** The innate and lifelong process of becoming an individual, the move towards wholeness through the integration of conscious and unconscious aspects of the personality.

**Psyche.** A term used by all dynamic theorists to refer to the idea that the mind functions as the centre of thought, emotion, and behaviour at both a conscious and unconscious level, adjusting or mediating the body's responses to the social and physical environment.

*Religious symbols indicate humanity's desire to find divinity and spiritual fulfilment.*

**Consciousness.** The range of experience of which one is aware. These experiences come together to form a sense of our continuity in time and place. Consciousness is a reflection of the ego, the 'I' of our being in the world.

**Ego.** The ego or 'I' is the centre of consciousness, and as such it constitutes the contents of consciousness. Consciousness is only aware of the experiences of the conscious ego. Post-analytic thinking has taken the concept further and postulates, like Freud, that ego is also partly unconscious.

**Ego-complex.** The term by which Jung indicates that the 'I' is the centre of consciousness.

**Personal unconscious.** The reservoir of our own forgotten or repressed experiences. Unlike Freud's 'unconscious', which contains the phylogenetically constituted id, Jung's concept is ontogenetically constituted and can, in principle, be made conscious.

**Phylogenetic.** Origin and development of the species.

**Ontogenetic.** Origin and development of the individual.

mind functions as the centre of thought, emotion, and behaviour at both a conscious and unconscious level, adjusting or mediating the body's responses to the social and physical environment. In Jungian terms psyche is seen as the place of conscious and unconscious processes. It is the centre of mind and soul and is thus the centre of experience and meaning. Therefore we see that the psyche is not the mind but rather an organising function that unites all the mental functions that make us human.

Jung (1983; 1986) considers the psyche as operating at three levels. Freud had also postulated three levels of functioning. Freud's structural model postulated the working of the id, ego, and superego. In Freud's model, the id constitutes the reservoir of the unconscious, the contents of which are the instinctual drives of the individual, which are never able to become conscious. The ego arises out of the id and acts as the mediator between the tensions of the id and the superego, which is the individual's conscience. These three levels are distinct but are dynamically interrelated in the resolution of drives. This means that Freud's model is a conflict model, based on the relationships (dynamics) between the three levels as they try to negotiate a process for psychic equilibrium around drive conflicts. Jung's concept of the structure of the psyche is quite different. His is not a conflict model, rather he sees the elements of the psyche as working together in a progressive journey of growth towards individuation.

## The three levels of the psyche

### Consciousness
**Consciousness** is the range of experience of which we are aware (Jung 1986). These experiences come together to form a sense of our continuity in time and place. Consciousness is a reflection of our **ego**, the 'I' of our being in the world. The 'I' is the centre of consciousness. Jung calls this the **ego-complex**. (We will discuss his idea of complexes when we look at the relationship between the complexes, the personal unconscious, and the archetypes.) The ego or 'I' is the centre of consciousness, and as such it constitutes the contents of consciousness. In other words, consciousness is only aware of the experiences of the conscious ego. Post-analytic thinking has taken the concept further and postulates, like Freud, that ego is also partly unconscious (Jung 1983; 1986).

### Personal unconscious
The **personal unconscious** is the reservoir of our own forgotten or repressed experiences. This is not the same concept as Freud's unconscious. Freud's unconscious contains the id – **phylogenetically** inherited material that can never be made conscious. Jung's version is **ontogenetically** constituted and can, in principle, be made conscious. Whereas Freud's phylogenetic unconscious is firmly located within humankind's historical development, within its cultural taboos, Jung's ontogenetic focus emphasises the individual's development. Jung's focus here is upon the personal context for what has become unconscious.

## Collective unconscious

The idea of the **collective unconscious** (Jung 1983) is Jung's unique contribution. By this concept he postulates an inherited part of the psyche, which is shared by all humans. It is a patterning of behaviours that occurs across cultures and races. He postulates this concept in an attempt to account for the striking structural similarities in behaviour and experience that we see across all cultures. Regardless of where one is in the world, there are human interactions and behaviours that are universally common. This suggests that there are organising principles that account for us being human. These are revealed in events such as the initiation rituals of birth, entry into adulthood, marriage, and death.

By definition then, the universality of the collective unconscious is of limitless extent and depth and possibility. We are born deeply unconscious and this experience provides the matrix out of which consciousness, and thus the ego, will develop. It is also the matrix to which we return in sleep. Sleep is the place of dreaming. Through the dream experience we are in contact with the wisdom of the collective unconscious. Jung's positive view of man's unconscious sets him apart from Freud and other psychoanalytic theorists. He postulates that forces within the collective unconscious guide a journey towards individuation. These ideas will unfold as we go along. Dreams, for Jung, are thus the fundamental processes through which personal growth occurs, as it is through our dreams that we have access to the guiding forces of archetypal energies – the wisdom and history of our ancestors.

## Complexes

The idea of **complexes** arose from Jung's work with word association. He found that individuals displayed specific identifiable themes, unique to

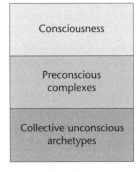

| Consciousness |
| Preconscious complexes |
| Collective unconscious archetypes |

**Figure 8.1** The three levels of the structure of the psyche.

**Collective unconscious.** An inherited part of the psyche, which is shared by all humans and which is responsible for the patterning of behaviours that occurs across cultures and races. Jung postulates this concept in an attempt to account for the striking structural similarities in behaviour and experience, which we see across all cultures.

## Symbols

The circle is the most universal of all symbols. The unbroken line represents perfection, eternity, and the never-ending cycle of creation, death, and regeneration.

The Tai-chi is a circle enclosing the yin and yang, the two opposing but complementary forces of creation. They are often thought of as male and female. Around the Tai-chi are the Eight Trigrams. In Chinese divination, these are the magic symbols used to determine the balance of cosmic forces.

The uroborus is a symbol of a dragon or a snake swallowing its tail. It is an ancient symbol that is found as far apart in the world as West Africa and central America. With the beginning (the mouth) and the end (the tail) at the same point, it represents an eternal cycle of destruction and simultaneous regeneration.

**Complexes.** The personalised psychic structures, found within the personal unconscious, which act as organising principles. A complex clusters the effects of several archetypal patterns with personal experience and affect (emotion).

each individual, in their associations to stimulus words (Jung 1986). The concept of the complex was Jung's way of linking some fascinating observations. He noted that there appear to be *universal themes* common to all humankind, such as loving, hating, desiring, raging, abandoning, engulfing, etc. He postulated that these strata of experiencing arose from a deeply unconscious level of experience, which is the *collective unconscious*. Jung also noted that each individual experienced these common themes in completely individual ways. Therefore a system was in place that allowed these collective themes to be expressed in an individual fashion. Thus he postulated that a personal unconscious exists and that the individual nature of these universal themes is expressed from this personal level of experiencing.

The personal unconscious is thus the centre from which the organisation of the complexes occurs. The complexes coordinate the personal dimension of being human with the collective dimensions of being human. Jung postulated that personal experiences throughout life cluster around *archetypal energies*. Events in childhood, and especially internal conflict, provide the personal aspects of the way the archetypal core is organised and experienced in adult life.

Thus we may define the complexes as the personalised psychic structures, found within the personal unconscious, which act as organising principles. A complex clusters together the effects of several archetypal patterns with personal experience and affect (emotion). Experience tends to gather round the complexes and it is mediated (organised and understood) through them. Complexes are the personalised and integrated psychic organising principles that emerge out of the relations between archetypal potentialities and the personal experiences of the personal unconscious. As a personalised and integrated psychic structure, a complex is an organising function that makes sense of particular archetypal energies in the themes of everyday life. Jung emphasises that the themes will accord with the experiences of an individual, that is, within a particular life experience. Thus a complex results from a blend of archetypal core experience and human experience and it is through the complex that meaning is given to certain archetypal energies.

This notion of the complexes links Jung with all other psychoanalytic theorists who postulate that there are central internal organising principles that influence the way we are able to live our lives and interact with others. For Freud, these were the influences of fixations, for Klein the relative strengths of the paranoid-schizoid and depressive positions, and for Winnicott the mediation of the false self. These concepts are explored throughout this psychoanalytic section.

In line with his positive view of humankind's potential, Jung saw growth as occurring through the process of bringing to consciousness the archetypal energies that organise or structure our existence. So long as the complexes remain unconscious they will exert unconscious influences on our lives and we will remain unaware of them. Jung maintains that an individual's most habitual complexes are the 'tender spots of the psyche, which react most quickly to an external stimulus or disturbance' (Jung 1990, 28). Free association or word association (his old research tool) will thus inevitably lead one to the 'critical secret thoughts' of the individual.

# Archetypes

Jung (1986) initially used the term 'primordial images'. His thinking included the idea that in the development of the human mind we still retained the fundamental biological, prehistoric, and unconscious aspects of archaic humanity. These archaic remnants would provide our most primitive but essential foundations of how to be human. He termed these remnants 'projected memories'. (Jung's concept of memories is similar to Klein's notion of phantasy, that is, a reservoir of innate knowledge of the object of the instincts, such as breasts, nipples, etc.). He conceptualised this archaic foundation as providing primordial or archaic tendencies to organise ourselves as human. These tendencies, he postulated, are observable as inherent tendencies to form representations or images or symbols about experience and behaviour. Importantly, it is not the representations that are inherited. What is inherited is a tendency to organise behaviour or experience in certain ways. Thus these tendencies influence each culture to form representations of what is essentially our primordial or archaic inheritance. The tendency to represent leads to images that indicate universal modes of experience and behaviour. He was later to term these influences **archetypes**.

Jung (1990) explains that, in archaic times, man did not reflect upon his symbols; symbols were lived and were unconsciously animated by their meaning. Think of any symbol that permeates your culture. You will find that once you start to investigate the mythology of the symbol, its origin proves to be rooted in some action or deed. These deeds were originally motivated by affect (emotion). For example, fear of a new guest at the supper table, who might stab you for your lands or your wife and child, led to the custom of placing all weapons on the right hand side of the eater. In that way any attempt to use the weapons would be visible. It is now customary in Western culture to place the table knife on the right hand side.

The closer the image is to an archetypal core, the greater will be the emotional impact. Perhaps one of the most emotionally charged archetypal behaviours is contained within the ceremonies of a wedding. Clear symbolic acts that are linked to the fears and anxieties of a tribe are revealed in the ceremonies. For example, the couple needs to be protected in their separation from the parents, hence the giving of gifts. The vulnerability of a woman in defending herself is symbolised in the vows exchanged in traditional marriages where the husband is expected to look after her. The woman must protect the working of the marriage for the peaceful continuance of the tribe, she thus makes vows of obedience and commitment to her husband and his will. Another rich example is death and its elaborate ceremonies that attempt to allay our fears of dying and confirm our hope in the afterlife. Here we see formalised partying, eating, and giving of gifts either from the dead person, as in bequests, or gifts to the dead as in the laying of flowers or funeral wreaths. All these actions symbolise our hopes and fears about dying.

By 1919, Jung was using the term *archetype* for the inherited, unknowable nucleus – for 'a system of readiness for action' (1983). The archetypes are the typical patterns of human adaptations that have been passed on through phylogenetic history. The actual form in which the

**Archetypes.** The typical patterns of human adaptations, which have been passed on through phylogenetic history. The actual form in which the archetype will be realised or lived is dependent upon the environmental and historical contexts of the individual. Thus, while the archetypes have unlimited universal potentialities, how they come to be lived in an individual's life is always defined by the culture and the particulars of that individual's personal life history.

archetype will be realised or lived is dependent upon the environmental and historical contexts of the individuals. Thus, while the archetypes have unlimited universal potentialities, how they come to be lived in an individual's life is always structured through the culture and the particulars of that individual's personal life history. The complex bridges the universal and the particular. Jung (1990) gives the example of two men he was seeing as patients. One of them, a shy young man, dreamed of jumping over a wide water channel. Other men in his dream fell into the water. The other, a convalescent old man, who was proving to be a very difficult patient, had a very similar dream of jumping over a water channel. Jung observes that the dream of the young man encourages him in the belief that he can do something that he consciously thinks he cannot. The dream of the old man, on the other hand, offers a different wisdom. The dream indicates that what he is doing is foolhardy in relation to his being an old man and that he is not acting in ways that are appropriate. It signifies that being a difficult patient is foolhardy.

A very important distinction that Jung (1983) makes is that there is a sharp distinction between the *archetype* and the *archetypal image*. The archetype, as such, is never knowable. It is part of the collective unconscious and offers only a *tendency* with regard to the organising of experience. The archetypal image, however, is knowable. It is the means whereby the tendency is given expression. This expression is made manifest through such media as ceremonies, behaviours, symbols, etc. An example of such an archetypal image is the family. The formation of the family is an archetypal tendency, seen in all cultures, which serves to protect and unite people for the procreation of the species or the tribe.

## Myth as archetypal tendency

In studying myths and folklore you will see that the same themes occur across all cultures. Myth is thought to capture humanity's attempts to tell the stories of its development. These stories present evolutionary themes about how people have managed to master and engage with their surroundings. In this they convey the archetypal themes that have patterned humanity's development. One such theme is the construction of the various myths about heroes or tricksters. They are usually stories about animals that have heroic characteristics but also tend to be cunning tricksters. Some examples of tricksters include the tale of the Praying Mantis who brought fire to humanity (South West Africa), the tale of Anansi, the spider trickster who, while his behaviour is not always moral, will usually manage to outwit his opponents (Dagomba people from West Africa), the Aboriginal myth of Malu, the red Kangaroo who left caves, rocks, and creeks to mark his journey across Australia, the Chinese Hare who mixes the elixir of life with his mortar and pestle, and the North American tale of Coyote who stole fire from the gods to give it to humans. Shakespeare's plays also contain the trickster in such characters as the clown in *Twelfth night*, Trinculo the jester in *The tempest* and Touchstone the clown in *As you like it*. These characters, while acting as fools or jesters, articulate the wisdom or moral of the play.

# Hierarchy of archetypes

Since archetypes provide the organising tendencies for being human, we can review the archetypal images by examining the developmental hierarchy of archetypal influences. The infant, initially, is absorbed within the total and unconscious *self archetype*. The self is thus the very centre of being. Out of this centre arises the *ego archetype*. The ego slowly develops out of the collective unconscious, that is, from the totality of the self. The ego emerges as fragments from the collective unconscious and gradually coheres with 'good-enough' interpersonal experiences. Such coherence entails the integration of psychic functions, the personalisation of archetypal images and themes, and the development of a personal identity and boundary. The ego comes to contain what is conscious and what is concerned with living with others in a shared world. The ego presides over the process of becoming conscious of thinking, knowing, and being able to live autonomously. The ego allows desire and ambition to be fulfilled and takes us into a world where we share the collective ideals of our culture (Jung 1983; 1986; 1990).

In childhood, archetypal images are related to in **projected form** and in a concrete way. The child is unable to see the mother in her unique personality. To the child, the mother is the archetypal mother; she is the incarnate of all that mothers ought to be. Much of the work in psychotherapy deals with the difference between what were the client's relations to images of the archetypal mother, and what were their actual relations to the real mother. It is sometimes the case that great disappointment in the mother is related to fantasies of the archetypal mother, who is experienced as all good or all bad. Once these archetypal influences have been worked through, the client is able to appreciate that the mother, while fallible, was still a loving mother.

**Projection.** The psychical process whereby qualities of the self are seen as embodied in another.

## Persona

Through development, the child must learn to conform to societal norms. The **persona** archetype is the social mask that develops in order to enable the containment of strong, primitive emotions and impulses. There is a need for the persona archetype, as it allows one to adapt to the demands and cultural needs of one's society and culture. The danger of the persona is that one can become too closely identified with the mask and act as if it were the real self. In such an instance one has become *inflated with the persona* and may lose the capacity to integrate the wholeness of one's self. (*Inflation* will be discussed when we look at pathology.)

**Persona.** This archetype is the social mask that develops to enable the containment of strong, primitive emotions and impulses.

## Shadow

In our attempt to adapt to our cultural norms, we also develop the **shadow** archetype. The shadow contains whatever is unacceptable to our culture and also to our self. These unacceptable aspects often entail moral issues such as greed, envy, prejudice, and racism. The shadow also often contains repressed aspects of instinctual life that are intended for survival, such as sexuality and aggression. These are perhaps aspects about which we are ashamed and which we attempt to hide, both from others and ourselves. As shadow aspects we often *project* them onto

**Shadow.** The archetype that contains whatever is unacceptable to one's culture and also to one's self, such as moral issues like greed, envy, prejudice, and racism. It also contains repressed aspects of instinctual life such as sexuality and aggression.

others, seeing others as the embodiment of those aspects that are too difficult for us to face in our selves. Life is full of examples of people who project their shadow onto others. Prejudice is a process whereby aspects repressed within one's own sense of self are projected onto another race or culture. You can come to know about your own shadow by taking note of any strongly held negative belief about other people. These negative beliefs are the basis of your own shadow, which you have projected onto others. The therapeutic process attempts to move away from judgemental attitudes towards the shadow and to try to integrate these qualities into the self. Integration of one's shadow is an aspect of the individuation process.

## Integration of the shadow

A dreamer dreams that she has been cornered in a cul-de-sac by a group of street children. Her immediate thoughts are that such children are dirty and are thieves. Further exploration reveals that she also sees that they show remarkable resilience in surviving their harsh lives. What finally emerges in her amplifications on the street children is that they have been fatally abandoned by their families and that they must suffer great despair. In relation to her own life, she too had shown remarkable resilience in overcoming severe childhood trauma. She had split off and projected onto the street children her own abandonment and despair. These were shadow emotions, which she had been too afraid to embrace in response to her own situation.

### Animus and anima

During childhood and adolescence, physiological and social pressures influence the development of sex role and gender identities. Jung (1983) postulates that these identities are intimately involved in archetypal male and feminine images. He proposes the concept of the contra-sexual archetypes: the **animus** and **anima** archetypes. Animus is Latin for mind or intellect, while anima is Latin for soul or breath. In Jung's adaptation, they are the masculine aspects in women (animus) and the feminine aspects in men (anima).

Animus/anima. The contra-sexual archetypes. Animus is Latin for mind or intellect, while anima is Latin for soul or breath. In colloquial usage (following Jung) they are the masculine aspect in women (animus) and the feminine aspect in men (anima).

The contra-sexual archetypes are based upon both the collective and the personal unconscious. Thus a man will carry with him images of the feminine arising from the archetypal tendencies of the collective unconscious. These could be typical images such as the 'virgin', the 'whore', the 'Madonna', 'the child girl', etc. He will also have his personal experiences of his mother, sisters, lovers, friends, and societal images of women. The same process holds true for women. It is possible that one's shadow can be projected as the qualities of our contra-sexual archetype. In such a situation you might experience your partner as containing the hated, despised aspects of your own rejected contra-sexual archetype. An example might be a man who fears being dependent and emotional. He projects these aspects onto women and then fears and hates them for what he sees as their emotionality and dependence. A passive woman might fear her dominant husband. She has projected her own assertive, aggressive abilities. Her shadow contains these potentially helpful quali-

PHOTO: CHA JOHNSTON

*The young hero forging his way in the world. The hero breaks ties with the mother archetype and goes out into the world of adventure.*

ties but she has rejected them and projects them onto her husband. Thus, while he may be a dominant man, she inflates his dominance into fearful proportions. What is important is that these projections comprise aspects of one's self. Therefore, while the projections might find likely 'hosts' for themselves (we will always find people who fit the projection in some way), they are not the truth about the other.

Another way in which the contra-sexual archetype tendency might be realised is through *identification* with the archetypal image. Identifying with archetypal images of the masculine and the feminine might result in stereotypical portrayals. An example might be an animus-possessed woman. She has become identified with the masculine and is 'more man than a man'. An anima-possessed man might be a 'screaming queen' in gay circles.

The contra-sexual archetypes themselves often appear in *projections* onto real men and women, thus potentially facilitating empathy and

## The variety of archetypes

Jung identified only a small number of archetypes. Post-Jungian writers have identified many more, such as the divine child, the eternal youth, the Oedipal child, the earth mother, the hero, death, birth and rebirth, the wise old man or woman, and the wounded healer. These archetypes are universal potentialities but their realisation occurs within a cultural context and is further differentiated by the particulars of family life and experience. These images are often the subject of stories, myths, and art. Read the myths of a number of cultures and you will find that they contain stories that have the same themes, such as creation, keepers of light and darkness, fertility stories, elements of nature, heroes and tricksters, death and rebirth. These myths chronicle humankind's continual quest to understand the organising principles that govern the condition of being human, or the *meanings* of life.

**Self.** The archetype of all archetypes, the self for Jung is the centre and the totality, the source and the goal of human life. Jung also saw the self as the prime agent in the production of deep, spiritual numinous symbols.

**Symbols.** The purposive, healing inventions of the self archetype.

**Teleological.** Purposive, indicating that something has a final cause.

**Opposites.** Archetypal themes occur as pairs of opposites such as outside-inside, self-other, male-female. Resolution of opposites brings about individuation. An example of such resolution would be the integration of the shadow and the persona, or of the animus and the anima.

understanding of the opposite sex. Integration of the animus in women allows a capacity for logical intellectual thought and assertion balanced with the feminine. Integration of the anima in men allows for the capacity for feelings and emotions balanced with the masculine. Some cultural norms make integration difficult. Some cultures or societies do not support the emancipation of women; neither do they support the notion of men being informed by their emotional side. The 'new age man' does not do well in a beer-drinking, rugby-oriented society, nor in an aggressive male dominated culture. In a similar way, an assertive, ambitious, logical woman does not do well in a culture that requires her to be submissive and subservient, where her place is 'children, kitchen, and church'. For growth to occur, the contra-sexual archetypes need to be balanced and integrated. Where this is missing, there is neglect of the whole self.

## Self

Jung (1990) saw the **self** as the archetype of all archetypes. By this he means that the self is the centre and the totality, the source and the goal, of human life. Remember that he sees the self as the initial unconscious state of the infant. Consciousness emerges out of this matrix of the unconscious by means of **symbols**, which for Jung are the purposive, healing inventions of the self archetype. The self has a **teleological** (purposive) healing function. Throughout life, the self is the overarching ordering tendency for all other archetypal experiences. The widening and deepening of consciousness, through progressive integration of archetypal energies, is the goal of the self. This integration is ultimately the progressive integration of the self. Thus the self is understood to be both the source and the goal of human life. In Jung's terms, the self is mysterious and divine. How else are we to understand this uniquely human capacity for self-realisation and movement towards a spiritual realm? Jung (1990) sometimes sees the self as the archetype whose special function is to balance and pattern, not only other archetypes, but all of a person's life in terms of purposes not yet considered nor lived. What raises the self above the patterning of other archetypes is its function as synthesiser and mediator of the **opposites** within the psyche.

PHOTO: CHA JOHNSTON

*The desire for spiritual wholeness is a universal phenomenon.*

**Numinous symbols.** Symbols of a self-regulatory and healing nature. A numinous experience verges on the sense of the inspirational or divine.

Jung (1990) also sees the self as the prime agent in the production of deep, awesome, **numinous symbols**. These symbols are of a self-regulatory and healing nature. A numinous experience verges on a sense of the inspirational or the divine. Such an experience is one that is powerful, awesome, mysterious, and not able to be described exactly. Such an experience could be the inspirational feeling some people have when standing on top of a mountain, or seeing a beautiful sunset, and moments that capture a sense of completeness and unity with the universe. Jung held a positive view of the potential of the self as an innate potential for growth and individuation as an integrated person. Thus Jung saw individuation as an instinct that will occur with or without the person's assistance. According to Jung, maturity is host to the many faces of the self which occur to consciousness.

# Dynamics of personality

## The role of opposites

Freud had postulated psychic motivation as dependent upon the conflicts inherent within the drives. Kleinian and later Object Relations theorists moved the conceptualisation of psychic motivation into a relational realm. At the time that Klein (and Fairbairn) was working out her theory, Jung was also postulating that the motivation for psychic activity was primarily relational (Jung 1986). The focus on relational motivations was one of the principal developments in post-Freudian thinking. This focus moved psychic motivation from a drive conflict model to an emphasis on relational dynamics. Jung postulated that relational needs express themselves through conflict and resolution of opposite archetypal tendencies.

## Psychic activity

Archetypes express built-in polarities between positive and negative aspects of experience and emotion. Consider for example the persona and the shadow, the animus and the anima. The impact of the archetypal image depends to a great extent on the way in which environmental experience blends with or mediates the archetypal imagery. In ordinary development, such mediation will prevent too extreme a concentration at one or other end of the polar continuum – either **inflation** or **alienation**. (We shall examine these conditions presently.) If real experience reinforces either extreme, the individual is hooked onto only one end of the range of archetypal possibilities. An example of this might be the belief that the persona is the real self. By contrast, the resolution of opposites brings about individuation. An example of such resolution would be the integration of the shadow and persona, or of the animus and anima. Jung (1986) maintains that difficult times in one's life are often turning points when one is working out archetypal activity towards a resolution.

**Inflated/inflation.**
Inflation develops when the environment has reinforced one extreme of the archetype. This is the situation in which the ego has become too identified with the archetypal energy; the identification is of such an extent that the ego is engulfed by the archetype.

**Alienation.** The situation in which the ego becomes detached from the life-giving archetypal energies and life loses its meaning.

# Individuation and the self

*Individuation* is the process of becoming an individual, the move towards wholeness through the integration of conscious and unconscious aspects of the personality. Conflict is an inevitable condition of the polarities of life. Individuation occurs through acceptance and integration of these polarities, such as the shadow and the persona, and the two contra-sexual aspects. Individuation for Jung was not an elimination of conflict, but rather an increased consciousness of conflict and its potential. The self becomes an image of a more complete person, as well as being the goal of life. This is the attaining or realising of one's self (Jung 1983; 1986; 1990).

In the process of individuation, the ego ideal is given up in favour of self-acceptance. Remember that the ego is the centre of consciousness. Thus the ego ideal is taken up with the ego archetype. It is concerned with the outer aspirations of the ego, with collective aspirations. These could be aspects such as ambition, achievement, family, and friends. With individuation, there is withdrawal from these collective foci of the ego. The collective ego norms are replaced with the self as an inner guide.

There are basically two stages of adult development – the *morning* and *afternoon* of life. The transition from one to the other is often, but not always, heralded by a *mid-life crisis*. In the morning of one's life the focus is on the development of the ego. The ego, the 'I', will establish a social identity (persona) and forge a place in the world, independent of parents. The ego has primacy and functions with a consciousness immersed in the collective consciousness of social conformity. The ego is thus taken up with collective norms. The morning of one's life lasts until about the mid-fifties or fifties (Jung 1983).

In the afternoon of life there is a move towards the realisation of the self, and the self becomes the new centre of psychological life. Individuation is often associated with this latter stage of life, for realisation of the self is its goal. As the depth of the collective unconscious is unfathomable and limitless, self-realisation is never complete and thus individuation, as a fixed or attainable state, cannot be achieved. One is always on the way towards individuation (Jung 1983).

The journey to the self – or individuation – will occur even if one is not consciously concerned with fostering one's own development. Clearly, however, there are great advantages in being consciously and actively aware of this striving towards growth and individuation. The process occurs through the workings of dreams and the integration of the archetypes.

There have been a number of people in our history whom we might consider to demonstrate having attained a high level of individuation. Gandhi and Mandela probably exemplify such people. They are people who have been able to hold true to their self in the face of enormous pressure from the outer world to conform to ego norms and aspirations.

## Stages in the individuation process

Nearly all Jung's work after 1916, when he first used the term *individuation*, was concerned with amplifications on this central theme (1983). The process of individuation can be represented along a chronological spectrum as follows. First there is birth and early childhood. Initially, archetypal themes are largely undifferentiated as pairs of opposites such as outside-inside, self-other, male-female. The self is largely experienced in relation to the *Great Mother archetype* that is projected upon the actual mother or the primary caregiver.

The role of the ego is dominant in early development and young adulthood. This is the time, as we have seen, when the individual is concerned with the establishment of identity and fitting in with societal

*We commemorate the dead through belief in a spiritual afterlife. Jung postulated that the quest for spirituality was the quest of the self archetype.*

norms and ambitions. The ego is thus concerned with what is conscious and collective in society. Throughout childhood, adolescence, and young adulthood, the ego develops, giving a sense of identity and growing autonomy to the individual. In order to achieve this autonomy, the Great Mother archetype must be overcome. The individual must break the tie to an archetypal mother. Thus the *hero archetype* must slay the dragon that keeps the hero young and afraid, and embark upon a journey of self-discovery.

The *father archetype*, as the *spiritual principle*, counteracts the regressive longings for the Great Mother and unconsciousness. The father opens up a world beyond the mother. Here Jung sees the significance of the Oedipus complex. Where a child is unfortunate enough to have an Oedipal victory, it is locked into pre-Oedipal primitiveness. The child then cannot afford to slay the dragon and move into the world, for there is no world beyond the mother. Negotiation of the Oedipus complex opens up the triumph of rationality over instinct and the child's appropriation of the human cultural order.

The development of the persona is the compromise that links identity with the needs of society. Where there is too close an identification, there is an immersion in the anonymity of collective life. True individuality and consciousness is founded upon dialogue with the self. Severe and persistent identification with the persona leads to crisis. Jung postulates that this crisis will tend to happen in mid-life when the individual realises that who they are in a world of collective consciousness is no longer fulfilling. Many individuals attempt to solve the crisis by changing their circumstances. This, however, does not solve the problem. It is just more of the same. Jung suggests that the crisis is actually the call to give up this immersion in a life of social consciousness – that is, the collective norms of the ego – and embark upon a journey of self-discovery. This is essentially a journey of aloneness, where one finds values and meanings that are personal and individual. The essence of these values and meanings, Jung postulates, will be spiritual in nature. This is based upon the notion that the self is indistinguishable from the God-image and the goal of individuation is spiritual wholeness.

# Theory of symbols

Jung (1990) viewed symbol creation as central to the understanding of human nature. He explored the correspondences between symbols arising from the life struggles of individuals and the symbolic images underlying religious, mythological, and magical systems of many cultures and eras.

Jung hypothesises that psychological functioning is largely the work of symbolic activity. Symbols of totality are symbols of the self. Characteristically, he postulates that the symbol expresses a conflict in a manner that also helps to resolve it. Some symbols operate consciously, but others require a symbolic attitude before they are perceived and experienced as symbols. Whether it is conscious or unconscious, Jung conceives symbolic activity as the content of psychological functioning. The symbolic nature of dreams thus gives us direct access to the content of psychological functioning. The symbol, according to Jung, is the best possible formulation of relatively unknown psychic contents which cannot be, or are not, known to consciousness. He describes symbolic experiences as *numinous*, which means that they are powerful, awesome, mysterious, and not able to be described exactly. Humanist psychologists would call these 'peak experiences'.

## Symbols of the self

As the self symbolises the infinitude of the archetypes, anything postulated to be greater than oneself can become a symbol of the self – for example Christ, or Buddha. Symbols of the self are often exemplified by the mandala, the 'magical circle'. The appearance of a mandala symbol in dreams is seen to express not only potential integration but also to contribute to the self-healing capacities of the psyche. This is an important concept. Jung postulates that healing and individuation occur through the workings of symbolic activity in our dreams, creativity, and daily life.

# Pathology

There are several possibilities for pathology, each of which reflects imbalance or lack of integration in the relationship to archetypal energy (Jung 1983).

## Inflation

Where the environment has reinforced one extreme of the archetype, *inflation* develops. This means that the ego has become too identified with the archetypal energy. The identification can be so complete that the ego is engulfed by the archetype. Psychosis would reflect this state, in which the ego is engulfed and fragmented, and at the mercy of archetypal powers. In psychosis the individual is so inflated with the archetype that contact with reality is lost. This is the condition seen in schizophrenia.

In less extreme forms of inflation, the person acts out the archetypal energies. These energies define the person and preclude the possibility of integrating the total person. An example that we may find in everyday life is the woman who has no life other than in her children. She is *inflated with the mother archetype* and is not connected to her larger personality or self. Another common example is the man who is a philanderer; he is unable to make commitments and may be *inflated with the peura eterna archetype* – the youth who never grows up. *Inflation with the persona* would indicate that one has become identified with the persona as the whole of the personality.

## Participation mystique

Jung's ideas offer a helpful approach to certain pathological phenomena such as cult involvement and cult leaders. He terms this pathology **participation mystique**. Participation mystique reflects a situation where the ego becomes fused with archetypal reality. Unlike inflation, where the ego is potentially *engulfed and disintegrated by* the archetype, in participation mystique the ego struggles to find an adequate differentiation between inner and outer reality. The ego becomes *fused with* the archetype. Thus the conscious capacities of the ego remain, but they are fused with the unconscious realities of the archetype. An example of participation mystique is a cult leader who becomes fused with (or *participates in*) a myth. The theme of the myth is usually about a saviour or a great leader. The cult leader becomes fused with this myth and lives as if he or she were this mythical leader.

**Participation mystique.** The situation in which the ego becomes fused with archetypal reality. The ego struggles to find an adequate differentiation between inner and outer reality. The conscious capacities of the ego remain but they are fused with the unconscious realities of the archetype.

## Neurosis

Freud sees **neurosis** as the ego's compromise between the strivings of the id and the censorship of the superego. As the id presses for discharge, anxiety signals the ego into action. When such action does not resolve the problem, the symptom then becomes the disguised means whereby the ego can satisfy both the id and the superego. The symptom thus holds the meaning of the conflict.

Jung's (1986) formulation is similar to Freud's. Jung also saw the symptom as holding the secret of cure in its meaning. However, Jung's formulation differs fundamentally over the nature of the psychic energy pressing for expression. Whereas Freud has the dangerous id pressing for discharge, Jung postulates archetypal energy pressing for expression. In the Jungian sense, archetypal energy is not of itself dangerous. It is in fact the seat of wisdom. *It is our relation to this archetypal energy that is the potential problem.*

For Jung, in neurosis, the ego misguidedly but heroically fights the changes that the archetypes are trying to bring about within the total per-

**Neurosis.** The concept of neurosis, for Jung, refers to the situation in which the ego misguidedly but heroically fights the changes that the archetypes are trying to bring about within the total personality structure. Through the ego's resistance of the changes that are indicated, the potentialities of the archetypal core are prevented from being realised.

sonality structure. Through the ego's resistance of the changes that are indicated, the potentialities of the archetypal core are prevented from being realised. In Jung's view of the innate strivings towards individuation, the changes that the archetype indicates and strives to bring about are steeped in wisdom, yet the ego is afraid of the power of the self and the archetype and resists these changes.

An example of such neurosis may be obsessive behaviour that indicates the struggle of the ego to keep chaos at bay. The ego cannot allow the experience of chaos to impart its wisdom and be integrated into the total personality. It may be that the individual's life had contained too much chaos either in the external or internal world. Now there is a desperate fight against allowing the chaos its expression. Thus, instead of integrating the potential wisdom of chaos, the individual must defend against it by obsessively tidying and ordering life's experiences.

## Alienation

In *alienation* the ego becomes detached from the life-giving archetypal energies and life loses its meaning. Jung believed that the plight of modern society is that we have become alienated from our collective unconscious and our spiritual domain. Suicidal people have become alienated from archetypal energies. They no longer feel that the patterns and organising symbols of life have any meaning. Adolescence is a time of potential alienation where adolescents question the received wisdom of the culture and society. Adolescence is the period of life when most suicides occur. The integrating of despair and alienation offers a renewed vigour and optimism about life as a young adult.

# Psychological types

Jung (1983) postulates that each individual can be characterised as either primarily outwardly or inwardly oriented. *Extroversion* and *introversion*, respectively, are his terms for these attitudes towards stimulation (or the world). Clearly it is rare for an individual to be only extroverted or only introverted. However, individuals may tend towards one or other habitual attitude.

## The extroverted type

The extroverted attitude is characterised in a person by an outward flow of libido, an interest in events, people, and things. The individual has a relationship with, and a dependence upon, these stimuli. When the attitude is habitual, this is the extroverted type – an individual who is motivated by outside factors and greatly influenced by the environment. Extroverted types may then be characterised by:

◆ qualities of sociability and confidence,
◆ a tendency to be active in trying to shape the world according to their patterns,

◆ superficiality,
◆ an inability or dislike for being alone,
◆ a tendency to find self-reflection morbid, hence possible lack of self-criticism or insight,
◆ typically being more popular with the world than with their own family, and
◆ a tendency to be conventional.

## The introverted type

This attitude is characterised by libido flowing inwards to subjective factors. The major motivation is *inner necessity*. When the attitude is habitual, this is the introverted type, which is characterised by:

◆ independent judgement and values,
◆ a tendency to be at their best when alone or in small groups,
◆ a preference for reflection rather than activity,
◆ a lack of confidence in relation to others,
◆ sensitivity to criticism, and
◆ a tendency to be overconscientious, pessimistic, and critical.

Each type undervalues the other, seeing mainly weakness. The extrovert sees the introvert as egotistical and dull. The introvert sees the extrovert as superficial and insincere. These attitudes clearly reflect the *shadow* aspects of each type. These differences may cause difficulties in relationships and marriages, especially as there seems to be a tendency to be attuned to the opposite type. If the relationship is to move beyond the 'being in love' phase, there will be inevitable difficulties. Merely being tolerant of one another is not the answer according to Jung. This will only lead to deadness and perhaps violent warfare between the couple. Jung proposes that what is needed is far reaching development of each personality. This would mean the integration of the split off and projected parts 'held' by the partner.

## Functions of psychological types

Each psychological type uses what Jung terms the *most developed function*. Jung postulates four functions that we use to orientate ourselves towards the world and also towards our own inner reality:

◆ *thinking:* organising meaning and understanding through thought,
◆ *feeling:* understanding through assessing and judging values,
◆ *intuition:* sensing future or past possibilities and organising information about the atmosphere that surrounds all experience, and
◆ *sensation:* perception through the senses.

Each function can be experienced in either an extroverted or an introverted way. Most people use one function, while more complex individuals use two. People who are highly individuated may use three while the use of all four functions lies in the domain of highly individuated people. These individuals have reconciled their opposing trends.

### Rational functions

The functions of thinking and feeling are rational functions that arise from the level of consciousness.

### Thinking

Where thinking is the dominant function, we may see the extroverted thinker as characterised by:

◆ the drawing of conclusions based upon facts,
◆ the use of formulae to express views,
◆ a life strategy based upon principles,
◆ a view of the self as rational, logical, and correct,
◆ a tendency to ignore things that do not fit,
◆ a fear of the irrational,
◆ the repression of emotions and feelings, and
◆ the tendency to neglect friendships, to be 'in and out' of relationships.

The unconscious takes revenge through a number of ways. The re-pressed feelings burst through in unfortunate love affairs with unsuitable partners. There may be moods that are denied; there may also be some-thing noble about the individual, but they lack warmth and tolerance.

By contrast we may see the introverted thinker as characterised by:

◆ a tendency to value ideas over facts, the inner over the outer, and
◆ a quality of being at odds with the world, especially since they often pay little attention to nurturing their general relationship to the out-side world.

The *inferior function* for the thinking type is feeling.

### Feeling

Jung has an interesting understanding of this: *feeling* is not emotion; rather it is a function by which values are weighed, accepted, or refused. (Any function can lead over to emotion, which is then a consequence, but not the function.) Thus to say, 'It feels right' is to be using the feeling function. Where feeling is the dominant function, we may see that the extroverted type is characterised by:

◆ a tendency to be well adjusted to the environment,
◆ a strong feminine principle,
◆ good personal relationships,
◆ charming, soothing qualities, a desire to help,
◆ (at best) being sympathetic, helpful, and charming, and
◆ (at worst) being superficial and insincere.

By contrast, the introverted type, where feeling is the dominant func-tion, is characterised by:

◆ a tendency to appear cold and reserved,
◆ being constant and reliable both in relationships and in work, and
◆ the capacity for deep love.

The *inferior function* for the feeling type is thinking.

## Irrational functions

The functions of sensation and intuition are the irrational functions as they arise from the level of the unconscious.

## Sensation

Where sensation is the dominant function, we may see the sensation type. These are those individuals who experience things as they are, without imaginative trimmings. What counts for the sensation type is the strength and pleasure of the sensation. They can be mistaken for rational because of their calm, even phlegmatic, natures. They are frequently easy and jolly with a great capacity for enjoyment. The danger lies in overvaluation of the senses. There is the danger of degenerating into unscrupulous and hedonistic pleasure seekers. For extroverted sensation types, the *object* is important. For introverted sensation types, the *experience* is important.

## Intuition

Intuition is a perception of reality that arises from the unconscious. Extroverted intuition types are characterised by the attitude that all things are possible, and by an intense dislike for what is known, familiar, safe, and well established. Extroverted intuitive types exhibit little respect for customs and typically show ruthlessness towards the feelings of others when they feel as if they themselves are 'onto something'. They are the classic 'sowers of seeds' but not the reapers; it is others who benefit from their energy and enterprise.

Introverted intuition types are characterised by a concern with the collective unconscious. They see visions, and often have prophetic dreams. They are often at risk of madness unless a way is found to relate experience to life. Such individuals are usually quiet about their experiences. They come across as odd but harmless, but may also be gripped by an inner vision that is powerful for good or evil. The experience of this type is highly contagious and may result in religious conversions, or mob violence, or cult or sect involvement.

## Jungian analytic therapy

In Jungian therapy, which deals extensively with dreams and fantasies, a dialogue is set up between the conscious mind and the contents of the unconscious. Patients are made aware of both the personal and collective (archetypal) meanings inherent in their symptoms and difficulties. Under favourable conditions they may enter into the individuation process: a lengthy series of psychological transformations culminating in the integration of opposite tendencies and functions and the achievement of personal wholeness.

# Dreams from a Jungian analytic perspective

For Jung (1986; 1990) the dream is the principal therapeutic method. It is the psychic phenomenon that affords the easiest access to the contents of the unconscious. Dreams are the language of the unconscious. Their images express the archaic potentialities in the collective unconscious. The self is seen as the source of dream images; it is the organising centre and has a regulating effect on the development of the psyche. One could say that one does not dream, but *is dreamed*.

The dream structure not only reveals the core of the neurosis or conflict, but it also has a purposeful structure, indicating an underlying intent or idea. The dream is seen as a natural psychic phenomenon, which is autonomous and purposive. The purpose may be unknown to consciousness, but is accessible to anyone who cares to engage with the dream. Freud maintained that the dream was a disguised wish fulfilment of instinctual desires. For Jung, the dream content *articulates exactly what the unconscious means* about a situation. The dream and its images are not seen as distortions of hidden content, as in Freud's approach.

## The functions of dreams

Jung (1986) postulated that we could think of dreams as having a number of purposes.

◆ The dream may convey a specific diagnostic message about the dreamer; it tells something about the dreamer's psychic state. The diagnosis may concern childhood issues, as well as a present-day assessment of psychic function.

◆ The dream may also be prognostic, that is, it tells you something about possible future outcomes.

◆ The dream can be considered as having a compensatory function. This means that the material of the dream (wisdom from the unconscious) is the opposite of the conscious attitude. Emotions or attitudes that are repressed by the rational consciousness demand expression through the dream formation. The dream then reflects the need for expression of the potentialities of the personality. (For example, a passive woman dreams of being full of rage and murderous intent. The dream suggests that she is one-sided and needs to integrate a more dominant assertive side.)

◆ Dreams also could have a purposive (or teleological) function. This derives from the compensatory function. It indicates the area in which the individual has repressed potential. The dream image is the unconscious showing us where the conscious attitude needs to be redressed. Here we must ask for what attitude the dream is compensating. (For example, a man dreams of having no hands. The dream suggests that he has lost the ability to take, give, or do. He must 'grow hands'.) This function is concerned with prospective possibilities that are indicated to assist in the integration of opposites.

◆ Dreams can also have a reductive function. In such instances the dream 'brings the dreamer down', as it were, to his mortal insignificance. An inflated individual may dream of being poor and insignificant.

◆ There are anticipating dreams. These are especially significant when embarking upon new ventures. The initial dreams in psychotherapy give valuable information about the therapeutic attitude and possible prognosis (outcome) of the therapy.

## Dream-work, or amplification

Jung conceptualises dreams as the psychic seat of wisdom. The dream is as much concerned with the direction in which we are going, as with the experiences from which we have come. The implication is that the unconscious is creative and that it contains a moral component. Dream symbols may have rich symbolic significance but this significance, Jung cautions, is personal. Dream-work, or **amplification**, is required to access the personal significance of a dream symbol. Amplification is a process of associations that are made to each of the dream images themselves. This process establishes, with great care, the context of the dream images. Amplification broadens and enriches the dream content with analogous images and personal associations of the dreamer and the therapist. Together they move towards establishing a correct interpretation which the dreamer finds convincing. Amplification is conducted first on the personal level. Only when the personal concerns and conflicts have been redressed, does it move to an archetypal focus. A knowledge of myths and symbolism is necessary for the therapist when working at this level of understanding.

> **Amplification.** The process whereby associations are made to each of the dream images so as to establish the context of the dream images. Amplification broadens and enriches the dream content with analogous images and personal associations of the dreamer and the therapist.

Jung maintains that *free association*, as used by Freud, will always reveal the complexes. However, it will not necessarily reveal those connected to the dream image. Therefore it is necessary to stay close to the dream images themselves.

Another source of amplification is a *series of dreams*. Over a series we are able to recognise important contents and themes. Every interpretation is only an hypothesis, but a degree of relative certainty can be achieved when working with a series of dreams where the dream continues like a monologue. The series can be conceptualised around the theme as a central point.

When the central point is revealed to consciousness, a new point arises. It is therefore important to keep dream books for recording dream-work, or amplification. In this way the continuity and meaning of dream processes are brought to consciousness. Jung observes that conclusions can seldom be drawn from a single dream. It is the series that reveals the context and meaning of the dream's guiding message.

**Figure 8.2** Conceptualising a series of dreams around a central point.

*Big dreams* have a special vividness and often occur in colour. They often have little relevance to events from conscious life and may reflect ancient or bizarre images or symbols. Such a dream arises from the collective unconscious and there is little close relation to the conscious concerns of the individual. Amplification is of little use here; it is knowledge of mythology and universal symbols and analogies that will assist in understanding the dream.

### Analysing dreams as drama

An interesting way of conceptualising and analysing dreams is to see them as classic dramas and to understand them from the perspectives of a drama:

1) What is the time and place of the setting? What thoughts might one have about why the dream needed to be placed in this setting? What wisdom is there in this setting? Are things still fantastical or are they more reality-based?

2) Who are the dramatis personae? What archetypal figures occupy the dream? What does this tell you about the psychic tensions and conflicts of the dreamer?

3) What are the characteristics of the archetypal figures? These are the amplifications of the archetypes. Are they inflated, alienated, etc?

4) What is the 'plot' or the 'problem' of the dream? Here the unconscious gives the archetype or complex a visible form that can be worked upon by the dramatis personae. How does this problem relate to the conscious problems of the dreamer? Why has the dream offered this 'problem'?

5) What is the quality of the 'play', the emotional tones, the weaving of the plot, the intensification of the events? Is the dream filled with affect (emotional appeal) or is it flat? Why does the 'problem' need to be approached in emotional ways?

6) Is there a development of a crisis, or a transformation, or a catastrophe? In offering a 'solution' to the 'problem', the dream provides some insight into one or more of its compensatory, purposive, reductive, or anticipatory functions.

7) What is the solution or resolution? The conclusion points to the needful transformation within the dreamer in terms of any of the compensatory, purposive, reductive, or anticipatory functions. When

> *'All human beings are also dream beings. Dreaming ties all mankind together.'*
>
> Jack Kerouac

PHOTO: CHA JOHNSTON

*By middle age to old age, collective ego ideals have given way to a more self-reliant sense of self. It is the time of the wise old man and woman.*

there is no conclusion, or it is unrealistic, the indications are that the ego is still in control and fearful. The ego blocks the wisdom of the self, which is the offering of the dream wisdom.

## A dream analysis

*'I am walking through a magical land. Every one is smiling and happy and there are many children running about. I feel as if they are all my children and that I am the perfect mother. Everything is beautiful. Suddenly I see a huge lion, it is a male lion and it wants to eat me. I run away, but it chases me. I realise that I have nowhere to run and that it will catch me. I stop and turn. I feel terrified but look at the lion. Suddenly the lion turns into a horse, a beautiful white horse. I get on the horse and we gallop over the land. I find myself at the office having a meeting with A, a work colleague. He usually frightens me but we are discussing things and I am very strong.'*

### Overarching understanding

This is a compensatory and purposive dream. It gives the woman insight into her unbalanced identification with the feminine (purposive aspect) and shows her what might be possible were she to integrate the masculine (compensatory aspect).

*'I am walking through a magical land.'* This is not based in the real world; it is a fantasy component. *'Everyone is smiling and happy and there are many children running about.'* This evokes a scene of motherhood and child bearing. It suggests a great mother archetype and identification with the feminine (anima).

*'I feel as if they are all my children and that I am the perfect mother. Everything is beautiful.'* Here is confirmation of the archetypal identification with the great mother and the anima. *'Suddenly I see a huge lion, it is a male lion and it wants to eat me.'* Masculine power and aggression are symbolised by the male lion. Instinctual

and shadow aspects here are primitive since the symbol is an animal. This indicates the lack of current integration of the animus, i.e. the animus is still at the instinctual level. Lack of integration is indicated in the desire to flee and in the fear of the lion, the shadow aspect.

*'I run away, but it chases me.'* This illustrates the dream's purposive function – if integration is run away from, it will follow and be destructive. *'I realise that I have nowhere to run and that it will catch me.'* Here is realisation and acceptance of the need for integration.

*'I stop and turn. I feel terrified but look at the lion.'* A moment of possible integration is attempted, even in fear. The dream's purposive function is showing what might be possible. *'Suddenly the lion turns into a horse, a beautiful white horse.'* A transformation occurs with the facing of the animus. The primitive and fearsome lion transforms into a horse, which is symbolic in evolutionary terms – it has assisted humankind to evolve and develop in ways not possible before its arrival. White indicates purity and the possibility of a transformation. White is symbolic of new beginnings.

*'I get on the horse and we gallop over the land'.* Here are newfound possibilities for covering new terrain and psychic ground. *'I find myself at the office having a meeting with A, a work colleague. He usually frightens me but we are discussing things and I am very strong.'* This is the compensatory function of the dream showing how, when integration of the animus occurs, there is the possibility of being strong and equal in relation to masculine energies, which are now no longer experienced as frightening.

## An example of thinking around a dream

A man's dream: *'I was going down into a cave or something like a dungeon. It was very dark and cold, with a strange smell. I didn't seem to feel scared or anything. In the corner I saw a woman. She was crouched down and looked very sick or was dying. I was repulsed by her and couldn't stay there. I ran out of the cave.'*

This dream appears to indicate a descent into some place that is unfamiliar and uninhabited. This might indicate a psychic place that is not inhabited and is neglected, has been neglected for a long time. Going down might indicate a descent into the unconscious. Certainly the space is small and lacks aliveness and light.

There are only two people in the dream, the dreamer and a woman. The man, being the dreamer, is probably the persona while the woman could be both the shadow and the animus.

The persona is initially unafraid but is then repulsed by the woman. The shadow/animus energies are sick or dying, indicating the degree to which the man has become alienated from these archetypes. He appears to be inflated with the persona. He is unafraid and uncaring for the plight of the woman. Significantly the man is not scared in a context that calls for some degree of fear or wariness.

He thus appears to be out of touch with the potentials of this place.

The plot is about finding a sick woman who needs care and rescuing. The sick or dying woman appears to represent a sick or dying aspect of his psyche, his animus. The dream indicates that the animus needs rescuing and that to neglect this task will result in serious repercussions for the psyche. His initial lack of response and his subsequent fleeing indicate that the ego is afraid to engage with the wisdom of the shadow and animus archetypes. The dream indicates the degree to which he has split off and neglected the animus qualities in his conscious life. His repulsion at the sight of the woman indicates the degree to which he is out of touch with qualities of the animus, perhaps empathy, concern, vulnerability, and death.

The dream seems to be a purposive dream offering the man insight into what he has to redress and what he is actually doing with his shadow and animus.

It would seem that the woman represents the abandoned animus that he has shut away in the cave. The invitation to rescue her is rejected and he flees, leaving her behind. The dream seems to indicate that he has projected the animus qualities onto the shadow archetype and that he needs to care for the animus and integrate this neglected aspect into his personality.

## Critiques of Jung

Clearly the same kinds of critiques that have been applied to Freud have been levelled at Jung's theories, though his have perhaps drawn more criticism because of their esoteric or spiritual postulations. The arguments that have been raised against Freudian conceptualisation could be applied to Jung. Look at the critiques of Freud (Chapter 5) and apply them to thinking about Jung's theories.

A number of post-Jungian theorists themselves argue that Jung's emphasis on the role of the self is an overemphasis (Samuels 1985). They claim that Jung's postulation of an innate growth-seeking potential does not provide a sufficiently complex understanding of psychopathology.

Further, the notion of integration of archetypal energies as a product of psychic wholeness has been rejected by some. This has resulted in the development of the Archetypal School of Analytic Psychology. Hillman is a major theorist within this tradition. As its name suggests, the focus is on the archetypes. This tradition rejects the notion of integration of the archetypes as symptomatic of a healthy psyche. Rather, they claim that we are most psychologically healthy when we are able to embrace our multiplicities of being.

The Developmental School has evolved to address Jung's lack of focus on a developmental psychology. Their allegiance is with the Object Relations tradition, since the idea of archetypes ties in well with Klein's postulation of innate knowledge of certain primitive images. Object relations theory has come to be the informing developmental theory of this school of thought.

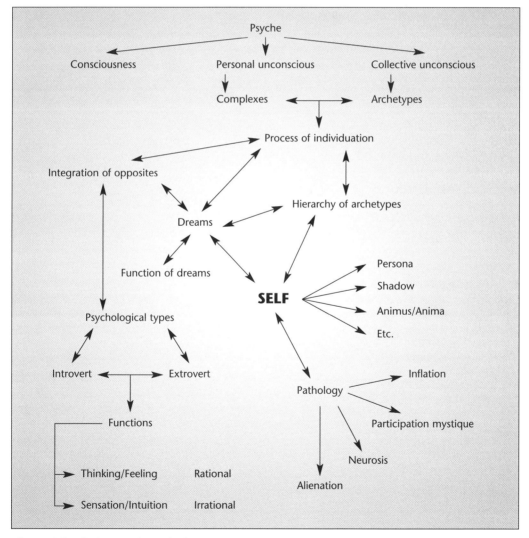

**Figure 8.3** Mind map of Jung's theory.

# Recommended readings

*(Brooke, Samuels, and Jung's collected works are probably for the more serious scholar of Jung, but they are worth a try. The other books make quite accessible reading.)*

Adler, G. (1967). 'Methods of treatment in analytic psychology'. In B. Wolman (ed.), *Psychoanalytic technique*. New York: Basic Books.
*(An overview of the methods and assumptions that underlie Jungian interventions. Interesting for those who are interested in entering a Jungian psychotherapy or in how psychotherapy works.)*

Brooke, R. (1990). *Jung and phenomenology*. London: Routledge.
*(This is a scholarly read. Brooke, in elucidating the assumptions of phenomenology, argues that Jung, far from being within a psychoanalytic paradigm, was a phenomenologist at heart. The book offers an in-depth and extensive coverage of Jungian concepts.)*

Jung, C. G. (1963). *Memories, dreams, reflections*. London: Routledge & Kegan Paul.
*(This is Jung's autobiography. It gives an insight into Jung's life and the particularities of his personality. There is a fascinating introduction by Donald Winnicott, which is a gem on its own.)*

Jung, C. G. (1972). *The Collected Works of Carl G. Jung*. 20 vols. (1953–75). London: Routledge.
*(Routledge published the first complete English edition of Jung's work. It is worthwhile going to the original works to follow Jung's own elucidation of his theory.)*

Jung, C.G. (1983). *Jung, selected writings*. Introduced by Anthony Storr. London: Fontana.
*(A wonderful selection of Jungian concepts that Storr brings together to elucidate the development of Jung's thought.)*

Jung, C. G. (1986). *Analytic psychology: Its theory and practice*. London: Ark Paperbacks.
*(This slim volume covers Jung's 1935 lectures to the Tavistock. They are published in their lecture format and give a wonderful sense of how Jung thought and spoke about his concepts.)*

Jung, C. G. (ed.) (1990). *Man and his symbols*. New York: Aldus Books.
*(A beautifully illustrated book with essays by Jung and others on various aspects of mythology and symbolism.)*

McGuire, W. and Hull, R. C. G. (eds) (1980). *Jung speaking: Interviews and encounters*. London: Picador.
*(The book presents interviews with a vast number of people who knew or met Jung, covering his whole life. A fascinating portrait of the man develops through the eyes of those who knew him.)*

Samuels, A. (1985). *Jung and the post-Jungians*. London: Routledge.
*(This book is a scholarly read but well worth the effort. Samuels takes us through the essentials of Jung's thought and then shows the progressive development of three post-Jungian schools of thought. These are the Classical Jungian School, building upon Jung's theory, the Developmental School, which has close ties with object relations theory, and the Archetypal School, which has developed Jung's thinking around the functions of the archetypes.)*

# Critical thinking tasks

## Specific tasks

1) Considering that Jung's theory is principally about adult development, how does it provide an understanding of the behaviours and motivations of Geldenhuys as presented in the case study? Think about the archetypal energies that might be involved and how, or if, these energies constitute a pathology in the case of Geldenhuys. You would need to consider the role of the complexes in trying to locate the workings of the archetypal energies in his personal life.

2) Consider what particular psychological function is dominant in Geldenhuys. Think about how the dominant function would interact with his inferior function to account perhaps for his behaviour.

3) Jung suggests that archaic man did not reflect upon his symbols, but rather lived them, and was unconsciously animated by their meaning. Investigate the origins of a symbol or symbolic behaviour within your culture. The symbol you choose, whether it is marriage, the Star of David, or initiation rites, is the link to archetypal organising energies. Consider how it was originally lived and what function it serves in ordering our humanity.

4) Consider the four major patterns of pathology and provide an example of people or events that illustrate Jung's understanding of each of these pathological possibilities.

## General tasks

1) Make a family tree of your family. Provide pseudonyms to ensure confidentiality. Identify what patterns emerge. It may be that the women or the men of the family follow similar patterns or have similar characteristics, or that particular events or characteristics are seen in the family. Trace these patterns and identify which of the archetypal images are being activated within this family. How do you understand this activation?

2) Consider the stages of the individuation process. Discuss where you are in this process and what archetypal themes may have already been integrated into your life and what still lies ahead. Remember that individuation is a lifelong process.

3) Describe your psychological type and which function is dominant for you. Which function are you most challenged to develop? Explain in your answer why you think these observations apply to you.

4) Keep a dream journal for a month. Trace the themes and symbols. You will probably find that the themes make sense of things happening in your life at the moment. If there are some strange symbols look them up in a book of symbols.

5) Think of an example of a leader of a religious cult (such as David Koresh, the charismatic cultist involved in the infamous Waco incident in the United States of America). Consider how Jung's concept of participation mystique may be applied in this case.

# Lacan's mirror stage

*Derek Hook*

This chapter introduces Lacan's theory of the mirror stage. It locates Lacan's theory in relation to certain basic principles of early Freudian psychoanalysis and presents the following concepts:

1. Prematuration.

2. The *corps morcele*: the body in pieces.

3. The image.

4. The body as *gestalt*.

5. The mental permanence of the 'I'.

6. Infant narcissism.

7. Image as 'instinctual trigger', and as enabling of the infant.

8. Mimicry.

9. Identification with, and 'captation' by, the image.

10. *Meconnaissance*: misknowing as the primary function of the ego.

11. The hated image and aggressivity.

12. Primal identification and rivalry.

13. Transvitism.

14. Alienation.

The chapter examines what for Lacan is both a key event in childhood development, and the fundamental structure of human subjectivity. The chapter also includes a series of practical applications of the theory.

*'The image is the first organized form in which the individual identifies himself so the ego takes its form from, and is formed by, the organizing and constitutive qualities of this image.'*

Benvenuto and Kennedy (1986, 55)

# Introduction

Jacques Lacan was perhaps the most controversial 'post-Freud' Freudian. Although a psychoanalyst and an advocate of a return to the original works of Freud, Lacan radically reinterpreted much of Freudian psychoanalysis and offered a number of complementary psychoanalytic notions that differed from traditional understandings. In fact it was exactly this 'radicalism' that ultimately resulted in his 'excommunication' from established psychoanalytic circles. By introducing to psychoanalysis certain important notions pertaining to French Structuralism and Linguistics, Lacan arguably extended the parameters of psychoanalysis, and in some ways 'modernised' and changed the face of the discipline.

Lacan rejected all popular attempts to explain Freudian ideas, and took from these ideas a model of mental life that was full of fracture and internal conflict (Ward 1996).

Jacques Lacan

Whereas certain versions of psychoanalysis suggested that the basic conflicts of mental life could be resolved, Lacan felt that they were, as Ward puts it, 'fundamentally irreparable: discord and fracture cannot be cleared away from the psyche because they *are* the psyche' (Ward 1996, 134). Not only did Lacan hope to deflect attention away from watered down and overly optimistic interpretations of Freud's original work, he also suggested that psychoanalysis should take an almost anthropological interest in the cultural and place less emphasis on biological-level explanations. Similarly, he suggested that less emphasis should be placed on the idea that the self-sufficient events within the individual mind are the source of dreams, word associations, Freudian slips, and so on, as these are affected primarily by cultural rather than personal factors (Ward 1996).

Lacan's popularity and importance has grown in recent years. Many of his works are notoriously difficult. However, his theorisation of the 'mirror stage' has proved extremely influential and we will briefly discuss the importance of this notion to child development.

# The source of the ego

Lacan saw himself as a faithful adherent to Freudian psychoanalysis; indeed, Freud's notions are basic and fundamental to many of the seemingly complimentary ideas that Lacan would go on to develop. *(Note that this chapter will assume a basic familiarity with the Freudian terms of ego, superego, id, auto-eroticism, sexual object, etc. as discussed in Chapter 5. For the most part the definitions of these key Freudian terms are to be found in the glossary for that chapter.)* The obvious connection-point to Freud, with regard to Lacan's mirror stage, is the notion of the ego, and the idea of the ego's development. For Lacan, the weak point in Freud's developmental theory was exactly this – his description of the initial formation of the ego.

Lacan maintains that for Freud the ego was not 'in-built', that is, was not present within the child from birth. Freud, in Lacan's view, did not sufficiently explain how this psychic apparatus came into existence. The superego was well explained as the internalisation of social values and morals through the identification with parental authority. Likewise the id, as the instinctual set of unconscious desires and drives innate to all human organisms, seemed adequately explained. From where, though, did the ego stem?

## Ego as mental projection of the body's surface

Freud did offer a number of possible answers. First, he noted, the ego was largely derived from bodily sensations, and chiefly those springing from the surface of the body (1966). In this way the ego *was like a projection of the surface of the body*:

> The ego is ultimately derived from bodily sensations, chiefly those springing from the surface of the body. It ... [is] a mental projection of the surface of the body ... representing the [surfaces] of the mental apparatus (Freud 1966, 26).

## Narcissism: the ego arising through self-love

This was not the only answer Freud gave though. According to Freud, the newly born child is in an 'auto-erotic' stage where it can, initially, obtain satisfaction from its own body without needing an external object. (A prime example of this is in the action of thumb sucking). The infant will obviously need move on from this auto-erotic state – as discussed in Chapter 5 – if it is to take on an adult sexuality, and focus its sexual instinct on an external object (another person). The only way that the infant will succeed in this goal is by first taking *itself* as its object of desire, and then transferring this self-desire onto other objects. According to Freud (1966, 60–61):

> There comes a time in the development of the individual at which he unifies his sexual drives (which have until now been engaged in auto-erotic activities) in order to obtain an [external] love object ... he begins by taking his own body as his love-object, and only subsequently proceeds from this to the choice of some person other than himself.

**Narcissism.** Narcissism is the (generally gratuitous) love of the self, as epitomised in the myth of Narcissus. In psychoanalytic terms, narcissism is the state in which one's libido is so strongly invested in one's own ego that it cannot properly involve itself in object-love (love of another).

In other words, if auto-eroticism is to cease, the child needs to go through a stage of **narcissism**, which will then lead to the process of making *external* object-choices. Presumably, the ego in this scheme, as Benvenuto and Kennedy (1986) put it, would be formed at this stage of narcissism, between the stages of auto-eroticism and object-love, *while being taken as a love-object*. Part of this stage of narcissism would be the gradual development of a sense of self and a sense of separateness from the external world, both of which would stem from processes of identification and incorporation. Freud, however, did not fully explain exactly how this state of narcissism came about, especially since it did not exist from the start of life. He noted that some 'new psychical action' would have to take place to constitute the ego, but did not, as Leader and Groves (1995) point out, say exactly what this action would be.

## Ego as outcome of transition from pleasure to reality principle

Another possible 'strand of development' that we may provide as a way of bolstering Freud's account of the emergence of the ego is through the development of the reality principle. This is that principle of mental functioning which modifies the pleasure principle and aims to adapt the instincts and impulses of the organism to the state and conditions of the objective and external world. (The pleasure principle, by contrast, always seeks first and foremost the most direct route to the satisfaction of instinctual needs; a route which can understandably get its subject into a considerable amount of trouble.)

In terms of this explanation, the ego – as that entity that needs to balance the rivalling forces of id and superego – comes into being exactly because of the need to moderate the pleasure principle, exactly as that psychical agency which will develop and implement the reality principle. In short, it is through learning to moderate the wishes of the pleasure principle and to obey instead the pragmatics of the outside social world that the reality principle – and more fundamentally its governing agency the ego – comes into being.

To translate this account more directly into Freud's own terms: one portion of the id undergoes a special development; a special organisation arises which from that point on 'acts as an intermediary between the id and the external world ... [that special organisation is] ... the ego' (Freud 1966, 145).

## Superego considerations

Freud also involved the superego in his explanation of the ego. Now whereas the superego cannot be in any way responsible for the emergence of the ego (as we know from the chapter on Freud, the superego only develops after the ego), the ego does contain certain elements within it that will make it a suitable place for the superego to arise. These elements give us an important clue as to the development of the ego. Benvenuto and Kennedy (1986, 51–52) provide an extremely helpful summary in this regard:

> The super-ego ... compromises both a critical, self-observing and punishing function, and also the setting up of ideal goals derived from the 'ego-ideal'. The notion of the ego-ideal ... brings into a basically persecuting and aggressive super-ego (with which it is difficult to identify) a narcissistic element, the love of one's own ideal. What the individual projects before him as his ideal is the substitute for the lost narcissism of his childhood in which he was his own ideal.

In other words, Freud has suggested that the superego contains, in the 'ego-ideal', a powerful element of narcissism, the love of one's own ideal. This powerful element of narcissism stems from the ego, a factor already alluded to above, but now reiterated. For these reasons, it now becomes crucial to involve an explanation of narcissism in the account of how the ego emerges. Lacan will go on to do just this. In fact, his explanation for the emergence of the ego will be able to account for both the elements of aggressivity and narcissism, which – following Benvenuto and Kennedy's (1986) thoughts above – will be strongly present in the incipient superego.

### Gaps in Freud's account

All of these explanations above were important to Lacan. They were able to tell us something about the ego, to offer important tentative contributions as to how the ego may have developed, but were, ultimately, not able to tell us properly how it came into existence. Although these various explanations are mutually supportive and generally coherent, they tell us a lot more about the 'whys' than about the 'hows' of ego development. Lacan hoped, with his *mirror phase* theory of development, to provide the definitive explanation of the formation of the ego.

## Challenges facing the newborn

Before we enter into a discussion of the exact 'mechanism' of the mirror stage, it is useful to familiarise ourselves with the physiological and psychological challenges facing the newborn infant. These 'challenges of survival' will, understandably, need to be overcome if the infant is one day to enter the adult world of identity, individuality, self-sufficiency, and autonomy. Having a clear sense of these challenges will give us a better sense of what it is that the mirror stage, that is, the formation of the ego, will come to enable within the child.

### 'Humans are always born prematurely'

**Prematuration.** The term Lacan uses to emphasise how biologically and psychologically 'incomplete' and dependent the human infant is at birth, especially in its lack of basic sensorimotor coordination and control of even its most rudimentary bodily functions.

Lacan repeatedly emphasised how helpless, dependent, and unprepared for the world human infants are at birth. The human infant is extremely dependent on external care, and takes a far longer time than any other animal to reach a reasonable level of self-sufficiency. As Leader and Groves (1995, 18) put it, 'Humans are born prematurely. Left to themselves they would probably die. They are always born too early. They can't walk or talk at birth; they have a very partial mastery of their motor functions and at the biological level, they are hardly complete'.

This **prematuration** is visible in a number of ways. Infants lack basic sensorimotor coordination, that is, they do not possess basic motor control of their limbs, which, within the first few months of life often move and twitch uncontrollably, independent of the infant's volition. Likewise, they have not yet attained control of their bodily functions such as defecating or urinating and as such have no real sense of agency over their own body. Understandably, given that the child is relatively uncoordinated, helpless, and dependent, the first months of life are full of anxiety, uneasiness, and 'discord' (Benvenuto and Kennedy 1986). The importance of this early period of anxiety and discord can barely be overestimated for Lacan. We as adults sometimes revisit this period of unease in later life, experiencing it as horrific, as we will go on to explain. The facts that the human infant's body is so immature relative to that of other mammals, that it takes such a long time to develop, and that the baby 'has a basic deficit, a lack of co-ordination and fragmentation of functions' (Benvenuto and Kennedy 1986, 54), make for a daunting set of challenges, but also for a unique *psychical* solution on the part of the human infant, as we shall see.

## Separation and individuation

The fragmentary, disconcerting, and helpless nature of the infant's early motor experiences has a profound impact on its psychical development. At this point, the infant can be described as a heterogeneous, shifting, and centre-less mass of needs and sensations (Burr 1995). It has no proper sense of being separate from the world or the mother, and certainly no sense of being a separate person in its own right. As Marini (1992) puts it, the child has only a very slowly dawning sense of distinction between the world, others, and itself. All sensation and experience have appeared, until now, as a complete whole for the infant, who is still bound up in a symbiotic relationship with the mother, lacking a fundamental sense of being separate from her (Burr 1995). (It is interesting here to speculate around the fact that babies cry not only when they have a painful or pressing physical stimulus – on the level of their own body – but also when their more general environment is disturbed. This might be taken to indicate that a more proper distinction between the two has yet to be drawn).

Developing the rudimentary distinctions between self and outside world, between self and mother, between internal and external forms of stimulus, will clearly prove central to the infant's psychological development, and to its formation of an ego. Without these rudimentary psychological adaptations the infant can be said not to possess an 'I', a basic sense of self, or a fledgling identity. Simply put, the baby understands itself, at this point, as neither psychologically nor physically distinct from the world around it.

## The 'hommelette': the 'little scrambled person'

Lacan is keen to emphasise here not only the disturbing or disconcerting nature of this early pre-separation-individuation experience, he is also keen to emphasise the fragmentary, shapeless, undifferentiated nature of the infant's sense of the world. The baby has no proper sense yet of where its body ends and where the world begins, of itself as a unified anatomical whole. Its limbs, not properly controlled by it, are not seen as necessarily its own, nor are they conceived of as parts of its own bodily whole. Hence Lacan refers to the child as the *'hommelette'* – the little scrambled person.

*Corps morcele.* Literally 'the body in pieces'; Lacan uses the term to refer to those primal (and largely unconscious) images of the fragmented body that remind us of our earliest experiences of bodily discord, before we had gained a sense of our body as a whole, singular unit.

## *Corps morcele:* the body in pieces

Given a moment of introspection, one can see how this experience, of not knowing where one's body ends and another begins, of perceiving a series of disconnected and separate limbs that may or may not be one's own, might be horrific or frightening, especially from the perspective of the adult who is used to being able to control his or her own limbs and to distinguish them from others. In fact, images of the body in pieces, what Lacan calls the *corps morcele* (or fragmented body), will always be disturbing to us as adults, because they remind us of the specific and fundamental relation each and every one of us has had to our own body. This primal relation is vividly enacted, for Lacan, in the playing of children, where the 'pulling off of the head and the ripping open of the belly are themes that occur spontaneously to their imagination, and ... [that are] ... corroborated by the experience of the doll torn to pieces' (Lacan 1977, 11).

PHOTO: MICHELE VRDOLJAK

For Lacan, the corps morcele *(body in pieces)* is vividly enacted in the games of children when they pull off the heads and limbs of their dolls.

These are the aggressive images and phantasies of dismemberment that are, as Bowie (1991, 29) puts it, 'the burden of all self-aware and membered creatures'. They crop up constantly in dreams and in analysis, precisely when the most archaic and fundamental fixations of the analysand are accessed. In Lacan's own words:

> The fragmented body manifests itself regularly in dreams when the movement of analysis encounters a certain level ... It then appears in the form of disjointed limbs, or of those of organs, represented in exoscopy, growing wings and taking arms up for intestinal persecutions (Lacan 1977, 5).

## The image of the self

Having gained something of a sense of the physiological and psychological challenges facing the newborn infant, it is now time to look at exactly *how* the infant overcomes them. The answer to these challenges – which is also Lacan's answer to the riddle of the formation of the ego – lies in the notion of *the image*, or more specifically, in the infant's accommodation of *an image of the self*. This is the fundamental activity of the mirror stage, a key developmental event, that, according to Lacan, occurs roughly between the ages of six and eighteen months, when the infant begins to recognise its image in the mirror.

This formative event has been well documented in various studies of early child and primate behaviour: the baby looks into a mirror, recognises the image – a recognition which is accompanied by great pleasure – becomes fascinated by it, and goes on to try and control or play with it. This is the moment, as Bowie (1991) puts it, that the child suddenly seems able to formulate, however roughly, the propositions 'I am that' and 'that is me'. A variety of important bodily and psychological changes accompany this event:

> At a certain point, around six months ... the infant becomes aware, through seeing his image in the mirror, of his own body as a totality, a total form or *Gestalt*. The mirror image is held together, it can come and go with a slight change in the infant's position, and his mastery of the image fills him with triumph and joy. The mirror image anticipates the mastery of the body that the infant has not yet objectively achieved. He falls in love with his image and, in contrast to the auto-erotic stage, in which he has an erotic relationship to his fragmented body, he now takes the image of his whole body as his love-object (Benvenuto and Kennedy 1986, 54–55).

This is a valuable and compact description of the major features of the mirror stage, which we will break down into a series of important developmental implications. Before we turn to this, however, we should first examine what might be meant by *the image*.

## Various media for the image, and the image as reflection of the self

Although Lacan uses the example of the mirror as the paradigmatic case through which the infant comes to recognise its own image, this is not the only medium in which the infant may perceive its own reflected image.

## 'Monkey business': Chimpanzees and the mirror stage

The 'mirror test' claims Evans (1996) was first described by the French psychologist and friend of Lacan, Henri Wallon in 1931:

> It refers to a particular experiment that can differentiate the human infant from his closest animal relative, the chimpanzee. The six-month-old child differs from the chimpanzee of the same age in that the former becomes fascinated with its reflection in the mirror and jubilantly assumes it as its own image, whereas the chimpanzee quickly realizes that the image is illusory and loses interest in it (Evans 1996, 115).

Benvenuto and Kennedy (1986) likewise make reference to the use of this 'mirror test' in early chimp experimentation, and quote at length the work of Kohler:

> Rana [a chimpanzee] ... gazed long and intently into the mirror, looked up and then down, put it to her face and licked it once, stared into it again, and suddenly her free hand rose and grasped as though at a body behind the mirror. But as she grasped emptiness she dropped the mirror sideways in her astonishment. Then she lifted it again, stared fixedly at the other ape, and again was misled into grasping into empty space. She became impatient and struck out violently at the mirror ... She held the mirror still in one hand, drew back the other arm as far as possible behind her back, gazed with an air of indifference at the other animal, then suddenly made a pounce with her free hand. However, she and the rest soon became used to this side of the affair, and concentrated all their interest on the image; this interest did not decrease ... but remained so strong that the playing with reflecting surfaces became one of the most popular and permanent of their fashions (Kohler, cited in Benvenuto and Kennedy, 1986).

Indeed, as might well be pointed out, not all infants have access to mirrors. Such an awareness of one's own image – an image that is as a reflection of self – may occur in different ways. One example lies in the infant's awareness of how the mother's gaze – or for that matter, the mother's voice – reflects its own current emotional state. In fact, intersubjective moments more generally, where individuals gain a sense of self through multiple kinds of interactions with others, are all an important source of reflected 'images' of self. The same holds for interactions with 'like' individuals, say children of the same basic age as the infant. As Bowie (1991) notes, a roughly equivalent experience to beholding one's mirror image is that of seeing one's own behaviours reflected in the imitative gestures of an adult or another child. The important point is that the child will come to understand itself as a coherent, unified being *via these reflected images of the self*. (This also occurs through the fact that parents, adults, and siblings treat the child as if it were a unified and coherent being. Hence it is sent messages about its coherence and unity, both bodily and psychologically, from the various responses of caregivers *in addition to glimpses of its own physical appearance in the form of visual reflections*.)

## The body becomes 'a whole'

Lacan characterises the sight of the infant before the mirror as a 'startling spectacle'. Even though the infant is as yet unable to walk, and has difficulty standing up, and in supporting itself, it nonetheless tries its best to overcome these obstructions in its eagerness to gaze at its own image. This of course can only happen when the perceptual apparatus is reasonably matured – although, importantly, this gazing into one's own image *takes place before the child has attained the maturity of basic motor and physical coordination*. This means that the body now becomes 'a whole' – as far as the infant is concerned – and, second, it means that a sense of the image of one's self always precedes the *actual* mastery of motor coordination.

The fact bears repeating here that the infant has, up to this point, never seen its body as a whole – as a composite organism of different parts. Indeed, how else is the child to 'see' its whole body – its face and eyes as attached and related to its torso, legs, and arms – apart from seeing an image of itself? This is indeed a momentous event for the child. It starts to have some understanding of how its body fits together, how it might control it, and where it ends and the world begins. A part of this is realising that whereas it can control its arm, for instance, it cannot control the breast, or other external objects. This control of the body, and its accompanying sense of separateness from the world, is something that we as adults typically take for granted. Hence it is certainly worthwhile considering, as we shall do, the *psychological* gains that are associated with these newfound levels of mastery.

## The body as *gestalt*

A vital part of what happens in the mirror stage (as indicated in the summary above by Benvenuto and Kennedy) is that the child comes to see its own body as 'a totality, a total form, or a *gestalt*'. We should be careful

*Gestalt.* An organised pattern, or more specifically, a visual pattern which is *perceived* as a unified whole. An image is only a *gestalt* in the sense that it has an effect which none of the component parts have in isolation; in a *gestalt*, the whole is always greater than the sum of the parts.

not to skip over this last word, because it proves to be a vital piece of the puzzle. What exactly is a *gestalt*? It is an organised pattern or, more distinctly, a visual pattern which is *perceived* as a unified whole. We should add here that an image is only a *gestalt* in the sense that it has an effect which none of its component parts have in isolation; indeed, *in a gestalt, the whole is greater than the sum of its parts*.

It is useful here to think for a moment of optical illusions. Think for example of a series of dots that are suggestively arranged somewhat like a circle. Even though this shape may not be properly formed – the circle may not be closed, for example, or the arrangement of dots may be somewhat irregular – we still perceive a circle. The importance of this for Lacan's mirror stage is that in perceiving our own image as *gestalt*, there is always the possibility that something is being added, that we are seeing something in addition to what is actually there. There is always the possibility for trickery and illusion, for the suggestion of a unity or closure that may not in fact exist at all. We shall return to this point presently.

## The statue that symbolises the mental permanence of the 'I'

The image of the infant's body is like a mirage, an external image that the mirror reflects back in reversed symmetry and perspective. As Benvenuto and Kennedy (1986, 55) put it, 'The infant's movements and bodily prematurity are reversed in the fixity of a big "statue" of himself'. Why do these authors, following Lacan, choose the metaphor of a statue? Well, because this image gives to the infant more than just a sense of unity and cohesion. It also gives it a sense of fixity and stature, a basic and solid sense of consistency, which can join together various moments of experience. It is in this way that the infant gains a consistent sense of self over time – a series of experiential moments joined together give some substance, no matter how illusory, to the ego. In Lacan's own words (1977, 2), 'This Gestalt ... in these two aspects [fixity and stature] of its appearing symbolises the ego's mental permanence'.

PHOTO: CHA JOHNSTON

*The image gives to the infant more than just a sense of unity and cohesion – it also gives it a sense of fixity and stature, a basic and solid sense of consistency, which can join together various moments of experience.*

Importantly then, the image not only unifies the perceptions and experiences of the body, it also unifies the psychological experiences of the infant, and substantiates 'the mental permanence' of the 'I'.

This notion of the statue as the means through which the infant projects its own mental and bodily permanence bears a strong resemblance to one of the explanations that Freud had offered for the development of the ego. As Benvenuto and Kennedy (1986) note, in Freud's later work the ego was regarded, in part, as a 'mental projection of the surface of the body'. This is compatible with the notion of the mirror image as a projection of the surface of the body.

**Aggressivity.** Lacan's notion of aggressivity is best understood by distinguishing it from the similar concept of aggression. Where the latter refers explicitly to violent acts, 'aggressivity' has a more fundamental meaning which indicates a wider range of acts and phenomena – even seemingly benevolent ones. Thus Lacan uses this term to define the fundamental *ambivalence* underpinning love and hate. Since the erotic-aggressive relationship with the mirror image is seen by him as *underwriting the basic structure of human subjectivity*, the term 'aggressivity' embraces the wide range of aggressive, rivalrous, and hating emotions and values that are present in any instance of identification, whether conscious or not.

# The beginning of narcissism: the infant falls in love with its image

Psychoanalysis is well renowned for its affinity for the myths of classical antiquity. The myths of Oedipus and Elektra were both taken up as emblems for primal phylogenetic developmental processes, as we have seen in the chapter on Freud. In the same vein, Lacan refers to the **myth of Narcissus** as a telling analogy for what happens in the mirror stage. Like the central figure in this myth, the human infant recognises the reflection of its own image and falls in love with it. In contrast to the earlier auto-erotic stage, in which the infant has an erotic relationship to its own fragmented body, it now takes the image of its whole body as its love-object. For Lacan, it seems, this is a fairly automatic, or instinctual, outcome of the child's exposure to its own image.

It is this activity that provides the answer to Freud's unspecified 'new psychical activity' that had to occur before (external) object-love could take place. It is important to note, as pointed out by Evans, that this narcissism has both an erotic and an aggressive character:

> It is erotic, as the myth of Narcissus shows, since the subject is strongly attracted to the *gestalt* that is his image. It is aggressive, since the wholeness of the image contrasts with the uncoordinated disunity of the subject's real body, and thus seems to threaten the subject with disintegration (Evans 1996, 120).

For Lacan the development of a stage of narcissism is, in this way, unavoidable. It is an absolutely fundamental aspect of human psychology across cultures and across history. The subjectivity of every single human being involves both elements of narcissism, including the **'aggressivity'** that this narcissism entails. For Lacan, these are both fundamental constituent elements of our ego's emergence. We will return to this point.

## The myth of Narcissus

In Greek mythology Narcissus was the handsome son of the river god Cephissus and the nymph Liriope. For rejecting the love of Echo he was punished by Aphrodite by being compelled to fall in love with his own reflection in a pool of water. Hopelessly enamoured with his own image, he was unable to pull himself away from it, and eventually pined away. His body was transformed into the flower of the same name, which was said to be the last flower plucked by Persephone, the goddess of fertility, before she was carried off to the underworld.

**Myth of Narcissus.** Famous Classical Greek myth of a god who falls in love with his own image (reflected in a pool of water) with tragic consequences.

# The enabling function of the image

Lacan almost always emphasises the degree to which the child's recognition of its own image fills it with triumph, jubilation, and joy. It seems that there may be a number of reasons for this. Since this is an experience that enables the child to unify its disturbing and fragmented sense of its body, and of its self, it is understandable why this might be such a triumphant event. Another reason why this is such a 'jubilant' moment is that from this point on, the child begins to achieve a far greater mastery of its various bodily functions (such as sphincter control) and its motor functions (movement). (Both of these reasons may also be seen as partly explaining why the infant seems so inevitably to fall in love with its own image).

One can start to understand that the exposure to the mirror image might result in a kind of mastery for the child. If a child is able to see the reflections of its physical movements, it may understand better the correspondence between its attempts to control its body and the movements its body actually makes. In this regard, the child's sense of the correspondence between what it is *trying to make its body do*, and what it sees *it doing* in the reflection, might be thought to accelerate the learning process.

It is this enabling function of exposure to the mirror image that Lacan is referring to when he notes that 'the mirror image anticipates the mastery of the body that the infant has not yet objectively achieved' (Lacan 1977, 20). The pivotal point for Lacan is that *the infant's imaginary mastery of the body always anticipates its biological mastery*. In short, our perceptions of ourselves and our abilities are always based on an image before anything else. In this way, as Benvenuto and Kennedy (1986) assert, '*any future relationship with reality will be marked by imaginary anticipation*'. There are a series of profound implications that stem from this position, which we will go on to discuss. Before we do this, though, it is important to consider how the image might be seen as enabling.

## The image as 'instinctual trigger'

The image as in some way 'enabling' is a theme that Lacan often returns to, and he elaborates on it in a number of ways. For a start, he considers the image of the self to act as a 'releasing mechanism' that triggers certain instinctual responses. For example, when an animal perceives a unified image of another member of its species, it responds in certain instinctual ways. Lacan's famous illustration in this regard describes the female pigeon that will not properly develop a gonad (that is, a specific reproductive organ) if it does not see another member of its species. Nevertheless, as Lacan notes, the sight of its own mirror reflection is enough to ensure this development. Lacan argues that for humans the body image also produces instinctual responses, especially sexual ones, such as triggering the end of auto-eroticism and the beginning of desire for an external object.

Another powerful example of the instinctual importance of the image is to be found in Lorenz's famous experiment of 'imprinting':

> Lorenz had put his Wellington boots next to duck eggs. As the ducklings hatched out and saw the boot, they became 'imprinted' with its image; wherever that boot went, the little ducks would follow. They mistook Lorenz's boot for their mummy. When Lorenz wore his Wellingtons he was slavishly followed by a trail of ducklings, each of whom [was] captivated by the image of the boot (Hill 1997, 11).

These ecological examples of the *instinctual* importance of exposure to the image at early phases of development certainly strengthen Lacan's argument. Just as in the case of the pigeon, or as in Lorenz's ducks, Lacan argues, the early exposure to the image – the image of the self – will be vital to the human child, and will trigger a series of uniquely human psychological processes which would not otherwise be initiated. (The vital psychical stage of narcissism, as explained above, is one example of this triggering.)

## Mimicry: learning and adaptation through the image

**Mimicry.** In the zoological or ethological sense this refers to the fact that certain beasts have the habit of assuming insignia and colouring that match their surroundings.

The image is also central to activities of **mimicry**, through which the young child learns by reproducing the movements and activities of others (or of its own reflected image). The role of mimicry in learning is vital to Lacan (1977), as, arguably, is its role in adaptation to a given environment. It is exactly through reproducing kinds of actions observed in the outside world, and in various images (whether of themselves or of similar others), that infants come to be able to control their bodies and progressively adapt to the world around them.

Mimicry, in the zoological or the ethological sense, refers to the fact that certain beasts have the habit of assuming the insignia and colouring of their surroundings. The obvious explanation for this phenomenon, as Leader and Groves (1995) point out, is that it protects the animal against predators. This is not always the case however, because as investigators found out, those animals that assumed an image were very often just as likely to be eaten as those that did not (Leader and Groves, 1995).

Mimicry, then, need not be confined to an adaptive activity, it may simply follow a natural law whereby people or animals within a certain

## Mirror anecdotes

There were pillars lined with full-length mirrors at the department store where I used to work. Young children always seemed drawn to the mirrors. I remember one little girl who kissed her reflection and pressed her face against the glass, forcing air out of her cheeks at the same time. Others would pull faces and make gurgling sounds, whilst playing with 'themselves' in the mirrors. There were nearly always little hand marks at the bottom of mirrors at the end of the day when I went home.

I remember a separate occasion when I shared Christmas with another family, who had two young boys, Ben (who was eighteen months old) and his brother Harry (a year older). Whilst we were opening presents, Ben started pointing at the full-length mirror which was balancing against the mantelpiece and excitedly identified 'Harry, Harry', even though Harry was at the other end of the room. Ben toddled up to the mirror and started to pull at it, trying to climb behind it, all this time calling Harry. Eventually I asked Ben, curious to see whether he was identifying with the mirror image, 'Where is Ben?' Ben then hid behind the couch, eventually peeking around the corner. 'Ben' he identified, pointing to himself, joining in the game. —*Michele Vrdoljak, University of the Witwatersrand* environment come to take on certain of its qualities, becoming 'captured in their environment'. Indeed, whether through the active learning of mimicry, or through less voluntary processes in which organisms become 'captured in their environment', the evolutionary or instinctual process of 'taking on an image' seems widespread across the animal kingdom. Lacan's implication is that this is an enabling activity that has an important function in the psychological development of the human infant: that of founding an ego.

## Identification with the image

If we bring together all of the explanatory elements discussed above – that the *gestalt* image enables a bodily and psychological permanence and unity not otherwise achieved, that it initiates the stage of narcissism, that it enables learning and adaptation through mimicry, as well as providing an important instinctual trigger – then we can start to appreciate the centrality of the image in developmental psychology for Lacan. However, there is one vital element missing in this description, an element that will strengthen Lacan's overall account, and amplify its explanatory ability. That element is **identification**. Indeed, this is the key – and the central process – in infants 'taking on an image'. In emphasising the importance of identification in this way, Lacan's account is much like Freud's. Indeed, identification should not be underestimated in the psychological development of the individual. For psychoanalysis, as Heaton (2000) notes, identification is the operation whereby the human subject is constituted. In a very fundamental way, we, as humans with identities of some psychological depth, do not exist without making identifications.

With this emphasis in mind, we can understand the full force of Lacan's assertion that the 'image is the first organized form in which the individual identifies himself so the ego takes its form from, and is formed by, the organizing and constitutive qualities of this image' (Benvenuto and Kennedy 1986, 55).

**Identification.** For Freud, identification is the process whereby a subject adopts one or more attributes of another subject for him- or herself. Lacan basically agrees with this definition, but adds to it the importance of the image, so that identification, for him, is a transformative process in which the subject 'assumes an image'.

## Implications of our identification with the image

There is one particular aspect of the mirror stage that Lacan never tires of repeating, and that is *that the ego is always formed on the basis of an imaginary relationship of the subject with his or her own body*. We know from the above discussion that identification with the image is an enabling factor, which gives the child increased control over its motor functions, among other things. But what does it mean that the ego is formed on the basis of an *imaginary relationship* with the body, and that all future engagements with reality will be marked by *imaginary anticipation*?

Here it is important to reconsider certain of the implications of the image as *gestalt* – that, for example, the *gestalt* lends a sense of completeness, closure, unity, and autonomy that is not necessarily there. In other words, there is always something imaginary, something illusionary, in our identifications with our own images, something deceptive, untruthful, and fictitious. Lacan hints at this in his descriptions of the mirror stage as a process of trickery, seduction, captivation, slavery, bondage, and so on.

## 'Captation' by the image

One cannot escape the fact that, for Lacan, something delusory is going on in front of the mirror. As Bowie observes:

> where the chimpanzee is able to recognize that the mirror is an epistemological void, and to turn his attention elsewhere, the child has a perverse will to remain deluded. The child's attention is seized [by the image] ... he or she is captivated (Bowie 1991, 23).

*The child is thought to be seduced by, and to fall in love with, its mirror image at the earliest stages of development. Lacan uses the term 'captation' to describe this process, implying both the sense of fascination and the sense of capture.*

It is in this sense that Lacan uses the term captation to describe what is going on. As Evans (1996) points out, the French term has two equally applicable meanings: it expresses the fascinating and seductive power of the image, on the one hand, and the idea of 'capture', the more sinister sense of an 'imprisoning' or 'disabling fixation' on the other. It is in this way that Bowie (1991) speaks of the mirror as that which, although so seemingly consoling and advantageous, nonetheless operates as a ruse, a trap, and a decoy. The idea is that 'falsehood and underhandedness are somehow ingrained into the ego during its first, formative moments' (Bowie 1991, 23). In other words, the ego, which may have been assumed as basically honest, is in fact integrally and fundamentally dishonest.

*Meconnaissance.* Literally 'misknowing'. Lacan uses this term to suggest what he sees as the primary ego function – the misleading and deceiving of its subject. For Lacan, people have an almost infinite capacity to deceive themselves.

## *Meconnaissance:* misknowing as the primary function of the ego

In this regard, Lacan's notion of the ego has powerful resonances with that of the early Freud. Both observe the ego's capacity to mislead and trick its owner. Lacan, if anything, would like to emphasise even more strongly this deceiving quality of the ego. Deception, for him, is the primary function of the ego. Hill (1997, 18) describes this deceptive function of the ego:

> This means that whatever the circumstances, and however much psychoanalysis a person has had, in matters of consciousness and judgement – especially reflexive ones in which people make judgements of themselves – the productions of the ego are suspect ... The deceptive function of the ego is something we are all stuck with. A deceptive ego that tells lies is a necessary part of our mental structure.

## Implications of *meconnaisance* for psychotherapy

Considering Lacan's characterisation of the ego's primary function as *meconnaissance*, what are the implications for psychotherapy? Well, if one makes the assumption that the ego is not to be trusted, then it stands to reason that Lacan was

> absolutely and fundamentally opposed to any idea that one should help the [patient] ... to strengthen his ego, or to help him adjust to society in any way, or that one should help him tolerate unconscious impulses by building up his ego. He was opposed to any notion that psychoanalysis is concerned with producing healthy, well-adjusted individuals who would be able to know what reality is, and who would be in possession of a

healthy tolerant ego. In addition, he considered that the individual was in permanent conflict with his surroundings, and that any notion of a unified, healthy individual who was happy with his adjustment to his surroundings was a meconnaisance of Freud's basic teachings (Benvenuto and Kennedy 1986, 60).

This is certainly a radical view, especially in Lacan's ardent opposition to *any* suggestion that psychotherapy should play a role in adjusting the individual to his or her social environment. Many of course would suggest that it is exactly this objective that constitutes one of the predominant functions of psychotherapy.

Lacan refers to the false judgements of the ego as *meconnaissance*, or misknowing. It is on this basis that he suggests that people have an almost infinite capacity to deceive themselves, particularly when they are making value judgements about themselves, or when they are contemplating their own image (Hill 1997). It is important to emphasise how different this understanding of the ego is to other versions of psychoanalysis or to American ego psychology. The latter 'philosophies' of the ego argue that it may be strengthened, or put more in touch with reality, by the construction of a 'conflict free zone' (Hill 1997). For Lacan this is not only idealistic, it is also simply false. The ego lies compulsively. It attempts to negotiate between unconscious desire and reality by covering up the necessary conflicts that life entails. Importantly then, not only does the ego twist and distort and censor unconscious impulses, it also twists, distorts, and alters our perceptions of external reality. As Hill (1997, 19) puts it, 'In other words, it bullshits, like any public relations department'.

## The return of the fragmented body

We know *why* the image is false, and hence *why our egos lie to us*. But what is achieved in this way? Why is it so important that this lying actually happens? It happens, first, as a way of covering up the real extent to which we lack a basic completeness, unity, or autonomy of the 'I' – of the ego. Second, it happens to cover up the great disparity between how we perceive and understand ourselves – via the image – and how we *actually* are. And third, it happens as a way of hiding the fact that we are continually threatened by disturbing images and feelings of fragmentation, disunity, and dislocation. These three answers stem, in fact, from a single central cause. This is how Evans (1996, 67) represents it:

In the mirror stage the infant sees its reflection in the mirror as a whole/synthesis ... [a perception which contrasts with] the perception of its own body ... as divided and fragmentary. The anxiety provoked by this feeling of fragmentation fuels the identification with the ... image by which the ego is formed. However, the anticipation of a synthetic ego is henceforth constantly threatened by the memory of this sense of fragmentation, which manifests itself in images of 'castration, emasculation, mutilation, dismemberment, dislocation, evisceration, devouring, bursting open of the body' which haunt the human imagination.

The less than unified ego needs to lie to us continually if it is sufficiently to hide the disparity between our *illusions* of autonomy and cohesion and what is actually the case. It has to hide from us the fact that our apparently unified senses of self and identity are always being threatened with collapse. Here Evans (1996, 67) makes a further crucial point:

In a more general sense, the fragmented body refers not only to images of the physical body but also to *any* sense of fragmentation and disunity ... Any such sense of disunity threatens the illusion of synthesis which constitutes the ego.

We are not only haunted by images of physical or anatomical dislocation and dismemberment, we are also continually threatened, on a psychological level, with the fragmentation of our seemingly solid senses of self and identity.

## The hated image and aggressivity

This *return of the fragmented body* has a profound implication in terms of how we take *ourselves* as our first and most primal rivals. In the discussion of infant narcissism we mentioned that narcissism is characterised by aggressivity, which stems from the contrast between the wholeness of the image and the uncoordinated disunity of the subject's real body. We can return to this understanding now, and elaborate it, again with reference to Evans (1996, 115): 'This contrast is first felt by the infant as a rivalry with its own image, because the wholeness of the image threatens the subject with fragmentation ... the mirror stage thereby gives rise to an aggressive tension between the subject and the image'.

## Instituting a primal rivalry with the self

Of course, the subject *must* identify with the image, because of the image's enabling function. In this way the infant ends up identifying with, and *internalising*, its most hated rival, the image of itself. Hence it is true to say that the infant is its own rival before being the rival of another. The image of the self that the subject comes to identify with is both *loved* and *hated*; such identification implies an ambivalent relation with the counterpart, involving both eroticism and aggression (as discussed in connection with narcissism). This 'erotic aggression' continues as the fundamental ambivalence underlying all future forms of identification. This is a fact that reiterates Freud's concept of **ambivalence**, that is,

**Ambivalence.** The co-existence of contradictory impulses or emotions towards the same object; the term usually refers to the co-existence of love and hate.

the notion that feelings of love and hate are powerfully interlocked and interdependent.

The erotic/aggressive identification with the mirror image will form the basic template for all future relations of love and hate. All future objects of love and hate will in some ways re-evoke these primal feelings of *self-love* and *self-hate*. At the beginning of this chapter we discussed how Freud's notion of the ego precipitated the superego by suggesting that the ego contained both self-loving qualities (the ego-ideal stemming from the individual's narcissistic childhood when they took themselves as their ideal) and aggressive qualities (self-punishing tendencies). We now see how both of these loving and hating qualities are foreshadowed by, and 'inbuilt' within, the ego. Lacan continues, in later writings, to elaborate on how the hated image of the self is thus always the source of our aggressive feelings for others.

## Primal identification and rivalry: the mirror stage and our interactions with others

The mirror stage hence signals the onset of two very basic yet also very fundamental psychological functions within the human infant: identification and aggressive rivalry. Both of these come to feature as powerful components in even our most ordinary interactions with others. The importance of the mirror stage lies not only in the fact that it conditions the way the infant sees and understands itself, it also powerfully affects *the way it sees and understands others*.

In fact, these qualities of identification and rivalry are generally far more a part of our day-to-day engagement with others than we might at first assume. As Benvenuto and Kennedy (1986, 58) observe, 'The primary conflict between identification with, and primordial rivalry with ... the image, begins a dialectical process that links the ego to more complex social situations'. In some ways (and this indicates how readily humans are 'seduced' by the image) humans are *overidentificatory* beings. In fact, identification with others seems to be a uniquely human characteristic. The implication of this is that we humans are always gratuitously identifying, not only in the sense of identifying personally with someone else, but also in the case of mistakenly identifying another person with a third party. Lacan humorously refers to this when he says that he loves his dog Justine because, unlike humans, she would never mistake him for anyone else. (Another obvious and classical psychoanalytic example would be the tendency to see your mother or father in your sexual partner.) This kind of overidentification, or 'domination by the image' is, of course, largely unconscious.

## Transvitism: the other as self

Lacan's attention to the importance of identificatory processes in early childhood enabled him to explain the fascinating developmental phenomenon of **transvitism**. Transvitism is that process, to quote Lacan (1977, 19), when 'The child who strikes another says he has been struck; the child who sees another fall, cries'. Transvitism is the overidentifica-

**Transvitism.** The over-identificatory practice in which the needs, desires, or emotions of the other are taken on as one's own.

tory practice in which the needs, desires, or emotions of the other are taken on as one's own. In this connection it is well documented how children find other children more interesting than adults, and how they engage more readily with other children – particularly of the same age – than with adults. Given that the identifications of self with the external image do not stem exclusively from the mirror, but also stem *from children's identifications with other children*, we can see how transvitism occurs. By overidentifying with the other who is structurally similar to the self, and by not yet having settled exactly where one's body ends and another's begins, the desire, need, or emotion of the other is taken on as that of the self. It is in this connection that Marini (1992, 32) comments, 'If there is a counter-part – an other who might be me – it is only because the self is originally other'.

## The deep-rootedness of rivalry and hatred: the self as other

We take on *the other as self* in the mirror stage, through overidentifying with people who, quite literally, are not part of ourselves (although at some level we act as if they are). We also do the opposite, *we project self as other*. Both of these are constituents of the intensive identificatory practices that occur around the mirror stage, and which, as much as we might deny it, continue to occur throughout our adult lives. The important consequence of this is that original elements of self-rivalry and self-hatred feature in all our interactions with others. His assertion of this fact enables Lacan to provide something of an explanation for the frequency of conflict, aggression, and hatred that so often characterises human relationships. It also suggests an explanation for the apparently deep-rootedness of particular forms of social prejudice and intolerance such as racism, sexism, and bigotry. These are all forms of hatred that are anchored in the very foundational structures of the human ego.

Make no mistake, Lacan warns: jealousy and hatred are emotions that exist even in the youngest infant. He derives the following anecdote from St Augustine's *Confessions*: 'I have myself seen jealousy in an infant and know what it means. He was not old enough to speak but whenever he saw his foster-brother at the breast, he would grow pale with an envious stare' (Lacan 1977, 20). Lacan presents this as an example of the infant involved in a confrontation with his counterpart, as if in front of the mirror. He continues to emphasise how aggressivity and narcissism are tightly bound to one another, suggesting that, 'They enter into action in every process of identification, whether it be with an image or oneself, with another person, or with fragments of oneself or another' (Benvenuto and Kennedy 1986, 59).

## Alienation through the image

We have spoken, in our discussion of the image as *gestalt*, of how the image always potentially 'adds something', how it includes qualities (kinds of unity, closure, autonomy, and so on) that are not necessarily there, within the subject. In this way, claims Lacan, while there are vitally important achievements to be gained by the recognition of the image of self, there is also a fundamental **alienation** in this act, by virtue of the fact that it must always, at some level, represent the inclusion of something *more than is actually there*. In other words, we might suggest that the action of identifying oneself with the image must always represent *the internalisation of something external*.

The infant's prospective mastery, through the mirror image, of basic motor and physical coordination must always come from *outside* of itself; it is not yet really the master of its own movements. It can only see its form as unified – as a more or less total image – in an *external* image. This external image is a virtual, alienated, ideal unity that cannot actually be touched (Benvenuto and Kennedy, 1986). Indeed, the mirror image is always a paradox; it is always two contradicting things at once. It seemingly *is* the child, by virtue of the fact that it is exactly the child's *reflection*. But by being a reflection, and a reflection *only*, it is also essentially *not* the child but something outside of it.

> There is ... a fundamental 'alienation' in this action [of the mirror stage]. The infant's mastery in the mirror image, is outside of himself ... his form [resides in] ... an external image ... that cannot be touched. Alienation is this lack of being by which his realization lies in another actual or imaginary space (Benvenuto and Kennedy 1986, 55).

## 'I is an other': alienation as human psychical destiny

Given that this recognition of the image of self is in some ways the founding point of the ego, then it stands to reason that there is always something fundamentally alien – something external, at the basis of the ego, at the basis of our most fundamental understandings of 'I'. For Lacan, we only ever realise ourselves through an external image or reflection, and accordingly there is an 'inbuilt' sense of alienation that cuts across all our self-understandings, no matter how deep or how arbitrary. This is perhaps one of the most profound implications of his understanding of how we are 'seduced' by the image. This is how that we 'take on board' something as being real and integral to ourselves, which in fact is quite external, quite other, and quite false. Indeed, it is at this point of the mirror stage where Lacan (1977) ironically notes that the instrumental intelligence of the ape very briefly surpasses that of the human infant of the same age. Where the chimpanzee, like the human being, appears briefly to confuse the image with reality, it eventually loses interest, recognises the image for what it is – merely an image – and moves on. The human being remains entranced, fascinated by the reflection, mistaking it for him or herself. This is the prototype of the self-alienation to which all human beings are damned, and which the ape manages to avoid.

Alienation is hence an inevitable consequence of the process by which the ego is constituted by identification with the counterpart. The attempt to gain a full or truly meaningful knowledge of oneself will always be doomed to failure. As Bowie (1991, 25) puts it, 'The "alienating destina-

**Alienation.** On a basic level the term refers to a fundamental split within the subject, in which she or he is estranged, distanced *from her or his self*. Alienation is the unavoidable result of the process by which the ego is constituted through identification with the external counterpart.

PHOTO: GILL HAIDEN

*For Lacan, we only ever realise ourselves through an external image or reflection, and accordingly there is an 'inbuilt' sense of alienation that cuts across all our self-understandings, no matter how deep or how arbitrary.*

tion" of the "I" is such that the individual is permanently in discord with himself'. Evans (1996, 9) makes a valuable allusion here to illustrate the point. Quoting Lacan, he notes, 'the initial synthesis of the ego is essentially an alter ego'. He extends this by referring to Rimbaud's assertion that 'I is an other'.

## Conclusion

The mirror stage describes the formation of the ego via the process of identification with an external image. The child identifies with an image outside itself, which may be a real mirror image or simply the image of another child. The apparent completeness of this image gives the child a new mastery over its body, a new awareness of its capacities, which, through a kind of mimicry, precipitates the child's actual control over itself. This identification with an external image or other party enables the child to do things that it could not do before. Importantly, this identification with an external image is more than a single moment in childhood: it is an organising principle of human development generally. As Evans (1996) emphasises, it is not simply a moment in the life of the infant, rather it represents a permanent structure of subjectivity – a structure in which the subject is permanently caught and captured by its own image.

However, this mastery of motor functions, this entry into the human world of space and movement, comes at a price: the subject is captivated by the image and becomes fundamentally deluded by it – with significant consequences for the rest of life. The image as *gestalt* possesses an illusory completeness and unity that the infant does not possess in terms of its physical or psychological conceptions of self. In fact, in total contrast to this, the infant exists in a disturbing state of fragmented and disconnected physicality, where it perceives its body as in pieces. Because the image enables it to gain a sense of the physical integrity of its body, along with a basic sense of 'this is me' apart from the outside world, it comes to love and identify with the image. This image is also the form of the first rival, however, because it contrasts with the uncoordinated disunity of the subject's real body. The image accentuates the subject's feelings of

*For Lacan, the mirror stage represents a permanent structure of subjectivity, a structure in which the subject is permanently caught and captured by his or her own image.*

PHOTO: GILL HAIDEN

fragmentation and gives rise to an aggressive tension and rivalry between the subject and the image. The erotic/aggressive identification with the mirror image will form the basic template for all future relations of love and hate.

Since the mirror image always comes from 'the outside in' – and since the recognition of the image of self is in some ways the founding point of the ego – it stands to reason that there is always something fundamentally alien, something external, at the basis of the ego, at the basis of our most fundamental understandings of self. In this way, a sense of identity only comes at the price of a fundamental alienation. We only come to know ourselves, and to develop our efficacy in the world, in terms of what is not us, in terms of something other, and apart from ourselves. Hence our sense of self is always imbricated (enmeshed, interwoven) with the other (the position of someone outside of us), just as the other is always imbricated in our sense of self.

PHOTO: CHA JOHNSTON

*In terms of Lacan's theory, our sense of self is always imbricated with the other, just as the other is always imbricated in our sense of self.*

The primary function of the ego then, based as it is on imaginary images, is deception, mis-knowing, *meconaissance*. It is not to be trusted, and treatment should not seek to strengthen or develop it, or to help the subject know him- or herself better. These attempts to find a unified and total person are futile, and doomed to end in failure. Mainstream developmental psychology has still to ponder the full implications of this intriguing theory for the psychosocial development of the child.

## Critiques of Lacan

Perhaps the chief criticism of Lacan is one that applies to virtually all of his writings, and not to the mirror stage alone. It is simply that Lacan seems almost perverse in the obscure and abstruse style in which he expresses his theories and ideas. He intentionally chose a writing style that was non-linear and opaque, and which, as Bowie (1991) notes, is typically frustrating, difficult, and ambiguous. At a literary level perhaps this might be rationalised as a style appropriate to its subject matter – to the unconscious flow of meaning. The problem, however, is that one is almost always at pains to know whether one is accurately interpreting his ideas.

The mirror stage has been an extremely influential theory. It has been widely lauded and even more widely applied in academic discourse, and has become emblematic of post-structural and post-modern debates about the fragmentation and multiplicity of self. (This fact is lamented by Sey (1999), who sees it as a misappropriation and 'domestication' of the theory.) Mainstream developmental psychology has still to engage properly with the ideas, and to assess their practical utility. Until then the popular jury is still largely 'out', at least regarding the critical evaluation of this theory.

# Recommended readings

Benvenuto, B. and Kennedy, R. (1986). *The works of Jacques Lacan: An introduction.* London: Free Association Press.
(*In a field filled with deliberately obscure styles of writing, this volume presents an invaluably accessible primer to Lacan's basic ideas. Highly recommended.*)

Bowie, M. (1991). *Lacan.* London: Fontana.
(*Almost as accessible as Benvenuto and Kennedy (1986). Bowie's book does a similarly admirable job of plotting out the general shape of Lacan's overarching psychoanalytic theory.*)

Evans, D. (1996). *An introductory dictionary of Lacanian psychoanalysis.* London: Routledge.
(*A clear and thorough explication of all the major terms and concepts of Lacanian psychoanalysis, which includes commentaries on how they have been developed and in some instances transformed across the whole span of Lacan's writings.*)

Hill, P. (1997). *Lacan for beginners.* London: Writers and Readers.

Lacan, J. (1977). *Ecrits.* London: Norton.

Lacan, J. (1979). *The four fundamental concepts of psychoanalysis.* London: Penguin.
(*It seems unusual not to recommend the original writings of the author to students, but as mentioned above, Lacan's original writings can be hair-raisingly frustrating and esoteric. Ecrits contains the mirror stage paper, and is probably the slightly easier of the two.*)

Leader, D. and Groves, G. (1995). *Lacan for beginners.* Cambridge: Icon Books.
(*Both of the above are colourful, user-friendly, comic-book style introductions to Lacan, which usefully illustrate many of his core concepts.*)

## Critical thinking tasks

1) Be on the lookout for the theme of mirror images in popular magazines, advertising, and popular culture generally. Try and collect a series of such examples. Carefully 'read' these examples according to your understanding of the mirror stage, and explore the various implications of Lacan's theory for each of them.

2) If possible, try to observe infants playing in front of mirrors. Do their actions seem to affirm or refute the basic mirror stage theory? Motivate your answer.

3) Is it true, in your opinion, that young children often 'play out' the theme of the *corps morcele*? (Think about games that you yourself played as a child). Give examples to support your answer.

4) How would you explain the disorder of anorexia nervosa in terms of the mirror phase? Do you think the theory has any useful application here?

# SECTION THREE
## Cognitive development

# Theories of cognitive development: Piaget, Vygotsky, and information-processing theory

*Kate Cockcroft*

---

This chapter provides a brief overview of the most influential theories of cognitive development:

1. Piaget's theory of cognitive development.

2. Criticisms of Piaget's theory.

3. Vygotsky's socio-cultural theory of cognitive development.

4. Criticisms of Vygotsky's theory.

5. The information-processing approach to cognitive development.

6. Criticisms of the information-processing approach.

---

## What is cognition and cognitive development?

Cognition is a collective term for the processes involved in acquiring, organising, manipulating, and using knowledge. These processes are not directly observable. Remembering, problem solving, imagining, creating, fantasising, and using symbols, for example, are all cognitive processes. Cognitive psychologists do not see people as passive recipients of information, but as active processors of information, constantly reorganising and changing the information they receive. **Cognitive development** refers to the ways in which people acquire various cognitive abilities and how these abilities change over time.

**Cognitive development.** The acquisition, development, and refinement of our mental abilities.

Although different aspects of cognitive development will be discussed in the chapters that follow, the cognitive system generally operates as a whole, and it is necessary to emphasise that each aspect must be viewed as related to the functioning of all the other parts. While the chapters may give the impression that aspects of cognitive development, such as language, intelligence, and memory, can be neatly compartmentalised, in reality this is not the case. Using a language, for example, requires that we draw on aspects of attention, perception, memory, and concept formation, to name a few of the cognitive processes involved. Due to the complexity of the cognitive system, it is easier to explain cognitive development by using these artificial distinctions.

## Theoretical approaches to cognitive development

As mentioned in Chapter 1, theories organise and give structure to information that may otherwise be unmanageable. They provide a framework within which we can formulate questions and understand behaviour. Each theory tries to develop a plausible explanation for why and how a particular behaviour occurs. It is worth knowing several theories of cognitive development, because one alone is unlikely to account for all aspects of development. Consequently, three of the main theoretical approaches in cognitive developmental psychology, namely Piagetian theory, social context theory, and information processing theory, will be discussed in this chapter.

## Piaget's theory of cognitive development

Jean Piaget (1896–1980), more than any other person, has laid the groundwork for many of our current beliefs about cognitive development. From a young age he was interested in the scientific study of nature. When, at ten years old, he found that his questions could only be answered by access to the university library, Piaget wrote and signed a short paper on the sighting of an albino sparrow, in the hope that this would stop the university librarian from treating him like a child and give him access to the library. It worked (Papert 1996). Later, Piaget trained as a biologist and before he was twenty years old, was well known in Europe for his work in this field. After completing a dissertation on molluscs and receiving his doctorate at the age of twenty-one, Piaget decided that he wanted more formal training in psychology. He became interested in psychoanalysis and attended Jung's lectures in Zurich. Shortly thereafter, he started working with Theodore Simon (who developed the Simon-Binet Intelligence Test). During this work, Piaget discovered that

Jean Piaget

whether a child was right or wrong on a particular intelligence test item was far less interesting than his or her reasoning in arriving at a particular answer, especially a wrong answer. Piaget concluded from examining children's answers and how they reached them that children's thinking was qualitatively different from adults and that it had its own special logic. Einstein called Piaget's discovery 'so simple that only a genius could have thought of it' (quoted in Papert 1996, 59). In one of his famous experiments, Piaget interviewed many children to reveal how they thought. One question that he asked them was: *'What makes the wind?'*

> *Julia:* The trees.
> *Piaget:* How do you know?
> *Julia:* I saw them waving their arms.
> *Piaget:* How does that make wind?
> *Julia: (waving her hand in front of his face):* Like this. Only they are bigger. And there are lots of trees (Piaget in Papert 1996, 60).

Piaget recognised that five-year-old Julia's beliefs, while not correct according to any adult criteria, are not strictly incorrect either. Another common belief that Piaget's research identified among seven-year-olds was the belief that going faster can take more time. Einstein was particularly intrigued by this, maybe because his own theories of relativity run contrary to common sense (Papert 1996).

While Piaget believed that the social context is important for development, most of his work focused on the role that individuals play in their own development. He referred to the developing child as 'a little scientist', making and testing hypotheses relatively independently in order to construct an understanding of the world, and said, *'children have real understanding only of that which they invent themselves, and each time we try to teach them something too quickly, we keep them from reinventing it themselves'* (Piaget in Papert 1996, 56). In addition, Piaget was concerned with explaining the universal aspects of cognitive development rather than individual differences between people. While the specific beliefs and ideas of different cultures may vary, Piaget believed that the stages of cognitive development unfold in the same sequence irrespective of cultural background (Piaget 1952).

Piaget devoted the rest of his life to investigating how *intelligence* develops. By *intelligence* Piaget meant more than just what is measured by intelligence tests. According to Piaget, intelligence influences all acts of thinking – perception, language, morality, to name but a few. This is why his theory is often called a theory of *cognitive*, rather than 'intellectual', development. Reflecting his past training, he saw the development of intelligence as a form of biological adaptation to the environment. Remaining a helpless baby, totally dependent on others for survival, is not adaptive. So, for example, through the process of adaptation, the baby gradually learns how to grasp a bottle and satisfy its hunger, thereby decreasing its dependence on others. The process of adaptation will be discussed in more detail later.

Piaget's theory is essentially a **constructivist** one which assumes the active building up of knowledge and cognitive processes from a very basic starting point, and that children at different developmental levels

**Constructivism.** The notion that reality is a construction based on the information from our environment and in our heads. So, each person constructs a different understanding of the world.

PHOTO: GILL HAIDEN

*Piaget viewed the child as a solitary explorer, discovering the world in a relatively independent manner.*

**Genetic epistemology.** The experimental study of the development of knowledge.

**Schemes.** Piaget's term for mental structures that process information from the external world. Schemes change as we develop.

**Operations.** Piaget's term for reversible mental actions. Operations combine to form qualitatively different stages of cognitive development.

construct different realities (Papalia and Olds 1998). Piaget referred to his approach as **genetic epistemology**, where the term *genetic* signifies growth and development, rather than the action of genes, and *epistemology* means the study of knowledge (Piaget 1952). Piaget developed a philosophy of *epistemological relativism* in which multiple ways of knowing are acknowledged and examined analytically and objectively.

# Basic concepts underlying Piaget's theory

## Schemes, operations, and adaptation

Piaget called mental structures **schemes**. Schemes, in this definition, are ways of processing information that change as we develop. There are two types of scheme: *sensorimotor schemes* (also known as action schemes) and *cognitive schemes* (also referred to as concepts). During the first two years of life, the infant's knowledge of objects and events is limited to various practical sensorimotor schemes such as grasping, sucking, and looking. Thus, for a ten-month-old baby, a fluffy teddy bear is not understood as a bear, but simply as an object that feels soft and can be cuddled or chewed. According to Piaget, the child only shows signs of cognitive schemes at about two years of age. Then the child becomes capable of solving problems and thinking about objects and events without having acted on them. This means that the child is able to represent experiences mentally and use these mental symbols to achieve certain objectives. Piaget (1962, 63) illustrates how his sixteen-month-old daughter, Jacqueline, formed a mental representation of the behaviour of a visiting child and reproduced his behaviour the following day:

> Jacqueline had a visit from a little boy (18 months of age) ... who, in the course of the afternoon, got into a terrible temper. He screamed as he tried to get out of a playpen and pushed it backward, stamping his feet. Jacqueline stood watching him in amazement, never having witnessed such a scene before. The next day, she herself screamed in her playpen and tried to move it, stamping her foot ... several times in succession.

Schemes are ultimately organised into **operations** (that is, reversible mental actions), which combine to form qualitatively different stages of cognitive development (Papalia and Olds 1998).

## Adaptation: assimilation and accommodation

Piaget believed that cognition develops as a consequence of two inborn intellectual processes, which he named **organisation** and **adaptation**. Organisation is the process whereby children combine existing schemes, or ways of understanding, into new and more complex intellectual structures (Shaffer 1996). For example, the baby who has the gazing, reaching, and grasping reflexes will soon learn how to organise these reflexes into a more complex structure called *visually directed reaching*, which enables the baby to reach out and grasp objects within his or her field of vision, and so learn more about those objects. Piaget believed that children are constantly reorganising their existing schemes into more complex and adaptive structures (Shaffer 1996).

The aim of *organisation* is *adaptation*, or the ability to adjust to the demands of the environment. Piaget separated adaptation into two complementary components called **assimilation** and **accommodation**. To explain these concepts, Piaget used a biological analogy: the ingestion and digestion of food. In eating, physical substances such as food are broken down and converted by the teeth, mouth, gastric juices, and other organs of the digestive system. In other words, something from the external, physical world is transformed and changed – it is taken in or assimilated to become part of the existing digestive system so that it can be beneficial to the person. A similar thing happens at the cognitive level – information that we receive from the environment is processed and assimilated into our cognitive systems. Each person will take in or assimilate information to a different degree since our cognitive systems vary in degree of sophistication. For example, while Einstein's general theory of relativity may be understood at some level by all of us, only those who are more intellectually or academically developed in the understanding of physics will grasp its intricacies. Assimilation thus refers to transforming new information so that it fits within existing ways of thinking (Piaget 1952).

The converse of assimilation is accommodation. Here, the structures themselves are changed. In terms of the biological example of the ingestion and digestion of food, the mouth must be reshaped to take in solid food instead of liquids or modified to be able to drink milk from a cup rather than a bottle or breast. Additional structures, such as teeth, emerge and allow for the ingestion of new types of food. Similarly, cognitive structures are altered and reorganised as a result of our experiences. For example, although you may not fully understand Einstein's theory of relativity, through exposure to it you may have changed the way you think about things. Accommodation refers to changing ways of thinking to integrate new experiences. Therefore, we assimilate new learning into existing mental structures and we change our existing mental structures to accommodate new information (Piaget 1952).

All cognition involves both assimilation and accommodation. They are complementary aspects of the need to adapt and their aim is to bring the cognitive system into equilibrium, or balance, with the environment. (Such a balanced state of affairs is called *cognitive equilibrium*, and the process of achieving it, **equilibration**). Piaget saw development as the formation of ever more stable equilibria between the child's cognitive system and the external world. He also suggested that equilibration develops in three stages. First, very young children are satisfied with their mode of thought and are therefore in a state of equilibrium. Soon, they become aware of shortcomings in their existing thinking and are dissatisfied. This constitutes a state of disequilibrium. Finally, they adopt a more sophisticated mode of thought that eliminates the shortcomings of the old one. That is, they reach a more stable equilibrium. Piaget conceptualised

**Organisation.** The process whereby children combine existing schemes, or ways of understanding, into new and more complex intellectual structures.

**Adaptation.** Piaget's term for the ability to adjust to the demands of the environment, a process during which schemes are elaborated, changed, and developed. Piaget separated adaptation into two complementary components called assimilation and accommodation.

**Assimilation.** The process of transforming new information so that it fits within existing ways of thinking.

**Accommodation.** Changing ways of thinking to integrate new experiences.

**Equilibration.** The basic process of human adaptation, according to Piaget. This involves seeking a balance between the environment and one's mental structures.

**Sensorimotor stage.**
Piaget's first cognitive developmental stage, during which the infant processes information through his or her senses and motor actions, thereby learning about the world.

**Preoperational stage.**
Piaget's second stage of cognitive development, which is initiated by symbolic representational ability. During this stage, the child's thinking tends to be concrete, irreversible, and egocentric.

**Concrete operational stage.** Piaget's third stage of cognitive development. Children are now able to perform reversible mental actions on real, concrete objects, but not on abstract objects. Thinking also becomes less intuitive and egocentric and more logical.

**Formal operations.**
Piaget's final cognitive developmental stage, which is characterised by increased abstract thinking and the use of metacognitive ability.

**Circular responses.** A specific form of adaptation in infancy, in which the infant accidentally performs some action, perceives it, and then repeats the action.

**Primary circular responses.** Circular responses involve the discovery of the baby's own body and occur between the ages of one to four months.

cognitive development as a gradual construction of self-contained operations (Piaget 1952).

# Piaget's stages of cognitive development

According to Piaget, there are four qualitatively different cognitive developmental stages. These are: **sensorimotor** (birth to two years); **preoperations** (two to seven years); **concrete operations** (seven to eleven years); and **formal operations** (adolescence onwards). Piaget argued that people pass through stages at different rates, and therefore the ages attached to them are not very important. However, everyone progresses through the stages in a fixed sequence. Each progressive stage reflects an increasingly more complex way of thinking than the previous one and thus the process of thinking at each stage is qualitatively different from the previous one. Preoperational thinking is different from concrete operational thinking because the former lacks the operations that are present in the latter. Similarly, concrete operational thinking, although logical, is still tied to concrete objects and lacks the abstract and hypothetical qualities of formal operational thinking (Crain 1992). Piaget also believed that the accomplishments of the lower stages become integrated into the subsequent new stage. For example, we still use the coordinations of the sensorimotor stage in activities such as playing tennis (Inhelder and Piaget 1958). These stages of cognitive development will be discussed briefly below.

## The sensorimotor period (birth to two years)

Piaget agreed with Darwin and Watson that the process of cognitive development begins from the most basic reflexive actions such as sucking and grasping. During this stage, basic sensory inputs and motor capabilities are coordinated to form sensorimotor schemes, which are the way the infant processes information from the environment during the first two years of life. From this limited set of primitive reflexes or schemes, basic programmes of intelligent behaviour develop, called *circular responses*, which eventually give rise to verbal intelligence and thought (Piaget 1952). Piaget identified different types of circular responses or reactions, which effectively separate the sensorimotor stage into six sub-stages. These sub-stages describe the infant's transition from a '*reflexive to a reflective organism*' (Shaffer 1996, 249).

## Sub-stages of the sensorimotor period
### Circular responses
**Circular responses** are a specific form of adaptation in infancy. According to Piaget (1952), much of what the young child learns begins by accident – the child accidentally performs some action, perceives it, likes it, and then repeats the action, assimilating it into her or his existing scheme. For example, the baby accidentally puts its thumb in its mouth, becomes aware that it is sucking it, finds this pleasurable and so repeats this action. This would be what Piaget called a **primary circular reaction or response**.

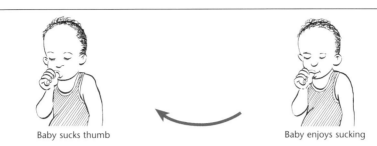

Baby sucks thumb      Baby enjoys sucking

(a) **Primary circular reaction:** action and response both involve infant's own body (one to four months)

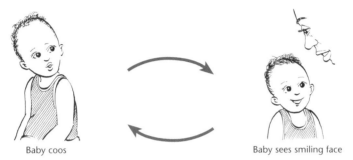

Baby coos      Baby sees smiling face

(b) **Secondary circular reaction:** action gets a response from another person or object, leading to baby's repeating original action (four to eight months)

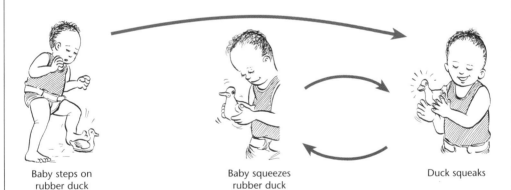

Baby steps on      Baby squeezes      Duck squeaks
rubber duck      rubber duck

(c) **Tertiary circular reaction:** action gets one pleasing result, leading baby to perform similar actions to get similar results (twelve to eighteen months)

**Primary, secondary, and tertiary circular reactions.** According to Piaget, infants learn to reproduce pleasing events they have discovered accidentally.

(a) **Primary circular reaction:** A baby happens to suck a thumb, enjoys sucking, and puts the thumb back into the mouth or keeps it there. The stimulus (thumb) elicits the sucking reflex; pleasure then stimulates the baby to keep on sucking.

(b) **Secondary circular reaction:** This involves something outside the baby's body. The baby coos; the mother smiles; and because the baby likes to see the mother smile, the baby coos again.

(c) **Tertiary circular reaction:** The baby tries different ways to reproduce an accidentally discovered response. When the baby steps on a rubber duck, the duck squeaks. The baby then tries to produce the squeak in other ways, perhaps by squeezing it or sitting on it.

**Figure 10.1** Primary, secondary, and tertiary circular responses. Adapted from Papalia and Olds (1998).

**Secondary circular responses.** Circular responses which involve goal-directed behaviour that gets a response from another person or object.

**Tertiary circular responses.** Circular responses that occur between twelve and eighteen months, when the baby experiments with different ways of reproducing an accidentally discovered response or of solving a problem.

**Symbolic representation.** The use of a picture, word, number, gesture, or some sign to represent past, present, or future events, experiences, and concepts.

Such responses are termed *primary* because they are the first motor habits to appear and *circular* because the pleasure that they bring stimulates their repetition (Shaffer 1996). Primary circular reactions involve the discovery of the baby's own body and occur between the ages of one to four months (Papalia and Olds 1998).

From four to eight months, the baby's circular reactions become more advanced and start to involve objects and people outside the baby's body. For example, the baby coos, the mother smiles, and this makes the baby feel good. It wants the mother to stay with it, so it coos again. This is a **secondary circular reaction or response**. Secondary circular responses involve goal-directed behaviours that get responses from another person or object.

From eight to twelve months the baby demonstrates *coordinated secondary circular reactions*, where he or she coordinates two or more actions to solve new problems. It will know, for example, to pick up a cup to look for something underneath it, or will look at a toy and feel it simultaneously. At this stage, the baby's behaviour starts to display *intentionality*, as in using a stick to pull a toy closer.

**Tertiary circular responses** occur between twelve and eighteen months, when the baby experiments with different ways of reproducing an accidentally discovered response or solving a problem. It accidentally steps on a squeaky toy, for example, likes the squeaky noise it makes and so picks it up and squeezes it, so that it squeaks again (Papalia and Olds 1998).

### Symbolic representation

During the period between eighteen months and two years, the child develops **symbolic representational** ability. Symbolic representation refers to the use of a picture, word, number, gesture, or some sign to represent past, present, or future events, experiences, and concepts. It is the ability to represent something that is not physically present. The earliest forms of representation are actions, such as 'waving bye-bye', and the ultimate form of symbolic representation is language. Symbolic representation is also manifest in the child's play, as in using a broomstick to represent a horse.

### Object permanence

The most important development of the sensorimotor stage, according to Piaget (1952) is **object permanence**. This is the awareness that objects continue to exist even when they are no longer visible. This is only fully developed at around eighteen months. Searching for hidden objects begins at about five months. Before that, the baby does not search for a hidden object, but seems to forget about it altogether. At a year, the child's object permanence is still not fully developed. If the child is used to finding a hidden toy in place A, she will carry on looking for it in place A, even if you show her that you are hiding it in a different place (place B). Object permanence is generally reached around eighteen months when the walking toddler is able to explore the world more actively, for example, when a ball rolls out of sight, she can follow it and see where it has gone.

*The earliest forms of symbolic representation are actions, such as 'waving bye-bye'.*

**Object permanence.** The awareness that objects continue to exist even when they are no longer visible.

However, some research suggests that object permanence may develop earlier than Piaget thought, because he tested its existence with activities that required motor actions of which the baby was not yet capable. For instance, the baby may remember that the object is under the pillow, but does not have the motor ability to move the pillow. Infants as young as three and a half months old act as if they remember an object that they cannot see, when tested with more age-appropriate procedures (Baillargeon and DeVos 1991). It is suggested that infants may have a more sophisticated knowledge of objects based on their perceptual development, but their motor development lags behind this (Baillargeon 1987).

### Imitation

Piaget believed that imitation plays an adaptive role in the child's development. Based on his observations of infants, Piaget believed that they are incapable of imitating novel responses until eight months of age. **Deferred imitation**, or the ability to reproduce the behaviour of an absent model, first appears around twelve to eighteen months of age. (Jacqueline's reproduction of her playmate's temper tantrum, mentioned earlier, is an example of deferred imitation.) It is only once a child is capable of forming mental symbols or images of another person's behaviour and of storing and retrieving these from memory, that he or she is capable of deferred imitation (Ginsburg and Opper 1969). Research has indicated that infants and children are capable of imitation and deferred imitation much earlier than Piaget proposed (Craig 1996). Some newborns are able to imitate an adult sticking out their tongue, but then lose this ability and do not recover it for several months (Craig 1996). Meltzoff (1988) found that nine-month-olds are able to imitate very simple acts such as pressing a button to activate a noise-producing toy, a day after observing a model producing such behaviour.

**Deferred imitation.** The ability to reproduce the behaviour of an absent model.

## Preoperations (two to seven years)

The period from two to seven years is a time of much intellectual curiosity, when children come up with all sorts of questions, such as 'What makes you stop growing?' or 'Why do you have to have a man and a lady to have a baby?' Piaget called this period the *preoperational* or *prelogical* stage because he believed that preschool children have not yet acquired the cognitive operations that would enable them to think logically or to interpret reality correctly. Piaget's descriptions of preoperational thinking focus mainly on the limitations of this stage (Piaget 1952).

The preoperational stage is divided into two parts: the **preconceptual stage** (from two to four years) and the **intuitive or transitional stage** (from five to seven years). The preconceptual stage is characterised by the increasing use of symbols, including language and symbolic play. For example, a child playing with a piece of wood as if it were a car is engaging in symbolic play. The use of symbols enables the child to think about things that are not only in its immediate environment. The child also has the power to name things that may not be immediately present. Children in the preconceptual stage still have difficulty distinguishing between mental, physical, and social reality. They may think, for example, that all

**Preconceptual stage.** The first phase of the preoperational stage of cognitive development. It is characterised by the increasing use of symbols, including language and symbolic play.

**Intuitive stage.** The second phase of the preoperational stage of cognitive development, also known as the transitional stage. During this phase the child becomes less egocentric and much better at classifying objects on the basis of perceptual categories such as size, shape, and colour.

**Transitional stage.** See intuitive stage.

**Animism.** The preoperational belief that all moving objects (and sometimes inanimate objects) are alive.

objects that move are alive, including cars and clouds. (This is called **animism**). The child may expect that the inanimate world will obey her or his commands, a trait stemming partly from the child's self-centred view of the world (or **egocentricity**). Most of these 'illogical' ways (by adult standards) of thinking about the world result from the child's *transductive reasoning*. **Transductive reasoning** entails reasoning from the particular to the particular. When any two events co-vary, the child assumes that one has caused the other. For example, when Piaget's daughter had missed her regular afternoon nap one day, she said, 'I haven't had a nap, so it isn't afternoon' (Shaffer 1996, 256).

**Egocentricity.** A view of the world that is centred on one's own perspective; a characteristic of preoperational thinking.

The transitional or intuitive stage begins around five years of age and the differences between the preconceptual and the intuitive stages are so slight, one wonders whether the preoperational stage actually warrants division into these two stages. The intuitive child is less egocentric and much better at classifying objects on the basis of perceptual categories such as size, shape, and colour. Piaget called the child's thinking at this stage *intuitive* because his or her understanding of objects and events still centres on their single most important characteristic, rather than on logical or rational thinking.

**Transductive reasoning.** Reasoning from the particular to the particular. Assuming, for example, that when any two events occur simultaneously, one has caused the other.

### How preoperational thinking differs from later cognitive stages

**Centration.** Focusing on only one physical aspect or dimension of an object or situation; a characteristic of preoperational thinking.

◆ Preoperational thinking tends to be **centred** on one physical aspect of an object or a situation. For example, when given six sticks of different lengths, the preoperational child can usually pick out the longest and shortest. But the child cannot line the sticks up from longest to shortest because this requires that he or she simultaneously judges that each stick is longer than the one before but shorter than the one after. This is because the child can only focus on one aspect or dimension of an object or situation at a time.

◆ The thinking of the preoperational child is concrete. He or she finds it difficult to deal with abstract concepts, such as honesty. Preoperational children's reliance on the concrete world for understanding often results in them confusing appearance with reality, as in thinking that non-documentary events on television are real.

**Irreversibility.** The belief that events and relationships occur only in one direction; a characteristic of preoperational thinking.

◆ The preoperational child's thinking tends to be **irreversible**. That is, events and relationships are believed to occur only in one direction. The child cannot imagine how things can return to their original state or go in two (or more) directions. According to Piaget, *reversibility* is the most clearly defined characteristic of intelligence. Lack of **reversibility** is illustrated in this excerpt from Piaget's child observation diary (Piaget 1952):

**Reversibility.** The ability to reverse an action by mentally performing the opposite action.

> *Piaget:* Do you have a sister?
> *Marie:* Yes.
> *Piaget:* What is her name?
> *Marie:* Stephanie.
> *Piaget:* Does Stephanie have a sister?
> *Marie:* No.

◆ Preoperational children tend to focus on present states of objects and not on processes of change. They judge things according to their present appearance and cannot understand how they came to be that way. An example of this is when the child is shown two identical balls of clay and one ball is transformed into various shapes, while the other is untouched. When the child is asked which ball has more clay, he or she may sometimes select the untouched ball, because it is fatter, and other times the transformed one, because it is longer or more spread out. The child never says that the two balls have the same amount of clay, although he or she is always shown how the one is changed. This is because the child is focusing on the current state of the object and not on the process of transformation. The child is also focusing on one dimension of the clay at a time such its 'flatness' or 'fatness'. This example also shows how the preoperational child's thinking is concrete, based on direct experience in the 'here and now', and it shows the irreversibility of the child's thinking – he or she is unable to reverse the clay ball back to its original state.

◆ Thinking tends to be egocentric or centred on the child's own perspective. For example, the child may think that other people cease to exist when they are not in sight. Research indicates, however, that young children may not be as egocentric as Piaget assumed and that he may have underestimated the ability of preschool children to understand events from another's point of view. Flavell, Everett, Croft, and Flavell (1981) showed three-year-olds a card with a picture of a dog on one side and a cat on the other. The card was then held in such a way that the child could see the dog and the tester could see the cat, and the child was asked which animal the tester could see. The three-year-olds answered correctly each time, indicating that they could assume the tester's perspective. Despite this and other findings (Ruffman, Olson, Ash, and Keenan 1993; Sodian, Taylor, Harris, and Perner 1991) that indicate that preoperational children are not as egocentric as Piaget believed, they tend nonetheless to rely on their own perspectives and therefore often fail when judging other people's motives. They often assume, also, that if they know something, others will too.

### Advances of the preoperational stage over the sensorimotor stage

*Symbolic representation* continues to develop in the preoperational child. Once children begin to use symbols, their thought processes become increasingly more complex. Pretend play, too, helps the child to understand the feelings and viewpoints of others. This increased sensitivity to others moves the child from egocentric thinking into more *sociocentric thinking*. Sociocentric thinking takes several years to develop, but has its roots in the symbolic representational abilities of the young child. In addition to symbolic representation, the preoperational child has an understanding of *cause and effect relationships*. Preoperational children are also able to classify objects into categories, for example, they know that mum and dad belong to the category of people.

Preoperational children begin to develop a rudimentary idea of numbers and what they represent. At some point, usually by three years of age, they understand *five basic principles of numeracy*:

♦ *The one to one principle*, that is, that you say only one number for each item being counted.
♦ *The stable order principle*, that is, that you say numbers in a fixed order.
♦ *The order irrelevance principle*, that is, you can start counting with any item and the total number will always be the same, for example, if counting 'Smarties', you can begin counting with any colour 'Smarty', and you will always reach the same total number (unless you eat some in the process, of course).
♦ *The cardinality principle*, that is, the last number name that you use is the total number of items.
♦ *The abstraction principle*, that is, that you can count all sorts of things, sweets, people, number of times jumping up in the air (Papalia and Olds 1998).

## Concrete operations (seven to eleven years)

Piaget saw the ages of five to seven as marking the transition from preoperational to concrete operational thought. At around seven years, the child moves into Piaget's stage of concrete operations. Piaget defined an *operation* as a *reversible mental action*. In the preoperational period, the child is unable to perform reversible mental actions, while in the concrete operations period, he or she can perform reversible mental actions on real, concrete objects, but not on abstract objects. Thinking now becomes less intuitive and egocentric and more logical, which is probably why most cultures choose this age for starting formal education (Papalia and Olds 1998).

**Figure 10.2** While the preoperational child may understand number concepts, the concept of conservation is not understood until the concrete operational stage.

### Advances of the concrete operational stage over the preoperational stage

A major difference between preoperational and concrete operational thinking is shown in the school-going child's use of logical inference. This is when a conclusion is reached through either seen or unseen evidence, as exemplified in Piaget's famous conservation of liquids experiment. In this experiment, preoperational children judge that a tall, narrow glass holds more water than a wide, short glass, although the liquid was poured into both containers from the same glass. Concrete operational children know that the differently shaped glasses contain the same amount of liquid. They realise how the liquid can be transformed by the shape of the container and remember how it appeared before it was poured into the glasses. These children display reversibility, or the ability to undo mentally the pouring process and imagine the water back in its original container, while preoperational children will point to one or the other glass as having more water.

Children in the concrete operational stage gradually master the concept of **conservation** in a series of stages. For instance, the conservation of number and weight is usually understood first (around seven or eight years) and conservation of area last (around eleven or twelve years). Piaget called this inconsistency in the development of a particular cognitive ability, such as conservation, *horizontal decalage*. Children in this stage find it difficult to transfer what they have learnt about one type of conservation to another type, such as from number conservation to length conservation, although the underlying principles are the same. One explanation for this is that problems of conservation, while appearing to be similar, actually differ in complexity.

The concrete operational child is able to understand **seriation** problems, that is, she or he can mentally classify objects by placing them in order according to one or more dimensions. This indicates **transitive inference** – the ability to mentally compare different objects and find similarities and differences between them. If, for example, Susan is shorter than Peter, and Peter is shorter than Mary, who is the shortest? It follows logically that Susan is the shortest, and the concrete operational child is able to understand the *transitivity* of these size relationships. The child is also able to focus on more than one feature of a problem simultaneously, an ability referred to as *decentration* (the opposite of centration).

Concrete operational children, unlike preoperational children, can theorise about the world. They can guess about things and test out their guesses, estimating for example how many breaths of air they can blow into a balloon before it pops or how many blue 'Smarties' it is necessary to eat for their entire tongue to turn blue. But this ability to theorise is limited to concrete objects that they can see. Children only develop theories about abstract concepts in the formal operations stage around eleven or twelve years of age.

The skills outlined above, which are characteristic of concrete operations, do not appear all at once or over a short period of time. Piaget (1952) maintained that operational abilities develop gradually and sequentially as the initial, basic skills are consolidated and reorganised into increasingly more complex mental structures.

## Formal operations (twelve years onwards)

Cognitive development at this stage is characterised by increased abstract thinking and the use of **metacognitive** skills (the ability to think about one's own mental processes). While younger children are more comfort-

**Conservation.** A cognitive capacity described by Piaget as particularly important during the concrete operational period. It refers to the ability to judge changes in amounts (liquid, area, volume, or mass) through logical deduction rather than on the basis of appearance.

**Seriation.** The ability to mentally classify objects by placing them in order (in series) according to one or more dimensions.

**Transitive inference.** The ability to mentally compare different objects and find similarities and differences between them.

**Metacognition.** The ability to reflect on one's own mental processes.

able with concrete, empirical facts, adolescents are able to think abstractly about possibilities and compare reality with things that might or might not be. Formal operational thought involves the ability to formulate, test, and evaluate hypotheses. It involves the manipulation of known facts as well as events contrary to fact. During this stage thinking becomes more systematic and the adolescent is able to plan and think ahead. In a study where tenth-graders, twelfth-graders, first-year college students and final-year college students were all asked to imagine and describe what they thought might happen to them in the future and to say how old they thought they would be when these events occurred, the older subjects could look farther into the future than the younger ones and their speculations about the future were far more specific (Greene 1990).

Formal operational thought is characterised as a *second-order process*. First-order processes of thinking entail discovering and examining relationships between objects. Second-order processes involve thinking about your own thoughts, looking for connections between relationships, and moving between reality and possibility. The three main characteristics of hypothetical-deductive formal operational thought are:

◆ the ability to combine all variables and find a solution to a problem,
◆ the ability to speculate about the effect one variable may have on another, and
◆ the ability to combine and separate variables in a logically formulaic manner, for example if X then Y (Piaget 1952).

Not all people are capable of thinking in formal operational terms – between one-third and one-half of American adults never attain this stage of formal operations, as measured by Piagetian tasks (Kohlberg and Gilligan 1971). This fact has lead many psychologists to believe that it should be considered an extension of concrete operations, rather than a separate stage (Piaget actually proposed this himself). Also, once formal operations have been attained, a person may not maintain them consistently. Many people, when confronted with unfamiliar problems in unfamiliar situations, will fall back on a more concrete type of reasoning (Piaget 1952). Does cognitive development then end with formal operations? Many theorists have proposed development beyond this final Piagetian stage.

## Post-formal operations

Research indicates that mature thinking may be far richer and more complex than is suggested by the abstract manipulations of formal operations (Labouvie-Vief 1985; Riegel 1984). **Post-formal thinking** (sometimes called **dialectic** or **relativistic** thinking) is flexible and adaptive, relying on intuition and logic. It is characterised by the ability to deal with uncertainty, inconsistency, contradiction, and compromise. Sinott (1984) proposed the following criteria of post-formal thought:

◆ the ability to shift between abstract reasoning and practical, real-life situations,
◆ awareness that most problems have more than one cause and more

**Post-formal thinking.** Also called dialectic or relativistic thinking, this refers to thinking that is flexible and adaptive, relying on intuition and logic. It is characterised by the ability to deal with uncertainty, inconsistency, contradiction, and compromise.

**Dialectic thinking.** See post-formal thinking.

**Relativistic thinking.** See post-formal thinking.

than one solution, and that some solutions may be more successful
than others,

◆ ability to choose the best of several possible solutions and to identify
the criteria upon which this choice is based, and

◆ recognition that a problem or solution involves inherent conflict.

Critics argue that the notion of a stage of post-formal thinking has no
research support. This means that future research needs to determine
whether post-formal thinking can be assessed by means of reliable and
objective measuring of its qualitative characteristics.

# Criticisms of Piaget's theory

Piaget's theory is one of the most enduring in the field of cognitive development since it has been in existence for over sixty-seven years, and continues to influence developmental psychologists today. However, much of
the interest in his theory now comes in the form of criticism. A few of the
major criticisms of Piaget's theory are outlined here.

## Cognitive development as a series of stages

Piaget held that his stages of intellectual development are holistic structures, or 'coherent modes of thinking that are applied across a broad
range of tasks' (Shaffer 1996, 274). However, the term 'stage' generally
implies that there are abrupt changes in intellectual functioning as the
child acquires higher-level abilities and progresses from one stage to the
next. Research indicates that transitions in intellectual ability actually
occur very gradually, and there is often a great deal of inconsistency in the
child's performance of tasks identified by Piaget to measure the abilities
that define a particular stage. For example, some concrete operational
children are capable of success in formal operational tasks, yet cannot
successfully complete all concrete operational tasks (Bjorklund 1995;
Flavell, Miller, and Miller 1993).

The issue of whether cognitive development occurs in stages is still
debated and much of this debate centres on the understanding of the
word 'stage'. Some theorists agree that cognitive development is coherent
and does progress through a series of stages (Flavell *et al.* 1993). Many
others, however, hold that cognitive development is a complex, multifaceted process in which children gradually acquire skills in a wide range
of areas such as visual spatial ability, mathematical reasoning, verbal reasoning, and so on (Bjorklund 1995). While development within each of
these areas may occur in a series of stages, one cannot assume consistency
across them. It appears that cognitive development does not occur in
stages that are as discrete or clear-cut as Piaget proposed.

## Underestimation of children's abilities

Piaget seems particularly to have underestimated the abilities of preoperational children. It has also been found that children who are not initially

capable of performing certain concrete or formal operational tasks can often be trained in these abilities. Four-year-old children, for instance, can be trained to perform successfully in conservation tasks (Bjorklund 1995). However, most of these training studies are limited to artificial training situations and the extent to which these skills can be generalised to everyday situations is as yet unknown.

## Competence versus performance

Piaget assumed that if a child failed on one of his tasks, it was because the child lacked the underlying competencies necessary to perform that task. However, this is an invalid assumption since there are many factors other than a lack of the underlying concepts that may undermine performance on a cognitive task. For example, young babies appeared to lack object permanence, because they were assessed on tasks that required them to perform motor actions which they were not yet capable of producing. When assessed with more age-appropriate methods, they display object permanence. Later on, Piaget (1972), realised that he may have been mistaken in this regard, when he discovered that adolescents are more likely to use formal operational thinking when solving familiar problems and concrete operational thinking when attempting to solve unfamiliar problems.

## Description or explanation of cognitive development?

Piaget does not clearly explain the underlying mechanisms that enable a child to move to progressively higher levels of intellectual functioning. Consequently, many researchers regard his theory as a detailed *description* of cognitive development as opposed to an *explanation* of how cognitive development occurs (Kuhn 1992).

## Failure to include social and cultural influences on cognitive development

Piaget did admit that cultural factors might influence the rate of cognitive development.

Research has shown that cultural factors may also influence *how* children think (Rogoff 1990). Piaget's theory gives insufficient attention to the ways in which children's social interactions with others may influence their cognitive development. Recall the image of the little scientist exploring the world, in relative isolation from everyone around her or him. It is now common knowledge that many of the child's competencies are gained through her or his interactions with peers, siblings, parents, and other caregivers. It was partly out of this area of shortcoming in Piaget's theory that Vygotsky's theory emerged, with its focus on socio-cultural influences on cognitive development.

# Vygotsky's theory of cognitive development

Lev Vygotsky (1896–1934) was born in the same year as Piaget, but died much younger, at the age of thirty-eight, before his theoretical work was complete. While he admired Piaget's work, Vygotsky felt that the latter had overlooked the impact of cultural context on development. Vygotsky's theory was strongly influenced by his Marxist background and he believed that interactions with others are essential for cognitive development. Vygotsky held that patterns of social interaction do not just 'assist' cognitive development, as Piaget believed, but that *social interaction determines the structure and pattern of internal cognition* (Vygotsky 1956). According to Vygotsky (1988, 74), 'the very mechanism underlying higher mental functions is a copy from social interaction; all higher mental functions are internalised social relationships'. The dominant theme of Vygotsky's theory is that cognitive development is inseparable from its *cultural context*. Some of the main aspects of Vygotsky's theory will be discussed below.

Lev Vygotsky

# Basic concepts underlying Vygotsky's theory

## Psychological tools

Vygotsky was influenced by the writings of Friedrich Engels, who explained how primitive people's development to the stage of tool use helped to increase their mastery over the environment. Vygotsky drew parallels between physical tools and symbolic, **psychological tools**. He proposed that people have psychological tools which help them to master their behaviour and their thoughts and which help to mediate their psychological processes. Vygotsky called these psychological tools *signs* and said that it is impossible to understand human thinking without examining the signs that cultures provide. The most important sign system or psychological tool that humans use to govern their behaviour is *speech*. It enables us to move from the present situation, to think about both past and future, and it enables the developing child to participate in the social life of his or her cultural group. Other important psychological tools are *writing and numbering systems*. Writing enables us to keep a permanent record of information, while numbering systems help us to quantify objects. These tools teach children how to use their basic mental abilities more adaptively as, for example, a school-age child may learn that she or he can remember things more efficiently by noting them down (Vygotsky 1956).

## Higher and lower mental processes

Vygotsky's chief concern was with those exclusively human cognitive abilities, which he referred to as **higher mental functions** as opposed to

**Psychological tools.** Vygotsky's term for cognitive abilities and strategies that enable us to use our mental abilities more adaptively. For example, mnemonics help us to remember information better.

**Higher mental functions.** Vygotsky's term for those sophisticated cognitive processes such as focused attention, deliberate memory, and symbolic thought, which evolve out of basic cognitive abilities such as reactive attention, associative memory, and sensory motor (lower mental functions) as a result of exposure to one's culture.

Through guided learning, the adult shifts the child's zone of proximal development to ever higher levels.

**Lower mental functions.** Vygotsky's term for those basic cognitive abilities such as reactive attention, associative memory, and sensory motor thought, which are eventually transformed by a person's culture into more sophisticated mental processes such as focused attention, deliberate memory, and symbolic thought (higher mental functions).

**lower mental functions.** Lower mental functions include reactive attention, associative memory, and sensory motor thought and are eventually transformed by a person's culture into more sophisticated mental processes (higher mental functions) such as focused attention, deliberate memory, and symbolic thought.

Higher mental functions are qualitatively different from the lower, natural processes of basic memory, attention, sensation, and perception. Perhaps the easiest way of making the distinction between higher and lower mental functions is to think of the higher order mammals: at some very basic level these mammals – like human infants – can remember, be attentive, and even in some rudimentary way, prove to be intelligent, or communicative. Nevertheless, these cognitive abilities are fundamentally limited. Animals do not have the variety of internal mental tools that adult humans do – they cannot use language, writing, counting, mnemonic devices, or sophisticated categories. These internal mental tools are largely language-based and it is these psychological tools that Vygotsky classified as higher mental functions.

In the early stages of cognitive development a child's operations with quantities are spontaneous and perceptual in nature. The child is not 'counting' in the proper sense of the word, but is rather 'immediately perceiving' the quantity before her or him. In older children this primitive type of 'arithmetic' is replaced by a more sophisticated approach that makes use of certain tools, such as fingers and self-directing speech.

## The zone of proximal development (ZPD)

**Zone of proximal development.** Vygotsky's term for tasks too difficult for children to master alone, but which can be mastered with the guidance and assistance of adults or more skilled, usually older, children.

The zone of proximal development is 'the distance between the actual developmental level as determined by independent problem solving and the level of potential development as determined through problem solving under adult guidance or in collaboration with more capable peers' (Vygotsky 1956, 86). The zone of proximal development is Vygotsky's term for tasks too difficult for children to master alone, but which can be mastered with the guidance and assistance of adults or more skilled, usually older, children. Thus, the lower limit of the ZPD is the level of problem solving reached by a child working independently. The upper limit is the level of additional problem solving that the child is capable of, given the assistance of an able instructor (this may be an older sibling, parent, caregiver, or teacher). The child's own knowledge develops from the assistance of adults or older children, who guide the child towards more sophisticated solutions in a task. Vygotsky's emphasis on the ZPD underscored his belief in the importance of social influences on cognitive development and the role of instruction in cognitive development, since it involves the child working together with others. He held that instruction

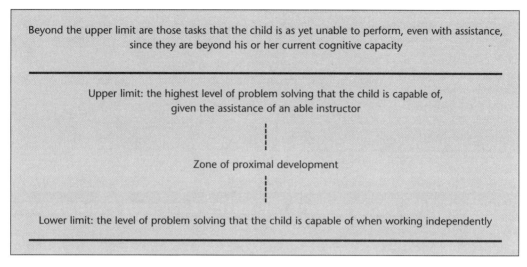

Beyond the upper limit are those tasks that the child is as yet unable to perform, even with assistance, since they are beyond his or her current cognitive capacity

Upper limit: the highest level of problem solving that the child is capable of, given the assistance of an able instructor

Zone of proximal development

Lower limit: the level of problem solving that the child is capable of when working independently

**Figure 10.3** Schematic representation of the zone of proximal development.

is essential for a child to reach the highest levels of thinking (Vygotsky 1988).

Like Piaget, Vygotsky saw the child as an active participant in his or her own learning. However, the two theorists differed in their view of the instructor's role in the learning process. Piaget saw a child's learning as a relatively independent process of self-discovery, whereas Vygotsky saw the teacher as an active participant in the child's learning, structuring the learning activity, providing hints and instructions that are appropriate to the child's current abilities, monitoring his or her progress, and gradually allowing him or her to perform more of the mental work (Shaffer 1996).

In an attempt to determine how effective Vygotsky's idea of guided learning is, Freund (1990) asked a group of children between the ages of three and five years to help a puppet decide which furnishings should be placed in each of six rooms of a doll's house. First, Freund assessed what the children already knew about the placement of furniture. Next, each child worked at a similar task, either alone (in the manner of Piaget's discovery-based learning) or with his or her mother (as in the manner of Vygotsky's guided learning). To assess what the children had learned, they were each given another, more complex, furniture-sorting task. The findings indicated that the children who had been assisted by their mothers were significantly better at the furniture sorting than the children who had worked independently. Similar positive effects have been found in children's problem-solving abilities when they collaborate with peers rather than working on a problem alone (Azmitia 1992). Although these findings indicate that children learn more effectively when given some guidance in the process, it is likely that a combination of guided and independent learning is necessary for effective learning to occur

Vygotsky's theorising about the ZPD shows that one of the primary contributions that his work makes is in the field of education, learning, and teaching. According to Vygotsky, teaching (whether formal or informal) often takes the form of a guided arrangement, especially in parent-child interactions, where the level of parental involvement is gradually

**Scaffolding.** Adjusting the guidance given during a learning session to fit the student's current performance level.

decreased as the child gains mastery over the task. Wood, Bruner, and Ross (1976) use the term **scaffolding** to describe the support provided by the parent or teacher that allows the child to extend skills to higher levels of competence, during which progression the scaffolding is gradually removed. Reuven Feuerstein, an Israeli professor of psychology and a student of Piaget's, developed the notion of mediated learning from Vygotsky's ZPD. Mediated learning occurs when a human mediator interposes him- or herself between the learning child and the world in order to interpret, guide, and give meaning to the child's experiences with the world (Mentis, Dunn, Durbach, Arnott, Mentis, and Skuy 1991).

# Feuerstein's construct of Mediated Learning Experience

Feuerstein's construct of Mediated Learning Experience (MLE) and his structured Instrumental Enrichment (IE) programme of cognitive development have been used successfully to improve the thinking skills of a range of populations, for example retarded adolescents, disadvantaged elementary school children, deaf students, learning-disabled students, and gifted, disadvantaged students (Skuy, Lomofsky, Fridjohn, and Green 1993).

In South Africa, MLE and IE have proven effective in improving the self-concept and academic and creative skills of disadvantaged students. In the study by Skuy, Mentis, Durbach, Cockcroft, Fridjohn, and Mentis (1995) the IE thinking skills programme was combined with teacher training in MLE skills, and carried out with three different primary school groups in the mining town of Lime Acres. The groups were a) Afrikaans- and English-speaking white children, b) coloured (mixed race) children and c) black children.

The children were pre-tested on a range of cognitive, creativity, and self-concept measures prior to the intervention, and they were post-tested on the same measures after a one-year intervention during which IE and MLE skills were incorporated into the school curriculum. On the cognitive level, all three groups showed significant improvement after the intervention, with the black children improving the most of all groups. The coloured and black children also improved significantly in terms of their self-concept and creative ability. Overall, the improvements for the black children were significantly greater than for the others, which was expected in terms of their educational deprivation under apartheid.

An important achievement of this study was to demonstrate the effectiveness of MLE and IE for different socio-cultural, ethnic, and language groups. This is an important achievement in view of South Africa's multicultural composition.

## Private speech

**Private speech.** Vygotsky's term for talking aloud to oneself. Piaget called this egocentric speech.

**Egocentric speech.** See private speech.

Anyone having contact with young children will have noticed that they talk to themselves a lot, sometimes more than they talk to others. This **private speech** is an essential part of cognitive development for all children. Vygotsky was the first psychologist to document its importance and there has been much debate about its purpose and value. Piaget called it **egocentric speech** because the child does not adjust her speech to the perspective of the listener, but egocentrically assumes that the listener's perspective is the same as her own. Further, Piaget said this type of speech reflects social and cognitive immaturity and has no positive role in normal cognitive development. Vygotsky, on the other hand, believed that private speech plays a special role as a guide to help the child master his or her actions, and it eventually fades away as the child becomes able to do this silently. Vygotsky also believed that children who engage in a large amount of private speech are more socially competent than those who do not use it extensively. He argued that private speech represents an early transition in becoming more socially communicative and that the development of private or **inner speech** is a process of internalising social interactions. This starts as an interpersonal process, occurring between the child and adult, usually the caregiver, and ultimately becomes an intra-psychic process, which occurs within the child. Vygotsky (1988) believed that this pattern – the development from interpersonal or social to intra-psychic or personal – occurs in all aspects of the child's cognitive development:

**Inner speech.** Vygotsky's term for the silent speech used to guide thought and behaviour.

> every function in the child's cultural development appears twice;
> first, on the social level, and later on the individual level; first,
> between people [inter-psychic], and then inside the child [intra-
> psychic]. This applies equally to voluntary attention, to logical
> memory, and to the formulation of concepts. All higher functions
> originate as actual relations between human individuals
> (Vygotsky 1978 in Lock, Service, Brito, and Chandler 1989, 57).

Research supports Vygotsky's interpretation of the usefulness of private speech in cognitive development. Berk (1986) attempted to discover whether all children engage in private speech, whether it really emerges from social communication, and whether it helps to guide the child's actions. Through observational studies of young children, he found that what Piaget referred to as egocentric speech (speech that is not addressed to anyone in particular nor adapted in any way so that another might understand it) seldom occurred. Most of the private speech that the children engaged in served to describe or guide the child's actions – consistent with Vygotsky's assumption that self-guidance is the central function of private speech. Berk also found that children talked to themselves more often when working alone on challenging tasks and also when their teacher was not immediately available to help them, that is, when the child needed to take charge of her or his own behaviour. In addition, Berk found evidence that private speech develops similarly in all children irrespective of cultural background, and that it arises from social experience, as Vygotsky had maintained.

Vygotsky believed that language plays a critical role in cognitive development, eventually becoming one of the most important 'tools' of intellectual adaptation. His and Piaget's views on the relationship between language and thought will be discussed in Chapter 12.

## Criticisms of Vygotsky's theory

Vygotsky's theory has not received the intense scrutiny that Piaget's has, partly because some of his works have only recently been translated from

Russian. The main criticism of his works is whether it is applicable to all cultures. Despite Vygotsky's claims that his ideas are culturally universal, Rogoff (1990) argues that the use of guided learning – which is heavily dependent on verbal instruction – may not be equally useful in all cultures or for all types of learning. In some cases, observation and practice may be more useful ways of learning particular skills.

# Information-processing theory and connectionist models

## Mind as computer

This approach to cognitive development is very different from the last two as it is based on a computer analogy for the way the mind receives, processes, and stores information received from the external environment. The information-processing approach attempts to identify what happens during these stages. The 'hardware' that information-processing theorists deal with is the cells and grey matter of the brain and the 'software' is the learned strategies for processing information. We are constantly processing information by selectively attending to and perceiving certain information above others and by operating or acting on that information. This information is also stored in our memories, to be retrieved when needed.

**Functionalism.** An approach to cognition that is concerned with how cognitive processes actually function or work.

## A functionalist approach

The information-processing approach developed as part of the reaction to behaviourism in the 1960s, which resulted in the foundation of cognitive psychology as a discipline. At that time, technological developments in telecommunications, human-factors engineering, and digital computers resulted in analogous developments in psychological theory, particularly with regard to the processing of information (Sternberg 1996). Analogies between the human mind and computers provided the framework used by information-processing theorists to explain how children take in information and use it to solve problems. There is no single information-processing theory of cognition, rather many models which attempt to explain different cognitive processes.

This approach is called a **functionalist** approach as it is concerned with how cognitive processes actually function or work (Sternberg 1996). Information-processing theorists hold that we are born with identical representational and computational systems that are genetically prestructured. However, each child is exposed to different environmental factors, which result in individual differences between us. As the child's brain and nervous system develops, and as he or she learns new problem-solving, attention, and memory

PHOTO: GILL HAIDEN

*A central tenet of the information-processing approach is that cognitive functioning can be likened in many ways to the processing of a computer.*

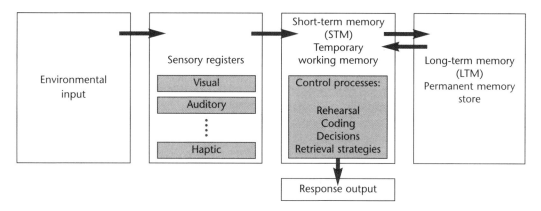

**Figure 10.4** Atkinson and Shiffrin's model of memory (1968).

strategies, the child becomes capable of performing cognitive tasks with greater speed and accuracy (Shaffer 1996).

Information-processing theorists that are interested in cognitive development study how children encode information, that is, how they identify key aspects of an object or event in order to form an internal representation of that object or event. They also formulate models to predict how we encode and process information. These models assume sequential stages of cognitive processing that are usually represented in the form of a flowchart. One of the most commonly known of these models is Atkinson and Shiffrin's (1968) model of how the human memory functions. (A more detailed discussion of this model is included in Chapter 13 on memory development.)

The main assumptions of information-processing theories are:

◆ People process information, that is, we mentally act on information in order to know it.
◆ People have limited processing capacity, that is, we can deal with only a certain amount of information at a given time.
◆ Information moves through the cognitive system, and the pathways between input, storage, and output can be depicted schematically as a flowchart.

More recently, it has been discovered that cognitive processes are unlikely to occur serially or in the orderly fashion as portrayed in flowcharts. This has led to the development of an approach called *connectionism*, which looks at the associations between knowledge and mental processes.

## Connectionism

**Connectionism** is an interdisciplinary approach that draws on ideas from artificial intelligence, psycholinguistics, cognitive psychology, and neuropsychology. This approach, often termed **parallel distributed processing** (PDP), is based on an understanding of the interconnections between the neurons in the brain. Each neuron is connected to many other neurons, forming large and complex neural networks. Neurons produce

**Connectionism.** An interdisciplinary approach that draws on ideas from artificial intelligence, psycholinguistics, cognitive psychology, and neuropsychology. Also referred to as parallel distributed processing, this approach models cognitive processes as interconnectioned patterns of activity.

**Parallel distributed processing.** See connectionism.

certain electro-chemicals that may either excite or inhibit other neurons, causing them to fire. Using this analogy, connectionist models conceive of information as being stored in a pattern of excited or inhibited elements called nodes, which are functionally similar to neurons.

Each node is connected to many other nodes. When a person's perceptual system is stimulated – by hearing a particular word for example – some nodes related to the perception and comprehension of that word will 'fire', while others that are not related to it will be inhibited. The connections between the 'firing' nodes are strengthened each time that word is perceived. There is some debate as to whether it is the pattern of connections that represents the knowledge (which may be concepts or any other type of information) or whether the specific nodes represent this knowledge (McClelland and Rumelhart 1985). The development of connectionist networks is affected by the stimulation received through the senses and continues throughout one's life. As more information becomes available, the system is extended and modified to assimilate or accommodate it.

The main difference between the information-processing and connectionist explanations concerns the level and the process of information storage. Information-processing models have information stored as 'symbols' or meaningful units in a long-term memory. Connectionist models store information as a pattern of excited and inhibited nodes in an interconnected network.

# Criticisms of the information-processing approach

Although information processing remains one of the dominant perspectives in cognitive development, its models are constantly being tested, challenged, and modified. The following are some of the main criticisms of this approach.

## The role of external factors

This approach gives little attention to the role of social and cultural factors in cognitive development. In view of Vygotsky's emphasis on these factors, their omission in the information-processing account appears as a major shortcoming.

## Fragmented view of the individual

Individual cognitive functioning is generally broken down into models depicting the functioning of different cognitive 'systems' and development is regarded as occurring at differential rates and manners in these systems. This is in contrast to Piaget's theory, which proposes that development occurs in a more or less homogenous way across different cognitive domains.

## Oversimplification of human cognitive functioning

The mind-computer analogy which information processing theorists draw on has been criticised for being too simplistic an explanation of human cognitive functioning. Unlike computers, human thinking is influenced by emotions and motivations. Unlike computers, humans are capable of creating, dreaming, and introspection. Psychologists are increasingly concerned with the biological bases of cognition and its development. This has not been a traditional concern of the information-processing approach, and critics argue that new theories must take into account the relationship between brain structure and cognitive processing when developing models of human cognition. Some of the challenges to the information-processing approach come from the developing field of *cognitive science*. This new approach combines traditional cognitive psychology with the fields of linguistics, artificial intelligence, evolutionary biology and neurobiology, among others, to give a much richer perspective of human cognition.

# Recommended readings

Bjorklund, D. F. (1995). *Children's thinking: Developmental function and individual differences.* Pacific Grove, CA: Brooks-Cole.

Flavell, J. H., Miller, P. H., and Miller, S. A. (1993). *Cognitive development.* Englewood Cliffs, NJ: Prentice Hall.

Kozulin, A. (1990). *Vygotsky's psychology: A biography of ideas.* Cambridge, MA: Harvard University Press.

Piaget, J. (1952). *The origins of intelligence in children.* New York: International Universities Press.

## Critical thinking tasks

### Specific tasks

1) What is the significance of symbolic representation for cognitive development?

2) Compare and contrast Piaget's and Vygotsky's theories. Focus on specific themes, for example, private speech, or the relationship between language and thought (see Chapter 12 on Language Development for more information on this aspect).

3) How does the information-processing approach to cognitive development reflect our technological society? Provide examples to illustrate and explain your answer.

### General tasks

1) How do cognitive theories help us to make predictions about development and behaviour?

2) Create your own theory of cognitive development by combining those aspects of the theories discussed above that you feel are most important for explaining cognitive development. Justify your choices.

# 11

# Intellectual development

*Kate Cockcroft*

---

This chapter provides a brief overview of the different approaches to intelligence and its development. It covers the following:

1. The psychometric approach to intelligence.

2. Criticisms of the psychometric approach to intelligence.

3. The cognitive approach to intelligence.

4. Criticisms of the cognitive approach to intelligence.

5. The concept of 'emotional intelligence'.

6. Changes in intelligence.

---

## Introduction

Often the terms *intellectual development* and *cognitive development* are used interchangeably. This is because intelligence generally encompasses all cognitive abilities (attention, perception, memory, language, concept formation, and problem solving all feed into our intellectual ability). This chapter explores how our intellectual competence increases as we develop. You will note, however, that a substantial portion of this chapter is devoted to explaining the different theories of intelligence. This is necessary in order to illustrate the extent to which the theories do or do not attempt to account for intellectual change over time. The chapter starts with an attempt to define what intelligence is. It then looks at the various approaches to intelligence and its development, and finally it considers a few of the more interesting topics that have been linked to intelligence, such as the concept of emotional intelligence and the links between intelligence and creativity.

## What is intelligence?

The short answer to this question is, as Pyle (1979) puts it, 'We don't know.' Intelligence has been given many definitions by different philosophers, psychologists, and researchers. Here are a few of them (from Pyle 1979, 3):

*Binet:* to judge well, to comprehend well, to reason well.
*Terman:* the capacity to form concepts and to grasp their significance.
*Wechsler:* the global capacity of the individual to act purposefully, to think rationally and to deal effectively with the environment.
*Piaget:* adaptation to the physical and social environment.

All of the theorists mentioned above stress the ability to reason as an important part of intelligence, but they each tend to focus on different aspects of intelligence – biologists, such as Piaget, stress the ability to adapt to the demands of the environment, while educationalists, such as Binet, stress the ability to learn. Debate about what exactly intelligence is continues even today. Detterman and Sternberg (1986), in an attempt to find a shared definition of intelligence, asked the main theorists in the field each to provide their own definition. The responses were then analysed for frequencies of mentioned attributes. Twenty-five attributes were mentioned, but only three of these, namely biological, cognitive/ motivational, and behavioural/environmental factors, were mentioned by twenty-five per cent or more of the theorists. One of the reasons why there is still no common definition of intelligence is because different theorists make different assumptions about the structure and stability of those attributes that they view as indications of intelligent behaviour (Shaffer 1996). The fact that 'intelligence' seems to mean different things to different psychologists has led to a recent suggestion that it is better understood, not as a fixed phenomenon existing within people, but as one created through social activities and represented between people as a social construct (Mugny and Carugati 1989).

## Intelligence as a social construct

According to Mugny and Carugati (1989), our social world provides certain 'signals' of intellectual inferiority or superiority, which we conceptualise as part of intelligence. These signals have been shown to include quite superficial aspects such as personal appearance (wearing glasses or having a high forehead), social class dialect, and self-presentation. We then attribute 'intelligence' differentially to people according to the extent to which they display the accepted signals. The task of a scientific study of intelligence as a social construct is to demonstrate how such representations are related to particular social contexts, and how they bear on children's development.

Francis Galton

# Perspectives on intellectual development

There are two main perspectives on intellectual development: the psychometric approach, begun by Sir Francis Galton, which led to the creation and use of intelligence tests, and approaches that focus on the cognitive processes underlying intelligence. (Piaget's theory, discussed in the previous chapter, fits in with the latter approach.) Each of the approaches is briefly discussed below.

**Psychometric approach.** Theories of intelligence which are based on the assumption that intelligence can be described in terms of mental factors, and that tests can be developed which measure individual differences in these factors.

# The psychometric approach to intelligence

The **psychometric approach** is concerned with attempts to measure intelligence (whatever it may be). This approach was initiated by Sir Francis Galton, a cousin of Charles Darwin, who, like Plato, favoured a eugenics breeding programme for the improvement of intelligence in society. Galton is credited with making the first scientific attempt to measure intelligence. Between 1884 and 1890, he ran a service at the South Kensington Museum in London, where, for a small fee, visitors could have their intelligence checked. For example, he invented a whistle, which, he claimed, could tell him the highest pitch a person could perceive. Other tests involved determining the weight of gun cartridges or how much pressure on the forehead was necessary to cause pain! When correlations were run to determine whether performance on Galton's 'intelligence tests' was related to school and college marks, the findings were unsurprisingly negative (Robinson 1981).

Alfred Binet

### The Binet-Simon Intelligence Test

The first real breakthrough in the measurement of intelligence was the work of Alfred Binet. He was commissioned to devise a test to predict school performance and, especially, to distinguish children who were genuinely mentally retarded from those who had behavioural problems, but whose mental processes were intact. Together with his colleague, Theodore Simon, Binet developed the Binet-Simon Intelligence Test. This test measured a range of abilities such as vocabulary, verbal comprehension, verbal relations, and repeating a sequence of numbers, and it summarised performance as a Mental Age (MA) score (Robinson 1981). The majority of eight-year-olds would manage the items at the eight-year-old level, and so could be said to have a Mental Age of eight. If an eight-year-old could only manage up to the six-year-old level of the test and no further, then, although his or her *chronological age* (CA) is eight, his or her **mental age** is said to be six. The idea of using MA and CA to determine a person's *intelligence quotient* (IQ) was developed in 1914 by Stern, who devised the following formula (Pyle 1979):

**Mental age.** Level of mental functioning (in years) as determined by the number of items passed on a test (usually an IQ test). Previously, mental age was used in the calculation of IQ scores, today deviation IQs are used.

$$\text{Intelligence quotient (IQ)} = \frac{\text{Mental Age (MA)}}{\text{Chronological Age (CA)}} \times 100$$

## Army Alpha and Beta Tests

During World War I, intelligence testing acquired greater importance as psychologists were required to develop a method to screen potential soldiers. This led to the development of the Army Alpha test (a verbal test for English speakers) and Beta test (a non-verbal test, with pantomimed instructions for non-English speakers). These tests could be administered in groups.

## The Stanford-Binet Intelligence Scale

Shortly afterwards, a series of tests was evolved to measure various kinds of achievements and abilities including IQ, scholastic aptitude, academic aptitude, and related constructs. In 1916, Lewis Terman of Stanford University published a revision of the Binet-Simon intelligence test, which was similar in structure to the original test, but included more items (ninety in total). This test, which became known as the Stanford-Binet Intelligence Scale, was so successful at predicting school performance that a revised version is still in use today, mainly in the United States (Robinson 1981).

Lewis Terman

## The Wechsler Adult Intelligence Scale

David Wechsler, an American psychologist, believed that the Stanford-Binet test was not very useful for assessing adults, and so devised the Wechsler Adult Intelligence Scale (WAIS) in the 1930s. Shortly afterwards, he also developed the Wechsler Intelligence Scale for Children (WISC) and the Wechsler Preschool and Primary Scale of Intelligence (WPPSI), both of which, in revised format, are still in use today. In South Africa, the Junior South African Individual Scales (JSAIS) were developed in 1979 to assess scholastic and intellectual functioning in English- and Afrikaans-speaking white children between the ages of three and seven years. The Senior South African Individual Scales - Revised (SSAIS-R), were first developed in 1964 to gauge intellectual functioning in white and Indian English- or Afrikaans-speaking children between the ages of five and seventeen years. Individual Scales have also been recently developed for each of the different cultural groups in South Africa, for example, Zulu, Xhosa, Tswana, and North and South Sotho. These are generally for school-age children and adolescents up to nineteen years old. The South African Wechsler Adult Individual Scale (SAWAIS) was modelled on the Wechsler-Bellevue Adult Intelligence Scale in 1969 for English- and Afrikaans-speaking white South Africans and is currently undergoing revision (Owen and Taljaard 1989).

**Factor analysis.** A statistical technique used to find clusters of IQ test items that are highly correlated with one another but unrelated to all of the remaining items in the test. The clusters of items are called factors, and each factor is believed to represent a distinct mental ability.

## Spearman's two-factor model of intelligence

Some psychometric theorists challenged the idea that all that is intelligence can be captured by a single IQ score, particularly since intelligence

Charles Spearman

**g (Spearman's g; general mental ability).** The idea that intelligence can be expressed as a single general mental ability that flows into performance on all cognitive tasks.

tests consisted of a range of sub-tests. These theorists proposed that these sub-tests might represent distinct mental abilities rather than a single, general ability. The performance of great numbers of individuals on intelligence tests was subject to a type of statistical analysis called factor analysis, in order to investigate whether intelligence is a single attribute or many different attributes. **Factor analysis**, very simply put, is a technique for finding clusters of test items that are highly correlated with one another but unrelated to all of the remaining items in the test. The clusters of items are called factors, and each factor is believed to represent a distinct mental ability (Shaffer 1996).

Charles Spearman developed factor analytic methods and used them to investigate relations among intelligence test scores. He found that children's scores were moderately correlated across a range of cognitive tasks, and so concluded that there must be a general mental ability, later designated as 'g', which flows into performance on all of these tasks. However, Spearman also noted that there were inconsistencies in intellectual performance, so that a person who excelled at most cognitive tasks may perform poorly on a particular test, such as mathematical reasoning. He proposed a *two-factor model of intelligence*, which stated that, in addition to general ability (*g*), intellectual ability also consists of specific abilities, designated as 's', which are specific to performance on a particular task (Pyle 1979). The best evidence for the existence of *g* is what has been termed the *positive manifold* – the frequent finding of high correlations among scores on sets of cognitive tasks that have little in common with one another in terms of content or strategies used (Bjorklund 1995).

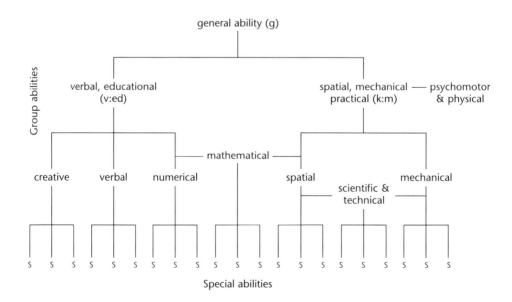

**Figure 11.1** Schematic representation of Spearman's two-factor model of intelligence.

## Thurstone's primary mental abilities

Several years later, Louis Thurstone factor-analysed the test scores of approximately fifty intelligence tests, and found seven factors, which he called **primary mental abilities**. These were spatial ability, perceptual speed (how quickly you can process visual information), numerical reasoning, verbal meaning (defining words), word fluency (how quickly you can recognise words), memory, and inductive reasoning (generating a rule based on partial information). All the primary mental abilities were held to be quite basic, with none assuming more importance than any other.

## Guilford's structure of intellect model

J. P. Guilford believed that a model of intelligence based on *g* or broad group factors was far too simplistic, and he proposed that there were at least 180 distinct mental abilities, if not more. He argued that to group them together under broad headings such as 'visuo-spatial ability' did not do justice to describing the richness and complexity of human intelligence. He based his 'structure of intellect' model on three facets: 1) content (what the person must think about, for example, letter symbols or numerical symbols), 2) operations (the kind of thinking the person needs to perform, for example, recognising information in symbolic form and holding it in memory), and 3) products (the kind of answer that is required, for example, speaking a word, or pressing a button). He proposed that there are five types of content, six possible operations, and six products, which allow for up to 180 primary mental abilities (5 X 6 X 6).

There is much respect for Guilford's attempt to broaden the view of intelligence. His model is based on evidence from genetics, neurology, the biological sciences, and experimental psychology. Guilford's next task was to construct tests to measure each of his 180 mental abilities, and to

**s (Spearman's s; specific mental ability).** The idea that intellectual ability consists of specific abilities (s), which are specific to performance on a particular task.

**Primary mental abilities.** Thurstone's seven mental factors, determined by subjecting IQ test scores to factor analyses. These basic abilities include spatial ability, perceptual speed, numerical reasoning, verbal meaning, word fluency, memory, and inductive reasoning.

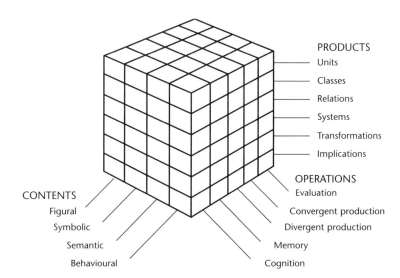

**Figure 11.2** Guilford's structure of intellect model.

date there are tests that assess over 100 of the mental abilities in his model. However, findings have indicated that scores on these tasks are often correlated, suggesting that the abilities they measure are not as independent as Guilford assumed (Brody 1992).

## Hierarchical models of intelligence

Many psychometricians today use a hierarchical model of intellect. In this model intelligence is viewed as consisting of a general ability factor at the top of the hierarchy, which influences performance on all cognitive tasks, as well as several specific ability factors (similar to Thurstone's primary mental abilities), which influence performance in particular areas of intellectual functioning, such as a test of numerical reasoning (Shaffer 1996).

## Fluid intelligence

**Fluid intelligence or $G_f$.** The ability to solve novel and abstract problems of the sort that are not taught and are relatively free of cultural influences.

The final psychometric approach is that of Raymond Cattell and John Horn. They proposed that Spearman's $g$ and Thurstone's primary mental abilities could be divided into two major dimensions, namely *fluid* and *crystallised intelligence* (Horn and Cattell 1982). **Fluid intelligence or $G_f$** is the 'ability to solve novel and abstract problems of the sort that are not taught and are relatively free of cultural influences' (Shaffer 1996, 336), such as verbal analogies. Fluid intelligence is a measure of the influence of biological factors. It is comparable to inherited ability and is believed to flow (hence the term 'fluid') into a wide variety of intellectual activities. In contrast, **crystallised intelligence or $G_c$** is 'the ability to solve problems that depends on knowledge acquired as a result of schooling and other life experiences' (Shaffer 1996, 336), such as general knowledge questions. Research indicates that $G_f$ and $G_c$, in reality, are difficult to separate.

**Crystallised intelligence or $G_c$.** The ability to solve problems that depends on knowledge acquired as a result of schooling and other life experiences.

# The Learning Propensity Assessment Device

Departing radically from conventional psychometric testing, with its static, product-oriented approach, Reuven Feuerstein has formulated a dynamic assessment and intervention model, called the Learning Propensity Assessment Device (LPAD). This model assesses an individual's learning processes, obtains a measure of learning potential, and provides the opportunity to modify the deficient cognitive functions that are identified. This approach to assessment, known as learning potential assessment or dynamic assessment, raises questions about traditional conceptualisa-

tions of intelligence, particularly since tests of learning potential do not correlate highly with traditional measures of intelligence. The response to this is that either IQ or learning potential is not a valid measure of intelligence. Given the controversy around the definition of intelligence, this is not surprising. All that can be concluded from the available evidence is that the two phenomena are different: IQ is not learning ability. 'Whether either or neither is "intelligence" remains to be studied and debated' (Lidz 1991, 4).

## Culture-fair intelligence testing

Culture-fair tests are tests that are designed not to be culturally biased. Some would argue that no such test exists, since it may be impossible to rule out the role of experience in relation to socio-economic and ethnic background. Many intelligence tests are clearly culturally biased, favouring urban dwellers over rural dwellers, people from high socio-economic backgrounds to those from lower socio-economic backgrounds, or white people over black, coloured, or Indian people. For example, one item on an intelligence test for children, which has subsequently been revised, asked, 'What would you do if you found a three-year-old child in the street?' The correct answer was, 'Call the police'. However, children who may have negative perceptions of the police are unlikely to choose this answer. Such an item does not measure the knowledge necessary to adapt to one's environment. Furthermore, cultural attitudes can affect how well a person does in a testing situation. For example, a person from a culture that stresses sociability and cooperation may be handicapped in taking a test alone, or a person from a culture that stresses slow, painstaking, and precise work, may be handicapped in a timed test (Kottak 1994). These factors are still seldom taken into account in testing situations.

**Culture-fair tests.** Tests that are designed not to be culturally biased, usually by removing the language component.

# Critical evaluation of the psychometric approach

Many difficulties have arisen out of the attempts to measure intelligence and some of these will be discussed here.

## Assessing infant intelligence

Testing infants' and toddlers' intelligence is difficult, mainly because most tests are language-based and very young children have limited language abilities and attention spans. Intelligence tests for infants tend to focus on motor abilities (what the child can do and what she or he is used to doing) and on developmental milestones, as in the Bayley Scales of Infant Development (Bayley 1993). This test calculates a Developmental Quotient (DQ) rather than an IQ, and compares it to the norm group. Generally, infants' (children under two years) intelligence test scores tend to be unreliable. That is, they tend to vary markedly from one test occasion to the next.

## Infant ability as a predictor of later IQ

Infant's IQ scores tend to be poor predictors of future functioning. It is not until a child is about three years old that the child's IQ score, as well as factors such as the parents' IQ and educational level, enable more accurate prediction of later intellectual ability. Of a group of toddlers who were tested at two and a half years and again at seventeen years, one in seven showed an increase of forty IQ points or more. Since an IQ score of 100 means an average IQ and 140 means a gifted IQ, this is quite a marked difference. Developmental scales have value in that they enable one to trace a baby's developmental progress and allow for the diagnosis of neurological and cognitive disorders, but they are also poor predictors of the child's later IQ or scholastic achievement (Rose, Feldman, Wallace, and McCarton 1989). The main reason for this discrepancy is that tests for very young children tend to focus on sensory and motor abilities, while tests for older children measure verbal, mathematical, and spatial reasoning (Bornstein and Sigman 1986).

## School-age IQ scores as predictors of later achievement

For school-going children, IQ test scores are quite good predictors of school performance. Conventional intelligence tests correlate between 0.4 and 0.6 (on a 0 to 1 scale) with school marks, which, statistically speaking, is quite a good level of correlation. However, a test that predicts performance with a correlation of $r = 0.5$ only accounts for about twenty-five per cent of the variation in individual performances, leaving seventy-five per cent unexplained. Therefore, there is much more to school performance than only IQ. The predictive validity of IQ tests decreases when they are used to forecast performance in later life, such as salary, job performance, or even the likelihood of obtaining a job. Generally, the correlations are slightly over $r = 0.3$, which means that the tests account for approximately ten per cent of the variation in people's performance, while ninety per cent remains unexplained (Ceci 1990). Further, IQ prediction is even less effective when populations, situations, or tasks change. Fiedler (in Ceci 1990) found that IQ positively predicts leadership success under conditions of low stress, but in high stress situations the tests negatively predict leadership success. Research has shown that the IQ scores of most students improve when they are taught to think analytically, creatively, and practically (Sternberg 1998). Despite this, the actual contents of IQ tests have changed very little since the beginning of the twentieth century.

What does an IQ represent then, if not one's intellectual ability? Many researchers in the field believe that an IQ score is just an estimate of a person's performance at one particular point in time – that is, when the test was taken (Shaffer 1996).

## Narrow definition of intelligence

Psychometric definitions of intelligence have been criticised for being too narrow. They focus predominantly on what the test taker 'knows', rather than on the process whereby this knowledge is acquired, stored, and manipulated in problem solving. More recently, tests such as The Kaufman Assessment Battery for Children (K-ABC) (Kaufman and Kaufman 1983) and the Cognitive Assessment System (CAS) (Das, Naglieri, and Kirby 1994) have been developed as attempts to assess these processes. However, although they are tests of intellectual ability, these tests do not fall strictly within the psychometric domain, as they are based on theories of cognitive processing. They form part of the growing group of tests developed as a reaction to the narrowness of the psychometric understanding of intelligence, and fall under the cognitive approach to intelligence.

# The cognitive approach to intelligence

The **cognitive approach** seeks to understand intelligence in terms of actual knowledge and underlying reasoning processes. Many of these theorists extend the basic information-processing assumptions described in Chapter 10, in an attempt to formulate models of intelligence or cognition. The two main cognitive theories of intelligence are those of Sternberg and Gardner, which will be discussed below.

## The triarchic theory of intelligence

Robert Sternberg (1985, 45) defines intelligence as 'mental activity directed toward the purposive adaptation to, and selection and shaping of, real-world environments relevant to one's life'. He claims that many theories of intelligence are not incorrect, but are incomplete, since human intelligence encompasses a much broader variety of skills than imagined by previous theorists. Sternberg believes that skills necessary for effective perform-ance in the real world are just as important as the more limited skills assessed by traditional intelligence tests. He proposes a **triarchic theory of intelligence** that, as its name implies, emphasises three interrelated components of intelligence. Sternberg presents these as the componential, experiential, and context-ual sub-theories.

Robert Sternberg

◆ The *componential sub-theory* addresses the mental processes that are emphasised by most theories of intelligence, namely the ability to acquire new knowledge and to solve problems effectively, that is, it looks at what happens inside a person's head when he or she thinks intelligently.
◆ The *experiential sub-theory* deals with the ability to adjust to new tasks, to use new concepts, to adapt creatively in new situations, and to use insight.
◆ The *contextual sub-theory* considers people's ability to select contexts in which they can excel, to capitalise on strengths and compensate for weaknesses, and to shape the environment to fit their strengths (Sternberg 1984).

### The componential sub-theory

The **componential sub-theory** is the most highly elaborated of the sub-theories. It considers the various types of *components* or mental operations that individuals use in problem solving. The component is the basic level of analysis in Sternberg's theory and is defined as 'an elementary infor-mation process that operates upon internal representations of objects and

**Cognitive approach.**
Theories of intelligence that seek to understand intelligence in terms of actual knowledge and underlying reasoning processes.

**Triarchic theory.**
Sternberg's theory of intelligence which emphasises three inter-related components of intelligence, designated as the componential, experiential, and contextual sub-theories.

**Componential sub-theory.** That part of Sternberg's triarchic theory of intelligence that considers the various types of 'components' or mental operations that individuals use in problem solving. This sub-theory includes three types of components: knowledge acquisition, performance, and metacomponents.

symbols' (Sternberg 1985, 97). Sternberg further specifies three broad kinds of component, which are interrelated:

**Metacomponents.** In the componential sub-theory of Sternberg's triarchic theory of intelligence, these components are involved in planning, monitoring, and evaluating the processing that occurs during problem solving.

◆ **Metacomponents** play a supervisory, decision-making role in problem solving. They are used to plan, monitor, and evaluate processing during problem solving. These components are responsible for allocating attentional resources to various aspects of task processing.

◆ **Performance components** carry out problem-solving strategies specified by the metacomponents. They can be subdivided into 1) encoding components, in which the sensory information is defined and represented in the information-processing system, 2) components involved in the combination of, or comparisons between, sensory stimuli, and 3) response components, which provide the necessary response to the problem.

**Performance components.** In the componential sub-theory of Sternberg's triarchic theory of intelligence, these components are involved in executing cognitive tasks.

◆ **Knowledge-acquisition components** selectively encode, combine, and compare information during the course of problem solving, thereby bringing about new learning (Sternberg 1984).

For example, when writing an essay, metacomponents help you to choose a topic, organise the paper, monitor the writing, and evaluate the final work. Knowledge-acquisition components enable you to carry out the research for the paper. Performance components are involved in the writing of the paper, in searching for appropriate words and phrases and retrieving them from memory.

**Knowledge-acquisition components.** In the componential sub-theory of Sternberg's triarchic theory of intelligence, these components are involved in the acquisition of knowledge, which entails selective encoding, selective combination, and comparison of information.

### The experiential sub-theory

The **experiential sub-theory** was developed to explain an aspect of intelligence that was missing from the componential sub-theory – the role of experience in intelligent performance. A given problem does not draw on the intelligent use of mental components to the same degree for all people. To a grade 0 child, for example, reading the word 'dog' may be a novel experience requiring a great deal of effort to sound out the letters and blend them together, while a literate English-speaking adult would find the word very easy to read and understand. Since a particular task may be new to one person or may be unfamiliar within a particular culture, the degree to which a problem requires intelligence will vary from person to person and from culture to culture. Sternberg maintains that experience with a particular task resides on a continuum from totally new and unfamiliar to completely automated. In relation to this, the experiential sub-theory proposes that intelligence is partly a function of two abilities – the ability to work through new tasks and situations, and the ability to automate information processing. The two abilities interact, since the more one is able to automate information processing, the more mental resources can be devoted to processing new tasks (Sternberg 1984).

**Experiential sub-theory.** That part of Sternberg's triarchic theory of intelligence which deals with the ability to adjust to new tasks, to use new concepts, to adapt creatively in new situations, and to use insight.

According to Sternberg (1984), the most important application of the experiential sub-theory concerns the selection of tasks for measuring intelligence. Tasks that are completely new or completely automated will not reveal much about a person's intelligence. If a task is completely novel, the testee will not have a frame of reference for handling the problem. Whereas, if it is completely automated, a task will not reveal much about a person's intelligence either, because such tasks bypass problem solving. Therefore, the best tasks to use in measuring intelligence are those that are relatively novel or are in the process of becoming auto-mated. Sternberg proposes that how people respond to novelty, and the ease with which they can automatise information processing, are impor-tant and universal aspects of intelligence.

## The contextual sub-theory

The **contextual sub-theory** holds that intelligence must be viewed in the context in which it occurs. Three kinds of mental process are central to the contextual sub-theory:

◆ adaptation,
◆ selection, and
◆ shaping of real-world environments.

These three kinds of mental process are hierarchically ordered. Adaptation is the adjustment of one's behaviour to achieve a good fit with one's environment. If adaptation to the environment is not possible, then the person will try to select a different environment in which they can adapt successfully. Alternatively, if a new environment cannot be selected, the person may shape the environment in order to achieve a bet-ter fit. For example, if a spouse is unhappy in a marriage, *adaptation* to the current circumstances may no longer be feasible. The spouse may then *select* a different environment by getting a divorce or separation or may try to *shape* the current unhappy relationship into something better by attending marital counselling (Sternberg 1984).

Although these three processes are universal features of intelligence, what is required for adaptation, selection, and shaping will vary among different groups of people, so that a single set of behaviours cannot be specified as intelligent for all individuals (Bjorklund 1995). Therefore the contextual sub-theory is culturally relativist; intellectual skills that are crucial for survival in one culture may not be as important in another.

## The development of intelligence

The information-processing approach has attempted to explain the development of intelligence in terms of the development of specific cog-nitive processes. These include the development of control strategies such as monitoring, 'chunking' of information, and selectivity of responses in problem solving; the increase in the amount of information that can be processed by the individual at any one time; the ability to analyse increas-ingly complex or 'higher order' relations; and the increased flexibility in thinking (Sternberg 1988). These processes are what Sternberg (1984) refers to as *components* in his triarchic theory. It has been suggested that general cognitive ability develops through increase in the size of a 'cen-tral computing space' (Pascual-Leone 1970). Also, as children get older, they tend to use more complex strategies of reasoning and to construct more complex mental models and better procedures for testing these models (see Piaget's theory in Chapter 10).

The greatest strength of the triarchic theory is that it brings together diverse aspects of intelligence: the componential sub-theory considers low

**Contextual sub-theory.** That part of Sternberg's triarchic theory of intelligence which considers the ability to select contexts in which the individual can excel, to capitalise on strengths and compensate for weaknesses, and to shape the environment to fit his or her strengths.

level explanations; the experiential sub-theory considers the role of experience and the contextual sub-theory addresses higher order views of intelligence.

## Multiple intelligences

Gardner's theory of **multiple intelligences** (MI theory) is less mechanistic than the triarchic theory. Gardner (1984) challenges the assumption that there is a single general intelligence or *g*, which is believed to be reflected by an individual's IQ. The basic tenet of the theory of multiple intelligences is, as its name implies, that human intelligence encompasses at least eight different kinds of competencies. These include what are traditionally regarded as intelligence, such as linguistic, logical-mathematical, and spatial abilities, as well as other less traditional conceptions of intelligence, such as musical and kinaesthetic capabilities. For Gardner, each form of intelligence represents a modular, brain-based capacity. These intelligences do not always reveal themselves in traditional paper-and-pencil tests.

Gardner's theory is based on extensive research into the nature of intelligence. In order to define the various intelligences possessed by humans, he developed the following set of conditions and criteria that each distinct intelligence had to meet:

Howard Gardner

- ◆ Potential isolation by brain damage. For example, there is evidence that damage to specified areas of the brain can either compromise or spare linguistic ability.
- ◆ The existence of prodigies (individuals with generally normal abilities in most areas and exceptional ability in one area), savants (individuals with low IQs who display a single and exceptional cognitive ability), and other exceptional individuals, who allow for the intelligence to be observed in relative isolation. Gardner believes that such exceptions reflect modular, brain-based skills, which must surely exist in the general population.
- ◆ An identifiable core operation or set of operations, for example, musical intelligence consists of a person's sensitivity to melody, harmony, rhythm, timbre, and musical structure.
- ◆ A distinctive developmental history within an individual, together with a definable nature of expert performance, for example, one can examine the skills of an expert athlete, as well as the steps that occur towards attaining such expertise.
- ◆ An evolutionary history and evolutionary plausibility. For instance, forms of spatial intelligence in mammals can be examined.
- ◆ Support from tests in experimental psychology. Researchers have devised tasks that indicate which skills are related to one another, and which are discrete.
- ◆ Susceptibility to encoding in a symbol system, such as language, arithmetic and maps (Gardner 1984).

**Multiple intelligences.** Gardner's theory of intelligence, which holds that human intelligence encompasses at least eight different kinds of competencies. These include linguistic, logical-mathematical, musical, naturalist, spatial, bodily-kinaesthetic, interpersonal, and intrapersonal abilities.

In 1983, Gardner concluded that there were seven abilities that met these conditions sufficiently well to be regarded as intelligences: linguistic, logical-mathematical, musical, spatial, bodily-kinaesthetic, interpersonal, and intra-personal abilities. The last two refer respectively to the ability to read other people's moods, motivations, and other mental states, and the ability to access one's own feelings and to draw on them to guide one's behaviour. Interpersonal and intra-personal intelligence may be considered as the bases for emotional intelligence (which we will discuss presently). In 1995, Gardner added an eighth intelligence – that of the naturalist, which permits the recognition and categorisation of natural objects, such as in the personalities of Charles Darwin and John James Audubon. He is currently considering a ninth intelligence, namely existential intelligence, which involves the proclivity to raise and ponder fundamental questions about existence and death and which is embodied by personalities such as the religious leader, the Dalai Lama, and the existentialist philosopher, Søren A. Kierkegaard (Gardner 1998).

Multiple intelligences theory makes two claims: that all humans possess these intelligences, and that each person has an individual profile of intelligences (Gardner 1998). Gardner argues that, since children enter school with distinctive profiles of intelligences, these should be cultivated through suitable activities in the curricula. He argues that the reliance on IQ tests to classify individuals in terms of their intelligence does a great disservice to them and to society. Since the focus of these tests is linguistic and mathematical abilities, children gifted in other areas, such as musically or manually, are often 'thrown on society's scrap heap' (Gardner 1984, 76).

# Critical evaluation of the cognitive approach

## Is the cognitive approach significantly different from the psychometric approach?

Gardner (1984) argues that Sternberg's account of intelligence is not very different from the psychometric account, in that it allows for a general intellectual factor similar to Spearman's g. Sternberg (1984) counters that it is too early to compare his and Gardner's theories because there have been no experimental tests of Gardner's theory. Furthermore, Gardner's theory has been described as an extension of Guilford's domain-specific theory of intelligence, and therefore not that different itself to the psychometric approach.

## Definition of intelligence

Gardner's theory has been criticised in particular for including human characteristics that are not typically considered to be mental operations, such as athletic ability and bodily control. This returns us to the question asked at the beginning of this chapter, 'What is intelligence?'

# Emotional intelligence

**Emotional intelligence.**
The term used to describe
qualities such as
understanding one's own
feelings, empathy for the
feelings of others, and the
ability to read social cues.

The phrase '**emotional intelligence**' was coined by Peter Salovey and John Mayer in 1990 to describe qualities such as understanding one's own feelings, empathy for the feelings of others, and 'the regulation of emotion in a way that enhances living' (Goleman 1996b, 4). Emotional intelligence, or EQ, was popularised by Daniel Goleman in his book on the subject (Goleman 1996b). Goleman maintains that IQ and standardised achievement tests may be less predictive of success than a person's emotional skill. EQ, however, is not the opposite of IQ. Some people are lucky enough to have a lot of both, some have a little of either.

The cornerstone to EQ seems to be 'metamood' or a sense of awareness of one's own emotions. Metamood is a complex skill since many emotions disguise others. For example, a person in mourning may know that they are sad, but they may not recognise that they are also angry with the deceased for dying, because this seems inappropriate. Goleman (1996b) believes that self-awareness is the most important factor in EQ, because it allows us to exercise some self-control over our behaviour.

Anger is possibly the most difficult emotion to control, probably because of its evolutionary role in priming people to action. The body's first response is a surge of energy that results from the release of neurotransmitters called catecholamines. If a person is already aroused or under stress, the threshold for release of these neurotransmitters is lower, which explains why people's tempers shorten during a difficult day. Anxiety also serves a useful function, as long as it does not become excessive. Worrying is a rehearsal for danger, where the mind is made to focus on a problem in order to search effectively for solutions. Problems occur when worrying blocks the ability to think efficiently.

People with higher EQs, as measured on Rosenthal's Profile of Nonverbal Sensitivity (PoNS), appear to have sufficient self-awareness to develop mechanisms for coping effectively with these emotions. Such people tend to be more successful in their work and relationships, while children who score well on the PoNS are more popular and successful, even though their IQs are often average (Goleman 1996b).

# Is global intellect rising?

Research indicates that IQ scores have been rising by approximately three points per decade and therefore by a full standard deviation (fifteen points) in the past fifty years (Flynn 1998). Since this change is too rapid to be accounted for by genetic factors, Ulric Neisser (in Flynn 1998) proposes that this increase may have to do with the increasing visual complexity of modern life. Images on television, billboards, and computers have enriched our visual experience, making us more capable at performing well on the visual-spatial aspects of intelligence tests. Others suggest that improved nutrition may be responsible for the rise in average levels of both IQ and height in developed countries (Flynn 1998).

# Intelligence and ageing

Brain imaging techniques such as PET scans and MRI indicate that the brain shrinks somewhat in old age, but not as much as was previously thought. Furthermore, this shrinkage, in a healthy brain, does not seem to result in a great loss of mental ability (Goleman 1996a). In the past it was believed that brain cells were lost every day. While some loss does occur with healthy ageing, it is not this dramatic. The amount of space between the ventricles and sulci of the brain does gradually increase with age, reflecting a loss in the overall mass of the brain. Between the ages of twenty and seventy years, the average brain loses approximately ten per cent of its mass. However, because there are so many interconnections among neurons, the brain can often compensate for this loss.

Analyses of the brain also reveal that older people use different parts of the brain from those used by younger people to accomplish the same task. People in their twenties, for example, tend to be quicker at recognising faces and tend to use more diverse areas of their brains than do people aged between sixty and seventy-five. However, in Goleman (1996a), the older group tested recognised faces with the same degree of accuracy as the younger group, only needing more time to do so. In the context of development, fluid intelligence is believed to increase gradually throughout childhood and adolescence as the nervous system matures. It levels off during young adulthood, and gradually declines with age (usually after sixty years). Crystallised intelligence is said to increase throughout the life-span, since it is the culmination of one's learning experiences (Schaie and Willis 1996).

## The damage of Alzheimer's disease

Some of the data about the ageing brain comes from the Nun Study, a longitudinal study of ageing and Alzheimer's disease which began in 1986 and is funded by the National Institute on Aging in America. The participants are 678 American members of the School Sisters of *Notre Dame* religious order who were between seventy-five and one hundred

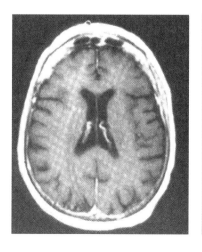 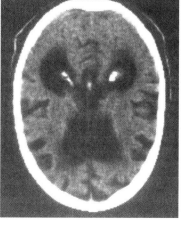

**Figure 11.3** Left: MRI scan of a normal adult brain. Right: MRI scan of a patient with Alzheimer's disease, showing the deterioration of the cerebral cortex. (Lahey, B. B. (2001). *Psychology: An introduction.* Boston: McGraw-Hill.)

and three years of age at the commencement of the study. Each sister in the study agreed to participate in annual assessments of her cognitive and physical functions, to undergo a brief medical examination, have her blood drawn, allow investigators full access to her archival and medical records, and to donate her brain at death for neuropathologic study. In 1990 David Snowdon, the research leader, restricted the focus of the study to examining Alzheimer's disease.

Alzheimer's disease is a progressive, irreversible brain disorder, characterised by gradual deterioration of cognitive functioning – particularly memory, reasoning, and language – and eventually, physical functioning. Autopsies reveal that the brains of Alzheimer's patients are filled with deposits known as plaques, formed from pieces of nerve cells and a protein, beta amyloid. The plaques accumulate at sites of nerve cell connections and prevent communication between nerve cells, and they also impair the ability of neurons to absorb glucose from the bloodstream. It is uncertain whether the plaques actually cause Alzheimer's or whether they are a secondary effect caused by other factors. Something also goes wrong with the neurotransmitter acetylcholine in Alzheimer's patients. (This chemical is important for memory and for the motor control of muscles). It is possible that the problems with acetylcholine production are due to a defective gene (Smith, Sayre, Monnier, and Perry 1995).

The Nun Study has revealed that there is a relationship between the occurrence of strokes and the severity of Alzheimer's disease. Many of the brains of deceased nuns revealed that they were living with advanced Alzheimer's, yet, even in their last years of life, these nuns managed to conduct themselves with clarity and coherence. It was found that none of these nuns had suffered from strokes, particularly the small strokes that occurr frequently in the elderly. Only fifty-seven per cent of the 'stroke-free' nuns developed dementia (deterioration of mental functioning), compared with ninety-three per cent of nuns with a history of mini-strokes (Nash 1997).

## Creativity and intelligence

Creativity is the ability to think about something in novel and unusual ways and to come up with unique solutions to problems (Goleman, Kaufman, and Ray 1993). Experts on creativity believe that intelligence is not the same as creativity and research indicates that creativity is only weakly related to IQ scores. A reason for this may be that intelligence tests tend to measure convergent thinking, where a person is required to produce one correct answer to a problem, while creativity entails divergent thinking, where a person produces many answers to the same question (Guilford 1967).

Amabile (1993) has been studying creativity in children for many years. Her research indicates that the following circumstances are most likely to destroy children's natural creativity:

◆ *Pressure.* Establishing huge expectations for a child's performance can inhibit creativity.

◆ *Surveillance.* When adults hover over children, they make the child feel that they are constantly being watched while they are working and risk-taking creative urges are diminished.

◆ *Rewards.* Excessive use of rewards (toys, stars, money) can stifle creativity by undermining any intrinsic pleasure that the child may derive from creative pursuits.

◆ *Overcontrol.* This is related to surveillance and involves telling the child exactly how to do things. This leaves the child feeling that any originality is a mistake and exploration a waste of time.

◆ *Restricting choice.* If an adult dictates which activities the child should engage in, without allowing the child to choose its interests, it is less likely to engage creatively in those activities.

Despite the links between intelligence (as measured by traditional IQ tests) and creativity being tenuous, children can benefit from the presence of creative people. Santrock (1999) describes how the poet Richard Lewis visits classes in New York City. He brings with him only a shiny marble that fills with a spectrum of colour when held up to the light. He shows this to the class and asks students to write about what they see. One student wrote that she sees the rainbow rising and the sun sleeping with the stars.

## Recommended readings

Brody, N. (1992). *Intelligence.* San Diego, CA: Academic Press.

Ceci, S. J. (1990). *On intelligence, more or less.* Englewood Cliffs, NJ: Prentice Hall.

Gardner, H. (1998). 'A multiplicity of intelligences', *Scientific American*, 9 (4), 19–23.

Sternberg, R. J. (1985). *Beyond IQ: A triarchic theory of human intelligence.* Cambridge: Cambridge University Press.

## Critical thinking tasks

1) What is the main difference between the psychometric and cognitive approaches to intelligence?

2) How do Sternberg's triarchic theory and Gardner's theory of multiple intelligences overlap?

3) How does creativity differ from intelligence? Think up some tasks that could be used to assess creativity.

# Language development

*Kate Cockcroft*

This chapter will introduce the main theories of language acquisition and the process of language development. The following aspects of language development will be discussed:

1. The main theories of language acquisition.

2. The process of spoken language acquisition.

3. The process of learning to read.

4. Disorders of language.

5. The relationship between language and thought.

The chapter also includes a brief section on the advantages and disadvantages of bilingualism and multilingualism.

## What is language?

Language involves the use of a shared set of symbols (letters, words, gestures, icons) for communicating information. Vygotsky (1962) described language as one of the primary mental tools that connects the human mind to the world. Learning to use this tool requires the child to master an extremely complex linguistic system. This task is particularly difficult because language is arbitrary, with often no overt connection between the symbol (the word) and the object or idea to which it refers. So, the meanings of words, particularly abstract ones, are often difficult for the child to discover. Having overcome this obstacle and discovered what certain words mean, the child then has to determine the complex ways in which particular words may be combined to form sentences. The child does not only have to learn how to produce sentences of his or her own, but also how to discover the meaning of sentences which other people use. Despite the difficulty of these tasks, most children learn to talk, and by five years of age, most children are able to use language with a great deal of skill.

B. F. Skinner

# Theories of language acquisition

There are several theories that attempt to explain how a child learns to speak. Five of the major approaches to language acquisition are discussed below. Few theorists today would support any of the extreme versions of these approaches. Rather, it seems that language is learned through a combination of the processes put forward by these approaches.

## Learning theory

B. F. Skinner (1957) extended his model of **operant conditioning** in order to explain language acquisition. (*Operant* is the term he uses to define behavioural responses of the subject (or child) that influence its environment. In other words, such responses are associated more with their consequences – their effect – than with their cause or origin; they may be seen as emitted rather than elicited responses. *Operant conditioning* is the process by which selected **operant responses** are reinforced by the caregivers.) Skinner claimed that children learn language through imitating their caregivers, who also shape the child's initially incorrect attempts at speech, through reinforcement, so that these eventually become 'adult-like'. According to Skinner, utterances that are not reinforced gradually decline in frequency until they stop occurring altogether. The remaining utterances are then shaped with reinforcers until they are correct. For example, as children grow older, parents may use shaping and insist on closer and closer approximations of the word 'chocolate' before supplying the requested treat.

> **Operant conditioning.** A term used by B. F. Skinner for responses that are reinforced by their consequences.

> **Operant response.** This is a kind of behavioural response – identified and defined by Skinner – which leads to a certain consequence. In other words, the emphasis, in such behaviour, is on its effect rather than on its cause.

Skinner did not believe that animals could be taught to speak through schedules of reinforcement, because animals use vocal expression in set ways to express emotional states such as fear or rage and they also lack the necessary articulatory organs for producing many of the sounds in human language (Skinner 1957).

It seems that, according to Learning Theory, most early vocabulary is learned through imitation, with the infant trying to copy the adult, saying for example 'airpha' for aeroplane. However, this approach fails to explain how the child comes up with novel and grammatically incorrect sayings that she or he could not have imitated from anyone else, for example 'that man *growed* outwards'. Also, when the child is very young, parents tend to reinforce all utterances, even the grammatically incorrect ones, tending to correct the content, rather than the grammar of what is being said. For example, the child may say 'That dog eated the food', and the parent may respond 'No, it's not a dog, it's a horse' rather than saying 'We don't say eated, we say ate' (Craig 1996).

## Nativism

Noam Chomsky (1959) held that language is creative. This means that a person who knows a language does not just know how to speak or understand a limited number of spoken, written, or signed messages. Rather, a language user knows how to produce and understand an infinite number of messages, including messages that they have never encountered

Noam Chomsky

previously and could therefore not have copied from their caregivers. The creativity in language is possible because the individual units of a language, namely words (which are finite in number), can be combined in an infinite number of ways.

Chomsky argued that Skinner's view of language acquisition did not explain how children are able to understand new utterances and why they make so many errors as in saying 'I *goed* to school'. Children can't imitate things they don't hear. Therefore, Chomsky held that children are born with certain innate linguistic skills, which he termed the Language Acquisition Device (LAD). The LAD allows the language user to discover the rules governing his or her language, starting with simple rules and progressing to more complex ones. Chomsky held that language is largely preprogrammed in our biological make-up, and is acquired as a result of maturation rather than learning. He also stressed that the rules of language could not be learned through reinforcement, as Skinner maintained, since adult language is often riddled with hesitations and grammatical errors, and thus serves as a poor model for children. According to Chomsky, language is innate because most children seem to acquire the complex skill of language quickly and effortlessly, and development in most children unfolds at approximately the same pace, even though there are vast environmental differences (Chomsky 1959).

Although Chomsky's theory does not deal with the actual processes people use to produce or understand sentences, it was the first theory to draw psycholinguists' attention to the syntactic rules of language. Chomsky outlined the process whereby children learn the rules of language, not specific verbal responses, as was the focus of Skinner's theory.

## Language acquisition as part of cognitive development

Piaget (1926) maintained that language couldn't be separated from general cognitive development, which he viewed as preparing the way for linguistic development. According to Piaget, during the first eighteen months of life the baby learns to interact with the world through sensory and motor activities. Piaget held that it is only once the sensorimotor stage nears its end, and the child acquires the ability to represent objects and events symbolically, that language appears. He argued that language acquisition is the result not of conditioning (Skinner) nor of maturation (Chomsky), but of the completion of the cognitive processes involved in sensorimotor development, such as object permanence and the capacity for symbolic representation. For example, once the child has fully acquired object permanence, he or she reflects those cognitive processes in speech with words such as 'bye-bye' and 'all gone'.

Piaget believed that the ability to conceptualise an idea develops before the ability to express it in words. So, the child would first understand the concept of 'bigger than' and 'smaller than' before using those words. The relationship between language and thought is discussed in more detail at the end of this chapter.

## Social interactionism

This approach is less clearly defined than the others mentioned so far. Lev Vygotsky and Jerome Bruner are both social interactionist theorists and stress the importance of the interpersonal context in which language appears. According to this approach, the baby learns about language through her or his exchanges with the mother or caregiver in a highly familiar context. While the caregiver may introduce new utterances to the child, the situations in which they are spoken are familiar. These familiar contexts provide an opportunity for the child to learn about concepts that she or he will later be able to express in language. For example, a child and caregiver may play games together and the caregiver will comment on their actions as they play. In this way the child learns about objects and the relations between objects and, through the caregiver's verbal comments, the child also learns a verbal way of expressing these concepts. Research confirms that the responsiveness of the environment is crucial for both intellectual and language development (Hoff-Ginsberg and Shatz 1982). Language is a social act, which requires practice. The more that caregivers talk with babies, the sooner babies can pick up the rules of speech.

## Connectionism

Connectionism has as its starting point the human neural system, which has the ability to form and retain networks. Babies are born with such a system, which continues to develop throughout life. According to the connectionist view, neural systems are constructed on the basis of what happens to the developing person's senses. As more sensory information becomes available, the neural system will be extended and modified to incorporate the new sensory material. An aspect of language that has been widely researched using connectionist models is the learning of the

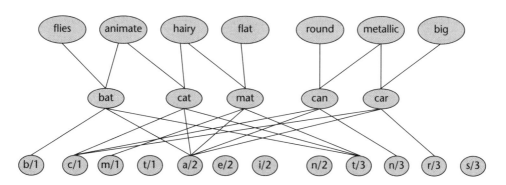

**Figure 12.1** An example of a three-layered connectionist network. The bottom layer contains the units that represent particular graphemes (written units) in particular positions within a word. The middle layer contains units that recognise complete words, and the top layer contains units that represent semantic features concerning the meaning of the word (Eysenck and Keane 1990, 230).

English tense system. The usual explanation is that children have to learn a rule that, in order to refer to the past, verbs must be given an '-ed' suffix. They must also learn that there are many irregular exceptions in English, for instance, 'go' becomes 'went', and 'see' becomes 'saw'.

Children have to learn and store the rule and its exceptions. Children in the early stages of learning English tend to overuse the rule and add '-ed' to both regular and irregular verbs. For example they may say 'goed' and 'seed' instead of 'went' and 'saw'. Rumelhart and McClelland (1986) constructed a connectionist model, which was given information about verbs as its input and was required to produce past-tense verbs as its output. The model produced the same pattern of verb usage as found in the language of young children. Importantly, the model produced this 'human-like' behaviour without learning a rule. Connectionist models are based on learning connections of various strengths between (in this case) the tenses of different words. This may indicate that although the language of young children appears to be rule-governed, there may be no need for the complexity of rule knowledge at all. Connectionist models of language and language development are currently an important area of research activity (Rumelhart and McClelland 1986).

## The process of language development

Language development has several aspects to it: learning to produce words (spoken and written), learning **semantics** (the meaning of words), and learning the grammatical rules of a language (how words can be combined into sentences to express ideas). A distinction is made between **receptive language**, which is your understanding of the language you hear or read, and **expressive** or **productive language**, which is the language you produce in writing or speech. Receptive language generally develops slightly before productive language ability. So, if the parent says to the one-year-old, 'go to your room and fetch your shoes', the child may be able to understand this instruction and carry it out, but cannot produce such a sentence him- or herself.

It was previously believed that language development only started when the child was around two years old. In fact, the word 'infancy', which refers to children under the age of two, derives from the Latin *infans*, meaning 'without language'. However, it is now apparent that language development begins from birth, or possibly even earlier.

**Semantics.** The meaning of words.

**Receptive language.** Our understanding of the language we hear or read. Receptive language generally develops slightly before expressive language ability.

**Expressive language.** The language we produce in writing or speech. Also called productive language.

**Productive language.** See expressive language.

### Before words

At birth, the most obvious vocalisations that the baby makes are crying, and by two months, also cooing. The baby's cooing contains the basic sounds of all languages, not just those of the baby's native language. By four to five months, the infant strings several sounds together to produce babbling. These sounds are the building blocks for later language development. Children born to deaf parents also babble, so that adult verbal interaction is not necessary for this aspect of language to develop (Lenneberg 1967).

## The language of animals:
## Do chimpanzees have a history?

Can chimpanzees have a meaningful, cross-generational cultural history? For Vygotsky the answer must be no. Why so? Because chimpanzees have a very limited linguistic ability. For Vygotsky, the idea that 'the limits of my language are the limits of my world' holds true in a very important way. In fact, the assertion that chimpanzees don't have a meaningful cultural history is reasonably easy to prove. Think for a moment of how one would record, or commit to memory, a statement of the sort: 'On 12 May 1924 the first chimpanzee set foot on the moon' *without the use of an oral or written language.* (Granted, this is a very specific kind of history, but it is precisely a history of this sort about which we are talking). Try to communicate this 'fact' to someone without using language, and you'll get a sense of how impossible it must be to record or 'archive' information of this sort without language. One should also bear in mind here that although chimps have certain communicative abilities – they can most certainly express basic emotions to one another – they cannot convey complex propositions to one another, such as the statement given above.

How do we know this? Well, chimpanzees do not have a grasp of the basic rules of language, the structuring elements of syntax and grammar, which make language use meaningful. After exhaustive experimentation, linguists found that even though chimpanzees could repeat fairly elaborate hand-gestures (apparently non-verbal language), ultimately this was merely the case of learned responses – associated or conditioned responses that would get them certain rewards. Despite the linguists' rigorous efforts, chimps were never able to use the language in the sophisticated sense of formulating statements that they had never heard before, or in the sense of properly grasping the rules of grammar and syntax. (Interestingly enough, human infants tend to do both with ease.)

The point of all this, for Vygotsky, is that our psychological (or cognitive) tools, such as speech and the ability to use written language, or numbering systems, greatly extend our abilities. Effectively then, we have far greater mnemonic skills (the ability to remember), both in terms of our own individual and our shared cultural lives. So it is not surprising that we cannot remember much from our first few years of life.

See Chapter 13 on memory for more about infantile amnesia. —*Derek Hook*

A few months later, the baby may string together the same sound, as in 'dadada'. The baby's babbling will also take on the inflections and speech patterns similar to his or her parents' language, and by six months, the infant is only producing the sounds contained in the language(s) he or she is exposed to. If there are no verbal interactions by this age, for example if the child is deaf, he or she gradually loses the ability to communicate verbally.

Between six months and a year, the infant's babbling includes pauses and changes in pitch that often make it sound like real speech. Psycholinguists call this **expressive jargon** since its intonation resembles adult speech, but its content is said to be meaningless.

**Expressive jargon.** A baby's babbling, which includes pauses and changes in pitch that often make it sound like real speech, while its content is meaningless.

## Infant-directed speech

**Motherese.** See infant-directed speech.

**Parentese.** See infant-directed speech.

Social learning theorists, such as Vygotsky and Bruner, were interested in how the child's caregiver helps the child's language development in several ways. For example, most adults generally tend to talk to infants in a different way than when they talk to other adults or to older children. This speech was initially termed **motherese**, then **parentese**, as fathers also talk to their infants in this way, and it is now called **infant-directed speech**, as most adults employ it when they talk to infants. There are several characteristics of infant-directed speech: the pitch is higher, it is slower, it contains much repetition, and it is grammatically simple. The pitch helps to gain the infant's attention and enables the infant to know that the adult is addressing him or her. The slow speech and repetitions help the infant to hear and learn the words. As the child's capacity for language advances, the parent gradually increases the complexity of verbal exchanges (Furrow, Nelson, and Benedict 1979). This is an example of scaffolding, which helps the child to move in his or her zone of proximal development with regard to language learning. (See Chapter 10 for a more detailed discussion of scaffolding.)

PHOTO: MICHELE VRDOLJAK

*Infant-directed speech serves a special purpose in helping infants to learn a language.*

**Infant-directed speech.** The form of speech most adults use when talking to young children. This is characterised by a high pitch, slow pace, and frequent repetition of words. It is also sometimes referred to as motherese or parentese.

Social learning theorists pointed out that it is not only the caregiver's verbal utterances that contribute to the infant's language development, but also the types of social exchanges engaged in with the infant. Much interest has centred on the game of 'peek-a-boo', and other give-and-take games played between infants and their caregivers. These games have some of the structural qualities of conversations, such as turn taking. As a note of caution, however, Vygotsky (1978) warned against over-intellectualising children's play. He made the point that children and parents often play for the sake of playing and not in order to advance intellectual or social development.

## Telegraphic speech

**Holophrases.** The young child's first 'sentences', which consist of single words such as 'up!' and 'more!'

Eventually that first magnificent word is uttered, at around a year of age. The first words are usually concrete nouns spoken in the presence of the objects they represent. During the next six to eight months, children build up a vocabulary of one-word sentences called **holophrases** such as 'up!' and 'more!' They may also compound words such as 'awgone' (all gone).

**Telegraphic speech.** The young child's stage of language development where simple sentences are formed. These sentences include only the most important words, for example 'Mommy give bopple'.

By the age of two years, the child is generally able to create two-word combinations such as 'Mommy gone', which are primitive sentences and which soon expand in length. The rules of syntax start to appear. English-speaking children always say 'see car' and not 'car see'. Brown (1965) found that children at this age seize on the most important parts of speech, those that contain the most meaning, called *contentives* (nouns, verbs, adjectives) and tend to omit inflections, auxiliary verbs, prepositions and articles, which he called *functors*. The result is what Brown (1965) called **telegraphic speech**, which omits less significant words and includes words that carry the most meaning, for example 'Mommy give bopple'.

## Pivot grammar and case grammar

Braine (1963) identified what he called **pivot grammar** during this two-word stage. At the two-word stage, the child's language consists of pivot words in combination with nouns, or nouns on their own. Since a pivot is 'a short staff or pin supporting something that turns' (Hanks 1989, 637), pivot words are usually verbs, prepositions, or possessives, which may appear on either side of a noun. So the sentence 'see cat' consists of the pivot 'see' and the noun 'cat'. Pivot words are not generally used on their own – they act as support or description to other words. Because the two-word sentence can have many meanings ('mummy up' may mean 'mummy pick me up', or 'mummy look up there') it must be interpreted in context. The child may change the word order to indicate different things: 'doggie play' may mean 'the dog is playing', and 'play doggie' may mean 'I want to play with the dog'. This is called **case grammar**, where word order is used to express different relationships in speech.

## Referential and expressive speech styles

Katherine Nelson (1973) found that the individual words and the category of early words that a child uses depend on the child's personal speech style. She found that speech style in young children could be divided into two types: **referential** and **expressive**. Children with a referential style tended to be object-oriented and predominantly to use nouns like 'bird' and 'plane' in their speech, while children with an expressive style tended to be more oriented towards people, including themselves, and to use mainly verbs and pronouns like 'go there' and 'give here' to express their feelings and needs. Expressive children also tend to create and use dummy words or words with no apparent meaning (except to the child, of course) to stand in for words they do not know, as in 'there's a flight-bit' (aeroplane). Nelson also found that children with a referential style tended to show faster vocabulary development than children with an expressive speech style. However, the children with an expressive style showed a faster rate of syntactic development. These differences have been confirmed by several later studies, for example Barrett (1979).

## The overextension error

Because the young child's vocabulary cannot yet encompass all he or she wishes to describe, the child quite skilfully overextends the meaning of words that he or she already knows, to cover things and ideas for which a new word is lacking. For example, the child may use the term 'dada' to refer to men other than his or her own father (this could be quite distressing to a proud new father), and a general term for any kind of four-legged animal could be 'doggy'. The term for this adaptation is **overextension error**. An overextension occurs when a child incorrectly uses a word to describe a wider set of objects or actions than it is meant

---

**Pivot grammar.** The name given to the use of single nouns with adjectives, adverbs, prepositions, or possessives on either side of the noun, typically during the two-word stage of language development. For example, 'big dog', 'dog bite'.

**Case grammar.** During the two-word stage of language development, word order is often used to express different relationships in speech; this is referred to as case grammar. Hence the child may change the word order to indicate different things: 'doggie play' may mean 'the dog is playing' and 'play doggie' may mean 'I want to play with the dog'.

**Referential speech style.** One of two speech styles found in young children. It is characterised by object-oriented speech with frequent use of nouns.

**Expressive speech style.** One of two speech styles found in young children. It is characterised by people-oriented speech and consists mainly of verbs and pronouns. Expressive children often create their own words to stand in for words they do not know, as in 'there's a small 'puter' (calculator).

**Overextension error.** When a young child incorrectly uses a word to describe a wider set of objects or actions than it is meant to, as in using the word 'moon' to refer to anything that is round.

**Alphabetic writing systems.** Are based on the association between letters and sounds in languages such as English, Afrikaans, Zulu, Xhosa, and Sesotho (in fact all of South Africa's official languages).

**Graphemes.** The smallest units of written language.

**Phonemes.** The smallest units of spoken language. For example /sh/ /oo/ /t/ are the three phonemes in the word 'shoot'.

**Phonics reading strategy.** A method of teaching children how to read by focusing on the sounds in words.

**Whole word reading strategy.** A method of teaching young children how to read by focusing on the learning of entire word representations, rather than the separate sounds that make up words. Often called visual reading.

**Sight-vocabulary stage.** The first stage of learning to read, which occurs roughly between four to six years of age. During this stage, the child is able to read aloud a small set of words whose visual appearance has been memorised, either through teaching or through the child's own observations of pairings of particular words and particular pronunciations, as seen for instance on television or on shop signs.

to describe. Often the child emphasises aspects of objects that adults may ignore when categorising them, for example, a child may use the word 'fly' as an overextension to refer to anything small.

The child's words and their meanings are generally linked to the concepts that she or he is learning about. A child who uses the word 'moon' for everything that is round has developed a concept of what roundness is. Some researchers, including Piaget (1962), believe that the concept is formed first and then the child learns the corresponding word for it. Others believe it works the other way around: the child first learns the name of an object and through naming the object, she or he learns about the category it belongs to and forms a concept of it. Probably the processes work both ways; the relationship between language and thought will be discussed in more detail at the end of this chapter.

After three years, children begin to fill in their sentences, for example 'Roy school' becomes 'Roy goes to school'. They start using the past tense as well as the present; they ask more questions and learn to employ 'why?' effectively (and sometimes monotonously). By four years they have mastered most of the grammatical rules of their language.

## Learning to read

In Western cultures, reading is highly valued. Young children in South Africa typically begin to learn to read when they are about seven years old. **Alphabetic writing systems**, such as English, Afrikaans, Zulu, Xhosa, and Sesotho, are based on the association between letters or **graphemes** (the smallest units of written language) and sounds or **phonemes** (the smallest units of spoken language). The first step in learning to read entails understanding this *alphabetic principle*. The alphabetic principle is based on grapheme-phoneme correspondence rules that relate letters or groups of letters to phonemes. For example, the word 'ship' has four graphemes, which relate to the three phonemes 'sh', 'i' and 'p'. In English, the grapheme-phoneme mappings are not always straightforward or regular, since there are only twenty-six letters and more than forty phonemes. Certain words such as 'choir', for instance, cannot be pronounced correctly by using the alphabetic principle and are better learnt by using a visual strategy where the arrangement of the letters and their corresponding pronunciation are remembered.

The stages through which the child progresses when learning to read may vary according to the language of instruction and whether the child is taught to read by means of a **phonics** or a **visual strategy** or a combination of the two. Phonics is based on using spelling-to-sound rules to read a word, while visual (sometimes called **whole word**) strategies entail learning direct correspondences between a letter string and its spoken representation. Several theories have been proposed to account for the development of the reading process. One of the most representative approaches to the development of reading is Harris and Coltheart's (1986) four phases in learning to read, which is based on ideas from Marsh, Friedman, Welch, and Desberg (1981), Seymour and McGregor (1984), Frith (1985), and Seymour and Elder (1985).

# Four phases in learning to read

## The sight-vocabulary stage

The first stage of learning to read, which occurs roughly between four to six years, is called the **sight-vocabulary stage**. During this stage, the child is able to read aloud a small set of words. The child is able to read these words because it has memorised their appearance either through teaching or through its own observations of pairings of particular words and particular pronunciations, for example on television or on shop signs. Even children as young as two years old have been found to possess sight vocabularies of a few hundred words. Harris and Coltheart (1986) conducted some informal studies with a four-year-old girl called Alice, who was in the sight-vocabulary stage of reading. Alice could read approximately thirty real words, but was unable to read unfamiliar words or nonsense (made-up) words. One example of a word that Alice had learned to read without being taught was the shop name 'Harrods' which she read from shopping bags.

A common proposal has been that children in the sight-vocabulary stage of reading recognise words in terms of their overall shape. This makes sense, because the words are clearly not read by using letter-sound rules, as children at this stage can't read words they have not seen before. So, perhaps the fact that the words are made up of letters is ignored and the words are treated as indivisible visual wholes or as single visual patterns. In order to test this, Alice was asked to read this item:

hArRoDs

This is a word-shape or visual pattern that Alice had never seen before. If she were reading by recognising words as visual wholes, she would not have been able to read this word, as it was entirely unfamiliar as a visual whole. She read the word correctly. This experiment was replicated with other words in Alice's sight-vocabulary, with the same results. Alice's performance indicates that the direct, visual procedure for reading which is used during the sight-vocabulary stage, does not necessarily depend on recognising words as wholes (by their overall shape, for example), because changing the word's overall shape did not prevent her from being able to read the word. Rather, the direct procedure during the sight-vocabulary stage appears to operate by recognising words as particular sequences of letters, even though the procedure does not involve translating these letters into sounds. Words seem to be analysed into their constituent letters in order that the words be recognised, and thus it is inappropriate to refer to the procedure as involving only whole word recognition.

## The discrimination-net stage

The second stage in learning to read is called the **discrimination-net stage**. The reason for this name is that the child now reads single words by discriminating or selecting from amongst the set of words that she or he can already read, that word which most closely matches the letter string that has been presented to read. Of course, the item presented to be read may be a non-word or a word outside the child's existing vocabulary,

PHOTO: ANDEE DEVERELL

*Learning to read starts long before learning the alphabet – exposure to books and paired reading are important from an early age.*

**Discrimination-net stage.** The second stage in learning to read. The child reads single words by discriminating or selecting from amongst the set of words that he or she can already read, the word which most closely matches the letter string that has been presented to read. For example, if the child knows the word 'dog' begins with a /d/, words such as 'doll' or 'dad' may also be read as 'dog'.

but the child does not consider these possibilities. For example, if the child knows that the word 'big' is short and begins with a /b/, she or he may read other short words beginning with a /b/, such as 'boy' or 'bag' as 'big'. This is not really reading in the strict sense – the child is actually collecting just enough information from the printed stimulus in order to discriminate suffciently between all the words in her or his existing reading vocabulary so as to decide (or guess) which word in this vocabulary should be produced as a response.

When the child has just entered the discrimination-net stage and still has a very small reading vocabulary, the amount of information from the printed stimulus that is used to select an item from the reading vocabulary can be very small. For example, the child may simply use word length and may read 'television' as 'children', explaining that she or he knew the word was 'children' because 'children' is a long word. Or the child may focus on certain letters and may read any letter-string containing /ll/ as 'yellow', because 'yellow has two stalks' (Harris and Coltheart 1986). If the child is reading words in a text, she or he will also use the surrounding context to decide what the unfamiliar word is. Thus the main feature of the second stage in learning to read is *selection*, which often occurs on the basis of minimal cues.

As the child's reading vocabulary expands, it becomes more difficult to read using discrimination-net techniques. It becomes more difficult for the reader to distinguish between words in her reading vocabulary on the basis of certain fragmentary features of the word she is trying to read, because the number of items in her reading vocabulary is getting to be rather large. It is this difficulty that prompts the child to move to the next stage of reading development, namely **phonological recoding**.

**Phonological recoding.**
The third stage in learning to read, where the child begins to learn how to map individual sounds onto letters and can sound out unfamiliar words.

### The phonological-recoding stage

Before entering this stage, the child is unable to read aloud written non-words, such as 'brillig' or 'loddernappish', because she is not able to map individual sounds onto individual letters. Rather, a non-word will be read as the closest existing word in her reading vocabulary, for example 'pib' may be read as 'pig'. Eventually, however, the child begins to learn how to map individual sounds onto letters, that is, the child learns how to recode (or translate) letters into sounds (or phonology), hence the term *phonological recoding*. This is based on learning the alphabetic principle discussed earlier. The child's responses are no longer only selected from his reading vocabulary, but may also be words that have not been learned directly or may even be non-words, as the child is now able to sound out words. This leads to a rapid expansion in the number of words the child is able to read aloud correctly. This behaviour indicates a move from the discrimination-net stage to the phonological-recoding stage. In the phonological-recoding stage, the child makes use of translating letters into sounds and also learns the visual representations of words where the spelling prevents them from being translated directly into the correct sounds, for example the words 'rough' and 'yacht'. Evidence shows that the tendency to translate letters into sounds dominates at this stage (Doctor and Coltheart 1980).

## The orthographic stage

Phonological recoding has certain advantages, as in allowing the reader to read completely unfamiliar new words, but it also has disadvantages. The first of these is that English has many *homophonic* words, or words that are spelled differently, yet pronounced the same, such as 'wear' and 'where'. A reader who relies on sounding out words in order to read would be unable to discriminate between homophone pairs. A second disadvantage is that exceptions or irregular words such as 'choir' or 'yacht' will not be read correctly using this approach. For these reasons, we know that phonological recoding is used when acquiring reading skills, but is not used by skilled readers who are able to distinguish between homophones and to read irregular words correctly.

Progress from being an effective beginner reader to being a skilled reader involves a progressive increase in reliance upon *orthographic or visual recoding* (Doctor and Coltheart 1980). Hence the final stage in reading development is called the **orthographic stage**, where skilled readers use a direct strategy of reading words as visual wholes, rather than by using phonological recoding. Phonological recoding may still be used during this stage when the reader is presented with a totally unfamiliar word. A process of analogy may also be used to read unfamiliar words, for instance, the non-word 'oftight' may be read by drawing analogies between it and the known words 'often' and 'light'.

There is some debate about whether learning to read occurs rigidly in the fixed sequence proposed by Harris and Coltheart's four phases. Seymour and Elder (1985) found that young children may employ sight-word and phonological recoding simultaneously when learning to read.

# Disorders of language

Not all children acquire language in the normal way. Children who acquire language more slowly or less completely than the majority are said to show a **developmental language disorder** (language disorders which result from injury to the brain are termed **acquired disorders** and will not be dealt with here). The term **learning disability** is often used to refer to developmental language disorders including **dyslexia** (impaired acquisition of reading), **dysphasia** (impaired acquisition of spoken language), and **dysgraphia** (impaired acquisition of writing).

Definitions for learning disabilities generally include several assumptions about the learning-disabled individual. The most common assumptions are that the individual:

◆ has at least average intellectual ability, that is, an IQ score of ninety or above (this helps to distinguish between children who are learning-disabled and those whose problems are related to low intelligence),
◆ has experienced adequate educational instruction,
◆ is not socio-culturally deprived,
◆ possesses some form of neurological dysfunction in the sense of atypical brain or central nervous system functioning, and
◆ experiences difficulty performing certain cognitive tasks.

**Orthographic stage.** The final stage in reading development, where skilled readers use a direct strategy of reading words as visual wholes (orthographically), rather than by using only phonological recoding.

**Developmental language disorder.** When language is acquired more slowly or less completely than by the majority of children at a particular age.

**Acquired language disorders.** Language disorders which result from injury to the brain.

**Learning disability.** A broad term used to refer to developmental language disorders such as the impaired acquisition of reading (dyslexia), impaired acquisition of spoken language (dysphasia), and impaired acquisition of writing (dysgraphia).

**Dyslexia.** Impaired acquisition of reading.

**Dysphasia.** Impaired acquisition of spoken language.

**Dysgraphia.** Impaired acquisition of writing.

# Language and thought
## Piaget

There has always been debate about which develops first – language or thought – and about the exact nature and degree of interdependence between them. According to Piaget, language is intimately related to the development of symbolic representation, which provides the capacity for mental representation, imagery, imitation, and pretend play, as well as spoken language. All new stages (language being one of them) must wait for the appropriate mental structures to develop and mature. Thought develops first, from sensorimotor activities, and creates the necessary mental structures for language development. Piaget thus believed that language is dependent on thought.

## Sapir and Whorf

**Linguistic determinism.** The idea that the way one thinks is dependent on (relative to) one's language.

**Sapir-Whorf Hypothesis.** The proposal that one's language determines the nature of one's thought; also called linguistic determinism.

**Balanced bilingual.** A person who is equally competent in two languages.

**Linguistic determinism** presents the opposite view, in which it is proposed that language determines the nature of thought. This is often called the **Sapir-Whorf Hypothesis** after Benjamin Whorf (1956) and his mentor, Edward Sapir, who first advocated this view. Whorf speculated that a particular language would dominate and shape its user's perceptions of reality, providing a total world view. The Garo people of Burma, for example, distinguish between many different kinds of rice, which is their staple diet and source of income, while the English language has just one word for rice. Whorf speculated that the Garo people perceive rice differently from English-speaking people. When the Garo thought about rice, they would perhaps view it with greater complexity of thought since they had more cognitive categories for it than English-speakers. In essence, the Whorfian hypothesis proposes that language shapes thought.

Some evidence for linguistic determinism comes from research among people who are **balanced bilinguals** or fluent in two languages. It has been suggested that bilinguals think about things somewhat differently in one language as distinct from the other. For example, in forming impressions of people, Chinese-English bilinguals have a social schema for characterising people that go to work that is formulated in English but not Chinese (Hoffman, Lau, and Johnson 1986).

The major problem with this view is that it sees infancy and early childhood as subject to a process of socialisation into a tightly defined world picture – a closed system of restricted thinking. It does not address the possibility of thought existing before language, or of types of thought that may exist without language.

## Vygotsky

Vygotsky adopted a position somewhere between those of Whorf and Piaget. Vygotsky proposed that thought and language are potentially present but separate at birth, and their subsequent development is not parallel but undergoes many changes (Vygotsky 1988). The earliest form

# Bilingualism and multilingualism

◆ South Africa's population of approximately forty million people speak more than twenty-eight different languages, of which eleven are officially recognised, namely Afrikaans, English, Ndebele, North Sotho, South Sotho, Swati, Tsonga, Tswana, Venda, Xhosa, and Zulu. Zulu and Xhosa are the most common home languages, spoken by twenty-two per cent and seventeen per cent of the population respectively. Afrikaans is spoken by fifteen per cent of the population and English is the home language of only nine per cent of the population (Raidt 1995). More than half of the country's population are bilingual or multilingual (Raidt 1995). Much controversy surrounds the issue of whether bilingualism is an advantage or disadvantage.

◆ Learning two languages is a complex task involving two systems of rules, two sets of vocabulary, special usage, and different pronunciation. Most bilingual and multilingual three-year-old children show little confusion between the languages they are learning, although they do sometimes substitute vocabulary from one language when speaking in another. This has led linguists to theorise that the young child initially uses a unitary language system, and only much later is able to distinguish two separate languages. A recent study suggests that when children learn two languages simultaneously from infancy, the languages share the same brain region (Broca's area) that is responsible for the execution of speech as well as for some grammatical aspects of language (Hirsch and Kim 1997). However, when a second language is learnt later in childhood or in adulthood, this brain region is divided, with a distinct area for the second language. These findings may account for the apparent ease with which a second language is learnt in early childhood.

◆ Does learning two languages instead of one during the preschool years hinder the child's language acquisition or cognitive development? Early studies in the United States of America and Great Britain found that learning two or more languages at a young age could have a detrimental effect on cognitive development, because multilingual children scored lower on standardised English tests than monolingual English-speaking children. However, none of these studies took into account differences in socio-economic or educational level of the children or their parents. It is possible that the scores of multilinguals may have been depressed for reasons other than their multilingualism, such as poverty, poor education, or lack of familiarity with the culture of test taking.

◆ More recent research indicates that learning more than one language in early childhood has cultural, linguistic, and cognitive advantages (Diaz 1985). Young children may be at a disadvantage while acquiring two (or more) languages, but once they have integrated the two languages, they often surpass their monolingual peers linguistically and cognitively (Goncz 1988). Studies have found that bilingual children are more adept at divergent thinking, are more creative both linguistically and cognitively, and are better at concept formation than their monolingual peers.

of thinking in infants is action-based and concerned with purposeful, but basic, problem solving such as reaching for food or toys, or opening a container. The earliest 'speech' consists of sounds produced by air leaving the lungs and passing through the throat, nose, and mouth. This often serves as a form of emotional release, as in cries of frustration, grunts of pleasure, and screams of anger. This 'speech' also serves a social function, since it keeps the infant in close contact with its caregivers and attracts attention and help. When a relatively high level of development has been reached in both preverbal thinking and pre-intellectual speech, around the age of two years, the two processes begin to combine and form a new kind of mental function, *verbal thinking* (Vygotsky 1988). The onset of verbal thinking is marked by the child's curiosity about words and the names of things, and the corresponding increase in the child's vocabulary. Language develops first in social interactions with adults or peers, with the sole objective of communicating. As language is mastered, it is internalised, in private speech, to support thought and inner speech dialogues. (See Chapter 10 for more about private speech.)

Vygotsky (1988) maintained that thought is largely the product of language. He believed that we could only really understand a child's mental processes through the psychological tools – such as language – that mediate them. This means trying to understand the cultural meanings of words and language, the unique context in which they are being used, and the range of previous experiences and motivations that lie behind them.

## Recommended readings

Bjorklund, D. F. (1995). *Children's thinking: Developmental function and individual differences.* Pacific Grove, CA: Brooks-Cole.

Harris, M. and Coltheart, M. (1986). *Language processing in children and adults.* London: Routledge and Kegan Paul.

Saunders, G. (1988). *Bilingual children: From birth to teens.* Clevedon: Multilingual Matters.

## Critical thinking tasks

1) Use the spellchecker on a computer word processor. How has it been organised, and which theory(s) of language acquisition discussed in this chapter is it based on?

2) Which of the theories of cognitive development discussed in Chapter 10 would be most useful in describing how a child learns to read? Motivate your answer by giving examples based on the theory.

3) Explain why phonological recoding is not the final stage of reading, even in languages that do not possess any irregular words.

4) Vygotsky saw language as a tool that helps us to organise and refine our thoughts. What are some of the ways in which language aids our thinking?

# Memory development

*Kate Cockcroft*

---

This chapter provides a brief overview of the major models of memory and the development of memory. The following topics are covered:

1. The multistore model of memory.

2. Schema theory.

3. Semantic networks.

4. The development of memory.

---

## What is memory?

> When I used to grieve for my mother, and later for my aunt, I told myself that although they were certainly as dead as they were ever going to be they were still mine, that they inhabited my interior world, which was at least as noisy and various as life itself. From early on I valued the gift of memory above all others. I understood that as we grow older we carry a whole nation around inside of us, with places and ways that have disappeared, believing that they are ours, that we alone hold the torch for our past, that we are as impenetrable as stone. Memory still seems a gift to me and I hold tight to those few things that are forever gone and always a part of me ... (Hamilton 1994, 39).

People often think typically of scenes from their past when thinking about 'memory'. However, these 'autobiographical' memories are not the only type of memory we possess. First, there is the well-known distinction between long- and short-term memory. An example would be looking up a telephone number and remembering it for just long enough to be able to dial it (**short-term memory**), as opposed to recalling an event from childhood (**long-term memory**) (Greene and Hicks 1984). Tulving (1972) distinguished between two types of long-term memory: **episodic memory**, which is memory for personal experiences and events that have happened in one's life, and **semantic memory**, which contains one's general knowledge.

**Short-term memory.** That memory system which stores information over very brief intervals of time (usually seconds).

**Long-term memory.** Information that is stored for longer than a few seconds.

**Episodic memory.** Memory for personal experiences and events that have happened in an individual's life.

**Semantic memory.** Memory of general knowledge or factual information.

# Models of memory

Most work on human memory has taken place within the information-processing framework. Information-processing theorists define memory as 'the capacity for storing and retrieving information' (Baddeley 1982, 11). This framework conceptualises memory as a series of complex, interconnected processes that take in, store, and retrieve information about the world. The process of taking in sensory information about the world and converting it into a memory is referred to as *encoding*. Storage is the way in which the information is represented in the brain and *retrieval* is how information in memory is made available to the individual. Failure to remember could be the result of a problem at any of these three stages: encoding, storage, or retrieval.

The distinction between long- and short-term memory led researchers to develop a **multistore model of memory**. It is called 'multistore' because it proposes several different stores within memory. The most common version is that of Atkinson and Shiffrin (1968), a basic information-processing model that conceptualises the memory system in terms of three main processes or stores (see Figure 13.1).

First, information that is perceived by the senses is held briefly in the **sensory store** (called **iconic memory** when referring to sensory *visual* memory, and **echoic memory** when referring to sensory *auditory* memory). The information here is in its raw state – the only thing that has been done to it is to convert it from information in the environment, such as sounds or light, into electrical activity in the brain. Information in this state is still relatively meaningless. Information from the eyes, for example, arrives in the brain in the form of 'blobs' and 'edges' of light and dark. Information that is selected for further processing enters the short-term store, where it is processed further. The *short-term store*, as its name implies, only holds information briefly, between six and twelve seconds. However, this can be extended by using various strategies such as rehearsal, where you repeat the contents of the short-term store either out aloud or mentally in your head. (Memory strategies and their development will be discussed later in this chapter.) The use of various strategies to increase memory retention results in the information being stored indefinitely in *the long-term store*. **Schema theory** provides a useful explanation for the understanding of long-term memory.

**Multistore model of memory.** An information-processing model of memory that proposes several different stores within memory.

**Sensory store.** Information that is perceived by the senses is held here very briefly. (Sensory memory is called iconic memory when referring to sensory visual memory, and echoic memory when referring to sensory auditory memory.)

**Iconic memory.** See sensory store.

**Echoic memory.** See sensory store.

**Schema theory.** Bartlett's theory that we construct schemata (units of information) about typical events, for example, we have a schema for a typical movie theatre and what occurs there.

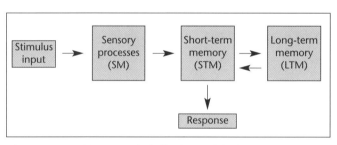

**Figure 13.1** Atkinson and Shiffrin's model of memory.

## Schema theory

Schema theory was proposed by Frederick Bartlett (1932) who proposed that memories are constructed, rather than being exact replicas of the information that is stored. The reconstructive nature of memory is evident when you think about how two people may have experienced the same event, yet their recollections of that event can show great deviations.

Memory **schemata** are discrete units of information that relate to a typical object or event. Schemata incorporate everything we know about a subject or object, for instance by now you should have a fairly well-defined schema about lectures, and how they typically proceed. In addition to supplying a base of knowledge, schemata also provide a framework within which new information can be processed. Schema-like memories for events (called **scripts**) influence how we remember events. A script for a restaurant might include information about food, waiters or waitresses, paying the bill, and so on.

**Schemata.** Discrete units of information that relate to a typical object or event.

**Scripts.** General remembered outline of a familiar repeated event, used to guide behaviour.

## Semantic network models

Schemata are not represented as separate from one another. Rather, they are depicted in memory as a massive interconnected web of information, called **semantic networks**. Collins and Loftus (1975) were interested in the *links between* concepts stored in memory, rather than the actual concepts, and this led to the development of a semantic network model of memory. In semantic networks, the connections between the concepts (or **nodes** as they are referred to) in the network specify the relationship between them. So, for example, the link between 'apple' and 'fruit' would be an 'is a' link. The links also have varying strengths, since concepts can be strongly, weakly, or moderately related to one another (with many gradations in between). Apples, for example, are always fruit, so the link between apple and fruit would be very strong. The link between 'apple' and 'green' would be weaker, since not all apples are green.

**Semantic network.** A large interconnected web of schemata.

**Nodes.** The concepts (words, numbers, ideas) that are linked in a semantic network.

Semantic networks illustrate the associative and interconnected nature of memory. All concepts are linked, and when one concept is activated (as in being mentioned, seen, or thought about), this in turn activates the other concepts to which it is linked in a process called *spreading activation*.

While semantic networks are often located within the traditional 'boxes and arrows' or modal model understanding of memory, they are actually somewhere between the traditional information-processing and connectionist explanations of memory. (See Chapter 10 for a review of these approaches.) The reason why semantic networks cannot fully be defined as part of the connectionist approach is because connectionist models attempt to make a neural analogy between memory functioning and brain processes, while semantic networks are hypothetical only. The commonality that schema theory and semantic networks share with the information-processing approach is that they are functional models of memory, since they attempt to explain what is happening in memory without saying what is happening in the brain.

## Connectionist models of memory

McClelland and Rumelhart (1985) describe a basic computational model of conceptual memory that explains how object schemata are represented in human memory. Their model illustrates some of the important aspects of connectionism. Just as sensory information is converted into electrical activity in the brain, so McClelland and Rumelhart's model processes information in a numerical way. The network consists of twenty-four units, each connected to the others by a link, which has a strength or weight. Concepts that are recognised by the network are converted into numbers, depending on what the concept is. Activation is also sent to all other units in the network that are related to the concept. Just as with neurons in the brain, the activation of the units can be either inhibitory or excitatory, depending on the relationship between them. For example, the concept 'apple' would excite activation with concepts such as 'fruit' and 'red', but would probably inhibit activation with concepts such as 'car' and 'shoe', which are unrelated to it. McClelland and Rumelhart provided a formula that is used by the network to calculate activation levels between the various units. Eventually the network will settle into a stable state, with the activation of all the units scarcely changing, and it is then said to have recognised the stimulus or concept. (This is how the network learns.)

The greatest criticism of these models of memory presented above is that they all focus on the similarities in human memory rather than on the differences.

# The development of memory

## Prenatal memory

Research suggests that memory for sound may be present even before birth. Studies show that three-day-old babies can distinguish their mothers' voice from that of another female. In one study, the baby was able to control which voice it heard by the rate of sucking on an artificial nipple (which did not provide any nourishment). Fast sucking made the mother's voice play on a tape recorder, while slow sucking made a stranger's voice play. Once the babies learned that they could control their environment in this way, the babies in the study sucked in such a way as to produce their mothers' voice most of the time. Since the babies had only spent about twelve hours since birth with their mothers – they were looked after by nurses in the hospital – it was concluded that each preferred his or her own mother's voice because they had grown used to it while still in the womb (Wertheimer 1961).

## Memory in infants

Most of the methods that are used to study memory in children and adults require the subject to verbalise his or her response, and are thus inappropriate for babies and infants. In order to assess memory in infants under two years of age, a method was needed that does not depend on language ability. One that is commonly used is called the **habituation-dishabituation paradigm** (Kail 1979). **Habituation** means a decrease in responding to a repetitive stimulus. **Dishabituation** means the recovery from habituation, that is, it means that responding returns to prehabitu-

**Habituation-dishabituation paradigm.** A method of assessing memory in babies. If the baby stops looking at a familiar pattern over a number of trials, this means that the baby has remembered it (become habituated to it) and chooses to look at something new and more interesting. If the baby is not shown the familiar pattern for a period of time, he or she will ultimately start looking at it again for the same length of time as when he or she first saw it. This means that the baby has forgotten it (dishabituation).

**Habituation.** A decrease in responding to a repetitive stimulus.

**Dishabituation.** The recovery from habituation when responding to a stimulus returns to prehabituated levels.

ation levels. Visual recognition is the most popular type of memory assessed using the habituation-dishabituation method.

A typical habituation-dishabituation experiment would involve presenting infants with the same pattern over a series of trials and recording the length of time they fixate on (look at) the pattern. Usually the infants show a decrease in the amount of time spent looking at the pattern over trials as it becomes familiar to them. This decrease is believed to reflect habituation, that is, the infants recognise the pattern from previous trials and choose to look at it less than before because it is no longer novel and interesting. By varying the amount of time between trials and observing the extent of habituation that may occur, it is possible to estimate how long infants can maintain their memories for the original pattern. If a long enough delay occurs between successive showings of the pattern, they will forget the pattern altogether. When this happens, the infants will inspect the pattern on subsequent presentation for approximately the same amount of time as they did when they first saw that pattern (Kail 1979).

Infants may choose to look at one pattern rather than another for several reasons that are unrelated to memory, for instance they may find certain patterns more interesting than others – three- to five-month-old babies have been found to prefer bull's-eye patterns to stripes (Fantz, Fagan, and Miranda 1975). To control for such preferences, the infants in the study were divided into two groups. The memory test for both groups involved a bull's-eye pattern paired with a picture of stripes. For one group, the bull's-eye pattern was the first one shown, followed by both patterns, while the other group was shown the stripes first, followed by both patterns. If both groups looked longer at the new pattern (stripes for the first group and bull's-eye for the second), there was evidence of infant memory, as they remembered the old pattern and became habituated to it.

## Memory in childhood

What is your earliest childhood memory, and when did it occur? Until quite recently, it was believed that most people are unable to recall specific events that occurred before their third birthday. This was called **infantile amnesia**. Freud (1953, 175), who coined the term *infantile amnesia*, said that the first years of life showed 'the remarkable amnesia of childhood ... the forgetting which veils our earliest youth from us and makes us strangers to it.' He believed that the experiences of the first years of life are not actually forgotten, but instead are merely inaccessible to our conscious awareness due to repression. According to Freud, many of our desires and fantasies are very erotic in nature at this age and these sexual feelings conflict with the realities of everyday life. To resolve this conflict, we repress this whole period of our lives into the unconscious mind. However, stripped of its psychoanalytic trimmings, Freud's view basically maintains that infantile amnesia is due to retrieval failure. The experiences are still represented in memory, but the individual cannot gain access to them. It is supposed that retrieval failure occurs because the context at the time of the original learning is very different from the context at the time of attempted retrieval (often decades later).

**Infantile amnesia.** Freud's term for the individual's inability to recall specific events that occurred before their third birthday.

**Encoding specificity principle.** The likelihood of retrieving information from long-term memory will be maximised if the conditions at retrieval match as closely as possible the conditions present during the original learning.

**Implicit memories.** Memories that can produce behavioural change without intentional recall or conscious awareness of the memory. Examples are how to kick a ball or drive a car.

**Explicit memory.** Memories for factual knowledge such as names of people and events.

**Recognition.** Refers to the ability to select from pictures, objects, words, or digits that are currently present, those that have been seen or heard before.

**Recall.** Refers to the ability to retrieve information about objects or events that are neither present nor current. It requires the generation of information from long-term memory without the object being in view.

It has also been suggested that young children organise, encode, and store information in very different ways from adults. For example, adults and older children use language to a much greater extent than do infants. For instance, if asked to recall your second birthday, you would probably have difficulty doing so because the memories were probably not originally encoded and stored verbally. In order to retrieve any information about your second birthday, you will need to reinstate some of the original context, to look, for example, at a photo or video of your party. This illustrates the **encoding specificity principle** (Tulving 1972), that is, that the likelihood of retrieving information from long-term memory will be maximised if the conditions at retrieval match as closely as possible the conditions present during the original learning. Remember this when studying for exams – make your study conditions as similar as possible to the exam conditions.

Children as young as two years old have been shown to have memories of events that occurred months earlier. Often, however, these memories do not last for a long time, because they are **implicit memories**, that is, memories that can produce behavioural change without intentional recall or conscious awareness of the memory. Examples of this are the knowledge of how to kick a ball or drive a car. It is thought that the brain structures necessary for implicit memory develop before those necessary for **explicit memory**, that is, memories for factual knowledge such as names of people and events. Consequently, most people are unable to retrieve explicit memories that occurred before the age of three. The rapid development of language from three to six years enables the child to store information for longer periods than previously, when information was stored mainly in a visual format.

## Assessing memory in older children and adults: recognition and recall

**Recognition** refers to the ability to select from pictures, objects, words, or digits that are currently present, those that have been seen or heard before. **Recall** refers to the ability to retrieve information about objects or events that are neither present nor current. It requires the generation of information from long-term memory without the object being in view.

Recognition is present at birth and develops considerably in the first six months. The onset of recall is more difficult to specify exactly. A typical way of assessing memory recall in adults and older children is to present a set of stimuli to be remembered, remove the stimuli, and then ask the subject to recall the set (Kail 1979). It is, obviously, impossible to give such tasks to infants. Instead, their search for objects is examined. By seven months, infants will look for objects that are out of sight (Ashmead and Perlmutter 1980). Requiring the infant briefly to wait seems to disrupt memory considerably as she or he will no longer search for the object after as brief a delay as five seconds. At eight months even a very short delay (eight seconds) makes it impossible for the infant to find a toy that has been placed under one of two identical cloths. However, by ten months, infants can wait as long as eight seconds and still find the hidden object. By sixteen to eighteen months, recall is possible after delays of twenty to thirty seconds (Diamond 1985).

The assumption in all of the studies of infants' recall is that their search for the hidden object is based on their ability to recall the experience of seeing the toy being hidden. The failure to find a hidden object does not imply that the infant lacks the capacity to recall. It is possible that they may not understand what is required of them, or that the experimenter's actions are too complex for the infant's motor skill level. Nevertheless, the research indicates that the ability to recall prior experiences seems to emerge in the first year of life and increases gradually thereafter.

While preschool children are readily able to recognise things, their recall is much poorer, but improves with age. In a recognition task, in which many objects were shown only once to children between the ages of two and five years, even the youngest could correctly recognise eighty-one per cent of the objects when placed with other objects, while the older children were able to recognise ninety-two per cent of the objects correctly. This shows that young children are able to encode and retain substantial amounts of information. In recall studies, when children between two and four were asked to name objects the experimenter had shown them, the three-year-olds could only name twenty-two per cent of the objects, while the four-year-olds could name forty per cent (Myers and Perlmutter 1978). This finding may reflect increasing vocabulary, which may be a confounding factor in this study.

Experiences early in life impact on how a person develops subsequently. But, experiences can only have impact if they are stored in memory. Consequently, infants with better memories should be able to learn from experience better than those with poorer memories. This line of reasoning led to the hypothesis that measures of early memory ability should be related to later cognitive development. In support of this hypothesis, Rose and Wallace (1985) found that recognition ability at six months was positively and significantly related to intelligence at two, three, and six years of age.

## Memory strategies

Memory strategies or **mnemonics** are purposeful and deliberate attempts to enhance memory performance. As such, mnemonics are controllable, deliberately implemented by the individual, and potentially available to consciousness (Harnishfeger and Bjorklund 1990). They may be used to acquire information, such as study skills learned at school, or to retrieve information from long-term memory. Memory strategies can either be executed at the time of learning (at input), or at the time of retrieval (at output). Input strategies include rehearsal (the repetition of selected information), organisation (grouping similar items together), and elaboration (the association of two or more items by creating a representation that connects them). Output strategies are simply retrieval strategies, which involve accessing information and bringing it into consciousness.

Mnemonics based on visual imagery go back a long way, in fact to the first century BC. Cicero, who wrote at that time, mentions the visual

**Mnemonics or memory strategies.** Purposeful and deliberate attempts to enhance memory performance.

mnemonics used by the Greek poet Simonides (about 500 BC). The story goes that a Greek who had won a wrestling match at the Olympic Games invited guests to a victory banquet at his house. Simonides was among the invited guests and gave a recitation in honour of the victor. Shortly after completing his eulogy, Simonides was called away. This was fortunate for him because shortly afterwards the floor of the banquet hall collapsed, killing and mutilating the guests. Many of the bodies were unrecognisable. Simonides, however, found that he could assist with the identification of the bodies by remembering where they had been at the time when he left. Consequent to this, Simonides speculated that since his visual memory appeared to be so good, why not use it to recall other material? He then devised a system in which he visualised a room in great detail, and then imagined various items in specific places in the room. Whenever he needed to remember what the items were, he would look into his room, and find them at the appropriate location. This system became very popular with classical orators such as Cicero, and has continued in use to the present (Baddeley 1982). Baddeley (1982, 196) illustrates how it works:

> First of all, think of ten locations in your home, choosing them so that the sequence of moving from one to the other is an obvious one – for example, front door to entrance hall, to kitchen, to bedroom, and so on. Check that you can imagine moving through your ten locations in a consistent order without difficulty. Now think of ten items and imagine them in those locations. If the first item is a pipe, you might imagine it poking out of the letterbox of your front door and great clouds of smoke billowing into the street. If the second is a cabbage, you might imagine your hall obstructed by an enormous cabbage, and so on.

Different cultures evidently differ in the extent to which they encourage particular memory strategies. Shaffer (1996) points out that strategies such as rehearsal, organisation, and elaboration are useful for school-age children living in Western urban societies, but not for unschooled children from more rural environments, whose important memory tasks may be recalling the location of objects in a natural setting, such as water, animals, poisonous or medicinal plants, or remembering instructions told to them in the form of proverbs or stories. This is in keeping with Vygotsky's notion that cognitive development is always *located within a particular cultural context*, which defines the problems that children are faced with as well as the strategies (which he called tools) that they develop for solving the problems.

## The development of mnemonic strategies

Age differences have been found in both the number of strategies that children of different ages use as well as the efficiency with which they use those strategies. One of the reasons why children under the age of six tend to be poor at recall tasks is that they do not spontaneously organise or rehearse information they want to remember as an adult would. If you were given a list to remember, with items such as 'cat', 'chair', 'aeroplane',

## Vygotsky's use of mnemonics

Vygotsky made use of mnemonics to help him remember information. His daughter wrote this about his ability:

> Right there, by the stove, Lev Semenovich would demonstrate to us his ability to remember large numbers of words. We would, working together, compile a list of 100 words and hand it over to Lev Semenovich. He would slowly read each word, return the list, and then offer to recite it in any order. To our amazement and joy, he would, without mistake, repeat all the words on the list from beginning to end, and then repeat them in the reverse order. Then we would ask him to reproduce the 17th,

43rd, 61st, 7th and so on, word, and he, without difficulty and without any mistakes, would do it. (Vygodskaia 1995, 58).

The secret to Vygotsky's amazing memory was his use of visual imagery. Not only could he easily create a wealth of images, he also made use of synaesthesia or the ability for a stimulus in one sense to evoke an image in another, for example associating high-pitched sounds with bright colours and low-pitched sounds with more sombre colours.

'dog', 'desk', 'car', you might first classify the items into groups such as 'animals', 'furniture', and 'vehicles', and then repeat them quietly to yourself before being asked to recall the list. In doing this, you are using the memory strategies of organisation and rehearsal to assist your recall. Preschool children tend to display a 'passive' or non-cumulative rehearsal style, because they only repeat one or two words of an entire list they are asked to recall. Children over the age of six years tend to show a 'cumulative' rehearsal style, because they rehearse as many words as possible when given a list of words to recall (Ornstein, Baker-Ward, and Naus 1978). However, the rehearsal capacity of ten-year-olds is only about eighty per cent that of adults. The reason for this may be that most ten-year-olds only speak eighty per cent as quickly as adults. It appears that the capacity of short-term memory is linked to the speed of speech. Therefore, the faster you can speak, the more information you can rehearse (Hulme and Tordoff 1989). Organisational strategies develop around nine or ten years.

Rehearsal serves to strengthen the memory trace, while organisation helps in two ways. First, it structures what is being learned, so that recalling partial information is likely to make the rest accessible, and second, it associates newly learned information with information you already have stored in your memory. This means that the richer your existing knowledge base is, the easier it will be to remember new information (Baddeley 1982). Thus children's memories improve as their knowledge base expands. The more you know about a topic, the easier it is to understand, integrate, organise, and remember new information concerning that topic. In addition, to remember something well, a person needs to be motivated to learn more about that topic. Children can show amazing memory abilities if motivated to learn about a topic. Chi and Koeske (1983) reported on the knowledge that a four-and-a-half-year-old boy had about twenty-one different dinosaurs. Although many young children have an interest in and some knowledge about dinosaurs, this child's interest bordered on the unreal. To support his consuming interest in the topic, his parents apparently read dinosaur books to him about three hours a week for one-and-a-half years prior to his testing. He owned nine books on dinosaurs and had many plastic models.

Contrary to what the previous passage indicates, young children do use memory strategies, but they are not the typical ones that adults would use. Instead they use what we would consider to be faulty strategies. For example, an eight-year-old may write a note to remind him- or herself to watch a favourite television show tonight, but then place the note inside a piggy bank for safekeeping.

## Metacognition

**Metacognition**. The sophisticated intellectual processes that enable people to be aware of and reflect on their own thinking, memory (metamemory), and language (metalinguistic) abilities.

Metacognition refers to the sophisticated intellectual processes that enable people to be aware of their own thinking, memory (metamemory), and language (metalinguistic) abilities. Between the ages of six to twelve, children develop **metacognitive** abilities, which they use to help them with problem solving and decision making. A simple example of this is a study where preoperational and concrete operational children were all given a group of items to study until they felt they could remember them perfectly. After studying the items for a while, the concrete operational children said they were ready, and they usually were. When tested, they could remember all of the items. The preoperational children did not perform so well, although they also assured the researchers that they knew all the items. Thus, their metacognitive abilities – or awareness of their own cognitive processes and ability to monitor these abilities – were poorer than those of the concrete operational children (Kail 1979).

## Memory in later life

Very little research exists on memory during later life, although some evidence does indicate that a decline occurs in the memory capabilities of forty- and fifty-year-olds, often at the time when careers make bigger memory demands (Parkin 1999). US President Bill Clinton, for example, in his defense over his affair with Monica Lewinsky, claimed that he had forgotten the details of his various encounters with her, because his memory was overloaded. Research into memory in later life has tended to focus on retirement age (post sixty-five years). Findings indicate that short-term memory remains relatively unaffected by advancing age. General knowledge about the world and vocabulary remain intact, although there is some evidence that older people access their memories more slowly.

The major change in memory with age is a decline in the ability to recall things explicitly. Therefore, memory for day-to-day events decreases considerably and older people, in laboratory experiments, perform poorly at the recall of lists of words or pictures. However, recognition memory does not show such dramatic declines with age. While explicit memory appears to decline with age, implicit memory appears to be intact in older people.

# False Memory Syndrome

In Missouri, USA, in 1992, a church counsellor 'helped' Beth Rutherford to remember during therapy that her father, a priest, had regularly raped her between the ages of seven and fourteen, and that her mother sometimes assisted, by holding her down. In therapy, she developed memories of her father twice impregnating her and forcing her to abort the foetus herself, using a coat-hanger. The father had to resign from his post as a priest after the allegations became public. Later medical examination of Beth revealed that, at twenty-two, she had never been pregnant and was still a virgin. The daughter sued the therapist and received a $1 million settlement (Loftus 1997). Rutherford's case was one of many instances of false memory reported in the USA in the 1990s. Some of the cases were based on abuse that occurred during the first year of life.

Loftus (1997) maintains that it is highly unlikely that an adult will be able to recall genuine episodic memories from the first year of life because the *hippocampus*, which plays a key role in the creation of memories, has not matured enough to form and store long-lasting memories that can be retrieved in adulthood. How is it possible, then, for people to acquire detailed and confident false memories? Research has

demonstrated that, under the right circumstances, false memories can be instilled quite easily in some people. False memories are most likely to be created, whether in an experimental setting, in therapy, or in everyday life, when certain external factors are present. The first comprises the social demands on the individual to remember. For example, the therapist may exert some pressure on a patient to recall instances of abuse. Second, memory construction through imagining events may be explicitly encouraged when people are having trouble remembering. Finally, individuals may be encouraged not to think about whether their memory constructions are real or not (Loftus 1997).

False memories are constructed by combining actual memories with the content of suggestions received from others. During this process, the individual may forget the source of the information. However, though experimental work on the creation of false memories raises doubt about the validity of long-buried memories, as in the case of repeated trauma, it does not disprove such memories. Without corroboration, there is little that can be done to help even the most experienced researcher to differentiate true memories from ones that were planted through suggestion.

At the simplest level, our memories fail with increasing age because we lose neurons, resulting in reduced processing capacity. In order to function effectively, our mental processes must attend to what we are doing and actively ignore irrelevant information (a process called *inhibition*). In relation to memory, a deficit in inhibition could impair memory, leading people to concentrate less effectively on what they are trying to remember. Ageing selectively causes neuron depletion in the frontal lobes of the brain, which are responsible for controlling inhibition (Hasher and Zacks 1988). Another theory of ageing and memory, the *processing speed hypothesis*, is that our memories become poorer because our brains just get slower at operating (Salthouse 1997). A problem with this hypothesis is that the tasks used to support it may only be measuring fluid intelligence (the ability to think flexibly and solve problems) and not crystallised intelligence (knowledge of language and basic concepts). Fluid

*While some memory loss is inevitable in old age, staying mentally active can considerably lessen this loss.*

**Senile dementia.**
Cognitive decline in old age resulting in confusion, forgetfulness, and personality change (also known as organic brain syndrome).

intelligence is known to decline markedly with age, while crystallised intelligence does not (Parkin and Java 1999).

A severe deterioration in memory in old age is often a precursor to **senile dementia** or *organic brain syndrome*, ultimately resulting in intellectual handicap. The forgetfulness may seem at first quite mild – forgetting where one has put objects, or the times or dates of appointments. It can, however, become so severe that the afflicted individual is unable to lead a normal life. Baddeley (1982, 141) cites the case of an old lady suffering from senile dementia who agreed to have a nurse stay with her at night, but then forgot all about this arrangement so that when the nurse arrived, she was treated with suspicion, locked out, and the police telephoned. Senile dementia is progressive and typically occurs shortly before death in very old people. Riegel and Riegel (1982) studied many elderly people, testing their intellectual and physical abilities over several years. They suggested that mental ability declined fairly gradually in old age up to a point approximately a year before death, when deterioration became rapid, a phenomenon referred to as *terminal drop*.

For those who are not afflicted with dementia, there is hope. Studies of animals suggest that an enriched environment results in the loss of fewer neurons as age progresses. A few studies have compared elderly individuals living in institutionalised settings with those living more active lives in the community. On various tests of memory, the active community-dwelling elderly showed better performance. The answer then seems to be: keep mentally active.

## Recommended readings

Baddeley, A. (1982). *Your memory: A user's guide.* London: Multimedia Publications.

Loftus, E. (1994). *The myth of repressed memory.* New York: St Martin's Press.

## Critical thinking tasks

1) Think of various strategies that an elderly person could use to prevent memory decline. Base your answer on the theory of memory as presented in this chapter.

2) What function does memory play in cultures with a strong oral tradition?

3) Think back to a memory of a shared event that happened at least five years ago, and write it down. Then speak to a person who shared that event and ask them to write down their memory of it. What does your comparison of the two recollections tell you about the reconstructive nature of memory?

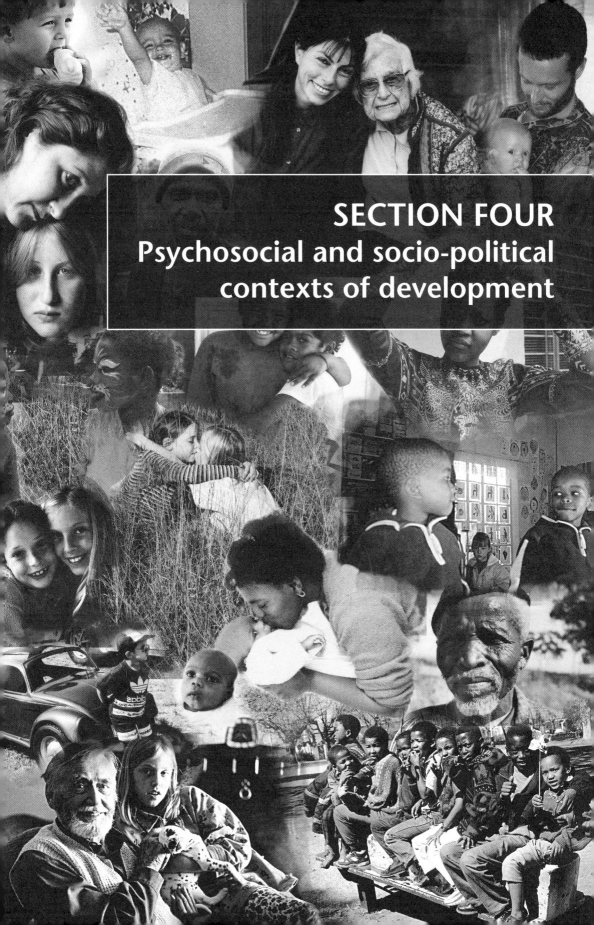

# SECTION FOUR
## Psychosocial and socio-political contexts of development

# Attachment theory

*Lee Senior*

This chapter presents a review of attachment theory, drawing largely on the ideas of John Bowlby and Mary Ainsworth. We introduce and discuss the following concepts central to attachment theory:

1. Attachment behaviour and the attachment behavioural system.

2. Attachment/exploration balance and the secure base phenomenon.

3. Internal working models.

4. Strange Situation laboratory procedure and patterns of attachment.

Attachment patterns tend to be enduring, and attachment in adulthood is thus briefly reviewed. Thereafter we explore the relationship between attachment and temperament, emotion regulation, and psychopathology. The implications of the AIDS epidemic for the attachment security and development of South African youth are highlighted. The chapter closes with a critique of attachment theory, including the question of its cross-cultural relevance.

## Introduction

Attachment theory concerns early caregiving relationships and the way that these relationships support the child's subsequent development. The nature of the parent-child relationship during early childhood is believed to be one of the central causal factors in personality development and interpersonal functioning, as well as having implications for psychopathology.

Mary Ainsworth

# Bowlby's attachment theory

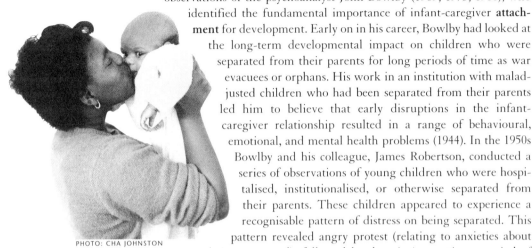

PHOTO: CHA JOHNSTON

*Attachment theory emphasises the critical role of the early caregiving relationship in the development of the child.*

Attachment theory and research initially emerged from the clinical observations of the psychoanalyst John Bowlby (1969; 1973; 1980), who identified the fundamental importance of infant-caregiver **attachment** for development. Early on in his career, Bowlby had looked at the long-term developmental impact on children who were separated from their parents for long periods of time as war evacuees or orphans. His work in an institution with maladjusted children who had been separated from their parents led him to believe that early disruptions in the infant-caregiver relationship resulted in a range of behavioural, emotional, and mental health problems (1944). In the 1950s Bowlby and his colleague, James Robertson, conducted a series of observations of young children who were hospitalised, institutionalised, or otherwise separated from their parents. These children appeared to experience a recognisable pattern of distress on being separated. This pattern revealed angry protest (relating to anxieties about being separated), followed by despair (suggesting a period of grief or mourning), and detachment when the separation was prolonged and the young children tried to protect themselves against the distress of losing a parent (Robertson and Bowlby 1952). Bowlby became increasingly aware of the importance of a close and continuous relationship with a primary caregiver.

Bowlby postulated that central to human motivation is an inborn, universal human need to form a primary attachment. He described attachment as a special type of social relationship involving an affective bond between infant and caregiver. Bowlby's formulations ran contrary to psychoanalytic thought predominant at the time, which maintained allegiance to a dual drive reduction theory of psychological development, and understood the infant's tie to the mother as a function of the mother satisfying the infant's hunger drive. As is apparent in the interpersonal nature of his theory, Bowlby was influenced by the object-relations tradition in psychoanalysis, which gives primacy to the need for, and the orientation toward, objects, but his theory also draws on concepts from evolution theory, ethology, control theory, and cognitive psychology.

**Attachment.** Strong emotional bond between infant and caregiver.

## Attachment behaviour

**Attachment behaviours.** Any behaviour designed to get children into a close, protective relationship with their attachment figure.

**Attachment behavioural system.** An organised system of attachment behaviours.

Bowlby theorised that attachment serves an evolutionary purpose, enhancing the survival of the species. Humans, like other primates, possess an evolutionary-adapted behavioural system, the goal of which is maintaining proximity to a caregiver, particularly when danger threatens, and thereby ensuring the vulnerable infant's protection from predators and ultimate psychological and physical survival. **Attachment behaviours** are thought to be organised into an **attachment behavioural system.** Human infants' attachment behaviours serve to activate maternal behaviour and bring the caregiver into close contact with the infant. An obvious early example of this is an infant crying when a mother leaves the room – a signal not easy to ignore and designed to bring the mother to the child. Other examples include smiling, babbling, grasping, the gesture of raising arms, clinging, and following. While some attachment behaviours, such as smiling or vocalising, may be characterised as signalling behaviours that alert the mother to the infant's interest in interaction, and thus to bring her to the infant, other behaviours, such as crying, are aversive behaviours, and bring the mother to the infant to terminate them. Some behaviours, such as approaching and following, are active behaviours that move the infant to the mother (Cassidy 1999). As the infant develops, he or she becomes increasingly effective in seeking and maintaining proximity to the preferred caregiver.

A central aspect of Bowlby's attachment theory is the hypothesis that attachment behaviour is organised by means of a control system within the central nervous system (Bowlby 1969; 1988). Bowlby described the workings of a thermostat as an example of a control system: when a room gets too cold, the thermostat activates the heater; when the desired temperature is reached, the thermostat turns the heater off. Similarly, when a separation from the caregiver becomes too great, the attachment system is activated until sufficient proximity has been achieved (Cassidy 1999).

The behaviours and emotions associated with attachment are likely to be triggered in situations of anxiety or distress:

◆ within the infant, such as feeling hungry or tired,
◆ within the environment, such as a frightening event, and
◆ within the attachment figure, such as a caregiver being absent, unresponsive, rejecting, or hostile.

## Perceptual predispositions towards attachment to mother in the newborn

Although Bowlby asserted that the infant-caregiver relationship builds over time, he did suggest that, from the outset, there are powerful biological forces directing the mother and infant towards mutual attachment. Research with newborns has confirmed the existence of perceptual biases in the newborn that facilitate the mother-infant bond. Newborns just a few hours old are able to recognise their mothers' voices. Newborns' heart rates and patterns of sucking behaviour have been shown to change in response to their mothers' voices. The basis for this recognition has been thought to be prenatal experience in hearing the mother's voice. The newborn infant has a visual accommodation of about twenty-five centimetres, which is just enough for the newborn to be able to recognise general features of the face, and the newborn prefers looking at human faces above any other stimulus. Newborn infants are able to differentiate between their own mother and another mother on the basis of smell. In one study, significantly more babies spent more time turning towards their own mother's breast pad than towards a clean breast pad at five days of age, and by six days of age were showing a differential response between their own mother's breast pad and another mother's breast pad. Breast-fed infants rapidly learn their mother's characteristic olfactory signature while sucking at her breasts and can subsequently recognise her by that unique scent.

While the set goal of the attachment system was initially regarded as physical proximity, Bowlby (1973) later refined his definition of the set goal of the attachment system. In this he emphasised the importance of the infant's belief that the attachment figure would not only be physically present, but be emotionally accessible and responsive if needed. Quality of care and sensitivity of the caregiver to the infant's signals became the central issues of infancy.

## Phases of the development of attachment

Attachment is a gradual developmental process that evolves from birth. Bowlby (1969) describes four phases in the development of an infant's attachment.

### Table 14.1 Bowlby's phases of the development of attachment

| Phase | Age | Behaviour |
|---|---|---|
| Pre-attachment | 0 to 2 months | Undiscriminating social responsiveness. Crying, smiling, babbling, grasping, and reaching. Tracking, listening, and responding to adult speech. |
| Attachment-in-the-making | 3 to 6 months | Discriminating social responsivenss. Ability to single out primary caregiver; selective social smile. |
| Clear-cut attachment | 7 months to 3 years | Active initiative in proximity and contact. Increasingly discriminating. Strangers treated with increasing caution. Use of newly developed language and locomotor skills to seek out and maintain contact with attachment figure. |
| Goal-corrected attachment | 3+ years | Begins to understand mother's point of view, feelings, plans, and motives, and to make inferences about her behaviour. Enters into a more complex relationship or partnership with caregiver. |

## Attachment/exploration balance and the secure base

According to attachment theory, the attachment figure is seen as providing a 'secure base' (Ainsworth, Blehar, Waters, and Wall 1978), allowing the infant to express an innate instinct to explore in order to grow progressively independent of the attachment figure. When danger seems unlikely, the attachment system recedes into the background and allows for exploratory activity. The infant who feels secure in the caregiver's availability and attentiveness may wander off to explore and play, returning at times to check that the caregiver is accessible, before venturing off again. If, however, the caregiver's proximity is questionable, independent exploration of the environment is dramatically reduced. The dynamic equilibrium between the complementary, yet mutually inhibiting, attachment and exploratory behavioural systems is thought to be crucial for development (Ainsworth 1972). An attachment-exploration balance ensures that while the child is protected by maintaining proximity to attachment figures, he or she is able nonetheless to learn about the environment through exploration.

## Internal working models

A basic assumption of attachment theory is that critical variations in the quality of one's early experiences with caregiving figures shape the formation of mental representations or **internal working models** of close relationships. Internal working models comprise:

◆ *self model* – containing perceptions of one's own worth and lovability, and
◆ *other model* – containing expectations regarding the essential goodness, trustworthiness, and dependability of important others in one's social world.

> **Internal working models.** Internal mental representations, developed in early close relationships between the self, attachment figure(s), and the environment.

Those who experience sensitive and emotionally available caregiving develop a sense of others as dependably available and supportive, a sense of themselves as competent and worthy of attention and affection, and generally positive expectations of intimate relationships. In contrast, when caregiving is inadequate, the individual develops deficiencies in feelings about self and others, and a negative set of expectations regarding relationships (Zeanah, Mammen, and Lieberman 1993).

PHOTO: CHA JOHNSTON

*Emotionally accessible and responsive caregiving and sensitivity to the infant's signals are central ingredients in a secure attachment.*

According to Bowlby (1973; 1988) a person's internal working models, once formed in early childhood, tend to persist and serve as a template for his or her subsequent close relationships. They become a central aspect of personality and are so taken for granted that they come to operate largely at an unconscious level. Internal working models may tend to become self-fulfilling in the sense that new relationships may be created in the light of expectations developed in earlier relationships. Internal working models may be resistant to change, even in the face of contradictory evidence, thus limiting the person's ability to learn from interpersonal interactions.

## Ainsworth's Strange Situation and the patterns of attachment

According to attachment theory, behavioural patterns of seeking care and nurturance emerge as a function of the primary caretaker's response to the child. A child learns, from an early age, which behaviours will elicit care from the primary caretaker, and which will not have this effect. Those that elicit at least limited security become preferred and safe ways of interacting with caretakers (Slade 1999).

Ainsworth, Blehar, Waters, and Wall (1978) attempted to investigate empirically whether the quality of maternal responsiveness is directly tied to patterns of infantile behaviour, particularly comfort-seeking and contact maintenance behaviour. Ainsworth *et al.* (1978) conducted a laboratory procedure known as the *Strange Situation*. This involved eight brief (three-minute) episodes that provided opportunities to observe a variety of the twelve- to twenty-four-month-old infants' responses to the stresses of a new environment and of separation from an attachment figure.

Ainsworth was able to distinguish three primary attachment classifications: *secure*, *resistant*, and *avoidant*. These patterns were linked to caregivers' success or failure in responding to, and meeting, the infants' needs. Typically, secure infants readily separated from the caregiver in the laboratory procedure and became easily absorbed in exploration. After being separated from the caregiver, secure infants simply sought proximity with the caregiver on her return and then felt comforted and returned to play. Securely attached children develop confidence that caregivers will be available, responsive, and helpful, should they encounter adverse or frightening situations. With this assurance, they feel competent and bold in their explorations of the world. This pattern is promoted by the caregiver being readily available, sensitive to the child's needs, and lovingly responsive whenever he or she seeks protection or comfort (Bowlby 1988).

## Table 14.2 Summary of Strange Situation procedure

| Episode | Events and procedures |
|---|---|
| 1 | The mother (or father) and infant are introduced into a sparsely furnished room containing toys for the infant and chairs for the mother and another adult. |
| 2 | The mother is non-participative while the infant explores. |
| 3 | An unfamiliar adult enters, sits quietly, then converses with mother and eventually engages the infant in play. |
| 4 | Mother is signalled to leave the room inconspicuously. First separation episode. |
| 5 | Mother returns and tries to engage the infant in play. First reunion episode. |
| 6 | Mother exits once more, leaving child completely alone. Second separation episode. |
| 7 | Stranger returns. |
| 8 | Mother returns. Second reunion episode. |

**SOURCE:** Adapted from Ainsworth *et al.* (1978).

Resistant and avoidant attachment classifications may both be placed within the broad category of *anxious* or *insecure attachment* (Ainsworth 1972; Ainsworth *et al.* 1978; Bowlby 1973). Infants who have anxious attachment relationships with their caregivers have not experienced consistent availability of, and comfort from, their caregivers when the environment has proved threatening (Ainsworth *et al.* 1978; Bowlby 1973). These infants are anxious about the availability of their caregivers, fearing that the caregivers will be unresponsive or ineffectively responsive when needed. As such, they may not be able to direct attachment behaviours at caregivers when appropriate, or may not be comforted by caregivers who have been unreliable in the past. Anxious attachment compromises free exploration of the world, which means that these infants cannot achieve the same confidence in themselves and degree of mastery of their environments as securely attached children (Weinfeld, Sroufe, Egeland, and Carlson 1999).

Within the Strange Situation laboratory procedure, *resistant* (also referred to as *ambivalent*) infants showed great distress at separation and manifested angry, tense, and clinging behaviour when the caregiver returned. These infants wanted to be comforted, but resisted their mothers' efforts to soothe them. They remained too distressed in the Strange Situation to be able to return to play. The resistant infant is uncertain whether the parent will be available or responsive or helpful when called upon. As a result of this uncertainty, the child is always prone to separation anxiety and is anxious about exploring the world (Bowlby 1988). This pattern tends to be promoted by inconsistent parenting, that is, when a parent is available and helpful on some occasions, but not others.

*Bowlby believed that the need to form emotional bonds is the central human motivation.*

PHOTO: CHA JOHNSTON

*Avoidant* behaviour was seen in infants who appeared less anxious during the separation and snubbed the caregiver on her return, avoiding eye contact or using toys to distract their attention away from the caregiver. These infants showed no preference for the mother or caregiver over a stranger. The child who evidences anxious avoidant attachment has no confidence that, when seeking care, there will be a helpful response, rather than rejection (Bowlby 1988). This pattern, in which conflict is more covert, results from a caregiver who constantly rebuffs the child when approached for comfort or protection. The most extreme cases result from repeated rejections.

In later research, Main and Solomon (1986; 1990) described a third insecure category, the *disorganised/disoriented* category. These infants had no coherent strategy whatsoever to deal with the experience of separation and showed disorganisation and dissociation upon reunion. Some appeared dazed or confused and exhibited atypical behaviours such as freezing of all movement; approaching the caregiver with head averted; rocking on hands and knees, moving away from the caregiver to the wall, rising to greet the caregiver, then falling prone on the face, mixing avoidant with resistant behaviours. Some instances of disorganised attachment are seen in infants known to have been physically abused or grossly neglected by the parent (Crittenden 1985), in infants of mothers who are still preoccupied with mourning a parental figure lost during the mother's childhood, and in infants of mothers who themselves suffered physical or sexual abuse as children (Main and Hesse 1990).

## Attachment in adulthood

There is growing evidence that these patterns of attachment, once developed, tend to persist and are remarkably stable across the life-span (Rothbard and Shaver 1994). Bowlby maintained that attachment behaviours 'characterise human beings from the cradle to the grave' (1979, 129), and that, 'while attachment behaviour is at its most obvious in early childhood, it can be observed throughout the lifecycle, especially in emergencies' (1989, 238). Classifications established in childhood persist through the end of childhood in the absence of substantial environmental change (Egeland, Kalkoske, Gottesman, and Erickson 1990; Erickson, Sroufe, and Egeland 1985). Adult attachment patterns appear to be developmental successors of childhood attachment patterns (Rothbard and Shaver 1994). Three major longitudinal studies (Hamilton, 1994; Main, 1997; Waters, Treboux, Crowell, Merrick, and Albersheim 1995) have shown a sixty-eight to seventy-five per cent correspondence between attachment classifications in infancy and classifications in adulthood.

Mary Main and her colleagues conducted research into adult attachment, utilising a semi-structured interview known as the Adult Attachment Interview (George, Kaplan, and Main 1985), in which adults are asked to describe childhood attachment relationships, as well as experiences of loss, rejection, and separation. Main discovered patterns of representation that were analogous to infantile patterns of behaviour in the Strange Situation: *autonomous* adults, like secure infants, had ready and coherent access to a range of positive and negative feelings about their early attachment experiences. While autonomous or secure adults' representations of early attachment experiences were coherent and flexible, *insecure* adults described such experiences in incoherent and contradictory ways. Whereas *preoccupied* adults seemed overwhelmed and flooded by the affect associated with early attachment experiences, *dismissing* adults idealised early relationship experiences and described painful events in a detached and often contradictory way. Preoccupied adults, like resistant children, were unable to contain and regulate memories and affects associated with early attachment. Dismissing adults, like avoidant children, minimised and overregulated affects that would disrupt their functioning (Slade 1999). Main classified subjects whose interviews revealed disordered thinking in the discussion of mourning or trauma as 'unresolved/disorganised with respect to mourning or trauma' (Main and Hesse 1990).

In another major line of work examining attachment patterns in adults, Hazan and Shaver (1987) extended the childhood paradigm of Ainsworth *et al.* (1978) to adult love relationships and developed a brief self-report measure to assess adult parallels of the three childhood patterns: secure, anxious-ambivalent, and avoidant. Using this measure, Hazan and Shaver (1987; 1990) asked adult respondents to characterise themselves as secure, anxious-ambivalent, or avoidant in romantic relationships, and asked them to respond to questions regarding their most important experience of romantic love, their mental models of self and relationships, their memories of childhood relationships with parents, and their experiences at work. Adults subscribing to the secure style agreed that they found it relatively easy to get close to others, were comfortable in depending on others and having others depend on them, and were not worried about being abandoned. Individuals selecting the ambivalent style agreed that others were reluctant to get as close to them as they would like, were worried that their partners did not really love them or want to stay with them, and wanted to get very close to their partners, although they were aware that this sometimes scared people away. Adults identifying with the avoidant style acknowledged being somewhat uncomfortable with closeness to others, found it difficult to trust others completely or to allow themselves to depend on them, and became nervous when love partners wanted to get too close. Bartholomew and Horowitz (1991) subsequently identified two subgroups of avoidant individuals: *fearful* avoidants who avoid intimacy because of a fear of rejection, and *dismissing* avoidants who take a detached stance towards close relationships.

## Attachment and temperament

Temperament may be defined as the inherited personality traits present at birth (Buss and Plomin 1984). Infants are believed to be born with characteristic levels of sociability and emotional styles, including levels of emotional reactivity to disturbances in the environment. Temperament theorists agree that individual differences along temperament dimensions carry implications for the frequency and quality of exchanges between a child and the significant people in the child's environment, and that these exchanges may, in turn, modify the characteristic expression of temperament (Vaughn and Bost 1999). There is some empirical support for the conclusion that temperament and attachment are related (Vaughn and Bost 1999). Two studies cited by Hetherington and Parke (1993) have found that infants with 'difficult' temperaments or less sociability have demonstrated more distress during separations and reunitings with caregivers than 'easy' or more sociable babies. Irritability during infancy has been found to increase the risk for later insecurity of attachment (Crockenberg 1981; Sussman-Stilman, Kalkoske, Egeland, and Waldman 1996; Van den Boom 1994; Waters, Vaughn, and Egeland 1980). Infant temperament may potentiate inadequate caregiving practices when caregivers themselves are stressed (Vaughn and Bost 1999). Mothers with irritable infants and poor social support have been found to be more likely to have anxiously attached infants (Crockenberg 1981). The influences of temperament and experience are difficult to disentangle – the nature of the development process is such that inborn differences in temperament and influences in early care interact to create the adaptation of the infant. Caregiving may well be influenced by the nature of the infant, and the infant's basic nature is transformed by the caregiving experience (Sroufe 1996).

## Attachment and affect regulation

Attachment theory has been regarded as a theory of affect regulation (Kobak 1986; Kobak and Sceery 1988; Sroufe and Waters 1977). Attachment implies an emotional bond between parent and infant. Attachment theorists regard the attachment relationship as the context within which the human infant learns to regulate emotion (Sroufe 1990; 1996). As an infant is not capable of regulating his or her own emotions, the assistance of a caregiver is required in modulating fluctuating emotions. A dyadic regulatory system evolves where the infant's signals of changes in state are understood and responded to by the caregiver, thereby becoming more regulated. The infant learns that becoming emotionally distressed in the presence of the caregiver will not lead to disorganisation beyond his or her coping capabilities. In states of uncontrollable arousal, the infant will come to seek physical closeness to the caregiver in the hope of soothing and the recovery of homeostasis (Fonagy 1999). Differences in the quality of care, including the responsivity of the caregiver, lead to differences in emotional arousal and the expression, modulation, and flexible control of the emotions by the child (Sroufe 1996). According to the degree that the caretaker is responsive, the child acquires confidence in his or her own ability to influence the environment as well as internal states. Poor quality and anxious attachment will be revealed in dysfunctional emotional regulation (Sroufe 1996).

For securely attached children, emotions are thought to operate in an integrated and smoothly regulated fashion to serve the inner organisation and the felt security of the child (Sroufe 1990). The experience of security is based not on the denial of negative affect or arousal, but on the regulation of affect and the ability to tolerate negative affect temporarily in order to achieve mastery over threatening situations (Carlson and Sroufe 1995; Kobak 1985). Securely attached children readily engage situations that have the potential for emotional arousal and they express their emotions directly. This ability is based on their expectations that others are available and will respond when they are emotionally aroused, that emotional arousal is rarely disorganising, and that should emotional arousal be disorganising, restabilisation is likely to be achieved quickly (Sroufe 1996). Emotions, especially negative emotions, are not experienced as threatening but are expected to serve a communicative function (Bowlby 1969; Sroufe 1979). Not only do secure children demonstrate an ability to tolerate negative affect while maintaining constructive engagement with others, but they are also able to display positive emotions that enhance social interaction and social competence (Sroufe, Schork, Frosso, Lawroski, and La Freniere 1984). Children who have participated in responsive and smoothly regulated attachment relationships are expected to carry forward a capacity for self-regulation and a sense of the self as competent in maintaining some degree of emotional regulation (Carlson and Sroufe 1995).

Resistant children are believed to have experienced intermittent caregiver responsiveness to signals of distress, contributing to a constant state of arousal in these children (Bowlby 1980; Sroufe 1990). Affect is not effectively modulated and the children remain chronically vigilant and may heighten expressions of distress in an effort to elicit caregiver response (Carlson and Sroufe 1995). They come to expect that the caregiver will not be consistently available or responsive to help manage high levels of tension and arousal and to believe that they are unworthy and lacking in personal resources to cope with distress (Bowlby 1973; 1980). These children view a range of situations as threatening and are prone to exaggerated emotional displays (Bell and Ainsworth 1972). They may develop low thresholds for threat, be preoccupied with having contact with the caregiver, and show signs of frustration regarding contact when distressed (Carlson and Sroufe 1995).

Children with histories of avoidant attachment are believed to have been exposed to an overly rigid style of emotion regulation and rejection of their attempts to gain reassurance (Bowlby 1980; Sroufe 1990). Heightened arousal is experienced as disorganising – the expression of distress and negative emotion is not experienced as effective in eliciting care, and as a result, these children may fail to seek contact in response to perceived threat, instead redirecting distress and withholding the desire for closeness (Carlson and Sroufe 1995). Certain vital emotions are experienced as unacceptable or confusing. In order to minimise the conflict aroused by such unacceptable feelings, the expression and, in time, the experience and perception of cues arousing such feelings are defensively restricted from awareness and there may come to be a separation between aspects of thought and feeling (Carlson and Sroufe 1995). These children tend to have an underlying anger or negativism that they have learned not to express at its source and generally develop individual styles that distance feelings and people (Sroufe 1983). Negative affect tends not to be acknowledged, particularly when it may heighten conflict and alienation (Cassidy and Kobak 1988; Kobak and Sceery 1988).

*Research has found that siblings with secure attachments have less antagonistic relationships than siblings with insecure attachments.*

## Attachment and psychopathology

From an attachment perspective, variations in the response to stressful life circumstances and the development of psychopathology are related to early experiences of caregiving and the quality of attachment (Carlson and Sroufe 1995). Disturbed attachment relationships may be seen as markers of an incipient pathological process or as a significant risk factor for later psychopathology (Sameroff and Emde 1989; Sroufe 1983). Secure attachment constitutes a protective factor in confronting stress and affords people a measure of psychological resilience (Morisset, Barnard, Greenberg, Booth, and Spieker 1990). People with an internalised sense of security in attachment are more able to handle distress and to react to everyday problems, as well as to deal with extreme levels of physical and psychological threat, with more contained negative emotional responses (Mikulincer, Horesh, Eilati, and Kotler 1999). According to Mikulincer and Florian (1998), this adaptational role may be derived from three sources: first, secure individuals' optimistic attitude towards life may act as a shield in the face of unexpected adversity. Second, secure individuals' positive self-image may allow them to confront life difficulties with a sense of self-efficacy. Third, their openness to new information may allow for greater adjustment to environmental change and the development of more realistic coping plans. Conversely, individuals who have

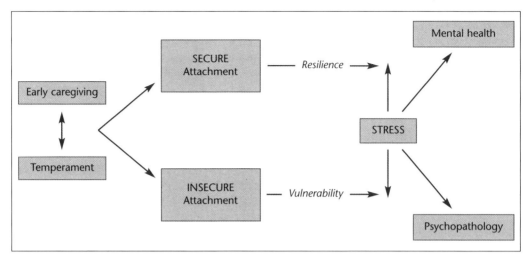

**Figure 14.1** The role of attachment in the development of psychopathology. As depicted above, temperament and early caregiving experiences interact in shaping attachment security. Attachment patterns, in turn, may act as protective factors, or risk factors, when facing adversity. Securely attached individuals tend to have better self-esteem and to engage their worlds with confidence, are more socially competent, independent and adaptable, and have been found to be better problem solvers. Securely attached individuals tend to be more resilient to the effects of subsequent life stress. Insecure attachment has negative implications for personality development and is associated with interpersonal difficulties and social isolation, poor self-esteem, and difficulty regulating emotion. Insecurely attached individuals tend to experience and respond to life stress more negatively, and are vulnerable to developing psychopathology.

adopted insecure strategies may be particularly vulnerable to stresses and adverse life events (Carlson and Sroufe 1995), and their insecure attachment strategies may negatively influence the way in which they appraise, and react to, life events (West, Livesley, Reiffer, and Sheldon 1986).

Attachment patterns may also influence an individual's ability to establish and utilise social networks, thereby affecting the availability of support at times of stress (West *et al.*1986). Based on experiences with caregivers who were unavailable or inconsistently responsive, insecurely attached individuals may be prone to forming relationships that are not supportive and may easily be disrupted. As stress is elevated, the avoidant individual may fail to signal directly a need for support from others and may remain isolated with his or her problems. The resistant individual may become excessively caught up in negative emotion and unable to remain engaged constructively in social relationships, developing patterns of relating to others based on heightened displays of emotion or extreme passivity (Carlson and Sroufe 1995). What begins as personal distress may be compounded by isolation, lack of support, and relationship dysfunction (Kobak and Shaver 1987).

Insecure attachment has been linked to the development of psychopathology in adulthood. Early experiences of major separation, loss of a parent, or disruption of the parent-child relationship have consistently been linked to greater risk for depression and anxiety in adolescents and adults and there is a growing body of empirical research relating personality disorders to attachment problems.

# Attachment and culture

Child rearing and parental interaction vary across socio-cultural contexts. Bowlby's emphasis on attachment as species-specific has led to criticisms about his assumptions regarding the universality of attachment across cultures. Concerns have also been raised about the extent to which attachment theory allows for the diverse ways in which specific cultures incorporate attachment relationships into prescriptions for family life (Bretherton 1997).

Much of the work that has been done in reviewing attachment and culture has focused on Ainsworth's Strange Situation procedure and questions about the generality of results across cultures and social contexts. While Ainsworth found two thirds of the North American infants in her research to be securely attached, researchers using the Strange Situation in other cultural groups have identified different proportions of secure, resistant, and avoidant classifications. Socialisation patterns and caregiving circumstances have an impact on the perceived stressfulness of the Strange Situation in different cultures (Harwood 1995). For instance, the high proportion of avoidant attachments identified by Grossman, Grossman, Spangler, Suess, and Unzer (1985) in a sample of German infants was understood to reflect an emphasis in German culture on fostering independence in one's offspring. In contrast, the high percentage of resistant classifications in a Japanese sample may be attributable in part to aspects of Japanese society that encourage the child's interdependence on family members (Miyake, Chen, and Campos 1985). Japanese babies are typically in constant physical contact with their mothers throughout the day and sleep in the same room at night, and the separation episodes of the Strange Situation are therefore totally alien to such infants, and thus likely to cause considerable distress. While secure attachment behaviour is associated with a variety of valued characteristics across many cultures, in some circumstances, resistant or avoidant attachments may equip children to grow up into adults who best fit the cultural norms (Harwood 1995). What is adaptive, competent, and responsive for one culture may not apply equally to others. Additionally, cultural systems of meaning influence the behavioural patterns that infants may show in the Strange Situation and the processes for measuring and labelling attachment in the Strange Situation may be qualitative judgements reflecting ethnocentric ideas (Takahashi 1990). An infant's responses to elements of the Strange Situation may not be an accurate indication of the actual intensity of the emotional bond between infant and caregiver.

## Monotropism

Another question is whether attachment theory adequately accommodates the use of multiple caregivers, a prevalent practice in some socio-cultural contexts. Bowlby stressed the importance of a continuous relationship with a primary caregiver for emotional health. While Bowlby stated that infants will, from the outset, form more than one attachment, often establishing a small hierarchy of attachments, he asserted that infants have a strong tendency to prefer a principal attach-

**Monotropism.** Theory suggesting that although infants have a small hierarchy of attachments, they evidence a bias for attaching themselves especially to one figure at the top of the hierarchy and will tend to seek out this figure during a crisis period.

ment figure for comfort and security, a phenomenon known as **monotropism**. Authors such as Jackson (1993) have conducted research in cultures in which a multiple caregiver arrangement is normative and question whether monotropy adequately describes attachment development in the multiple caregiver context. Van Ijzendoorn (1993) asserts, however, that even in contexts where infants have multiple caregivers and develop multiple attachments, a special infant-mother bond exists and infants are likely to prefer proximity to their mothers in stressful situations.

While the distribution and manifestation of secure and insecure attachment may differ among various cultural groups, the link between early care and infant security appears to hold across cultural contexts. Posada, Gao, Fang *et al.* (1995) found evidence of secure base phenomena in all seven of the cultures they studied. Posada, Jacobs, Carbonell *et al.* (1999) reported strong correlations between maternal sensitivity and infant secure base behaviour in two different samples of Columbian infants. This relationship was evident in both a middle class and a very poor sample, suggesting that the association between maternal sensitivity and infant security is not specific to middle class sectors of the population. Waters and Cummings (2000) argue that while attachment theory does assume that sensitivity to infant signals, cooperative interaction, availability, and responsiveness are important in the development of attachment, attachment theory does not assume that these are equally prevalent in every culture. They believe that attachment theory is able to accommodate differing cultural contexts.

# The impact of AIDS on childhood development in South Africa

With a total of 4.2 million infected people, South Africa has the largest number of people living with HIV/AIDS in the world, as well as one of the world's fastest-growing epidemics. In South Africa, by the end of the year 2000, one woman in four between the ages of twenty and twenty-nine was infected with the virus (UNAIDS 2000b). As more HIV infections develop into AIDS cases, the epidemic, with its dire social and economic consequences, is becoming increasingly visible. A less well-known but equally calamitous effect of the AIDS pandemic is the effect of the disease on the emotional well-being of South Africa's children. The majority of those dying from AIDS tend to be people in the prime of their lives who are often parents. The disease poses a threat to the psychological development of South African children both in terms of the impact for the millions who live with a parent or parents with AIDS, and in terms of the huge number who have been, and stand to be, orphaned by the disease.

Women with AIDS are at risk of compromised mother-infant interactions that may impede the establishment of secure attachment and render these infants vulnerable to subsequent difficulties. Prolonged or severe illness in the family of origin may contribute to attachment style in that this affects the quality of parenting – rendering parents unavailable, or inconsistently available, to their children both physically and emotionally (Stuart and Noyes 1999). Prolonged illness and associated factors such as physical debilitation, separations due to hospitalisation, and depression may interfere with the development of an attachment bond to a parent infected with AIDS. Healthy spouses may be equally unavailable to children in their bid to care for the ill and in their absorption with their own loss. Parental illness may also result in the parenting relationship becoming inverted, with children, increasingly perceived by seriously ill parents as sources of support, assuming caregiving roles. Equally, children who are themselves infected with AIDS may have attachment difficulties. Young children with specific chronic medical conditions were shown to be less secure as infants than children in a matched control group. Minde (1999) argues that not only will children with existing attachment difficulties prior to contracting a serious medical condition be further compromised in their attachment status by events associated with illness, but also a chronic illness is likely to stress significantly the attachment system of many well-attached children.

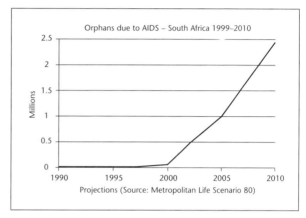

**Figure 14.2** Orphans due to AIDS in South Africa, 1990–2010 (UNAIDS, 1999).

Insecure attachment puts these children at risk of developing behavioural and social problems, poor self-esteem, and general adjustment difficulties, particularly when there is no improvement in the subsequent caregiving environment.

The number of children orphaned by AIDS in South Africa may reach one million children by 2004, with fourteen per cent of South African children having lost their parents by 2005. It is believed that one in every three of such children will be under the age of five.

Clearly, loss of parents due to AIDS is likely further to disrupt attachment for these children – the association between loss of a parent during childhood and a marked degree of insecure attachment has been well documented in the literature. From an attachment theory perspective, the long-term developmental impact of these early upsets and losses is potentially dire, and these orphaned children may be vulnerable to a range of behavioural, emotional, and mental health problems. Early loss of a significant caregiver may render them more susceptible to the effects of stress and influence the way they interpret future relationships and experiences. However, opportunities for change remain, particularly if these orphaned children are afforded stable and responsive care over an extended period of time.

A common strategy in AIDS-affected households is to send one or more children away to extended family members to ensure that they are fed and cared for. Such extended family structures have been able to absorb some of the stress for increasing numbers of orphans, particularly in Africa. However, urbanisation and migration for labour, often across

*Developmental psychologists in South Africa have an important role to play in examining the psychology of the AIDS orphan.*

borders, are destroying those structures. As the number of orphans grows and the number of potential caregivers shrinks, traditional coping mechanisms are stretched to breaking point (UNAIDS 2000a).

The impetus for the development of attachment theory came from Bowlby's investigations of the mental health of homeless children in post-war Europe, and Bowlby's work had a significant impact on social policy regarding the placement and care that was most likely to foster healthy psychological development. Similarly, developmental psychologists in South Africa have an important role to play in examining the psychology of the AIDS orphan, in informing society and policy makers about the developmental sequelae of this phenomenon, and in making recommendations about how best to intervene in supporting these children and fostering their psychological growth.

## A critique of attachment theory

Bowlby revolutionised thinking about the mother-infant relationship and about the importance and function of close relationships (Bretherton 1997). Attachment theory has emerged as a major domain of inquiry among researchers interested in human development and has been empirically productive, generating an enormous body of research focused on understanding the social, emotional, and interpersonal development of children. Although the Strange Situation has been criticised for not reflecting cultural variation in cross-cultural studies, it has provided researchers with an excellent tool for measuring attachment security in infants. There is substantial empirical evidence that supports the existence of the core elements of attachment theory, including the secure base phenomenon and internal working models. Attachment theory has also been valued for having the potential for predictive power, based on findings of continuity between early quality of attachment and later socio-emotional development (Harwood 1995).

Bowlby took issue with the emphasis placed by psychoanalysis on the child's inner fantasy world, rather than on actual life events and inter-actions. Bowlby chose to emphasise external reality and the importance of environmental influence in psychological development. Consequently he has been accused by the psychoanalysts of not taking sufficient account of the child's inner world (Holmes 1995) or of distortions in the child's per-ceptions of the external world (Fonagy 2000).

Bowlby was aware of the importance of societal supports for the development of secure relationships in childhood and later life and had a keen interest in social policy throughout his career (Bretherton 1997). He championed the rights to love and care of children who were innocent victims of war and social disruption (Holmes 1995). Many of the revolu-tionary changes in childcare of the post-war period were partly a result of Bowlby's efforts. These include allowing parents into hospital with their sick children, the emphasis on foster, rather than institutional care, and political acceptance of the need for childcare benefits paid to mothers. Bowlby has, however, been criticised for placing undue emphasis upon the role of the mother, and the concept of maternal deprivation has led mothers to feel anxious about the potentially damaging effects of even brief separations from their children. These concerns appear to stem from a misunderstanding of the concept of monotropism to mean that only the mother would do.

# Recommended readings

Bowlby, J. (1969). *Attachment and loss (Vol. 1): Attachment.* London: Hogarth Press.

Bowlby, J. (1973). *Attachment and loss (Vol. 2): Separation: Anxiety and anger.* London: Hogarth Press.

Bowlby, J. (1980). *Attachment and loss (Vol. 3): Loss, sadness and depression.* London: Hogarth Press.
(*The original Bowlby trilogy presenting his theory of attachment. The first volume examines the nature of the child's ties to the mother, focusing on instinctive behaviour and the development of attachment behaviour. The second volume focuses on separation and separation anxiety. The third volume looks at the effects of a death in the family on the lives of children and adults. Bowlby's writing is fairly accessible.*)

Cassidy, J. and Shaver, P. R. (1999). *Handbook of attachment: Theory, research and clinical applications.* New York: Guilford Press.
(*A comprehensive volume, with contributions from the pre-eminent authorities in the field, presenting the current state of knowledge about attachment, and the continuing development of attachment theory and its clinical applications. Highly recommended for those with a particular interest in broadening their knowledge within this field.*)

Holmes, J. (1993). *John Bowlby and attachment theory.* London: Routledge.
(*Jeremy Holmes has written several commentaries on Bowlby's work. In this book, he provides some detail on Bowlby's life and work, examines the origins of Bowlby's ideas, and presents the main features of attachment theory and their relevance to contemporary psychoanalytic psychotherapy.*)

(*Peter Fonagy's articles comparing attachment and psychoanalytic theory may be of interest. He has written a chapter in Cassidy and Shaver's* Handbook of attachment, *entitled 'Psychoanalytic theory from the viewpoint of attachment theory and research'. Alternatively, his paper entitled 'Points of con-vergence and divergence between psychoanalytic and attachment theories: Is psychoanalytic theory truly different?' may be downloaded at http://www.psychol.ucl.ac.uk/psychoanalysis/confpapers.html.*)

# Critical thinking tasks

1) Skinner and Swartz (1989) conducted research in the Western Cape examining the psychological sequelae for the preschool child of a parent's detention as a political prisoner. These authors found that children whose parents had been detained in the 1985–1986 State of Emergency in South Africa suffered a range of developmental and emotional difficulties, including separation anxiety.

   1.1) Drawing on attachment theory, account for the difficulties experienced in this circumstance.
   1.2) Discuss other phenomena prevalent in apartheid South Africa (such as urbanisation, migrant labour, domestic workers), which are likely to have impacted on the development of attachment among South Africans.

2) Consider the AIDS epidemic in South Africa and the enormous number of children orphaned by the disease. If, like Bowlby, you were called upon to comment on the mental health implications of the problem and to make recommendations to the government regarding a policy of intervention, what issues would you emphasise and what suggestions would you make?

3) Given the increasing number of women entering the workforce, a substantial number of children are receiving non-parental care, including that offered by crèches or day care centres, from a very early age. What are your feelings about this trend and its impact on attachment?

4) Can you identify the common grounds, and the points of major theoretical divergence, between attachment theory and psychoanalysis?

5) Refer for your answers to the case study of Kobus Geldenhuys given in Chapter 3.

   5.1) How would Kobus Geldenhuys be classified in terms of his attachment security?
   5.2) Comment on the implications of Geldenhuys's mother's parenting style for the establishment of an attachment-exploration balance during childhood.
   5.3) Give a brief sketch of the nature of the internal working models that you imagine Geldenhuys developed within the context of his early caregiving relationships. Remember to comment on both his self model and other models.
   5.4) Discuss the impact that Geldenhuys's attachment difficulties are likely to have had on his personality development and later actions. In formulating your answer, consider the following:

   ◆ Insecure attachment has been found to be associated with criminality and violent behaviour, including coercive sexual behaviour.
   ◆ Poor social adjustment and a failure to achieve intimacy in adulthood have been cited as playing a role in sexual aggression.
   ◆ Insecure attachment is believed to result in deficits in empathy.

# Erikson's psychosocial stages of development

*Derek Hook*

---

This chapter presents the psychosocial theory of Erik Erikson. We shall discuss the following concepts:

1. The epigenetic approach to development.

2. Developmental 'virtues' and 'vices'.

3. The idea of ongoing and cumulative lifelong development.

4. The psychological impact of physical needs and effects.

5. The psychosocial stages of:
   - trust versus mistrust
   - autonomy versus shame and doubt
   - initiative versus guilt
   - industry versus inferiority
   - identity versus role confusion
   - intimacy versus isolation
   - generativity versus stagnation
   - integrity versus despair.

We include some considerations of Erikson's theory in the South African context of psychosocial development, and the chapter concludes with a review of critiques of this theory.

---

Erik Erikson

## Introduction: differences between Freud and Erikson

There are a significant number of continuities between the developmental theories of Sigmund Freud and Erik Erikson. In fact, in many

**Ego.** The 'executive' or adaptive agency of the mind, which mediates between the demands of reality, the superego, and the id. The ego arises from the need to master instinctual impulses, to operate independently of parental figures, and from the self-preservative imperative for the id to adapt to the conditions of objective reality.

**Crises.** Key challenges or turning points of maturation through which one can trace the pattern of an individual's personality. Each step in the cycle of life presents the individual with a new adaptive psychosocial life task, which the individual needs to resolve if further healthy development is to occur.

**Epigenetic approach to development.** The view that psychosocial development follows a 'ground-plan', a predetermined schedule, in terms of which each part of a developing organism will have a special time of ascendancy.

ways Erikson's first five stages are a reformulation and an expansion of Freud's psychosexual stages (Maier 1988). There are also, however, vital differences between the theories, and it is worthwhile, by way of introduction, to focus briefly on some of these theoretical divergences.

Freud emphasised the role of the unconscious, and hence the id, in determining behaviour. He also prioritised the sexual level of development, and viewed the developing child within a tight focus on the child-mother-father Oedipal triangle. Erikson, by contrast, focused on the adaptive abilities of the **ego**, and prioritised the social level of development. Instead of an ongoing, lifelong struggle between conscious and unconscious processes, he considers how personal and social **crises** provide the necessary challenges for healthy growth to occur within the individual. In short, although Erikson, like Freud, held a psychoanalytic view, it would be true to say that he converted Freud's *psycho-sexual* account of development into a properly *psychosocial* theory of development.

A further difference between the theorists lies in the fact that Erikson seems to adopt a far more optimistic view of development than Freud does. In this respect it is significant that Freud's developmental theory may be seen as oriented towards explaining the causes of psychopathology. In fact, to make a general distinction between the theories of Freud and Erikson, one might say that whereas Freud's theory is a 'map of how things can go wrong', Erikson's is a 'map of how things go right' in the life of the child. Erikson's optimism is also reflected in the fact that, unlike Freud, he felt that a great deal of important development takes place after the first six years of life. Rather than following Freud's determinism, which allows for very little, if any, deviation from the fundamental behavioural and interactional patterns set in early life, Erikson (1980) asserts that fundamental developmental changes occur across the entire life-span. In stark contrast to Freud, he sees people as problem solvers who move towards constructive and progressive resolutions of life problems.

# Basic assumptions of Erikson's theory

## The epigenetic approach

Erikson favours an *epigenetic* approach ('epi' meaning 'upon', 'genetic' meaning 'emergence') to the study of human development. This, in short, means that everything that grows has a 'ground-plan', a predetermined schedule, in terms of which each part of a developing organism will have a special time of ascendancy. This time of ascendancy is a critical period in which maturational growth must take place, failing which detrimental effects will follow. A decisive turn one way or another is unavoidable here – these are moments of decision between progress and regression, integration and retardation (Erikson, 1963). Having said this, it is important to be clear that the various stages do, however, all exhibit a tendency to *overcome* their respective developmental challenges.

For Erikson (1963; 1980), growth occurs in a regular and sequential fashion, moving in an orderly and cumulative manner from one developmental stage to the next, until each part of the individual has developed. The outcome of this 'maturational timetable' is a wide and integrative set of life skills and abilities that function together within the autonomous individual. Each stage of the maturational timetable ties a key social life-challenge (or crisis) to a crucial point of physiological development. As Erikson puts it, each human being is at all times a biological organism, an ego, and a member of society, and is involved as such in three processes of development. The outcome of human development then is 'the ego's successful mediation between the physical stages and social institutions' (Erikson 1963, 54). Hence Erikson, like Freud, powerfully links psychological development (and socialisation generally) to biological maturation. (It should be noted, however, that Erikson places far more emphasis on specific social structures than does Freud, to the point that he even implicates social institutions in the outcome of his developmental stages).

## Virtues and vices

Although Erikson refers to his developmental stages as *crises*, these are not crises in the fatalistic or catastrophic sense, but are rather critical times in the developmental sense of challenges – turning points of maturation – through which we can trace the pattern of an individual's personality. Each step in the cycle of life presents the individual with a new life task, a set of choices and tests, which are prescribed by the structure of the culture and society in which he or she lives (Erikson 1963). The successful resolution of such challenges leads to the gaining of what Erikson calls **virtues**, a term which should be understood not as an evaluation of the individual, but as an indication of growing **ego strength**. In this way growth, for Erikson, may be understood in terms of the achievement of integration – both of new psychosocial abilities within the ego, and of the individual into the structures and values of society. The completion of each stage of life means, in Erikson's words, that a 'new strength is added to a widening ensemble of life-skills' (1969, 52). One should note here that the opposite of a *virtue* is not a vice, an 'evil', but is rather a developmental deficit, a disorder or dysfunction, that manifests wherever an individual has been hindered in the activation and perfection of *virtues* (Erikson 1968).

**Virtues.** The psychosocial values of hope, will, purpose, skill, and fidelity that are the outcome of the healthy resolution of developmental crises. These virtues should not be understood as an evaluation of the individual, but rather as an indication of growing ego strength.

**Ego strength.** The term used to describe the ability of the ego to moderate and deal with the effects of the opposing forces of the id, the superego, and reality.

## Ongoing and cumulative development

Although certain crises become critical at certain points of the life cycle (at which point they will be more important than other related crises), and although they require the resolution of certain tasks and conflicts, these crises are all presented throughout the life of the individual (Erikson 1963; 1980). Throughout life, for example, people will need to test and revisit the degree to which they can trust others. In this way none of the stages is ever fully complete, or absolutely resolved. We will continue, for instance, both to trust and mistrust throughout our lives, and indeed knowing how to mistrust is frequently as important as it is to trust.

Because Erikson's is a cumulative account of development, each developmental stage is reliant, to a degree, on the successful negotiation of earlier stages. The resolution of earlier developmental crises and their integration into the ego is in a sense the necessary preparation the child will need to tackle the next developmental stage. (Each resolved step is also, in some ways, a reintegration of previous steps). Nevertheless, although Erikson claims that the lack of resolution of an earlier stage will adversely affect how the individual attempts to resolve later stages (because the later stages will have a foundation which has not been completely built), he does allow for the possibility that adjustments made at one stage can in fact be altered or even reversed later. Craig (1996, 59) describes this as follows:

> ... children who are denied attention in infancy can grow to normal adulthood if they are given extra attention at later stages ... adjustments to conflicts play an important part in the development of personality. The resolution of these conflicts is cumulative; a person's manner of adjustment at each stage affects the way he or she handles the next conflict.

Although each developmental crisis manifests around a biological focus and has a social dimension (not to mention a powerful effect on the eventual personality of the child), it is important to understand that each stage crystallises around an *emotional conflict*. This is why Erikson refers to each stage as *an opposition*. Erikson is predominantly a theorist of affect; it is emotions in their productive and resolving capacities that make up the building blocks of human behaviour, and ultimately, individual personality. In what follows we will discuss Erikson's eight stages of psychosocial development, with a particular focus on the first five stages, all of which are applicable to childhood.

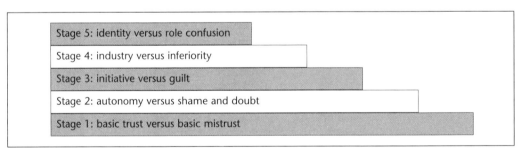

**Figure 15.1** For Erikson each stage forms the basis for the next; the successful resolution of each stage forms the foundation for the next stage of development (Carver and Scheier 1988).

# The eight stages of psychosocial development

## Stage 1: basic trust versus basic mistrust

After a regulated life of warmth and protection in the womb, the newly born infant arrives in the outer world as a helpless, vulnerable, and absolutely dependent creature. Understandably, its first emotional task is learning how to trust the primary caregiver, without whom the infant would not survive. This trust is reliant on the baby's developing sense of the world as a good and safe place. It is also reliant on a sense of physical comfort and on a minimum amount of (physiological) uncertainty and doubt. As Maier (1988, 90) describes it:

> Maintaining the bodily functions of respiration, ingestion, diges-
> tion and motor movements are the only concerns of young organ-
> isms ... these functions comprise their immediate purpose for
> interacting with their environment. Thus, bodily experiences pro-
> vide the basis for a psychological state of trust.

It is in this way that Erikson notes that the first demonstration of social trust in the baby is 'the ease of his feeding, the depth of his sleep, the relaxation of his bowels' (1963, 247).

## The psychological impact of physical needs and effects

A basic sense of mistrust stems from unsatisfactory physical experiences, from the sense that one's needs are being unmet. A fundamental goal of this stage is the attainment of a kind of equilibrium – the mutual regula-tion of the baby's increasingly receptive capacities with the maternal tech-niques of provision (Erikson 1963). It is this regulation that helps the child balance the discomfort caused by the immaturity of the homeosta-sis with which it was born (Erikson 1963). In its increasing waking hours the child comes to develop a greater sense of familiarity, which coincides with a feeling of inner goodness. In this sense it is understandable that Erikson (1963, 247) calls the infant's first social achievement its 'willing-ness to let the mother out of sight without undue anxiety or rage'.

A rudimentary trust begins to develop here – a sense of inner cer-tainty as well as of outer predictability. Indeed, this basic growing bud of ego identity depends on the recognition that there 'is an inner population of remembered and anticipated sensations and images which are firmly correlated with the outer population of familiar and predictable things and people' (Erikson 1963, 247). Consistency and sameness are important values for the child, and need to be experienced both on the 'inside' and on the 'outside' so that the child can learn to trust and rely on its providers, and so that it can trust the self and the capacity of its own organs to cope with urges (Erikson, 1963).

Erikson, like Freud, feels that the mouth is the primary bodily focus of this stage of development. Accordingly, he suggests that teething is a crucial testing phase here, where the child is set the challenge of trying to moderate the internal stimulus of pain without giving in totally to the only action which promises some relief – biting (Erikson 1963, 248). Biting of the breast of course may result in the breast being withdrawn, hence this inner sensation may affect the child's outer-world relations. Erikson claims that teething may have a prototypical significance, and that masochistic tendencies later in life may stem from just this tendency to 'assure cruel comfort by enjoying one's hurt when unable to prevent a significant loss' (1963, 248).

### The possibility for psychopathology

This is the most foundational of all the stages; indeed, its resulting virtue – *hope* – is the basic ingredient of all ego strength to follow. Given the founding importance of this essential constituent of the ego, it is unsurprising that Erikson notes that a great variety of psychopathologies would have their origin at the unsuccessful resolution of this early stage of development. He observes:

> we do find in potentially psychotic people that the first relationships in earliest childhood seem to have been severely disturbed. We could speak here of a psychosocial weakness which consists of a readiness to mistrust and to lose hope in rather fundamental ways (Erikson 1963, 248).

In addition to masochism and depression, schizoid behaviour (that is, social detachment and a strongly conflictual or restricted emotional disposition) may stem from this early developmental phase. Each of these disorders, for Erikson (1963), relates to the absence of a basic trust in self and the world.

**Identity.** For Erikson the idea of identity refers to a sense of being at one with oneself as one grows and develops; it refers to an affinity between the individual and his or her social roles and community ties. Identity for Erikson is only attained through the integration of previous identifications.

### The importance of parental care

Although the various crises of trust versus mistrust ultimately need to be dealt with in the child's newly developing ego, they are first a task for maternal care. Indeed the quality of the maternal relationship here is vital – it is mothers who create a sense of trust in their children by administering to their needs in a way that combines sensitive care of the baby's individual needs with a firm sense of personal trustworthiness (Erikson 1963). This maternal care forms the basis in the child of a sense of **identity** which will later combine 'a sense of being "all right", of being oneself, and of becoming what other people trust one will become' (Erikson 1963, 249). As Erikson (1963) puts it, good maternal care results in the baby learning once and for all to trust the mother, to trust him- or herself, and to trust the world.

Erikson is optimistic about the abilities of infants to learn to trust, and claims that there are very few frustrations that the child cannot endure if ultimately their frustration leads to 'greater sameness and stronger continuity of development, toward a final integration of the individual life cycle with some meaningful wider belongingness' (Erikson 1963, 249). It is important to note that the care of the child does not begin and end with the mother. Other adults in the household will also play some caring role in the development of the infant, as will the extended family into which the child is born. Moreover, society's recognition of the family as one of its basic institutions, and the relevant culture's guarantee for the continuation of fundamental societal mores and values, will likewise influence

PHOTO: GILL HAIDEN

*For Erikson, one of the child's first developmental challenges is learning to trust the external world. The role of the parents, as principal caregivers, in consoling the child in times of misfortune, disappointment, or physical pain, is of utmost importance here.*

the developing child (Maier 1988). What is important here is that Erikson places the infant squarely within its socio-cultural context. Therefore, although he has aimed to design a theory that is a generalisable and even universal account of human development, he still suggests that we should, indeed *must*, 'fill in the blanks' by looking carefully at the socio-cultural and political circumstances underpinning development.

### Institutional correlatives to development

For Erikson, each successive developmental crisis corresponds to a social institution, for the simple reason that the human life cycle and society's institutions have evolved together (Erikson 1963). The social institution corresponding to this first stage of development is religion, an institution that powerfully demonstrates the human ability to hope and trust (Erikson 1963).

## Stage 2: autonomy versus shame and doubt

With the development of a basic sense of trust in their caregivers, in their environment, and in themselves, infants begin to realise that they can determine their own behaviour, and this ability is the basis of a growing sense of autonomy (Erikson 1963; 1980). Infants are still very much dependent on caregivers, however, and this continued reliance means that they experience doubt about their capacities and about their own autonomy (Erikson 1963). The infant's contrasting feelings about its self-capacity and autonomy stem from the range of activities it is involved in at this stage. It is at this stage that toddlers have a budding awareness of their body and how to control it. At this stage they are involved in a very wide range of day-to-day activities like eating, dressing, 'toileting', and moving about.

### The importance of rudimentary mobility and muscular maturity

The toddler at this stage is mastering movement and mobility; reaching, walking, climbing, and holding are all important new exploratory activities (Maier 1988). Similarly, this is the stage where children become able to regulate their own toiletry activities through increased muscular maturity (Erikson 1963). All of these activities can lead either to a sense of accomplishment, self-control, and self-confidence if successfully carried out, or to a sense of self-doubt if unsuccessfully executed. Parental supervision accompanies all of these activities, and the parent's role is absolutely vital in encouraging and affirming certain accomplishments, and in correcting failures. Parental approval inevitably boosts the child's sense of self-esteem and competence in the case of 'a job well done'; failures, on the other hand, particularly in toilet training, may be accentuated (Erikson 1963). This is especially the case if the child is punished or labelled as messy, sloppy, or bad, and creates a situation where the sense of shame and self-doubt may become very strong and may have detrimental effects on the emotional development of the child (Erikson 1963).

Given that toilet training and sphincter control are the most important physiological challenges at this stage of development, it is hardly surprising that the two most basic and abstract concepts that come to prominence within the child at this stage are those of 'holding on' and 'letting go' (Erikson 1963). Virtues and vices can both be read into these relations:

> ... to hold can become a destructive and cruel retaining or restrain-ing, and it can become a pattern of care: to have and hold. To let go, too can turn into an inimical letting loose of destructive forces, or it can become a relaxed 'to let pass' and 'to let be' (Erikson 1963, 251).

### A budding sense of volition and independence

It is at this stage of the infant's life that it comes to possess, in the most powerful way so far, the prerogative of choice – to 'hold on' or to 'let go' – and this is its route towards 'standing on its own feet', to deciding for itself or, on the other hand, to clinging fearfully to the parents. A sense of autonomy then stems not only from the child's sense of accomplish-ment in toilet training, and in a variety of exploratory activities, it also comes from the child's *sense of independence*, from its limited but growing ability *to choose and act for itself.* Accordingly, the virtue of this stage is that of possessing one's own *will.* The development of such a will calls for sensitive parenting, because this is the 'me do' phase where toddlers begin to try and do almost everything themselves. This is where parents have to strike a balance between granting the child gradual independ-ence, letting it try certain things, while still maintaining firm limits, and disallowing it from trying others. It is important here that a give-and-take relationship is established between child and parent, because it is through a balanced relationship of this sort that autonomy is fostered and self-doubt diminished within the child.

The inadequate resolution of this stage can lead to detrimental out-comes in the individual. If it is the case that children are denied the grad-ual and well-guided experience of the autonomy of free choice, they will turn against themselves all these urges to manipulate and discriminate (Erikson 1963). They will *overmanipulate* themselves, and develop a precocious and excessive self-consciousness, which for Erikson (1963) is the source of senseless repetitiveness, obsessiveness, stubbornness, and obsessive-compulsive behaviour. Intolerance and irrational fear may like-wise be seen as the result of such a lack of confidence and self-assurance.

### The implications of self-doubt and shame

Doubt and shame are the chief factors that threaten the development of autonomy. Erikson characterises shame as an extreme form of self-con-sciousness – as being highly visible without wanting to be visible (Erikson 1963). This 'being seen' against one's own wishes, this being caught 'with one's pants down' is like a rage that would like to 'destroy the eyes of the world', or alternatively it is a 'rage turned against the self' (Erikson 1963, 253). In this connection one might consider how formative childhood experiences of shame play a part in influencing the development of sui-cidal tendencies, or antisocial personality disorders. Doubt is 'the brother of shame' according to Erikson (1963). It results as a personality trait if the child is consistently dominated by the will of others, if what they do is constantly questioned or criticised. For Erikson (1963) this stage becomes decisive in determining the individual's interpersonal ratios of cooperation or wilfulness, self-expression or self-suppression, and love or hate. As he puts it, 'From a sense of self-control without loss of self-esteem comes a lasting sense of good will and pride; from a sense of loss of self control and of foreign overcontrol comes a lasting property for doubt and shame' (Erikson 1963, 254).

### The institutions of law and order

Just as the first developmental crisis was tied to a fundamental social institution, so this stage is tied to 'the lasting need of the individual to have his will reaffirmed and delineated within an adult order of things which at the same time reaffirms and delineates the will of others ... [under] the institutional safeguard [of the] ... *principle of law and order*' (Erikson 1963, 254). Erikson also suggests that the pattern of child training established at this stage determines the eventual form of political authority that the child will prefer as an adult.

## Stage 3: initiative versus guilt

Having gained a rudimentary sense of autonomy, children now build on their limited explorations of the previous phase by moving on to a new set of environmental conquests in widening social and spatial spheres (Maier 1988). This is an optimistic period of growth for Erikson (1963), who remarks how children seem to be in possession of surplus energy that enables them to forget failures quickly and to approach new activities with undiminished enthusiasm. This is the stage in which the social environment of children challenges them to be active and directed in mastering specific tasks. The virtue that correlates to these challenges is *purpose*. It is at this stage that children are asked to assume an increasing amount of responsibility – for themselves, for their own bodies, and even, occasionally, for their siblings.

### Children's widening exploratory potential

Having mastered the skills of reaching, grasping, climbing, and holding, children are now learning better how to walk and run, two newfound mobilities that quickly extend the child's exploratory abilities (Erikson 1963). Similarly, children have a better grasp of language and can ask enquiring questions about what they do not understand. They are fascinated by how the world works, and how they may be able to influence it. In many ways, children at this stage are testing their new skills and abilities, 'feeling out' their potentials. Children also have an active fantasy life at this stage; for them the world contains both real and imaginary things and people, and they fantasise actively about what they might become 'when they grow up' (Erikson 1963). These imaginative abilities are important in stimulating learning and creativity in the child.

Children at this stage have an enormous thirst for experience and exploration, an enthusiasm for initiative that can easily get them into trouble, or lead them into danger. As Maier (1988) explains, children are reaching out with both language and locomotion at this stage, expanding their fields of experience and of imagination, but some of these possibilities frighten them. Certain boundaries and rules have been put in place by caregivers, and the child has to decide whether to respect these restrictions, or whether to explore beyond them.

### Guilt and self-regulation

Guilt is the emotion that arises to limit these explorations, to stake out reasonable from unreasonable areas of investigation. Maier (1988, 100–1) claims that, 'Permissiveness towards such trying out, daring, and investigating is an essential feature of development – as is the establishment of certain boundaries to circumscribe just what *is* permissible'. It is the child's task to balance these two options. Given that Erikson's developmental stages are largely mapped upon those of Freud, it is not surprising to discover that the exploratory activities of this stage also revolve around the discovery of the genitals as a zone of pleasure. Similarly, the guilt of this stage is intricately intertwined with the content of the Oedipus complex and, in boys, the phobias of castration anxiety.

The conflict of initiative versus guilt is to a large degree the process by which children learn to take on a parental role over themselves (Erikson 1963; 1980). This is the stage where children face the universal crisis of turning from an attachment to their parents to the slow process of becoming a parent, of *becoming one's own parent* and supervising one's self (Erikson 1963). Through the processes of the Oedipus complex, through strong identification with the same-sex parent, and through a greater awareness and respect for parental authority, the child now becomes able to do just that – to take on, in part, a parental role over itself. The conscience of the superego now comes into operation. Erikson's suggestion here is that there is a split in the child 'where the infantile body and mind now become divided into an infantile set which perpetuates the exuberance of growth potentials, and a parental set which supports and increases self-observation, self-guidance and self-punishment' (Erikson 1963, 256).

### Moral development

Erikson (1963) suggests that moral development in children occurs primarily at this stage, and contends that its source (the early superego) can be cruel and overcontrolling – overconstricting to the point that children develop an over-obedience more literal than the one the parent has wished them to develop. In fact, Erikson argues that some of our deepest regressions and longest resentments stem from parents who themselves did not live up to the ideals of this new conscience: 'One of the deepest conflicts in life is the hate for a parent who served as the model for the superego, but who ... was found trying to get away with the very transgressions which the child can no longer tolerate in themselves' (Erikson 1963, 257).

The adult problems that can stem from this phase of development are inhibition, impotence, or denial – the kinds of paralysis that result from an individual being too scared to 'stick their neck out' (Erikson 1963). On the other hand, we may find recklessness, showing-off, and gratuitous risk-taking behaviour in those who are trying to overcompensate for such inhibitions (Erikson 1963).

# The effects of domestic violence on psychosocial development in children

South Africa is a violent society characterised by high levels of brutal crime and physical political conflict. An often-neglected form of South African violence is that of domestic abuse. As Angless and Shefer (1997) note, the home – far from being a safe place for children – is often riddled with various forms of familial violence, with physical and sexual abuses, which can understandably cause a range of emotional difficulties in child development. The effects of witnessing violence committed against a family member by another family member, or of being abused oneself, vary widely for different children.

In Erikson's psychosocial developmental theory it is easy to see that a violent parent, or violence in the home more generally, would pose a threat to the child's ability to resolve, in particular, the crisis of *trust versus mistrust*, but also the crises of *autonomy versus shame/doubt* and of *initiative versus guilt*. If children live largely in the shadow of fear of an abusive parent, it will be very difficult, if not impossible, for them to form a strong sense of trust in that parent. In this connection, Angless and Shefer (1997) report that children exposed to domestic violence often live with terrible anxiety and uncertainty, and exhibit symptoms of emotional distress such as restlessness, nervousness, and a variety of related somatic complaints. In addition to being not able to trust their basic home environment – or abusive parent(s) – such children often experience the suspicion that they may ultimately not be able properly to trust or control *themselves*. Abused children observe parents who cannot control their own anger and subsequently become concerned that they may not be able to control themselves. Guilt and anxiety, and *auto-phobia* (fear of their own behaviour) are generally characteristic features of this state of fundamental mistrust.

Guilt is a major problem for abused children. As Angless and Shefer (1997) suggest, an alarming number of children who live with the threat of domestic violence feel that such violence is *their* fault, and come to blame themselves for 'causing the problem'. This can have detrimental effects on the self-esteem of such children, in the form of shame and feelings of 'badness'.

Social isolation is a frequent outcome for children who witness or suffer domestic abuse. Angless and Shefer (1997) quote a variety of figures suggesting that the children of battered women are often alienated from their peers, and do not relate to their common interests and activities. Similarly, children who have been abused themselves often have great difficulties in social adjustment, in 'fitting in' at school and in maintaining productive social interactions more generally. Difficulties in concentration, poor academic results, school phobia, fighting with peers, and general rebelliousness against adults and authority figures may all stem from a violent home background (Angless and Shefer 1997).

The formation of strong role models and positive gender identifications are both also extremely problematic for children who come from violent homes. While children do not want to identify with the abuser, they equally do not want to identify with the victim and as such they may equate maleness with violence and hurting women, and femaleness with being hurt by men (Angless and Shefer 1997).

Perhaps most disturbing of all is the contention that frequent exposure to violence, both as a witness and as a victim, appears to be a predisposing factor in future violence. This is an ominous suggestion, particularly considering the current 'culture of violence' in South Africa, where a climate of brutal violence is so well established in the history of the country.

The moral conscience (or superego) is built up not only from parental prohibitions, but also from the child's socio-cultural heritage. Cultural values, the tastes, class standards, characteristics, and traditions of a society all contribute to the child's sense of morality (Erikson 1980). Many of the child's wildest fantasies are now repressed and inhibited through this new capacity for guilt, and the predominant challenge here is to balance a newfound sense of moral order with an ongoing thirst for initiative. The child has to negotiate the tension between an ever-present sense of moral surveillance and the desire to gain social experiences and knowledge. Like Freud (1991) though, Erikson (1963) suggests that the new superego of the child not only restricts the horizon of the permissible, but also fosters positive goals; it sets the direction in which the dreams of childhood might be attached to the goals of an active adult life.

### The child becomes 'a unit of social interaction'

The energetic learning of this stage is matched by a new willingness to share and cooperate, to associate with, and enter the lives of others. The child at this stage, according to Erikson (1963), learns quickly and avidly, and is eager to combine with other children, to profit from teachers, and to emulate ideal prototypes. Indeed, sociability is certainly a core component of this stage – here the child starts to become a social unit, an integrated personality, a social being in relationship to other beings (Maier 1988). Children begin to take note of and understand role and sex differences among those within their environment. They come to experience themselves as a boy or a girl – a gender identity that is grasped and understood in a social manner through a sense of membership with a particular social grouping.

### Gender and social role development

Overt gender differences become apparent at this stage. Erikson (1963) sees boys as indulging in intense motor activities, and as participating in directed problem-solving practices where curiosity and urgent exploration fuel investigations into the unknown. Boys' activities at this age are marked with an intrusive quality; the earlier emphasis on experiences with people shifts increasingly to a preoccupation with the world of actions and things (Erikson 1963). By contrast, the activity of girls at this age is characterised by an inceptive quality, a willingness to include others, and to be involved in the lives of others. These are the qualities that will go on to prepare girls for their future maternal role (Erikson 1963). Erikson adds here that cultural values and roles are imposed on developing children, and therefore one should allow a certain amount of cultural latitude for the way that boys and girls will be gendered into social roles. In whatever way such roles may be assigned however, Erikson (1963) does emphasise that they will be well practiced by the child at this stage of development.

As children become increasingly socially competent, they also come to be aware of differences between discrete families and social groups. They are also involved with a variety of different social institutions: nursery schools, kindergarten, the earliest grades of primary school, church, and, of course, their own family (Erikson 1980). Their sense of social role and placement becomes increasingly well defined and they gradually become aware of the opportunities and responsibilities that they may be able to, or have to, take on as adults (Erikson 1980). The social institution that correlates to this stage of development is economic endeavour, an institution which takes root through the adoption of ideal role models that children will go on to emulate as they become active participants in the economic life of a society (Erikson 1963).

## Stage 4: industry versus inferiority

This stage corresponds to Freud's period of latency and is, accordingly, a relatively calm period where children need to consolidate the rapid advancements made in the three previous stages. In many ways this is the stage in which the child 'fills in the gaps' of those psychosocial skills, social roles, and levels of physical growth already achieved. Although the child is now rapidly approaching the age where it is able to be parent (in the most rudimentary psychological and biological terms), it must first become a worker – a productive member of society and a potential provider (Erikson 1963). In short, the child must develop the virtue of *industriousness*.

### A wider sphere of social interactions

According to Erikson (1963), the child has now resolved, at some unconscious level, that there can be no workable future within the 'womb of the family', and it must now spread its skills and initiatives across a wider social realm. Children at this stage are developing an increasing number of skills and abilities at both home and school. They are preoccupied by the goal of gaining competence, proficiency, and mastery in certain key tasks assigned to them by parents and teachers (Erikson 1963). Energies once expended in play are now devoted to honing physical and perceptual skills, and children are eager to apply themselves to task-oriented activities, to becoming an absorbed unit of a productive situation (Maier 1988).

It is at this stage that the child's peer group comes to act as an extra-familial source of identification, and subsequently this group quickly becomes one of the most important influences on the developing personality of the child. The ability to communicate and productively to engage with peers becomes highly valued, as does gaining the recognition and positive acknowledgement of the peer group. This means of social identification is a

*At Erikson's fourth stage, industry versus inferiority, energies once expended in play are now devoted to honing physical and perceptual skills, and children are eager to apply themselves to task-oriented activities, such as those involved in education.*

highly competitive one, and children accordingly focus a great deal of energy on trying to excel at whatever activity they are involved in (Erikson 1963). Children are almost constantly 'sizing one another up', measuring their own skills and worth in comparison to a group norm. A great deal of emphasis is placed on who is the best, the funniest, the

PHOTO: GILL HAIDEN

*In many ways the school environment becomes 'a little culture by itself', as Erikson (1963) puts it.*

strongest, the fastest in the group, and in many ways the school environment becomes a little society of its own, 'a little culture by itself', as Erikson (1963) expresses it.

### Evaluation of self relative to group norms

The threat here lies in the danger of the child's sense of *inadequacy* and *inferiority* relative to this social group. Because comparison with peers at this stage is so important, a negative evaluation of self (relative to one's peers) is especially damaging at this time. In this way, the developmental crisis of this stage occurs precisely around the need of the child to find a strong sense of identity *apart from the nuclear family, within a receptive and affirming peer group* (Erikson 1963; 1980). Should the child fail in this quest, and in the related quest to gain the necessary technical competencies relevant to its culture then an abiding sense of inferiority and ineptness is what awaits him or her. For Erikson (1963), inferiority complexes, feelings of unworthiness, inability, and low self-esteem are rooted in this stage of development.

PHOTO: MICHELE VRDOLJAK

*At the fourth stage of development the child's imagination is increasingly submitted to the laws of the 'three Rs' (reading, writing, and arithmetic). This stage is also characterised by training, by systematic forms of instruction that teach children the basic fundamentals of technology – how to handle necessary tools and utensils.*

### Technological proficiency

This stage is characterised by training, by systematic forms of instruction that teach children the basic fundamentals of technology, how to handle the utensils, the tools, and household appliances handled on a day-to-day basis by 'big people' (Erikson 1963). Teaching the child to read and write, and application to practical educational tasks become important focal points at this stage, because these are the means through which the widest possible range of careers is made open to the child. Indeed, success at education is an important priority at this stage, no matter where the child is being raised. In this way, the exuberant imagination of children becomes increasingly tamed and harnessed, as Erikson (1963) puts it, to the laws of the 'Three Rs' (reading, writing, and arithmetic). The child's sense of self is enriched by the realistic development of certain competencies; it begins to appreciate the pleasures of work-completion through steady attention and persevering diligence (Erikson 1963). The child is now becoming a little adult with abilities that mirror and reflect the abilities of adults. At this point childhood ends and young adulthood begins. The ideal virtues that reflect this stage of development are technological skill and industriousness, and the social institution is technology.

## Stage 5: identity versus role confusion

Puberty brings about rapid bodily growth and a number of significant anatomical changes. The mastery of the body previously accomplished must now in a sense be 're-accomplished' as the child enters adulthood. The same holds for a variety of psychosocial skills: the adolescent must now face up to increasingly strong sexual urges, and must relocate him- or herself within a very different social matrix to the one inhabited as a child (Maier 1988). The doubts of childhood must now be re-negotiated; all the sameness and continuity relied upon in earlier stages must now be questioned (Erikson 1963). The entire developmental span of childhood must now be left behind, and a whole new set of challenges must be met if the adolescent is successfully to become an adult (Maier 1988).

*Answering the question 'Who am I?' – securing a solid base identity made up of various roles, talents, skills, and preferences – is the key challenge for individuals to face at Erikson's fifth stage of development.*

Just as the quality of *basic trust* was the platform upon which the child could forge new childhood experiences, so the establishment of *identity* (and the process of *identity formation*) will now prove fundamental if the adolescent is going to be able to enter the adult community. For Erikson (1963) the idea of identity refers to a sense of being at one with oneself as one grows and develops, and to an affinity between the individual and his or her social roles and community ties. Identity for Erikson (1963; 1980) is only attained through the integration of previous identifications. This integration is more than the sum total of all childhood identifications. It is the accrued experience of *all* identifications hitherto made

PHOTO: MICHELE VRDOLJAK

– all libidinal investments (that is investments of the sexual instincts), taken along with the aptitudes developed out of endowment and the opportunities offered in social roles (Erikson 1963). Skills and technical competencies gathered at the previous stage are also integrated into the developing sense of identity at this point. A key challenge here is in the way that these abilities may be cultivated within the occupational prototypes of the day (Erikson 1963).

### Integrating all aspects of self

In this phase, the dominant challenge in substantiating a secure sense of identity is to bring together the various facets of one's ego – those identifications and object-choice decisions, along with talents, skills, and multiple social roles. The key tension at this stage of development lies in holding together this diffuse and dispersed array of possible identifications, in trying to assemble and integrate the disparate rudiments of an identity. As observed by Craig (1996), it is typical these days for children to learn a number of roles: student, friend, sibling, athlete, musician, boy/girlfriend, etc. They have to sort out these various roles in some consistent way that allows for a basic similarity of attitudes and values, often a difficult task. It is made all the more difficult because a feeling of wholeness and self-consistency has to be coordinated with an ever-increasing perception of self as distinct and separate from others (Erikson 1963).

There are many life choices to be made here that will impact on the identity of the individual. These concern the individual's choice of career, the nature of personal alliances they will be prepared to enter into with others, the degree of mutuality they will share with peers, and their placement relative to their social roles, and with reference to the predominant socio-political issues of the day. The formation of identity requires a number of hallmarks of stability, and these stabilities are provided in terms of sameness and continuity – the qualities that are needed to hold together both one's past history and one's possible future and career. It is these qualities that lend a sense of confidence to the developing identity of the adolescent (Erikson 1963).

**Role confusion.** Inability to settle on an occupational career, a sexual object-choice, or a fundamental social role, leading to the inability to form a secure identity.

**Role confusion** can surface in various ways. Strong previous doubts about sexual orientation can lead to delinquent or psychotic episodes (Erikson 1963), whereas milder forms of confusion stem predominantly from the inability to settle on an occupational career, and from overidentifying practices (Erikson 1963).

### In- and out-group identifications

**Overidentification.** Adoption of a group identity that threatens to totally eclipse one's own sense of identity.

**Overidentification** for Erikson (1963) refers to that overzealous adoption of a group identity that threatens to totally eclipse one's own sense of identity. Here he means the excessive emulation of heroes or idols, involvement in particular cliques or crowds, or blind adherence to varieties of dress codes, or youth conventions. Overidentification is itself part of falling in love which, Erikson (1963) claims, is by no means simply a sexual matter at this age: 'To a considerable extent adolescent love is an attempt to arrive at a definition of one's identity by projecting one's diffused ego image on another and by seeing it thus reflected and gradually clarified' (Erikson 1963, 262).

Stability of identity is likewise secured through a consistency in the way that others variously understand, receive, and perceive one (Erikson 1963). For Erikson (1963), young adults at this stage are remarkably sensitive to, and aware of, the way that they appear in the eyes of others. This increased awareness of how one is viewed by the social world can complicate the process of identity formation, because one is involved in the attempt to *define* and *distinguish* oneself as *precisely distinct* from the rest of the social world generally. The danger at this stage is that of role confusion.

Erikson (1963) notes how youngsters at this age of development can be remarkably cruel to those who are 'out' – who are 'different' in race or cultural background, in tastes and gifts, in dress and gesture. This stage of development is characterised by the selection of the signs of the 'in-group' and the 'out-group'. The intolerance of youths towards 'out-groupers' is in large part, according to Erikson, a 'defence against [their

## Black adolescent identity development in apartheid South Africa

Drawing on Erikson's psychosocial theory, Stevens and Lockhat (1997) have attempted to explore how black South African adolescents may be attempting to negotiate the developmental challenges facing them within the changing socio-historical contexts of post-apartheid South Africa. Correctly reflecting the central challenge of Erikson's fifth stage, Stevens and Lockhat (1997) suggest that the primary task here is the development of congruence between the self-image and role expectations of the individual's social and emotional world. This, the authors suggest, may have been hampered in many black adolescents in apartheid South Africa because of contradictory role expectations encouraged through capitalist ideology on the one hand, and a racist ideology on the other:

> Black adolescents have been exposed to the imagery, symbols and values that encouraged individual achievement and social mobility, but simultaneously have been refused access to any significant material resources that allowed for this ... these contradictions have impeded the development of healthy self-concepts ... and healthy levels of independent judgement among black South Africans (Stevens and Lockhat 1997, 252).

Moreover, the widespread destruction of black family relations has also contributed to 'increased emotional insecurity among black adolescents ... [to] difficulties related to emotional independence during and after adolescence' (Stevens and Lockhat 1997, 252). In addition, these authors question whether the majority of black adolescents at this time were in a position to enjoy a moratorium period, especially considering that economic independence was, almost without exception, unattainable, and that entrance into a restricted job market would mean almost instant 'material enslavement' rather than a rich array of career options.

Rather than simply portraying black adolescents as victims in this way, Stevens and Lockhat argue that involvement in one or another kind of political activism – whether whole-hearted or merely peripheral – enabled a powerful way of resolving this stage of development:

> Politicisation provided a framework in which to generate meanings for social experience and to challenge them, and simultaneously offered a 'home' to many black adolescents who had originally experienced a disintegrated family life. It ... promoted a common social identity, through identification of common oppressive experiences, a common 'enemy', and broad, common objectives. In addition it fostered various counter-ideologies, a culture of collectivity, democratic participation, mature and socially independent judgement (Stevens and Lockhat 1997, 252).

own] sense of identity confusion' (1963, 262). If children were impressionable at the previous stages, they are in a sense more so now, because identity formation has become such an overriding focus. Indeed, Erikson (1963) notes that simple, cruel, and totalitarian doctrines often have appeal to the youths of countries and classes that are in the process of losing their more traditional group identities. The mind of the adolescent is an 'ideological mind', 'eager to be affirmed and to be confirmed by social rituals, creeds, and programmes which delineate what is evil, uncanny, and inimical, along with what is socially valued, prized, and idealised' (Erikson 1963, 263). This search for identity also means that youths often end up appointing well-meaning people in the role of adversaries. Youths are, as Erikson puts it, 'ever ready to install lasting idols and ideals as guardians of a final identity' (1963, 261).

### The importance of peers

Peers are important intermediaries between the developing individual and society at this stage. In a sense, the task of establishing a firm identity needs to happen fundamentally *through such peers*, and if possible, through a cooperating partner, someone with a place, a social career, and a perception of the future (Maier 1988). According to Erikson (1963, 262), 'adolescents ... help one another temporarily through much discomfort by forming cliques and by stereotyping themselves, their ideals, and their enemies'. Peer groups, friends, and close associates are generally the best indication here of the life path that the individual will follow. Key relationships with significant adults are also able to stabilise the identity and social role of the adolescent.

### Moratorium

**Moratorium.** A time of experimentation with different ideologies and careers, which will ultimately be resolved with a firm choice of identity.

This stage is also characterised by the transition from the general and abstract morality learned by the child to the applied and pragmatic ethics to be adopted in the day-to-day life of the adult (Erikson 1963). Similarly, it is this psychosocial stage that is most indicative of the transition between childhood and adulthood. The mind of the adolescent is essentially a mind of **moratorium** (a time of experimentation with different ideologies and careers which will ultimately be resolved with a firm choice of identity). It is in this way that Maier (1988) suggests that society should ideally offer adolescents sufficient time, space, and social freedom to experiment with their forming identities, yet without denying them its ultimate range of control and guidance. Failure to integrate a central identity, to bring one's moratorium to a productive close, or to resolve major conflicts between roles with opposing value systems can lead to **ego diffusion**, the inability to settle on a stable and well-founded sense of self. Likewise, inability to enter or properly to resolve a psychosocial moratorium might lead to identity **foreclosure** – the situation in which self-definition is attained without exploring different possible identities. Foreclosure is the status of a person who has made identity commitments with little evidence of a crisis, without experimenting with other identity possibilities. An example of someone who is foreclosed – as provided by Carver and Scheier (1988) – is a young man who is committed to becoming a surgeon because his father and grandfather were surgeons.

**Ego diffusion.** Inability to settle on a stable and well-founded sense of self, which stems from failure to integrate a central identity, to bring one's moratorium to a productive close, or to resolve major conflicts between roles or with opposing value systems.

**Foreclosure.** The status of a person who has made identity commitments with little evidence of a crisis – without first experimenting with other identity possibilities.

### Negative identifications

**Negative identity formation.** The choosing of an identity opposite to the one suggested by society. A lack of identity resolution is often evident in the behaviours of substance abusers and antisocial personalities such as violent criminals.

Ego diffusion, a particularly severe form of role confusion, can lead to social alienation – to the social withdrawal and isolation of those who are unable to integrate themselves within the social structure and values of their home culture. The lack of resolution at this stage may be linked to the behaviours of substance abusers and antisocial personalities such as violent criminals. For Erikson (1980) these are roles of deviance and extreme non-conformity that suggest **negative identity** formation, or the choosing of an identity opposite to the one suggested by society.

## Table 15.1 Schematic representation of Erikson's first five stages of development

| Stage | Trust vs Mistrust and Doubt | Autonomy vs Shame | Initiative vs Guilt | Industry vs Inferiority | Identity vs Role Confusion |
|---|---|---|---|---|---|
| Age | birth to 12–18 months | 12–18 months to 3 years | 3 to 6 years | 6 to 11 years | Adolescence |
| Corresponding Freudian stage | Oral stage | Anal stage | Phallic stage | Latency | Genital |
| Virtue | Hope | Will | Purpose | Industriousness and skill | Fidelity |
| Predominant activity | Intake of food, eating. Oral sensory activities. | Development of muscular control, particularly anal control. | Locomotion and genital activity. Exploration and play. | Child is typically engaged in forms of systematic instruction and education. | Adolescent decides on occupation, significant other, and identity. |
| Goal of stage | Reduction of tension. Attainment of basic equilibrium, both of inner biological need, and between inner and outer worlds. | Attaining a basic sense of independence, free choice, and will from accomplishment of rudimentary tasks and exploratory activities. | Reaching out; meeting the challenges of the social environment in a directed and purposeful way; being able to take responsibility for self. | Technological proficiencies; abilities to use tools. | Integration of ego identifications, personal aptitudes and social opportunities into solid identity. |
| Possible developmental mal-adaptations | Psychosocial weaknesses. Masochistic, depressive, schizoid personality (social detachment and restricted emotional disposition), psychosis. | Aggressivity, cruelty, intolerance, irrational fears, obsessiveness, stubbornness, antisocial personality disorder. | Rigidity, overdeveloped superego, inhibition, self-consciousness, social impotence; alternatively, recklessness, showing-off, gratuitous risk-taking. | Inferiority complexes, low self-esteem, feelings of unworthiness and incompetence. | Social withdrawal and isolation, psychotic episodes, delinquency, substance abuse, antisocial personality disorder. |
| Radius of significant persons | Maternal person | Paternal person | Basic family | Neighbourhood and school | Peer groups, in- and out-groups. Models of leadership. |
| Period of childhood | Infancy | 'Toddlerhood' | Early childhood | Late childhood | Adolescence |
| Corresponding social structure | Religion | Law and order | Economic structures | Technology | Ideology |

**SOURCE:** Table assembled from various sources (Maier 1988).

*More fully individual and more fully social*

As the adolescent moves towards the resolution of this stage he or she becomes increasingly a member of society, and yet also an autonomous person in their own right (Erikson 1963). In Maier's formulation (1988), the gradual growth and transformation of the adolescent comes increasingly to make sense to them, just as it makes increasing sense to others. An ever-wider social sphere of identifications now becomes important, where the identities of individuals are jointly informed not only by peers, friends, and family, but by their neighbourhood, school, work, and by their ethnic, national, or community ties. The integration of identity is therefore characterised by a 'two-way pull' – one comes increasingly to be an individual, distinct from the social mass, yet also more fully a member, more fully a part of one's society (Maier 1988). This situation reiterates the fact that identity development is *both psychological and social* (Erikson 1980). Considering the importance of role-defined behaviour and self-identity here, Erikson (1963) nominates *fidelity* as the characteristic virtue of this stage.

The social institutions that correlate to this stage of development are those of social value, meaning, and identity, which correspond to *ideology* (Erikson 1963).

## Stage 6: intimacy versus isolation

The search for the prospective *significant other* takes centre stage at this developmental phase. What individuals are looking for here is more than sexual intimacy (although this does play a strong role). Individuals are

## The role of racism in psychosocial development

Louw, Louw, and Schoeman (1995) have called attention to the influence of the black child-minder on psychosocial child development. Given that a large number of white South African families use black 'domestic workers' or 'nannies' as child-minders, it has become a pressing research question as to what the effects of such an arrangement would be upon white children. Indeed, in such a historically racially divided society, it may have been proposed that this was a situation that lent itself to a form of racial integration. In view of the fact that the 'nanny' was taking on a partly maternal role in caring for the children of a family, one may have supposed that strong affectional bonds may have been exhibited by children in ways that

transcended the apartheid imposition of racial boundaries. Similarly, in view of the fact that such 'nannies' were entrusted with the children of a family, and charged with their care, one might suppose that the family as a whole (parents included) would come to form close emotional ties with her.

Ultimately, however, research into the influence of black child-minders (Straker 1990; Wulfsohn 1988) on white children supported neither of these suppositions. It was, as Louw *et al.* (1995) note, markedly not the case that extended contact between white child and black child-minder meant that such white children exhibited greater acceptance of other race groups in South Africa.

(continued)

Similarly, such consistent daily exposure to a member of another culture did not significantly influence white children in the sense that they became better versed in the values of a different culture, or less entrenched in the values of their own culture. The black child-minder was not a central figure in the life of the child, particularly not in the emotional sense and, as Straker notes (cited in Louw *et al.* 1995), had no power, status, or real importance in the eyes of children. In many ways the perception of the child seems to have been that the child-minder had a contractual and not an emotional bond to the family. This is a view corroborated by many of such children's actions, where they were content to 'let the nanny do it' rather than do it themselves (as in the case of cleaning up a mess left by the child).

It seems in this way that even fairly young children were responsive to socio-political factors in their developmental environment, and aware of social role positions and disparities of power in their immediate social spheres. Erikson (1963) predicts this in his third stage, where he warns that the increasing social competence of the child enables their awareness of a variety of social institutions, social roles, and standings in society. Bronfenbrenner (1979) likewise would find the results of the above study unsurprising in the sense that macrosystem influences, like broad socio-political values and ideolo-

gies such as racism, would permeate all the way down to the more immediate levels of development such as the microsystem sets of face-to-face 'nanny' and child relationships.

Another significant fact stemming from the above research is that parental influence on children is not always benign or positive. Parents cannot take responsibility for all social values learnt, especially when there is no doubt that the environment into which the child is developing is a social one informed by a particular history, and populated with certain popular (or predominant) values, standpoints and ideologies. Nevertheless, parents certainly can take responsibility for socio-political values that are the norm *at home*. Given the foundational nature of immediate familial relationships within the context of home life (in Freud, Erikson, and in Bronfenbrenner) it seems that racism might well 'start in the home' so to speak, and that parental influence would have a lot to answer for in the psycho-social development of racism in the child. This is certainly an area in which more research is needed, particularly in view of the fact that a psychosocial developmental account of racism would seem to be able to explain not only the tenacity of the phenomenon, but also its 'deep-rootedness' – the way it seems to function at such an intuitive, immediate, almost 'naturalised' level within people.

seeking to invest in others, to forge important romantic relationships, to find a healthy, well-balanced, and developed sense of love – a fact reflected in Erikson's assertion that love is the key virtue at this stage of development. As Craig (1996) observes, the central objective at this stage is to share oneself with another, and to do so without the fear of losing one's own identity. The success at this stage depends largely on the individual's success at identity formation at the previous stage. This is because the individual now needs to take chances with identity, which, in the previous stage, was precisely what was most precious and vulnerable (Erikson 1963). Indeed this is perhaps the stage that most crucially relies upon the successful resolution of prior crises, because if they have not previously been resolved, they are likely to reoccur here.

### The importance and risks of intimacy

Most young adults emerge from the search for identity with a willingness to fuse their identities with others, with an enthusiasm for intimacy, and with the rudimentary ethical strength that they will need in order to abide by the emotional commitments they make to potential significant others at this stage. The ego needs to be strong in this phase, so as to fend off the fear of ego loss in the case of close friendships, in the case of inspiration by teachers, in the orgasms of sexual union, and in various close affiliations (Erikson 1963). The consideration here is the necessity to maintain the integrity of the ego and not to let it be incorporated wholesale into something or someone else. Such ego losses may lead to a deep sense of isolation and subsequent self-absorption. (It is understandable, by this rationale, why suicide might occur with particular prevalence at this stage of life).

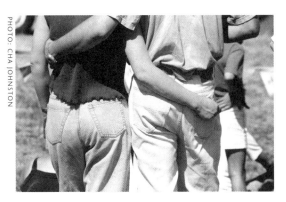

PHOTO: CHA JOHNSTON

*The search for the prospective significant other is central to Erikson's sixth stage.*

### Distantiation and competitiveness

*Distantiation* (distancing those around one) is the counterpart of intimacy. What frequently occurs here is a willingness to destroy and isolate those forces and people who seem to threaten the ego. Prejudices early learned may be consolidated and strengthened at this stage. The danger here is that often the sharp and cruel distinctions between the familiar and the foreign that so characterise this stage are experienced with and against the very same people with whom intimacy is being sought (Erikson 1963). Competitive, combative, and intimate kinds of interaction are hence often part of the same relationship at this stage. The *competitive encounter* and the sexual embrace do, however, become more distinct and separate as full adulthood begins.

### Orgasmic and genital sexuality

The physical focus of this phase of development is on genitality. It is here that true, mutually interactive, and heterosexual genital sexuality can begin to occur in a way distinct from the phallic or vaginal strivings of earlier development where the sex life was largely concerned with building identity (Erikson 1963). The search for and substantiation of gender is now well and truly over. The emphasis now is towards achieving an 'orgastic potency so free of pregenital interferences that the genital libido ... is [exclusively] expressed in heterosexual mutuality, with full sensitivity of both penis and vagina' (Erikson 1963, 265).

Erikson recalls, in paraphrase, Freud's curt response to the question as to what a healthy, normally functioning individual should be able to do well. Freud's response was 'to love and work'. Erikson takes this formula as a summary of the goals of this stage: the ability to formulate a mature love that may be acted upon with a genital sexuality, and the ability to express a general work-productiveness that compromises neither this genital focus nor this capacity for being a loving person (Erikson 1963).

In many ways Erikson (1963, 265) presents the prospects of sexual union as something of a curative force:

> the total fact of finding via the climactic turmoil of the orgasm, a supreme experience of the mutual regulation of two beings in some way takes the edge off the hostilities and potential rages caused by the oppositeness of male and female, of fact and fancy, of love and hate. Satisfactory sex relations thus make sex less obsessive, overcompensation less necessary, sadistic controls superfluous.

For Erikson (1963, 266) the 'utopia of genitality' should include the following elements:

1) mutuality of orgasm,
2) with a loved partner,
3) of the other sex,
4) with whom one shares a mutual trust,
5) with whom one can work, procreate, and relax, and
6) so as to secure offspring to the successful stages of development.

Despite Erikson's implicit suggestion that this is the normative pattern of development, one cannot escape the heterosexual bias that seems so dominant within his theory and that seems to marginalise any image of healthy homosexual development and mutuality. We will return to this point in discussing critiques of Erikson towards the end of this chapter.

## Stage 7: generativity versus stagnation

Erikson begins his description of this stage by saying that:

> ... the fashionable insistence on dramatizing the dependence of children on adults often blinds us to the dependence of the older generation on the younger one. Mature man needs to be needed, and maturity needs guidance as well as encouragement from what has been produced and must be taken care of (Erikson 1963, 266–7).

The idea is that adults by now have often largely resolved earlier life-stage conflicts and are hence free to direct their attention to the assistance of others, particularly their own children (Craig 1996). Generativity refers chiefly to the tasks of establishing and guiding the next generation. Recognising that not all individuals will have children, this generativity also refers broadly to values of productivity and creativity, although neither of these can ever be a proper replacement for the guidance of offspring (Erikson 1963). Craig (1996, 60) succinctly states that 'parents sometimes find themselves by helping their children'. It follows that *caring* is the virtue of this middle adulthood stage of development.

Failure to provide such guidance and assistance (and through them self-enrichment) can lead to a sense of stagnation and self-impoverishment (Erikson 1963). Here Erikson locates those adults who seem to gain their only pleasures through self-indulgence, who are preoccupied with

PHOTO: CHA JOHNSTON

themselves, and who treat themselves, basically, as their 'only child'; whose early invalidism – physical and psychological – becomes their chief vehicle of self-concern (1963).

This stage is also characterised by a sense of community, a 'belief in the species' as Erikson (1963) puts it, a willingness to direct one's energies, without conflict, to the solution of social issues. 'As to the institutions which safeguard and reinforce generativity, one can only say that all institutions codify the ethics of generative succession' (Erikson 1963, 267).

*For Erikson, the role of peers, friends, and colleagues remains an important influence throughout the stages of psychosocial development.*

## Stage 8: integrity versus despair

'Ego integrity' is the name that Erikson gives to the ripening rewards of having resolved all previous stages of development – 'it is the ego's accrued assurance of its proclivity for order and meaning' (Erikson 1963, 268). Attaining 'ego integrity' involves a love for the human ego – not of the self – as an experience that conveys world order and spiritual sense. It is normal here for individuals to look back over their lives and judge them. In looking back, if one has a sense of meaning and involvement – a sense of acceptance – then one has this sense of integrity. If not, if one's life seems to have been a series of misdirected energies and lost chances, one is left with a sense of despair (Craig 1996).

Dealing with the fear of death represents an important challenge at this stage of development. On the one hand the individual may accept that theirs is not the one and only 'life within life' so to speak; on the other hand despair arrives, by virtue of the realisation that time is too short now to start a new life, to try out alternative routes to integrity (Erikson 1963). The virtue of dignity is something of an index of ego integrity:

> ... the possessor of integrity is ready to defend the dignity of his own life style against all physical and economic threats ... he knows that an individual life is the accidental coincidence of but one life cycle with but one segment of history ... In such final consolidation, death loses its sting (Erikson 1963, 268).

Disgust on the part of aging adults can often function in trying to hide despair, even if only in the form of 'a thousand little disgusts that cannot add up to one big remorse' (Erikson 1963). In reaching this final developmental stage, each individual must have developed to some extent all the previously mentioned ego qualities; they must have resolved all the foregoing developmental crises, although each cultural location requires a particular combination of these resolved conflicts (Erikson 1963). Moreover, this final integrity is only really achieved if the individual knows, understands and, to some extent, participates in the various social institutions of his or her society – the religion, the politics, the economic order, the technology, and the arts and sciences which make up their home culture (Erikson 1963). 'Ego integrity implies an emotional integration which permits participation by followership as well as acceptance of the responsibility of leadership' (Erikson 1963, 269).

# Black adolescent identity formation in post-apartheid South Africa

Stevens and Lockhart (1997) assert that post-apartheid South Africa also poses significant challenges to black adolescent identity development. While apartheid capitalism no longer exists, 'racial capitalism', they argue, most certainly does. Hence many black adolescents are presented with prescribed roles that are consistent with a capitalist framework, yet which, given the historical legacy of apartheid, are still unattainable for them. Likewise, the common enemy that provided such a crucial rallying point for collective (oppositional) self-definition is no longer so visible, or so obvious, in the post-apartheid state (Stevens and Lockhat 1997). As Stevens and Lockhat express it, many black adolescents have had to change their life scripts virtually overnight, from 'young lions' to 'young entrepreneurs'.

The increased prominence of Western ideologies and role models – through the expanding influence of American popular culture – has led to the promotion of the values of American competitive individualism and wealth-creation. This makes a strong contrast with the collective identity of shared political consciousness that challenged and resisted a pervasive racist ideology. Stevens and Lockhat (1997, 245) refer to this as the ascendant influence of 'Coca-Cola' culture – a situation in which 'Western ideological symbols' are present at 'all levels of the social fabric, through language, dress codes, recreational facilities and so on'. The problem here is that choosing an identity appropriate to this socio-historical period may mean adopting one that also marginalises and alienates the adolescent from his or her social reality. This is a situation where role confusion emerges, instead of the desired integration of identity.

In fact, for Stevens and Lockhat (1997, 253), the current South African situation is anything but facilitative for identity development among black adolescent youth:

> The cynicism related to not being able to experience tangible benefits in the 'new' South Africa, the double-bind as a result of confusing and contradictory role prescriptions, the lack of structural containment and programmes to allow for the development of healthy independence and judgement; have all contributed to even fewer healthy options for black South African adolescents ... What we now also encounter, is a proliferation of gangsterism, substance abuse, anti-social behaviour ... and an emerging ethnic separatism ...'

Nevertheless, this author feels that the creativity of much contemporary youth culture in post-apartheid South Africa should not be underestimated. Exposure to the 'Coca-Cola culture' of 'first-world' entertainment role models does not simply lead to a kind of dead-end or derivative culture of alienation and marginalisation. Rather, these kinds of influence might prove to be valuable resources from which vital South African youth movements and cultures may emerge. Kwaito music seems a good example; to consider kwaito merely an alienating cardboard cut-out of American rap and dance music would seem to miss the vibrancy and originality of this new style.

In some ways this last stage of development links up with the very first stage, of trust, particularly since trust is sometimes defined as 'the assured reliance on another's integrity'. Accordingly, Erikson concludes with the observation that 'it seems possible to ... paraphrase the relation of adult integrity and infantile trust by saying that healthy children will not fear life if their elders have integrity enough not to fear death' (1963, 269). The virtue at this late adulthood stage of development is wisdom.

# Criticisms of Erikson's theory

## More description than explanation

While Erikson's theory is certainly a good *description* of psychosocial development, it appears, unlike Freud's theory, to lack a fundamental *explanation* of why changes occur. It is, in short, better at accounting for *how* than for *why* in respect to developmental changes. Shaffer (1996) argues that Erikson's theory is often vague, and that it does not have the ability to explain the enormous personality differences that exist among people. Moreover, Shaffer (1996) argues that Erikson is not clear enough about how the resolution of each stage impacts on *individual* personalities. In this connection, it seems that Erikson's failure to involve more centrally the dynamic personality structure of Freud's id, ego, and superego has limited the degree to which his theory is applicable in idiosyncratic, specific, individual, or atypical contexts.

## Idealism

Whereas Freud has been criticised for a seemingly pessimistic view of development, Erikson's theory, it has been argued, is frequently too *optimistic* and idealises descriptions of typical development (Maier 1988). What place is there for human tragedy in his theory? And, likewise, are there not emotional conflicts that lead in no 'healthy' direction at all? It would seem that the very essence of certain crises is that they lead to no productive resolution, and in fact constitute a 'waste' of human feelings and impulses. One needs to ask whether Erikson, in avoiding Freud's theoretical tendency to focus on 'how things can go wrong', has not perhaps given us an idealised rather than a realistic or a pragmatic account of psychosocial development.

In a similar vein, approaches like that of Lacan (1977) would suggest that, while Freud may appear deterministic and reductionist, Erikson, by contrast, overvalues the adaptive and integrative functions of the ego. For Lacan (1977) it is decidedly *not* the case that the ego is a basically honest mechanism that is congruent with reality, and that places the individual in an ever more healthy and adaptive relationship to society. For him, many of the primary functions of the ego remain unconscious, fundamentally deceptive, and connected to external reality in a basically illusionary manner. This view makes a stark contrast to Erikson's positive understanding of ego-adaptation and development.

## Allegations of sexism

Erikson, like Freud, has been criticised for treating the male as the standard of human development, with the female featuring only as a

variation, or even deviation, of the normal path of psychosocial development. As Maier (1988) contends, Erikson can reasonably be criticised for
suggesting that the development of 'humankind' is in fact the development of *male*kind. Not only is it the case that Erikson's writings reflect a
male bias and dominance, it is also the case that his clinical and historical
research subjects are all male (Maier 1988). For this reason, Erikson's theories may be seen as not only a limited means of accounting for female
development, but also as a *demeaning* account of female development. His
later stages strongly prioritise the procreative and maternal qualities that
he sees as endemic to femininity; these qualities are indicative to Erikson
of both necessary social roles and personality development within women
(Erikson 1963). As an extension of this view, women have, within
Erikson's theory, typically been conceptualised as more dependent and
less assertive or active than men. This induces the suggestion that it is
only through intimate relations that women come properly to find their
identity – a precondition that does not hold for men (Maier 1988). In this
vein, and quoting Erikson to substantiate her critique, Weisstein makes
the following observation:

> Erikson ... upon noting that young women often ask whether they
> can 'have a identity before they know whom they will marry, and
> for whom they will make a home,' explains ... that: 'Much of a
> young woman's identity is already defined in her kind of attrac-
> tiveness and in the selectivity of her search for the man ... by
> whom she wishes to be sought...' Mature womanly fulfilment, for
> Erikson, rests on the fact that a woman's '... somatic design har-
> bors an "inner space" destined to bear the offspring of chosen
> men, and with it, a biological, psychological, and ethical commit-
> ment to take care of human infancy' (Weisstein 1973, 391).

## Cultural bias

If Freud can be accused of cultural bias, then so can Erikson. Erikson's
theories may seem less biased to us purely because they are not as historically or culturally distant to us as are Freud's. However, they exhibit a
number of strong late twentieth century capitalistic American values,
which may limit the universality of his theory, or its cross-cultural applicability. Certain of Erikson's virtues, like *independence* (the virtue of his
third stage), *initiative*, and *industriousness* sound more like the individual
qualities that are specifically desirable within a competitive and capitalistic society than the universal virtues of healthily developing children. In
this connection, Sampson (1992) takes issue with Erikson's approach,
which, according to him, is a model of human development that insidi-
ously inserts a series of dominant American cultural and ideological
idealisations. These idealisations are chiefly those of self-contained individualism, economic profitability, and self-responsibility, all of which
contribute strongly to the social, political, and economic order of late
twentieth century America.

A similar criticism here is that Erikson has, despite his protestations
to the contrary, implicitly *moralised* development, by pinpointing a series
of 'virtues' as developmental necessities. The obvious implication is that

those who do not develop the required (and culturally specific) virtues specified by Erikson are 'sinful' – lacking in some basic moral fibre. This becomes a particularly important concern if Erikson's virtues are in fact specific to his own cultural location but are nonetheless imposed cross-culturally.

## Overly prescriptive developmental values

A danger of Erikson's theory that he himself (1964) was well aware of, is that it may be taken as overly prescriptive. Rather than as a theory of phases of development, Erikson was concerned that his work might be taken as an ineluctable piece of science, as an ascending list of developmental challenges that would be 'eagerly accepted by some as a potential inventory for tests of adjustment or as a new production schedule in the manufacture of desirable children, citizens or workers' (Erikson 1964, 59). This concern parallels those of Rose (1991) and Burman (1994) who point out that theories of developmental psychology may often function as evaluative norms against which deviance may be identified and stigmatised. It is seemingly in this connection that Erikson (1980) claims to have no interest in proposing a new set of norms that would facilitate the giving of 'good or bad grades in mental health' (Erikson 1980).

Rose (1991) and Burman (1994) also express reservations about how developmental theories such as Erikson's may inform professional practices such as health, law, education, and welfare. They argue that these theories are applied in an overly standardising or 'normalising' manner. In such an application, not enough attention is paid to class, race, and gender variables, and the standards of white, male, heterosexual, upper class, and American development are uniformly imposed on all children. This is a process that has the tendency to 'pathologise' differences across demographic categories (Rose 1991; Burman 1994).

# Recommended readings

*Erikson's theory has proved to be an influential and popular staple of developmental psychology, and as such it features in virtually every developmental psychology textbook. If you are interested in Erikson's theories though, it is worthwhile engaging directly with Erikson's own writings, which are generally accessible, and contain far more textured and nuanced detail than most textbook summaries of his thinking. The two central texts to try are:*

Erikson, E. H. (1963). *Childhood and society.* New York: Norton.

Erikson, E. H. (1968). *Identity, youth and crisis.* New York: Norton.
*Both these texts provide useful perspectives and elaborations on his psychosocial stage theory. Also interesting are the following texts, which essentially extend and apply the theory:*

Erikson, E. H. (1964). *Insight and responsibility.* New York: Norton.

Erikson, E. H. (1969). *Gandhi's truth.* New York: Norton.

Erikson, E. H. (1980). *Identity and the life cycle.* New York: Norton.

*If you're interested in tackling a good critical commentary on Erikson – and it is a good idea to read someone other than Erikson on Erikson, because, regrettably, some of his understandings of race and gender have dated badly – then try the relevant sections of:*

Maier, H. W. (1988). *Three theories of child development.* Third edition. New York: University Press of America.

## Critical thinking tasks

### Specific tasks

1) Reflect briefly on how a punitive upbringing with frequent corporal punishment would influence a child's acquisition of basic trust.

2) What parenting styles would ideally promote the development of autonomy in the young child? Similarly, give some thought to the kinds of life events that would threaten the development of basic autonomy in the child.

3) In terms of Erikson's theory, how would blindness, or lack of mobility, as in the case of the handicapped child, impact on child development within the first three stages?

4) Try and 'rewrite' Erikson's description of the fifth stage of development in the terms of your own personal life experiences at this age.

5) Trace a series of parallels, where possible, between the first five stages of development as conceptualised by both Freud and Erikson.

6) This chapter provides a tabular breakdown of the first five of Erikson's developmental stages. Following the same format, try to generate a similar table highlighting the key aspects of the last three developmental stages.

### General tasks

1) By systematically working through the first five stages of Erikson's theory of psychosocial development, compile a list of the developmental challenges that Kobus Geldenhuys appears to have been unable to meet.

2) What are some of the developmental 'virtues' that Geldenhuys did not attain, and how do you see this failure as impacting on his individual personality development?

3) What kinds of interventions or crucial differences in Geldenhuys's life could have helped to prevent his actions? What plausible life events may have aided him in repairing early developmental deficits?

4) Whose theory, Freud's or Erikson's, do you feel has the greatest explanatory power with regard to the Geldenhuys case? Explain your answer, giving concrete examples.

5) How can the theories of Freud and Erikson, with their different focuses, be used in a complementary way? Can you use them to build on one another, to 'fill in each other's gaps', in explaining developmental phenomena in the Geldenhuys case?

# Kohlberg's theory of moral reasoning

*James Grant*

This chapter will introduce and explain Kohlberg's theory of moral development. The following topics are covered:

1. The cognitive developmental approach.

2. Piaget's influence.

3. Kohlberg's stages of moral development.

4. Critiques of Kohlberg's theory:
   - Methodological concerns.
     - Invariance of sequence and cross-cultural universality.
     - Gilligan's critique of 'justice reasoning'.
     - The relationship between moral reasoning and action.

   We conclude by considering some of the primary critiques of Kohlberg's theory.

## Introduction

How does one decide what one ought to do in circumstances of moral significance? Are there certain clear rules that one must obey: don't steal, cheat, or spend quality time with your neighbour's partner? Above all, don't kill. Is it that simple? Would you observe the principle not to kill if you were attacked and the only way to defend yourself was to kill? That is, would you avail yourself of the well-recognised right to self-defence? The year 2001 saw the United States of America kill Timothy McVeigh and Botswana kill South African Marietta Bosch in the most premeditated fashion. But these were bad people? Well then, what about abortion? South African law permits abortion (Choice on

Lawrence Kohlberg

Termination of Pregnancy Act), but prohibits the death penalty (*State v. Makwanyane* 1995). Is this inconsistent? Can we *sometimes* kill?

What about theft? Is that not simpler? Yet here we must ask whether Robin Hood is immoral. In the following scenario we must contemplate what 'Heinz' should do:

> In Europe, a woman was near death from a special kind of cancer. There was one drug that the doctors thought might save her. It was a form of radium that a druggist in the same town had recently discovered. The drug was expensive to make, but the druggist was charging 10 times what the drug cost him to make. He paid R400 for the radium and charged R4 000 for a small dose of the drug. The sick woman's husband, Heinz, went to everyone he knew to borrow the money and tried every legal means, but he could only get together about R2 000, which is half of what it cost. He told the druggist that his wife was dying, and asked him to sell it cheaper or let him pay later. But the druggist said, 'No, I discovered the drug and I'm going to make money from it.' So having tried every legal means, Heinz gets desperate and considers breaking into the man's store to steal the drug for his wife (Colby, Kohlberg, Speicer, Hewer, Candee, Gibbs, and Power 1987).

*Morality is not something we are born with; rather it is something that we have to learn. Moreover, if Kohlberg is correct, our level of moral reasoning is dependent on the level of our cognitive functioning.*

Here we see the rule not to steal manifested in the law, together with the rights of someone to his property, in conflict with the right to life of another. What should Heinz do, should he steal the drug?

Lawrence Kohlberg found that people offered different answers to questions such as these (which always set an individual in a dilemma in having to chose some rule or right over another). Thus, there seemed to be no one right answer. More particularly, there appeared no significant relationship between an individual's knowledge of moral rules or declared morality in the sense of what someone ought to do in a morally significant circumstance, and their ultimate conduct (Kohlberg 1964; 1968; 1969). What he did find, however, was that the way people reasoned about the problem tended to correlate with their ages and degree of cognitive development, so that generally individuals of similar age and cognitive development considered moral problems in the same manner. Thus Kohlberg's interest in posing dilemmas, such as that of 'Heinz', was to elicit the reasons for the solutions that his subjects proposed. His concern became the structure of cognition behind the individual's notions of right and wrong.

## The cognitive developmental approach

Kohlberg's thesis is that morality may be variously conceived. He distinguished six different modes of apprehending the moral course of conduct – of *moral reasoning* – which he structured into a developmental stage theory of moral reasoning: *Kohlberg's cognitive developmental theory*.

Although cognitive development is considered as a necessary factor for the development of moral reasoning, it is recognised in itself to be insufficient (Kohlberg and Kaufman 1987). Research supports the argument that cognitive abilities alone do not translate into moral reasoning capacities. Proficiency in cognitive tasks, for instance, does not translate into proficiency in moral reasoning (Rest 1983). Cognitive development *precedes* moral development and allows for the subsequent development of moral reasoning with the child's interaction in social environments (Bee 1992). It is only after the application of cognitive processes to social problems that moral development occurs (Kohlberg and Kaufman 1987). *Cognitive and social challenges, then, produce moral development.*

## Alternatives to the cognitive developmental approach

◆ Blasi (1980) considers learning theories and psychoanalysis as assuming in common (though otherwise being very different) that moral action is produced out of behavioural action tendencies and the interplay between these.

◆ By contrast he considers the cognitive developmental theories of Piaget and Kohlberg as assuming instead that moral action is cognitively mediated.

◆ According to behaviourism and cognitive-social theory, one learns what one ought to do by conditioning or modelling. Forbidden conduct becomes conditioned with emotions such as anxiety.

◆ Cognitive-social theory gauges moral development as indicated in pro-social behaviour.

◆ Psychodynamic theory postulates that an individual's conscience (the superego) develops by identification and internalisation (first as external rules and later as personal guides), and is enforced primarily by guilt avoidance.

## Piaget's influence

Kohlberg's observations led him to elaborate upon the two-stage cognitive model of children's moral judgement presented by Piaget (1932; 1965) whose theories fascinated and inspired him (Crain 1992). Piaget had conceived his theory by observing children's treatment of rules when playing games such as marbles. Moral development, Piaget theorised, took the form of a progression from *heteronomous* (subject to external rules) to *autonomous* (internal) moral reasoning. **Heteronomous moral reasoning** is the reasoning initially adopted by children and is characterised by strict adherence to rules and duties, and obedience to authority. Rules are regarded as fixed and absolute, deriving from some supreme commandment (adults, parents, or a deity even). One cannot break or amend these commandments, regardless of whether they are inconvenient, or even unfair. This is the reasoning of children younger than about ten years old (it is also the reasoning of some civil servants: the rules are the rules). This reasoning results from three factors. The first is due to a problem of 'realism' (the difficulty the child experiences in distinguishing rules from real objective phenomena). The second is due to the egocentric nature of the young child's cognitive structure in that she or he cannot take a different perspective. The third results from the power relationship between adults and children in that children are subject to adult authority. The heteronomous orientation is characterised by the child's respect for the unquestionable authority of adults or parents.

**Heteronomous moral reasoning.** Piaget's notion that the reasoning adopted by children is initially characterised by strict adherence to rules and duties, and by obedience to authority. Rules are regarded as fixed and absolute, deriving from some supreme commandment (adults, parents, or God). (*Heteronomous* means according to various external laws or principles, that is, laws and principles that are imposed on one from without.)

The **autonomous moral reasoning** orientation develops out of interaction with other children and is characterised by an ability to consider rules critically, and selectively to apply these rules based on the goals of mutual respect and cooperation. If the rules of one's game of marbles are inconvenient or unfair they can be altered with the agreement of the participants. Kohlberg elaborated Piaget's model into a six-stage theory. In this he proposed a *heteronomous orientation* (marked by the first stage) as a child's initial morality, and an *autonomous orientation* (marked by the later stages) as the ultimate development of moral reasoning.

**Autonomous moral reasoning.** Piaget's second stage of moral reasoning, which is no longer dependent upon respect for norms as supreme commandments. Children's moral reasoning in this stage is characterised by an ability to consider rules critically, and selectively to apply these rules based on the goals of mutual respect and cooperation. (*Autonomous* means having one's own laws, making one's own rules, making internal independent judgements.)

# Kohlberg's stages of moral development

According to Kohlberg (Kohlberg and Kauffman 1987), children progress sequentially from lower to higher stages out of recognition that a higher stage of moral reasoning provides a better mechanism for the resolution of moral issues. Each new stage represents a *qualitative* reorganisation of the individual's pattern of thought, which becomes more complex, differentiated, and adaptive. The child is not just smarter and more caring, his or her morality is qualitatively advanced. Progress occurs through engaging with others in debate over moral issues, and in social experience that challenges one to evaluate one's moral reasoning. Such challenges motivate one to develop new and more comprehensive moral conceptions that equip one better to resolve moral problems. Progression requires understandings gained at previous stages, so development proceeds in a predictable sequence without skipping stages. Subjects are regarded, therefore, as able only to represent the stage of moral reasoning actually attained, since a subject is not able to internalise higher stage thinking or produce higher level responses than the level of development actually achieved.

Thus development is determined by the individual's own concerns with moral problems and not by biological imperatives (genetic clockwork) or socialisation agents (such as parents or teachers) (Kohlberg 1969; Crain 1992). While he opposed the notion that children are taught morality, Kohlberg did, however, consider it possible to promote moral development by challenging people to consider the aptness and efficacy of their present orientation (Blatt and Kohlberg 1975; Kohlberg 1981).

Kohlberg's six stages are structured in three levels, each of which comprises two stages that describe the sequence of moral development within each level. The full sequence (Kohlberg 1969, 379–82) is presented below, with illustrative exemplar statements in respect of the Heinz dilemma, both in favour of (for) and opposed to (against) Heinz stealing the drug (Bukatko and Daehler 1995; Crain 1992; Kohlberg 1969; 1981; Kohlberg and Kauffman 1987; Papalia, Olds, and Feldman 1998).

**Preconventional/ premoral morality.** Kohlberg's first level orientation in which morality resides externally, determined by norms and principles that are imposed from 'above'. It is dependent upon consequences since the individual is concerned with the avoidance of punishment or the attainment of reward.

## Level 1

Morality in Level 1 is referred to as **preconventional** or **premoral morality**. This means that morality resides externally: norms and principles are imposed from 'above'. It is dependent upon consequences, since the individual is concerned with the avoidance of punishment or the attainment of reward.

### Stage One

The first stage is the *obedience and punishment orientation* (or *heteronomous morality*) in which right is determined by the avoidance of punishment.

> **For:** He should steal the drug. It isn't really bad to take it. It isn't as though he didn't ask to pay for it first. The drug he'd take is only worth R400; he's not really taking a R4 000 drug. Or: if you let your wife die, you will get into trouble. You'll be blamed for not spending the money to save her and there'll be an investigation of you and the druggist for your wife's death.

> **Against:** He shouldn't steal the drug; it's a serious crime. He didn't get permission; he used force and broke and entered. He did a lot of damage, stealing a very expensive drug and breaking up the store, too. Or: you shouldn't steal the drug because you'll be caught and sent to jail if you do. If you do get away, your conscience would bother you thinking how the police would catch up with you at any minute.

### Stage Two

The second stage is the stage of *individualism, instrumental purpose, and exchange* and is determined by how one can attain reward as opposed to avoiding punishment. The concern remains 'preconventional' in that moral reasoning is that of an individual rather than a member of society. The orientation is represented well by the notion, 'You scratch my back and I'll scratch yours'.

> **For:** It's all right to steal the drug because she needs it and he wants her to live. It isn't that he wants to steal, but he has to use this way to get the drug to save her. Or: if you do happen to get caught you could give the drug back and you wouldn't get much of a sentence. It wouldn't bother you much to serve a little jail term, if you have your wife when you get out.

> **Against:** He shouldn't steal it. The druggist isn't wrong or bad; he just wants to make a profit. That's what you're in business for, to make money. Or: he may not get much of a jail term if he steals the drug, but his wife will probably die before he gets out so it won't do him much good. If his wife dies, he shouldn't blame himself, it wasn't his fault she has cancer.

## Level 2

Level 2 is referred to as the level of **conventional** or **role conformity morality** in which norms have become internalised and the individual is concerned with his or her reputation – how she or he is perceived by others. Moral values are determined by conforming to majority norms, maintaining the conventional social order, and fulfilling the expectations of others.

**Conventional/role conformity morality.** Kohlberg's second level orientation in which norms have become internalised and the individual is concerned with his or her reputation – how they are perceived by others. Moral values are determined by conforming to majority norms, maintaining the conventional social order, and fulfilling the expectations of others.

## Stage Three

The third stage is oriented by *mutual interpersonal expectations, relation-ships, and interpersonal conformity* (also called the *good-boy/good-girl orientation*). Morality is now determined by an attitude of approval-seeking and is attained by fulfilling the expectations of others close to one – being 'good' and 'nice'. *Concerns shift from consequences to inten-tions* in that 'meaning well' prevails over the possible consequences of conduct. It is a morality of love, empathy, and caring for one's significant others.

> **For:** He should steal the drug. He is only doing something that is natural for a good husband to do. You can't blame him for doing something out of love for his wife; you'd blame him if he didn't love his wife enough to save her. Or: no one will think you're bad if you steal the drug but your family will think you're an inhuman husband if you don't. If you let your wife die, you'll never be able to look anybody in the face again.

> **Against:** He shouldn't steal. If his wife dies, he can't be blamed. It isn't because he's heartless or that he doesn't love her enough to do everything that he legally can. The druggist is the selfish or heart-less one. Or: it isn't just the druggist who will think you're a crim-inal, everyone else will too. After you steal it, you'll feel bad thinking how you've brought dishonour on your family and your-self; you won't be able to face anyone again.

## Stage Four

The fourth stage's orientation is in *social system and conscience* (or *author-ity and social-order-maintaining*). It is directed by a sense of the value in maintaining the conventional social system as a duty. In contrast to Stage Three reasoning, in which the individual's moral focus is his or her sig-nificant others such as family and friends, at Stage Four the individual becomes concerned with society and 'the institution'. The orientation is represented well by the notion that the system is supreme and that one cannot simply do what one thinks is right if it conflicts with what the sys-tem requires, because then there would be chaos.

> **For:** You should steal it. If you did nothing you'd be letting your wife die, and it's your responsibility if she dies. You have to take it with the idea of paying the druggist. Or: if you have any sense of honour, you won't let your wife die because you're afraid to do the only thing that will save her. You'll always feel guilty that you caused her death if you don't do your duty to her.

> **Against:** It's a natural thing for Heinz to want to save his wife but it's still always wrong to steal. He still knows he's stealing and tak-ing a valuable drug from the man who made it. Or: you're des-perate and you may not know you're doing wrong when you steal the drug. But you'll know you did wrong after you're punished and sent to jail. You'll always feel guilty for your dishonesty and lawbreaking.

# Level 3

**Postconventional/
principled morality.**
Kohlberg's third level
orientation in which
morality becomes internal
and autonomous, and
norms are determined on
the basis of principles of
justice, fairness, and
dignity, independent of
conventions such as
national laws.

Level 3 is the level of **postconventional** or **principled morality** in which
morality becomes internal and *autonomous*. Norms are determined upon
the basis of principles of justice, fairness, and dignity, independent of conventions such as national laws.

## Stage Five

This stage's orientation is in *social contract or utility and individual rights*.
Moral norms are now defined in terms of laws or institutionalised rules
for their social utility. *Now the concern is with a good society.* This sets it
apart from Stage Four reasoning in which the focus was simply on maintaining the system. An autocracy that functions smoothly would not
impress a Stage Five reasoner. A good society is defined as one born of
consensus (the social contract), while at the same time respecting certain
rights, such as life, as inviolable on the premise that respect for these
rights is universal. (Agreement in this respect is assumed.)

> **For:** The law wasn't set up for these circumstances. Taking the
> drug in this situation isn't really right, but to do it is justified. Or:
> you'd lose other people's respect and not gain it, if you don't steal.
> If you let your wife die, it would be from fear, not from reasoning
> it out. So you'd just lose self-respect and probably the respect of
> others too.

> **Against:** You can't completely blame someone for stealing, but
> even extreme circumstances don't really justify taking the law
> into your own hands. You can't have everyone stealing whenever
> they get desperate. The end may be good, but the ends don't jus-
> tify the means. Or: you would lose your standing and respect in
> the community and violate the law. You'd lose respect for yourself
> if you were carried away by emotion and forgot the long-range
> point of view.

## Stage Six

The sixth stage is the morality of *universal ethical principles* in which
morality is directed by self-chosen ethical principles – not dependent
upon consensus – which are assumed to found the law, but which pre-
dominate where the law conflicts with these personal principles. Stage
Six's existence as a separate stage above and beyond the scope of Stage
Five is questionable. It is not provided for in the most recent edition of
the instrument for the attribution of stages to subjects (Colby and
Kohlberg 1987; Colby *et al.* 1987). The distinction between Stages Five
and Six is not all that clear as both are concerned with what constitutes a
good society and both respect individual rights. The difference seems to
be that rights, in Stage Five, are respected on the assumption that they are
dictated by consensus. In Stage Six, however, rights are respected irrespective of consensus; they are apparently taken as rules of natural law
(Crain 1992). All post-conventional thought is now assessed, however, as
Stage Five reasoning (Colby *et al.* 1987).

**For:** This is a situation that forces him to choose between stealing and letting his wife die. In a situation where the choice must be made, it is morally right to steal. He has to act in terms of the principle of preserving and respecting life. Or: if you don't steal the drug and you let your wife die, you'd always condemn yourself for it afterwards. You wouldn't be blamed and you would have lived up to the outside rule of the law, but you wouldn't have lived up to your own standards of conscience.

**Against:** Heinz is faced with the decision of whether to consider the other people who need the drug just as badly as his wife. Heinz ought to act not according to his particular feelings toward his wife, but in considering the value of all the lives involved. Or: if you stole the drug, you wouldn't be blamed by other people but you'd condemn yourself because you wouldn't have lived up to your own conscience and standards of honesty.

The stages are dependent upon the structure of an individual's reasoning rather than on the content of that reasoning (Kohlberg and Kauffman 1987). That is, the stage at which an individual is reasoning is determined by the relationship between her or his ideas; it is determined by the form of thought rather than by the conclusions reached. Any decision concerning the proper course of action may be justified by alternative means. It may, for example, be an egocentric justification or a justification concerned with the maintenance of individual rights. These alternative justifications represent the underlying form or structure of moral reasoning, which is the concern of Kohlberg's theory.

Kohlberg asserts that his stages are invariant in their sequence, as presented above, in that every child must go step by step through each stage and that, moreover, the invariant stage sequence applies universally and cross-culturally, that is, to every society (Kohlberg 1969; Kohlberg and Kauffman 1987).

This description of the levels and stages is presented in definitive form in Table 16.1 overleaf.

## Task: Classifying stages of moral reasoning

Classify the following statements:

1) Heinz should not steal because the owner worked hard for what he has and you shouldn't take advantage.
2) Heinz should steal the drug because certain rights have been agreed upon or defined by us through social process or social contract.
3) Heinz should steal the drug because his wife might be a very important person.
4) Heinz shouldn't steal because it's selfish or deceitful to steal.
5) Heinz should steal the drug because of the marital responsibility he accepted.

*Stage scores are shown at the end of the chapter.*
*Remember: 'Don't cheat'.*

## Table 16.1 Kohlberg's stages of moral reasoning

| Level and stage | Content of stage | | Social perspective of stage |
|---|---|---|---|
| | **What is right** | **Reasons for doing right** | |
| **Level 1 – Preconventional**<br><br>*Stage One:*<br>*Heteronomous Morality* | To avoid breaking rules. Backed by punishment, obedience for its own sake, and avoiding physical damage to persons and property. | Avoidance of punishment, and the superior power of authorities. | Egocentric point of view. Does not consider the interests of others or recognise that they differ from the subject's; doesn't relate two points of view. Actions are considered physically rather than in terms of psychological interests of others. Confusion of authority's perspective with one's own. |
| *Stage Two:*<br>*Individualism, Instrumental Purpose, and Exchange* | Following rules only when it is to someone's immediate interest; acting to meet one's own interests and needs and letting others do the same. Right is also what's fair, what's an equal exchange, a deal, an agreement. | To serve one's own needs or interests in a world where you have to recognise that other people have their interests too. | Concrete individualistic perspective. Aware that everybody has his or her own interest to pursue and these conflict so that right is relative (in the concrete individualistic sense). |
| **Level 2 – Conventional**<br><br>*Stage Three:*<br>*Mutual Interpersonal Expectations, Relationships, and Interpersonal Conformity* | Living up to what is expected by people close to you or what people generally expect of those in your role as child, sibling, friend, etc. 'Being good' is important and means having good motives, showing concern about others. It also means keeping mutual relationships, such as trust, loyalty, respect, and gratitude. | The need to be a good person in your own eyes and those of others. Your caring for others. Belief in the Golden Rule. Desire to maintain rules and authority that support stereotypical good behaviour. | Perspective of the individual in relationships with other individuals. Aware of shared feelings, agreements, and expectations that take primacy over individual interests. Relating points of view through the concrete Golden Rule, putting themselves in the other person's shoes. Does not yet consider generalised system perspective. |
| *Stage Four:*<br>*Social System and Conscience* | Fulfilling the actual duties to which you have agreed. Laws are to be upheld except in extreme cases where they conflict with other fixed social duties. Right is also contributing to society, the group, or institution. | To keep the institution going as a whole, to avoid the breakdown in the system 'if everyone did it'. The imperative of conscience to meet one's defined obligations (easily confused with Stage Three belief in rules and authority). | Differentiates societal point of view from interpersonal agreement or motives. Takes the point of view of the system that defines roles and rules. Considers individual relations in terms of place in the system. |

# Table 16.1 Kohlberg's stages of moral reasoning (continued)

| Level and stage | Content of stage | | Social perspective of stage |
|---|---|---|---|
| | What is right | Reasons for doing right | |
| **Level 3 – Postconventional or principled** <br><br> *Stage Five:* <br> *Social Contract or Utility and Individual Rights* | Being aware that people hold a variety of values and opinions, and that most values and rules are relative to your group. These relative rules should usually be upheld, however, in the interest of impartiality and because they are the social contract. Some non-relative values and rights like life and liberty, however, must be upheld in any society and regardless of majority opinion. | A sense of obligation to law because of one's social contract to make and abide by laws for the welfare of all and for the protection of all people's rights. A feeling of contractual commitment, freely entered upon, to family, friendship, trust, and work obligations. Concern that laws and duties be based on rational calculation of overall utility: 'the greatest good for the greatest number.' | Prior-to-society perspective. Perspective of a rational individual aware of values and rights prior to social attachments and contracts. Integrates perspectives by formal mechanisms of agreement, contract, objective impartiality, and due process. Considers moral and legal points of view; recognises that they sometimes conflict, and finds it difficult to integrate them. |
| *Stage Six:* <br> *Universal Ethical Principles* | Following self-chosen ethical principles. Particular laws or social agreements are usually valid because they rest on such principles. When laws violate these principles, one acts in accordance with the principle. Principles are universal principles of justice: the equality of human rights and respect for the dignity of human beings as individuals. | The belief as a rational person in the validity of universal moral principles, and a sense of personal commitment to them. | Perspective of a moral point of view from which social arrangements derive. Perspective is that of any rational individual recognising the nature of morality or the fact that persons are ends in themselves and must be treated as such. |

**SOURCE:** Colby and Kohlberg (1987).

# Critiques of Kohlberg's theory

Criticisms have been made of Kohlberg's theory in respect of method, of his claim of invariant stage sequence and cross-cultural universality, of his conception of the moral domain (as concerned with 'justice reasoning'), and of moral reasoning's relationship with moral behaviour. Each of these will be considered in turn.

## Methodological concerns

Kohlberg's method for scoring (assessing) moral reasoning, the *Moral Judgment Interview* (MJI), relies upon a subject's free responses to questions concerning his or her moral reasoning about moral dilemmas such as that of Heinz above. The MJI has attracted criticism for its reliance upon an interpretative scoring system, which has been said to incur serious threats of scorer subjectivity. The elaborate scoring system is cumbersome, and to the extent that subjects do not offer clear stage-related responses (due to the freedom given them to answer), inferences must be drawn from what is said in order to identify the responses with a particular stage or stages. The present MJI (Colby and Kohlberg 1987; Colby *et al.* 1987) claims 'semi-standardisation' while conceding complexity and that it may appear 'at first unwieldy'. An aspirant interviewer is warned to set aside a minimum of a month or two of concentrated study and practice to learn how to score an MJI. Thus, while the threat of subjectivity may have been reduced, the MJI remains a complex and somewhat tortuous instrument to administer and score. One may apprehend the difficulties inherent in scoring by considering the statements in the box on page 301 and attempting to attribute each to a Kohlbergian stage.

In response to the criticisms levelled at Kohlberg's MJI, Rest developed the *Defining Issues Test* (DIT) as an objective and simpler measure of moral reasoning (Rest 1974; Rest, Narvaez, Bebeau, and Thoma 1999). Using Kohlberg's moral stages, statements were compiled which exemplify the characteristics of the various stages. Subjects are scored on the importance they attach to each of these statements. The DIT, now in its second edition (DIT2), is probably the better instrument (The Centre for the Study of Ethical Development 2000).

PHOTO: CHA JOHNSTON

*Is Kohlberg warranted in suggesting that lower class rural populations are less likely to develop principled and autonomous morality? This seems an unusually prejudiced contention to make, which is in need of critique. The findings of Tudin, Straker, and Mendelsohn (1994) seem to suggest that Kohlberg may have been mistaken in this regard.*

## *Invariance of sequence and cross-cultural universality*

Kohlberg's rather grand assertions in this respect have attracted much controversy and it is impressive that these assertions have endured empirical scrutiny. Snarey (1985) reviewed forty-five studies of moral development throughout twenty-seven countries and found the notion of invariant stages well supported. Snarey attributed the apparently rare occurrence of stage skipping and regression to measurement error. Universality of stages was found in respect of Stages One to Four while the development of principled morality (Stages Five and Six) appears to be biased in favour of complex urban societies and middle class populations as opposed to simple, rural, lower class populations who are therefore less likely to develop principled and autonomous morality. This bias is not entirely unpredicted by Kohlberg, in his belief that moral development follows from opportunities for thinking and that such opportunities may be lacking in rural communities and lower socio-economic classes owing to their relative social and cognitive simplicity. Nisan and Kohlberg (1982) explain that in isolated villages and tribal communities, Stage Three moral reasoning (mutual interpersonal expectations, relationships, and interpersonal conformity) may be a perfectly proficient orientation for the personal relations inherent in such societies, so that nothing motivates further moral reasoning development.

Some evidence has recently appeared, though, which questions the relationship implied by Kohlberg between low socio-economic class, or rural circumstances, and delayed or underdeveloped moral reasoning (Tudin, Straker, and Mendolsohn 1994). This later study demonstrates that the cognitive and social challenges that foster moral development might exist in lower socio-economic classes. Essentially, however, Kohlberg's prediction that cognitive and social challenges foster moral development remains intact, and his claim of invariant universal stage development appears well-founded – with the caveat that some societies do not progress all the way.

## Gilligan's critique of 'justice reasoning'

Kohlberg's theory of moral reasoning is concerned with *justice reasoning*. An individual's development is traced against her or his progress in considering moral dilemmas from the perspective of what an impartial social contract would demand, based on universal rights and equality (Kohlberg and Kauffman 1987). Gilligan (1982) argues that Kohlberg ignores the feminine moral orientation of the *morality of care*, a morality of responsibility and caring based on non-violence. She proposes that this alternative 'morality of care' predominates in women, whereas justice reasoning predominates in men, and that Kohlberg's theory is therefore biased in terms of gender in that 'the thinking of women is often classified with that of children' (Gilligan 1982, 70).

Kohlberg can be said to have brought this controversy upon himself in that in his initial sample – the data from which served as the basis of his theory – comprised only boys aged between ten and sixteen years (Kohlberg 1958).

Gilligan's claims raise two questions:

1) whether men and women are differently oriented: men to justice and women to the morality of care, and
2) whether Kohlberg's theory is gender-biased in that it relegates women to lower (less adequate) levels of reasoning.

In respect of whether men and women are differently oriented in terms of moral reasoning, there seems to be little or no evidence to suggest that different genders do actually subscribe to one orientation more than another, as orientations have not been found to be gender specific

*Gilligan (1982) criticises Kohlberg for not taking into account the possibility that the 'caring morality' of women may differ fundamentally from the morality of men.*

(Walker, de Vries, and Trevethan 1987). Men and women seem equally to utilise both orientations. Further, Kohlberg does regard other incidental orientations as included in his concept of justice reasoning:

1) general and normative order, or impartial following of rules and normative roles,
2) utilitarian maximising of the welfare of each person,
3) perfectionistic seeking of harmony or integrity of the self and the social group, and
4) fairness, balancing of perspectives, maintaining equity, and social contract (Kohlberg and Kauffman 1987).

It appears that Gilligan's morality of care may well be subsumed under the justice orientation.

On the issue of whether women's moral reasoning is devalued within Kohlberg's scheme, again the answer seems to be 'no'. Gilligan's suspicions have not been confirmed by research, in the fact that no discernible difference in moral reasoning has been observed between males and females (Bee 1992; Bourne and Felipe Russo 1998; Rest, Narvaez, Bebeau, and Thoma 1999). For example, Thoma (cited in Rest *et al.* 1999) found that education accounted for fifty-two point five per cent of the variance in moral reasoning, whereas gender accounted for only nought point two per cent. Walker (1984, 688) found such scant evidence for the proposition of gender bias that she lamented that energy would be better spent wondering 'why the myth that males are more advanced than females persists in the light of so little evidence'. The weight of evidence appears not to support the claim that Kohlberg's scheme is biased against women (Lapsley 1996).

Yet Gilligan and Wiggins (1987) persist. They point to the discrepancy between men and women in terms of moral behaviour – that men are responsible for the majority of violence and antisocial conduct and that prison populations are overwhelmingly male – and they ask: 'If there are no sex differences in empathy or moral reasoning, why are there sex differences in moral and immoral behaviour?' (Gilligan and Wiggins 1987, 279) Could the answer to their question just be that men are the ones who get caught because they are dumb? However, Gilligan and Wiggins present a very good question, which needs to be considered within the framework of the multiplicity of complex factors at play in the production of conduct in a morally significant context. We shall turn to this matter after considering briefly the criticism levelled at Kohlberg in this respect.

## The relationship between moral reasoning and action

One should be clear at the outset that Kohlberg was far less concerned with moral action (that is, action in a morally significant context) than with an individual's deliberations of what he or she ought to do in the circumstances and, more particularly, his or her reasons for this (Westen 1996). Further, Kohlberg's theory is but one possible perspective (of how individuals consider what they ought to do) of one possible component (of what is required of individuals ultimately to do what they ought) (Rest 1983; Westen 1996).

Nevertheless, as we have mentioned, Kohlberg's theory has attracted criticism for having no direct correlate with moral behaviour. He did not propose, however, that such a correlation would exist. His assumption in this respect is not that moral judgement will match or be matched by behaviour:

> [Kohlberg's theory assumes] that the subject's thinking about moral questions and interpretations of right and wrong are important determinants of moral conduct. This is not to say that people always do what they think is right. The relation of moral judgment and conduct is complex and incompletely understood. No doubt the causality is bi-directional: Our overt behaviour can influence our moral beliefs just as our moral beliefs can influence the course of our behaviour. But our present point is that judgment is an integral component of action and that moral judgment must be assessed if moral conduct is to be understood (Kohlberg and Kauffman 1987, 2).

Research has demonstrated an impressive correlation between the degree of development of moral judgement and moral conduct when interpreted from Kohlberg's perspective: that the higher the level of reasoning, the stronger the link ought to become between what the individual considers to be the right course of action and his or her behaviour (Blasi 1980; Kohlberg 1968).

Some studies may illustrate the point well:

◆ Only eleven per cent of subjects who associated themselves with principled morality cheated in an experimental situation, whereas half of those at a conventional level of morality cheated (Kohlberg 1968).
◆ Whereas seventy-five per cent of morally principled subjects (reasoning at a principled level) refused to administer increasing levels of electric shocks to an experimental 'victim', only thirteen per cent of the other subjects (those not reasoning at a level of principled morality), refused to shock the 'victim' (Kohlberg 1968).
◆ The study by Kohlberg and Candee (1984) found that of those individuals who concluded that it was morally correct to participate in a student protest, approximately seventy-five per cent of those reason-

ing at Stages Four and Five participated while only about twenty-five per cent of those reasoning at Stage Three participated.

Blasi (1980) reviewed seventy-five studies concerning the relationship between moral judgement and behaviour and found in seventy-six per cent of the studies that moral judgement correlated with behaviour. He concludes that the body of research appears to support the hypothesis of a statistical relationship between moral reasoning and moral action in the sense of the subject doing what she or he considers to be moral.

What might be argued is that the small positive correlation that Kohlberg claims – and that seems empirically supported – leaves much to be explained, so that its value may be questioned as being negligible. But this argument overlooks the complexity of the precedents of moral conduct in implying that *one factor* should offer a clear insight into the moral nature of conduct that is expected from individuals. Kohlberg clearly considered that a variety of other factors mediate between an individual's moral reasoning capacities and his or her ultimate conduct. He recognised that moral reasoning or principles in themselves do not direct behaviour, but that principles (moral reasoning) are a basic component for moral action:

> The prediction from stages or principles to action requires that we take account of intermediary judgments that an individual makes. One does not act directly on principles, one acts on specific content judgments engendered by those principles. We hypothesize that moral principles or 'structures of moral reasoning' lead to two more specific judgments, one a judgment of deontic choice, the other a judgment of responsibility. The first is a deontic decision function, judgment of what is right. The second is a follow-through function, a judgment of responsibility to act on what one has judged to be right (Kohlberg and Candee 1984, 517).

Rest (1983; 1986), a student of Kohlberg's, offers a framework that may explain how other factors beyond moral judgements may be responsible for a failure to act morally. The framework allows for some insight into the complexity of factors that may produce moral behaviour, considering that moral reasoning explains only twenty per cent of conduct in a morally significant circumstance (Rest *et al.* 1999). Rest proposes that moral behaviour depends on four components. (Note that he does not assert that moral behaviour is produced out of a linear process of the components, and he cautions that components are interrelated in such a way that each component may influence the outcome of other components.) His framework assumes that the following components produce moral behaviour:

◆ *Component One – moral sensitivity:* involves the interpretation of the situation in terms of how other people's welfare may be affected by the subject's actions and what courses of action are available to the subject.

◆ *Component Two – moral judgement:* concerns what ought in the circumstances, identified in Component One, to be done. This is the realm of moral judgement in its **deontic** (ethically binding) sense. It is

**Deontic.** Ethically or morally binding. It describes that which is an ethical obligation, or duty.

## Moral reasoning and criminal conduct: the case of Moses Sithole

Moses Sithole's life is littered with violations of the law and of the rights of those who have encountered him. His previous convictions begin, at the age of thirteen years, for housebreaking. For this he admits guilt. At the age of twenty he was again convicted of housebreaking and again he admits guilt. At twenty-two years, and again at twenty-five, he was convicted of fraud; he admits guilt in both these instances. At the age of twenty-five he was also convicted of a rape; he insists he is not guilty of this crime, however (Sithole 1996).

He was arrested again at the age of thirty, on suspicion of being a serial rapist and killer responsible for forty rapes, thirty-eight murders, and six robberies.

On 4 December 1997 he was convicted on all counts and the following day sentenced to die in prison, which was the Judge's express will in handing down a sentence of 2410 years in prison with eligibility for parole arising at 1460 years.

Grant (1997)* examined Sithole's moral reasoning from a Kohlbergian perspective and was surprised that Sithole, the worst serial killer and rapist in South African history to date, demonstrated post-conventional moral reasoning and may appropriately be assigned to that level.

In the face of this finding, it appears doubtful that moral reasoning can be taken as a direct indicator of an individual's prospective conduct in a morally significant context.

(*The assistance of Merle Friedman was invaluable to this project and greatly appreciated.)

the realm in which Kohlberg's theory may contribute as a factor. Another factor is the impact of social norms that may be internalised or learnt, which makes it also the realm of behaviourist, cognitive-social, and psychodynamic theory.

◆ *Component Three – moral motivation:* involves the selection of which value or domain or motive – such as moral, personal (self-interest), or conventional (arbitrary rules) – will inform the subject's intentions for action. This is the component of competing claims or values.

◆ *Component Four – moral character:* concerns the execution and implementation of what one intends to do (as conceptualised in terms of Component Three).

Failure to behave morally may then be attributed variously to deficiencies in one, some, or all of the components. Where there is insensitivity to the needs of others, or the circumstances are too ambiguous for interpretation, the subject may fail to act morally (deficiency in Component One). Where a subject fails to appreciate what ought morally to be done in the circumstances, action may fail to be moral (deficiency in Component Two). Where moral values are compromised or displaced by other values or motives (such as self-interest), the subject may again fail to act morally (deficiency in Component Three). If the subject, who has decided upon and intends a moral action, loses sight of his or her goal, is distracted, or just wears out, there may again be a failure to act morally (deficiency in Component Four) (Rest 1983). Component Two may be identified with Kohlberg's domain of moral reasoning, since it is the component in which what ought and ought not morally to be done is considered (Rest 1986).

It may be possible now to consider an answer to Gilligan and Wiggins's question: 'If there are no sex differences in empathy or moral reasoning, why are there sex differences in moral and immoral behaviour?' The answer may be that the difference lies anywhere in the other factors within the moral judgement component or any of the other components required for moral conduct.

It appears that many factors collaborate to produce behaviour of moral significance. Kohlberg's claim is that the domain of moral reasoning is only one such factor; though he does assert that it is an integral factor. (Blasi (1980) concurs in this assertion.) Rest's component analysis offers some insight into how these factors may need to collaborate in order to produce moral behaviour.

## Conclusion

Kohlberg's method is so cumbersome and at risk of error that James Rest's DIT has probably superseded the MJI as the instrument of choice for measuring moral reasoning development. Also, while Kohlberg's theory seems lacking in respect of its ability to explain behaviour directly in a morally significant context, he never claimed that it would, and his theory stands as an explanation of an integral factor of what is required for moral conduct. Further, his claims of invariant sequence and universality appear to have withstood empirical scrutiny (save that in some societies development is restricted for reasons Kohlberg seems to explain). Finally, Gilligan's critiques have not found empirical support and seem misplaced.

Kohlberg's realisation that moral reasoning develops alongside cognition has allowed for an appreciation that what determines what one ought to do in a morally significant context may not simply be concerned with the internalisation of set rules. His theory has explicated and confirmed Piaget's speculations that morality develops qualitatively. Moreover, he has illuminated the fact that the appropriate moral course has different meanings for different people and that 'wrong' doesn't have just one meaning. Ultimately it must be recognised that the understanding of morality has clearly been advanced by his theory and his rich research tradition.

## Recommended readings

Kohlberg, L. and Kauffman, K. (1987). 'Theoretical introduction to the measurement of moral judgment'. In A. Colby and L. Kohlberg (eds), *The measurement of moral judgment. Volume 1.* Cambridge: Cambridge University Press.
*(This provides the most recent and comprehensive exposition of Kohlberg's theory, on the authority of Kohlberg himself.)*

Rest, J. R. (1983). 'Morality'. In P. Mussen, J. H. Flavell, and E. M. Markman (eds), *Handbook of child psychology. Volume 3.* Fourth edition. New York: John Wiley.
*(An accessible rendition of Kohlberg's theory and a detailed discussion of Rest's component analysis of moral conduct.)*

## Critical thinking tasks

### Specific tasks

1) What stage of moral reasoning do *you* adopt when resolving morally significant problems?

2) What does it mean to say that someone *knows* that what they are doing is wrong, particularly in the case of a child? Similarly, what does Geldenhuys mean when he says, 'I knew what I did was wrong'? (See the case study in Chapter 3.)

### General tasks

1) Consider the significance of Geldenhuys's (supposed) and Sithole's moral reasoning capacities for Kohlberg's theory.

2) Discuss the relation between Moses Sithole's capacity for moral reasoning and his ultimate conduct in the light of Rest's (1983) component analysis.

3) What do you suppose can explain the way people conduct themselves in a morally relevant context?

## Stage scores for the task on classifying stages, according to the MJI manual (Colby *et al.* 1987)

Statement stages:
1) Stage 3 (p. 74).
2) Stage 5 (p. 55).
3) Stage 1 (p. 12).
4) Stage 3 (it is scored as an equivalent of statement (1) above) (p. 74).
5) Stage 4 (p. 42).

# Bronfenbrenner's ecological theory of development

*Derek Hook*

This chapter presents Bronfenbrenner's theory of **ecological development**. We will introduce and discuss the following concepts:

1. The importance of a contextual approach to development.

2. Multiperson systems of interaction.

3. The dyad as basic unit of analysis.

4. The importance of the perceived environmental context.

5. The microsystem, mesosystem, exosystem, macrosystem, and chronosystem spheres of influence.

6. A new approach to developmental interventions.

7. The notion of ecological transitions.

The chapter also features a brief historical study of apartheid's effects on development, before closing with a critique of Bronfenbrenner's theory.

**Ecological development.**
Development approached from a strongly contextual basis, which prioritises the influence of the individual's various social environments.

## Introduction: contexts of development

Urie Bronfenbrenner (1977; 1979) offers a welcome corrective to those accounts of psychosocial development that do not properly engage with the overarching *socio-political context* in which development occurs. Bronfenbrenner's is an original contribution to psychosocial developmental psychology for a number of reasons. For a start, he accords relatively equal importance to both the environment of development and the developing person; for him development is effectively the evolving interaction between these two variables. This twofold emphasis on the *inter-*

*play* between individual and environment fixes on the mutual accommodations that occur between individual and environment. In this way it prioritises the reciprocity of relations (Bronfenbrenner 1979).

Second, Bronfenbrenner sees the laboratory and testing room of experimental psychology as limited and insulated contexts for the study of psychosocial development (1977, 1979). He attempts to extend the scope of the developmental psychologist increasingly outwards, to the consideration of ever-wider social spheres of influence. For Bronfenbrenner the developing child never exists in social isolation, nor does the child exist outside of an acutely unique socio-political, historical, and ideological set of circumstances.

Urie Bronfenbrenner

Furthermore, for Bronfenbrenner, psychosocial development does not centre on the traditional psychological processes of perception, motivation, thinking, and learning perceived at the isolated level of the individual. He focuses rather on the *content* of these functions, on *what* is perceived, desired, feared, thought about, or acquired as knowledge, and on 'how the nature of this psychological material changes as a function of a person's exposure to an interaction with the environment' (Bronfenbrenner 1979, 9). In this way Bronfenbrenner (1979) defines development as the person's *evolving conception of the* **ecological environment**, their relation to it, as well as their *growing capacity to discover, sustain, or alter its properties*. For Bronfenbrenner there are no questions of psychology that are not also questions of context, and this would be particularly true for developmental psychology.

# The role of the individual in development

However, having suggested that context is never a minor element in any reasonable account of development, (development for Bronfenbrenner is always *development-in-context*), it is important to emphasise that the individual remains always a proactive feature of the environment. The developing person is not merely a *tabula rasa* on which the environment makes its impact, but is rather a growing dynamic entity that progressively moves into and restructures his or her social milieu (Bronfenbrenner 1979). Individuals are in fact capable of adapting their imagination to the constraints of objective reality, and even of refashioning their environment so that it is more compatible with their abilities, needs, and desires. In this sense Bronfenbrenner takes a strong *anti-deterministic approach* to development, and to the social factors impinging upon individual development. In fact, he sees the growing capacity to remould reality in accordance with human requirements and aspirations as representing the highest level of development (Bronfenbrenner 1979).

**Ecological environment.** The ecological environment is a series of successive layers, each surrounding a smaller sphere of environmental influences. Bronfenbrenner maintains that the ecological environment contains five such environmental systems: the microsystem, the mesosystem, the exosystem, the macrosystem, and the chronosystem.

# Systems of influence

In attempting to determine the fundamental environmental influences on development, Bronfenbrenner (1979) claims to break from the traditions of developmental research psychology. Rather than attempting to isolate the influence of linear variables, Bronfenbrenner's approach is to conceive development in *systems terms*, where any given variable is linked to a whole ecological chain of associated influences. In other words, Bronfenbrenner thinks in terms of **systemic forms of influence**. If a child's mother becomes sick, for example, or is fired from her job, this sets up a reverberating series of influences, which impact not only on the child's relationship with its mother, but on its relationships within the immediate family more generally, on its school life, on the familial resources available to it, etc. Thus the healthy development of the child is intricately entwined with factors such as role demands and stresses placed on the parents, the flexibility of the parents' job schedules, adequacy of childcare arrangements, the presence of family friends and neighbours, the quality of health and services, neighbourhood safety, etc. (Bronfenbrenner 1979).

> **Systemic forms of influence.** Where any given variable is linked to a whole ecological chain of associated influences.

Bronfenbrenner's conception of environmental influences on development is not only a systemic approach, it also recognises the fact that environments are non-static forms of influence that exist in a changing state of flux. Bronfenbrenner recognises that what can be said of a given developmental environment today may not necessarily be true of that environment tomorrow. It is also important to understand that the developing individual is very possibly an agent of change within a given environment. Likewise, larger environmental spheres exert their influence on smaller environments. This fact, in Bronfenbrenner's view (1977), is rarely dealt with satisfactorily in psychosocial developmental studies. In this way Bronfenbrenner (1979) argues that to understand human development sufficiently one needs to examine **multiperson systems of interaction** that are not limited to a single setting, and that take into account aspects of the environment beyond the immediate situation containing the subject.

> **Multiperson systems of interaction.** An awareness of the complex and multifaceted nature of patterns of interaction within groups of people.

# Connections between different settings of development

Interconnections between various environmental settings can be as instrumental in influencing development as can discrete events taking place within separate settings (Bronfenbrenner 1979). The example that Bronfenbrenner gives here is education, suggesting that effective learning requires effective parental support, supervision, and encouragement, in addition to school tuition. Such interconnections include joint participation, communication, and the existence of information in each setting about the other. Bronfenbrenner suggests, moreover, that the child can be profoundly influenced by events that take place even in settings in which they are not present. In many ways this seems an obvious assertion, but it draws attention to the fact that these forms of influence have not typically been considered as of any great importance in the history of developmental psychology. The example that Bronfenbrenner (1979) draws on here involves the conditions of parental employment, which altogether exert a powerful influence on the developmental context of the child.

Despite the varying scale of these various settings they frequently exhibit marked similarities within a given culture or subculture (Bronfenbrenner 1979). In fact, within a given culture, there are generally more similarities than differences across these various levels, and fundamental disparities only appear in cross-cultural comparisons. This circumstance leads Bronfenbrenner to speculate on the existence of a blueprint for the organisation of every type of setting, a blueprint that if changed will effect corresponding changes in other spheres of behaviour and development:

> research results suggest that a change in maternity ward practices affecting the relation between the mother and the newborn can produce effects still detectable five years later ... a severe economic crisis occurring in a society is seen to have positive or negative impact on the development of the child throughout the life span, depending on the age of the child at the time that the family suffered financial duress (Bronfenbrenner 1979, 4).

*Interconnections between various settings can be instrumental in influencing development. Take for example the case of effective education, which would seem to require more than simply going to school, or a good teacher, but also parental support, encouragement, and supervision.*

## The dyad

The basic unit of analysis for Bronfenbrenner (1979) is the **dyad**, or two-person system, a fact which itself indicates his commitment to not viewing the subject of development in social isolation. Dyads are dynamic structures characterised by reciprocal relations, where the parties are able mutually to affect the nature of interaction to the extent that Bronfenbrenner asserts that 'if one member of the pair undergoes a process of development, the other does also' (1979, 5). Dyads extend into larger structures: *triads*, *tetrads*, and larger interpersonal systems of interaction. In this sense Bronfenbrenner warns that the presence and participation of third parties, such as relatives, friends, neighbours, or work colleagues, can influence the child's immediate setting:

> If such third parties ... play a disruptive rather than a supportive role, the developmental process, considered as a system, breaks down; like a three-legged stool, it is more easily upset if one leg is broken, or shorter than the others (Bronfenbrenner 1979, 5).

**Dyad.** Dynamic structure of the two-person relationship characterised by reciprocal relations, where both parties are mutually able to affect the nature of the interaction.

## The perceived environment

Bronfenbrenner's theory (1979) also has a pronounced phenomenological quality in the sense that the environment is conceived not in a realist or

*Perhaps the most basic and fundamental example of a dyad is the mother-child bond in earliest childhood.*

objective sense, but as *how the subject perceives and experiences it*. This subjective approach arises from Bronfenbrenner's certainty of the:

> impossibility of understanding ... behaviour solely from the objective properties of an environment without reference to its meaning for the people in the setting; the palpable motivational character of environmental objects and events; and ... the importance of the unreal, the imagined ... (1979, 24).

**Microsystem.** The microsystem is the complex of face-to-face, bi-directional relationships between the developing person and important figures such as caregivers, parents, siblings, friends, classmates, and teachers. It is the smallest environmental system in Bronfenbrenner's ecological theory of development. The microsystem is assembled from three basic building blocks: the *activities*, *roles*, and *interpersonal relations* experienced by the developing person.

# The ecological environment

Like concentric onion peels, the ecological environment is a series of successive layers, each surrounding a smaller sphere. The example Bronfenbrenner uses is a collection of Russian dolls, which is a set of nested structures, each inside the next, enclosing a succession of formally similar yet smaller containers. For Bronfenbrenner, each such container can be likened to a different-level environment , a different environmental system of development. The smallest such environmental system is the **microsystem.**

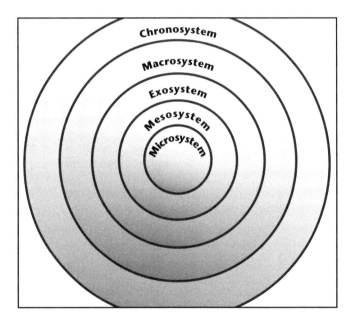

**Figure 17.1** Bronfenbrenner's ecological theory of development. The concentric spheres of micro-, meso-, exo-, macro-, and exosystem make up the five environmental systems.

## The microsystem

The microsystem is *the immediate situation that directly affects the developing person* (Bronfenbrenner 1979). It is the realm of face-to-face bi-directional relationships where influences flow back and forth so that a new baby will affect the lives of its parents, just as their attitudes will affect the baby (Papalia, Olds, and Feldman 1998). The microsystem is the complex of relations between the developing person and important figures such as caregivers, parents, siblings, friends, classmates, and teachers. It is important to understand that this complex of relations includes the connections across various people within the immediate setting, so that the relationship between the child's father and the child's grandfather will also ultimately exert an amount of influence on the child.

PHOTO: GILL HAIDEN

Bronfenbrenner's microsystem is assembled from three basic factors, comprising the pattern of *activities*, *roles*, and *interpersonal relations* experienced by the developing person (1979). By 'role' he means the set of behaviours and expectations associated with a position in society such as that of mother, baby, teacher, friend, and so on. He strongly ties the microsystem to particular concrete settings, such as the home, the day-care centre, the school playground, etc.

To get a sense of the next environmental system of development – the mesosystem – we need to 'zoom out' a little and take a slightly broader overview of the developmental context by looking at interrelations among microsystems.

*The sphere of the mesosystem also accommodates linkages and interconnections between the different facets of microsystems. These include influences across home and school, and across peer and family groups.*

## The mesosystem

The **mesosystem** is a system of microsystems, which is formed whenever the developing person moves into a new setting (Bronfenbrenner 1979). (Remember that a *setting*, for Bronfenbrenner, is a place where people readily engage in face-to-face interaction). The bi-directional interactions of the microsystem are now enlarged to the extent that we are now looking at slightly higher order environments, such as the school as a whole, the home taken to the level of neighbourhood, the *extended* family, and social relationships on the level of peer groups. The sphere of the mesosystem also accommodates linkages and interconnections between the different facets of microsystems. This means that influences across home and school, peer and family groups, work and recreational settings, are also considered. A case in point here is how parents and teachers may collaborate in educational planning for the child (Craig 1996).

**Mesosystem.** A system of microsystems, formed whenever the developing person moves into a new setting. The sphere of the mesosystem also accommodates linkages and interconnections between the different facets of microsystems.

## The exosystem

The **exosystem** refers to the social setting or organisation beyond the individual's immediate experience that nevertheless affects her or him. Examples may range from formal settings like a parent's workplace, community, welfare health systems, or the activities of the local school board, to less formal organisations like the parent's network of friends or the school class of an older sibling (Bronfenbrenner 1979). Bronfenbrenner defines the exosystem as:

**Exosystem.** The social setting or organisation beyond the individual's immediate experience that nevertheless affects him or her. It is an extension of the mesosystem, embracing other specific social structures, both formal and informal, that impinge upon the immediate settings in which that person is found.

*Whereas a specific church – a particular congregation, building, or grouping of people – would represent an exosystem variable for Bronfenbrenner, the broader institutional pattern (for example the Roman Catholic Church), would represent a macrosystem variable.*

**Macrosystem.** The macrosystem refers to the overarching institutional patterns of the culture or the sub-culture, such as the economic, social, educational, legal, and political systems, of which macro-, meso-, and exosystems are the concrete manifestations. The laws, values, traditions, and customs of a particular society are to be found at this level.

An ... extension of the mesosystem embracing other specific social structures, both formal and informal, that ... impinge upon or encompass the immediate settings in which that person is found, and thereby influence, delimit, or even determine what goes on there. These structures include the major institutions of the society, both deliberately structured and spontaneously evolving, as they operate at a concrete level. They encompass, among other structures, the world of work, the neighbourhood, the mass media, agencies of government, the distribution of goods and services, communication and transportation facilities and informal social networks (Bronfenbrenner 1977, 515).

## The macrosystem

We noted earlier that there is a good deal of consistency and similarity across different settings within a culture. Bronfenbrenner (1977) points to this similarity as evidence of the existence of the macrosystem. He notes that micro-, meso-, and exosystems all function in similar ways and appear 'to be constructed from the same master model' (Bronfenbrenner 1979). The **macrosystem**, as the 'master model', refers to the overarching institutional patterns of the culture or the sub-culture (such as the economic, social, educational, legal, and political systems) of which macro-, meso-, and exosystems are the concrete manifestations (Bronfenbrenner 1977, 515). The laws, values, traditions, and customs of a particular society are to be found at this level.

This is the level at which we might locate those very broad cultural patterns of ideology, dominant economic and political systems, general and popular discourses, values, laws, and customs. Bronfenbrenner (1977; 1979) warns that macrosystems should be conceived and examined not only in structural terms, but should be seen also as carriers of information and discourse that, both explicitly and implicitly, endow meaning and motivation to particular agencies, social networks, roles, activities, and their interrelations. In this connection, Craig (1996) valuably notes as an example that laws providing for the inclusion of handicapped children in mainstream school classes are likely to affect profoundly the education and social development of both disabled and normal children who are students in these classes. Craig (1996) goes on to suggest that the success or failure of this 'mainstreaming' may encourage or discourage other governmental efforts to integrate the two groups.

## The chronosystem

Bronfenbrenner (1979) also counts the dimension of time as a fundamental influence on the direction of psychosocial development. His implication of time applies in two ways within ecological theory. Time is important as it entails the patterning of environmental events and transitions over the life course, and as it refers to the unique socio-historical placement of the individual. An example in the first instance here would be the effects of the divorce of parents, which, while very severe around the first year of the event, appear, like the effects of the death of a loved one, to decrease as time passes (Santrock 1999).

In the second instance of ecological application, that of socio-historical contextualisation, time constitutes a very broad level of ecological influence. It includes factors as diverse as change in family size, place of residence, employment, dominant socio-political values (such as the current importance of democracy as a political system in most 'first-world' Western countries today, as opposed to 300 or 400 years ago), and larger scale cultural changes such as those caused by wars or economic cycles. One important example (Santrock 1999) of a chronosystem change that particularly influences the development of women is an increasing culture of women's rights, which means that women today are less likely to be discouraged from pursuing careers than they would have been thirty years ago.

## Examples of the environmental systems in the South African context

Characteristic examples of these systems in contemporary South Africa would, on the level of the chronosystem, include a history of apartheid, along with large-scale recent democratic political change.

Examples on the level of the macro-system might include the discourses of 'Truth and Reconciliation', of 'the African Renaissance', 'the new South Africa', and the values of racial equality, non-sexism, and tolerance towards diverse religious beliefs. The fundamental ideals of South Africa's new Constitution would belong here. Unfortunately many less positive values would also feature at the macro-system level, including the facts of ongoing racism in South Africa, the culture of violence and crime, and the strongly racialised lines of poverty and affluence.

Notable exosystem examples might include governmental policy and its practical implementation in the lives of South African citizens, as in the cases of affirmative action and outcomes-based education.

## Making developmental interventions

Bronfenbrenner differs from many developmental psychologists in the sense that the recommendations he makes for inducing productive and beneficial changes in the developing individual are not necessarily limited to the level of the microsystem. In fact, Bronfenbrenner's suggestion is that developmental interventions should occur preferably at the level of the *macrosystem*, because macrosystem changes impact on all lower levels of development.

Bronfenbrenner (1979) is a notable example amongst prominent developmental theorists in suggesting that developmental intervention should take the form of political lobbying for relevant changes in governmental policy. This form of implementing developmental change obviously has important bearing on the South African context. Indeed, one only needs to consider the macro role of apartheid in influencing all other spheres of development contained within it, particularly in the life of the black child. Indeed, the influence of such a system of government

*One of the most important political (macrosystem) challenges facing contemporary South African society is racial integration, from even the earliest of ages.*

**Ecological transition.** An ecological transition occurs whenever a person's position in the ecological environment is altered as a result of a change in either role or setting, or in both concurrently. An ecological transition can occur throughout the life-span and can occur at any of the four levels of the ecological environment.

did not stop at the macrosystem and exosystem levels of racist ideology and segregation (respectively), but spread also to mesosystem and microsystem levels where families were broken up by pass-laws and migrant labour, where police violence and intimidation reached into township homes and schools, and where racialised poverty and subsequent problems like malnutrition and inadequate education ensured development deficits at the smallest levels of development.

## Ecological transitions

Considering the importance of the ecological setting of development for Bronfenbrenner, it is not surprising that **ecological transitions** assume such an important place in his theory. In many ways, it is largely through such ecological transitions that one can trace the key life events and life changes of an individual. An ecological transition occurs whenever a person's position in the ecological environment is altered as a result of a change in either role or setting, or in both concurrently (Bronfenbrenner 1979). An ecological transition can occur throughout the life-span and can occur at any of the four levels of the ecological environment. Examples of an ecological transition include the arrival of a baby sibling, the beginning of school, the establishment of a secure relationship with a significant other, graduating from school or an institution of tertiary education, getting or losing a job, marrying, moving, or even a change in government.

*Role changes* are nodal points in the developmental history of the individual, because they correspond to a change in self-perception and a change in what behaviours are socially expected from an individual. For Bronfenbrenner (1979), role changes have an almost magical quality, which alters how a person is treated, how they act, what they do, and even what they think and feel. The social influence and presence of others is also paramount in tracing an individual's developmental progress. Exposure to, and active engagement with, important and influential individuals can lead to the adoption of certain behaviours and habits on the part of the individual. A child is 'more likely to learn to talk in a setting containing roles that obligate adults to talk to children or that encourage ... other people to do so' (Bronfenbrenner 1979, 7).

## Apartheid's effects on childhood development

Post-apartheid South Africa has found it difficult to assess the full extent of the damage of apartheid's large-scale and governmentally institutionalised forms of racism on South African society. In many ways, of course, the impact that this form of government has had, particularly on the lives of black South Africans, remains unquantifiable, and it is precisely this fact that has proved such a 'sticking point' for the reparations committee of the recent Truth and Reconciliation Commission. While it obviously cannot quantify the damage of apartheid, Bronfenbrenner's model of developmental influence can be used to trace a series of possible develop-

(continued)

mental deficits stemming from the implementation of the apartheid system.

On the level of the microsystem, one needs to bear in mind that the lives and upbringing of many black children were fundamentally affected by the absence of parents. Segregated living arrangements, created by the old 'homelands' system, and by the pass-law system, meant that parents frequently had to work in places far removed from where they lived, which, as in the situation of migrant labour, or of a 'domestic' worker living in 'white South Africa', frequently led to the disintegration of the nuclear family. Furthermore, the division of privilege with regard to public service amenities meant that it was far more difficult for black families to access services such as public health, and even when they did, the facilities typically were vastly inferior to those available for white South Africans.

At perhaps an even more fundamental level, the fact of racialised poverty – the effect of, amongst other things, poor 'Bantu' education and white job-reservation – meant that black families did not have the financial support for childcare that the majority of white families did. Such economic disempowerment made for a pervasive influence that affected almost all levels of development, even down to questions of basic nutrition and availability of food. As Chikane (cited in Duncan and Rock 1997, 139) notes:

> being born into apartheid South Africa
> meant, for most black children, the depri-
> vation and violence associated with living
> in the ghettos created for those not
> classified as white ... inferior education ...
> discriminatory social security ... parents
> [exploited by] local enterprises [or as] ...
> migrant labourers ... communities
> constantly destabilized as a result of
> forced removals.

Duncan and Rock (1997) call attention to the fact that, during the apartheid state's various 'states of emergency', the

security forces were given far-ranging warrants and prerogatives, which meant that they were able to disregard all legislation promulgated to protect children. No one was exempt from repressive measures such as the military occupation of black residential areas, house arrest, and indiscriminate attacks on black citizens. Members of the police force could at any time enter a township house, forcibly remove any children and detain them in prison for indefinite periods, without giving any indication when they would be released. The security forces also frequently added to the punishment of incarceration by torturing such children in a wide variety of ways (Duncan and Rock 1997).

Education was a particularly important developmental focus of apartheid repression, as signalled by the Soweto uprisings in 1976. So-called 'Bantu' education was to turn black children into productive and subservient menial labourers who could work for whites. Security forces were also active in breaking up social gatherings on even the smallest scale, even when of a religious nature. Apartheid also worked on a strong ideological level, and mass-media reports were dramatically slanted towards supporting the National Party government, whereas dissenting voices were quickly silenced. The educational system for whites, in the form of 'Christian National Education', was an ideological basis of instruction that prioritised strongly conservative, nationalistic, and racist values.

Clearly then, the influence of the apartheid system made itself felt in virtually every conceivable aspect of Bronfenbrenner's model of developmental influence, from the base level of the health of the child, through to the levels of the family, the neighbourhood, the church, the school, the community, basic public amenities and resources, recreational and health facilities, the mass media, commerce, industry, religion and fundamental social values, beliefs, discourse, and ideology.

# Concluding the ecological perspective

In conclusion then, Bronfenbrenner's theory is intended to offer a conceptual framework for analysing psychological life in terms of three predominant factors: *activity*, *role*, and *relation*, as they manifest across different levels of social influence. In this way it draws attention to the importance of individual differences in development, and implicitly supports the need for an increasing amount of cross-cultural and localised developmental research.

Bronfenbrenner's model provides, in total, a strong theoretical and research means through which the influence of the environment as a whole can be factored into individual or social accounts of human development. Furthermore, it seems that this ecological theory of development can be used in conjunction with other explanatory accounts, typically as a complementary level of explanation with which to supplement more isolated individualist accounts of psychosocial development.

# Critiques of Bronfenbrenner's ecological theory

Bronfenbrenner's ecological model is a very recent one, and the field of developmental psychology has, at the time of writing, offered few real critiques of his approach. There are, however, two basic criticisms one might be able to level against this theory. The first is that, while Bronfenbrenner has plotted an account that does not seem to underestimate the complexity of development, it does appear that it may be a difficult explanatory model to apply. There are two main reasons for this. First, Bronfenbrenner requires an extensive scope of ecological detail with which to build up and substantiate an adequate developmental account. The breadth of his model would seem to suggest that almost *everything* within the individual's developmental environment could potentially play some role in their development. While this may well be true, and while this level of detail and complexity may be necessary for an adequate developmental account, we need to ask at what point one has enough detail and information to mount a tentative explanation for behaviour or personality.

Second, whereas earlier developmental accounts sought the answers to developmental outcomes in immediate familial or social surroundings (as in Freud and Erikson respectively), Bronfenbrenner's scope of developmental influences seemingly knows no bounds, and this makes his model difficult to apply in a balanced way. It is often difficult to collect so much information, and when one has so much information, it becomes difficult to hierarchise according to the relative importance of developmental influence.

Another problem stems from this contention: if Bronfenbrenner is right that we need to conceptualise developmental influences only in systems terms, then the smallest factor of influence needs to be understood only as a part component of a complex and multifaceted system of influence. Because all factors of development are mutually and systemically influential, it seems that we need to take all such factors into account when trying to establish the significance of even the smallest developmental variable. This fact once again makes the complexity of Bronfenbrenner's model practically unwieldy. The same holds for his argument that development is always a two-way process: the sophistication and complexity of his model, which prevents it from being reductionist, also makes it very difficult and complicated to implement practically.

## Recommended readings

Bronfenbrenner, U. (1977). 'Towards an experimental ecology of human development'. *American psychologist*, 32 (7), 513–531.
*(The original paper that summarised Bronfenbrenner's new metatheoretical approach to developmental psychology.)*

Bronfenbrenner, U. (1979). *The ecology of human development.* Cambridge, MA: Harvard University Press.
*(Essentially a more involved and elaborated version of the above; important if you're looking for a more detailed presentation of the ideas.)*

## Critical thinking tasks

### Specific tasks

1) How do you see the ecological model in terms of your own childhood? Draw a developmental 'map' based on Bronfenbrenner's diagram of the various spheres of psychosocial influence. Identify at least six prominent examples from each of the five spheres of ecological influence that were foundational to your own development. In doing so give special thought to whom you are, to how you understand yourself, and to your own sense of identity. Use little icons and diagrams as part of your developmental 'map'.

2) Considering that Bronfenbrenner prioritises macrosystem changes as the most effective level of implementing beneficial developmental interventions, what particular recommendations would you make, if you were in the position to make suggestions to the South African government?

3) Using Bronfenbrenner's theory, try and provide a developmental account for Kobus Geldenhuys that is able to offer some explanation for his murderous actions. Pay particular attention to Geldenhuys's social, cultural, and institutional memberships and roles. Pay careful attention also to the various ecological transitions he experienced before his crimes began.

### General tasks

1) The American sociologist Michael Kimmel tells a revealing anecdote about one of his first graduate classes in Women's Studies in which he heard a dispute going on between a white and a black women. The white woman was arguing that the universal oppression of women by men bound white and black women together in a common plight. The black

woman disagreed and asked, 'When you wake up in the morning and look in the mirror, what do you see?' 'I see a woman' the white woman replied. 'That's precisely the problem' said the black woman. 'When I wake up in the morning and look in the mirror, I see a black woman. My race is visible to me every day because I am not privileged in this culture. Because you are privileged, your race is invisible to you'. Kimmel was very much struck by this exchange because he realised that when he looked in the mirror he saw neither his whiteness nor his masculinity. All he saw was a simple human being (Kimmel, in Wetherell and Griffin 1991, 365).

1.1) When you look in the mirror what do you see? How do you account for the 'invisibility' of Kimmel's masculinity and whiteness in the above example, and what can this tell us about the influence of socio-political factors on the development of our senses of self and identity?

1.2) At what points of the ecological model of development would you place such forms of influence? And how do you imagine this would impact on childhood development?

2) Can Bronfenbrenner's theory be linked to Erikson's theory in any way, and if so, in what ways would these theories usefully complement one another?

3) How do you feel Bronfenbrenner's theory measures up in relation to Freud and Erikson's theories? Which types of explanation would suit which theory? (And which would expose their relative limits?) Would it be possible in any way to use all three theories in conjunction?

# Gender identity formation

*Gill Haiden*

This chapter will explain the process of, and the theory behind, gender identity development. We will discuss the following concepts:

1. Gender.

2. Gender stereotypes.

3. The process of gender formation.

4. Gender constancy and gender valuing.

5. Explanations of gender identity formation.

6. Gender and the law in South Africa.

## Introduction

This chapter focuses on several aspects of the existing literature concerning the study of gender. It consists of three parts.

We will begin by defining the relevant concepts for the study of gender. These concepts include sex, gender, and gender identity. The notion of societal and theoretical *gender lenses* will then be introduced. This is discussed in terms of the concepts of *androcentrism*, *gender polarisation*, and *biological essentialism*. These gender lenses are manifested in the use of gender stereotypes; for this reason, gender stereotypes will be discussed in terms of stereotypical constructions of **masculinity** and **femininity**.

In the second part of the chapter we locate the study of gender within a developmental framework. We shall discuss the process of **gender identity formation** in terms of the norms of development, and in this we shall consider how the concepts of stereotyping and gender identity formation may be linked. This attempt will centre on the concepts of gender constancy, gender valuing, and gender stereotyping.

Finally, we shall consider how these gender concepts relate to socio-economic factors in terms of a possible relationship between gender identity development and social class. In order to locate this discussion further within a developmental framework, we shall present a series of

**Masculinity.** Socially constructed characteristics of males.

**Femininity.** Socially constructed characteristics of females.

**Gender identity formation.** Development of the sense of being masculine or feminine.

**Gender.** Social, cultural, and psychological differences between men and women.

**Sex.** Biological and anatomical differences between men and women.

explanations of gender identity formation. These explanations include those offered in terms of biological considerations, Freudian concepts, cognitive developmental notions, and social learning and environmental influences.

# Defining gender

**Gender** is a categorisation that is universally present (Kendall 1993). Many theories have been postulated in the attempt to define and understand why this category exists. Kendall (1993, 1) defines the progression of understanding as follows: 'Our biology assigned separate functions to the male and female of Homo Sapiens. Our evolution strengthened and refined those differences. Our civilisation reflected them. Our religion and education reinforced them.'

In order to gain a more complete understanding of what is meant by gender we need to examine some conceptual differences in terminology. First, the word **sex** is used to denote the concept of biological or anatomical differences between men and women (Giddens 1992).

PHOTO: CHA JOHNSTON

Second, the word *gender* denotes the conceptual understanding of the social, cultural, and psychological differences between men and women (Giddens 1992). This distinction between *sex* and *gender* is essential because many of the differences found between females and males do not arise from biological considerations. Accordingly, the identification of the self as either male or female, and the attitudes and values that are attached to this identification, depend on how one was labelled as a child. In most cases, this identification label corresponds to biological differences in chromosomes and hormones. Therefore, biological differences can be conceptualised as a signal for (although not a cause of) gender differences in social roles (Giddens 1992).

*From the minute we are born we are assigned a gender label which determines how society understands us, and how we understand society.*

Third, **gender identity** is the sense of being either masculine or feminine. This sense involves how one's interests, behaviour, and psychological characteristics conform to one's own internalised definition of masculinity and femininity. These individual definitions are usually the definitions which society has prescribed, and which the individual accordingly adopts (Mussen, Conger, Kagan, and Huston 1990).

**Gender identity.** The sense of being either masculine or feminine.

## The role of the social structure

As the previous paragraph implies, it is necessary to examine social contexts in order to understand gender identity. It is important to contextualise our understanding of a society within an understanding of its **social structure**. The social structure can be defined as the relatively stable manner in which individuals in a particular culture are organised to carry out their roles and functions in their particular society. It is this organisation that gives the society its basic character, which distinguishes it from other societies, and which forms the lives of its individual members. The contents of culture are strongly linked to this.

**Social structure.** The relatively stable manner in which individuals in a particular culture are organised to carry out their roles and functions in their particular society.

We can conceptualise the contents of culture as the mutual products of human endeavour and learning (Fishbein 1984). These products comprise the standards for deciding *what exists*, and *what can be*, *how one feels* about these circumstances, and *what to do* about how one feels, and the standards for determining how we should act in this (Goodenough 1963, in Fishbein 1984). Our experience of the world, our perceptions, and our concepts give form to *what exists*, and these factors are acquired through social interaction. What *can be* consists of our own beliefs and propositions through which we are able to explain our experiences. Our values determine *how we feel* about this existence (Fishbein 1984).

## Gender lenses

One of the ways in which we assimilate *what exists* is through gender. In terms of gender, we have to make sense of *what exists*, *what can exist*, *how we feel* about this, and *how to deal* with these feelings. The mechanism through which this process occurs can be conceptualised as our **gender lenses**. It is these gender lenses that shape the way we perceive, conceive, and discuss our social reality. These gender lenses are embedded within our social institutions and therefore they mould material practices (such as gender discrepancies in monetary remuneration). Thus our social reality is constituted. There are three gender lenses that have been postulated in modern society, and which are thought to be our mechanisms for defining gender: *androcentrism*, *gender polarisation*, and *biological essentialism* (Bem 1993).

**Androcentrism** is thought to be embedded within our cultural discursive practices, individual psyches, and social institutions. This lens defines the norm or the neutral standard as the definition of the male and male experience. The female and female experience is positioned as a deviation from that norm, which is sex-specific. Therefore, males are not viewed as superior, and females as inferior, but rather, males are conceptualised as *'human'* and females as *'other'*.

The lens of **gender polarisation** incorporates the perceived difference between males and females as the central organising principle for the social life of a particular culture. Virtually every facet of human experience (for instance social roles, dress codes, expressing emotion, and sexual desire) is affected by the differences between females and males.

The lens of **biological essentialism** is a **secularised framework** of a particular religion's teleological scheme of existence. This secularised framework is constructed through a substitution of religious principles with scientific ones. Consequently, explanations involve an evolution of a teleological creation (Bem 1993).

These three gender lenses may be considered as operating simultaneously in society.

## Mutually exclusive scripts for males and females

Psychological theories have for the most part located their conceptualisations in the lens of gender polarisation. Thus mutually exclusive **scripts** for males and females have been defined. Traits that are thought to be

**Gender lenses.** Mechanisms for the assimilation of what exists, which shape how we perceive, conceive, and discuss our social reality in terms of gender.

**Androcentrism.** Where the male and male experience is defined as the norm or neutral standard.

**Gender polarisation.** A social organising principle in which the perceived differences between male and female are central.

**Biological essentialism.** Where biological differences between males and females are central to the organisation of a society.

**Secularised framework.** A manner of understanding in which religion loses its influence over the various facets of social life.

**Scripts.** Organised sets of knowledge that detail what individuals know about common activities.

*Our gender lenses function like masks. They determine our perceptions of ourselves and those around us.*

characteristic of one sex or another are identified as either masculine or feminine characteristics. This understanding has two implications. First, it is believed that either men or women possess a particular characteristic. This is a descriptive notion – it helps us to describe what men and women should do. Second, it is believed that either men or women should possess this characteristic. This is a normative idea and provides the rules for how men and women should behave.

Any discussion of the differences between males and females is complicated by more general assumptions and speculations about cognitive and emotional development. An example of this would be the nature versus nurture debate. This debate centres on the question of whether individuals are born with certain characteristics, or whether social interaction moulds the individual into the characteristics that he or she possesses. What is generally noted, however, is that each society has its own views about which traits belong either to males or females, which means, therefore, that physical differences are associated with mental ones (Fuchs Epstein 1988). An implication of this is that any individual who deviates from prescribed gender scripts is labelled as being problematic. The effect of this definition and its implications is both to construct and to naturalise the gender polarising link between biological sex and the character of the individual psyche (Bem 1993). This lens of gender polarisation may become conflated with the lens of androcentrism, with the consequence that scripts for the male and female are valorised, the male stereotype being positioned as the 'norm' and the female stereotype as the 'other'.

## Gender stereotypes

Common ideas about gender role stereotypes, and about the types of psychological characteristics associated with them, influence the extent of sex differences that different psychologists and psychological frameworks identify (Archer 1980).

A **stereotype** may be defined as a structured set of expectations and beliefs about the personal qualities, attributes, and characteristics of a group of individuals (Nelson, Acker, and Manis 1996). Within the framework of psychology, stereotypes are traditionally understood in neutral terms, as one type of categorisation that shares many of the facets of other cognitive categories (Deaux 1987). The process of gender stereotyping can be understood as the portrayal of the ideal or typical characteristics of males and females. Stereotyping, therefore, is the mechanism through which the prescriptive process for ideas of 'normal' behaviour is actualised. It is through this process that the concepts of femininity and masculinity become opposites (Sharpe 1978).

Our *gender belief system* can be seen as our internal site of gender stereotypes. This system is composed of our beliefs and opinions about females and males, and the qualities of femininity and masculinity. This belief system includes attitudes towards prescribed behaviours and roles, and attitudes towards those individuals who differ from our internalised notions (Deaux and Kite 1987). This belief system also impacts upon our gender attributes, which may be divided into three classes: *defining characteristics* (which focus on biological explanations), *identifying characteristics* (which focus on externally visible signs), and *ascribed characteristics* (which focus on adjectives describing traits) (Aube, Norcliffe, Craig, and Koestner 1995).

**Stereotype.** Structured set of expectations and beliefs about the personal qualities, attributes, and characteristics of various kinds of people.

## No universal definitions of masculine and feminine personalities

Mead (1950, in Sharpe 1978) investigated the construction of gender from an anthropological perspective. She found that there was no universal definition of the masculine and feminine personalities. Accordingly, certain historical groupings of people either displayed characteristics that were undifferentiated by sex, or displayed stereotypes that were the reverse of those seen in modern industrialised societies. Therefore, differentiation between the sexes and the surrounding values and attitudes

PHOTO: CHA JOHNSTON

*Gender neutrals or 'tomboys' are able to cross the gender divide successfully.*

of this differentiation are greatly influenced by the economic structure of a given society, and by the society's division of labour. An example of this is a culture in which the economy is dependent on the constant care of animals or the tending of crops. In this society, both genders are taught to be responsible, obedient, and compliant. These are characteristics that are described as feminine in Western industrialised societies. In societies in which hunting or fishing is central to the economy, both sexes are encouraged to be self-reliant, achievement-oriented and assertive. In industrialised societies these characteristics form part of the masculine gender identity (Sharpe 1978).

## Cross-culturally generalisable stereotypes

Although there is no universally adopted manner in which the two genders are defined, different societies hold similar stereotypes about gender. Comparisons between a typically Western industrialised society, the United States of America, and other countries reveal similarities and differences in gender stereotypes. William and Best (1982, in Deaux 1987) reviewed the gender stereotypes of thirty countries. Cross-culturally generalisable stereotypes included notions of males as strong, active, autonomous, achievement-oriented, and aggressive, and notions of females as weak, passive, affiliation-oriented, nurturing, and deferent. Although the manner in which stereotyped traits are labelled may differ, gender differences usually fall into this paradigm of expressive (female) versus instrumental (male) traits (Aube *et al*. 1995). Therefore masculine and feminine stereotypes are typically viewed as opposite ends of one continuum. Thus, by definition, what is masculine is not feminine, and vice versa. This idea is formulated in the English language through such phrases as the 'opposite sex' (Maccoby 1987).

## 'Fuzzy sets'

The perspective from which the understanding of masculinity and femininity is constructed is important because these constructs both endure and change. This is because our language, by which we delimit and define such constructs, changes according to the usefulness of the constructs within a given society at a particular time. Often there is no evidence of actual differences between the genders in terms of such constructs as, for example, achievement-orientation, self-esteem and sociability, nurturance, and dominance (Deaux 1987). Considering this shifting perspective, it is important to acknowledge that our ideas of what is masculine and feminine are located as 'fuzzy sets'. This means that there are no universal definitions of masculinity and femininity. Definitions of these constructs primarily consist of associated characteristics that relate to them in varying degrees of probability. It is important to acknowledge the points of confusion and lack of clarity which are inherent in the concepts of gender and which evolve within a particular social context (Maccoby 1987).

# The process of gender identity formation

Psychological gender is extremely difficult to alter after the child is two years old (Kate 1979). Thus it is thought that a rudimentary gender identity develops between the ages of eighteen months and three years. Therefore, children correctly label themselves and others as either male or female at this time (Louw 1991). In observations of child's play and sex role development between the ages of one and three years, children display a great deal of interest in gender-typed activities and play. Accordingly, in home observations, the girls played with dolls, soft toys, and dress-up clothes and danced more, while the boys played with blocks and transportation toys (Santrock and Yussen 1987). This difference may not necessarily be biological in nature, but due to the fact that parents may purchase gender-specific toys, thereby limiting the child's choice.

## Stereotypes and social expectations of gender

During the preschool years, the child's understanding of gender identity may be somewhat limited, for children do not necessarily display **gender constancy** (the understanding that gender does not change) at this time.

**Gender constancy.** The understanding that gender does not change.

Mussen *et al.* (1990) postulate that during the preschool years, the child's gender stereotypes are absolute prescriptions for what is considered to be appropriate behaviour. Children may thus enforce these stereotypes with more rigidity than adults would enforce them (Santrock and Yussen 1987).

PHOTO: CHA JOHNSTON

Between the ages of three and seven years, the child's understanding of gender constancy develops further. The child will increasingly enjoy spending time with peers of the same sex. Her or his knowledge of gender stereotypes increases, and both personal and social attributes of gender are further developed. These stereotypes include the masculine stereotypes of strength, dominance, and aggression, and the feminine stereotypes of gentleness, submission, and the ability to express emotion (Papalia and Olds 1993).

*Society has certain expectations of how both girls and boys should behave. These expectations are reflected in the toys and clothing that are purchased for children.*

During the period of middle childhood, children continue to define their understandings of the social expectations of gender, and their thoughts about gender stereotypes become less rigid than they were in early childhood (Mussen *et al.* 1990). During this time, girls do not display an increase in feminine activities, but show a stronger preference for masculine activities and interests (Santrock and Yussen 1987).

## The importance of critical periods for gender role development

Money (1965) postulated that biology and culture combined to form **critical periods** in gender identity development. A critical period may be defined as a brief time in life when biological changes combine with

**Critical period.** A brief time in life when biological changes combine with environmental events to produce virtually irreversible gender role patterning.

environmental events to produce virtually irreversible gender role patterning (Crain 1992). There are two critical periods for gender role development: in the first three years, and during adolescence. It is during these
two critical periods that the individual is faced with rapid physiological
changes that influence his or her gender role development, after which
one of several outcomes is possible.

First, the individual may develop an adaptive concept of masculinity
or femininity, which is in accordance with her or his biological category.
Second, the individual may be confused about the psychological characteristics of gender that are associated with the biological category. Third,
the individual may settle on some mixed gender role, for example, a
female role and a male body (Santrock and Yussen 1987). Thus the study
of gender identity development is meaningless unless the first critical
period has occurred. It is also important to note that congruence between
role and body may not necessarily be psychologically healthy, as girls
increasingly assume more masculine characteristics in order to cope in a
capitalistic society.

## Gender identity formation and stereotyping in childhood

The gender of other individuals is an important and salient criterion by
which children formulate their responses to their environments (Maccoby
1988). The process through which gender identification and stereotyping
occurs is useful for us to consider because this identification occurs within
a specific context. We will now look at this process in greater detail,
briefly examining gender constancy, gender valuing, and gender stereotyping, within the contextual framework of economic factors.

### Gender constancy

When determining whether or not children uphold gender stereotypes, it
is necessary to determine whether or not the children in the sample are
gender constant. For a child to be gender constant, he or she has to have
a biological understanding of gender. This involves an understanding
that gender does not change, an understanding that is acquired in three
stages. First, the child will acquire a rudimentary gender identity as
either a boy or girl. Second, the child will learn that genitalia do not
change. This occurs at about four years. Third, the child will understand
that gender remains the same regardless of changes in clothing, appearance, or activities. This occurs at about five to six years.

In the United States, by the age of three years, children were able to
classify males and females correctly, and were aware of the social expectations surrounding each gender, for example, girls wear dresses and boys
do not. Between the ages of four and five years, children possess a knowledge of the stereotypes for adult occupations, for example, women are
nurses and men are doctors (Mussen *et al.* 1990).

### Gender valuing

An important part of the awareness of the social categories of gender is
that children often value the categories to which they ascribe themselves

and devalue those categories to which they do not belong (Powlishta, Serbin, Doyle, and White 1994). It is often considered important that children value their particular category in order fully to formulate a gender identity (Turner and Gervai 1995). It is important to acknowledge that this facet of valuing may be more complex for girls because the masculine identity is generally more valued in societies such as South Africa.

### Gender stereotyping

An important part of the acquisition of gender **labelling** and identity is a developing awareness of gender stereotypes. Some children who are as young as two years old have acquired gender stereotypes around toys and activities (Mayes 1986) and adult occupations (Weintraub, Pritchard Clemens, Sockloff, Ethridge, Gracely, and Myers 1984). Other important gender stereotypes include appearance (Edelbrock and Sugwara 1978), peers (Benenson, Apostoleris, and Parnass 1997; Newcomb and Bagwell 1995), and media figures (Santrock and Yussen 1987). An examination of the development of social skills around gender has to consider the notion that mothers and fathers interact differently with boys and girls (Best, House, Barnard, and Spicker 1994). Boys are generally more sex-stereotyped than girls and show more negative reactions to female-preferred activities than girls do to male-preferred activities. This is thought to occur because girls receive more latitude in terms of constructing themselves around gender stereotypes (Fagot 1977).

**Labelling.** Attaching a meaning to an object or an individual, which helps individuals to order their world.

## Socio-economic factors

Cross-cultural studies in which data is analysed by gender are too rare to allow us to conclude that gender segregation is a universal norm in social development (LaFreniere, Strayer, and Gauthier 1984). Most evidence for the development of gender identity has arisen from a United States context. Evidence of the development of gender identity and adherence to gender stereotypes is sparse within a South African context (see the box on page 335). When attempts have been made to determine gender identity formation differences between societies, culture has been utilised as a framing mechanism. The use of culture has had, and continues to have, far-reaching and often negative consequences in South Africa because culture has often been the site of discrimination.

There is evidence for differences between economic groups in terms of adherence to gender stereotypes. Expectations of the self and of others are developed through the experience of interactions with primary caregivers, particularly during infancy and early childhood. It is these expectations that predispose children to respond selectively to later experiences (Bowlby 1980). MacKinnon-Lewis, Volling, Lamb, Dechman, Rabiner, and Curtner (1994) found that economic difficulties form the setting in which coercive parent-child interactions occur. Part of this coercive interaction may be strict adherence to gender stereotypes.

### Gender socialisation

Differences in gender socialisation have been found between economic groups. Accordingly, children from the higher income group (people who work in professional and managerial positions, and usually have some form of tertiary education) (Giddens 1992) are generally exposed to a greater emphasis on individuality. They have fathers who are more involved with them, and they experience discipline that is based on reasoning and shame (Lewis 1987). In contrast, children from the lower income group (people who work in blue collar or manual occupations, such as skilled and unskilled workers) (Giddens 1992) are generally exposed to an emphasis on conformity to social roles, especially gender roles. These children generally come from larger nuclear and extended families in which more specialised family roles are prevalent, and they experience more physical discipline (Lewis 1987).

Men in the lower economic category generally have jobs requiring heavy physical work, and provide little care for the children and the house, while women have jobs which involve housekeeping or menial tasks. Thus gender models and roles are clearly defined. In the higher economic group, which is a heterogeneous category (Giddens 1992), both men and women are teachers, lawyers, doctors, etc., and wives handle the family finances and drive family cars with equal frequency (Lewis 1987). Thus gender models are less distinctive. Therefore there is a difference between different economic groups in terms of how gender socialisation occurs and the degree of emphasis and importance that gender stereotypes hold (Lewis 1987). Boys from the lower income category have been found to be highly gender stereotyped, while girls from the higher income category are the least gender stereotyped (McCandless 1967).

# Explanations of gender identity formation

Many explanations about the formation of gender identity have been proposed. These include explanations concerning biological differences, a psychoanalytic explanation from Freud, cognitive development, and social learning and environmental theory.

## Biological explanations

Gender identity formation has been explained through the physiology or biology of girls and boys. Accordingly, the child's physiological composition as either a boy or a girl will automatically and naturally determine his or her masculine or feminine gender identity (Craig 1996). This explanation, however, does not receive much support and evidence has been produced which dictates that physical sex has little to do with psychological gender. Accordingly, Money, Erhardt, and Masica (1968, in Papalia and Olds 1993) examined subjects who were chromosomally male (that is, they had testes and not ovaries), but looked like females, and were raised as girls. These children were all stereotypically female and played with dolls and other girls' toys. Money and Tucker (1975, in Sarafino and Armstrong 1980) reported a male who was raised as a female. During a circumcision procedure at seven months, one identical twin's penis was irreparably damaged. At seventeen months, doctors advised the parents to raise the child as a girl. The child's genitalia were modified and she/he

## Barbie and beyond: An example of gender identity research in South Africa

With the changes in the political dispensation in South Africa, a new pattern of social thought has become dominant. We now have a Constitution that guarantees equal rights to all citizens. One of these rights is equality in terms of gender. What this means is that there should be no discrimination against either males or females. The Constitution should reflect the attitudes of the people; we can assume, therefore, because it is in the Constitution, that South African people believe in gender equality. If this assumption is correct, then we should be raising our children to believe in gender equality.

This notion was scrutinised in relation to a group of six-year-old girls. These girls were asked about their beliefs regarding gender and gender stereotypes. All the girls could correctly label themselves as girls. They valued being a girl because girls perform better academically (even though they were all still in preschool). They all would choose to be girls because girls are not naughty or aggressive.

In terms of appearance stereotypes, most of the girls believed that '[girls] ... have dresses on ... they have long hair ... and they do ballet ... and they wear skirts' (Haiden 1998, 56).

The following dialogue presents answers in terms of activity and toy stereotypes:

*Question:* What do girls do when they play?
*Answer:* They like to do all kinds of stuff. They like Princess ...

*Question:* How do you play Princess?
*Answer:* Princess ... there's like the queen and the princess, the wicked witch and stuff ... The wicked witch treats Cinderella like rubbish ... and like isn't very, very nice. The princess, she cleans up the floor and stuff like the ugly witch tells her to ...
*Question:* What makes toys be for girls?
*Answer:* Toys is Barbies and like talking dolls and ... clothes. Barbie clothes and the most important thing that I like in the whole wide world is Barbie. I've always asked my Mommy and Daddy for Christmas.

Gender stereotyping for activities is less strictly socially prescribed for girls than it is for boys (Fagot, 1977). This was evidenced in the following girl's answers:

*Question:* Can girls play with guns and cars?
*Answer:* No ... I don't play with cars. Because it isn't right for them to. They have to play with Barbies and stuff. If they haven't got anything to play with then they can, but it's not right for them.
*Question:* Can boys play with dolls?
*Answer:* No ... they just can't. They can play with Kens, but not Barbies (Haiden and Zietkiewicz 1999).

Thus, even though we have a Constitution that guarantees gender equality, are children are still being raised with gender stereotypes and rules for gender behaviour?

Considering evidence presented here and your own childhood experiences, what do you think is the ideal way to raise children in terms of gender socialisation?

underwent hormone treatment. The parents changed the child's name, clothing, and hair accordingly. At three years, the child's gender identity was diverging from her twin brother's. At five years, she preferred wearing frilly dresses, and asked for a doll for Christmas, in short, she was conforming to a feminine stereotype (Money and Tucker 1975, in Sarafino and Armstrong 1980). Thus the examination of gender identity formation cannot occur without consideration of social factors.

## Freud's psychoanalytic explanation

**Anaclitic identification.** Identification that occurs because of threatened withdrawal of parental affection.

Freud identified two processes of identification: **anaclitic** and **aggressive** identification. In terms of anaclitic identification, the individual is motivated to reproduce the behaviour of the parent because of the threatened withdrawal of parental affection. Both girls and boys form an anaclitic bond with their mothers. This form of identification is more important for girls because its pattern is maintained, while boys shift to identifying with the father as a model (Parke 1979). Aggressive identification involves the adoption of parental behaviour through fear of punishment. This, according to Freud, facilitates the shift of boys towards the father as a role model and occurs at the resolution of the Oedipus complex (Parke 1979). (See Chapter 5 for more detail.) It has been argued, however, that Freud's explanation does not adequately account for the acquisition of gender stereotypes and assumes that the child will automatically assume his or her same sex parent as a gender role model (Santrock and Yussen 1987). Freud's explanation may also be seen as not properly accounting for gender identity formation in single-parent or same-sex parent households (Mussen *et al.* 1990).

**Aggressive identification.** Identification that occurs because of fear of punishment.

## Cognitive development

Kohlberg (1966) postulated that gender typing arose in the child as a result of the child's cognitive developmental changes. Accordingly, children achieve gender identity (classifying themselves as girls or boys) as part of a general tendency of thought in terms of categories. Once this gender identity has been established, the child will actively seek out behaviour, activities, and values that distinguish boys from girls. Children begin to value patterns of behaviour and activities that are associated with their own gender. This process is considered to be complete when the child achieves gender constancy; it is accompanied by Piaget's notion of concrete operational thought (Crain 1992). (See Chapter 10 for more detail.)

Block (1973) expanded Kohlberg's theory in terms of stages of gender stereotyping. First, very young children will possess undifferentiated gender role concepts. Second, in the preschool years, the child will conform to conventional and rigid gender roles. Third, during early adolescence, this rigidity will be at a maximum. Finally, during adulthood, a stronger androgyny emerges (Mussen *et al.* 1990). It should be noted, however, that not all children place a high value on the roles that have been prescribed for their gender, and this theory does also not explain individual differences in the nature and strength of gender typing (Mussen *et al.* 1990).

**Schema (pl. schemata).** The manner in which we arrange our knowledge and memory about people and things. (See Chapter 13: Memory development.)

## Gender schema theory

**Schemata** may also be utilised to explain gender typing in terms of gender schemas. Schemata can be understood as the manner in which we arrange our knowledge about people and things (Sabini 1995). People are more likely to remember information that is consistent with their existing schemas than information that is in contradiction to them. Thus information is absorbed on the basis of existing knowledge structures. The information in memory is often organised around our schemas (Craig 1996). Thus, once the child has acquired a gender role schema, she or she will interpret events in terms of this schema. If events are in violation of this schema, the child may fail to notice or remember them. Examples would be a girl who plays with action men, or a boy with long hair. Gender schema theory is an example of the meeting of cognitive and social theories. This is because it assumes that in societies that are gender polarised, this internalised lens facilitates the developmental process of conventionally gendered perceptions. This theory, therefore, rests on two fundamental tenets: first, that gender lenses are entrenched in societal **discourses** and practice, and internalised by children; and second, that once these lenses have been internalised, the child is then predisposed to construct his or her identity in a manner that is congruent with this lens (Bem 1993). This aspect of cognitive development in terms of gender identity formation does not, however, explain how the child acquires a gender role schema and how the schemas may differ from child to child.

**Discourse.** A set of language practices relevant to a particular position in a specific context. The discourse adopted indicates the writer or speaker's positional values.

## Gender salience

**Gender salience** may be a further aspect of cognitive development to offer an explanation for gender identity formation. Gender may be more salient or important to some children than it is to others. Some children may view and interpret the world through gender-based lenses, while others may interpret it through different categories (Papalia and Olds 1993). An example of the impact of gender salience may be as follows. A group of children are playing with a ball in a park. Child A, who is gender salient, may ask herself whether or not playing with a ball is an activity in which girls participate, or whether other girls are playing. Child B, who is not gender salient, may ask herself whether she will look foolish or clumsy if she participates (Mussen *et al.* 1990). Although this theory may provide insight into individual differences in gender identity formation, it does not explain how some children possess gender salience, while others do not.

**Gender salience.** Where gender is considered an important organising principle for the individual.

An important aspect to remember in the formation of gender identity is the role of language in this process. The English language contains many gender biases, for example, *man* and *he* are used to refer to all humans, both male and female. Sexist thought and gender stereotyping may thus be the product of years of exposure to sexist language (Santrock and Yussen 1987). Although there may be some merit in this explanation, it does not explain the fact that people of all languages, and not merely those who speak English, conform to gender stereotypes. This theory also does not consider the political correctness in contemporary society, in which there is a move away from sexist language.

## Social learning and environmental influences

The process of social learning would occur through instrumental conditioning and observation. Accordingly, a child is reinforced or punished for different stereotypical behaviours from early childhood. This reinforcement or punishment may come from several sources, such as parents, peers, teachers, and the media (Louw 1991).

## The role of parents

First, in terms of the role of parents in the formation of gender identity, one has to consider the gender stereotypes which the parents themselves hold, and to which they will expose their children. Provenco and Luria (1974, in Sarafino and Armstrong 1980) interviewed parents of newborns on the first day of their children's lives. Male and female babies were matched for general health, weight, and size, but both mothers and fathers described the sexes in differentially gendered terms. Girls were described as being smaller, softer, and less attentive, while boys were described as being stronger, firmer, better coordinated, and more alert. Thus the expectations of the parents were based on societally gendered notions of the different sexes. Lamb (1981) found that, in terms of parental roles, mothers assumed more responsibility for physical care and nurturance, while fathers fulfilled the role of providing playful interaction, and were more demanding and exacting in seeing that the child conformed to societal norms. McCandless (1967) found that parents engaged in selective reinforcement of gender-appropriate behaviour. Consequently, fathers were rougher in play with their sons than with their daughters, and generally a mother's form of play was gentler. In terms of toys, parents bought toys such as guns, transportation toys, and footballs for boys, while girls received toys such as tea sets, dolls, and doll furniture (McCandless 1967).

Rheingold and Cook (1975, in Sarafino and Armstrong 1980) examined the bedrooms of middle class preschool children and found that the rooms of boys were decorated with animals and the rooms of girls were decorated in florals and frills. In terms of household chores, girls were assigned tasks such as washing dishes and dusting, while boys had to wash the car and take out the dustbin (Sarafino and Armstrong 1980). Thus it is the actions and gender stereotypes of parents themselves that are vital in the formation of a child's gender identity. It is through this process that gender stereotypes are perpetuated from generation to generation.

Parents also tend to socialise boys more intensely than girls, and there is pressure on the boy to act like a 'real boy and not like [a] girl' (Papalia and Olds 1993, 391). Girls are allowed more freedom in terms of clothing, games, play, and playmates. Fathers appear to be a major influence in gender stereotyping, appearing more concerned about this than mothers. Fathers become more easily upset when their sons engage in cross-gender play (Biller 1993). In terms of single-parent homes, it is usually the mother who is the single parent. Children from these homes tend to hold less stereotyped views because the mother is a more androgynous role model (Kate 1979). In these homes, boys show a more feminine patterning of behaviour, but this does depend on the attitude of the mother (Lamb 1981).

PHOTOS: CHA JOHNSTON

*Children prefer playmates of the same gender.*

## The role of peers

Second, peers may influence gender identity formation. In preschool, peers reward play that occurs in a gender-appropriate activity. Children who engage in cross-gender activities are generally either criticised by their peers or left to play alone. Perhaps successful tomboys are the best example of 'gender bilinguals' (Santrock and Yussen 1987,492), who are successful in both same- and cross-gender play, and are not ostracised by their peers. These girls are able to switch patterns of talk, naming, touch, and space as they cross the divide between the genders. They have access to the segregated activity of boys, depending on their verbal and athletic skills, and willingness to fight. They maintain access to girls' activities by claiming friendship with the most popular girl and guarding the play of girls from the invasion of boys (Santrock and Yussen 1987).

## The role of the media

Third, the media contribute to the formation of gender identity in terms of exposing children to stereotypes. In the United States, most children watch an average of three to five hours of television each day. Many programmes on television portray roles that are distinctly either masculine or feminine (Perloff, Brown, and Miller 1978, in Santrock and Yussen 1987). Occupational stereotypes are also highly prevalent, for instance, the male is a member of the workforce and the female is the romantic interest of the male and/or a housewife. In advertising, stereotypes are even more prevalent. Women appear in advertisements for home appliances and beauty and cleaning products, and men appear in advertisements for cars and liquor (Santrock and Yussen 1987). Thus the media serve as a potential source of gender-role stereotypes, which children may incorporate into their own gender identities.

# Gender and the law in South Africa

With the change in political dispensation, gender equality was entrenched as a constitutional right of all South Africans. The founding provisions in Chapter One state:

The Republic of South Africa is one sovereign state founded on the following values:

(b) Non-racialism and non-sexism (Republic of South Africa 1996a).

Chapter Two of the Constitution is concerned with the fundamental rights of the citizens of South Africa. Section Nine of Chapter Two sets out the equality provisions among citizens:

S9 (3) The state may not unfairly discriminate directly or indirectly against anyone on one or more grounds, including race, gender, sex ....

S9 (4) No person may unfairly discriminate directly or indirectly against anyone on one or more grounds in terms of subsection (3). National legislation must be enacted to prevent or prohibit unfair discrimination (Republic of South Africa 1996a).

Thus what is important to note here is that gender/sex equality is a constitutionally entrenched right. What this means is that discrimination, either in law or in social practice, is illegal in South Africa. It is worth noting that 'gender' and 'sex' are recognised as two distinct constructs. It is, however, unclear how this demarcation is exercised in practice.

## Entrenching gender rights

This change in South African law is important for several reasons. One would assume that a change in law, or societal rules, reflects societal attitude. What this implies is that South African citizens themselves feel the need to entrench gender rights in our pervasive and most important laws. Thus, if society itself calls for legal gender equality, then changes, even if they are subtle, should be reflected in social thought about gender. Gender stereotypes are an aspect of this social thought, and we should thus be conveying changing stereotypes, or no stereotypes at all, to our children.

However, notions of gender equality are not yet widely entrenched in society (Horn 1991). There is evidence from different sources that appears to support the notion that the removal or addition of legislation does not necessarily imply a movement in social thought. This is rather confusing if one considers that the government is supposed to be the representative of its people. Thus the flow of social change may appear to be reversed.

The following examples illuminate the gap between legislated and historically provided opportunity and the reality of social existence for women in the twentieth century. First, Sweden has the most progressive legislation concerning gender equality. However, few women hold top positions in the business world (Scriven 1984, in Giddens 1992). Second, when franchise rights for women were initially achieved, women did not vote in large numbers. In Britain, in the first general election in which women were allowed to vote (1929), only one third of women, compared to two thirds of men, exercised their new right (Giddens 1992). Third, World War 2 brought about changes to women's secondary status as, in

*Even though gender equality is a constitutionally entrenched right, there are still differences between men and women in terms of careers, place in society, and societal expectations.*

the absence of men, they fulfilled traditionally male roles in the workplace. However, the end of the war and the subsequent return of men negated this advance (Coppock, Haydon, and Richter 1995). Fourth, Anderson and Zinsser (1984, in Coppock *et al.* 1995) examined the development of equal gender rights and the disillusionment experienced by women that followed the growing realisation that little change had occurred in their lives.

Liberal and social feminists focused their energies on political issues such as maternity benefits, childcare provision, housing, education, and medicine (including abortion and contraception). However, many of these women came to distance their positions from feminist issues. Those who challenged both patriarchy and capitalism, and who were both politically active and independent, were stereotyped as being '... manhating, hysterical, anarchic aberrations' (Coppock *et al.* 1995).

These examples demonstrate that one of the stumbling blocks to gender equality is deeply entrenched social divisions and perceptions.

## Conclusion

In this chapter we have examined the broader context in which the study of gender may be conducted. We have located the study of gender in terms of both a development framework and a wider societal context. In terms of a developmental framework, several theoretical positions have been examined, including biological, Freudian, cognitive developmental, and social learning theories. It is important to understand that decisions regarding the relevance of these theories have to be located within a wider South African context.

# Recommended readings

Bem, S. L. (1993). *The lenses of gender.* New Haven: Yale University Press.

Nicholson, L. J. (1990). *Feminism/postmodernism.* New York: Routledge.

Reinisch, J. M. (1987). *Masculinity/femininity: Basic perspectives.* New York: Oxford University Press.

Wood, J. T. (1994). *Gendered lives: Communication, gender and culture.* Belmont: Wadsworth.

## Critical thinking tasks

1) What are the three best and three worst things about being the gender you are? Provide justification for each one.

2) Do you think that gender roles should exist in society? Give reasons for your answer.

3) Examine the ways in which you think that your culture impacts on your gender identity.

4) Refer to the Kobus Geldenhuys case study in Chapter 3. We have discussed several explanations of gender identity formation, namely biological, Freudian, cognitive developmental, and social learning theories. Think about how each of these theories could be used to understand Kobus Geldenhuys. You also need to think about the shortcomings of these theories in terms of understanding his gender identity formation.

5) Critically examine the relationship between gender identity (that is, the feeling of masculinity or femininity) and sexual identity (as an identifying criterion, such as heterosexual or homosexual).

    5.1) Do you think the two identities are related or not?

    5.2) Provide justifications for your answer in 5.1.

    5.3) Think about your own gender identity and sexual identity. Are they the same thing? How do the two identities relate to and influence one another?

6) 'Men are perpetrators of crime. Women are victims of crime'. Answer the following questions, using concepts contained in this chapter, and drawing on your own experience:

    6.1) Do you agree with this statement? Give reasons for your answer.

    6.2) When do you think that this particular dichotomy – that men are criminals, and women are victims – exists?

# Critical issues in developmental psychology

*Derek Hook*

In this chapter we examine a series of critiques and interrogations of developmental psychology. First we consider a brief overview of different historical conceptualisations of childhood, according to the following topics:

1. The 'invention' of childhood.

2. Philosophies of the child.

3. Changing families.

4. The 'invention' of adolescence.

5. Cultures and contexts of development.

We shall then discuss the broader themes of critical questioning as they are presented in Erica Burman's influential book, *Deconstructing developmental psychology* (1994):

1. Developmental psychology as means of social control.

2. The 'normalising' effects of developmental psychology.

3. The 'blameworthy mother'.

4. An isolated focus on the child.

5. Blaming the victims.

The chapter includes a series of boxes focusing on the ways in which the AIDS pandemic in South Africa affects the lives of the country's children.

# Taking up a critical perspective

Having surveyed a wide range of developmental theory, it is time now, by way of conclusion, to engage with a number of general criticisms of the field. One of the most accessible critical voices within the field is that of the feminist scholar Erica Burman, whose influential *Deconstructing developmental psychology* (1994) will be the source of many of the ideas presented and discussed in this chapter. She has drawn together in this book a number of diverse critical perspectives on developmental psychology. Before engaging with these critical themes, however, it seems useful to review briefly some different historical approaches to the understanding of childhood. Indeed, an important way of critiquing developmental psychology is to question what are its most commonplace assumptions. Different historical perspectives on childhood are able to provide us with a critical vocabulary of rival conceptions, which can be useful in this way. Some of the most important concepts that we will call into question here are the notion of *the innocent child*, the idea of the *historically unchanging family*, and certain aspects of *how we typically view adolescence*.

# The 'invention of the child'?

There are few assumptions that more naturally attach to the study of developmental psychology than that of the qualitative difference between the child and the adult. Surprising as it may seem, however, the category and the understanding of 'the child' as qualitatively different from the adult are, historically, fairly new ones. According to the French historian Aries, it was not until 1600 that European societies accorded any special status to children. Before that they were simply considered smaller, less intelligent, and weaker than adults (Aries 1962, 6).

Rather than conceived as inherently different, with age-specific qualities and properties, the body of the child was, prior to the Renaissance, the same as that of the adult, with the obvious exception of size. In fact the questions of size and scale seem the only salient differences in medieval depictions of adults and children, where the latter, with proportionately smaller heads, are typically posed and dressed in the same way as their larger adult counterparts. Western twelfth-century paintings consistently portray children as miniature adults, complete with mature facial structure and features (Aries 1962). Likewise, when depicted naked, the body of the child possesses the musculature of the adult; the male infant is typically depicted, even shortly after birth, with the abdominal and pectoral muscles of a man (Aries 1962). This dearth of properly 'realistic' representations of the child leads Aries to the hypothesis that at this point in history 'representation did not know childhood', that the image of childhood at this point had no reality (1962, 31). Here is a later expansion on this thought:

> In medieval society the idea of childhood did not exist; this is not to suggest that children were neglected, forsaken or despised. The idea of childhood is not to be confused with affection for children:

it corresponds to an awareness of the particular nature of child-hood, that particular nature which distinguishes the child from the adult, even the young adult. In medieval society, this aware-ness was lacking ... [A]dult society ... was partly made up of chil-dren and youths. Language did not give the word 'child' the restricted meaning we give it today ... The infant who was too fragile as yet to take part in the life of adults simply 'did not count' (Aries 1973, 125).

## The 'non-existence' of childhood?

Such a revisionist history of childhood is not based solely on representa-tions of children. Aries (1962) points out that, prior to 1600, children in European societies were not accorded any special status, and as such were expected, when physically able, to work long hours, and to enjoy many of the same pleasures as adults. Children were simply smaller, less intell gent, and weaker than adults. As Craig (1996) notes, children at the time were treated to adult conversation, food, music, jokes, and other forms of entertainment. This is in sharp contrast to today where the effort is often made to protect the child from the excesses and sins of the adult world. Similarly notable is the fact that children were not thought to share as strong emotional bonds with their parents as they are thought to today (Santrock 1999). What becomes noticeable here is that rather than pos-sessing more rights and privileges than adults – as it seems is the case in the modern world – children were significantly less *important* than adults. Aries (1962) notes the fact that the grave of a child who had died prior to a certain arbitrary age would not even be marked by a tombstone.

By 1600, childhood increasingly came to be considered a distinct category of humanity, and moreover, (perhaps via the frequency of the depiction of the Christ-child) childhood began to be considered as a *period of innocence*. From this point children were less often seen as anonymous members of a clan or a community and more as individuals within the family. It was not until the 1800s, however, that this attitude became popularised and children began to be treated as persons with a special status of their own (Craig 1996).

## The sexuality of the child in different historical times

One of the easiest ways to demonstrate how understandings of childhood have changed over the course of history is to look at how the *sexuality* of children has been differently understood. In Western Europe in Shakespeare's time it was quite reasonable for an older man to marry a girl who was twelve or thirteen, as Shakespeare himself did. In Classical Greek times, as Foucault (1980) notes, the age of young boys (between approximately twelve and sixteen), with whom it was common for older distinguished men to have sexual relations, could present a problem. This was not because the boys were *too young*, but because they might be *too old*. That is, they might be too old (from seventeen and eighteen upwards) to be subservient sexual partners, and old enough to be men who should find their own lovers rather than serving an older partner!

It should be noted that there is historical work that counters many of Aries's suggestions, but we should nonetheless be aware that childhood is a special conceptual category, and that the concept *changes* historically. The patriarchal view of 'women and children' as particularly vulnerable, and the idea that a crime committed against a child is worse than a crime committed against an adult both suggest that 'the child' today is treated somewhat differently from the child in early times. Indeed, such an intense interest in children, particularly as represented in developmental psychology, is a fairly recent historical phenomenon, and it tells us much, not only about our culture, but also about how we have come to *talk about*, *treat*, and *interact with children*. It tells us that how we *care for*, *parent*, *know*, and ultimately *protect* and *control* our children today is different from behaviours in previous historical eras. Basically, the ways in which we act on and perpetuate these understandings of childhood cause us to 'produce' children in ways that are historically unprecedented.

## Philosophies of the child

**Original sin.** A view of childhood in which children were perceived as being basically bad, born into the world as evil beings, and in which the goal of child rearing was salvation, to remove as far as possible all sin from the child's life.

*Tabula rasa.* A view of childhood in which children are viewed as a 'blank tablet' that will be written on, shaped and moulded through their experiences.

**Innate goodness.** The view of childhood that considers children to be innately good and that they should be permitted to grow naturally with little monitoring or constraint.

Santrock (1999) provides three (historical) philosophical views of the child: those of **original sin, tabula rasa**, and **innate goodness**. Through the perspective of *original sin* children were perceived as being basically bad, born into the world as evil beings. The goal of child rearing was salvation, to remove as far as possible all sin from the child's life (Santrock 1999). Parenting was seen as a struggle against the child, and we find comments on child rearing like the following from Susanna Wesley, 'Break his will now and his soul will live' (cited by Burman 1994, 51).

The *tabula rasa* view maintained that, instead of being 'bad', children were like a 'blank tablet' that would be written on, shaped and moulded through their experiences (Santrock 1999). They would acquire characteristics through experience and growth, which would lead to their characters as adults. From this point of view it started to become more important for parents to spend more time with their children, to help them develop in the best and most advantageous ways. The child was basically innocent and in need of stimulation and education. The view of *innate goodness* stressed that children were in fact innately good and that they should be permitted to grow naturally with little intervention, monitoring, or constraint (Santrock 1999).

## Implications of these understandings of childhood

These different philosophies of the child suggest that we protect our children far more today than in previous eras. (We also treat them as intense focal points of study and observation). We understand our children as a *different class of person* from adults, a special class that needs *particular* love, care and attention. Some commentators would suggest that even though the end of institutions like that of child labour may have been a good thing, children are far more intensely and carefully monitored and controlled today than ever before. Hendrik (1990) suggests that the idea of children as dependent and of childhood as a period of helplessness emerged as a largely ideological position. He suggests that it may be politically linked to initiatives for channelling children into the class-rooms of mass education – as a rationale for controlling a particular social group capable of political insurrection and rebellion within a given social order. Understandings of the child as ignorant and in need of education and socialisation furthered these objectives, by keeping children in schools where they could be morally educated and restrained from less productive social activities (Hendrik 1990). The British government's Education Act of 1870, which made schooling compulsory for all, could be taken as a specific example of this kind of political initiative.

Many of Hendrik's (1990) views might be taken as radical, and some may be countered by the suggestion that education may well be in the best interests of the public good, and therefore prevalent understandings of the child *are* in society's best interests. Nevertheless he does make some important points. He is of course talking predominantly about juveniles, and not so much about young children, and it seems that this may well be a part of the population able to create a measure of disorder of even a criminal kind within a given society. The following point gives some force to Hendrik's (1990) arguments that the predominant understand-ings of children are used to control and regulate them: in many modern countries young men of sixteen are treated as too young to vote or to marry without permission, but are, as Burman (1994) points out, consid-ered eligible to kill or be killed for their country.

## Changing families

Just as we can question and refresh our assumptions of what it means to be a child, we can also interrogate our assumptions about the modern family:

> Attitudes about family size, structure and function have ... changed over the years. Until the 1920's [sic], American families were large, usually including members from three or more gen-erations. Grandparents, parents and children frequently lived under the same roof and shared the same kind of work. Children were expected to stay close to home because their parents needed

PHOTO: CHA JOHNSTON

*There is a huge amount of historical variation in what constitutes a 'normative' family. What, in your opinion, is an ordinary size family in South Africa? What are ordinary ages for parents, and so on?*

help in running the farm, store, or household. Parents produced numerous children because birth control was not widely practiced and because infectious diseases ... killed so many ... While in the eighteenth century 35% of American families had seven or more members, today only 3.5% do ... Children receive a great deal of individual attention in small families, and parents, in turn, make greater psychological investments in them (Craig 1996, 20–21).

# AIDS orphans and child-headed households in South Africa

The changing shape of families and the changing responsibilities of children are brought into dramatic perspective by the effects of the HIV/AIDS epidemic. A recent report (June 2001) by the Nelson Mandela Children's Fund (NMCF) asserts that South Africa has the fastest growing rate of HIV/AIDS in the world:

With a total of 4.2 million infected people, the country has the highest rate of people living with HIV/AIDS in the world – about 19.9% of its adult population ... An estimated 1 500 people are infected daily and 250 000 people die each year from the disease ... in 10 years time, AIDS is expected to claim 635 000 people every year in South Africa (NMCF 2001, 12).

One of the tragic effects of AIDS is the vast number of children orphaned by the disease. It is estimated that by the end of 2001, a cumulative total of 13.2 million children (ninety per cent on the African continent) will have lost one or both parents to AIDS, 10.4 million of whom will be under the age of fifteen (NMCF 2001). Projected figures suggest that by 2005 there may be as many as 800 000 AIDS orphans within South Africa. As the report suggests, the extended family structure has traditionally operated as a

Child activist Nkosi Johnson did much to sensitise the world to the plight of child HIV/AIDS sufferers. He died of AIDS in 2001.

primary support mechanism in African societies – 'a social safety net for children that has remained resilient over the years' (NMCF 2001, 13). However, the capacity of communities and households to cope has been undermined by the growing number of AIDS orphans. The extended family as social support network is also being undermined by a range of factors including social upheavals, rapid urbanisation, poverty, and overstretched resources:

Along with the high number of adults dying from AIDS, and reduced capacity of communities to support and care for children, is a changing family structure and care-giving patterns where the burden of care falls on those who have the least capacity to provide parenting, support and care for the affected children, i.e. the elderly and the young. Hence the disturbing scenarios of grandparent-headed households and adolescent/child/sibling-headed households (NMCF 2001, 5).

Some of the results of this crisis are that the social, mental, and emotional needs of children remain unmet; likewise children lack a protective social environment in which to grow up. A key problem is the deprivation of parental love, guidance,

(continued)

support, and protection; similarly the emotional trauma associated with parental loss often goes unaddressed. Growing up without an environment of consistently applied rules and values, in the absence of a positive role model, may lead children to adopt less desirable values. These problems are further compounded by the challenges faced by child heads of families in having to cope with adult responsibilities (like becoming the household provider) at an age when they are not emotionally mature. Food security has been identified as the foremost problem, this being the first thing that AIDS-orphaned children ask for whenever they seek help. The NMCF report quotes a UNICEF researcher who claims that:

> AIDS orphans are at greater risk of malnutrition, illness, abuse and sexual exploitation than children orphaned by other causes. They grapple with the stigma and discrimination so often associated with AIDS, which can even deprive them of basic social services and education (NMCF 2001, 15).

In addition to the responsibilities of having to take care of their siblings, the problems faced by orphan heads of households include:

- shortage of income to fulfil basic needs, including food and clothing,
- obstacles to their and their siblings attendance at school, including inability to pay school fees and to purchase school materials and uniforms,
- stigmatisation and rejection by community members,
- lack of access to health care, and
- lack of moral support (NMCF 2001, 15).

Such children are highly vulnerable to physical and sexual abuse by neighbours and relatives, to poor health status due to physical and emotional neglect, and to the

likelihood of being drawn into prostitution and criminal acts as a means of survival. Many AIDS orphans appeared helpless and unable to think of ways of fending for themselves, tending instead to look up to the child head to 'make a plan' especially in terms of providing food. Some survival strategies included:

- child heads performing piece work (washing cars, polishing shoes, selling vegetables) in order to support their siblings,
- running errands for sympathetic neighbours,
- begging for food on a daily basis,
- attending church and then asking the pastor for food,
- in the case of teenage girls, attempting to commit themselves to early marriages in order to survive, and
- resorting to prostitution, at ages as young as eight to ten years (NMCF 2001, 26).

Stigmatisation is still a huge problem:

> The community often isolates [AIDS orphans] and they respond by isolating themselves from the community; parents discourage their children from playing with kids from child-headed families because they are believed to also have AIDS; the children who go to school tell us that their friends don't want to play with them as they might infect them (NMCF 2001, 21).

As one child even reported, 'My teacher said I will also die of AIDS; neighbours talk bad about us – saying our house is the AIDS house' (NMCF 2001, 22). AIDS orphans have to deal with the humiliation of begging food from neighbours, and the frustration of being unsuccessful. This is the report of another respondent in the study:

> 'I feel bad because when there is no food my younger brothers and sisters look at

(continued)

me and that worries me; at times I travel all the way to my aunt to ask for food and not find nothing – it frustrates me even more to think that I still have to tell the others that I went to my aunt for nothing' (NMCF 2001, 22).

Many of these children speak about being ridiculed by teachers and other

children because they do not have school uniforms, or because their parents have died of AIDS. In fact, according to the NMCF Report, many claim that school authorities insisted on them paying school fees even though their situation was well known to the teachers.

## The 'invention of adolescence'?

Predominant understandings of adolescence represent another range of developmental assumptions that may themselves be faulty:

**Storm-and-stress view.** An understanding of adolescence that sees this as a time of particular turbulence, conflict, and mood swings.

In 1904, American psychologist Hall wrote [a] ... scientific book on the nature of adolescence. The **storm-and-stress** view [was his] *concept that adolescence is a turbulent time charged with conflict and mood swings.* Thoughts, feelings, and actions oscillate between conceit and humility, good and temptation, and happiness and sadness ... As we move to the close of the twentieth century, experts on adolescence are trying to dispel the myth that adolescents are abnormal and deviant ... Too often all adolescents are stereotyped and described in sweeping generalizations based on a small group of highly visible adolescents ... [Other investigations have] documented that the vast majority of adolescents are competent human beings who are not experiencing deep emotional turmoil ... (Santrock 1999, 7).

It is becoming increasingly important in developmental psychology to acknowledge the role of context and culture in the development of the individual. The **inventionist view**, for example, states that – despite the fact that there are biological bases to adolescence – socio-historical conditions contribute to the emergence of the concept of adolescence, or to the way that adolescence is understood by a culture (Santrock 1999, 7). As Santrock notes (1999, 7–8):

**Inventionist view.** The idea that socio-historical conditions contribute to the emergence of certain concepts, such as that of the developmental psychology idea of 'adolescence'.

*American society may have 'inflicted' the status of adolescence on its youth through child-saving legislation.* By developing laws for youth only, adults placed young people in a submissive position that restricted their options, encouraged dependency, and made their movement into the workforce more manageable ...

## The powerful effects of developmental psychology

What we are pointing to then is the fact that concepts and categories generated within developmental psychology have an impact on how individuals live their lives, are raised and treated, and how they think of themselves. Moreover, these concepts translate into laws and legal identities. All states in the United States of America now have special laws for youths between the ages of sixteen and twenty-one (Santrock 1999). Of course these developmental norms are imported to other countries, often with problematic results. Burman (1994, 50–51) is critical of this circumstance:

> What we have here are features of white middle-class US society mapped onto models of development which are then treated as universal ... Are these [norms] as culture-free as they are represented? What kinds of injunctions do they make to parents?

What can we tell from all of this? Well, perhaps the first thing that we have learned is that developmental psychology, like our understanding of the child, is replete with social and political meanings which reflect our current times and beliefs rather than being timeless and universal values.

> Whether cast in terms of nostalgia or repugnance, the category of childhood is a repository of social representations that functions only by virtue of the relationship with other age and status categories: the child exists in relation to the category 'adult' ... [a] distinction ... given as a basis ... for granting additional rights ... and ... for restricting both the enjoyment of certain rights and the exercise of certain obligations ... (Burman 1994, 47–49).

We should continually be aware in this way of how childhood is used as a category of knowledge, intervention, and recommendation. Moreover, we should be aware of *whose* interests these understandings serve.

## Imposing adult categories of experience onto how we understand children

We have emphasised how historically relative our present-day notions of childhood are, and we have considered the effects of 'constructing' childhood as a qualitatively different concept from adulthood. It is important also to be aware of the opposite tendency, *that of assuming too much of a similarity between adults and children.* Whereas emphasis on the difference between adults and children seems the far more dominant tendency in developmental psychological thinking, it is important also not to interpret childhood on the basis of adult experience. We should be aware that how we experience the world now may be radically different from how we experienced the world as

toddlers. For instance, we should be aware of the tendency to project adult categories of experience and understanding onto the phenomenological world of the child.

Piaget (1926), for example, held firmly to the belief that in many ways children were qualitatively different to adults. For him the difference was principally in the realm of cognition (those psychological facets of intelligence, memory, language use, and so on). In fact he provided powerful evidence that children think and reason in qualitatively different ways from adults (see Chapter 10). For example, children tend to be more egocentric in their thinking, and are less able to concentrate on more than one dimension of a problem

(continued)

PHOTO: CHA JOHNSTON

*We should be aware of assuming that children and infants perceive and understand the world in the same way that adults do.*

at a time (Piaget 1926). Likewise, it would seem that children have less difficulty in believing in imaginary worlds, friends, and figures, which corroborates the popular notion that children have more active imaginations than adults. Children also appear to make moral decisions on a different level to that of most adults (see Chapter 16 on Kohlberg and moral reasoning).

Piaget's belief in the qualitative difference between the cognitive abilities of adults and children should be understandable, especially since language use is such a large part of what we typically consider to be cognition. Children have had a far shorter exposure to spoken language and hence are far less competent language users. This fact, in Vygotsky's view (1962), impacts dramatically on the ability of children to have, store, and make active use of memories. Similarly, the more competent one is in language use, the more one can enquire into what one does not understand – one has a better-equipped 'tool-box' for making sense of the world. Of course the paradox here is that children, for the most part, are so dramatically superior to adults in the speed at which they acquire a new language.

The importance of emphasising these differences is to suggest that certain very basic concepts that seem so innate and so

intrinsic to us need in fact to be learnt. These are concepts such as the notion of having a self, being an 'I' separate from the outside world, and having a gender, Much of what we assume to be 'pre-packaged' often needs painstakingly to be learnt.

We would also have to grant that on the phenomenological level (the level of an individual's *received sensations and experiences*) being physically smaller leads to a very different exposure to the world. Not being able to walk, crawl, or run would obviously limit the exploratory abilities of a child – what they are able to do, the various forms of stimuli they may be exposed to, and so on. Likewise, the social world responds very differently to you if you are in the body of a child or a baby. Moreover, the senses of a child are not always the same as that of an adult. Sometimes they are sharper and more accurate (children often have better eye-sight than their parents); at other times their senses are not as accurate (it takes a newborn infant some time to adjust to bifocal vision and its earliest images of the world are probably very blurred and incoherent).

In this way the world of the child, like its imagination and its various cognitive abilities, seems to be quite different from that of the adult. It is important to bear this in mind, not so that we can accentuate gratuitously the qualitative difference between children and adults, but rather so that we can guard against assuming certain similarities in trying to understand what it means to be an infant, a toddler, and a child. In fostering critical skills in our approach to developmental psychology it will be useful both to emphasise similarities between adults and children (for instance, in arguing that children are often actively disempowered in modern society), and to emphasise differences in order to avoid projecting adult categories of experience onto children.

# Five basic critiques of developmental psychology

One of the most accessible critical voices within the field of developmental psychology is that of the feminist scholar Erica Burman, whose influential book, *Deconstructing developmental psychology* (1994), will be the source and the reference for most of the discussion that follows. Burman has drawn together a number of diverse critical perspectives on developmental psychology and divided them into five general themes. We shall examine each of these in turn.

## Developmental psychology as regulatory means of social control

It is easy to underestimate the magnitude of developmental psychology's influence on the lives of real children. We should be under no illusions however:

> Developmental psychology, more than any other variety of psychology, has a powerful impact on our everyday lives and ways of thinking about ourselves. Its effects are so great that they are often almost imperceptible, taken-for-granted features about our expectations of ourselves, others, parents, children and families ... Part of the imperceptibility lies in the ways developmental psychology has structured the standards and even the forms of modern state intervention that accompany welfare policies of protection and care. Acknowledging these issues means going beyond the representation of developmental psychology research as scientific and benign in its effects (Burman 1994, 2).

## The 'power of psychology'

As early as 1953 Eysenck was publishing his concerns on how regulative the industries of psychology were proving to be in modern society. Consider the views he presents here, and their ramifications for the critique of developmental psychology:

> In one way or another almost everyone has come up against the mixed blessings which applied psychology bestows on humanity. Decisions regarding the child's future education are being made on the basis of intelligence tests applied at the tender age of eleven or twelve; indeed the whole modern system of education is based on [developmental] psychological discoveries and theories that are relatively recent. The soldier's allocation to a particular arm or trade inside the service, as well as his advancement to officer status, is determined by [such methods and theories] ... our new rulers, the upper ranks of the Civil Service, are being selected by 'new type' selection methods; vocational guidance and occupational selection are affecting the everyday working lives of thousands ... [These theories and methods] ... some of them carried out by Government agencies ... help to lay the foundations for legislation and policy-making ... Even old age is not safe from the ... scrutiny of [psychologists]; the intellectual and emotional development of old people is being studied more and more intensely, and action based on the results. This brief and incomplete survey shows to what extent psychology is already taking part in transforming our lives ... (Eysenck 1953, 7–8).

Developmental psychology has participated in social initiatives explicitly concerned with the comparison, regulation, and control of social groups and societies (Burman 1994). In fact, developmental psychology can barely be separated from the establishment more generally of tools of mental assessment and psychometric procedures that aim to classify abilities and develop norms through which people may be effectively separated, grouped, and regulated. Developmental psychology is vital in this way to the state's regulation of people, and of children in particular. As Burman (1994, 5–6) notes:

> Developmental psychological knowledge informs a number of professional practices, such as health, education and welfare, which touch everybody's lives. In particular, it forms part of the knowledge base for health visiting and social work, as well as education and law. For example, on what basis do law courts arrive at an understanding of what constitutes a child's 'best interests'? What underlies an education welfare officer's opinion that a child's 'social and emotional needs' will be better catered for outside mainstream school? What criteria do adoption agencies use in evaluating whether or not adoption is likely to be successful?

None of this is to suggest that developmental psychology is morally questionable; it is merely to suggest that the knowledge generated by developmental psychology is put to *powerful use* in the regulation of populations, and that its healthy prescriptions, like its errors and mistakes, reverberate 'beyond the theory or the experimental laboratory, as well as beyond the pages of child advice magazines and toyshops' (Burman 1994, 6). In short, we should not underestimate the power or the effects of developmental psychology. Likewise, we should maintain a strong critical and ethical awareness of the impact of its repercussions, wherever possible.

## Developmental psychology 'normalises'

Drawing on the work of Foucault, Nikolas Rose (1991) has written extensively about the way that individual psychology plays an important role in the classification and surveillance of individuals. He argues that, in order to control and regulate potentially unruly, wayward, or unproductive social elements, 'disciplinary societies' (Foucault 1977) developed a kind of monitoring, and psychology helped to provide this by producing **norms**. Norms were averages of growth, development, work-rate, and ability observed across populations, and each individual could now be assessed in relation to such norms. To quote from Burman (1994, 14):

> The psychological individual was a highly specified and studied entity whose mental qualities and development were understood by virtue of comparison with the general population. So knowledge of the individual and the general went hand in hand: each required the other, and each was defined in terms of the other. The division of the mad from the sane, the criminal from the lawful and the educable from the uneducable, shifted from moral-

**Norms.** Averages of growth, development, work-rate, or various other abilities observed across populations. It is important to be aware of the difference between statistical norms (a mathematical average drawn from a sample of a population) and the evaluative implications in talk of norms (implications of that which is ideal, 'normal', 'natural', or socially desirable).

# Selecting to war: The use and misuse of IQ tests in the military

Just as Eysenck (1953) was critical of the regulative functioning of applied psychology within society, he also pointed critical attention to the usefulness of intelligence testing:

> The new scientific discoveries of Binet, Spearman, and Stern in the field of intelligence testing were put to the crucial test of practical application by the American Army during the First World War; their triumphant success there established psychology once and for all as an indispensable adjunct to all selection procedures. It may be of interest to quote the directive setting out the tasks which the Army authorities expected the intelligence test to perform. The test was to 'designate and select men whose superior intelligence indicated the desirability of advancement for special assignment; to select and recommend for 'developmental battalions' such men as were so inferior intellectually as to be unsuited for regular military training; to enable officers to build up organizations of uniform mental strength, in accordance with definitive specifications concerning mental requirements; to select men for various types of military duty or for special assignments; to eliminate men whose intelligence was so inferior as to make it impossible to use them at all ...
>
> The very success of the intelligence test in this difficult assignment became the reason for subsequent disappoint-

ment. Thousands of enthusiasts ... eager to cash in on the new fad, invaded the field and tried to apply the Army testing procedures in industrial and commercial institutions ... Uncritical enthusiasts, fired by the conviction of righteousness given them by some 'system' or other, are trying to extend these methods to fields where they may not be appropriate ... (Eysenck 1953, 8–9).

This quote is of interest in revealing the indispensable use of psychology in the making of armies (and, for that matter, the making of war). It also suggests how these tests may go wrong and may lead, through misapplication and misuse, to the discarding of those people who might have been *suitable* for a given job and to the retention of those who may be *unsuitable*. This example also suggests how such tests may implicitly be used to separate upper and lower classes across a division of labour between the more dangerous and more menial jobs, on the one hand, and those that are safer and more desirable, on the other. (It would be interesting to question in this regard whether these tests were not at some level implicitly selecting on the basis of class rather than on the basis of 'pure' intelligence.)

political criteria to the equally judgemental, but scientific, evaluation of mental testing.

## Development and its relationship to abnormality

As Rose (1991) notes, a **developmental norm** was a standard based upon the average abilities or performances of children at a certain age. Such norms not only presented a picture of what was normal for children at such an age, they also enabled the 'normality' of any child to be assessed by this norm (Rose 1991). Children could now be rated and assessed through reference to all manner of detailed developmental norms, which could grade their performance between the poles of 'normal' and 'abnormal'. It is this attention to what is the 'normal', and to the **normalisation** of children, that made 'abnormality' possible, that is, 'abnormality' in the sense of a coherent category or conceptualisation of people (Burman

**Developmental norm.** A standard based upon the average abilities or performances of children of a specified age. See norms.

**Normalisation.** The attempt, through typically interventionist, curative, rehabilitative, punitive, or educational means, to make the 'abnormal' subject conform more closely to the norms of a population or society.

1994). The danger of these scientific categories of 'normal' and 'abnormal' is that they become very loaded terms. Certain critics suggest that it is personally damaging to be labelled 'abnormal', and that such labelling practices lead to social stigmatisation. Others, like Foucault, suggest that this scientific language is doing little more than replacing notions of good/bad, and right/sinful with the new categories normal/abnormal. Burman (1994) suggests that these kinds of practice endowed a scientific legitimating upon practices of social regulation and reform. Moreover, she argues that the 'normal' is a purely conceptual construct:

> The normal child, the ideal type, distilled from the comparative scores of age-graded populations, is ... a fiction or myth. No individual or real child lies at its basis. It is an abstraction, a fantasy, a fiction, a production of the testing apparatus that incorporates, that constructs the child (Burman 1994, 16–17).

Burman contends that what is especially problematic about the normalising standards of developmental psychology is that the moral evaluation underlying them is rendered invisible and *incontrovertible* through the apparent impartiality of statistical norms. Administration through the power of institutions can hence enforce statistical description as moral-political *prescription*:

> [N]ormative descriptions provided by developmental psychology slip into naturalised prescriptions. Developmental psychology makes claims to be scientific. Its use of evolutionary assumptions to link the social to the biological provides a key cultural area in which evolutionary and biologist ideas are replayed and legitimized. Closely associated with its technologies and its guiding preoccupations has been its use to classify and stratify individuals, groups and populations so as to maintain class, gender and racial oppression (Burman 1994, 4).

## The political value of 'normality'

According to Eysenck (1953, 177), 'Normality is a term which recurs with disturbing frequency in the writings of psychologists.' The reason for Eysenck's concern here is that there is no single agreed definition of the term. There are, however, at least two concepts of 'normality', which ('no matter how poorly', according to Eysenck) may be implied by the term:

> We may mean by normal that which characterizes the conduct of the majority

of people; this is what we may call the *statistical* definition of normality. A person of normal weight is one who is neither heavier nor lighter than the majority of people of his own height. This usage of the term is perfectly clear, straightforward, and intelligible. It does however present certain difficulties when we consider certain traits such as intelligence, or beauty or health ... This ambiguity of the term comes out strongest in relation to health. The normal person is the one who has an average number of illnesses and fractures and whose life is ended by one of the more common diseases. The person who is completely

(continued)

healthy and lives to a ripe old age, without any kind of physical disease, would be exceedingly abnormal from this point of view ... This is not a usual method of looking at health or beauty or intelligence. We tend to substitute for the *statistical* norm an *ideal* norm. We call a person normal the more [they] approach the ideal, whether it be ideally high intelligence, good looks, or uninterrupted health. But the ideal norm may be one which is statistically very infrequent, or which is not found at all in the population examined.

Confusion between the these two uses of the term is ... common, particularly with respect to mental health. When the psychoanalyst declares that no one is normal, [they have] ... in mind the ideal concept of normality (Eysenck 1953, 178).

The socially evaluative use of the term 'normality' is more often than not a false exploitation of a neutral, scientific, and statistical description. The evaluative function of the term – the way it is used to designate social ideals – becomes apparent in the seeming incongruence of notions like that of 'abnormal beauty' or 'abnormal intelligence'. The denigratory function of the term becomes apparent here.

Eysenck extends this argument by specifying a third implication of normality (which is of particular relevance to psychological descriptions): the conflation of 'normal with the concept of the 'natural':

we [often] call normal that which we consider to be *natural*. Thus ... [some might] consider it 'normal' for the male to be dominant and the female to be submissive; we consider heterosexual attraction 'normal', homosexual attraction 'abnormal'. [One might] hold these views even though it could be shown that in some communities, among the ancient Greeks, say, homosexuality was statistically more frequent than heterosexuality, or that among some nations, say the ancient Egyptians, women tended to be more aggressive and males more submissive (Eysenck 1953, 178).

Eysenck's examples are revealing – not only of the fact that certain politically implicated values (such as chauvinism and homophobia) are often embedded in the designations of what is 'normal' or 'natural' – but also of *how these values change historically*. Few academics today would venture such propositions as in the above paragraph; yet at the time of Eysenck's writing neither seemed to be particularly controversial, so much so that he thought to use them as examples of how we use 'normal' to designate what is in fact supposedly *natural*. Clearly Eysenck's attempt here is to show us that we frequently use the term 'normal' to refer to something that we consider to be somehow biologically or essentially innate, something *natural*. What his example shows us is that what is taken to be *normal*, just as what is taken to be *natural*, changes over time, and therefore supposed descriptions of normality should be seen as neither universal nor ahistorical. It is clear that assertions of universal and ahistorical verity are implicit in aligning the supposed 'norm' with an understanding of what is natural.

The point is that not only do so-called norms possess an evaluative and denigratory function, they often take on the form of dominant social prejudices, which try to present themselves as natural and universally applicable. Given these problems, it is difficult to understand why one would want to continue using the term 'normality' to refer to statistical averages, especially since its various implications, of the *ideal*, or of the *natural*, do not necessarily hold in this context. The statistical average is not *ideal*, nor need it be *natural* (as far as that term is even relevant here). Indeed, we should also be cautious of using the notion of the statistical average, because to a large extent it retains the evaluative implications of 'the normal'. Think of the value judgement implied, for

(continued)

example, by being categorised as 'well below average intelligence'.

Perhaps Eysenck's most important point here is that socio-political ideals often masquerade as 'norms'; that when we call something 'normal' we are making a politically loaded statement (one thoroughly invested with social values), rather than a value-neutral objective statement. Eysenck (1953, 189) ends his commentary by calling our attention to the fact that 'no ... universal norms of behaviour exist'. He substantiates this fact with reference to Kinsey's massive study of American sexuality. Kinsey reported such great diversity and conflict of opinions (related to topics such as masturbation, pre- and extra-marital intercourse, the illicitness of certain sexual acts, etc.) across areas, age groups, and communities that no overarching norms could be found. He quotes Kinsey's findings to substantiate his conclusion:

> The data now available show that patterns of sexual behaviour may be strikingly different for the different social levels that exist in the same city or town, and sometimes in immediately adjacent sections of the single community. The data show that divergences in sexual patterns of such social groups may be as great as those which anthropologists have found between the sexual patterns of different ... groups in remote parts of the world (Kinsey, cited in Eysenck 1953, 184).

### The 'colonialism' of normalisation

The standardisation and conformity that these processes of normalisation suggest are not always healthy for children. The fact, for example, that one child takes longer to talk than another is no guarantee that there is a problem. 'Late-talkers' sometimes become far more linguistically proficient than early talkers, and the same holds for late developers across almost all spheres of development. The danger of these kinds of norm becomes even more patent when one considers their source. Since most developmental research psychology originates in the United States of America, it is not surprising to discover that most of these developmental psychological norms have been influenced by strongly American values. Burman (1994) provides the example of the cultural value placed on maturity and autonomy within the United States (as compared especially to developing nations). This value, she indicates, has produced a research bias in which variations in child-rearing practices suggest that American children have more secure attachments than, for example, African children. Such norms necessarily reflect poorly on children in other countries with different social and ideological values. Two other examples are to be found in what are considered developmental problems for American developmental psychology, namely 'childhood obesity' and 'teenage pregnancy'. Burman (1994) points out that the majority of the world's children are born to mothers under twenty (and as such teenage pregnancy is not so much a problem as a natural occurrence in these parts of the world), and that most of the world is starving and struggling to survive (hence invalidating the universality of the problem of 'childhood obesity').

### Normality and power

Rose (1991) amplifies these foregoing critiques, possibly in even more condemning terms than Burman:

Our conceptualizations of normality are not simply generalizations from our accumulated experience of normal children. On
the contrary, criteria of normality are elaborated by experts on the
basis of their claims to scientific knowledge of childhood ... And
this knowledge of normality has not, in the main, resulted from
studying normal children ... It is around pathological children –
the troublesome, the recalcitrant, the delinquent – that conceptions of normality have taken shape. It is not that a knowledge of
the normal course of development of the child has enabled experts
to become more skilled at identifying those unfortunate children
who are in some way abnormal. Rather, expert notions of normality are extrapolated from our attention to those children who
worry the courts, teachers, doctors, and parents. Normality is not
an observation but a valuation. It contains not only a judgement
about what is desirable, but an injunction as to a goal to be
achieved. In so doing, the very notion of 'the normal' today
awards power to scientific truth and expert authority (Rose 1991,
131).

Rose not only casts a severe shadow of doubt upon the reliability of
norms, in that norms are largely generated around the study of the apparently 'abnormal', he also argues that they are almost always developed as
part of the agenda of social control, and that they are inseparably attached
to the maintenance of hegemony within societies.

# Norms and clinical treatment: The prospects of damage

Eysenck examines the dangers of using
norms in applied contexts, as in psychology. He notes that what essentially
occurs is that select persons (typically
advantaged white males):

> lay down the law, or try to ... help peo-
> ple from [historically disadvantaged] ...
> classes ... In clinical practice ... therapy ...
> and help in the sexual sphere are based
> essentially upon concepts of marriage
> and sexual conduct which agree with the
> norms obtaining among the [dominant
> or controlling classes] ... from which the
> practitioner comes, but which may be
> quite inappropriate to the norms of
> the ... person to whom [help] ... is being
> given (Eysenck 1953, 190).

Although Eysenck uses the example
here of sexual norms, the value of his
comments should not, obviously, be
restricted to this context alone. He is wary
here of the problem of perpetuating one
very select set of social values above and

beyond all others. That is to say, he is wary
of how the norms adopted by the mental
health professions may champion the values only of those in dominant social
positions. Moreover, he is wary of the
damage that this perpetuation may cause.
If a patient is seeking a psychotherapist's
help because of falling short in some way
of a social 'norm' – say, for example, that
of 'normal sexuality' – then any treatment
schedule that, however subtly, reiterates
this 'abnormality' will be damaging.
(Consider here that *homosexuality* used to
be considered psychopathological for this
very reason.) Such treatment will in effect
reinforce and perpetuate the very social
problem (in this case homophobia) that
had caused the problem in the first place.
In short, notions of 'normality', once
carried into the sphere of something like
clinical psychology, can in fact be actively
damaging.

PHOTO: CHA JOHNSTON

*One of the key criticisms of developmental psychology centres on 'mother blaming', the tendency to hold the mother responsible for a wide variety of supposed developmental deficits.*

## The 'blameworthy mother'

Feminist perspectives on developmental psychology suggest that in many ways mothers have replaced children as the primary focus for developmental psychological investigation, at least in terms of *the regulation of development*. Mothers frequently become the scapegoats for any developmental problems; they are the ones seen as bearing almost full responsibility for the healthy development of children. The notion of the 'bad mother' is important here; indeed there is no lack of traditional developmental theory that implies that 'a woman's place is in the home' and that children suffer if they are not in the full-time care of their mothers (Burman 1994). Likewise popular in developmental theory is the notion that children who have personal or behavioural problems in their later lives have been inadequately mothered; later moral or psychological aberrations exhibited by the child are then attributable to the mother. In this regard, Burman (1994, 3–4) argues:

> It is the adequacy of mothering that developmental psychology is called upon to regulate and legislate upon, and the continuity with which this issue crops up across the range of topics in developmental psychology is a manifestation of the widespread and routine subjection of women to the developmental psychological gaze.

Not only does this mean that mothers (women) are disproportionately more responsible for the healthy upbringing of their children than fathers (men), it also means that they are frequently held responsible for developmental problems, which may in many instances stem from contextual or political factors beyond their control, such as poverty and the resultant problem of undernourishment. As Singer (1992, 99) suggests, 'Through the child, the mother was made responsible for violence and social chaos in the world outside the family, a world from which she was more or less excluded'.

## Blaming the working mother

The great majority of developmental psychology research conforms to dominant familial and patriarchal assumptions of the nuclear family containing a male breadwinner and female child carer (Burman 1994). Almost by definition then, a working mother cannot be a good mother. Developmental psychology contains many such assumptions. Speaking on the work of Bowlby for instance, Burman (1994, 82) states that, basically, '[a]ny woman who asserts her right to have an existence independent from her child is dismissed as abandoning her, with a clear dichotomy set up between women who put childcare first and those who will not.' The developmental psychological notion of 'maternal deprivation' works in the same way. Winnicott (particularly with his concept of 'the good-enough mother') and Bowlby were responsible for making bold pronouncements for women's economic and social roles. Indeed, both posed near impossible demands on the conscientious mother who needed always to be available and attentive at the risk of producing far-reaching ill-effects in her children (Burman 1994).

Close on the heels of these kinds of understanding of motherhood are very particular definitions of femininity, definitions which characterise motherhood as women's ultimate fulfilment, something they should necessarily pursue at the cost of much else. Idealising motherhood in this way, and making the primary caregiver gendered in this way perpetuates asymmetrical gender relations and pathologises women who fail to conform to these ideal standards of mothering. Burman claims that the lack of greater preschool childcare provision in the workplace is symptomatic of these problems:

> Provision is structured around the assumption that children are primarily to be cared for by their mothers ... Not only are mothers disenfranchised from participating in the productive sphere of paid work by employers' expectations of their engagement in full-time childcare, but those who out of financial necessity do work are correspondingly positioned as morally *reprehensible*. Even where these assumptions are starting to be eroded, with childcare provision so minimal, those for whom it is provided are thereby designated as inadequate. How much more pathological a mother must be if she needs to be taught what is supposed to 'come naturally'! (Burman 1994, 81).

## An isolated focus on the individual child

> '[A]n exclusively child-centered focus is limited. Child development is not the whole of developmental psychology' (Goodnow and Collins 1990, 10).

Why should the individual and isolated child necessarily be the focus of developmental psychology? Although this question might sound a little strange, considering the extent to which we naturalise 'the child' as the immediate and commonsense focus of developmental psychology, it is a question that is worth considering. As Burman (1994, 4) states, the 'selection of children as objects of developmental psychological enquiry leads to a failure to theorise the psychological context they inhabit'. We need to ask ourselves about the consequences of considering the child as the single or predominant focus of development: what is left out in accounts of such focus, and what is the result of these omissions?

Why is it, for example, that the child of developmental accounts is overwhelmingly a 'he'? Following Burman (1994) we need to ask: *whose* development are we talking about here? Is it one that reflects all cultures, or is it simply a limited vision of development that reflects a specific culture – the culture of those who control the production of developmental psychology? Is the developmental psychology we learn a psychology of both men's *and* women's experiences? What are the consequences for developmental psychology of its forgetting of gender as a structuring dimension of development?

## Blaming the victims

Looking at development in isolation from socio-political factors frequently leads to individualistic interpretations of socially structured phenomena that can then lapse into victim blaming. Take, for example, the situation where mothers are treated as responsible for the social ills of the world in which they are trying to rear their children (Burman 1994). Consider likewise the situation where 'underprivileged' sectors of society are blamed for their own poverty or lack of education. Failures and problems in development often stem from causes greater than that of the individual child, or of the individual style of mothering. Class, culture, and other socio-political factors are often responsible for failures in child development or education, and we need to ask ourselves why this field of influence has not received more attention within the realm of developmental psychology (Burman 1994).

One important focus of attention here is parents, that is, parents *themselves*, beyond just the question of parenting styles. As Goodnow and Collins (1990) comment, parents are interesting in their own right, and their attitudes and values (political or otherwise) along with their general habits, preferences, tendencies, and lifestyles can exert a huge influence on children, for better or worse. The poet Philip Larkin is one of those who holds a rather negative view of the ways in which parents are able to influence their children, and expresses this in a stanza from his poem *This be the verse*:

> They fuck you up, your mum and dad.
> They may not mean to, but they do.
> They fill you with the faults they had.
> And add some extra just for you.
> (Larkin, in Jones 1988, 56)

There are numerous foci for developmental psychology that would take researchers away from the isolated individual child. Burman (1994, 9) argues that the unit of development under investigation should be seen as variable: 'We could be concerned with the development of a process, or a mechanism, rather than an individual'. This suggests an interesting direction for future and possibly more multidisciplinary approaches to the study of human development.

## The child as both familial individual and as subject

Hayes (1989) draws our attention to the fact that the child has both an individual familial role within a particular family, and a greater political role within the structural powers of a given society:

> Parents respond to the child as both an individual and a subject. The child is a subject for the parents in so far as there is social meaning attached to 'having children', and rearing children. The parent's relationships to their child are not always individual and emotional, but are often determined by social factors. For example, child-rearing practices, the social standard of acceptable behaviour which is often class determined, the morality that is promoted in the educational (school) system and so on.
>
> It is these social and ideological factors that intervene between parents and their children and which **interpellate** children not as individuals, but as subjects. In the complex societies of contemporary capitalism parents do not experience their children in an innocent and immediate way, and it is argued that a factor like ideology and its functioning can contribute significantly to explaining why the relationship between parents and children is often tense, contradictory, and in conflict. In other words, parents experience their children for what they are, as they appear, and also as subjects

that are constituted by multiple determinations. In this sense ideology interpellates individual children as subjects for parents (Hayes 1989, 89–90).

Hayes's point here is essentially that the bond between parent and child is not purely familial in nature, that it is infiltrated and invested by politics and social values in all its aspects. He uses Louis Althusser's concept of *interpellation*, which, in short, refers to how we are each socially situated as subjects of various types of power (Althusser 1971). The example often provided for this hegemonic mechanism of interpellation is that of an individual walking down a road who is hailed by a police officer. In turning around and answering this hail, the individual is immediately placed in a particular position which is underwritten with structural power and meaning; thus in this very act he or she *becomes a subject of power*. The mechanism of interpellation shows how we are not perhaps as free as we typically assume: it emphasises how we are placed in particular roles within society in largely unavoidable ways.

## Conclusion

In this chapter we have examined both a series of historical perspectives on childhood, and a variety of major criticisms of the field in general. It has been important to consider some philosophical questions about the nature of childhood, adolescence, and the family. This is because commonplace and seemingly 'natural' assumptions about what a child is, or should be, are powerful forms of knowledge. These are the kinds of knowledge that affect the way we raise children and *treat* them, *understand* them, *teach* them, and *discipline* them, and we should be aware of

**Interpellation.** A term invented by Louis Althusser (1971) for the ideological construction – through a process of 'hailing' or 'recruiting' – of the individual as a participatory subject of social or political power.

how historically relative they are. Put differently, what we learn in developmental psychology affects children in a powerful way, and hence the development of children and of adults can come to be affected by the ideas, principles, and theories that we deal with *here*.

Regarding the overarching critiques collected by Burman (1994), it is important to emphasise that these do not imply that we should do away with developmental psychology altogether, that we should reject all developmental theory offered up to now. Rather, we must understand that they highlight important issues of power and equality (or inequality), which should be given prominence in the developmental theory of the future. In assimilating important traditions and theories of developmental theory, it is vital that we be aware of their shortcomings, and that we involve critique as an active part of our learning.

## Children and power in modern society

Rose (1991) shares Burman's concern for traditional developmental psychology's neglect to analyse power in the study of childhood. He argues that childhood is the most intensely governed sector of personal existence:

> In different ways, at different times, and by many different routes varying from one section of society to another, the health, welfare, and rearing of children have been linked in thought and practice to the destiny of the nation and the responsibilities of the state. The modern child has become the focus of innumerable projects that purport to safeguard it from physical, sexual, or moral danger, to ensure its 'normal' development, to actively promote certain capacities of attributes such as intelligence, educability, and emotional stability (Rose 1991, 121).

Rose observes that the recent history of childhood has been one of multiple anxieties concerning children, which have occasioned any number of programmes to conserve and shape them. He observes that the child, both as an idea and as a target, has become inextricably connected to the aspirations of the authorities. The environment of the growing child is to be regulated legislatively and financially, and educational programmes are likewise carefully monitored and developed.

PHOTO: ©JESPER STRUDSHOLM/iAFRIKA PHOTOS

*The prevalence of war on the African continent points to the frequency of the use of child soldiers.*

Legislative obligations are imposed upon parents, requiring them to carry out social duties from the registration of their children at birth to ensuring that they receive adequate education up to their teens ... Child protection legislation has

(continued)

imposed powers and duties upon local authorities, requiring them to evaluate the standards of care being provided to children by their parents through the agencies of social work, and to intervene into the family to rectify shortcomings, utilizing legal means where necessary (Rose 1991, 121).

In accordance with these concerns, and with the correlative implementation of institutional mechanisms *within* the lives of children, the last hundred years have seen an increasing rise in the 'rights' of the child. Scathingly critical about how this idea of the rights of the child has been put to use, Rose (1991) notes:

> ... the extension of social regulation to the lives of children actually had little to do with the regulation of their rights. Children came to the attention of social authorities as delinquents threatening property and security, as future workers requiring moralization and skills, as future soldiers requiring a level of fitness – in

other words on account of the threat which they posed now or in the future to the welfare of the state. The apparent humanity, benevolence, and enlightenment of the extension of protection to children in their homes disguised the extension of surveillance and control over the family ... The upsurges of concern over the young – from juvenile delinquency in the 19th Century to sexual abuse today – were actually moral panics: repetitive and predictable social occurrences in which certain persons or phenomena come to symbolize a range of social anxieties concerning threats to the established order and traditional values ... (Rose 1991, 123).

Childhood, in short, has become intensely regulated by political power. Moreover, if we follow Rose's arguments, both childhood itself, and the ideas and initiatives around the promise of its protection, have become key terms in how a given social or political order is governed, maintained, and extended.

# Recommended readings

*This chapter has been based on three central texts:*

Burman, E. (1994). *Deconstructing developmental psychology.* London: Routledge.
(*Burman's book is the most accessible, and arguably the most important of those listed here, for an overall critique of developmental psychology. Highly recommended.*)

Eysenck, H. J. (1953). *Uses and abuses of psychology.* London: Penguin.
(*Eysenck's book was useful for its time, as the lengthy extracts above suggest. However, it has since dated somewhat, and the author's critical claims are in retrospect diluted by the remainder of his work which is in certain respects notably uncritical of psychology.*)

Rose, N. (1991). *Governing the soul: The shaping of the private self.* London: Routledge.
(*Rose's text is a critical* tour de force *through the history of psychology. Hard to match for pure critical incisiveness, although it is by no means focused on developmental psychology alone.*)

## Critical thinking tasks

1) If indeed children were treated and understood differently in past European cultures, consider what may have been the case traditionally or historically in African societies.

2) Which of the various basic philosophies of childhood is, in your opinion, predominant in the way in which we understand children and infants today? Give reasons for your answer.

Look for images of childhood in popular magazines or television advertisements to substantiate your answer. Similarly, consider which trends within the different philosophies of the child remind you of trends within psychology.

3) How do you understand your own adolescence? Do you find that the storm-and-stress view has any relevance in describing your experiences of this process?

4) If it is true that developmental norms are developed by experimental psychologists from small groups whom they study, then what do you suppose might be the origin of these studied groups, and how legitimate do you think the results would be when applied to 'adolescents' in other socio-cultural environments?

5) What familial factors do you think have a strong influence on the psychological development of children?

6) To what extent, and in what ways, do you think that children are controlled in modern Western society? Do you feel that these kinds of control are warranted, and what do you think are the other activities that juveniles might get up to if they did not attend school?

7) Give some thought to the developmental theories covered in the preceding chapters. Which theories exhibit certain of the tendencies criticised by Burman? Furthermore, if you do have a preferred or favourite theory, give particular thought to how it might be criticised in terms of the arguments Burman presents.

8) Thinking beyond the realm of psychological developmental theory itself, consider how certain of the tendencies mentioned by Burman are apparent in our day-to-day assumptions about human development. Provide examples to support your answer.

9) How might one 'customise' Burman's critiques to human development in the South African context?

10) Draw up a list of stereotypes around the idea of 'mothering'. Do the same around the idea of 'fathering' and then contrast and compare them. Reflect on how these parenting roles have been strongly gendered, and on the different types of responsibilities and activities implied by each.

11) If it is indeed limiting to maintain a (relatively) exclusive child-focused approached to development, what other important areas of focus could we use to widen our understanding of human development?

12) Consider the notion of normalisation: what kind of children/parents/families/homes would have been the basis for developmental norms in apartheid era South Africa, and which would have been routinely 'problematised' (considered deviant, problematic, 'pathological') in terms of these norms?

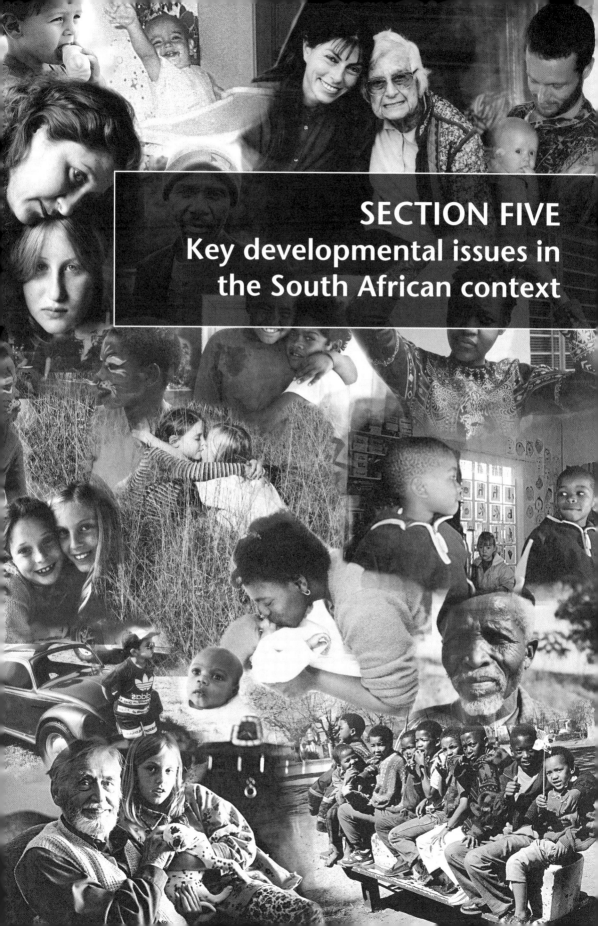

# SECTION FIVE
## Key developmental issues in the South African context

# Race, culture, and psychological theory

*Mambwe Kasese-Hara*

This chapter looks at race, culture, and psychology, with a focus on the influence of historical factors, culture, and ethnicity in shaping contemporary developmental theory. A range of issues in cognitive and social development is discussed. We start with some of the early debates surrounding the issue of 'cognition and culture' from a Euro-American context, and finish with a proposed model of human development in an African context. The following topics are covered:

1. Introduction.

2. Events surrounding the birth of psychology as a discipline.

3. Psychology and culture:
   ◆ The reductionist approach.
   ◆ Early debate about culture and cognition.
   ◆ A broader view of culture and cognition.

4. Psychology in a multiracial society.

5. Human development: a West African conceptual framework.

6. Conclusion.

## Introduction

The student initially experiences undergraduate psychology as though it were an imitation of some form of natural science – as though it were a pure science born and nurtured in a neutral environment, without the bias of class, culture, or creed. Most psychology classes introduce the discipline with concepts and phenomena, such as Wilhelm Wundt's 'reaction time', Thorndike's 'law of effect', and Skinner's 'operant condition-ing' (Gleitman 1991) so that from the onset we tend to assume that the discipline of psychology that we are about to study is a 'science' of human behaviour concerned mainly with physiological processes in interaction with environmental experiences.

Although the environment could be anything and everything that bears relevance to the individual or group, psychological theory has tra-ditionally been based mainly on a particular kind of environment, which is largely European and middle class (Nsamenang, 1992; Liddel, Kvalsig, Shabalala, and Masilela 1991). As such, when it comes to the social, cul-tural, and ethnic contexts in which individuals develop, traditional psy-chological theory is found to be lacking, as its evolution has to a large extent excluded other social and cultural experiences. This chapter is aimed at providing students of psychology with some insights into race, ethnicity, and culture as central features in the evolution of psychologi-cal theory, mainly as points of inclusion or exclusion. We shall consider how psychological theories may reflect common belief systems in society, and how they may help foster these, especially in relation to culture and ethnicity.

## Events surrounding the birth of psychology as a discipline

The birth of psychology as a discipline is traced back to late nineteenth-century Europe (Cole 1993). Although some of the concepts and phe-nomena in psychology can be traced back to philosophers before this, there was no distinct discipline prior to this that could be clearly defined as a humanistic science until the emergence of anthropology and psy-chology. In historical terms, the period preceding this was also the period during which Europe was extending her interests in the rest of the world in exploration, trade, the spread of religion, and the subsequent colonisa-tion of foreign lands. During this period, Europe saw itself as the centre of civilisation and culture, while the rest of the world was mysterious ter-ritory to be explored and conquered, and Africa was seen as the 'dark' continent inhabited by 'primitive beings'.

Thus psychology as a discipline emerged out of an era and context that was highly polarised along socio-cultural, racial, and geographical lines. Within European society itself, a preoccupation with culture and socio-economic status crystallised around the notion of 'civilisation' which became highly debated, with the general thinking being that these factors were linked to mental abilities, and that all of these were geneti-cally endowed. As though it were an endorsement of such prejudice, Darwin's evolutionary theory linking human evolution to that of the ape was highly influential, and so – in addition to the hierarchical ranking of people according to class – all living things were ordered in ranks with humans (white) at the top of the evolutionary scale. Anthropologists even argued that black humankind was the 'missing link' between humanity (white) and ape in the 'great chain of being' (Mosse 1999).

Racist ideology, whose legacy the social sciences and society in general continue to battle with, was conceived, nurtured, and consolidated in seventeenth- and eighteenth-century Europe (Mosse 1999). It was exported to the 'new world' (Australia and the Americas) and Africa by the settlers and colonial administrators, who established a social order comprising satellites of the 'mother society' back in Europe. Thus racist ideology became consolidated, and further enhanced, by the challenges of having to live in close proximity, and to share land and other resources with a people Europeans knew little about except in terms of highly distorted stereotypes. The colonial societies established by Britain, France, Spain, and Portugal had socio-economic, cultural, and political hierarchies with white settlers at the top. This was reflected, for instance, by the immigration policies of Australia and the United States of America, which excluded non-Europeans from citizenship (Castles and Vasta 1999; Omi and Winant 1999). Contemporary society still bears social and psychological burdens from these historical social structures, so that the world our children (black, yellow, or white) are expected to thrive in today, is still a world polarised along socio-economic, ethnic, and cultural lines. This presents special challenges for developmental psychology, some of which will become more apparent later on in this chapter.

# Psychology and culture

## The reductionist approach

With this brief background on the developments in European society surrounding the birth of psychology as a discipline, we may now turn more directly to developments in psychological theory. Early developments in psychology were characterised by a drift towards 'reductionism', which refers to the notion that all the sciences can be arranged hierarchically from the highest to the lowest, and each science is reducible to a more basic science, until we arrive at physics, the most basic science (Leahey 1987). Accordingly, psychological concepts of individual behaviour can be reduced to the concepts and laws of neurophysiology, or the functioning of individual bodies.

At the turn of the twentieth century, Hall (1904) and other genetic psychologists adopted **recapitulation theory** in their attempt to explain individual development over the life-span. Consequently they proposed that biogenetic law reproduces forms of thought and behaviour in the individual's development (*ontogeny*) that correspond to the various stages of cultural evolution (*phylogeny*). According to this theory, the white Western child passes through earlier and lower stages to arrive at 'civilisation', while on the other hand the individual in traditional societies retraces only part of this ancestral cultural history and remains arrested at one of the lower levels.

Spencer (1886), one of the major proponents of this theory, postulated the idea of *cultural* stages and concluded that societies developed over history, becoming increasingly complex and more highly organised, with each stage marked by more advanced forms of thought. This reasoning

**Recapitulation theory.** This refers to a broad-based nineteenth-century approach to individual development in which it was suggested that individuals reflect in themselves the historical development of their culture or 'civilisation' (Flugel and West, 1964).

supported the commonly held belief that culture, civilisation, and mental activity were closely interlinked. Obvious differences in technological advancement between peoples living in different parts of the world prompted some of the debate, but in theorising about the possible sources of these differences certain assumptions were made which shaped both theory and commonly held beliefs. The first assumption was that it would be possible to study the history of humanity by studying different peoples in contemporary society, who were at different 'levels of progress'. The second was that there was no major distinction between 'mind' and 'culture'. The reasoning for this was that, since culture provided experience – and it was supposed that some cultures provided a greater diversity of experience than others – there should be a direct relationship between cultural development and mental development (Cole 1993).

## Early debate about culture and cognitive development

Thus, the debate about culture and cognition was born, and many theorists have since argued against the reductionist perspective, including Vygotsky, Boas, Cole, and Scribner. Lev Vygotsky (1896–1934) was among the first to offer a counter-argument on culture and cognition (that is, mental activity). Proposing a 'socio-historical approach', he attempted to theorise the role of socio-cultural and historical factors in shaping the cognitive development of individuals and the subsequent advancement of societies (Glassman 1994). Although based on the same

## Racist characterisations of the mental abilities of 'non-Europeans'

Consider the following example from Franz Boas's classic, *The mind of primitive man* (1911), which repeats evidence used by Spencer to make generalisations about properties of 'primitive' mind:

In his description of the natives of the west coast of Vancouver Island, Sproat says, 'The native mind, to an educated man, seems generally to be asleep ... On his attention being fully aroused, he often shows much quickness in reply and ingenuity in argument. But a short conversation wearies him, particularly if questions are asked that require efforts of thought or memory on his part. The mind of the savage then appears to rock to and fro out of mere weakness.'

Boas produces an anecdote of his own:

I happen to know through personal contact the tribes mentioned by Sproat. The questions put by the traveller seem mostly trifling to the Indian, and he naturally soon tires of a conversation carried on in a foreign language, and one in which he finds nothing to interest him. As a matter of fact, the interest of these natives can easily be raised to a high pitch, and I have often been the one who was wearied out first. Neither does the management of their intricate system of exchange prove mental ineptness in matters which concern them. Without mnemonic aids to speak of, they plan the systematic distribution of their property in such a manner as to increase their wealth and social position. These plans require great foresight and constant application (Boas 1911 in Cole 1993, 194).

theoretical question of culture, class, and cognition, Vygotsky's own position was that any society that had attained the use of language was in essence developed to the 'civilised stage' and, accordingly, the adult in traditional (non-industrialised) society must not be considered as cognitively equivalent to the child in industrialised society.

According to Franz Boas (1911) (who himself carried out some observational studies with non-European cultures), some of the misconceptions about the mental abilities of people from non-European cultures were based on deeply flawed evidence, which was apparently supportive of evolutionary schemes (see the box on page 372).

## A broader view of culture and cognition

Culture is indeed a part of the environment that shapes cognition, but arguing that culture equals cognitive development as in the Spencerian view is rather simplistic, and contemporary theory gives a much broader view. In more recent years greater interaction between psychology, anthropology, and history has greatly enhanced the scope of the study of human development (Liddell *et al.* 1991). Consequently, human development is seen as a complex process that takes place in an ecosystem jointly structured by the physical environment and a cultural community with a socio-political history (Bronfenbrenner 1979; Serpell 1993). This means that the environmental forces that determine the child's behaviour or development are mediated by mental processes which come about through conscious interaction among the persons that constitute a social group; and this interaction is in turn mediated by that group's accumulated cultural stock and cognitive resources, their language, theories, and technology (Serpell 1993). Furthermore, in the case of non-European cultures such as African cultures, which have been subjected to evaluation and interpretation from a Euro-American perspective (Nsamenang 1992), any value the culture may potentially have is devalued. The Euro-American inclined theorist or researcher is prevented through bias from seeing any enhancing properties in the culture.

PHOTO: CHA JOHNSTON

*Many traditional African cultures have ceremonies which often involve masking of faces. In modern-day society this has become incorporated into fun events such as children's parties.*

Take for instance the traditional African practice of carrying the baby on the back (or indeed the front), closely secured to the mother's body by a long sash or blanket. This behaviour was generally frowned upon in the early days of colonialism and seen as 'primitive' and 'uncivilised'. More recently, however, psychological research has established some of the enhancing qualities of the close physical contact that comes about as a result of this practice, particularly with regard to infant sensory and motor development, as well as 'attachment' (Brazelton, Koslowski, and Tronick 1993). These findings would not be possible if researchers continued to maintain the early Western misconceptions about African parenting styles.

## Psychology in a multiracial society

We have established above how theories of human development have been influenced by, and have themselves influenced, notions about ethnicity and cultural differences. The world today is characterised by racial prejudice and tension, whether in South Africa (still dealing with the social and economic heritage of apartheid), or North America, Europe, and Australia, which otherwise claim to be egalitarian societies (Kasese-Hara 2000). Race and ethnicity, therefore, become central issues in theorising human development in the African context, and indeed in any context throughout the world where multiracial communities are to be found. In studying human development in African societies, the experience of colonisation and subsequent forms of socio-political oppression such as imperialism, neo-colonialism, and globalisation is important to consider. All of these conditions perpetuate the subordination of African cultural experience, as well as the subordination of socio-economic hierarchies that are based on socio-cultural experience and ethnicity. Similarly, the historical role of psychology in colonial and post-colonial Africa, which has been mainly to rationalise and perpetuate racial differences, must give way to approaches and perspectives that are less prone to bias (Seedat 1997; Nsamenang 1992).

## Human development: a West African conceptual framework

The search for culturally informed theories of developmental psychology reflects a growing awareness among theorists that their endeavours are situated in a cultural matrix (Serpell 1994). Nsamenang (1992) asserts that, due to psychology being an ethnocentric science cultivated mainly in Western Europe and North America, theories of psychology overwhelmingly reflect Western socio-cultural ethos as if the rest of the cultural world has nothing to offer the discipline. Firmly believing that the rest of the scientific world deserves to know how other cultural contexts – especially family environments – shape human development, Nsamenang (2000) laid out a conceptual framework of human development in

## Some examples of psychology used to impact negatively on blacks

Psychological theory was used to provide a scientific rationale for slavery in the early nineteenthth century. The rationale was based on the prevailing beliefs about Africans lacking in intelligence (Bulhan 1981). These arguments obviously, did not prevent the Anti-Slavery Act being passed in 1809.

The notion of racial differences on standardised IQ tests, which persisted through the early twentieth century, was later discredited by mainstream psychology as racist, only to resurface again in the 1990s, and has continued to be backed by psychological 'findings' (including Yerkers 1923; Jensen 1969; Herrnstein and Murray 1994). The findings that over time have helped support the notion that blacks are intellectually inferior to whites, and that the differences are likely to be genetically determined, have tended to be methodologically flawed and biased. For example, observations have been made that the so-called scientific studies done with black Americans were biased in ignoring the cultural, linguistic, and socio-economic status of samples from the black community. Moreover, scientists, though claiming to be impartial, intrinsically believed blacks to be intellectually inferior to whites and tried to rationalise away any evidence of superior black performance, such as performance on rote memory tasks, making rhymes, naming words, and in time orientation (Grubb 1986).

On the African continent psychological tests provided a basis upon which assessment for positions in colonial and apartheid administrations was based, mainly to ensure inferior positions for blacks and Africans in organisations and companies (Bulhan 1981). Here again, the notion that Africans were only fit for lower, technical, and manual positions, rather than higher managerial posts that involved greater mental capacity, continued to be reinforced through psychological tests which have tended to be developed on the basis of Western cultural norms.

According to Moosa et al. (1997), early psychological research in South Africa tended to focus on blacks simply as victims of overwhelming socio-economic and political forces which undermined their psychological functioning individually and collectively, thus oversimplifying the role of the individual (black person) in responding and confronting the dilemmas they faced. The past few decades have seen psychological literature that supports a much broader view of marginalisation. This view basically contends that, whereas marginalisation according to race, language, or culture may bring with it disadvantage in terms of access to resources and knowledge, it may equally have enhancing properties. Bilingualism, for example, which was traditionally seen as a 'handicap', is now considered rather as an opportunity for broader linguistic experience (Mohanty and Perregaux 1997).

African societies, with a focus on West African societies. The following are the main concepts of Nsamenang's model.

## Familial context

This is an important part of the child's social world. Because the family, the child, and the environment constantly interact, and therefore influence each other, the family context plays a determinant role in what is normal and what facilitates or hinders development. Thus children's search for meanings, competence, and the 'right way' of the world begins in the family, long before they go to school (Nsamenang 2000). In the African context, parental actions and regulatory behaviours are embedded in a familial ethos that extends beyond the parents to include siblings, relatives, and other mentors, especially peer mentors of the extended African family networks and neighbourhoods.

## World-view

*World-view* is a shared frame of reference or psychological outlook by which members of a particular culture perceive or make sense of the universe and the fate of the human in it. It is an integral part of the social representations through which a given culture makes sense of human existence. The indigenous West African world-view is marked by a set of social realities, cultural traditions, and existential imperatives. This world-view constitutes a different frame of reference from that which informs contemporary developmental psychology.

## Virtue-based versus rights-based social relationships

Social relationships and factors in cultural institutions such as the family (broadly defined) are the primary forces in forming and shaping the norms and values that regulate behaviour, and that set limits on the developing person. According to Nsamenang (2000), the relationships and competencies that sustain life and energise development in African cultures are *virtue-based* rather than *rights-based*. The individual's character is thus configured not through his or her private psychological characteristics and experiences, but through the community and through activities of a collective or social nature. Thus, in the West African community, the worth of the individual's motives and actions is judged on the basis of the common good, whereas in Western culture, the motives and actions of the individual are primary. Because seeing oneself as secondary to the *common good* is virtuous, cognition (which is otherwise a personal attribute) is deployed less for personal gain than to serve social purposes. Thus, the relationship between the individual and the collective is the key to understanding African behaviours.

## African participatory education

In traditional African society, education is linked directly to daily life, as training takes place through social acts (such as production) and social relationships (such as in family or peer groups). Nsamenang identifies three stages of African participatory learning: *observation*, *imitation*, and *creative action*. The child observes first before imitating, and then 'takes perspective and acts creatively, to exercise his or her trade or art' (Nsamenang 2000). Children are expected to observe, with little or no instruction, to think or build mental pictures by themselves, and to imitate or rehearse whatever they observed during their play activities.

The primary role of the parents and peer mentors (and the anticipated role of teachers) is:

1) to provide appropriate guidance to the children,
2) to communicate standards of valued behaviour and virtue, and
3) to provide an environment that enables children to participate and acquire the desired knowledge and skills.

Because participatory learning is socially designed to fit each child's emerging capacities and competencies, it helps the child gradually to discover his or her talents and limitations and to improve on them.

## The role of the peer group

Peer group activities in traditional African society help to bridge the gap between play and productive work. Nsamenang (2000, 5) describes the importance of such play as follows:

> ... in creating their own playthings or making miniature replicas of common objects from available materials (Bokombo 1981; Nsamenang and Lamb 1993), children learn how to plan work, to organise tools and materials, to measure, and to conceive of objects in multiple dimensions (Segall *et al.* 1999). These constructions express remarkable creativity and when recognised as 'products' boost children's self-esteem and nourish their mental growth. The onus to learn rests on the child, who is frequently reminded of and almost immediately experiences the consequences of failure to learn.

PHOTO: CHA JOHNSTON

*In African societies peer group activities blur the boundaries between play and productive work (Nsamenang 2000, 5).*

## Conclusion

In this chapter we have dealt with issues of race and culture and ways in which culture and ethnicity have influenced psychological theories of human development. More importantly, we have considered how developmental psychology may begin to deal with these issues in order to avoid bias and the drawing of erroneous conclusions. Such an endeavour will enhance the capacity for psychology as a social science that is concerned with peoples of various cultural, ethnic, and socio-economic backgrounds worldwide, and in particular in sub-Saharan Africa.

## Recommended readings

Bulmer, M. and Solomos, J. (eds) (2000). *Racism*. Oxford: Oxford University Press.

Moosa, F., Moonsamy, G., and Fridjon, P. (1997). 'Identification patterns among black students at a predominantly white university'. *South African journal of psychology,* 27 (4), 256–260.

Nsamenang. B. A. (1992). *Human development in cultural context: A third world perspective.* Newbury Park, CA: Sage.

Scribner, S. (1985). 'Vygotsky's uses of history'. In J. V. Wertsch (ed.), *Communication and cognition: A Vygotskian perspective.* Cambridge: Cambridge University Press.

Serpell, R. (1993). *The significance of schooling: Life-journeys in an African society.* Cambridge: Cambridge University Press.

## Critical thinking tasks

1) How different do you think psychology would be if it had been developed in a different culture and era, such as in Ancient China or in Shaka's Zulu empire?

2) Identify the common elements between Nsamenang's West African framework of human development and mainstream psychological theory, such as, for instance, Vygotsky's socio-historical approach.

# Theory and South African developmental psychology research and literature

*Catriona Macleod*

In this chapter we shall examine the theoretical assumptions that drive developmental psychology research and literature in South Africa.

The basic underlying models utilised in developmental research are presented here as follows:
◆ mechanistic
◆ organismic
◆ contextual
◆ social constructionist.

A description of the fundamental premises of each of these will be followed by examples of research that uses the particular approach. Some of the controversies that plague developmental psychology research will be included in the discussion.

## Introduction

The questions that form the basis for this chapter are:
◆ What are the theoretical frameworks utilised by South African researchers and authors in developmental psychology?
◆ How are these theories put to work to illuminate issues in people's lives in the South African context?
◆ What are some of the criticisms that could be levelled at the theories used?

These questions are important with regard to the dominance of Euro-American research in our textbooks and in many developmental psychology courses.

*A life-span approach to human development means that research on people in middle to late adulthood should be included in any review of developmental psychology.*

**Mechanistic.** A philosophical approach to studying humans that maintains that all phenomena may be understood in terms of cause and effect, and that basic universal laws may be established.

**Organismic.** Theoretical approaches that emphasise the need to approach people as a total entity with a multitude of interrelated processes.

It must be made clear from the outset, however, that this chapter is not intended as a comprehensive review of developmental psychology research and literature in South Africa, for two reasons. First, defining the boundaries of what counts as developmental psychology, and what does not, proves to be difficult. For example, collecting research on children only is not satisfactory, given the life-span developmental theories. Focusing on work that specifically studies individual development is also not adequate, given the emphasis on the meso-, exo- and chronosystems of Bronfenbrenner's (1979) approach. Asking the questions, 'Which studies concerning children, adolescents, adults, and the aged are relevant, and which not?' and 'Which studies on the family, the school, race, class, cultural issues, etc. are relevant and which not?' becomes a tedious, and perhaps not very useful task. Second, researchers in South Africa, contrary to popular belief, are relatively prolific. Collating and summarising all the research in developmental psychology exceeds our present scope. In this chapter, therefore, we shall take a broad view of the field in the decade following 1990, discussing the main theoretical trends, and illustrating each with examples of research or theoretical writing.

The structure for this chapter has been guided by Overton and Reese's distinction between **mechanistic** and **organismic** models of development (1973, cited in Widdershoven 1997) as well as by Lerner's (1986) and Widdershoven's (1997) extension of this to the **contextual** and **narrative** models respectively.

In 1973 Overton and Reese identified two basic metaphors or models that underlay theorising in developmental psychology at the time. What they meant by this is that all the theories of human development could be broadly divided into two categories in terms of their underlying philosophical assumptions about the nature of development and the nature of the developing person. These two categories they called *mechanistic* and *organismic*. (What is meant by each of these will be explained in more detail in the relevant sections below.) In response to further developments in the field, Lerner (1986) introduced a further category, the *contextual model*. At a later stage, Widdershoven (1997) discusses a *narrative* approach to developmental psychology. Although Widdershoven (1997) introduces an important new element to the broad understanding of the basic models underlying developmental theorising, his use of the word 'narrative' is perhaps less than inclusive. Narrative theory is just one approach among many that are broadly identified with the social constructionist movement in psychology. Thus, for the fourth model we shall propose a **social constructionist** model.

A number of controversies have plagued work in developmental psychology from its inception. These are usually posed in the form of dualisms: nature versus nurture; continuity versus discontinuity; universality versus relativism; activity versus passivity; risk versus resilience. The questions evolving from these controversies essentially are: To what extent is human development due to biological and hereditary forces or to environmental and social influences? Is human development an additive process that occurs gradually and continuously, or are there a series of abrupt changes in which the person is elevated to a new and more advanced level of functioning? To what extent do developmental sequences apply to all 'normal' people in all cultures, and to what extent do specific cultural or sub-cultural factors affect development? Are children active in determining the outcome of their development or are they passive recipients of environmental and genetic influences? Are all children exposed to difficult circumstances vulnerable or at risk of developing problems or do some cope well without being negatively affected? These controversies have been debated in the literature for some time now. Many times, however, a researcher may merely assume one or the other position. In this chapter we shall consider how some of these controversies have been taken up in the South African literature.

**Contextual.** An approach to the study of psychology that proposes that behaviour must be studied in relation to the context within which it occurs. Interpreting behaviour outside the context is misleading.

**Narrative theory.** Emphasises the central role of language and meaning creation in the formation and structuring of self, identity, and the other.

**Social constructionist.** Theoretical approaches that view knowledge, language, and the human personality as dynamically constructed and reconstructed through constant social interrelation and interaction. The role of language and narrative myth construction are prominent factors in this approach.

# Mechanistic approaches

In mechanistic approaches human development is seen as a collection of elements, each of which can be causally explained (much like the working of a machine). Events are seen as causally related to prior events, and under the same set of circumstances equal causes will have equal effects. Humans are seen as passive in that they develop as a result of outside influences. Development is continuous, with change happening

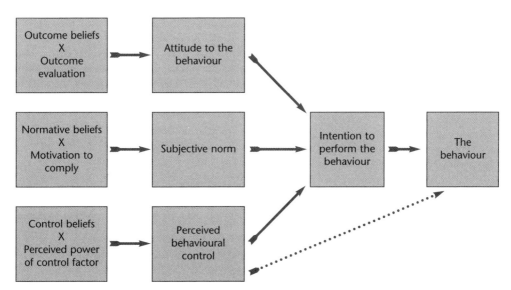

**Figure 21.1** Each box in the diagram represents a discrete and identifiable attribute, or the interaction of two attributes. The arrows indicate causal (one-way) relationships between these discrete elements (Morojele 1997, adapted from Ajzen and Madden 1986).

gradually as new elements (such as new behaviour patterns) are added or subtracted. Behaviourism, with its emphasis on learning theory, represents the most striking example of a mechanistic approach.

The mechanistic approach to developmental psychology seems not to be a popular one in South Africa, and exists only in isolated examples. This may have to do with the declining popularity of behaviourist approaches generally in psychology, as well as with an overall recognition within developmental psychology in South Africa that contextual issues need to be given a primary focus.

Morojele's (1997) discussion of adolescent use and abuse of alcohol provides an example of a mechanistic approach. He discusses Ajzen's theory of planned behaviour, which is based on a rational decision-making model of behaviour referred to as the theory of reasoned action. He modifies an illustrative diagram from Ajzen and Madden (1986, cited in Morojele 1997), which is reproduced in Figure 21.1 on page 381.

## Organismic approaches

In organismic approaches the processes of human development are viewed as an organised whole. In other words, development is seen as a totality rather than as a collection of parts. Instead of causal explanations, theorising centres on the final goal or the function of development (much like the systems of a living organism). The principles of **epigenesis** and **equifinality** apply. Epigenesis refers to the irreducibility of later forms from earlier ones. In other words, new characteristics emerge at higher levels, making development discontinuous in nature. Equifinality means that goals may be reached along different lines. In other words, although tendencies may be described, predictions may not be made (compare this to the mechanistic model). Organismic models see the individual as active in the process of development, with change occurring because of the unfolding of internal forces. Examples of theories fitting into the organismic model are Freud's psychoanalytic theory of development and Piaget's cognitive developmental theory. In each it is assumed that, given reasonably optimal conditions, human beings will progress through invariant and discontinuous stages of development as directed by forces lying within them.

Turning to South African research, Broom and Doctor's analysis of children's reading difficulties illustrates some of the central premises of the organismic approach. They assert that, 'When children are learning to read, competence at one developmental stage depends on transmission of information from a previous stage, so impaired development of a previous stage will affect development of subsequent skills' (Broom and Doctor 1994, 219). Development thus proceeds through the unfolding of a series of **invariant stages**. Each stage requires the mastery of particular skills (such as emotional, cognitive, or social). Failure to do so has implications for development at a later stage. This type of stage theorising has certain implications. The first is that it allows for the development of tools to measure the appropriateness of a particular individual's development as calibrated against the **norms** of others in the same developmen-

**Epigenesis.** The emergence during development of new characteristics at various stages, making development discontinuous in nature.

**Equifinality.** The notion that goals may be reached along different lines.

**Invariant stages.** Developmental stages that follow one another. People progress through the stages in predictable order (stages are not skipped).

**Norms.** Statistically speaking, any measure of central tendency that is representative of a group and which may be used as a basis for comparison of individual cases.

PHOTOS: CATRIONA MACLEOD

tal stage. Thus, for example, Broom and Doctor (1994, 219) state that 'a battery of psycholinguistic tests appropriate for English-speaking South African children was devised to identify the preceding [reading] strategies which a child has and has not acquired'. The second implication, linked to the first, is that it allows for particular children to be categorised as developmentally delayed, thereby necessitating intervention programmes. Broom and Doctor (1994), for example, recommend in cases of developmental dyslexia (as assessed by the above-mentioned tests) an intervention programme aimed at the development of orthographic reading skills.

*Organismic approaches assume that people progress through invariant stages of development. Environmental factors (such as school or home) merely enhance or impede the progression.*

The problem with organismic models is that, because of the emphasis on internal factors, researchers may ignore the political, social, gendered, and cultural context within which development is taking place. An example of this is research by Ackerman (1990), who uses refinements of Erikson's psychosocial stage theory in his research with white Afrikaans-speaking secondary school adolescents in a semi-urban area. Erikson proposed that the central developmental crisis facing adolescents is the attainment of identity versus role confusion. He initially emphasised occupational identity issues and ideology as central concerns in identity development. Various researchers added further domains in later research. Ackerman (1990) assesses the relative importance of thirteen of these domains (including, for example, life goals and ideals, gender role, choice of dating partner, etc.) for the participants in his research. All thirteen domains were found to be important, but with some sex and age differences in six of the domains. However, there is no discussion in the paper of gender or cultural issues, nor is there acknowledgement that the thirteen domains referred to may be rooted in particular gendered and cultural understandings of what it is to be human.

This type of de-contextualisation is not necessarily a feature of research that utilises organismic frames. For instance, in the section under contextual theories and research we shall discuss a paper by Gibson (1993) who integrates a psychoanalytic framework (usually associated with organismic models) and a contextual approach concerning violence.

Another example of organismic research that takes context into account is the paper by Tudin, Straker, and Mendolsohn (1994). They investigate the relationship between Kohlberg's stages of moral development and exposure to political and social complexity amongst a group of South African university students. Thus, although they accept Kohlberg's assertion that there are universal principles that guide moral reasoning and that there are basic, invariant developmental stages in moral reasoning, their research revolves around the influence of social context on the development of this moral reasoning.

# Contextual theories and research

In these approaches human development is theorised in relation to or in transaction with the environment or context. Thus, development is seen as a dynamic interplay between person and environment. These models allow for 'both/and' rather than 'either/or' thinking. For example, the individual can be seen as both active in his or her developmental processes, as well as being influenced by the environment. How well theories manage to explain the 'both/and' of various developmental controversies differs, however, as we shall see later with the individual versus society debate. In contextual models, the embedded quality of various systems (the family, the school, ideological frameworks, etc.) is emphasised, with change at one level promoting change at another level.

It appears that a contextual approach is currently the most popular in developmental psychology research in South Africa. Speculations as to why this should be the case could include: 1) the particular social and political circumstances in South Africa, and 2) the self-inspection that psychology in South Africa underwent in terms of its contextual relevance in the mid to late 1980s (see, for example, Dawes (1986) and Gilbert (1989) amongst others).

We shall now discuss various approaches that fall under the broad banner of contextual models. The first is a **positivist** approach. In many respects positivism may be classed as mechanistic as it isolates various elements and explores the relationship between them. Nevertheless, all the research discussed here has one key feature, and that is a commitment to understanding the influence of contextual issues on children's responses. The other approaches discussed include a developmental-contextual approach, cultural psychology, a public health perspective, and a political approach.

## Positivist approaches

Much research in South Africa that attempts to understand the relation between individual children and the environment is premised on positivist principles. In positivism relevant **variables** are identified and **operationalised**, controls are set up to obviate the influence of **extraneous variables**, quantitative data is collected, and statistical tests of **probability** are run. In this way it is hoped to gain insight into the influence of the environment on the child. Importantly, though, the child and the social

---

**Positivist.** An approach to science that argues that it is not possible to go beyond the objective world, and that only those questions that can be answered from the application of scientific method are valid.

**Variables.** Properties that change or vary over time or between particular categories of people.

**Operationalise.** To give definition to variables and procedures utilised in research.

**Extraneous variables.** Variables that interfere with (that are not central to) the main relationships being studied.

**Probability.** The calculation of the likelihood of an event occurring using proportional frequency.

context are treated as two distinct realities that are **ontologically** separate while they also affect each other (Dawes and Donald 1994).

One of the aims of positivism is to build up a cumulative knowledge base that is objective and based on universal truths. A key concept here is **generalisability**, which means that results in one situation will hold true in another. Barbarin and Richter (2001), for example, test the cross-national generalisability of the relationship between community violence, poverty, and psychological difficulties in children. They find that, as in the United States, community danger in South Africa is linked to a variety of psychological problems, including anxiety, depression, aggression, opposition, and low affability in children, but that socio-economic status is not related to behavioural and emotional adjustment.

Positivist research allows for comparative work. This is different to the notion of generalisability discussed above. Comparative research is not interested in establishing universal laws or truths, but rather with providing an in-depth description of two groups identified as different in some ways and as similar in others. A good example of this is Liddell's research on the interpretations of six pictures by eighty South African and eighty British children in their second and third year of schooling. Liddell (1996) starts her paper by exploring how pictures may: 1) provide a bridge into literacy for children, 2) enrich the meaning of texts, 3) provide contextual information in text, and 4) assist children in retaining information. She reviews the literature from developed countries in which it is shown that children follow a predictable developmental sequence in their picture interpretation skills. But then she asks the question whether the same patterns 'manifest themselves in children from homes where literacy skills amongst parents are poorly developed, where picture books do not exist, where teacher-child ratios mean that one teacher assists forty to fifty children in the classroom, and where children at school are exposed to – at most – four illustrated readers in a year' (Liddell 1996, 356). This question is important as it provides the framework within which the comparative research is located. Too often with comparative research the implication is that differences noted are owing to some intrinsic characteristics of the groups compared. Here Liddell (1996) invokes structural-contextual issues, not to explain the differences, but to frame her question. Her results show differences in the way rural South African and rural British children interpret pictures, as well as different patterns of change as the two groups progress in school. She discusses this in the light of the possible different functions of literacy in the two communities.

One of the greatest achievements of positivist research is the development of statistical models that allow for prediction. Liddell, Lycett, and Gordon (1997) utilise such a model to predict children's early school achievement in rural South African schools. They found that if children master basic elements of the curriculum and behave in ways that allow them to survive crowded and under-resourced rural classrooms, they will do well in Grade Two. They admit, however, that some of the variables used in predicting success are not quick or cheap to measure, thereby putting into question the usefulness of utilising this type of research in widespread programmes.

**Ontology.** Metaphysical inquiry concerned with the question of existence.

**Generalisability.** Where a factor can be judged as applicable to an entire class or category of people, events, or phenomena.

One of the potential difficulties with positivist research is that researchers enter into too little critical analysis of how terms are operationalised. For example, Cherian and Malehase investigate the relationship between parental control and children's scholastic achievement. They state that an 'objective estimate' of parental control was obtained via a questionnaire. The questionnaire items, we are informed, measured 'parental order and control of children, parental supervision of daily activities of children, parental involvement in proper control and supervision of school tasks, parental time spent on children's school work, and parental communication with their children' (Cherian and Malehase 2000, 666). The actual items of the questionnaire are not provided so we are not able to judge exactly what questions elicited responses in these various areas. Nevertheless, there is no indication that the choice of words such as 'proper control and supervision', 'parental order', and 'parental involvement' is political, and implies the valuing of particular parental activities over others. Instead these practices take on the aspect of naturalness – correct and good parental actions. This point is taken up by Rose (1989), who points out that scientific and professional descriptions of good parental practices gain their power by appearing to be universally valid and natural. In a similar paper, Cherian and Cherian (1997) examine the relationship between what they call 'parental interest and life status' and the academic achievement of their children. In order to measure the latter they utilise the aggregate of marks awarded to their participants in seven subject areas in the Grade Nine examinations. Again there is no problematisation of these tests in such areas, perhaps, as measuring convergent thinking only, or promoting education as domestication (some of the several critiques that could be made about educational processes in South Africa). Instead they are seen as unproblematic calibrations of academic achievement.

## Developmental-contextual perspectives

Developmental-contextual approaches take an overtly 'both/and' perspective. In other words, researchers attempt to include both individual and social factors into their theorising, rather than one or the other. For example, in his discussion on special educational needs, Donald (1994, 151) calls for 'ecologically sensitive research that clarifies the interactional relationship between various disabilities and their socially and structurally determined contexts'.

Stead (1996) utilises a developmental-contextual model to analyse career development in black adolescents in South Africa. This perspective emphasises the dynamic interaction between an individual and his or her proximal (such as family or peer group) and distal (such as economic or socio-cultural) contexts. He discusses career development in black adolescents in relation to education, the family, the economy, culture, and identity development. Stead (1996) states that the developmental-contextual approach 'overcomes (a) an inordinate focus on either the individual or the individual's environment and (b) an emphasis on a unidirectional relationship between the self and context'. However, his analysis does not make it clear how this is done. Indeed, his discussion devolves on either

PHOTOS: CATRIONA MACLEOD

the environment (the family, education, etc.) or the individual (identity development) without theorising exactly *how* one relates to the other. Merely saying that individual development is influenced by context is insufficient. This point is important, because theorising precisely what the interrelationship is between the individual and society is one of the crucial aspects of a contextual approach. It is on this level that we may start to differentiate between adequate and inadequate contextual (and other) analyses of development.

Gibson (1993) raises this issue in her article on the influence of violence on children. She argues that questions should be asked 'within a psychological theory which can explain the complexity of the relationship between an external event and an individual's response' (Gibson 1993,167). In her article, she discusses the question of whether violence begets violence, critiquing approaches that posit a linear causal relationship between external events and violent behaviour, as well as interactionist approaches that merely add additional internal and external variables to the equation. Neither of these approaches answers the fundamental question of 'How is it possible that violence may arise out of violence?' Answering this question requires a perspective that theorises the complex interrelationship between the **intra-psychic** world and social factors. She invokes the psychoanalytic concept of traumata or 'facts' that interconnect the psychological state of the subject, social circumstances, and psychic conflict, and she utilises a combination of Freudian and Kleinian theory in an attempt to answer the above question ('how it is possible that violence may arise out of violence?'). A paper by Len Bloom (1996), entitled 'The emotional damage of apartheid: A psycho-analytic view', attempts a similar project, though it focuses more on the psychological effects of apartheid: 'a social system that demeaned and diminished adults and children' (Bloom 1996, 55). What is interesting here is how both authors have utilised a theory usually associated with an organismic approach and harnessed it to provide interesting theoretical insights into the transaction between the individual and the social context.

*Contextual approaches theorise the interaction or transaction between individual development and context. Consider the similarities and differences between the developmental contexts depicted in these photographs (commercial farming in a former 'white' area of South Africa, right, and a rural village in a former 'homeland', left).*

**Intra-psychic.** Of elements that are assumed to arise or take place within the mind (a psychoanalytic term).

**Cohort.** A number of people possessing common characteristics, especially being born in a particular year.

Another important aspect in contextual theorising is the acknowledgement of historical effects. Finchilescu and Dawes' (1998) paper on South African adolescents' socio-political orientations following the rapid social change of the early to mid-1990s is an excellent example of the importance of taking **cohort** effects into account. Their work was partially informed by a generational approach to the study of the influence of political context on human development. From a generational perspective, particular generational groups will share a political consciousness, which is shaped by exposure to particular events occurring during the sensitive developmental period of youth. Thus, Finchilescu and Dawes (1998) talk of the Resistance cohort, the Negotiation cohort, and the Democracy cohort, referring to people who entered adolescence prior to 1990, during the time of the political negotiations, and after the elections of 1994 respectively. Each of these generational cohorts contains sub-generational units based on the racial groups defined by apartheid. This approach clearly links contextual issues to historical effects, effects that are obviously more clearly seen in times of rapid change, but which should always feature in our thinking about developmental psychology.

## Cultural approaches

**Cross-cultural research.** An experimental method in which different cultures are evaluated and compared on different cultural dimensions.

That there are diverse cultures in South Africa is probably a truism that few people would dispute. This is reflected in developmental psychology research where culture features relatively strongly. However, the way in which culture is conceptualised and the uses to which it is put differ markedly. In the first place, there is **cross-cultural research** in which culture is viewed as a variable that can be separated from other variables, and that can be used in explanation of observed differences or similarities. Second, 'culture' is used as a broadly defining, static, and overarching feature of human existence. Third, there are those studies that locate themselves within the *cultural psychology* tradition. Cultural psychology employs a dynamic conceptualisation of culture as social practices and traditions that permeate, transform, and regulate human behaviour. Cultural psychology thus studies the meaning of the cultural worlds we inhabit, their historicity, and the interpersonal maintenance of the practices on which they are premised.

An example of cross-cultural research is the paper by Akande (1999) entitled 'Intercultural and cross-cultural assessment of self-esteem among youth in twenty-first century South Africa'. He hypothesises that perceptions of the self differ from one cultural context to another. Therefore, using culture as the variable, he compares the means obtained on the 'Self-Description-Questionnaire-1' by South African, Australian, Zimbabwean, Kenyan, Nigerian, and Nepalese children. Liddell, Kvalsig, Shabalala, and Qotyana (1994) are critical, however, of studies that assume that 'cultures' represent distinct and homogeneous units that can meaningfully be measured. While maintaining a positivist focus, these authors believe that a range of ecocultural factors should be investigated simultaneously. This, they assert, will allow for the most salient aspects of culture to be discerned. In their study they compare the predictive validity, with regard to children's behaviour, of three 'cultural descriptors' (ethnicity, degree of urbanicity, and individual community) in conjunction with factors pertaining to the child's household (socio-economic status, household size, and reliance on subsistence agriculture). They conclude that, taken as a whole, the model predicted significant amounts of variance in children's behaviour, but that some factors such as crowding, socio-economic status, and ethnicity are less powerful in predicting children's behaviour.

The second sense in which culture is used is as a static and **essentialist** feature of human existence. This approach is evidenced in Stead's discussion of career development in black adolescents. In this article, Stead (1996) seems to see culture as a possession – something that describes or identifies groups of people in a definitive sense. Note the following passage:

> Whites are generally considered to identify with a Western lifestyle that emphasizes independence, individuality, self-actualization, and competitiveness. In this respect they tend to differ from Blacks, who follow a traditional African lifestyle that emphasizes cooperation; Blacks tend to be community oriented and be dependent on the wishes of significant others when making decisions (Stead 1996, 272).

Thus, 'whites' equal 'Western' and 'blacks' equal 'traditional', with all the attendant characteristics. The use of the qualifying words 'generally' and 'tend' does not detract from this equation, as there is no indication of any of these cultural characteristics as dynamic and fluid.

It is this static and essentialist view of culture that cultural psychology has attempted to counter, while still maintaining the explanatory power that may be gained by considering cultural issues in developmental psychology. Gilbert, Van Vlaenderen, and Nkwinti (1995), for example, locate their research within cultural psychology. They study the role of local knowledge in the process of socialisation in rural families. They define local knowledge as 'the presuppositions used to interpret immediate experience borne out of action in the local environment' (Gilbert *et al.*1995, 229). This conceptualisation illustrates the dynamic nature of a cultural psychology perspective, in that local knowledge is a product of day-to-day actions and hence is constantly being constructed and re-constructed while still having a historicity. This makes a significant contrast to the notion of 'traditional knowledge', which has the connotations of stasis and preservation. The theorising of socialisation as a dynamic process allows for a dialectical understanding of the 'active versus passive' debate. Gilbert, Van Vlaenderen, and Nkwinti (1995) indicate that socialisation is both a conservative and a creative process. They utilise a combination of the Vygotskian *zone of proximal development* (the space between what a child can do on its own and what it can do with the help of a more knowledgeable member of the culture) and Geertz's view of culture as a set of control mechanisms used for governing behaviour. In other words, culture simultaneously structures children's lives so that they internalise the available cultural rules and instructions *and* allows the space for children to construct their own meaning.

Issues of universality and relativism tend to be raised when 'culture' is invoked. Magwaza (1997) provides an interesting summary of this

**Essentialist.** Viewing phenomena (such as culture) as having an absolute reality, existence, or essence.

dilemma in her discussion of child sexual abuse. She presents Schechter and Roberge's definition of sexual abuse as 'the involvement of dependent, developmentally immature children and adolescents in sexual activities they do not fully comprehend and to which they are unable to give informed consent, and which violate the social taboos of family roles' (1976, cited in Magwaza 1997, 161). But then she asks whether this definition does not raise questions from a cultural perspective. For example, at what stage can a person be judged to be sufficiently competent to consent to a sexual relationship? Magwaza (1997) believes that many African post-pubertal children may lack essential knowledge of sexual activities and their consequences. She thus calls for an acknowledgement of cultural diversity in our attempt to understand sexuality across societies and cultures. However, she tempers this with an appeal to 'universal standards of sexuality' (Magwaza 1997, 162). Exactly what these universal standards are is not spelt out. What is important to note, however, is how Magwaza (1997) attempts to integrate a cultural relativist perspective (recognising and theorising about difference) while at the same time maintaining moral universalism (the view that there are particular benchmarks against which we can judge particular actions, such as sexual abuse, as reprehensible).

Dawes and Donald (1994), in their discussion of the 'universalism versus relativism' issue, observe that some of the difficulties in this debate stem from the essentialist views of culture that are used in psychological theorising. They suggest making a distinction between developmental processes that could be shown to have universal relevance, and the content and norms of behaviour that may be culturally specific. Drawing the boundaries around each of the distinctions proposed by Magwaza (1997) and Dawes and Donald (1994), and making decisions about what practices fit into what category, appears to be a difficult but necessary endeavour in developmental psychology.

## Public health approach

Most Euro-American textbooks of developmental psychology assume a certain basic level of health and hygiene in children. For example, in a recent textbook on child development (in its ninth edition), thirty-six pages are devoted to 'physical development in childhood and puberty' (Santrock 2001). Only two of these pages discuss illness and health in children, and this is divided into sections on the illness and health of children in the United States and those in the rest of the world. The health concerns listed in the former section include exposure to parental tobacco smoke, birth defects, cancer, and heart disease. In the latter section diarrhoea, acute respiratory diseases, under-nutrition, the timing of births, and hygiene are mentioned. The health issues that face North American children and that affect development are very different to those facing the majority of children in South Africa.

In contrast with the tendency described above, there is a strong public health focus in many South African writers' work in developmental psychology. This acknowledges the fact that general health issues and children's development are strongly interconnected. The focus on public health shifts the definition of health away, first from an individual focus, and second, from something attended to by medical practitioners in clinics and hospitals. Instead, public health 'targets all points where matter, energy, and information are exchanged between people and their human, social, and physical environments, for it is through this exchange that individual and group health status is determined' (Butchart and Kruger 2001, 215). Duncan (1997), for example, illustrates how the causes of malnutrition, a condition linked to poor developmental outcomes, cannot be located in individuals' shortcomings (such as parental ignorance concerning nutrition), but rather in broader social processes. Combating malnutrition will, according to Duncan (1997), require broad-ranging interventions, including employment generation programmes and projects aimed at making diversified nutrition and basic health facilities available to all. Richter and Griesel (1994), in a thorough review of malnutrition research, strongly criticise simplistic comparisons of low birth weight and malnourished children with control groups. They propose a transactional model of malnutrition that includes a variety of factors that operate in environments of poverty, including fragmented family life, unstable and disrupted child care practices, high levels of life stress, social isolation, and infant vulnerabilities (such as temperament, illness, sex), etc.

Much of the public health debate is framed within the human rights discourse. Authors draw on documents such as the United Nations Declaration of Children's Rights (Duncan 1997), and the World Health Organisation and South African Government documents on disability rights (Van Niekerk 1997). Strong arguments are made for the recognition of the rights and aspirations of groups marginalised by developmental psychology and government policy decisions, such as mentally handicapped children (Parekh and Jackson 1997).

The 'risk versus resilience' debate has mostly been framed within a public health discourse. Initially, in the spirit of prevention (a fundamental aim of primary health care), factors that put children at risk of the development of particular problems were analysed. The rationale was that if we could identify these factors, then we could perhaps do something to prevent them. This approach was questioned in the mid-1980s (Rutter 1985) and the idea of resilience in the face of adversity became popular. The key reasoning here is that some children, despite difficult circumstances, manage to cope well and do not develop any problems. A host of research was initiated, which studied the protective factors and the coping strategies that assisted in making children resilient. The resilience thesis gained a fair amount of credence in South Africa in the light of the poor socio-economic conditions and the political violence that characterises many South African children's young lives. Instead of seeing children as victims of their circumstances (at risk of developing a range of psychosocial and physical disorders), the resilience hypothesis allowed researchers to emphasise positive aspects of children's environments as well as the children's agency in developing coping mechanisms. The issue of resilience has been revisited by some researchers, however, because, as Duncan (1997) points out, the resilience argument has one serious defect: that it could lead to complacency on the part of those in power in ensuring conditions that promote the optimal development of children. An article that treads the middle path in the risk and resilience debate, indicating the relative contribution of both, is one by Donald and Swart-Kruger (1994) in which they discuss street children. They find, on the one hand, evidence of developmental risk and vulnerability, and on the other hand, resourcefulness, adaptability, and coping.

## Political issues

**Social accountability.**
Responsibility to society
for consequences arising
out of research actions.

Liddell and Kvalsig (1990) examine the issue of **social accountability** in developmental psychology in South Africa. They ask first whether developmental psychology can claim to be neutral in the research that it conducts, and second, whether our research has no impact in the real world. Their analysis reveals a number of practices in South African developmental psychology that militates against it being proclaimed a neutral discipline:

> Failure to become involved in lobbying procedures for issues which research has revealed as being urgently in need of strategies of intervention, ethnically biased attribution of causal factors in dealing with factors such as underachievement, failure to provide a balanced image of both areas of competence and failure in black South African children, and the under-representation of children from black communities in published research (Liddell and Kvalsig 1990, 5).

In answer to the second question, they state that there is evidence that South African developmental psychology is used and, at times, abused in the real world. It is not clear whether all their conclusions still stand eleven years later, and a further analysis of the kind undertaken by Liddell and Kvalsig is probably due. Nevertheless, their central points remain valid: that scientific neutrality is not an option for South African developmental psychology, and that developmental psychologists (among other people) are socially accountable for children's psychological well-being and for children's image in society. They argue that developmental psychologists need to engage with government in ensuring maximum benefits for children.

The paper by Stevens and Lockhat (1997) is an example that deals directly with the effects on development of socio-political issues in South Africa. Whether this paper meets the criteria for social accountability as outlined by Liddell and Kvalsig (1990) is a matter of debate. As we shall see, the authors' attempt to integrate diverse theoretical approaches seems to lead them into both a theoretical dead end, and a position that prompts the pathologisation of black adolescents.

Stevens and Lockhat (1997) argue that a combination of Erikson's psychosocial theory of adolescent development and Bulhan's analysis of identity development within oppressed social groups may be used to analyse the impact of apartheid-capitalism as well as post-apartheid politics on black adolescent identity development. In addition, they invoke at times a post-structuralist understanding of subjectivity as 'dynamic, adaptive and dialectical' (1997, 252), but then contradict themselves by uncritically assuming 'healthy levels of identity congruence' (1997, 250). Exactly what constitutes this healthy identity is not made clear. What is clear, however, is that the authors see black adolescents as having few 'healthy options' (1997, 253) for identity development, owing to a combination of apartheid-capitalism and what they call the dominance of Western ideologies in post-apartheid South Africa. Their conclusion rests on an uncritical usage of Erikson's theory. For example, they indicate that Erikson's concept of adolescence as a *psychosocial moratorium* does not apply to the majority of black adolescents. (Erikson's term refers to a period in which society allows adolescents to experiment with various identities). Furthermore, in choosing between capitulation and assimilation into the dominant (white) culture on the one hand, and radicalisation on the other, the authors see black adolescents as experiencing what Erikson called *identity foreclosure*.

The authors do not problematise the theoretical concepts of psychosocial moratorium and identity foreclosure as linked to particular socio-historical circumstances. Instead they accept the legitimacy of these concepts and utilise them to suggest that there are 'potentially negative psychological consequences' (1997, 252) and a 'long-term impact' (1997, 253) associated with the lack of a psychosocial moratorium and with identity foreclosure. The net result is the (probably unintended) pathologisation of black adolescents. Aware of this potential, the authors spend some time discussing the debate on 'risk versus resilience' in South Africa, stating that adolescents should not merely be seen as victims. Their own theorising allows for little more, however, and merely asserting resilience does not compensate for this.

This article has been analysed in some detail because it illustrates the importance of careful theoretical work in analyses that attempt to integrate socio-political issues into our thinking on development.

## Social constructionist analyses

Social constructionism is a fairly diverse field and is not easily summarised in a few short sentences. Nevertheless, there are some basic commonalities. Burr (1995) summarises some of the basic premises as follows:

◆ A critical stance is taken regarding taken-for-granted knowledge. Social constructionists question the assumptions made in psychology and indicate how these are frequently used to serve particular dominant interests.

◆ There is an emphasis on the social and historical specificity of human characteristics and interactions. This links up with the above point as it highlights that there is nothing fundamental or necessary in the way that we view things, but rather that our knowledge of the world is socially and historically constructed.

◆ Knowledge is viewed as constructed in interactions between people. Social action and knowledge are intricately linked.

PHOTO: CATRIONA MACLEOD

*Social constructionists question the taken-for-granted assumptions of developmental psychology, such as the assumption that mothers are necessarily the primary caregivers of infants.*

◆ Binary logic (male/female, active/passive, nature/nurture, etc.) is rejected and a focus on multiple layers of difference employed.

Social constructionist work contributes in two ways to the critique of mainstream developmental psychology. In the first place, the basic assumptions underlying theorising and research in developmental psychology itself are questioned. Second, the nature of the child, the adolescent, the mother, and the family as (mostly) spoken about in developmental psychology is called into question.

Examples of the first contribution are to be found in Bozalek (1997), Parekh and Jackson (1997), Shefer (1997), and Levett (1994). Bozalek (1997) locates the origin of developmental psychology in Western Europe and North America during the rise of industrial capitalism. As such, developmental psychology has been based on research that 'normalised and universalised white, middle-class, heterosexual values and experiences' (Bozalek 1997, 7). She indicates how developmental psychology has been used to inform many social practices relating to health, psychology, education, and welfare, but in disparate ways depending on the race of the child. Parekh and Jackson (1997, 41) argue that 'children with mental handicap are subjected to, constrained and marginalised by psychological developmentalist talk'. They question the assumption that mental handicap means the same thing for one group as for another, and they question the prioritisation of the cognitive and intellectual as hallmarks of childhood development. Shefer (1997) observes how developmental psychology's approach to gender ignores the social, historical, and political context of gendered identity development and presents development from a male perspective. She uses a social constructionist perspective to analyse the ways that gender (as a social construction) has an impact on our development from the moment we are identified as male or female. Levett (1994) criticises research on child sexual abuse for glossing over issues connected to the social construction of male sexuality, gendered identity, and patriarchal power.

Bozalek (1997) provides an example of the second contribution – questioning developmental psychology's underlying assumptions in theory and research. She shows how textbooks assume a particular family form (the nuclear family with two heterosexual parents) as universal, an assumption that she highlights as erroneous given the lived realities of many South African children and adolescents. Furthermore, the *functional systems* perspective of families that dominates textbooks disregards power relations that exist within families. This allows for wife and child abuse to be seen as symptoms of family pathology rather than as part of differential power relations based on discourses surrounding gender and child relations within the family.

Social constructionism is not just about critique, however. An increasingly popular social constructionist approach in areas such as therapy is *narrative theory*. Narrative psychology emphasises the central role of language and the creation of meaning in the formation and structuring of self, identity, and the other (Crossley 2000). Laubscher and Klinger (1997) utilise a narrative approach to explain the development of self-definition or what is more commonly called 'personality'. They contend that 'all people are story-tellers and create a particular story about themselves that defines who they are, that captures their essential and evolving self' (1997, 67). They explore how the personal myth begins in infancy when infants learn about narrative tone – the *qualitative* mood or feeling of stories. This tone may permeate the entire life cycle. Through the use of narrative tone, imagery, theme, mythic characters, and the contextual ideological setting, we create and re-create our self-defining myth. Laubscher and Klinger (1997) claim that a narrative approach to development simultaneously acknowledges individuality and social factors, thereby overcoming the individual/society divide characteristic of more traditional theories.

Mkhize and Frizelle (2000) utilise a narrative approach to explicate cultural and historical issues in career development work. They argue that every culture develops an indigenous psychology, which they define as the shared understanding of what it means to be human. The primary vehicles of this indigenous psychology, they argue, are narrative or cultural tales, passed on from generation to generation through language, myths, fairy tales, histories, and stories. To develop into a competent member of a society requires developing an appreciation for and knowledge of the multiple and complex range of meanings developed by that society over time. This does not imply narrative determinism, as individuals enter into dialogue with the multiplicity of voices and perspectives available in context.

Another key feature of a social constructionist approach is the theorising of subjectivity or identity as multiple rather than unitary. Dawes (1994) utilises this feature in his discussion of the emotional impact of political violence on children. He notes that children's psychological trauma is not analogous to physical trauma; a one-to-one correspondence between trauma and reaction cannot be made. Dawes (1994) postulates that children subjected to political violence 'potentially occupy a range of frequently contradictory positions, as they respond with their own history of internalisations of invested subjectivities which have developed in the context of their learning of social codes and significations of events' (1994, 192). Thus children may move between their traumatised and other selves, displaying frightened, dependent behaviour in one instance, and brave, independent behaviour in another.

## Conclusion

It is clear that a range of theoretical approaches and models have informed developmental psychology research in South Africa. Resulting from this there has been disagreement between researchers regarding what constitutes adequate theorising in this field. For example, Bloom (1996) takes Dawes (1994) to task for his interpretation of the contribution that psychoanalytic theory can make.

Two central questions are: Why is it important to take stock of our theoretical orientations? And why is it vital that a forum for the discussion of theory in developmental psychology remains open when there are clearly pressing issues facing children and adolescents (as well as parents, adults, and the elderly) in South Africa?

We hope that the answers to these are at least partially provided in this chapter. To summarise, the basic philosophical and theoretical assumptions that we make have implications in terms of 1) how we view the nature of the developing person; 2) what factors we consider in our research and how we conceptualise their linkages; 3) the questions we ask in conducting our research; 4) how we undertake our research; 5) the usages we envisage for our research; and finally 6) how interventions proceed in the lives of children, adolescents, and parents. This latter point is made very strongly in a book edited by Donald, Dawes, and Louw (2000), in which they discuss various community-based programmes that have attempted to address adversity in children's lives.

*(Acknowledgements: Thank you to Desmond Painter for reading and commenting on an earlier draft of this chapter.)*

## Recommended readings

*There are three excellent South African books of relevance to developmental psychology. The first two provide reviews of research done in a variety of areas relating to developmental psychology, while the third addresses interventions with children.*

Dawes, A. and Donald, D. (eds) (1994). *Childhood and adversity: Psychological perspectives from South African research*. Cape Town: David Philip.

De la Rey, C., Duncan, N., Shefer, T., and Van Niekerk, A. (eds) (1997). *Contemporary issues in human development: A South African focus*. Johannesburg: Thomson.

Donald, D., Dawes, A., and Louw, J. (eds) (2000). *Addressing childhood adversity*. Cape Town: David Philip.

## Critical thinking tasks

1) Which of the above-mentioned models provides the most promising approach to studying developmental psychology in South Africa? By what criteria would you decide this?

2) Do you think that South African developmental psychologists should take an overtly political stance in their work, or do you think that there is a place for scientific neutrality and objectivity? Is there a middle ground? Do you think there is a way of integrating the two stances, and if so, how?

3) Do you think that 'culture' should be included in our thinking about developmental psychology? If so, how should it be conceptualised?

4) Imagine yourself as a researcher in developmental psychology in South Africa. What would your research priorities be? What sort of approach would you want to take in investigating the issues? What do you think should be done with the results of your research (that is, how should they be utilised)?

# References

## A

Abraham, K. (1927). 'The influence of oral eroticism on character formation'. In K. Abraham (ed.), *Selected papers on psychoanalysis*. London: Hogarth Press.

Ackerman, C. J. (1990). 'Identiteitsontwikkeling tydens adolessensie: 'n Groep sekondêre skoolleerlinge se evaluering van die belangrikheid van lewensterreine'. *South African journal of education*, 10, (4), 283–290.

Adler, G. (1967). 'Methods of treatment in analytic psychology'. In B. Wolman (ed.), *Psychoanalytic technique*. New York: Basic Books.

Ainsworth, M. D. S. (1972). 'Attachment and dependency: A comparison'. In J. L. Gerwitz (ed.), *Attachment and dependency*. Washington, DC: V. H. Winston.

Ainsworth, M. D. S., Blehar, M. C., Waters, E., and Wall, S. (1978). *Patterns of attachment: A psychological study of the strange situation*. New Jersey: Erlbaum.

Akande, A. (1999). 'Intercultural and cross-cultural assessment of self-esteem among youth in twenty-first century South Africa'. *International journal for the advancement of counselling*, 21 (3), 171–187.

Althusser, L. (1971). *Lenin and philosophy and other essays*. London: New Left Books.

Amabile, T. (1993). 'Commentary'. In D. Goleman, P. Kaufman, and M. Ray, (eds), *The creative spirit*. New York: Plume.

Angless, T., and Shefer, T. (1997). 'Children living with violence in the family'. In C. de la Rey, N. Duncan, T. Shefer, and A. van Niekerk, *Contemporary issues in human development: A South African focus*. Johannesburg: Thomson.

Appignansi, R. and Zarate, O. (1992). *Freud for beginners*. London: Icon.

Aries, P. (1962). 'The discovery of childhood'. In Santrock, J. W. (1999), *Life-span development*. Boston: McGraw-Hill.

Aries, P. (1973). *Centuries of childhood*. London: Jonathan Cape.

Archer, J. (1980). 'The significance of sex differences in developmental psychology'. In J. Saints (ed.), *Developmental psychology and society*. London: Macmillan.

Ashmead, D. H. and Perlmutter, M. (1980). 'Infant memory in everyday life'. In M. Perlmutter (ed.), *New directions for child development*. San Francisco: Jossey-Bass.

Atkinson, R. C. and Shiffrin, R. M. (1968). 'Human memory: A proposed system and its control processes'. In K. W. Spence and J. T. Spence (eds), *The psychology of learning and motivation. Volume 2*. London: Academic Press.

Aube, J., Norcliffe, H., Craig, J-A., and Koestner, R. (1995). 'Gender characteristics and adjustment-related outcomes: Questioning the masculinity model'. *The personality and social psychology bulletin*, 21 (3), 284–295.

Azmitia, M. (1992). 'Expertise, private speech and the development of self-regulation'. In R. M. Diaz and L. E. Berk (eds), *Private speech: From social interaction to self-regulation*. New Jersey: Erlbaum.

# B

Baddeley, A. (1982). *Your memory: A user's guide.* London: Multimedia Publications.

Baillargeon, R. (1987). 'Object permanence in three-and-a-half and four-and-a-half-month-old infants'. *Developmental psychology*, 23 (5), 655–674.

Baillargeon, R. and DeVos, J. (1991). 'Object permanence in young infants: Further evidence'. *Child development*, 62, 1227–1246.

Barbarin, O. A. and Richter, L. (2001). 'Economic status, community danger and psychological problems among South African children'. *Childhood: A global journal of child research*, 8 (1), 115–133.

Barrett, M. D. (1979). 'Semantic development during the single-word stage of language acquisition'. Unpublished doctoral thesis, University of Sussex, Hove.

Bartholomew, K. and Horowitz, L. M. (1991). 'Attachment styles among young adults: A test of a four-category model'. *Journal of personality and social psychology*, 61, 226–244.

Bartlett, F. (1932). *Remembering.* Cambridge: Cambridge University Press.

Bayley, N. (1993). *Bayley scales of infant development.* Second edition. San Antonio: Psychological Corporation.

Bee, H. (1992). *The developing child.* Sixth edition. New York: Harper Collins.

Bell, S. and Ainsworth, M. (1972). 'Infant crying and maternal responsiveness'. *Child development*, 43, 1171–1190.

Bem, S. L. (1993). *The lenses of gender.* New Haven: Yale University Press.

Benenson, J. F., Apostoleris, N. H. and Parnass, J. (1997). 'Age and sex differences in dyadic and group interaction'. *Developmental psychology*, 33 (3), 538–543.

Benvenuto, B. and Kennedy, R. (1986). *The works of Jacques Lacan: An introduction.* London: Free Association Press.

Berk, L. E. (1986). 'Private speech: Learning out aloud'. *Psychology today*, 20 (5), 34–42.

Best, D. L., House, A. S., Barnard, A. E., and Spicker, B. S. (1994). 'Parent-child interactions in France, Germany and Italy: The effects of gender and culture'. *Journal of cross-cultural psychology*, 25 (2), 181–193.

Best, S. and Kellner, D. (1991). *Postmodern theory: Critical interrogations.* Hong Kong: Macmillan.

Biesheuvel, S. (1987). 'Psychology, science and politics: Theoretical developments and applications in a plural society'. *South African journal of psychology*, 17, 1–8.

Biller, H. B. (1993). *Fathers and families: Paternal factors in child development.* Westport: Auburn House.

Bion, W. (1962). *Learning from experience.* New York: Basic Books.

Bion, W. (1967). *Second thoughts.* New York: Jason Aronson.

Bjorklund, D. F. (1995). *Children's thinking: Developmental function and individual differences.* Pacific Grove, CA: Brooks-Cole.

Blasi, A. (1980). 'Bridging moral cognition and moral action: A critical review of the literature'. *Psychological bulletin*, 88 (1), 1–45.

Blatt, M. M. and Kohlberg, L. (1975). 'The effects of classroom moral discussion upon children's level of moral judgement'. *Journal of moral education*, 4, 129–161.

Block, J. H. (1973). 'Conception of sex-roles: Some cross-cultural and longitudinal perspectives'. *American psychologist*, 28, 512–516.

Bloom, L. (1996). 'The emotional damage of apartheid: A psycho-analytic view'. *Psycho-analytic psychotherapy in South Africa*, 4 (20), 55–71.

Boas, F. (1911). *The mind of primitive man.* New York: Macmillan.

Bonn, M. and Webley, P. (2000). 'South African children's understanding of money and banking'. *British journal of developmental psychology*, 18 (2), 269–278.

Bornstein, M. H. and Sigman, M. D. (1986). 'Continuity in mental development from infancy'. *Child development*, 57, 251–274.

Bourne, L. E. J. and Felipe Russo, N. (1998). *Psychology: Behaviour in context.* New York: Norton.

Bowie, M. (1991). *Lacan.* London: Fontana.

Bowlby, J. (1944). 'Forty-four juvenile thieves: Their characters and home life'. *International journal of psycho-analysis*, 25, 19–52 and 107–27.

Bowlby, J. (1969). *Attachment and loss (Vol. 1): Attachment.* London: Hogarth Press.

Bowlby, J. (1973). *Attachment and loss (Vol. 2): Separation: Anxiety and anger.* London: Hogarth Press.

Bowlby, J. (1979). *The making and breaking of affectional bonds.* London: Tavistock.

Bowlby, J. (1980). *Attachment and loss (Vol. 3): Loss, sadness and depression.* London: Hogarth Press.

Bowlby, J. (1988). *A secure base: Parent-child attachment and healthy human development.* New York: Basic Books.

Bowlby, J. (1989). 'The role of attachment in personality development and psychopathology'. In S. Greenspan and G. Pollock (eds), *The course of life. Volume 1: Infancy.* Madison, CT: International Universities Press.

Bozalek, V. (1997). 'Representations of the family and South African realities'. In C. de la Rey, N. Duncan, T. Shefer, and A. van Niekerk (eds), *Contemporary issues in human development: A South African focus.* Johannesburg: Thomson.

Braine, M. D. S. (1963). 'The ontogeny of English phrase structure: The first phase'. *Language*, 39, 1–13.

Brazelton, T. B., Koslowski, B., and Tronick, E. (1993). 'Neonatal behaviour among urban Zambians and Americans'. In M. Gauvain and M. Cole (eds), *Readings on the development of children.* Oxford: W. H. Freeman.

Bretherton, I. (1997). 'Bowlby's legacy to developmental psychology'. *Child psychiatry and human development*, 28 (1), 33–43.

Brody, N. (1992). *Intelligence.* San Diego, CA: Academic Press.

Bronfenbrenner, U. (1977). 'Towards an experimental ecology of human development'. *American psychologist*, 32 (7), 513–531.

Bronfenbrenner, U. (1979). *The ecology of human development.* Cambridge, MA: Harvard University Press.

Brooke, R. (1990). *Jung and phenomenology.* London: Routledge.

Broom, Y. M. and Doctor, E. A. (1994). 'Developmental dyslexia: contrasting patterns of performance on a diagnostic psycholinguistic assessment'. *South African journal of psychology*, 24 (4), 219–228.

Brown, R. (1965). *Social psychology.* New York: Free Press.

Bukatko, D. and Daehler, M. (1995). *Child development.* Second edition. Toronto: Houghton Mifflin.

Bulhan, H. A. (1981). 'Psychological research in Africa: Genesis and function'. *Race and class,* 23 (1), 25–40.

Bulmer, M. and Solomos, J. (2000). *Racism.* Oxford: Oxford University Press.

Burman, E. (1994). *Deconstructing developmental psychology.* London: Routledge.

Burr, V. (1995). *An introduction to social constructionism.* London: Routledge.

Buss, A. H. and Plomin, R. (1984). *Temperament: Early developing personality traits.* New Jersey: Erlbaum.

Butchart, A. and Kruger, J. (2001). 'Public health and community psychology: A case study in community-based injury prevention'. In M. Seedat (ed.), *Community psychology theory, method and practice: South African and other perspectives.* Oxford: Oxford University Press.

# C

Carlson, E. A. and Sroufe, L. A. (1995). 'Contribution of attachment theory to developmental psychopathology'. In D. Cicchetti and D. J. Cohen (eds), *Developmental psychopathology.* New York: John Wiley.

Carver, C. S. and Scheier, M. F. (1988). *Perspectives on personality.* Boston, MA: Allyn and Bacon.

Cassidy, J. (1999). 'The nature of the child's ties'. In J. Cassidy and P. R. Shaver (eds), *Handbook of attachment: Theory, research and clinical applications.* New York: Guilford Press.

Cassidy, J. and Kobak, R. (1988). 'Avoidance and its relation to other defensive processes'. In J. Belsky and T. Nezworski (eds), *Clinical implications of attachment.* New Jersey: Erlbaum.

Castles, S. O. and Vasta, E. (1999). 'Multi-cultural or multi-racist Australia?' In M. Bulmer and J. Solomos (eds), *Racism.* Oxford: Oxford University Press.

Ceci, S. J. (1990). *On intelligence, more or less.* Englewood Cliffs, NJ: Prentice Hall.

Cherian, V. I. and Cherian, L. (1997). 'Relationship between parents' interest, life status and the academic achievement of Xhosa children in South Africa'. *Journal of psychology in Africa,* 2, 54–66.

Cherian, V. I. and Malehase, M. C. (2000). 'The relationship between parental control and scholastic achievement of children from single- and two-parent families'. *The journal of social psychology,* 140 (5), 665–667.

Chi, M. T. H. and Koeske, R. D. (1983). 'Network representation of a child's dinosaur knowledge'. *Developmental psychology,* 19, 29–39.

Chodorow, N. (1978). *The reproduction of mothering: Psychoanalysis and the sociology of gender.* Berkeley: University of California Press.

Chomsky, N. (1959). 'Review of *Verbal behaviour* by B. F. Skinner'. *Language,* 35, 26–58.

Cloninger, S. C. (1996). *Theories of personality.* Second edition. Upper Saddle River, NJ: Prentice Hall

Colby, A. and Kohlberg, L. (1987). *The measurement of moral judgment. Volume 1.* Cambridge: Cambridge University Press.

Colby, A., Kohlberg, L., Speicer, B., Hewer, A., Candee, D., Gibbs, J., and Power, C. (1987). *The measurement of moral judgment: Standard issue scoring manual. Volume 2.* Cambridge: Cambridge University Press.

Cole, M. (1993). 'Mind as a cultural achievement: Implications for IQ testing'. In M. Gauvain and M. Cole (eds), *Readings on the development of children.* Oxford: W. H. Freeman.

Collins, A. M. and Loftus, E. (1975). 'A spreading activation theory of semantic processing'. *Psychological review,* 82, 407–428.

Coppock, V., Haydon, D., and Richter, I. (1995). *The illusions of 'post-feminism': New women, old myths.* London: Taylor and Francis.

Craig, G. J. (1996). *Human development.* Seventh edition. Upper Saddle River, NJ: Prentice Hall.

Crain, W. (1992). *Theories of development: Concepts and applications.* Third edition. Englewood Cliffs, NJ: Prentice Hall.

Crittenden, P. M. (1985). 'Social networks, quality of child rearing, and child development'. *Child development,* 56, 1299–1313.

Crockenberg, S. B. (1981). 'Infant irritability, mother responsiveness, and social support influences on the security of infant-mother attachment'. *Child development,* 52, 857–865.

Crossley, M. L. (2000). *Introducing narrative psychology: Self, trauma and the construction of meaning.* Buckingham: Open University Press.

# D

Dale, M., De'ath, R., Evans, T., Thompson, Q., Georgi, G., and Spencer, P. (1998). *The human body.* London: BBC Films in association with the Learning Channel.

Das, J. P., Naglieri, J. A., and Kirby, J. P. (1994). *Assessment of cognitive processes.* Boston: Allyn and Bacon.

Dawes, A. (1986). 'The notion of relevant psychology with particular reference to Africanist pragmatic initiatives'. *Psychology in society,* 15, 55–61.

Dawes, A. (1994). 'The emotional impact of political violence'. In A. Dawes and D. Donald (eds), *Childhood and adversity: Psychological perspectives from South African research.* Cape Town: David Philip.

Dawes, A. and Donald, D. (1994). 'Understanding the psychological consequences of adversity'. In A. Dawes and D. Donald (eds), *Childhood and adversity: Psychological perspectives from South African research.* Cape Town: David Philip.

Deaux, K. (1987). 'Psychological constructions of masculinity and femininity'. In J. M. Reinisch, L. A. Rosenblum, and S. A. Sanders (eds), *Masculinity/femininity: Basic perspectives.* New York: Oxford University Press.

Deaux, K. and Kite, M. E. (1987). 'Thinking about gender'. In B. B. Hess and M. M. Ferree (eds), *Analysing gender: A handbook of social science research.* Newbury Park: Sage.

De la Rey, C., Duncan, N., Shefer, T., and Van Niekerk, A. (eds) (1997). *Contemporary issues in human development: A South African focus.* Johannesburg: Thomson.

Detterman, D. K. and Sternberg, R. J. (1986). *What is intelligence? Contemporary viewpoints on its nature and definition.* New York: Ablex.

Detterman, D. K. (1987). 'What does reaction time tell us about intelligence?' In P. A. Vernon (ed.), *Speed of information processing and intelligence.* New York: Ablex.

Diamond, A. (1985). 'Development of the ability to use recall to guide action, as indicated by infants' performance on AB'. *Child development*, 56, 21–52.

Diaz, R. M. (1985). 'Bilingual cognitive development: Addressing three gaps in current research'. *Child development*, 56, 1376–1388.

Doctor, E. and Coltheart, M. (1980). 'Phonological recoding in children's reading for meaning'. *Memory and cognition*, 80, 195–209.

Donald, D. (1994). 'Children with special education needs: The reproduction of disadvantage in poorly served communities'. In A. Dawes and D. Donald (eds), *Childhood and adversity: Psychological perspectives from South African research.* Cape Town: David Philip.

Donald, D., Dawes, A., and Louw, J. (eds) (2000). *Addressing childhood adversity.* Cape Town: David Philip.

Donald, D. and Swart-Kruger, J. (1994). 'The South African street child: Developmental implications'. *South African journal of psychology*, 24 (4), 169–174.

Duncan, N. (1997). 'Malnutrition and childhood development'. In C. de la Rey, N. Duncan, T. Shefer, and A. van Niekerk (eds), *Contemporary issues in human development: A South African focus.* Johannesburg: Thomson.

Duncan, N. and Rock, B. (1997). 'The impact of political violence on the lives of children in South Africa'. In C. de la Rey, N. Duncan, T. Shefer, and A. van Niekerk (eds), *Contemporary issues in human development: A South African focus.* Johannesburg: Thomson.

# E

Edelbrock, C. and Sugwara, A. I. (1978). 'Acquisition of sex-typed preferences in pre-school aged children'. *Developmental psychology*, 14 (6), 614–623.

Egeland, B., Kalkoske, M., Gottesman, N., and Erickson, M. F. (1990). 'Preschool behaviour problems: Stability and factors accounting for change'. *Journal of child psychology and psychiatry and allied disciplines*, 31(6), 891–909.

Epstein, C. F. (1988). *Deceptive distinctions: Sex, gender and the social order.* New Haven: Yale University Press.

Erdelyi, M. H. and Goldberg, B. (1979). 'Let's not sweep repression under the rug: Toward a cognitive psychology of repression'. In J. F. Kihlstrom and F. J. Evans (eds), *Functional disorders of memory.* New Jersey: Erlbaum.

Erickson, M. F., Sroufe, L. A., and Egeland, B. (1985). 'The relationship between quality of attachment and behaviour problems in preschool in a high-risk sample'. *Monographs of the Society for Research in Child Development*, 50 (1–2), 147–166.

Erikson, E. H. (1963). *Childhood and society.* New York: Norton.

Erikson, E. H. (1964). *Insight and responsibility.* New York: Norton.

Erikson, E. H. (1968). *Identity, youth and crisis.* New York: Norton.

Erikson, E. H. (1969). *Gandhi's truth.* New York: Norton.

Erikson, E. H. (1980). *Identity and the life cycle.* New York: Norton.

Evans, D. (1996). *An introductory dictionary of Lacanian psychoanalysis.* London: Routledge.

Eysenck, H. J. (1953). *Uses and abuses of psychology.* London: Penguin.

Eysenck, M. W. and Keane M. T. (1990). *Cognitive psychology: A student's handbook.* Hove: Erlbaum.

# F

Fagot, B. (1977). 'Consequences of moderate cross-gender behaviour in pre-school children'. *Child development*, 48, 902–907.

Fantz, R. L., Fagan, J. F., and Miranda, S. B. (1975). 'Early visual selectivity'. In L. B. Cohen and P. Salapatek (eds), *Infant perception: From sensation to cognition.* New York: Academic Press.

Fenichel, O. (1945). *The psychoanalytic theory of neurosis.* New York: Norton.

Finchilescu, G. and Dawes, A. (1998). 'Catapulted into democracy: South African adolescents' socio-political orientations following rapid social change'. *Journal of social issues*, 54 (3), 563–583.

Fishbein, H. D. (1984). *The psychology of infancy and childhood: Evolutionary and cross-cultural perspectives.* New Jersey: Erlbaum.

Fisher, S. and Greenberg, R. P. (1977). *The scientific credibility of Freud's theories and therapy.* New York: Basic Books.

Flavell, J. H., Everett, B. H., Croft, K., and Flavell, E. R. (1981). 'Young children's knowledge about visual perception: Further evidence for the level 1-level 2 distinction'. *Developmental psychology*, 17, 99–103.

Flavell, J. H., Miller, P. H., and Miller, S. A. (1993). *Cognitive development.* Englewood Cliffs, NJ: Prentice Hall.

Flavell, J. H. and Wellman, H. M. (1977). 'Metamemory'. In R. V. Kail and J. W. Hagen (eds), *Perspectives on the development of memory and cognition.* New Jersey: Erlbaum.

Flugel, J. C. and West, D. J.. (1964). *A hundred years of psychology.* New York: Basic Books.

Flynn, J. R. (1998). 'Intelligence considered'. *Scientific American*, 9 (4), 7–11.

Fonagy, P. (1999). 'Attachment, the development of the self, and its pathology in personality disorders'. In J. Derksen, C. Maffei, and H. Groen (eds), *Treatment of personality disorders.* Dordrecht: Kluwer/Plenum.

Fonagy, P. (2000). 'Points of convergence and divergence between psychoanalytic and attachment theories: Is psychoanalytic theory truly different?' Paper presented at the Michigan Psychoanalytic Institute, 2–9 April.

Foucault, M. (1977). *Discipline and punish: The birth of the prison.* London: Allen Lane.

Foucault, M. (1980). *The history of sexuality. Volume 1: An introduction.* London: Vintage.

Freud, S. (1953). 'The interpretation of dreams'. In J. Strachey (ed.), *Standard edition of the complete works of Sigmund Freud. Volumes 4 and 5.* London: Hogarth Press.

Freud, S. (1977). 'Three essays on the theory of sexuality'. In A. Richards and A. Dickson (eds), *The Penguin Freud Library. Volume 7 on sexuality: Three essays on the theory of sexuality and other works.* London: Penguin.

Freud, S. (1978). *The interpretation of dreams.* London: Penguin.

Freud, S. (1982). *Introductory lectures on psychoanalysis.* London: Hogarth Press.

Freud, S. (1991). 'The ego and the id'. In D. Richards and A. Dickson (eds), *The Penguin Freud Library. Volume 11 on metapsychology.* London: Penguin.

Freund, L. S. (1990). 'Maternal regulation of children's problem-solving behaviour and its impact on children's performance'. *Child development*, 61, 113–126.

Frith, U. (1985). 'Beneath the surface of developmental dyslexia'. In Patterson, K., Coltheart, M., and Marshall, J. (eds), *Surface dyslexia.* Hove: Erlbaum.

Fromm, E. (1980). *Greatness and limitations of Freud's thought.* New York: Harper and Row.

Fuchs Epstein, C. (1988). *Deceptive distinctions. Sex, gender and the social order.* New Haven: Yale University Press.

Furrow, D., Nelson, K., and Benedict, H. (1979). 'Mother's speech to children and syntactic development: Some simple relationships'. *Journal of child language*, 6, 423–442.

# G

Gardner, H. (1984). 'On being judged "intelligent" '. In P. S. Fry (ed.), *Changing conceptions of intelligence and intellectual functioning*. Amsterdam: North Holland.

Gardner, H. (1998). 'A multiplicity of intelligences'. *Scientific American*, 9 (4), 19–23.

Gay, P. (1988). *Freud, a life for our times*. London: Papermac.

George, C., Kaplan, N., and Main, M. (1985). 'Adult attachment interview'. Second edition. Unpublished manuscript, University of California, Berkeley.

Gibson, K. (1993). 'The effects of exposure to political violence on children: Does violence beget violence?' *South African journal of psychology*, 23 (4), 167–173.

Giddens, A. (1992). *Sociology*. Cambridge: Polity Press.

Gilbert, A. (1989). 'Things fall apart? Psychological theory in the context of rapid social change'. *South African journal of psychology*, 19, 91–100.

Gilbert, A., Van Vlaenderen, H., and Nkwinti, G. (1995). 'Planting pumpkins: Socialization and the role of local knowledge in rural South Africa'. *South African journal of psychology*, 25 (4), 229–235.

Gilligan, C. (1982). *In a different voice: Psychological theory and women's development*. Cambridge, MA: Harvard University Press.

Gilligan, C. and Wiggins, G. (1987). 'The origin of morality in early childhood relationships'. In J. Kagan and S. Lamb (eds), *The emergence of morality in young children*. Chicago: University of Chicago Press.

Ginsburg, H. and Opper, S. (1969). *Piaget's theory of intellectual development*. Englewood Cliffs, NJ: Prentice Hall.

Glassman M (1994). 'All things being equal: The two roads of Piaget and Vygotsky'. *Developmental review*, 14, 186–214.

Gleitman, H. (1991). *Psychology*. Third edition. New York: Norton.

Goldman, D. (ed.) (1993). *In one's bones: The clinical genius of Winnicott*. London: Tavistock.

Goleman, D., Kaufman, P., and Ray, M. (1993). *The creative spirit*. New York: Plume.

Goleman, D. (1996a). 'Studies suggest older minds are stronger than expected'. *New York Times*, 26 February, 1–10.

Goleman, D. (1996b). *Emotional intelligence*. London: Bloomsbury.

Goncz, L. (1988). 'A research study on the relation between early bilingualism and cognitive development'. *Psychologische Beiträge*, 30 (1–2), 75–91.

Goodnow, J. and Collins, W. (1990). *Development according to parents: The nature, sources and consequences of parents' ideas*. Hove: LEA.

Gormly, A. V. (1997). *Lifespan human development*. New York: Harcourt Brace.

Grant, J. S. (1997). 'The morality of Moses Sithole'. Unpublished honours dissertation, University of the Witwatersrand, Johannesburg.

Greenberg, J. K. and Mitchell, S. A. (1983). *Object relations in psychoanalytic theory*. London: Harvard University Press.

Greene, A. L. (1990). 'Great expectations: Constructions of the life course during adolescence'. *The journal of youth and adolescence*, 19, 289–303.

Greene, J. and Hicks, C. (1984). *Basic cognitive processes*. Milton Keynes: Open University Press.

Grosskurth, P. (1986). *Melanie Klein: Her world and her work*. London: Jason Aronson.

Grossmann, K., Grossmann, K. E., Spangler, S., Suess, G., and Unzner, L. (1985). 'Maternal sensitivity and newborn attachment orientation responses as related to quality of attachment in Northern Germany'. In I. Bretherton and E. Waters (eds), *Growing points of attachment: Monographs of the Society of Research in Child Development*, 50 (1–2), Serial No. 209.

Grubb, H. J. (1986). 'The black prole and whitespeak: Black English from an Orwellian perspective'. *Race and class*, 27 (3), 69–80.

Guilford, J. P. (1967). *The structure of intellect*. New York: McGraw-Hill.

# H

Haiden, G. A. (1998). 'An exploration of gender stereotypes in pre-school girls: Barbie and beyond.' Unpublished masters thesis, University of the Witwatersrand, Johannesburg.

Haiden, G. A. and Zietkiewicz, E. (1999). 'Non-Barbie and beyond: Pre-school girls' definitions of themselves in terms of a lack'. Paper presented at the Third Annual Qualitative Methods Conference, Johannesburg.

Hall, G. S. (1904) *Adolescence: Its psychology and its relations to physiology, anthropology, sociology, sex, crime, religiona and education*. London: Sidney Appleton.

Hamilton, C. E. (1994). 'Continuity and discontinuity of attachment from infancy through adolescence'. *Dissertation abstracts international*, 55 (2), 217.

Hamilton, J. (1994). *A map of the world*. New York: Anchor.

Hanks, W. F. (1989). *Word and image in Mayan culture: Explorations in language, writing and representation*. Salt Lake City: University of Utah Press.

Harnishfeger, K. K. and Bjorklund, D. F. (1990). 'Children's strategies: A brief history'. In D. F. Bjorklund, *Children's strategies: Contemporary views of cognitive development*. New Jersey: Erlbaum.

Harris, M. and Coltheart, M. (1986). *Language processing in children and adults*. London: Routledge and Kegan Paul.

Harwood, R. L. (1995). *Culture and attachment: Perceptions of the child in context*. New York: Guilford Press.

Hasher, L. and Zacks, R. T. (1988). 'Working memory comprehension and ageing: A review and a new view'. *Psychology of learning and motivation*, 22, 193–225.

Hayes, G. (1989). 'Psychology and ideology: The case of Althusser'. *South African journal of psychology*, 19 (2), 84–90.

Hazan, C. and Shaver, P. R. (1987). 'Romantic love conceptualised as an attachment process'. *Journal of personality and social psychology*, 52, 511–524.

Hazan, C. and Shaver, P. R. (1990). 'Love and work: An attachment-theoretical perspective'. *Journal of personality and social psychology*, 59, 270–280.

Heaton. J. M. (2000). *Wittgenstein and psychoanalysis*. London: Icon.

Hendrik, H. (1990). 'Constructions and reconstructions of British childhood: An interpretative survey, 1800 to the present'. In A. James and A. Prout (eds), *Constructing and reconstructing childhood: Contemporary issues in the sociological study of childhood*. Basingstoke: Falmer.

Herrnstein, R. and Murray, C. (1994). *The Bell curve: Intelligence and class structure in American life*. New York: Free Press.

Hetherington, E. and Parke R. (1993). *Child psychology: A contemporary viewpoint*. Fourth edition. New York: McGraw-Hill.

Hill, P. (1997). *Lacan for beginners*. London: Writers and Readers.

Hirsch, J. and Kim, K. (1997). 'New views of early language'. *Nature*, 103, 1141–1143.

Hoff-Ginsberg, E. and Shatz, M. (1982). 'Linguistic input and the child's acquisition of language'. *Psychological bulletin*, 92 (1), 3–26.

Hoffman, C., Lau, I., and Johnson, D. R. (1986). 'The linguistic relativity of person cognition: An English-Chinese comparison'. *Journal of personality and social psychology*, 51, 1097–1105.

Holmes, J. (1993). *John Bowlby and attachment theory*. London: Routledge.

Holmes, J. (1995). 'Something there is that doesn't love a wall: John Bowlby, attachment theory, and psychoanalysis'. In S. Goldberg, R. Muir, and J. Kerr, (eds), *Attachment theory: Social, developmental, and clinical perspectives*. New York: Analytic Press.

Horn, J. L. and Cattell, R. B. (1982). 'Whimsy and misunderstanding of $G_f$ – $G_c$ theory: A comment on Guilford'. *Psychological bulletin*, 91, 623–633.

Horn, P. (1991). 'The way forward towards the emancipation of women'. *Agenda*, 10, 53–66.

Horney, K. (1967). *Feminine psychology.* New York: Norton.

Hulme, C. and Tordoff, V. (1989). 'Working memory development: The effects of speech rate, word length and acoustic similarity on serial recall'. *Journal of experimental child psychology*, 47, 72–87.

# I

Inhelder, B. and Piaget, J. (1958). *The growth of logical thinking from childhood to adolescence.* London: Routledge & Kegan Paul.

Isaacs, S. (1948). 'The nature and function of phantasy'. In M. Klein (ed.), *Contributions to psycho-analysis, 1921–1945.* London: Hogarth Press.

# J

Jackson, J. F. (1993). 'Multiple caregiving among African Americans and infant attachment: The need for an emic approach'. *Human development*, 36, 87–102.

Jensen, A. (1969). 'How much can we boost IQ and scholastic achievement?' *Harvard educational review*, 39, 1–23.

Jones, G. R. (ed.) (1988). *The nation's favourite poems.* London: BBC.

Jung, C. G. (1963). *Memories, dreams, reflections.* London: Routledge & Kegan Paul.

Jung, C.G. (1983). *Jung, selected writings.* Introduced by Anthony Storr. London: Fontana.

Jung, C. G. (1986). *Analytic psychology: Its theory and practice.* London: Ark Paperbacks.

Jung, C. G. (ed.) (1990). *Man and his symbols.* New York: Aldus Books.

# K

Kail, R. (1979). *The development of memory in children.* New York: W. H. Freeman.

Kasese-Hara M. C. (2000). 'Historical contexts of developmental research: The experience of sub-Saharan Africa'. Paper presented at the Fifth Biennial Africa Regional Workshops of the ISSBD, 25–30 September, Kampala, Uganda.

Kate, P. A. (1979). 'The development of the female identity'. In C. B. Kopp and M. Kirkpatrick (eds), *Becoming female: Perspectives on development.* New York: Plenum.

Kaufman, A. S. and Kaufman, N. C. (1983). *The Kaufman assessment battery for children.* Circle Pines, MN: American Guidance Services.

Kendall, F. (1993). *The SeXY Factor: Gender differences at home and at work.* Norwood: Amagi.

Klein, L. and Hickman, D. (1994). *Baby it's you.* London: Channel 4 Television.

Klein, M. (1926). 'The psychological principles of early analysis'. *International journal of psycho-analysis*, 8, 25–37.

Klein, M. (1932). *The psycho-analysis of children.* London: Hogarth Press.

Klein, M. (1946). 'Notes on some schizoid mechanisms'. *International journal of psychoanalysis*, 27, 99–110.

Klein, M. (1948). 'Mourning and its relation to manic-depressive states'. In M. Klein (ed.), *Contributions to psycho-analysis, 1921–1945.* London: Hogarth Press.

Klein, M. (1957). *Envy and gratitude: A study of unconscious forces.* New York: Basic Books.

Klein, M. (1975a). *Love, guilt and reparation and other works, 1921–1945.* London: Hogarth Press.

Klein, M. (1975b). *Envy and gratitude and other works, 1946–1963.* London: Hogarth Press.

Kobak, R. R. (1985). 'Attitudes towards attachment relations and social competence among first-year college students'. Unpublished doctoral dissertation, University of Virginia, Charlottesville.

Kobak, R. R. (1986). 'Attachment as a theory of affect regulation'. Unpublished manuscript, University of Denver, Denver, Colorado.

Kobak, R. R. and Sceery, A. (1988). 'Attachment in late adolescence: Working models, affect regulation, and representations of self and others'. *Child development*, 59, 135–146.

Kobak, R. R. and Shaver, P. (1987). 'Strategies for maintaining felt security: A theoretical analysis of continuity and change in styles of social adaptation'. Paper presented at the Conference in Honour of John Bowlby's Eightieth Birthday, London.

Kohlberg, L. (1958). 'The development of modes of thinking and choice in the years 10 to 16'. Unpublished doctoral dissertation, University of Chicago, Chicago, Illinois.

Kohlberg, L. (1964). 'Development of moral character and moral ideology'. In M. Hoffman and L. Hoffman (eds), *Review of child development research*. New York: Russell Sage Foundation.

Kohlberg, L. (1966). 'A cognitive developmental analysis of children's sex-role concepts and attitudes'. In E. E. Maccoby (ed.), *The development of sex differences*. Stanford: Stanford University Press.

Kohlberg, L. (1968). 'Moral development'. In D. L. Sill (ed.), *International encyclopaedia of the social sciences*. London: Crowell, Collier and MacMillan.

Kohlberg, L. (1969). 'Stage and sequence: The cognitive developmental approach to socialization'. In D. A. Goslin (ed.), *Handbook of socialization theory and research*. New York: Rand McNally.

Kohlberg, L. (ed.) (1981). *The philosophy of moral development: Moral stages and the idea of justice. Volume 1*. Cambridge: Harper and Row.

Kohlberg, L. and Candee, D. (1984). 'The relationship of moral judgment to moral action'. In L. Kohlberg (ed.), *Essays on moral development. Volume 2*. New York: Harper and Row.

Kohlberg, L. and Gilligan, C. (1971). 'The adolescent as philosopher: The discovery of the self in a postconventional world'. *Daedalus*, 1051–1086.

Kohlberg, L. and Kauffman, K. (1987). 'Theoretical introduction to the measurement of moral judgment'. In A. Colby and L. Kohlberg (eds), *The measurement of moral judgment. Volume 1*. Cambridge: Cambridge University Press.

Kohon, G. (ed.) (1986). *The British school of psycho-analysis: The independent tradition*. London: Free Association Books.

Kottak, C. P. (1994). *Cultural anthropology*. New York: McGraw-Hill.

Kozulin, A. (1990). *Vygotsky's psychology: A biography of ideas*. Cambridge, MA: Harvard University Press.

Kuhn, D. (1992). 'Cognitive development'. In M. H. Bornstein and M. E. Lamb (eds), *Developmental psychology: An advanced textbook*. New Jersey: Erlbaum.

# L

Labouvie-Vief, G. (1985). 'Intelligence and cognition'. In J. E. Birren and K. W. Schaie (eds), *Handbook of the psychology of ageing*. New York: Van Nostrand Reinhold.

Labuschagne, I. (1999). 'Personal communication'. Presentation to students, University of the Witwatersrand, Johannesburg, 16 May 1999.

Labuschagne, I. (2000). 'Criminological evaluation of Kobus Geldenhuys'. Unpublished manuscript, Pretoria.

Lacan, J. (1979). *The four fundamental concepts of psychoanalysis*. London: Penguin.

Lacan, J. (1977). *Ecrits*. New York: Norton.

LaFreniere, P., Strayer, F. F., and Gauthier, R. (1984). 'The emergence of same-sex affiliative preference among pre-school peers: A developmental/ethological perspective'. *Child development*, 55, 1958–1965.

Lahey, B. B. (2001). *Psychology: An introduction*. Boston: McGraw-Hill.

Lamb, M. E. (1981). 'Fathers and child development: An integrative overview'. In M. E. Lamb (ed.), *The father's role in child development*. New York: John Wiley.

Laplanche, J. and Pontalis, J. B. (1973). *The language of psycho-analysis.* London: Hogarth Press.

Lapsley, D. K. (1996). *Moral psychology.* Boulder, CO: Westview.

Laubscher, L. and Klinger, J. (1997). 'Story and the making of the self'. In C. de la Rey, N. Duncan, T. Shefer, and A. van Niekerk (eds), *Contemporary issues in human development: A South African focus.* Johannesburg: Thomson.

Lazarus, J. (1993a). 'Would you have raped and killed me too?' *Sunday Star*, 26 September, 7–8.

Lazarus, J. (1993b). 'What makes a man become a beast to women?' *Sunday Star*, 26 September, 7–8.

Leader, D. and Groves, G. (1995). *Lacan for beginners.* Cambridge: Icon.

Leahy, T. H. (1987). *A history of psychology: Main currents in psychological thought.* Second edition. Englewood Cliffs, NJ: Prentice Hall.

Lenneberg, E. (1967). *Biological foundation of language.* New York: John Wiley.

Lerner, R. M. (1986). *Concepts and theories of human development.* New York: Random House.

Levett, A. (1994). 'Problems of cultural imperialism in the study of child sexual abuse'. In A. Dawes and D. Donald (eds), *Childhood and adversity: Psychological perspectives from South African research.* Cape Town: David Philip.

Lewis, M. (1987). 'Early sex role behaviour and school age adjustment'. In J. M. Reinisch, L. A. Rosenblum, and S. A. Sanders (eds), *Masculinity/femininity: Basic perspectives.* New York: Oxford University Press.

Liddell, C. (1996). 'Every picture tells a story: South African and British children interpreting pictures'. *British journal of developmental psychology*, 14, 355–363.

Liddell, C. and Kvalsig, J. (1990). 'Science and social accountability: Issues related to South African developmental psychology'. *South African journal of psychology*, 20 (1), 1–9.

Liddell, C., Kvalsig J., Shabalala, A., and Masilela P. (1991). 'Historical perspectives on South African children'. *International journal of behavioural development*, 14 (1), 1–19.

Liddell, C., Kvalsig, J., Shabalala, A., and Qotyana, P. (1994). 'Defining the cultural context of children's everyday experiences in the year before school'. In A. Dawes and D. Donald (eds), *Childhood and adversity: Psychological perspectives from South African research.* Cape Town: David Philip.

Liddell, C., Lycett, J., and Gordon, R. (1997). 'Getting through Grade 2: Predicting children's early school achievement in rural South African schools'. *International journal of behavioural development*, 21(2), 331–348.

Lidz, C. S. (1991). *Practitioner's guide to dynamic assessment.* New York: Guilford.

Lock, A., Service, V., Brito, A., and Chandler, P. (1989). 'The social structuring of infant cognition'. In A. Slater and G. Bremner (eds), *Infant development.* Hove: Erlbaum.

Loftus, E. (1994). *The myth of repressed memory.* New York: St Martin's Press.

Loftus, E. (1997). 'Creating false memories'. *Scientific American*, September, 70–75.

Louw, D. A. (1991). *Human development.* Pretoria: HAUM Tertiary.

Louw, D., Louw, A., and Schoeman, W. (1995). 'Developmental psychology'. In D. A. Louw and J. A. Edwards (eds), *Psychology: An introduction for students in Southern Africa.* Johannesburg: Lexicon.

# M

Maccoby, E. E. (1988). 'Gender as a social category'. *Developmental psychology*, 24 (6), 755–765.

Maccoby, E. E. (1987). 'The varied meanings of "masculine" and "feminine" '. In J. M. Reinisch, L. A. Rosenblum, and S. A. Sanders (eds), *Masculinity/femininity: Basic perspectives.* New York: Oxford University Press.

Macfarlane, F. (2001). 'A serial killer – why he kills: An attempt to understand the motives behind the actions of Jacobus Petrus Geldenhuys'. Unpublished honours thesis, University of the Witwatersrand, Johannesburg.

MacKinnon-Lewis, C., Volling, B. L., Lamb, M. E., Dechman, K., Rabiner, D., and Curtner, M. E. (1994). 'A cross-cultural analysis of boys' social competence: From family to school'. *Developmental psychology*, 30, 3, 325–333.

Magwaza, A. (1997). 'Sexual abuse: A socio-cultural developmental perspective'. In C. de la Rey, N. Duncan, T. Shefer, and A. van Niekerk (eds), *Contemporary issues in human development: A South African focus*. Johannesburg: Thomson.

Maier, H. W. (1988). *Three theories of child development*. Third edition. New York: University Press of America.

Main, M. (1997). 'Attachment narratives and attachment across the lifespan'. Paper presented at the Fall meeting of the American Psychoanalytic Association, New York.

Main, M. and Hesse, E. (1990). 'Lack of mourning in adulthood and its relationship to infant disorganization: Some speculations regarding causal mechanisms'. In M. T. Greenberg, D. Cicchetti, and E. M. Cummings (eds), *Attachment in the preschool years: Theory, research and intervention*. Chicago: University of Chicago Press.

Main, M. and Solomon, J. (1986). 'Discovery of a new, insecure-disorganized/disoriented attachment pattern'. In T. B. Brazelton and M. Yogman (eds), *Affective development in infancy*. Norwood, NJ: Ablex.

Main, M. and Solomon, J. (1990). 'Procedures for identifying infants as disorganized/disoriented during the Ainsworth Strange Situation'. In M. T. Greenberg, D. Cicchetti, and E. M. Cummings (eds), *Attachment in the preschool years: Theory, research and intervention*. Chicago: University of Chicago Press.

Malinowski, B. (1927). *Sex and repression in savage society*. New York: Humanities Press.

Marini, M. (1992). *Jacques Lacan: The French context*. New Brunswick, NJ: Rutgers University Press.

Marsh, G., Friedman, M., Welch, V., and Desberg, P. (1981). 'A cognitive-developmental theory of reading acquisition'. In G. E. MacKinnon and T. G. Waller (eds), *Reading research: Advances in theory and practice*. New York: Academic Press.

Martin, C. L. and Parker, S. (1995). 'Folk theories about sex and race differences'. *The personality and social psychology bulletin*, 21 (1), 45–57.

Mayes, P. (1986). *Sociology in focus: Gender*. New York: Longman.

McCandless, B. R. (1967). *Children: Behaviour and development*. Second edition. New York: Holt, Rinehart and Winston.

McClelland, J. L. and Rumelhart, D. E. (1985). 'Distributed memory and the representation of general and specific information'. *Journal of experimental psychology: General*, 114, 159–188.

McClelland, J. L. and Rumelhart, D. E. (1988). *Explorations in parallel-distributed-processing: A handbook of models, programs and exercises*. Cambridge, MA: MIT Press.

McGuire, W. and Hull, R. C. G. (eds) (1980). *Jung speaking: Interviews and encounters*. London: Picador.

Meltzoff, A. N. (1988). 'Infant imitation and memory: Nine-month-olds in immediate and deferred tests'. *Child development*, 59, 217–225.

Mentis, M., Dunn, M., Durbach, F., Arnott, A., Mentis, M., and Skuy, M. (1991). *Mediated learning experience working manual*. Johannesburg: University of the Witwatersrand.

Meyer, M. (2001). 'The Norwood serial killer: A discourse analytic review'. Unpublished honours thesis, University of the Witwatersrand, Johannesburg.

Mikulincer, M. and Florian, V. (1998). 'The relationship between adult attachment styles and emotional and cognitive reactions to stressful events'. In J. A. Simpson and W. S. Rholes (eds), *Attachment theory and close relationships*. New York: Guilford.

Mikulincer, M., Horesh, N., Eilati, I., and Kotler, M. (1999). 'The association between adult attachment style and mental health in extreme life-endangering conditions'. *Personality and individual differences*, 27, 831–842.

Minde, K. (1999). 'Mediating attachment patterns during a serious medical illness'. *Infant mental health journal*, 20 (1), 105–122.

Miyake, K., Chen, S. J., and Campos, J. J. (1985). 'Infant temperament, mother's mode of interaction, and attachment in Japan: An interim report'. *Monographs of the Society of Research in Child Development*, 50 (1–2), 276–297.

Mkhize, N. and Frizelle, K. (2000). 'Hermeneutic-dialogical approaches to career development: An exploration'. *South African journal of psychology*, 30 (2), 1–8.

Mohanty, A. K. and Perregaux, C. (1997). 'Language acquisition and bilinguals'. In J. W. Berry, P. R. Dasen, and T. S. Saraswathi (eds), *Handbook of cross-cultural psychology*. Boston: Allyn and Bacon.

Molon, P. (2000). *Freud and false memory syndrome*. Cambridge: Icon.

Money, J. (1965). 'Psychosexual differentiation'. In J. Money (ed.), *Sex research: New developments*. New York: Holt, Rinehart and Winston.

Moosa, F., Moonsamy, G., and Fridjon, P. (1997). 'Identification patterns among black students at a predominantly white university'. *South African journal of psychology*, 27 (4), 256–260.

Morojele, N. (1997). 'Adolescent alcohol misuse'. In C. de la Rey, N. Duncan, T. Shefer, and A. van Niekerk (eds), *Contemporary issues in human development: A South African focus*. Johannesburg: Thomson.

Morris, C. (2000). (Dir.) *Criminal minds*. Johannesburg: M-Net Television.

Morris, C. G. and Maisto, A. A. (1998). *Psychology: An introduction*. Englewood Cliffs, NJ: Prentice Hall.

Morisset, C. T., Barnard, K. E., Greenberg, M. T., Booth, C. L., and Spieker, S. J. (1990). 'Environmental influences on early language development: The context of social risk'. *Development and psychopathology*, 2, 127–149.

Mosse, G. (1999). 'Eighteenth century foundations'. In M. Bulmer and J. Solomos (eds), *Racism*. Oxford: Oxford University Press.

Mugny, G. and Carugati, F. (1989). *Social representations of intelligence*. Cambridge: Cambridge University Press.

Murray, C. and Herrnstein, R. J. (1994). *The Bell curve: Intelligence and class structure in American life*. New York: Free Press.

Mussen, P. H., Conger, J. J., Kagan, J., and Huston, A. C. (1990). *A child's world: Infancy through adolescence*. Sixth edition. New York: McGraw-Hill.

Myers, N. A. and Perlmutter, M. (1978). 'Memory in the years from two to five'. In P. Ornstein (ed.), *Memory development in children*. New Jersey: Erlbaum.

# N

Nash, M. (1997). 'Gift of love'. *Time*, 24 March, 43–44.

Nelson, K. (1973). 'Structure and strategy in learning to talk'. *Monographs of the Society for Research in Child Development*, 38, 1–2.

Nelson Mandela Children's Fund. (2001). *Report: A study into the situation and special needs of children in child-headed households*. Johannesburg: Nelson Mandela Children's Fund.

Nelson, T. E., Acker, M., and Manis, M. (1996). 'Irrepressible stereotypes'. *Journal of experimental social psychology*, 32, 13–38.

Newcomb, A. F. and Bagwell, C. L. (1995). 'Children's friendship relations: A meta-analytic review'. *Psychological bulletin*, 117, 2, 306–345.

Nicholson, L. J. (1990). *Feminism/postmodernism*. New York: Routledge.

Nisan, M. and Kohlberg, L. (1982). 'Universality and variation in moral judgment: A longitudinal and cross-sectional study in Turkey'. *Child development*, 52, 865–876.

Nolen-Hoeksema, S. (1988). *Abnormal psychology*. Burr Ridge, IL: McGraw-Hill.

Nsamenang, B. A. (1992). *Human development in cultural context: A third world perspective*. Newbury Park, CA: Sage.

Nsamenang, B. A. (1994). 'Cultural organisation of human development within the family context'. In S. C. Carr and J. F. Schumaker (eds), *Psychology and the developing world*. Westport, CT: Praeger.

Nsamenang, B. A. (2000). 'African view on social development: Implications for cross-cultural developmental research'. Paper presented at the Fifth Biennial Africa Regional Workshops of the ISSBD, 25–30 September, Kampala.

Nsamenang, B. A. and Lamb, M. E. (1993). 'The acquisition of socio-cognitive competence by Nso children in the Bamenda grassfields of northwest Cameroun'. *International journal of behavioural development*, 16 (3) 429–441.

# O

Omi, M. and Winant, H. (1999). 'Racial formation in the United States'. In M. Bulmer and J. Solomos (eds), *Racism*. Oxford: Oxford University Press.

Ornstein, P. A., Baker-Ward, L., and Naus, M. J. (1978). 'Rehearsal processes in children's memory'. In P. A. Ornstein (ed.), *Memory development in children*. New Jersey: Erlbaum.

Osborne, R. (1993). *Freud for beginners*. London: Writers and Readers.

Owen, K. and Taljaard, J. J. (eds) (1989). *Handbook for the use of psychological and scholastic tests of IPER and the NIPR*. Pretoria: Human Sciences Research Council.

# P

Papalia, D. E. and Olds, W. S. (1993). *A child's world: Infancy through adolescence*. Sixth edition. New York: McGraw-Hill.

Papalia, D. E., Olds, S. W., and Feldman, R. D. (1998). *Human development*. New York: McGraw-Hill.

Papert, J. (1996). 'Piaget's history'. In B. J. Wadsworth (ed.), *Piaget's theory of cognitive and affective development: Foundations of constructivism*. White Plains, NY: Longman.

Parekh, A. and Jackson, C. (1997). 'Families of children with a mental handicap'. In C. de la Rey, N. Duncan, T. Shefer, and A. van Niekerk (eds), *Contemporary issues in human development: A South African focus*. Johannesburg: Thomson.

Parke, R. D. (1979). 'Sex-role development: Introduction'. In R. D. Parke (ed.), *Readings in social development*. New York: Holt, Rinehart and Winston.

Parkin, A. (1999). *Memory: A guide for professionals*. New York: John Wiley.

Parkin, A. and Java, R. I. (1999). 'Determinants of age-related memory loss'. In T. Perfect and E. A. Maylor (eds), *Theoretical debates in cognitive aging*. London: Oxford University Press.

Pascual-Leone, J. (1970). 'A mathematical model for the transition rule in Piaget's developmental stages'. *Acta psychologica*, 32, 301–345.

Peterson, L. M. (1980). 'Why men have pockets in their pants: A feminist insight (or, if Freud had been a woman)'. *Society for the Advancement of Social Psychology newsletter*, 6, 19.

Piaget, J. (1926). *The language and thought of the child*. London: Kegan, Paul, Trench and Trubner.

Piaget, J. (1932/1965). *The moral judgement of the child*. New York: Free Press.

Piaget, J. (1952). *The origins of intelligence in children*. New York: International Universities Press.

Piaget, J. (1962). *Play, dreams and imitation*. New York: Norton.

Piaget, J. (1972). 'Intellectual evolution from adolescence to adulthood'. *Human development*, 15, 1–12.

Pistorius, M. (1999). 'Serial killers'. In R. Marsh (ed.), *With criminal intent: The changing face of crime in South Africa*. Kenilworth, Cape Town: Ampersand Press.

Pistorius, M. (2000a). Personal communication. Personal interview conducted on 21 March 2000, Johannesburg.

Pistorius, M. (2000b). *Catch me a killer.... Serial murders: A profiler's true story*. Natal: Penguin.

Popper, K. (1960). *The logic of scientific discovery*. London: Hutchinson.

Posada, G., Gao, Y., Fang, W., Posada, R., Tascon, M., Schoelmerich, A., Sagi, A., Kondo-Ikemura, K., Ylaland, W., and Synnevaag, B. (1995). 'The secure base phenomenon across cultures: Children's behaviour, mothers' preferences and experts' concepts'. In E. Waters, B. Vaughn, G. Posada, and

K. Kondo-Ikemura (eds), *Caregiving: Cultural and cognitive perspectives on secure-base behaviour and working models: New growing points of attachment theory and research. Monographs of the Society for Research in Child Development*, 60 (2–3), Serial no. 244, 133–145.

Posada, G., Jacobs, A., Carbonell, O. A., Alzate, G., Bustamante, M. R., and Arenas, A. (1999). 'Maternal care and attachment security in ordinary and emergency contexts'. *Developmental psychology*, 35 (6), 1379–1388.

Powlitsha, K. K., Serbin, L. A., Doyle, A. B., and White, D. R. (1994). 'Gender, ethnic and body type biases: The generality of prejudice in childhood'. *Developmental psychology*, 30 (4), 526–536.

Pyle, D. W. (1979). *Intelligence.* London: Routledge & Kegan Paul.

# R

Raidt, E. H. (1995). 'German speakers in South Africa, with special reference to KwaZulu-Natal'. In R. Mesthrie (ed.), *Language and social history.* Cape Town: David Philip.

Reinisch, J. M. (1987). *Masculinity/femininity: Basic perspectives.* New York: Oxford University Press.

Republic of South Africa. (1996a). *The Constitution of the Republic of South Africa, 1996.* Act 108 of 1996. Cape Town: Government Printer.

Republic of South Africa. (1996b). *Choice on Termination of Pregnancy Act*, No. 92 of 1996. Cape Town: Government Printer.

Rest, J. R. (1974). *Manual for the defining issues test: An objective test of moral judgment development.* Minneapolis: University of Minnesota.

Rest, J. R. (1983). 'Morality'. In P. Mussen, J. H. Flavell, and E. M. Markman (eds), *Handbook of child psychology. Volume 3.* Fourth edition. New York: John Wiley.

Rest, J. R. (1986). *Moral development: Advances in research and theory.* New York: Praeger.

Rest, J. R., Narvaez, D., Bebeau, M. J., and Thoma, S. J. (1999). *Postconventional moral thinking: A neo-Kohlbergian approach.* New Jersey: Erlbaum.

Richards, A. and Dickson, A. (eds) (1977). *The Penguin Freud Library. Volume 7 on sexuality: Three essays on the theory of sexuality and other works.* London: Penguin.

Richter, L. and Griesel, R. (1994). 'Malnutrition, low birth weight and related influences on psychological development'. In A. Dawes and D. Donald (eds), *Childhood and adversity: Psychological perspectives from South African research.* Cape Town: David Philip.

Riegel, K. (1984). 'Beyond formal operations'. In M. L. Commons, F. A. Richards, and C. Armon (eds), *Beyond formal operations: Late adolescence and adult cognitive development.* New York: Praeger.

Riegel, K. F. and Riegel, R. M. (1972). 'Development, drop and death'. *Developmental psychology*, 6, 306–319.

Robertson, J. and Bowlby, J. (1952). 'Responses of young children to separation from their mothers'. *Courr. Cent. Int. Enf.*, 2, 131–142.

Robinson, D. N. (1981). *An intellectual history of psychology.* New York: Macmillan.

Rogoff, B. (1990). *Apprenticeships in thinking: Cognitive development in social context.* New York: Oxford University Press.

Rose, N. (1991). *Governing the soul: The shaping of the private self.* London: Routledge.

Rose, S. A., Feldman, J. F., Wallace, I. F., and McCarton, C. (1989). 'Infant visual attention: Relation to birth status and developmental outcome during the first five years'. *Developmental psychology*, 25, 723–737.

Rose, S. A. and Wallace, I. F. (1985). 'Visual recognition memory: A predictor of later cognitive functioning in preterms'. *Child development*, 56, 843–852.

Rothbard, J. C. and Shaver, P. R. (1994). 'Continuity of attachment across the lifespan'. In M. B. Sperling and W. H. Berman (eds), *Attachment in adults: Clinical and developmental perspectives.* New York: Guilford Press.

Ruffman, T. K., Olson, D. R., Ash, T., and Keenan, T. (1993). 'The ABCs of deception: Do young children understand deception in the same way as adults?' *Developmental psychology*, 29, 74–87.

Rumelhart, D. E. and McClelland, J. L. (1986). 'On learning the past tense of English verbs'. In J. L. McClelland and D. E. Rumelhart (eds), *Parallel distributed processing: Explorations of the microstructure of cognition. Volume 2: Psychological and biological models*. Cambridge, MA: MIT Press.

Rutter, M. (1985). 'Family and school influences on cognitive development.' *Journal of child psychology and psychiatry*, 26, 683–704.

# S

Sabini, J. (1995). *Social psychology*. Second edition. New York: Norton.

Salthouse, T. A. (1997). 'The processing speed theory of adult age differences in cognition'. *Psychological review*, 103, 403–428.

Sameroff, A. and Emde, R. (1989). *Relationship disturbances in early childhood*. New York: Basic Books.

Sampson, E. E. (1992). 'The deconstruction of self'. In J. Shotter and K. J. Gergen (eds), *Texts of identity*. London: Routledge.

Samuels, A. (1985). *Jung and the post-Jungians*. London: Routledge.

Santrock, J. W. (1999). *Life-span development*. Boston: McGraw-Hill.

Santrock, J. W. (2001). *Child development*. Ninth edition. Boston: McGraw-Hill.

Santrock, J. W. and Yussen, S. R. (1987). *Child development: An introduction*. Third edition. Iowa: W.C. Browns.

Sarafino, E. P. and Armstrong, J. W. (1980). *Child and adolescent development*. Glenview, Illinois: Scott Foresman.

Saunders, G. (1988). *Bilingual children: From birth to teens*. Clevedon: Multilingual Matters.

Schaie, K. W. and Willis, S. L. (1996). 'Psychometric intelligence and ageing'. In F. Blanchard-Fields and T. M. Hess (eds), *Perspectives on cognitive change in adulthood and ageing*. New York: McGraw-Hill.

Scribner, S. (1985). 'Vygotsky's uses of history'. In J. V. Wertsch (ed.), *Communication and cognition: A Vygotskian perspective*. Cambridge: Cambridge University Press.

Seedat, M. (1997). 'The quest for liberatory psychology'. *South African journal of psychology*, 27 (4), 261–270.

Segal, H. (1964). *Introduction to the work of Melanie Klein*. New York: Basic Books.

Seltzer, M. (1998). *Serial killers: Life and death in America's wound culture*. New York: Routledge.

Serpell, R. (1993). *The significance of schooling: Life-journeys in an African society*. Cambridge: Cambridge University Press.

Serpell, R. (1994). 'Negotiating a fusion of horizons: A process view of cultural validation in developmental psychology'. *Mind, culture and activity*, 1 (1–2), 43.

Sey, J. (1999). 'Postmodernism: A critical practice?' In M. Terre Blanche and K. Durrheim (eds), *Research in practice: Applied methods for the social sciences*. Cape Town: University of Cape Town Press.

Seymour, P. H. K. and Elder, L. (1985). 'Beginning reading without phonology'. *Cognitive neuropsychology*, 1, 42–83.

Seymour, P. H. K. and McGregor, C. J. (1984). 'Developmental dyslexia: A cognitive-experimental analysis of phonological, morphemic and visual impairments'. *Cognitive neuropsychology*, 1, 43–82.

Shaffer, D. R. (1996). *Developmental psychology*. Fourth edition. Pacific Grove, CA: Brooks-Cole.

Sharpe, S. (1978). *Just like a girl. How girls learn to be women*. Middlesex: Penguin.

Shefer, T. (1997). 'The making of the gendered self'. In C. de la Rey, N. Duncan, T. Shefer, and A. van Niekerk (eds), *Contemporary issues in human development: A South African focus*. Johannesburg: Thomson.

Singer, E. (1992). *Child-care and the psychology of development.* London: Routledge.

Sinott, J. D. (1984). 'Postformal reasoning: The relativistic stage'. In M. L. Commons, F. A. Richards, and C. Armon (eds), *Beyond formal operations: Late adolescence and adult cognitive development.* New York: Praeger.

Sithole, M. (1999). Personal communication. Personal interviews conducted by James Grant with Moses Sithole in Pretoria Central Prison.

Skinner, B. F. (1957). *Verbal behaviour.* New York: Appleton Century Crofts.

Skinner, D. and Swartz, L. (1989). 'The consequences for preschool children of a parent's detention: A preliminary South African clinical study of caregivers' reports'. *Journal of child psychology and psychiatry,* 30 (2), 243–259.

Skuy, M., Lomofsky, L., Fridjohn, P., and Green, L. (1993). 'Effectiveness of instrumental enrichment for the preservice teachers in a disadvantaged South African community'. *International journal of cognitive education and mediated learning,* 2 (2), 92–108.

Skuy, M., Mentis, M., Durbach, F., Cockcroft, M., Fridjohn, P., and Mentis, M. (1995). 'Crosscultural comparisons of effects of instrumental enrichment on children in a South African mining town'. *School psychology international,* 16, 265–282.

Slade, A. (1999). 'Attachment theory and research: Implications for the theory and practice of individual psychotherapy with adults'. In J. Cassidy and P. R. Shaver (eds), *Handbook of attachment: Theory, research and clinical applications.* New York: Guilford Press.

Smith, M. A., Sayre, L. M., Monnier, V. M., and Perry, G. (1995). 'Radical ageing in Alzheimer's disease'. *Trends in neuroscience,* 18, 172–176.

Smuts, S. (1993a).'Norwood rapist "not schizoid" '. *The Star,* 23 September, 5.

Smuts, S. (1993b). 'Rapist-murderer did it "for thrills" '. *The Star,* 23 September, 4.

Snarey, J. (1985). 'Cross-cultural universality of social-moral development: A critique review of Kohlbergian research'. *Psychological bulletin,* 97 (2), 202–232.

Sodian, B., Taylor, C., Harris, P. L., and Perner, J. (1991). 'Early deception and the child's theory of mind: False trails and genuine markers'. *Child development,* 62, 468–483.

Solms, M. (1995). 'Is the brain more real than the mind?' *Psychoanalytic psychotherapy,* 9, 107–20.

Solms, M. and Saling, M. (1990). *A moment of transition: Two neuroscientific articles by Sigmund Freud.* London: Karnac Books.

Spencer, H. (1886). *The principles of psychology. Volume 5.* New York: D. Appleton.

Sproat, G. M. (1868). *Scenes and studies of savage life.* London.

Sroufe, L. A. (1979). 'Socioemotional development'. In J. Osofsky (ed.), *Handbook of infant development.* New York: John Wiley.

Sroufe, L. A. (1983). 'Infant-caregiver attachment and patterns of adaptation in preschool: The roots of maladaptation and competence'. In M. Perlmutter (ed.), *Minnesota symposia in child psychology. Volume 16.* New Jersey: Erlbaum.

Sroufe, L. A. (1990). 'An organizational perspective on the self'. In D. Cicchetti and M. Beeghly (eds), *The self in transition: Infancy to childhood.* Chicago: University of Chicago Press.

Sroufe, L. A. (1996). *Emotional development.* New York: Cambridge University Press.

Sroufe, L. A., Schork, E., Frosso, M., Lawroski, N., and LaFreniere, P. (1984). 'The role of affect in social competence'. In C. Izard, J. Kagan, and R. Zajonc (eds), *Emotions, cognitions and behavior.* New York: Cambridge University Press.

Sroufe, L. A. and Waters, E. (1977). 'Attachment as an organisational construct'. *Child development,* 48, 1184–1199.

*State v. Makwanyane* 1995 (2) SACR 1 CC.

Stead, G. (1996). 'Career development of black South African adolescents: A developmental-contextual perspective'. *Journal of counselling and development,* 74, 270–275.

Sternberg, R. J. (1984). 'Towards a triarchic theory of human intelligence'. *Behavioural and brain sciences,* 7, 269–315.

Sternberg, R. J. (1985). *Beyond IQ: A triarchic theory of human intelligence.* Cambridge: Cambridge University Press.

Sternberg, R. J. (1988). 'Intellectual development: Psychometric and information-processing approaches'. In M. H. Bornstein and M. E. Lamb (eds), *Developmental psychology: An advanced textbook.* New Jersey: Erlbaum.

Sternberg, R. J. (1996). *Cognitive psychology.* Fort Worth: Harcourt Brace.

Sternberg, R. J. (1998). 'How intelligent is intelligence testing?' *Scientific American*, 9 (4), 12–18.

Stevens, G. and Lockhat, R. (1997). ' "Coca-Cola kids": Reflections on black adolescent identity development in post-apartheid South Africa'. *South African journal of psychology*, 27(4), 250–255.

Storr, A. (2000). *Freud: A very short introduction.* Oxford: Oxford University Press.

Straker, G. (1990). 'Violence against children'. In B. McKendrich and W. Hoffman (eds), *People and violence in South Africa.* Oxford: Oxford University Press.

Stuart, S. and Noyes, R. (1999). 'Attachment and interpersonal communication in somatisation'. *Psychosomatics*, 40 (1), 34–43.

Sussman-Stilman, A., Kalkoske, M., Egeland, B., and Waldman, I. (1996). 'Infant temperament and maternal sensitivity as predictors of attachment security'. *Infant behaviour and development*, 19, 33–47.

# T

Takahashi, K. (1990). 'Are the key assumptions of the "strange situation" procedure universal? A view from Japanese research'. *Human development*, 33, 23–30.

The Center for the Study of Ethical Development. (2000). *Defining issues test – 2.* Published at website, http://edpsy.coled.umn.edu/PSYCHF/CSED/.

Tudin, P., Straker, G., and Mendolsohn, M. (1994). 'Social and political complexity and moral development'. *South African journal of psychology*, 24 (3), 163–168.

Tulving, E. (1972). 'Episodic and semantic memory'. In E. Tulving and W. Donaldson (eds), *Organisation of memory.* New York: Academic Press.

Tulving, E. and Donaldson, W. (eds) (1972). *Organisation of memory.* London: Academic Press.

Turner, P. J. and Gervai, J. (1995). 'A multidimensional study of gender typing in preschool children and their parents: Personality, attitudes, preferences, behaviour and cultural differences'. *Developmental psychology*, 31 (5), 759–772.

# U

UNAIDS. (1999). *Orphans due to AIDS, South Africa 1990–2010.* Published at website, http://www.unaids.org/publications/graphics/addis/sld016.htm.

UNAIDS. (2000a). *Report on the global HIV/AIDS epidemic, UNAIDS, June 2000.* Published at website, http://www.unaids.org/epidemic_update/report/index.html.

UNAIDS. (2000b). *Aids epidemic update – December 2000.* Published at website, http://www.unaids.org/epidemic_update/report_dec00/index_dec.html#full.

# V

Van den Boom, D. C. (1994). 'The influence of temperament and mothering on attachment and exploration: An experimental manipulation of sensitive responsiveness among lower-class mothers with irritable infants'. *Child development*, 65, 1457–1477.

Van Ijzendoorn, M. H. (1993). 'Commentary on Jackson (1993), "Multiple caregiving among African Americans and infant attachment: The need for an emic approach" '. *Human development*, 36, 103–105.

Van Niekerk, A. (1997). 'Traumatic spinal injury among youth'. In C. de la Rey, N. Duncan, T. Shefer, and A. van Niekerk (eds), *Contemporary issues in human development: A South African focus.* Johannesburg: Thomson.

Vaughn, B. E. and Bost, K. K. (1999). 'Attachment and temperament: Redundant, independent, or interacting influences on interpersonal adaptation and personality development'. In J. Cassidy and P. R. Shaver (eds), *Handbook of attachment: Theory, research and clinical applications.* New York: Guilford Press.

Vygodskaia, G. L. (1995). 'Remembering father'. *Educational psychologist*, 30 (2), 57–59.

Vygotsky, L. S. (1956). *Selected psychological investigations.* Moscow: Izdstel'sto Akademii Pedagogicheskikh Nauk.

Vygotsky, L. S. (1962). *Thought and language.* Harvard, MA: MIT Press.

Vygotsky, L. S. (1978). *Mind in society: The development of higher psychological processes.* Cambridge, MA: Harvard University Press.

Vygotsky, L. S. (1988). 'The genesis of higher mental functions'. In K. Richardson and S. Sheldon (eds), *Cognitive development to adolescence.* Hove: Erlbaum.

# W

Walker, L. J. (1984). 'Sex differences in the development of moral reasoning: A critical review'. *Child development*, 55, 677–691.

Walker, L. J., de Vries, B., and Trevethan, S. D. (1987). 'Moral stages and moral orientations in real life and hypothetical dilemmas'. *Child development*, 58, 842–858.

Ward, G. (1996). *Teach yourself postmodernism.* London: Hodder and Stoughton.

Waters, E. and Cummings, E. M. (2000). 'A secure base from which to explore close relationships'. *Child development*, 71 (1), 164–172.

Waters, E., Treboux, D., Crowell, J., Merrick, S., and Albersheim, L. (1995). 'From the strange situation to the adult attachment interview: A 20-year longitudinal study of attachment security in infancy and early adulthood'. Unpublished manuscript, State University of New York at Stony Brook, New York.

Waters, E., Vaughn, B. E., and Egeland, B. (1980). 'Individual differences in infant-mother attachment relationships at age one: Antecedents in neonatal behaviour in an economically disadvantaged sample'. *Child development*, 51, 208–216.

Weinfeld, N. S., Sroufe, L. A., Egeland, B., and Carlson, E. A. (1999). 'The nature of individual differences in infant-caregiver attachment'. In J. Cassidy and P. R. Shaver (eds), *Handbook of attachment: Theory, research and clinical applications.* New York: Guilford Press.

Weintraub, M., Pritchard Clemens, L., Sockloff, A., Ethridge, T., Gracely, E., and Myers, B. (1984). 'The development of sex-role stereotypes in the third year: Relationship to gender labelling, gender identity, sex-typed toy preference, and family characteristics. *Child development*, 55, 1493–1503.

Weisstein, N. (1973). 'Psychology constructs the female'. In P. Brown (ed.), *Radical psychology.* New York: Harper and Row.

Weiten, W. (1991). *Psychology: Themes and variations.* Pacific Grove, CA: Brooks-Cole.

Wertheimer, M. (1961). 'Psychomotor co-ordination of auditory-visual space at birth'. *Science*, 134, 1692.

West, M., Livesley, W. J., Reiffer, L., and Sheldon, A. (1986). 'The place of attachment in the life events model of stress and illness'. *Canadian journal of psychiatry*, 31, 202–207.

Westen, D. (1996). *Psychology: Mind, brain and culture.* New York: John Wiley.

Western, D. (1998). 'The scientific legacy of Sigmund Freud: Toward a psychodynamically informed psychological science'. *Psychological bulletin*, 124 (3), 333–371.

Western, D. (1999). 'The scientific status of unconscious processes: Is Freud really dead?' *Journal of the American Psychoanalytic Association*, 47 (4), 1061–1112.

Wetherell, M. and Griffin, C. (1991). 'Feminist psychology and the study of men and masculinity: Part 1: Assumptions and perspectives'. *Feminism and psychology*, 1, 361–93.

Whorf, B. L. (1956). 'Science and linguistics'. In J. B. Carroll (ed.), *Language, thought and reality: Selected writings of Benjamin Lee Whorf*. Cambridge, MA: MIT Press.

Widdershoven, G. (1997). 'Models of human development'. In W. van Haaften, M. Korthals, and T. Wren (eds), *Philosophy of development: Reconstructing the foundations of human development and education*. Dordrecht: Kluwer.

Winnicott, D. W. (1958). *Collected papers: Through paediatrics to psycho-analysis*. New York: Basic Books.

Winnicott, D. W. (1964). *The child, the family and the outside world*. London: Penguin.

Winnicott, D. W. (1965). *Maturational processes and the facilitating environment*. New York: International Universities Press.

Winnicott, D. W. (1971). *Playing and reality*. New York: Basic Books.

Winnicott, D. W. (1974). 'Fear of breakdown'. *International review of psychoanalysis*, 1, 103–107.

Wolheim, R. (1977). *Freud*. Glasgow: Fontana Modern Masters.

Wood, D. J., Bruner, J. S., and Ross, G. (1976). 'The role of tutoring in problem-solving'. *Journal of child psychology*, 17, 89–100.

Wood, J. T. (1994). *Gendered lives: Communication, gender and culture*. Belmont: Wadsworth.

Wulfsohn, D. (1988). 'The impact of the South African nanny on the young child'. Unpublished doctoral thesis, University of South Africa, Pretoria.

Wundt, W. (1874/1904). Principles of physiological psychology. Leipzig: Englemann.

# Y

Yorkers, R. M. (1923). 'Testing the human mind'. *Atlantic monthly*, 131, 358–370.

# Z

Zeanah, C. H., Mammen, O. K., and Lieberman, A. F. (1993). 'Disorders of attachment'. In C. H. Zeanah (ed.), *Handbook of infant mental health*. New York: Guilford.

# Index